Corrections
An Introduction

Third Edition

Richard P. Seiter
Saint Louis University

Prentice Hall

Boston Columbus Indianapolis New York San Francisco Upper Saddle River
Amsterdam Cape Town Dubai London Madrid Milan Munich Paris Montreal Toronto
Delhi Mexico City São Paulo Sydney Hong Kong Seoul Singapore Taipei Tokyo

Editor in Chief: Vernon Anthony
Acquisitions Editor: Eric Krassow
Development Editor: Elisa Rogers
Editorial Assistant: Lynda Cramer
Director of Marketing: David Gesell
Marketing Manager: Adam Kloza
Senior Marketing Coordinator: Alicia Wozniak
Senior Managing Editor: JoEllen Gohr
Project Manager: Jessica H. Sykes
Senior Operations Supervisor: Pat Tonneman
Operations Specialist: Laura Weaver
Senior Art Director: Diane Ernsberger
Text and Cover Designer: Rokusek Design
Manager, Visual Research: Beth Brenzel

Photo Researcher: Jerry Marshall
Manager, Rights and Permissions: Zina Arabia
Image Permission Coordinator: Debbie Latronica
Manager, Cover Visual Research & Permissions:
   Karen Sanatar
Cover Art: Sagel & Kranefeld/Corbis
Media Editor: Michelle Churma
Lead Media Project Manager: Karen Bretz
Full-Service Project Management: Karpagam Jagadeesan
Composition: GGS Higher Education Resources,
   A Division of Premedia Global, Inc.
Printer/Binder: Quebecor World Color/Versailles
Cover Printer: Coral Graphics
Text Font: Sabon, 11/13

Library of Congress Cataloging-in-Publication Data

Seiter, Richard P.
   Corrections : an introduction / Richard P. Seiter.—3rd ed.
      p. cm.
   Includes bibliographical references and index.
   ISBN-13: 978-0-13-506082-7 (alk. paper)
   ISBN-10: 0-13-506082-6 (alk. paper)
   1. Corrections—United States. I. Title.
   HV9471.S45 2009
   364.60973—dc22

                              2009044095

10 9 8 7 6 5 4

Prentice Hall
is an imprint of

www.pearsonhighered.com

ISBN 10:   0-13-506082-6
ISBN 13: 978-0-13-506082-7

Contents

part **Correctional Challenges 497**

Preface

As an author, I am very excited about this introductory textbook on corrections. Having spent most of my life working in the correctional field, I have had the opportunity to work in many different situations and with many dedicated people. I am pleased to be able to pass on some of the experiences and information gathered over twenty-five years to students studying corrections and perhaps considering corrections as a career.

As such, the goal of this textbook is to provide students with a practical understanding of today's operations of corrections. The text includes correctional history and theory; however, the text concentrates on what we do in corrections, why we do it, and what challenges face contemporary correctional staff and administrators. The text also presents case studies, information on careers, and real examples of situations to provide students with an understanding of the practical aspects of working in corrections.

The third edition of *Corrections: An Introduction* has been updated to provide faculty and students with state-of-the-art information on the operations of the various elements of corrections and the issues faced by correctional policymakers and practitioners. These updates include the most recent data regarding correctional populations and costs, as well as new research and findings that have had an impact on correctional policy. The following are sections that are either new or substantially expanded and updated for the third edition.

New to This Edition

- **Creative Sentencing Options—Mental Health Courts:** In Chapter 2, the section titled "Creative Sentencing Options" includes a discussion of Mental Health Courts as well as Drug Courts. The section on Drug Courts has also been updated.

- **Prisoner Reentry—Recent Progress in Prisoner Reentry:** In Chapter 6 in the section titled "Prisoner Reentry," there is a new section regarding Recent Progress in Prisoner Reentry. This section addresses the passing of the Second Chance Act by the U.S. Congress and includes other new developments and research findings in prisoner reentry.

- **Prisoner Reentry—A Systems Approach to Prisoner Reentry:** Also in Chapter 2, this new section includes an example of how the State of Washington has provided an outstanding model of how to integrate reentry into the overall sentencing, classification, and inmate management process by the Department of Corrections.

- **Life for a Correctional Officer—Recruiting and Retaining Correctional Officers:** In Chapter 12, the challenge of recruiting and retaining professional and competent individuals as correctional officers is addressed. Issues of negative perception, pay, and staff development are explored as well as the impact of the recession on recruitment.

- **The Impact of Budgets on Correctional Policy:** In Chapter 15, a new section examines the impact of the recession and reduced state revenues on correctional agencies. This section looks at both the challenge of cutting budgets and how states are reexamining their "tough on crime" sentencing policies, and considering alternatives to incarceration that are less expensive without undermining public safety.

- **Private Prisons:** Also in Chapter 15 is a new section that expands the material on private prisons that was in the second edition. This section addresses both the controversies of private operations of prisons as well as updates new research on the effectiveness and cost impact of privatization.

- **Correctional Technology:** In Chapter 16, several technological applications are described and the potential impact on the way that correctional agencies go about their work is addressed. With significant budget dollars going toward funding corrections, it is a prime target for technological innovations.

- **Updated Legal Decisions:** Throughout the textbook, there are updates to federal court decisions that affect current practices. This is most significant in Chapter 14 in the type and number of inmate lawsuits, religious freedoms and faith-based programming in prisons, and significant decisions and changes in public attitudes regarding the death penalty.

The third edition of *Corrections: An Introduction* has five parts and sixteen chapters. In Part I, students will learn theories of crime and how society responded to crime prior to the eighteenth century, the development of formal correctional practices, and the theories that are embraced by various correctional approaches. As well, students will be presented with the processes (pretrial diversion, bail, jail, and finding of guilt) that lead up to sentencing, various sentencing approaches and options, postsentencing processes for managing offenders, the activities and decision points regarding the actual sentencing decision, and creative sentencing options.

In Part II, students learn how the various elements of the correctional processes operate, including jails and detention facilities, probation and intermediate sanctions, prisons, and parole and prisoner reentry. Chapter 3 addresses the operations and issues surrounding contemporary use of jails. Included are issues of management, jail crowding, legal liabilities, and offender issues such as suicide prevention, mentally ill offenders, and classification. Chapter 4 reviews the operation of probation, including conditions, supervision styles, and revocation, and the entire range of intermediate sanctions between probation and prison is described and issues addressed. The chapter on prisons deals with the role and mission of prisons, the increasing reliance on prisons as a criminal sanction and the resulting challenge of increased capacity and crowding, and the various prisons systems within the United States. Included are descriptions of the various levels of security and operations within American prisons. Chapter 6 reviews the various mechanisms for release from prison. The history and current operations of parole, preparation for release, challenges facing ex-prisoners as they return to the community, supervision requirements, revocation processes, and successful completion from supervision is described.

In Part III, the perspectives regarding various categories of correctional clients is presented. In Chapter 7, general background information regarding male and female adult offenders is provided. This chapter "paints a picture" of the offenses they commit, the needs they have, and the special circumstances they face during the fulfillment of their sentence. Chapter 8 describes the system and processes for handling juvenile offenders separate from the adult system. The history, theories, practices, and issues of the juvenile correctional systems are presented. Chapter 9 covers offenders with special characteristics that require management or processing "out of the norm" of typical correctional operations. Included are descriptions of these issues as they relate to drug offenders, the mentally ill, aging and violent offenders, sex offenders, and offenders with a serious infectious disease.

In Part IV, the life within prison is described through the eyes of inmates and staff, while addressing how correctional administrators organize and manage prisons, how custody and treatment are provided, how legal rights of inmates have been developed and are managed, and how the death penalty is carried out in the United States. In Chapter 10, the overall approach that administrators take to create a prison environment that is safe, secure, and provides rehabilitative opportunities is presented. In Chapter 11, the world of inmates is described, and many issues such as violence, drug use, homosexuality, and the inmate culture are discussed. Chapter 12 presents the life faced by those that work in a prison, and the challenges and stresses they deal with on a daily basis. In Chapter 13, the sometimes-conflicting areas of custody and treatment are explained. And Chapter 14 details the historical development of legal rights for inmates, citing legal cases and illustrating the way case law has built the modern expectations for standard operations within prisons. The controversial use of the death penalty is also presented, including its history in the United States, the legal debates, the processes used to carry out the death penalty, and the pros and cons of the death penalty as a sentencing option.

Finally, in Part V, the challenges facing corrections now and in the future are presented. Chapter 15 addresses issues around the management of correctional processes, including accreditation, privatization, staff diversity, overcrowding, tightening budgets, program effectiveness, and political intervention. In Chapter 16, the future challenges that face correctional administrators over the next several years are presented. In this chapter, students are asked to reflect on issues regarding our current sentencing approach, rehabilitation as a correctional goal, community supervision, technology, the need for a new paradigm, prisoner reentry, and corrections as a career.

To give students a realistic and practical understanding of modern corrections, this textbook includes several features and approaches that are designed to heighten the learning process and make it interesting for students. Chapters include realistic experiences and insights into the real world of today's correctional operations. Some of these features that should make this book interesting and informative include the following:

- Each chapter includes a brief segment on history and theory, but focuses on the actual operations of prisons, community corrections, and jails. Students are able to experience the challenges that correctional workers face and the practical applications they use to meet these challenges.

- There are several case studies of real issues that have confronted staff who try to manage today's correctional populations. These examples provide students the opportunity for "A Look Into" the world of prisons, jails, and community corrections. Some of these describe how certain people look at their jobs or issues facing them, and others are a brief interview with someone working in the field described in the chapter.

- Students will enjoy and benefit from a feature entitled "Your Career in Corrections." Every chapter includes descriptions of jobs that students may carry out as a specific correctional application is described. For instance, in a discussion of halfway houses, there is a career box that notes the types of jobs available to staff entering this field, what they do, the requirements of the job, and the possible pay and work conditions they will face.

- Another interesting feature for students is "You Make the Decision." Included at the end of every chapter, this feature presents real situations that someone working in the field may encounter. For instance, in a discussion of probation, students have to struggle with the decision as whether to revoke a probationer for failing to follow all conditions of supervision. The chapter regarding parole presents several scenarios for prisoners appearing before the parole board, and students must make a decision whether to recommend parole or not.

- A valuable learning approach of the book is to focus on the policy implications of different theories and perspectives regarding corrections. All chapters address the practical issues of modern correctional policy development, and some chapters include a feature entitled "A Question of Policy." By addressing policy, students receive insight into the critical policy challenges that result from today's practice of corrections. The dilemmas that face elected officials and correctional administrators in creating a policy that is most effective and efficient and that contributes significantly to the accomplishment of correctional goals are presented.

- To take advantage of the many years of practical experience by the author, there is a feature in every chapter entitled "An Insider's Experience." You can find this feature on the *MyCrimeKit* website that accompanies this book. In this unique feature, the author describes events or circumstances that he had to address during his career and shares some very personal thoughts and observations.

- To provide a variety to perspectives from other key players in the correctional system, a feature entitled "An Interview With" provides personal accounts of correctional administrators, correctional officers, and inmates. These interviews add another touch of realism to the practical approach taken in this textbook.

- Each chapter also includes "Key Terms," "Chapter Objectives," and "Review Questions." As students begin to read a chapter, it will be helpful for them to read the objectives, and after reading the chapter, to use the questions to reinforce the most important aspects of the chapter.

Supplements

The *MyCrimeKit* companion website (www.mycrimekit.com) includes numerous media and tools to assist the student in understanding career choices in corrections, reviewing material contained in the chapters, and observing simulations relating to the duties of a corrections officer in the field. Margin notes throughout the book's chapters mark videos, simulations, and other media on *MyCrimeKit* that relates to the chapter material. A box at the end of each chapter lists the study tools and resources available for that chapter on MyCrimeKit.

Other supplements that accompany the text include an Instructor's Manual with Test Bank (ISBN 0-13-507813-X), TestGen test generator (ISBN 0-13-507851-2), and PowerPoint presentations (ISBN 0-13-507852-0), as well as a CourseSmart electronic version of the text (ISBN 0-13-507855-5).

To access supplementary materials online, instructors need to request an instructor access code. Go to www.pearsonhighered.com/irc, where you can register for an instructor access code. Within 48 hours after registering, you will receive a confirming e-mail, including an instructor access code. Once you have received your code, go to the site and log on for full instructions on downloading the materials you wish to use.

It is the author's hope that students enjoy this textbook, find it easy to read and study, and that the practical perspectives motivate students to consider a career in corrections. Even if students decide that corrections is not a career opportunity for them, corrections is such an important component in today's criminal justice system that an understanding of how programs operate and how much they cost is important to taxpayers who must support their operation.

Richard P. Seiter, Ph.D.

Acknowledgments

Writing and updating a book is a tremendous undertaking that could not be accomplished without the help of many people. I would first like to thank the many correctional colleagues that assisted me by granting me interviews, providing me advice, and giving me information that was used both for the general book information and to make the book come to life for students through their personal stories and situations. It is not easy to recall some memories of unpleasant situations, but through their candor and openness, readers will get a true understanding of what corrections is really like.

I thank the criminal justice and marketing group at Pearson Education. Elisa Rogers was the Development Editor who worked with me throughout the preparation, reviews, and revisions of the manuscript. I also thank the following reviewers selected by Pearson whose feedback guided this edition of the book: Carla Anderson, College of the Midland; Alton Braddock, University of Louisiana, Monroe; James D. Cunningham, State Fair Community College; Ken Egbo, Edinboro University of Pennsylvania; Randall Fesperman, South Plains College; Arnett Gaston, University of Maryland; Dorothy M. Goldsborough, University of Hawaii, Manoa; Marie L. Griffin, Arizona State University; Martha Henderson Hurley, The Citadel; M. Scott Henrie, College of Eastern Utah; Carly Hilinski, Grand Valley State University; Elizabeth C. McMUllan, University of North Florida; Kristine Miller, Southern Illinois University; Cassandra L. Renzi, Keiser University; Cort Tanner, Western Texas College; and Sheryl Van Horne, Pennsylvania State University. Their advice was always thoughtful, on-point, and helpful in improving the text, adding important topics, and making it more readable and useful for students of corrections.

I also thank the correctional agencies that were so helpful in giving me the opportunity to take pictures of their programs and facilities. Of greatest assistance was the Ohio Department of Rehabilitation and Corrections. Several individuals helped arrange the taking of photos and cooperated as I took pictures. Anne Diestel, archivist at the Federal Bureau of Prisons, provided several pictures for that agency. And staffs at the Correctional Corporation of America, David L. Moss Criminal Justice Center, and the Cimarron Correctional Facility were extremely helpful and cooperative. I also appreciate the assistance of the St. Louis County Justice Center and the St. Louis City Jail for allowing pictures to be taken of their facilities.

Most important in updating this revision was Dr. Michael Montgomery, Associate Professor, Department of Criminal Justice at Tennessee State University. Dr. Montgomery is an experienced correctional administrator in his own right and is an outstanding teacher and scholar as well. Mike did much of the research for the updates on material for this edition, and his advice on improvements to help both teaching faculty and students was outstanding.

Finally, I thank my family and friends who encouraged and supported me throughout the process. My wife, Riffi O'Brien, has been an important part of this book development and progress, and I thank her for her love, support, and encouragement. My son, Matt, has been through this process with me before and continues to provide his commonsense advice and humor as I get bogged down in the work of preparing a book of this magnitude. And, his personal work ethic is a constant motivation when I think I am working too hard.

Thanks to all of you. You made the third edition of *Corrections: An Introduction* a reality.

Richard P. Seiter, Ph.D.

About the Author

Richard P. Seiter is a career correctional professional, having worked in prisons and for correctional agencies for more than twenty-five years. Following receipt of his Ph.D. in Public Administration from the Ohio State University, he was a research associate and Assistant Director of the Crime and Delinquency Center at OSU. In 1976, he began a career with the Federal Bureau of Prisons (BOP) and worked in two federal prisons (the Federal Correctional Institution in Dublin, California, and the U.S. Penitentiary in Leavenworth, Kansas). He was Director of the BOP Staff Training Center in Denver, Colorado, and became the first Chief of the NIC National Academy of Corrections in Boulder, Colorado. He served as warden of two federal prisons (the Federal Prison Camp in Allenwood, Pennsylvania, and the Federal Correctional Institution in Greenville, Illinois). He also served as both Assistant Director for Industries, Education, and Training and Chief Operating Officer of Federal Prison Industries, with sales of over $400 million per year of prison-made products.

Dr. Seiter was Director of the Ohio Department of Rehabilitation and Correction for almost six years. In this position, he was responsible for all Ohio prisons, the parole board and parole supervision, and many community correctional programs. He managed an annual budget of $400 million and a staff of 8,000, and he oversaw the construction of more than 10,000 prison beds at a cost of $500 million.

After retiring from the Federal Bureau of Prisons, he became Professor and Director of Criminal Justice at Saint Louis University. During this time, he wrote two textbooks, published several articles, and expanded the program and course offerings at SLU.

In 2005, he became Executive Vice President of Corrections Corporation of America, the largest private prison company in the United States. In this position, Dr. Seiter oversees the operation of the sixth largest prison system in the country, with 63 prisons, 17,000 staff, and 75,000 inmates.

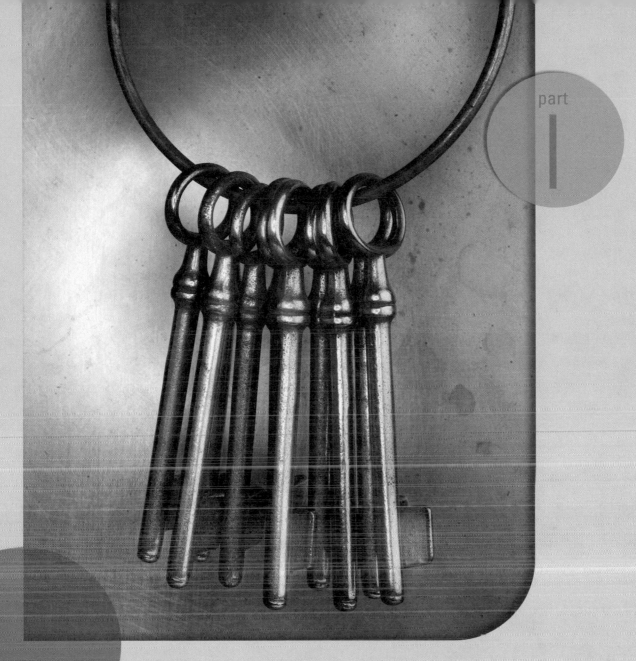

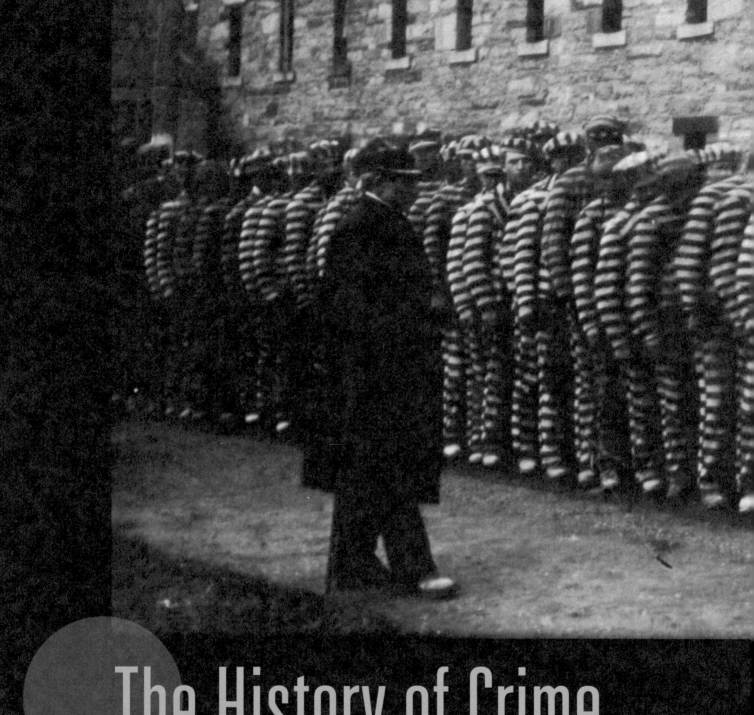

The History of Crime
and Corrections

After reading this chapter, you should be able to:

1. Define the term *corrections* and know how correctional agencies fulfill their mission of protecting society.

2. Identify how corrections can affect the crime rate by understanding the concept of the correctional funnel.

3. Outline the growth of corrections over the past two decades and describe why the scope of correctional budgets, staffing, and clients makes it important for students to study corrections.

4. Contrast the Classical School with the Positive School of criminology.

5. Describe the role of William Penn and the Pennsylvania Quakers in the development of the use of prisons in the United States.

6. Describe the operations of the Walnut Street Jail, the first American prison.

7. Compare the Pennsylvania system with the Auburn system of imprisonment.

8. Explain how the Irish penal system contributed to the development of the Reformatory Era of prison operations in the United States.

9. List the acts of Congress regarding the sale of prison-made products and describe their impact on the end of the Industrial Era of prison operations.

10. Describe the Rehabilitative Era and the medical model of corrections, and explain how this era evolved into the Reintegrative Era.

11. Identify and explain the five goals of corrections.

12. Define the theories of specific and general deterrence.

Introduction

What is corrections, how does it relate to the other components of the criminal justice system, how does it operate, how well does it work, and why should it be studied? This textbook is designed to answer these questions. Although these questions are worded as if "corrections" is a clearly defined and well-bounded activity, this is far from the case. Corrections includes a wide variety of activities, each with a wide variety of emphases and goals; some of the components have direct relationships with other correctional or criminal justice activities, and others operate almost independently. Corrections has been described as a system of fully integrated services and functions, and it has been described as a nonsystem with no coordination or shared mission by any of its components.

Throughout this text, students will learn how government, private, and not-for-profit agencies all contribute to corrections and the correctional process. The text covers history, theories, operations, costs, and effectiveness. It goes beyond providing students a historical perspective, an encyclopedia of terms, and general information regarding corrections. In addition, the text emphasizes practice as well as theory; the challenges to accomplishing the mission of correctional agencies; and the roles of the people who work in, are supervised by, or are affected by the correctional process. The goal of this textbook is to help students understand (1) how various factors throughout the historical development of corrections influenced the basic operating foundations of today, (2) the linkage of theory and practice, and (3) the difficulty in carrying out the functions of correctional agencies in a cost-efficient manner.

Defining Corrections

What is meant by "corrections"? Why do we even use the term *corrections* to refer to the legal punishment of criminal offenders? Does the use of the term *corrections* mean that it is the principal function of the management of criminals after sentencing? In this section, we define *corrections;* address these questions; and look at the historical development of terms, titles, and corresponding philosophies as our current practices evolved from the earliest approaches to punishing criminals. Terminology in any discipline usually comes from the role, mission, and expectations of the activities that are described. For our study of corrections, we examine the use of various terminologies over time, how they relate to the mission of corrections, and how corrections fits into the larger activities of the criminal justice system.

What Is Corrections?

Corrections is an interesting term to use to describe the punishment of offenders for the crimes they have committed. However, *corrections* offers a broader perspective on how agencies deal with criminal offenders. Previously, the term **penology** was used instead of corrections. *Penal* is defined as pertaining to or imposing punishment and is derived from the Latin term *peonalis,* meaning "punishment." Penology is simply the study of punishment. Until the 1950s, the functions, components, and actions of carrying out criminal sanctions regularly used the term *penal,* and penal institutions (prisons) and penal systems (organizations to carry out punishment) emphasized the principal function of implementing punishment for agencies handling criminal offenders after their sentencing.

However, ever since the founding of the United States and the creation of the prison as a method for punishment in the late eighteenth century, prisons and

penology
the study of the use of punishment for criminal acts

other correctional agencies have played a broader role. The Walnut Street Jail, established in 1790 as the first prison designed to house sentenced offenders in the United States, had reformation of the offender as its primary objective. Inmates were expected to read the Bible, reflect on their wrongdoing, and do penance for their crimes. Hence, **penitentiary** was established as the term used for secure facilities used to hold offenders serving a criminal sentence.

Penology is the study of punishment. However, this term generally included a much broader focus than simply punishment and effectively covered the theories, activities, and operations of carrying out the criminal sentence, whether in a prison or in the community. During the 1950s, the nation's penal system evolved such that the rehabilitation of offenders replaced punishment as its primary objective. This philosophical change affected theory and practice, and the term *penology* was replaced by the term **corrections**. For purposes of this textbook, *corrections* is defined as the range of community and institutional sanctions, treatment programs, and services for managing criminal offenders. As such, corrections includes functions such as the supervision and monitoring of offenders in the community, the secure holding of inmates in prisons, the provision of treatment for problems such as drug addiction or mental illness, and residential and other services provided to inmates as a transition from prison to the community.

In most diagrams of the criminal justice system, corrections is illustrated as the functions for dealing with criminal offenders after a court sentences them. However, the boundaries of corrections have expanded, and corrections now also relates to the detention in jails of offenders charged with crimes, as well as pretrial services such as supervising offenders released on bail. This broader characterization of corrections acknowledges that correctional agencies are often required to deal with offenders who have not yet been found guilty and sentenced to a punishment. This broader definition also makes the establishment of a mission for corrections difficult and complex.

penitentiary
the term first used to describe secure facilities used to hold offenders serving a criminal sentence; still used today for some older or highly secure prisons

corrections
the range of community and institutional sanctions, treatment programs, and services for managing criminal offenders

The Mission of Corrections

A mission is the statement of what an organization is to accomplish. Eadie defines the mission of an organization as "a statement of its basic purposes, often in terms of broad outcomes that it is committed to achieving or the major functions it carries out."[1] The mission of corrections has traditionally been to implement court-prescribed sentences for criminal violators or to carry out the sentence of

Corrections includes counseling and offender treatment programs, as well as prisons, concrete, and bars. Photo by Richard P. Seiter.

One of the earliest known bodies of penal codes is the Code of Hammurabi, created during King Hammurabi's reign of Old Babylon, ca. 1780 B.C. The code is best known from this carved stone, now in the Louvre Museum in Paris. Photo by Matthew Seiter.

the court. This mission statement is rather narrow and seems to indicate a lack of control or initiative by correctional agencies as to their functions and how they are to carry them out. However, most contemporary correctional administrators recognize a much broader mission and responsibility. The more complete mission of corrections is to protect society. Protection of society is accomplished through a combination of surveillance and control of offenders, of treatment and rehabilitative services, and of incapacitation during the service of a prison sentence.

In practice, correctional agencies fulfill their mission by assisting courts in the decision to grant bail, by providing the courts with information to guide sentencing, by supervising offenders in the community under court jurisdiction, by imprisoning offenders who receive a sentence of incarceration from the courts, and by overseeing inmates' reentry to the community. The short-term protection of society occurs as correctional agencies either detain offenders in jail or incarcerate them in prison, thus separating them from society and keeping them from further victimizing citizens in the community. The longer-term protection of society results from correctional agencies providing treatment and services to help offenders become less likely or less motivated to return to a life of crime and more likely to become productive and law-abiding citizens.

Corrections as a Part of the Criminal Justice System

Figure 1.1 is an illustration of the criminal justice system. There are generally thought to be three major components of the criminal justice system: police, courts, and corrections. In the ideal process of criminal justice, the police investigate

THE CRIMINAL JUSTICE SYSTEM

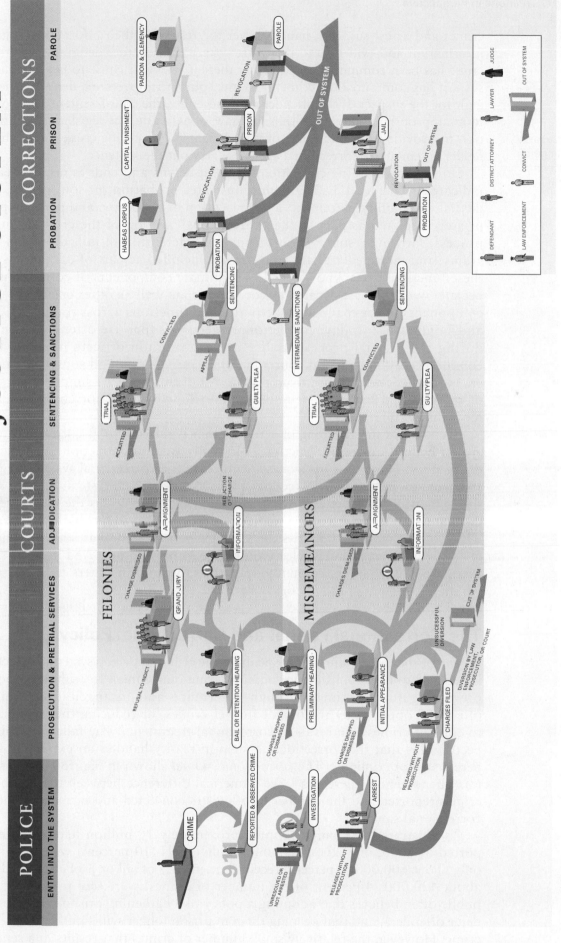

FIGURE 1.1 The Criminal Justice System

crimes and arrest suspects, handing over the results of their efforts (investigative information and evidence) to the court system. Prosecutors determine whether a crime has been committed and whether there is probable cause to believe that the suspect has committed the crime. If so, the courts then oversee a determination of guilt for the suspect. If the offender is found guilty, the courts sentence him or her to an appropriate sentence within the state **penal code,** the legislative authorization to provide a specific range of punishment for a specific crime. Once the offender is sentenced, correctional agencies carry out the sentence.

However, where the correctional system begins and ends is not as clear as indicated in Figure 1.1. The figure illustrates probation, prison, parole, residential community placement, and revocation of probation and parole, appropriately depicted as part of the "corrections" section of the criminal justice process. However, supervision during bail, detention in jail, diversion programs, and intermediate sanctions are not included as part of corrections. Yet these functions are acknowledged as legitimate components of corrections, especially over the past decade, as corrections (as well as other criminal justice components) has expanded its activities and functions across traditional lines and boundaries. Today, correctional agencies supervise offenders released during the pretrial process; police assist probation officers in supervising community offenders; and courts maintain jurisdiction and supervise offenders even after their release from prison. All of this makes a simple illustration of the criminal justice system and delineation of the major components almost impossible.

Even within the grouping of activities that is referred to as corrections, there are differences among jurisdictions. No one system of corrections exists across the country. There are three governmental levels of correctional systems: federal, state, and thousands of local (county and city) correctional systems. In each state, the role distinctions between what is done at the state versus the local level are different. Some state correctional systems operate all probation activities, whereas in other states counties carry out probation. Some states have a sentencing structure that includes release on parole; others do not. And in some states there are statewide or regionally operated jails, and in others jails are solely within the domain of the city or county.

The Correctional Funnel and Correctional Policy

As one of the three major components of the criminal justice system, corrections is believed to be responsible for administering punishment to criminals, thereby preventing future crimes through deterrence and incapacitation, limiting offenders' opportunity to commit further crimes, or reducing their inclination to commit crimes as a result of correctional treatments. The fallacy in this expectation is that the correctional system in reality handles an extremely small percentage of criminals. The *correctional funnel* shown in Figure 1.2 illustrates this phenomenon; there is a large numerical difference between the number of crimes reported and the number of offenders convicted and facing any specific correctional sanction.

As illustrated in Figure 1.2, of approximately 10 million felony crimes reported in 2000, only about 1 million individuals (10 percent) were convicted, only about 600,000 (6 percent) received a sentence of jail or probation, and only about 400,000 (4 percent of the number of crimes) were sent to prison.[2] The public often believes that adopting a policy of lengthening prison sentences will deter offenders, and that keeping them in prison longer will significantly reduce crime. However, the relatively small number of crimes that results in a sentence

penal code
a legislative authorization to provide a specific range of punishment for a specific crime

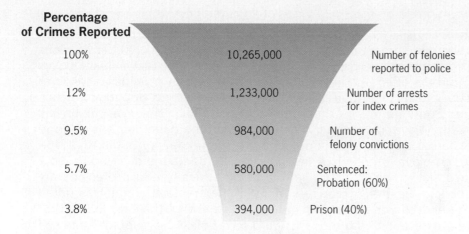

Percentage of Crimes Reported		
100%	10,265,000	Number of felonies reported to police
12%	1,233,000	Number of arrests for index crimes
9.5%	984,000	Number of felony convictions
5.7%	580,000	Sentenced: Probation (60%)
3.8%	394,000	Prison (40%)

Source: Adapted from Bureau of Justice Statistics, *Sourcebook of Criminal Justice Statistics, 2001* (Washington, D.C.: U.S. Department of Justice, 2003); and Matthew R. Durose and Patrick A. Langan, *Felony Sentences in State Courts, 2000* (Washington, D.C.: U.S. Department of Justice, Bureau of Justice Statistics, June 2003). Derived from Gerald Rainville and Brian Reeves, *Felony Defendants in Large Urban Counties, 2000* (Washington, D.C., 2003).

FIGURE 1.2 The Correctional Funnel

of imprisonment makes it unlikely that even major modifications of prison sentences will have a significant impact on crime rates.

The last few sections included a description of the mission of corrections, the role of corrections within the criminal justice system, and a discussion of the correctional funnel. These three topics do not, at first reading, appear to have a common theme among them. However, they all relate to correctional policy development. The development of correctional policy, for discussion purposes in this text, is the process that includes considering the mission and role, relevant information, and the best interests of the public (in terms of issues such as safety and cost), and then deciding what broad approaches to take to best meet the goal of protecting society. The correctional funnel is a good example of how, with thoughtful examination, it can be seen that extending sentences significantly may have a deterrent and incapacitative effect on those in prison. However, since they represent such a small percentage of the overall population that commits crimes, the direct impact on a reduction of crime rates is questionable.

Throughout this textbook, the "A Question of Policy" boxes encourage discussion of some of the difficult policy issues facing public officials and correctional

Your Career in Corrections

Policy Analysts

It may seem odd to start out the "Your Career in Corrections" boxes by describing the job of a policy analyst. Students seldom consider this job, and seldom do they begin a career track to achieve it. However, it is very important to good government that correctional policy be thoughtfully considered with full information regarding cost, effectiveness, and impact. In 2006, American taxpayers contributed $68.7 billion to maintain our correctional system, while much of what we do is not based on such a consideration. This textbook emphasizes the

policy choices that must be made as we reform, modify, and update correctional practices, and policy analysts can play a key role in this process.

A policy analyst who works on correctional issues can work for a variety of agencies. Most state (and some large county) correctional departments have a policy and research bureau. Its job is to conduct research and gather statistics that can assist the agency in making policy decisions, provide justification for funding, and assist in creating future

...continued

strategies and directions for the agency. Legislative bodies always employ policy analysts, and some are assigned to criminal justice or correctional committees. They also conduct research on the effectiveness of correctional programs, usually to aid the legislative body in funding decisions. Some nonprofit agencies employ analysts to examine correctional issues. Groups that are interested in issues such as drug treatment, sentencing, or employment issues for offenders conduct studies to assist in their lobbying efforts to urge that certain policies be implemented. Finally, universities or other research groups often receive grants to conduct correctional research and employ researchers and analysts to examine an issue and write reports as requested by the funding agencies.

There are no reports regarding how many people work in these areas. However, at any one time, easily more than a thousand people are doing the work we have described. Depending on the sophistication of the issue, some will have a doctorate and be experts in research methodology, possibly with some educational emphasis in corrections or criminal justice

research. Many others have a master's degree in sociology, criminal justice, business, or public administration and have skills to develop research and policy analysis criteria to be able to provide answers to questions regarding effectiveness or budget impact.

These jobs are not highly visible, yet can have a tremendous impact on the development of good public policy and save taxpayers millions of dollars. A key criterion for someone desiring to work in this field is to be ethically and professionally grounded. Many of the employing agencies noted above may have an "answer" they are looking for to move forward on a policy they would like to see adopted and only want the analyst to give them evidence to use in their arguments in favor of their preferred policy. However, it is critical for analysts to be above justifying a preferred position, without the true data and information to do so. Research and policy analysis should be unbiased and show the true impact of a program or practice. Truly professional analysts will never short-cut their examination or not cite evidence contrary to their agency's desired outcome.

administrators. Staff that work in corrections to aid in the policy development process are correctional policy analysts. These positions represent interesting and valuable potential jobs for students majoring in criminal justice and corrections. The "Your Career in Corrections" box presents the role of policy analysts.

Why should Students Study Corrections?

The criminal justice system and corrections is a booming business. The number of clients processed and managed by the system continues to climb every year. The amount of money directed to criminal justice agencies has expanded exponentially. The availability of jobs for those seeking a profession in the criminal justice system has increased significantly. And the interest in corrections by the general public and elected officials has grown tremendously. Today, few citizens of the United States do not have some understanding and knowledge of the criminal justice system, and almost everyone has an opinion on how the system should operate or be changed. Crime and corrections have gone through a metamorphosis from an almost invisible public function to one that seems to be on the minds of almost all members of society.

The number of clients under the supervision of correctional agencies has been increasing for the past three decades. The number of offenders on probation, in prison, and on parole has increased significantly. By the end of the twentieth century, more than 6 million offenders were either in prison, in jail, or under supervision in the community. Table 1.1 illustrates the growth from 1980 until 2007, during which there was a 260 percent increase in the number of offenders on probation, a 235 percent increase in the number of offenders in jail, a 211 percent increase in the number of inmates in prison, and a 267 percent increase in the number of offenders on parole.

TABLE 1.1   Correctional Populations

	Number of persons under correctional supervision				
	Probation	Jail	Prison	Parole	Total[a]
1980	1,118,097	183,988	319,598	220,438	1,842,100
1981	1,225,934	196,785	360,029	225,539	2,008,300
1982	1,357,264	209,582	402,914	224,604	2,194,400
1983	1,582,947	223,551	423,898	246,440	2,476,800
1984	1,740,948	234,500	448,264	266,992	2,690,700
1985	1,968,712	256,615	487,593	300,203	3,013,100
1986	2,114,621	274,444	526,436	325,638	3,241,100
1987	2,247,158	295,873	562,814	355,505	3,461,400
1988	2,356,483	343,569	607,766	407,977	3,715,800
1989	2,522,125	395,553	683,367	456,803	4,057,800
1990	2,670,234	405,320	743,382	531,407	4,350,300
1991	2,728,472	426,479	792,535	590,442	4,537,900
1992	2,811,611	444,584	850,566	658,601	4,765,400
1993	2,903,061	459,804	909,381	676,100	4,948,300
1994	2,981,022	486,474	990,147	690,371	5,148,000
1995	3,077,861	507,044	1,078,542	679,421	5,342,900
1996	3,164,996	518,492	1,127,528	679,733	5,490,700
1997	3,296,513	567,079	1,176,564	694,787	5,734,900
1998	3,670,441	592,462	1,224,469	696,385	6,134,200
1999	3,779,922	605,943	1,287,172	714,457	6,340,800
2000	3,826,209	621,149	1,316,333	723,808	6,445,100
2001	3,931,731	631,240	1,330,007	732,333	6,581,700
2002	4,024,067	665,475	1,367,547	750,934	6,758,800
2003[b]	4,120,012	691,301	1,390,279	769,925	6,924,500[b]
2004	4,143,792	713,990	1,421,345	771,852	6,995,000
2005	4,166,757	747,529	1,448,344	780,616	7,051,900
2006[c]	4,215,361	766,010	1,492,973	799,058	7,181,500
2007[d]	4,293,163	780,581	1,512,576	824,365	7,328,200

[a]Because some offenders may have multiple statuses (i.e., held in a prison or jail but remain under the jurisdiction of a probation or parole authority) totals in 2000–04 exclude probationers held in jail or prison; totals in 2005–06 exclude probationers and parolees held in jail or prison; and the total in 2007 excludes probationers and parolees held in jail or prison, probationers who were also under parole supervision, and parolees who were also under probation supervision. For these reasons, details do not sum to total.

[b]The 2003 probation and parole counts were estimated and may differ from previously published numbers.

[c]Illinois did not provide prison or parole data for 2006; therefore, all prison and parole data for Illinois were estimated. See *Methodology* in Prisoners in 2006 (PDF file 308K) and Probation and Parole in the United States, 2006 (PDF file 400K)

[d]Illinois, Maine, and Nevada did not provide prison data for 2007; therefore, all prison data for these states were estimated. See *Methodology* in Prisoners in 2007 (PDF file 195K). Oklahoma did not provide probation or parole data for 2007; therefore, all probation and parole data for Oklahoma were estimated. See *Methodology* in Probation and Parole in the United States, 2007–Statistical Tables (PDF file 355K)

Source: Bureau of Justice Statistics Correctional Surveys (The National Prisoner Statistics Program, Annual Survey of Jails, Annual Probation Survey, and Annual Parole Survey). Found at www.ojp.usdoj.govb/bjs/glance/tables/corr2tab.htm (accessed July 26, 2009).

Number of Adults

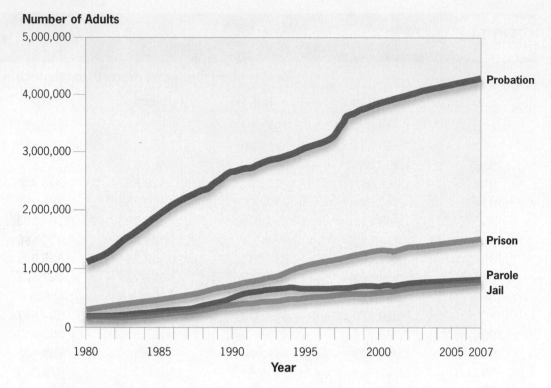

Source: Bureau of Justice Statistics, U.S. Department of Justice, Corrections Facts at a Glance, *The Number of Adults in the Correctional Population Has Been Increasing.* http://www.ojp.usdoj.gov/bjs/glance/corr2.htm (accessed September 15, 2009).

FIGURE 1.3   Adult Correctional Populations, 1980–2008

This growth has been very dramatic over the past five years (see Figure 1.3) and is expected to continue to grow, but at a slower pace, over the next decade. This continued growth in the number of offenders under correctional supervision will generate a comparable growth in the amount of money required to operate correctional agencies.

The Pew Center on the States provides some demographics on who is actually behind bars in the United States.[3] In 2008, 1 in every 100 adults was behind bars. Examine the following chart to see the demographics of the incarcerated population:

Males
White men ages 18 or older—1 in 106
All men ages 18 or older—1 in 54
Hispanic men 18 or older—1 in 36
Black men 18 or older—1 in 15
Black men ages 20–34—1 in 9

Females
White women ages 35–39—1 in 355
Hispanic women ages 35–39—1 in 297
All women ages 35–39—1 in 265
Black women ages 35–39—1 in 100

Source: Pew Center on the States (2008). *One in 100: Behind Bars in America, 2008*, p. 6.

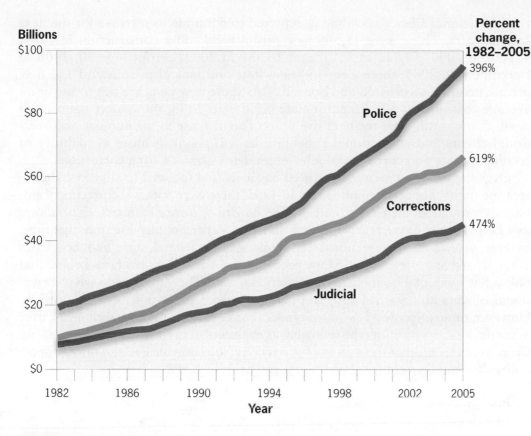

Billions

Percent change, 1982–2005

FIGURE 1.4   Direct Expenditure by Criminal Justice Function, 1982–2005

Source: Bureau of Justice Statistics, U.S. Department of Justice, Expenditure Facts at a Glance, *Direct Expenditures for Each of the Major Criminal Justice Functions (Police, Corrections, Judicial) Has Been Increasing.* http://www.ojp.usdoj.gov/bjs/glance/exptyp.htm (accessed September 15, 2009).

In fiscal year 1991, state and federal adult correctional agency budgets totaled about $40.6 billion. By fiscal year 2006, these budgets more than doubled to $105 billion.[4] Figure 1.4 illustrates the direct expenditure for all criminal justice functions from 1982 through 2005. Spending for police increased 396 percent, and spending for the judiciary increased 474 percent. However, expenditures for corrections increased 619 percent, far exceeding the increase in police and judicial spending. It is interesting to note the factors driving the increase in overall spending for adult correctional agencies. Inflation and increases in employee salaries and benefits cause some of the budget increase. During the period of 1990 to 2007, the inmate population for these agencies increased nearly 100 percent; from 1,148,702 to 2,293,157.[5] The increase in demand for services (housing more inmates) has almost entirely triggered the increased costs.

Just as budgets for prison operations have increased, the budgets for probation and parole functions have also increased. The average budget for state probation and parole agencies more than doubled from $34.3 million in 1992 to $82.9 million in 2002, and it is estimated that over $9 billion will be spent to supervise offenders in the community 2007.[6] In 2007, these state agencies supervised 5.12 million offenders on probation or parole[7] at an average cost per day of community supervision of $3.42 for 2008.[8] These average costs include regular probation and parole supervision, intensive supervision with more contacts by the officer with the offender than regular probation, special supervision with programs such as a boot camp, substance abuse treatment, and electronic monitoring of offenders using such devices as an ankle bracelet or some other electronic technology used to determine the offenders' whereabouts.

Correctional agency spending is expected to continue to increase for the next several years. There were 41,368 new prison beds under construction in 1999, 47,476 in 2000, 58,422 in 2001, and 26,869 in 2002.[9] From June 30, 2000 to December 30, 2005, there were 153 new state and federal prisons and 151 new private prisons constructed and opened.[10] As these new beds are put to use at an average cost of over $78.95 per inmate per day in 2008, the budget figures will climb dramatically over the next five years. The increase in the number of correctional clients and correctional expenditures will result in more availability of criminal justice and correctional jobs for students now studying corrections.

Over the past two decades, the need has increased for staff to supervise the increasing number of criminal offenders. In 1992, there were 556,500 correctional employees throughout the United States.[11] The *Bureau of Justice Statistics, Expenditure and Employment Extracts 2005* reports almost a 36 percent increase since that time, as there were 755,239 correctional staff working at the federal, state, and local levels in the United States in 2005.[12] Many people unfamiliar with corrections believe that only a few types of jobs are held by correctional staff. They understand what correctional officers and wardens do, and perhaps even a probation or parole officer. However, those are only a few of the types of jobs available to those seeking a career in corrections. Spertzel lists the following as examples of correctional jobs.[13] It is obvious from this list that the variety of correctional jobs is extensive and offers opportunities for employment for students in many fields of study.

> Budget administrator
> Chaplain
> Computer specialist
> Correctional officer
> Employee development specialist
> Facility manager
> Financial manager
> Food service manager
> Health system administrator
> Industrial specialist
> Institution administrator
> Juvenile caseworker
> Medical officer
> Ombudsman
> Personnel manager
> Probation/parole officer
> Psychologist
> Recreation specialist
> Safety manager
> Teacher
> Training instructor

mycrimekit

Media—Video: Career Opportunities.

Citizens and elected officials continue to increase their interest in and oversight of the criminal justice and correctional systems. Much of this is due to the misperception that crime is increasing. From 1991 to 2007, crime decreased significantly. The violent crime rate per 100,000 citizens in 1991 was 758.2 and the property crime rate was 5,140.2, whereas in 2007 the violent crime rate was 466.9 and the property crime rate was 3,263.5. This represents a drop in the violent crime rate of about 38 percent and a drop in the property crime rate of nearly 36 percent from 1991 to 2007.[14] However, thanks to continuous media coverage of crime and criminals, when citizens were asked in polls conducted over the past

TABLE 1.2	Attitudes Toward the Crime Level in the United States: Selected Years, 1989–2007

Gallup Polling Question: "Is There More Crime in the U.S. Than There Was a Year Ago, or Less?"

	More (%)	Less (%)	Same (volume) (%)	No Opinion (%)
2007	71	14	8	6
2006	68	16	8	8
2005	67	21	9	3
2004	53	28	14	5
2003	60	25	11	4
2002	62	21	11	6
2001	41	43	10	6
2000	47	41	7	5
1998	52	35	8	5
1997	64	25	6	5
1996	71	15	8	6
1993	87	4	5	4
1992	89	3	4	4
1990	84	3	7	6
1989	84	5	5	6

Source: The Gallup Organization, *The Gallup Poll* (*Online*). http://www.gallup.com/pol/indicators/indcrime.asp.2 (accessed March 15, 2009).

ten years whether there is more crime in the United States now than one year ago, they indicated a belief that crime is increasing (see Table 1.2).

Because of citizens' general concern about crime, public officials will continue to legislate or regulate responses to the perceived crime problem. They will expand penalties for offenders, increase the numbers of police, and authorize more money to be spent by the criminal justice system. This increased activity results in increased visibility for criminal justice agencies. As crime and corrections remain on the minds of the public and their elected officials, and there are demands to improve the system and find new ways of operating, those who work in the field will have to create new paradigms to make the system more efficient and enhance the level of support from the citizens whose tax dollars support it.

The question of why we should study corrections makes me recall my own career in corrections. Every chapter of this textbook contains a box titled "An Insider's Experience," in which students get a firsthand look at issues that I had to confront while working in correctional institutions and settings for more than twenty years. The first "An Insider's Experience" located in *MyCrimeKit* is an overview of this career, with some hindsight on things that relate to why we should study corrections. As you read later features on this topic, you will better understand the jobs I had and the issues I faced.

mycrimekit

Insider's Experience: Twenty-Five Years of Correctional Work

Theories of Crime and Punishment

To begin a study of corrections and its historical development, it is important to understand the evolution of theories of crime and its causes. If the purpose of the punishment is to "correct," the punishment must adequately match the reasons

Cesare Beccaria
an Italian theorist who in the eighteenth century first suggested linking crime causation to punishments and became known as the founder of the Classical School of criminology

Classical School
the theory linking crime causation to punishment, based on offenders' free will and hedonism

Jeremy Bentham
creator of the hedonistic calculus suggesting that punishments outweigh the pleasure criminals get from committing their crime

hedonistic calculus
the idea that the main objective of an intelligent person is to achieve the most pleasure and the least pain and that individuals are constantly calculating the pluses and minuses of their potential actions

why the person committed the crime. There has been considerable thinking and speculation regarding crime and the response to it over the years. Many authors note the contribution of the French thinkers Montesquieu and Voltaire for encouraging thinking about crime and the then-brutal response to it.[15] However, **Cesare Beccaria,** an Italian theorist, first suggested linking crime causation to punishments in the eighteenth century, and his 1764 book *An Essay on Crimes and Punishments* is often credited as the driving force in shaping contemporary thinking about crime and corrections.

Beccaria is known as the founder of the **Classical School** of criminology, the first organized theory of crime causation linked to appropriate punishments. Beccaria suggested that the purpose of punishment is utility, or the prevention of crime. Included in his principles are that crime is an injury to society, that prevention (deterrence of crime) is more important than punishment, that the accused have the right to speedy trials and humane treatment, that there should be no secret accusations or torture, that certainty and swiftness of punishment (more than severity) best deter crime, and that imprisonment should be more widely used as a punishment.

Underlying Beccaria's principles was an emphasis on free will and hedonism. For punishment to deter, individuals must have freedom to choose their actions of committing crime or not. As well, they would judge the impact of the punishment on their own well-being and make a choice regarding the seeking of pleasure and avoidance of pain (hedonism). Building on these principles, **Jeremy Bentham** (1748–1832) created the concept of **hedonistic calculus,** the idea that the main objective of an intelligent man is to achieve the most pleasure and the least pain and that individuals are constantly calculating the pluses and minuses of their

Jeremy Bentham. Courtesy of Hilton Archive/Getty Images.

Cesare Lombroso. ©Bettmann/
CORBIS. All rights reserved.

potential actions, Bentham therefore theorized that to prevent crime criminal laws should be organized so that the punishment for any act would outweigh the pleasure that would be derived from the act. Potential offenders would therefore (in line with the Classical School idea of free will) consider the consequences of their actions and be deterred from the commission of crimes.

In reaction to the development of the Classical School emphasizing free will, others began to suggest that not every criminal has complete choice over his or her criminal actions. The **Positive School** was created by **Cesare Lombroso** (1835–1909), with the suggestion that people sometimes commit acts beyond their control. Lombroso, an Italian physician, conducted research into the links between criminality and physical traits. He concluded that criminals had traits that made them throwbacks to earlier stages of evolution: they were not sufficiently developed mentally and had long arms, large amounts of body hair, prominent cheekbones, and large foreheads. This **atavism,** or the existence of features common in the early stages of human evolution, implied that criminals are born, and criminal behavior is *predetermined.*

While several later tests failed to prove Lombroso's theories of atavism, some still support the idea that some factors result in a level of predetermination (not total free will) that influences the chance that someone will commit crimes. Proponents of this approach cite the early works by Dugsdale and by Goddard suggesting that there are "criminal families" with a high number of members involved in crime, indicating the possibility of bad genetic influences;[16] the identification by Sheldon of certain body types that are most prone to aggression and violence;[17] or several studies addressing the possibility that chemical imbalances in the body contribute to crime.[18]

Positive School
the belief that criminals do not have complete choice over their criminal actions and may commit acts that are beyond their control

Cesare Lombroso
the Italian physician who in the nineteenth century founded the Positive School

atavism
the existence of features common in the early stages of human evolution, implied the idea that criminals are born, and criminal behavior is *predetermined*

A more recent theory that has developed somewhat as a compromise to the Classical and Positive Schools is the **Neoclassical School** of criminology. Suggested by Gabriel Tarde in 1890, the Neoclassical School recognized there was much ground between total free will and determinism. Tarde argued that no one has complete free will and is uninfluenced by factors such as gender, age, or social and economic environments, yet everyone is still the "author" of his or her own action.[19] The key factors are that, although the Classical School approach to holding offenders accountable makes sense, there should be some consideration of mitigating and aggravating circumstances in consideration of the criminal activities of any individual. Some authors suggest that the current "get tough" philosophies and transition to determinate sentences are most illustrative of the Neoclassical School in practice today.[20]

Modern theories seem to include a variety of factors that influence people toward criminal behavior. Several theories address the importance of psychological and social factors in determining criminality.[21] Today, however, policy regarding how to punish criminals most often follows the Classical School, emphasizing free will. It is generally believed that offenders must be held accountable and receive just punishments for their crimes. The underlying concept behind this approach is that offenders choose to commit crimes and that punishments must be dire enough to make them consider the result (in both pleasure and pain) of their criminal behavior.

Early Responses to Crime

The types of public responses to crime varied based on the beliefs regarding the causes of crime. The earliest responses to crime were extremely brutal and included torture, beatings, branding, and mutilation. These corporal punishments were often an attempt to relate the punishment as closely as possible to the crime. For instance, liars had their tongues ripped out, thieves had fingers or a hand cut off, and adulterers had a scarlet A branded on their foreheads to reduce their attractiveness and discourage any further adultery. Besides corporal punishment, removing the offender from the group was regularly used. Banishing someone from the tribe into the wilderness not only resulted in no likelihood of a repeat of the offense, but also often resulted in death, because the person could not survive alone in the wilderness. Another way to remove offenders from society was through **transportation** or deportation. Transportation started in England and was used throughout the seventeenth and eighteenth centuries to send undesirables to the colonies in America.

The first response to crime in the American colonies was based on the English criminal codes and incorporated the Puritans' linking of crime with sin in developing a rigid and strict system of punishments. Violations of expected community behavior were dealt with severely, using corporal and capital punishment carried out in public to deter both individual offenders and the broader community. Whipping at the town center whipping post or placement in stocks and pillories was common punishment for minor offenses such as drunkenness, slander, or stealing something of minor value. *Pillories* were wooden frames with holes for offenders' hands and head. Offenders had to stand while their hands and head were secured. *Stocks*, similar to pillories, allowed offenders to sit while their hands, head, and feet were all secured in the wooden frame. These punishments were not just for ridicule, as passersby often threw rotten vegetables or even rocks at the offender to aid in the punishment.

Historical punishments were both painful and shameful. Stocks and pillories were used both as physical punishment and to ridicule offenders in front of their fellow townspeople, in the hopes that they would end their criminal ways. Courtesy of Corbis/Bettmann.

Branding was also a popular way to punish offenders; the forehead, face, or hands would be branded, labeling the offender as a certain type of criminal. Adulterers had the letter A carved into their foreheads; thieves had a T carved on their hands; blasphemers were stamped with a B, or perhaps had a hole drilled in their tongues. Torture could also include cutting off a hand or finger of thieves or pickpockets; placing gossips in a *brank*, similar to a birdcage placed over their head with a sharpened shaft with barbs placed in their mouths; or subjecting other minor violators to the *ducking stool*, in which they were lowered underwater until they almost drowned. More serious offenses resulted in brutal torture, such as stretching and breaking the offender's body on the rack, or in capital punishment by hanging or burning at the stake.

In colonial times, prisons were not yet developed as punishment for crimes. The colonists did use jails, copying the English system of *gaols*, for holding defendants awaiting trial or those already convicted and waiting for their corporal or capital punishment to be carried out. These jails had deplorable conditions, in which poor men, women, and children all lived together in filth, with little food or sanitary conditions. Offenders who could afford it could avoid jail via the *fee system*, an early bail system that enabled the rich to pay a fee and be released. The conditions in both English and colonial jails during the 1600s and 1700s was so deplorable that few doubted the need for reform.

The most famous jail reformer was **John Howard,** who was the sheriff of Bedfordshire, England. Howard himself, while on an English ship, was taken captive by a French privateer and subsequently imprisoned. He was later paroled to England, but never forgot the horrendous conditions resulting in the death of several English prisoners. Once he became sheriff, he was responsible for the operation of the jail and was disturbed over the conditions and the fact that some people were there for weeks because they were unable to pay the fee required for

John Howard
the sheriff of Bedfordshire, England, who encouraged reform of English jails in the late 1700s

John Howard (1726–1790) was one of the earliest prison and jail reformers. He was appointed sheriff of Bedfordshire in 1773 and pushed for the passage of the English Penitentiary Act of 1779 to require minimum standards for jail conditions. Courtesy of the American Correctional Association.

release. He encouraged legislation to do away with the fee system and became a reformer, visiting gaols throughout England to observe conditions. In 1777, he wrote *The State of the Prisons in England and Wales,* which educated the public and Parliament to the problem. As a result, Parliament passed the Penitentiary Act in 1779, providing for "secure and sanitary structures, systematic inspections,

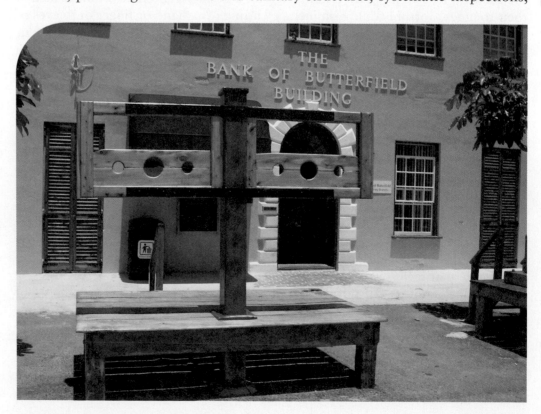

This replica of a pillory is in St. George, Bermuda. Photo by Richard P. Seiter.

abolition of fees for basic services, and a reformatory regime."[22] Howard coined the term *penitentiary* to emphasize the purpose of offenders doing penance while reflecting on their sins, rather than simply being punished brutally. These ideas not only had an effect on gaols in England, but also influenced the development of penitentiaries in the United States.

The Development of the Prison

As a result of the brutality and extensive use of corporal and capital punishment, some were dissatisfied with these methods of responding to criminal behavior. One reform-minded individual was William Penn, the governor of Pennsylvania. The Quakers, who settled Pennsylvania, were hardworking and economical people. They realized that the criminal codes were both inhumane and inefficient in that judges often did not follow the criminal codes because they did not want to inflict more severe punishments on relatively minor offenders. The Quakers had also been the victims of religious persecution, and freedom to choose their way of life was the reason they came to America and settled the Pennsylvania colony. Under the leadership of Penn, the Quakers replaced the current criminal code with a new one that included the following:

- The abolition of capital punishment for all crimes other than homicide
- The substitution of imprisonment at hard labor for bloody corporal punishments
- The provision of free food and lodging to inmates
- The replacement of the stocks and pillory with houses of detention[23]

The Walnut Street Jail

In the late 1700s, Dr. Benjamin Rush (one of the original signers of the Declaration of Independence) became leader of the Philadelphia Society for Alleviating the Miseries of the Public Prisons. He revived the Quaker code, which had been repealed when Penn died in 1718, and the Philadelphia Society established the first prison in the United States in 1790 by converting a wing of the Walnut Street Jail for use in housing sentenced offenders as an alternative to corporal punishment. As in John Howard's concept of the penitentiary, the **Walnut Street Jail** created a regimen of hard work and doing penance for their offenses.

Inmates were kept in individual cells and had to remain silent in order to avoid moral contamination among prisoners. Administrators of the jail did not want prisoners to even know the identity of other inmates and often put masks on inmates as they moved through the prison to avoid identification that would detract from the reform of prisoners in case they met each other after release. Prisoners were given work such as making handicrafts in their cells during the day, and were encouraged to read the Bible and do penance in the evenings. The overall operating theme was one of hard labor, strict discipline, solitary and silent confinement, and religious study.

Walnut Street Jail
the first penitentiary in the United States

The Pennsylvania System

When the state of Pennsylvania opened its first two prisons (the Western State Penitentiary in Pittsburgh in 1826 and the Eastern State Penitentiary in Cherry Hill just outside Philadelphia in 1829), the Walnut Street Jail served as the model

This hallway in the Eastern State Penitentiary shows the solid doors that prevented inmates from seeing other inmates as they moved through the hallway. Photo by Mary Nienaber Foster.

Pennsylvania system

the "separate and silent" system of prison operations emphasizing reformation and avoidance of criminal contamination

for their design and operation. The Western Penitentiary was an architectural nightmare, built in an octagon with small, dark cells inside the cellblocks to provide solitary confinement and no labor. It was soon modified in 1833 to provide cells on the outside of the blocks to allow light in through windows and increased cell size to allow for inmate labor within the cell. The mistakes of the Western Penitentiary influenced and improved the design of the Eastern Penitentiary, built with seven cellblocks extending from a hub in the center of the prison walls. Each cellblock was long and narrow, with cells on the outside and a corridor down the middle. The cells had a door through the wall into a small recreation yard, in which prisoners had brief exercise periods by themselves each day.

The basis of these two prisons' operation was the same as the Walnut Street Jail: to emphasize the opportunity for prisoners to reform themselves through hard work while reflecting on their crimes. The **Pennsylvania system** was known as the "separate and silent" system, with silence enforced and inmates not allowed to see or talk with each other. Through this approach, it was believed that offenders would not be morally contaminated and be trained in crime by other prisoners. There were several problems with the Pennsylvania system. First, it was almost impossible to keep inmates from seeing and communicating with each other. Second, it was very expensive to operate, as the requirement to keep inmates separate increased the number of staff needed. Third, there was very limited productivity by inmates, as the requirement to work alone in their cells did not allow for as much production of goods for resale as was desired. Fourth, opponents of the operation of the Pennsylvania prisons suggested that the solitude imposed on inmates made many of them mentally ill. Finally, the planned operation was modified almost immediately. Two inmates were placed in a cell together so one could learn a trade from the other and increase the production of goods. The warden of the Eastern Penitentiary, Samuel Wood, used inmates as servants in his home and allowed them to communicate. The Pennsylvania system seemed doomed from its beginning and forced prison operators in other states to search for new approaches to overcome the problems. Although there was great interest in the Pennsylvania system, only two states (New Jersey and Rhode Island) adopted its "separate and silent" system. However, both soon abandoned the Pennsylvania system in favor of the improved system that was created in Auburn, New York.

The Auburn System

New York opened a prison in Auburn in 1817 that was originally designed around the Pennsylvania model. Cells were back to back and stacked five tiers high to make it easier to keep inmates separate. However, this design did not allow for the use of individual recreation yards, as did the Eastern Penitentiary. The Auburn prison originally adopted the "separate and silent" system of Pennsylvania, but soon determined that the problems that plagued Pennsylvania were too serious to overcome. In 1823, a modification of the prison began, to change its unwieldy design and make it more efficient to operate.

The major change was in the Pennsylvania emphasis on keeping inmates separate. Auburn officials determined that they would continue to keep inmates in separate cells at night; however, they would allow them to congregate during the day to work in factories to improve the production of goods, which would be resold to cover some of the prison operational costs. The **Auburn system** became known as the "congregate and silent" system, as officials continued to reduce the spread of criminal ideas by inmates through silence and strict discipline. Barnes and Teeters describe the enforcement of the system through lockstep marching with eyes downcast, hard work and activity while outside cells, and prohibitions of inmates even being face to face.[24]

After the operation of Auburn was copied at Sing Sing prison in New York, as well as at prisons in other states, the Auburn system was recognized as better than the Pennsylvania system. The prisons were cheaper to build and operate, the congregate style allowed production of goods and more income for the state, and fewer inmates developed mental health problems. Other prisons being built across the country adopted the Auburn system. The operation of prisons for sentenced offenders received international attention, and many countries sent representatives to examine the operation of both the Pennsylvania-style and Auburn-style prisons. Although the Pennsylvania style of prisons was seldom favored in the United States, most international visitors found advantages in both, and many preferred the Pennsylvania system because of its effort to avoid contamination among prisoners. During the first half of the nineteenth century, the Auburn style of silence, hard labor, separation at night, congregation during the day to maximize production of goods, and strict discipline was the approach used for most American prisons.

Auburn system
the congregate and silent operation of prisons, in which inmates were allowed to work together during the day, but had to stay separate and silent at other times

Prisons Throughout the Last Two Centuries

During the first half of the 1800s, several large prisons were built and operated on the Auburn model. However, driven by a need to respond to the overcrowding of prisons by building new ones, U.S. prison administrators began to look for

During the Reformatory Era, prisons were often built using imposing "gothic" style architecture, to remind inmates of their need to reform their ways.

Courtesy of the Ohio Department of Rehabilitation and Correction.

reform and watched the early work of Captain Alexander Maconochie, who in 1840 took over the British penal colony on Norfolk Island, and Sir Walter Crofton, who built on the ideas of Maconochie as head of the Irish penal system. These two men used the concept of indeterminate sentencing, emphasizing preparing offenders for release, giving inmates an opportunity to gradually reduce control and work their way to a less restricted environment, and releasing offenders on a conditional basis when administrators determined that they were prepared to return to the community (the first effort to have conditional release, which led to the development of parole). This operation of the **Irish system** was seen as more humanitarian, placing an emphasis on training and preparation for release, and was believed to do more to return offenders to the community with a greater chance for success.

In 1870, a group of prison administrators, politicians, and interested citizens met in Cincinnati and formed the National Prison Association, now known as the American Correctional Association. They adopted the principles of the Irish system, emphasizing reformation rather than suffering, rewards for good behavior, and the use of indeterminate sentences to release prisoners when they were best prepared to become industrious free citizens.[25] At this point, corrections entered the **Reformatory Era,** which lasted from 1870 to 1910. To replace the emphasis on punishment and reflection on the past as with the Auburn system, the Reformatory Era provided an environment that expanded education and vocational programs and focused offenders' attention on their future.

As sensible as the Reformatory Era seemed, tremendous growth in the U.S. prison population forced another change after the turn of the century. During the first three decades of the twentieth century, the number of inmates in U.S. prisons grew more than 170 percent,[26] resulting in the construction of several new prisons designed to hold large numbers of inmates in harsh work-oriented environments. The emphasis was on having inmates work and produce products that could help make the prisons economically self-supporting. Using their free labor, prisons became very successful at this, prison management emphasized production as much as security and rehabilitation, and the volume of prison-made products sold on the open market increased considerably. Thus the **Industrial Prison Era,** from 1910 to 1935, led to the first major interest in the management of prisons by external parties.

Irish system

a four-stage system of graduated release from prison and return to the community; the stages were solitary confinement, special prison, open institutions, and ticket of leave

Reformatory Era

an environment emphasizing reformation that expanded education and vocational programs and focused offenders' attention on their future

Industrial Prison Era

prison operations with emphasis on having inmates work and produce products that could help to make the prisons self-sustaining

Prisons built and operated in the first part of the 1900s were designed to hold large numbers of inmates, in tiers of cells stacked one on top of another.
Courtesy of the Federal Bureau of Prisons.

The production and sale of prison-made products resulted in challenges to these practices from organized labor. As the country entered the Great Depression with the crash on Wall Street in 1929, Congress passed two laws to restrict competition from inmate-made goods with the private sector. The Hawes–Cooper Act in 1929 and the Ashurst–Sumners Act in 1935, amended in 1940, severely limited the sale of prison-made products on the open market. These statutes tolled the death knell for industrial prisons, which suddenly had no marketplace for their goods. Thousands of inmates who had previously been working were idled, and prison administrators had to find another approach to operating prisons.

From 1935 until 1960, corrections entered the **Period of Transition,** during which enforced idleness, a lack of professional programs, and the excessive size and overcrowding of prisons resulted in an increase in prisoner discontent and prison riots. Between 1950 and 1966, more than one hundred riots and major disturbances occurred in U.S. prisons.[27] Prison managers were constrained in what they could do with the large facilities designed to maximize production they had inherited, and they struggled to find alternative approaches to maintain control of large concentrations of idle prisoners. This era was greatly affected when the U.S. Supreme Court decided *Cooper v. Pate* (1964) and ended its **hands-off doctrine,** which had restricted judicial intervention in the operations of prisons and the judgment of correctional administrators. By accepting inmate-filed cases alleging cruel and inhumane punishment under the Fourteenth Amendment to the U.S. Constitution, the Court opened Pandora's box, and federal courts were flooded with requests by inmates to improve the conditions in most prisons.

Resulting reforms included the professionalizing of staff through recruitment and training and implementation of many self-improvement programs to take the place of the industrial work programs, ushering in the **Rehabilitative Era** (1960–1980). In the early 1960s, corrections adopted what was called the **medical model,** which became the dominant theory influencing prison and other correctional practices. Under the medical model, offenders were believed to be "sick," inflicted with problems that caused their criminality; they needed to be diagnosed and treated, and rehabilitative programs would resolve their problems and prepare them for release as "well" into the community, able to be productive and crime-free.

Period of Transition
an era of prison operations in which enforced idleness, lack of professional programs, and excessive size and overcrowding of prisons resulted in an increase in prisoner discontent and prison riots

hands-off doctrine
an avoidance by the U.S. Supreme Court of judicial intervention in the operations of prisons and the judgment of correctional administrators

Rehabilitative Era
an era of prison management emphasizing the professionalizing of staff through recruitment and training and implementation of many self-improvement programs of prison management

medical model
a theory of corrections that offenders were sick, inflicted with problems that caused their criminality, and needed to be diagnosed and treated, and that rehabilitative programs would resolve offenders' problems and prepare them for release into the community able to be productive and crime-free

reintegration

a belief that after offenders complete their treatment in prison they need transitional care, and that the community must be involved in their successful return to society

A minor "adjustment" to the medical model was the recognition of the need to strengthen the links between prisons and the community. **Reintegration** was added to the emphasis on rehabilitation. After offenders completed their treatment in prison, they needed transitional care. Reintegration includes the community in the medical model, with recognition that the transition from prison to free citizen is difficult. Community correctional programs were expanded, and halfway houses and special parole programs became important elements in the correctional process.

The medical model came under attack during the 1970s. In the early 1970s, Robert Martinson and his colleagues completed a review of correctional research to determine "what worked."[28] In the review of more than two hundred studies, the researchers concluded that, although there were a few isolated correlations between a treatment program and a reduction in recidivism, no consistent findings indicated that any single treatment program significantly reduced recidivism. Therefore, the Martinson review concluded that **"nothing works."** For public officials looking for a way to reduce costs and make corrections more punitive, this study provided statistical support and was the death knell for the medical model. Rehabilitative programs lost funding, and parole was eliminated in several states.

"nothing works"

a conclusion by Robert Martinson that no correctional treatment program reduces recidivism; it effectively spelled the end to the medical model

With the increase in crime, especially violent crimes, over much of the 1980s, crime and corrections became very important to the public and elected officials. Throughout the 1980s and 1990s, constant media coverage of violent crime created fear and anger toward the crime issue. Political rhetoric emphasized holding offenders accountable for their acts, and the current **Retributive Era** came into being, emphasizing the need to be tough on criminals while keeping them isolated from law-abiding citizens and making them serve "hard" time. With this model, correctional sanctions are tough, offer few amenities, and emphasize public safety over all else. The Retributive Era is also a return to the Classical School of criminality, in which offenders have free choice to commit their crimes, and a response of lengthening and toughening punishments is believed to deter and prevent crime.

Retributive Era

an era of corrections that emphasizes holding offenders accountable for their acts and being tough on criminals while keeping them isolated from law-abiding citizens and making them serve "hard" time

During the Retributive Era, some prisons and jails returned to making inmates wear stripes, a tradition that goes back to the 1800s. Although the argument was for security in case of escape, the real reason was to punish inmates in every way legally allowable.

Courtesy of the Maricopa County (Arizona) Sheriff.

A Look Into...

Prison Reforms through the Twentieth Century

T. Don Hutto is a legend in prison administration and reform from the 1960s through the 1990s. He started as a correctional officer in Texas in 1964, and three years later was the warden of the Ramsey Unit, one of the largest Texas prisons. At the age of 36, he became director of the Arkansas Department of Corrections, just after the incidents around its operation led to the movie *Brubaker*. Hutto moved to reform both the Ramsey Unit and the Arkansas prison system, ending racial segregation and the use of building tenders (inmates who acted as armed guards over other inmates). He also dealt with reforms needed to move Arkansas from the unconstitutional system it was found to be in *Holt v. Sarver*. The following is a segment of a speech Hutto gave to the North American Wardens and Superintendents Association in Memphis, Tennessee on April 10, 2009.

For as long as they have existed, prisons have reflected (although not always accurately) the culture in which they were spawned. Over a period of time, we have coined the term "corrections" to describe the broad process of carrying out the decisions of the courts in a manner which seems to best serve society's interests.

Spanning the generations in our profession, the metamorphosis of terminology has been agonizingly slow, often amusing, and sometimes painful, but the terminology itself has changed far more rapidly than have the actual practices. As too often happens in other endeavors, when we don't know exactly what we ought to be doing or how, we simply change the names. The term "penal," as in "penal system," survived for generations as did its namesake, "penitentiary," which was derived from the word "penitent," based on the vain hope that given enough time and solitude, the offender would somehow see the error of his or her ways (repent, if you will) and be fit to become a law-abiding member of society. In a cultural effort to find an acceptable name for what would preferably be "out of sight and out of mind," we tried "workhouse," "debtors' prison," "prison," "penitentiary," "colony," "camp," "farm," "institution," "center," "facility," and just plain "house." Meanwhile, we were busy redefining our charges as "convicts," "prisoners," "inmates," "offenders," "detainees," "residents," "patients," and even "students."

And, oh yes! We were at various times in the business of "reform," "rehabilitation," *"punishment," "incarceration," "treatment," and of course, "reintegration." "Reform" has been a buzzword regarding prisons and corrections for as long as I, and probably any of you, can remember. The New Oxford American Dictionary says that reform means to "make changes in order to improve something." "Reform" is a useful catchword, as, according to someone or some group, just about every societal or cultural institution, needs to be "reformed." Today, the word "change" is more in vogue but "change" means making something different, not necessarily better. The term "change" is neutral and can be either positive or negative. Transform, on the other hand, means to make a thorough or dramatic change, and the radical changes which have taken place in Southern corrections in the last fifty years suggest that "transformed" is the word that applies, but for convenience sake, I will talk about "positive change."*

I mentioned earlier that prisons developed as reflections of the culture in which they existed. Southern prisons certainly fit that pattern. With a few exceptions, the South was an agrarian society, deeply rooted in the plantation and slavery mentality. The large plantation-like prisons which developed in rural areas, particularly in Alabama, Mississippi, Texas, Louisiana, Arkansas and to a lesser extent Oklahoma, Georgia and Virginia, were logical extensions of the prevailing civilization and culture. West Virginia and Kentucky, recognized as border-states during the Civil War, were, in fact more akin to their neighbors, Pennsylvania and Ohio and developed accordingly. The coastal states of North Carolina and South Carolina were influenced heavily by the Piedmont and Appalachian mores and traditions. Florida, with two-thirds of its border being coastline, developed somewhat different traditions. So, when we speak of The South, we are not speaking of one cohesive entity. Nevertheless, it is fair to say that Southern prisons had a tendency to develop along the lines of plantation prisons or roadwork stations known for their "chain" gangs, and these usually widely scattered road station locations were anchored by one or more larger "penitentiaries." Virginia provides an example of a state which developed a combination; road stations, large farms and a penitentiary.

Up until the nineteen seventies, not much changed.

The Sentencing Goals of Corrections

The sentencing goals of corrections are punishment, deterrence, incapacitation, rehabilitation, and restitution. As one might imagine, it is very difficult to attempt these seemingly conflicting goals at the same time. Can corrections punish at the same time as it rehabilitates? Can prisons incapacitate offenders and at the same time try to get them to repay the victim or society for the damage they have done? Even though correctional officials may admit that these conflicting demands create a management challenge, society continues to expect corrections to pursue all five of these goals.

Punishment

punishment

the correctional goal
emphasizing the infliction of
pain or suffering

Although different correctional goals have been emphasized in varying degrees over time, the most dominant correctional goal has historically been **punishment,** the infliction of pain or suffering. As a society, we believe that punishment for inappropriate behavior is not only allowable, but also advisable. We use punishment to teach children right from wrong. We believe that punishment helps maintain moral order, with the focus on society rather than on the individual who committed the crime. Criminal offenders are brought to justice by the state, acting for society. Through punishment, society can maintain order and show fairness to those who do not violate the law. Some think of the role of punishment within society as a catharsis, a way for society to feel good about the punishment of offenders. People need to see that those who demonstrate inappropriate behavior receive their "just deserts," or what is coming to them.

retribution

infliction of punishment on
those who deserve to be
punished

Punishment for criminal acts is sometimes referred to as **retribution,** which implies the infliction of punishment on those who deserve to be punished. The idea of *lex talionis* (Latin for "law of retribution") is similar to the biblical adage of "an eye for an eye" and indicates that offenders get the punishment they deserve. The idea of punishment and retribution is primarily focused on the past, in that it is in exchange for the commission of a criminal violation. However, it is closely linked to more future-oriented correctional goals, such as deterrence or rehabilitation. Punishment is necessary for deterrence, and the presence of punishment encourages rehabilitation. Punishment is also reactive in that it focuses on the act or crime, rather than on the offender's particular circumstances or needs. Society believes that it is only fair and just that criminal offenders receive punishment for their crimes.

A good example of an approach to implement the "retributive" goal of corrections along with a public support for "getting tough on crime and criminals" is the following interview with Sheriff Joe Arpaio of Maricopa County (Phoenix), Arizona.

An Interview With...

The Toughest Sheriff in America

Maricopa County (Arizona) Sheriff Joe Arpaio touts himself as the "toughest sheriff in America." He was first elected and assumed the office of Sheriff in 1993 and has managed his jail to earn his reputation. He believes that inmates' jail experiences should not be something they enjoy, but something unpleasant enough that they do not want to come back.

...continued

Some of what he does is extremely controversial, such as housing inmates in tents even during hot Arizona summers, serving only one hot meal a day, and requiring them to wear pink underwear. Although prisoner support groups complain about his tactics, many conservatives cite his methods as right on target. The sheriff believes this is the right way to run a jail and that he is doing what his constituents want. In the following interview, the sheriff describes some of his approaches and the reasons he uses them.

Question: Sheriff, can you describe your background and how you created the jail management approach you use?

Sheriff Arpaio: Before becoming sheriff, I had no previous experience in corrections. I was a cop in Washington, D.C. and Las Vegas and worked for over 25 years for the U.S. Drug Enforcement Agency (DEA). With the DEA, I worked in Mexico, South America, and Turkey and saw how tough and unpleasant the jails were in those countries. I retired from the DEA in 1982, spent ten years in private business, and then ran for Sheriff. I had no predetermined notions about running a jail before, but just decided to put up tents because we needed to have plenty of beds so that we had room to lock up people. We called these CONtents, short for "convict tents."

Question: What other "get tough" things did you do?

Sheriff Arpaio: I did away with smoking by inmates. I couldn't see allowing inmates to smoke and having our officers have to breathe their sidestream smoke. I cut the number of sick calls by 32 percent as a result. I took coffee away from inmates and saved $100,000 per year. I did not allow inmates to watch R-rated movies and did not allow *Playboy* or *Hustler* magazines. The pink underwear idea was not to embarrass inmates, but because they were stealing socks and underwear. By dying it pink, they did not steal it. When people heard about it, everyone wanted to buy pink underwear, so we started making pink underwear with my badge and name and raised money for our volunteer posse

and to fight crime. We started a chain gang to make inmates work and do public service.

Question: What do you do next?

Sheriff Arpaio: I am running out of ideas. Our jail population is growing. We now have 10,700 inmates and are the second largest jail system in the country. We opened our Tent City in 1993 and have since expanded. We have more than 2500 inmates living in tents now. We do many of the things we do for cost efficiency. We went to two meals per day, a brunch and an evening dinner. We serve cold baloney sandwiches for some meals. Our meal costs are only 14 or 15 cents per meal.

We did recently take all radios away from inmates. We don't want them listening to certain music or radio shows, but want them to listen to the things that are educational or religious in nature. We are rebuilding our jail radio station, K-JOE, where we can control the programming and music. We will do some fun things on it, like have Inmate Idol rather than American Idol; it will be a real CONtest.

We put inmates in striped uniforms and issue them pink underwear. We also started female chain gangs for the same reason as the male chain gangs. Women inmates were violating my policies, so this was a way to punish them, but give them a chance to work their way back to live in tents. We also recently added a juvenile chain gang.

Question: I understand the public supports your "tough on crime" approach.

Sheriff Arpaio: All of this is to make jail an unpleasant stay and keep the costs down for the taxpayers of Maricopa County. The citizens of our county love these programs. I was just reelected to my fourth term of office as sheriff. Opponents from both sides (Republicans and Democrats) came after me, but I still won by twelve percentage points. The people that elected me support my approach to jail management and think I am doing my job. Recent polls gave me a seventy-seven percent approval rating. I care about serving the public; I don't care about politics or politicians. I am doing what I was elected to do and will continue to do so as long as the voters continue to support me.

It is difficult for a democratic society to determine how much punishment is necessary for the commission of a crime. The U.S. Supreme Court addressed this issue in *Bell v. Wolfish*, when the Court established the "punitive intent standard."[29] The case dealt with conditions and practices at a federal jail for short-term offenders in New York City. Inmates alleged that overcrowded conditions and restrictive security procedures were a violation of the Eighth Amendment, which states that "Excessive bail shall not be required, nor excessive fines imposed, nor cruel and unusual punishment inflicted." The Court ruled that the case should turn only on whether the practices in question violated detainees' right to be free from punishment, using a standard of whether the individual restrictions were punitive or merely regulatory restraints; whether the practice is reasonably related to a legitimate goal other than punishment; and whether it appears to be excessive in relation to the alternative purpose.

test of proportionality
the result of the 1983 case of *Solem v. Helm;* a test used to guide sentencing based on the gravity of the offense and consistency of the severity of punishment

The Court also addressed punishment and created the **test of proportionality** in the 1983 case of *Solem v. Helm,* by declaring that "a criminal sentence must be proportionate to the crime for which the defendant has been convicted . . . and be guided by objective criteria, including (i) the gravity of the offense and the harshness of the penalty; (ii) the sentences imposed on other criminals in the same jurisdiction; and (iii) the sentences imposed for commission of the same crime in other jurisdictions . . ."[30]

Deterrence

Deterrence is a correctional goal focused on future actions (or the avoidance of certain actions) by both individuals and society. The expectation is that, as a result of offenders receiving punishment, both they and others will be deterred or discouraged from committing crimes in the future. Jeremy Bentham, in his 1789 concept of hedonistic calculus, argued that, if the sanction for committing a crime inflicted a greater amount of pain than the pleasure resulting from the offense, crime would be prevented. When an individual commits a crime and receives a punishment, the punishment is designed to result in **specific deterrence** of that offender from committing further crimes. The idea is that the punishment the offender received created such an unpleasant situation that he or she will not want to experience it again. This certainly seems logical, but requires that offenders receive punishment that is swift, certain, and specifically linked to the criminal act. Unfortunately, justice today often does not end with these results.

specific deterrence
the effect of punishment on an individual offender that prevents that person from committing future crimes

Deterrence philosophies are also expected to have an effect on the general society. **General deterrence** presumes that others in society will not commit crimes, because they see that there is a punishment for such acts and that individuals do receive the prescribed punishments. For general deterrence to be effective, the punishment must be visible and the public must believe that if they commit a crime they will be caught and punished, the punishment will be carried out uniformly, and the benefits of the crime will not outweigh the punishment. This requires logic and rationality. The theory often breaks down, as criminals do not believe they will get caught, think they can get out of trouble with a good lawyer, or do not fear the available punishment enough for it to deter them from the criminal act.

general deterrence
the recognition that criminal acts result in punishment, and the effect of that recognition on society that prevents future crimes

Over the past two decades, legislators have operated under a misconception that if they continue to enhance (increase) penalties for certain crimes, the commission of these crimes will go down. Public relations campaigns have sought to educate potential criminals regarding the penalties for drug offenses or for using a gun in the commission of a crime. However, research has failed to indicate that such penalty modifications have a significant deterrent effect. However, those who increasingly favor using prison rather than probation and increasing the length of current prison sentences argue that, even if such enhancements do not have a deterrent effect, they will have an incapacitative effect.

Incapacitation

Incapacitation is thought of as reducing offenders' ability or capacity to commit further crimes. Correctional sanctions restrict offenders' opportunity to continue their criminality and, through this restriction, society is protected from potential criminals. Some suggest that incapacitation is reactive in that it is a punishment for past crimes. Others contend that "sentences based on incapacitation are future oriented, . . . [as they look] at the offender's potential future actions."[31] Others imply that incapacitation is both reactive and proactive. Carlson and colleagues argue, "Like retribution, incapacitation is reactive, and yet, like deterrence, it attempts to predict and influence future behavior."[32]

Blumstein suggests that there are two ways to define and view the correctional goal of incapacitation. "The most narrow is that incapacitation (through a sentence of imprisonment or death) makes it literally impossible for offenders to commit future crimes. In this view, incapacitation serves to [avert crimes] in the general society by isolation of the identified offenders during periods of incarceration."[33] Thus incapacitation is believed to reduce crime by focusing on the offender who is being incapacitated or imprisoned, while the person is under control of the authorities carrying out the punishment. Incapacitation is based on the belief that most criminals commit several crimes over their lifetimes and therefore, during the time of their criminal sanction, crime is being prevented by their reduced opportunity. Blumstein notes that incapacitation operates on the assumption that "punishment can take a slice out of an individual criminal career."[34] However, even a person who is in prison or on death row is capable of committing crimes against victims. In prison, inmates commit crimes of assault against other inmates or prison staff. Offenders in prison still use or deal in drugs. However, society is protected, even while those who work or live in prison are still potential victims of crime.

The second way to consider incapacitation is under a broader definition whereby offenders' opportunities to commit further crimes are lessened by the imposition of the criminal sentence. For instance, house arrest using electronic monitoring to ensure that an offender remains at home at prescribed times reduces the opportunity for criminal activity. Whenever an offender serving a sanction while in the community is under the supervision or monitoring of correctional staff, his or her opportunity to commit crime is reduced.

As noted above, incapacitation is based on a belief that most criminals repeat their criminality. Several studies, beginning with Wolfgang and Sellin's classic work on cohort groups in Philadelphia, have shown that most offenders commit more than one crime, and a small group of offenders commit a large percentage of crimes. A review of this work found the following:

> *Career criminals, though few in number, account for most crime. Even though chronic repeat offenders (those with five or more arrests by age 18) make up a relatively small proportion of all offenders, they commit a very high proportion of all crimes. . . . In Wolfgang's Philadelphia study, chronic offenders accounted for 23% of all male offenders in the study, but they had committed 61% of all crimes. Of all crimes by all members of the group studied, chronic offenders committed: 61% of all homicides; 76% of all rapes; 73% of all robberies; and 65% of all aggravated assaults.*[35]

These findings led to efforts to identify offenders with the greatest potential of committing a high number of crimes and sentence them to long prison terms, an approach referred to as **selective incapacitation**. During the 1980s, the RAND Corporation, recognizing that prison cells were an expensive and therefore scarce

incapacitation
reducing offenders' ability or capacity to commit further crimes

selective incapacitation
incarceration of high-risk offenders for preventative reasons based on what they are expected to do, not what they have already done

resource, created the concept of selective incapacitation. In this work, Greenwood argued that, in order to maximize the incapacitating result (preventing future crimes) of imprisonment, scarce prison and jail space should be reserved for the most dangerous, violent, and repeat offenders.[36] It had earlier been concluded that, if selected offenders who commit repetitive crimes were imprisoned and incapacitated for three or even five years, significantly fewer crimes would have been committed.[37] Therefore, a model of selective incapacitation advocates incarcerating, for preventive reasons, high-risk people for what they are expected to do, not for what they have already done.

Selective incapacitation remains hotly debated and has several critics. Gottfredson and Hirschi have challenged the methodological approach and conclusions of the RAND studies.[38] Others have raised the issue of "false positives" and the fairness of incarcerating for long periods of time those who are wrongly expected to commit future crimes. As Allen and Simonsen noted, "The evidence is that we would probably incarcerate numerous noneligible (a 'false positive' problem) persons and release to lesser confinement many of those eligible (a 'false negative' problem) persons. Whatever benefits might accrue to this sentencing doctrine have thus far eluded corrections."[39]

Rehabilitation

rehabilitation

a programmed effort to alter the attitudes and behaviors of inmates and improve their likelihood of becoming law-abiding citizens

recidivism

the state of relapse that occurs when offenders complete their criminal punishment and then continue to commit crimes

The next goal of corrections is to rehabilitate offenders, that is, return them to society better able to avoid criminality and less likely to commit further crimes. **Rehabilitation** means returning someone to a prior state. It is assumed that this refers to the life of offenders before they began to commit crimes. However, for most offenders, rehabilitation does not take them back, but to a new and better state, one in which they are self-restrained and not motivated to commit crime. The emphasis of rehabilitation is clearly proactive and focused on preventing future crimes. Correctional officials believe this may be their most important function, protecting society in the long term by reducing **recidivism** (a return to crime). However, it is questionable whether the effectiveness of correctional programs should be judged solely by the recidivism rate. No person or program can force offenders to change their behavior or to make good decisions to avoid crime, especially months after they leave the supervision of correctional officials. The situations and environments facing offenders differ from case to case. Even though recidivism may not be the most appropriate measure of the success of rehabilitation programs, it is likely to remain the one most often examined and used.

Corrections attempts to rehabilitate offenders in many ways. First, correctional programs are aimed at trying to reduce offenders' motivation to commit further crimes. Although there are many reasons why people commit crimes, correctional agencies offer psychological counseling to help offenders understand the factors that trigger certain behaviors, anger management and other programs to help offenders recognize dangerous situations in which they may act wrongfully, and sensitivity training to get offenders to understand the impact of their criminal actions on victims and their families. Second, correctional programs try to build competencies in offenders that may help them avoid problems that heighten their likelihood of committing crime. Such programs are designed to help offenders to increase their educational level, develop a vocational skill, or reduce the use of drugs or alcohol. Finally, correctional programs may simply have a goal of improving offenders' decision making. Why do offenders choose selling drugs over getting a legitimate job? Why do offenders choose to act out violently rather than avoid confrontation or seek nonviolent resolutions to problems? Or why do offenders steal others' property to try to make an easy buck? Some correctional programs help offenders improve their decision-making skills while considering the values and potential outcomes of their criminal actions.

Although the importance of rehabilitation has experienced ebbs and flows throughout the history of corrections, public attitudes have consistently supported rehabilitating criminal offenders. In the National Opinion Survey of Crime and Justice, respondents indicated support for rehabilitative programs; 93 percent support prisoners' learning a skill or trade and 94 percent support requiring offenders to be able to read and write before release from prison. Similarly, 88 percent support inmate work programs to construct buildings, make products, or perform services.[40]

Restitution

The first four goals of corrections are acknowledged by almost every author and in almost every textbook. Less mentioned, but currently gaining in popularity, is the goal of **restitution,** or making right by repaying society or victims for the wrongs created by offenders. This is not a new goal in the way it is carried out. Criminal sentences have historically included fines and victim restitution. And it can be argued that the chain gangs of the early twentieth century were public works programs in which inmates had to build roads or clear trails to improve the public good. During more contemporary times, the principle of *restoration* of the damage resulting from crime has increased in importance, and many more criminal sentences include the opportunity for restitution as the sanctions are carried out.

As society took over responsibility for bringing a criminal to justice and removed victims from the process to avoid their seeking revenge, the pendulum swung too far, and the victim became the forgotten participant in the criminal justice process. After police took victims' statements, victims often did not hear anything else official unless they were required to testify at trial. Victims played no role in sentencing, few sentences sought to repair the damages they incurred, and they seldom received any progress reports, such as when a criminal would appear before a parole board or was to get out of prison.

As the **victims' movement** became popular during the 1980s, the criminal justice system made many adjustments to include victims. Victim assistance programs advised them during the adjudication process and sometimes even arranged transportation to the trial if necessary. Sentencing decisions often considered victims'

restitution
acts by which criminals make right or repay society or their victims for their wrongs

victims' movement
the criminal justice system's recognition that victims should be involved in the process of sentencing criminals

Offenders are regularly required to do some type of community service to help pay back society for their crimes. Courtesy of the Ohio Department of Rehabilitation and Correction.

statements of their losses. Notifications regarding a change in status in the sentence of a criminal (such as a move from one prison to another) were initiated. Victims were informed of parole hearings and told how they could provide input if desired. And the plan for an inmate after release would be provided the victim to ensure that the victim saw no conflicts or felt threatened by the proposed release.

restorative justice
models of sentencing that shift the focus away from punishment of the offender and emphasize the victim by holding offenders accountable for the harm they caused and finding opportunities for them to repair the damage

All these activities were positive in getting offenders to repay the state or the victim for the damage done by their crimes. However, they still failed to satisfy the needs of most victims, the community, and even the offender. Over the past two decades, an alternative to traditional criminal sentencing, called **restorative justice,** emerged; it more fully implements the overall philosophy of the goal of restitution. Described more fully in Chapter 16, restorative justice models of sentencing shift the focus away from reactive, punishment-oriented sentencing, without concern for the victim. These models emphasize involving the victim while holding offenders accountable for the harm they caused and finding opportunities for them to repair the damage. Freeman describes restorative justice as "a process that focuses on the injury resulting from the crime and works to repair the injury by shifting the role of the offender from passive recipient of punishment to active participant in reparation."[41] Meanwhile, public opinion surveys conclude that "the process of mediating conflict between crime victims and offenders provides many benefits to the parties involved, the community, and the justice system."[42] Because of the current recognized value of holding offenders responsible for "making right" the harm they have done with their crimes and the importance of involving the victim in the criminal justice process, restitution is now recognized as a goal of corrections with importance comparable to the other four goals. In fact, and because of these reasons, this goal will probably continue to be seen as important in sentencing criminal offenders.

The "You Make the Decision" box asks you to compare and contrast the five goals of sentencing. Although these goals can all be accomplished in any jurisdiction's penal code and sentencing practices, the exercise makes students think about the relative importance they put on each goal.

Summary

CHAPTER REVIEW

This chapter includes several topics as we begin our study of corrections. Students receive an overview of what corrections is, how it links to the rest of the criminal justice system, and why it is important to study corrections. As the criminal justice system has expanded over the past several decades, the correctional system has grown at the most rapid pace, with elected officials authorizing extensive funds and resources to meet the growing demand for services. As this demand has grown, employment and advancement opportunities have increased, and more students are considering corrections as a career field.

The causes of crime are presented, from the earliest theories based on a range of beliefs that offenders exhibit "free will" to the idea that some offenders are "predetermined" and have no choice in becoming involved in crime. More modern theories, while not discounting any possible cause of crime, emphasize holding offenders accountable and weighing more heavily on the free will concepts than on predetermination. Understanding the theories regarding the causes is critical to determining how to respond to crime. Early approaches included severe corporal punishment, torture, and public humiliation; capital punishment for several crimes; and removing offenders by transporting them out of society. Today we have settled on the use of prisons to punish, deter, incapacitate, and rehabilitate criminals.

The Quakers of Pennsylvania, who opened the Walnut Street Jail in Philadelphia as the first penitentiary for convicted offenders in 1790, are credited with the creation of prisons to house sentenced offenders in the United States. For over two hundred years since that time, prisons have undergone many transitions regarding their emphasis on varying correctional goals, from punishment to rehabilitation. Each correctional goal is described in the chapter, and students can realize how correctional practices and various sentences emphasized certain goals over others during various eras of prison and community correctional operations.

The purpose of this chapter is to create a foundation of history and theory so that, as current policies and practices are described, students can link these to theories and goals in order to critically consider the overall effectiveness and public value of correctional policy. In the next several chapters, the operations of the major components of the correctional system are described, beginning with a description of the types of sentences that offenders receive. In Chapter 2, the first stage of correctional operations, including the processes (pretrial diversion, bail, jail, finding of guilt) that lead up to sentencing, is described, as well as various sentencing approaches and options and postsentencing processes for handling the offender and making the actual sentencing decision.

Key Terms

penology	Period of Transition
penitentiary	hands-off doctrine
corrections	Rehabilitative Era
penal code	medical model
Cesare Beccaria	reintegration
Classical School	"nothing works"
Jeremy Bentham	Retributive Era
hedonistic calculus	punishment
Positive School	retribution
Cesare Lombroso	test of proportionality
atavism	specific deterrence
Neoclassical School	general deterrence
transportation	incapacitation
John Howard	selective incapacitation
Walnut Street Jail	rehabilitation
Pennsylvania system	recidivism
Auburn system	restitution
Irish System	victims' movement
Reformatory Era	restorative justice
Industrial Prison Era	

Review Questions

1. How did the term *corrections* evolve from the earlier use of the term *penology*?

2. What is the mission of corrections?

3. Describe the correctional funnel.

4. What has driven the growth of corrections over the past twenty-five years?

5. What types of jobs are available in corrections?

6. List the principles of the Classical School of criminology.

7. What is Bentham's hedonistic calculus?

8. List the principles of the Positive School of criminology.

9. What reforms were needed that lead to the creation of prisons in the United States?

10. Describe the operation of the Walnut Street Jail.

11. Describe the differences in the Pennsylvania and Auburn systems.

12. How did the Irish system contribute to modern correctional operations in the United States?

13. What legislative acts influenced the changing operations of prisons?

14. How did abandonment of the "hands-off doctrine" affect prison operations?

15. In what ways does corrections attempt to rehabilitate offenders?

16. How does reintegration differ from rehabilitation?

17. Differentiate between specific and general deterrence.

18. What is selective incapacitation?

19. How has the victims' rights movement affected correctional policies and operations?

20. Describe restorative justice.

You Make the Decision...

Rating the Importance of Correctional Goals

No jurisdiction has to formally rate the importance of the five goals of corrections; however, the following exercise asks students to do just that. It can be done individually, but will be more fun and a better learning exercise in a small group.

Your instructions are to consider each of the five goals of sentencing and create a list of the favorable and unfavorable consequences of focusing on each one. For instance, someone might suggest that focusing on punishment can slowly undermine society's emphasis on fair and just treatment. Or, emphasizing incapacitation may result in positively affecting the crime rate, as incapacitated offenders cannot commit crimes in the community. After creating and discussing the list for each goal, go about the difficult task of rating the importance of each goal. There are no guidelines as to what "importance" means, and this should be a very individual decision. Does one person believe that the most important purpose of a criminal sanction is to punish an offender, whereas another believes it should first focus on rehabilitation? Each person should create his or her list, and then the group should discuss the lists and come to a group conclusion about the rating of goals by importance to society. The discussions, debates, and even arguments that result from this exercise should be both fun and a valuable learning opportunity.

Chapter Resources on mycrimekit™

Go to mycrimekit.com to explore the following study tools and resources specific to this chapter:

- **Practice Quiz:** multiple-choice, true/false, short-answer, and essay questions to help students test their knowledge
- **WebQuests:** learning activities built around Web searches
  - The Eastern State Penitentiary: www.easternstate.org

- **Insider's Experiences:** "Twenty-Five Years of Corrections Work"
- **Seiter Videos:**
  - See experts discuss career opportunities
  - See experts discuss sentencing policies
- **Flashcards:** Thirty-nine flashcards to test knowledge of the chapter's key terms

Sentencing and the Correctional Process

After reading this chapter, you should be able to:

1. Explain the operation of pretrial activities and understand how they can be considered a part of corrections.
2. Specify the reasons for preventive detention and describe the forms of release from jail pending trial.
3. Discuss how the Manhattan Bail Project operates and how it expands the number of offenders eligible for release on recognizance.
4. Identify the role that plea bargaining plays in criminal sentencing.
5. List the purposes of the presentence investigation.
6. List and describe the six sentencing options available as criminal sanctions.
7. Compare indeterminate and determinate sentencing models.
8. Explain the use of sentencing guidelines.
9. Suggest how drug and mental health courts are positive developments in the sentencing of criminal offenders.

Introduction

sentencing
the imposition of a criminal sanction by a judicial authority

Once a criminal offender has either pleaded guilty or been found guilty of a crime, a judge must determine the sentence to be received. **Sentencing** is the imposition of a criminal sanction by a judicial authority. Before a judge can prescribe a sentence, the range of allowable sanctions must be enacted by the legislature and listed in the state or federal penal code. Each year, hundreds of thousands of criminals appear before judges to be sentenced for their crimes. This chapter describes the process, the correctional activities that accompany the process, and the sentencing options and approaches available to judges.

felony
crime that is punishable by a year or more of incarceration

misdemeanors
crimes that are punishable by less than a year of incarceration

Sentencing descriptions are primarily for **felony** offenses, or those punishable by one year or more of incarceration. **Misdemeanors** are crimes punishable by less than one year of incarceration and have a significantly shorter process for handling offenders. Misdemeanor (lower) courts usually handle all the steps in the court process in one hearing and are often referred to as "assembly-line justice." Offenders charged with a misdemeanor appear in court for their preliminary hearing, usually plead guilty, and receive a sentence of a fine, probation, community service, a short jail term, or a combination of some or all of these. The entire court process may take only a few minutes.

Felony sentencing is much more complicated because the potential sanctions are much more severe. Correctional activities begin even prior to the determination of guilt, as offenders are evaluated for potential release from jail on bail or under some alternative release mechanism. After a finding of guilt, a process of information gathering begins to provide judges with a more complete picture of offenders and the crimes they committed. At the time of sentencing, judges must consider complicated sentencing laws for each individual case and offender. Today, judges have significantly less discretion in sentencing options than in the past. Mandatory minimum sentences, three-strikes laws, and sentencing guidelines frequently require specific sentences, with little consideration of personal factors regarding offenders, their crimes, and the victims. Various sentencing options and approaches usually available in today's criminal courts are presented next.

Pretrial Correctional Activities

The criminal justice system is said to have three major components: the police, who investigate crimes and arrest suspects; the court system, which includes prosecutors who determine whether to charge suspects with crimes and negotiate plea bargains, and courts that oversee the trial process and sentence guilty offenders; and corrections, which carries out the sentences imposed by the courts. Typically, corrections is considered to begin after the sentencing of criminal offenders. However, the past thirty years have seen many innovations and improvements in the criminal justice management of offenders just after the booking (the formal identification of a suspect arrested for a crime) and the first appearance (at which charges against suspects are read, suspects are advised of their rights, and they are afforded the opportunity for bail), but before the trial or a guilty plea and sentencing. These innovations include diversion from the criminal justice system, alternatives to traditional bail, and other nontraditional handling of those charged with crimes prior to their sentencing.

These innovations to the pretrial and presentence activities within the criminal justice system have expanded the traditional boundaries of corrections. Today, many consider the diversion of offenders from the criminal justice system into treatment and supervision programs a correctional practice. As well, pretrial services activities, including investigating the potential for offenders' release from pretrial detention on bail, release on recognizance, other alternatives to bail, and supervision in the community of those not detained in jail, are also considered part of corrections. Some authors describe these activities as part of a chapter on probation. However, these functions are pretrial and have a great effect on the sentencing process and decision. Therefore, pretrial activities are discussed in conjunction with, and described in terms of how they lead to, the sentencing decision in this chapter.

Diversion from the Criminal Justice System

Pretrial diversion provides the opportunity for a criminal offender to be diverted from processing in the criminal justice system by suspending criminal processing while offering offenders the chance to participate in treatment programs and avoid further criminal activity. Diversion occurs without (before) a finding of guilt; therefore, if offenders are successful in the diversion program, the charges against them are dismissed and they will not have a formal criminal record of the offense. Diversion programs are usually used for minor offenders of laws against public intoxication or minor property crimes who have little if any prior criminal record and appear to be candidates for some type of treatment in the community.

Pretrial diversion programs are sometimes referred to as *deferred prosecution* or *probation without adjudication*. Many court systems have bail and diversion staff, separate from the probation staff, who interview suspects in jail and then recommend to the court whether they should get bail or release on recognizance or whether they are good candidates for diversion. If offenders are charged with a nonviolent crime, have a limited prior criminal record, and possibly have a treatment need, such as for drug or alcohol abuse, the pretrial staff are likely to recommend that the judge grant the offender the opportunity for diversion. The recommendation will also include certain conditions that must be met over a specified period of time for the offender to successfully complete the diversionary program. Pretrial conditions are very similar to those for probationers (avoiding additional criminality, reporting to the supervising officer as required, maintaining employment, and participating in the identified treatment program). Pretrial services staff then supervise the diverted offender in the community while making periodic reports to the court.

The following practices are considered to define a pretrial diversion program:

- It offers people charged with criminal offenses alternatives to traditional criminal justice or juvenile justice proceedings.
- It permits participation by the accused only on a voluntary basis.
- The accused has access to defense counsel prior to a decision to participate.
- It occurs no sooner than the filing of formal charges and no later than a final adjudication of guilt.
- It develops service plans in conjunction with the defendant that address the needs of that defendant and are structured to assist that person in avoiding behavior likely to lead to future arrests.
- It results in dismissal of charges or the equivalent if the divertee successfully completes the diversion process.[1]

pretrial diversion
the suspension of criminal process while the offender is provided the chance to participate in treatment programs and avoid further criminal activity

One of the first and most notable diversion programs was Treatment Alternatives to Street Crimes (TASC).[2] TASC is focused on offenders with a drug problem that is believed to be the cause of their criminal involvement. With these types of programs, offenders may participate in a drug treatment program and avoid traditional processing through the criminal justice system. TASC and other diversionary drug treatment programs operate under the philosophy that, if offenders become involved in a treatment program for their addiction and successfully deal with their drug problem, their chance of avoiding future criminal activity is improved.

There are no conclusive data to indicate that pretrial diversion programs are more effective than formal criminal processing, even though diverted individuals typically have a lower recidivism rate than those who are not diverted. However, this is to be expected, as they are less serious offenders, and few evaluations control for the different levels of seriousness when examining such program models.[3] However, diversionary treatment programs have three advantages:

1. They reduce the demands on the court and prosecutors to process the case as a criminal activity. When an offender is diverted from criminal handling, prosecutors save considerable time by not having to prepare the case for trial and not having to assemble evidence to prove the offender guilty beyond a reasonable doubt. Even if the crime is likely to result in a plea bargain instead of a trial, it still reduces the prosecutors' time requirements. In addition, it eliminates several appearances before the court and clogging of the court docket.
2. They cost considerably less than criminal justice processing. Diversion generally moves the offender into community treatment programs (mental health, drug treatment, alcohol treatment) instead of more costly correctional-based programs. The reduction of prosecution and court time previously described also represents considerable cost savings.
3. Offenders avoid the stigma associated with a criminal conviction. For the type of offenders involved in pretrial diversion (nonviolent and usually first-time offenders), this is a significant advantage. It is generally believed that the further offenders penetrate into the correctional process (from probation to imprisonment) the more likely they are to be involved in crime in the future.

For these reasons, pretrial diversion programs are experiencing a resurgence of interest from criminal justice and court agencies that cannot keep up with their workloads. Today's emphasis on punishment and accountability of offenders has resulted in overcrowded jails and prisons and has overextended the resources available to justice agencies. The emphasis of diversionary programs on rehabilitation and reduction of recidivism is considered a bright light in the otherwise dreary environment of the criminal justice system. The National Association of Pretrial Services Agencies Diversion Committee writes:

> *Pretrial diversion is a strong, viable alternative that provides an important service for defendants and the communities in which they live. For defendants, diversion provides an opportunity to make significant changes in their lives and prevent further penetration into the criminal justice system. For communities, the programs assist the courts, prosecutors, and victims in addressing serious problems caused by growing criminal and juvenile justice populations through reducing reliance on traditional case processing and working to stem the "revolving door" syndrome.*[4]

Pretrial Detention in Jail

After arrest, booking, and a reading of their charges, many offenders are detained in jail until their trial or guilty plea. This occurs even though our justice system is based on the belief of "innocent until proved guilty," and there has yet to be a finding of guilt. Offenders are detained for one (or both) of two reasons. First, they are detained if considered a flight risk to ensure that they will appear at all future court proceedings. Second, they are detained if considered dangerous, in order to protect the public from their committing further crimes.

There are many alternatives to pretrial detention. It is generally believed that a variety of bail options (such as pledging money or property) will work for most individuals to reduce the likelihood of flight and ensure their appearance at court processes. The issue of danger and avoidance of risk to the community is much more difficult to predict and manage. Theoretically, we regularly hold charged yet still innocent offenders in jail for crimes they may possibly commit. This **preventive detention** is detaining an accused person in jail to protect the community from crimes he or she is likely to commit if set free pending trial.

In an effort to reduce the release from jail of high-risk offenders, the 1984 Comprehensive Crime Control Act authorized holding allegedly dangerous suspects in jail without bail if a judge finds no conditions that would ensure that the defendant will appear at trial and at the same time ensure the safety of the community. And the U.S. Supreme Court, in the 1987 decision of *United States v. Salerno,* upheld the ability of a magistrate to confine an offender on a presumption that he or she was dangerous.[5] Although some question holding defendants in custody for something they *may* do as a violation of their due process rights, most states have established laws that allow it to occur. Preventive detention can be criticized both in terms of violating one's right to due process and in terms of its effectiveness. Of all defendants released while awaiting trial, only 16 percent are arrested and less than half of those are convicted of a new crime committed during the release period.[6] And there is a strong correlation between denial of bail and a conviction.

If not granted bail, offenders are held in jails, temporary holding facilities that primarily house offenders before trial. At any time, more than half of the inmates housed in jails are not yet convicted of the crime for which they are being held.

preventive detention
detaining an accused person in jail to protect the community from crimes they are likely to commit if set free pending trial

The St. Louis County Jail holds more than eight hundred inmates, most there on pretrial detention, because they either do not have the funds to make bail or are too high a risk to release to the community pending trial.

Photo by Richard P. Seiter.

Almost every county in the United States has a jail, and many municipalities also operate jails. In the next chapter, operations and issues surrounding contemporary use of jails, jail management, jail crowding, legal liabilities, and offender issues such as suicide prevention, mentally ill offenders, and classification are described.

Release from Pretrial Detention on Bail

After criminal suspects are arrested and booked, they (usually within hours of their arrest) have a *first appearance* before a judge or magistrate, the charges against them are read, they are advised of their rights, and they are considered for bail or some other method of release from detention. In most cases, release requires the use of **bail,** the pledge of money or property in exchange for a promise to return for further criminal processing. Offenders on bail remain under the jurisdiction and supervision of the courts and must stay in the community while they await adjudication, but in most circumstances they have no contact with court personnel other than at formal hearings.

bail
the pledge of money or property in exchange for a promise to return for further criminal processing

The history of pretrial release programs can be traced to medieval England, when those accused of crimes were often detained for months in local jails until the traveling magistrate arrived for trial. These early jails were not designed to hold offenders securely for long periods of time; problems of idleness, sanitation, and disruptive behavior resulted, and many offenders escaped. To avoid these problems, when the offenders were not charged with a serious crime or seen as dangerous, sheriffs began to turn defendants over to willing friends, relatives, or employers. These third parties would offer themselves or money as **surety** (a person who is legally liable for the conduct of another) for the accused person's appearance in court. If the defendant did not appear, the surety could be imprisoned or forced to pay a sum of money to the sheriff. The concept of releasing a defendant before trial with a personal or financial guarantee thereafter developed into today's concept of bail.

surety
a person who is legally liable for the conduct of another; someone who guarantees the accused person's appearance in court

Unfortunately, the practice of bail was often abused and misused from its inception. Therefore, in 1275, specific offenses in England were established as "bailable" and other crimes as "not bailable." Furthermore, the authority to set bail was moved from the sheriff to justices of the peace. To discourage unreasonably high bails, the English Bill of Rights in 1689 stated that excessive bail should not be required, a stipulation later incorporated into the U.S. Constitution, which states in the Eighth Amendment (ratified in 1791) that excessive bail may not be required.

Many times, offenders, their families, or their friends do not have personal funds or property to pledge as bail. As a result, the posting of bail bonds moved away from friends and family and became commercialized, as the bond amount could be purchased for a fee. *Bail bond agents* are independent businesspeople who usually charge a fee of from 5 to 10 percent of the bond to provide it as bail. If offenders fail to appear for future criminal proceedings, the bond is forfeited. If they do appear, the full bond is returned to the person or business placing it. However, the percentage of the bond given to the commercial bond agent is not returned to the individual if he or she appears; it is just a fee for the posting of the bond.

There are many problems with the system of bail as a requirement for release. First, the availability of financial resources and the ability to "make bail" is not related to the risk of the offender or the chance of successful criminal processing. Second, the bail process discriminates against the poor. A survey found that of all offenders for whom bail was allowable yet who did not post bail, 94 percent remained incarcerated only because they could not afford bail or even the bond agent's fee.[7] Finally, many find the idea that "freedom can be bought for a price" unfair and antithetical to our system of justice for all. Because of these problems, several alternatives to financial bail developed.

Alternatives to Bail

To respond to the concerns noted previously, several options to traditional bail have been created. For minor offenses such as misdemeanors, summonses are used instead of arrest warrants. A *summons* is a legal order for an individual to appear at a future court proceeding. For felonies, a variety of bond options have been created. Options used by U.S. courts include the following:

- *Personal recognizance:* The defendant is released upon personal or own recognizance (promise to appear in court) without an appearance bond.
- *Unsecured bond:* The defendant is released on an unsecured appearance bond with a monetary amount that is secured only by the signature of the defendant.
- *Percentage bond:* The defendant is required to execute an appearance bond in a specific amount with the clerk of the court, in cash or other security as directed by the judicial officer.
- *Surety bond:* The defendant is required to execute a bail bond by the deposit of cash or the posting of a bail bond.
- *Collateral:* The defendant is required to execute the bail bond by posting property of a value equal to or greater than the bail set by the judicial officer.
- *Third-party custody:* The court may place the person in the custody of another person or organization.

With the first three options, individuals do not have to place the entire bond amount, but only an unsecured bond or a percentage of the bond required. A recent survey found that 75 percent of offenders were released at arraignment on either bail or personal recognizance, another 7 percent were later released on bail, another 4 percent later released on personal recognizance, and only 14 percent were detained until deposition of their cases.[8]

Pretrial Service Programs

The most frequent mechanism for releasing from jail offenders awaiting trial is **release on recognizance (ROR),** or with the defendants' personal promise to appear. Historically, not many felony offenders were granted this level of trust, and by the middle of the twentieth century, jails were becoming increasingly overcrowded with unsentenced offenders. To improve this situation, the Vera Institute of Justice in New York City created the **Manhattan Bail Project (MBP)** in the 1960s. The purpose of the MBP was to help judges identify individuals who were good candidates to be released on their own recognizance without commercial or monetary bond. The Vera Institute had determined that, even though judges had the authority to release offenders without bail, it was not being used to a great extent.

The staff of the MBP interviewed defendants in jail and contacted their references to verify interview statements. They worked on the assumption that offenders with strong community ties were most likely to appear for trial, and they created criteria to "score" offenders and recommend to judges those who they believed were most suitable for release on recognizance. Because of its positive impact on the

release on recognizance
release from jail based only on the defendant's promise to appear for further court procedures

Manhattan Bail Project
a program started in the 1960s to assist judges in identifying individuals who were good candidates to be released on their own recognizance without commercial or monetary bond

Inmates are placed in a holding cell while booked into jail until a decision is made as to whether they should be granted bail or released on recognizance.
Reprinted with permission of the Corrections Corporation of America.

supervised pretrial release programs
supervision of offenders released on their own recognizance, similar to supervision while on probation

detention and bail process, the MBP was replicated by many jurisdictions across the United States. By the 1980s, more than two hundred cities had such pretrial release programs to reduce jail crowding. Their goal was to decrease the number of offenders detained in jail awaiting trial while providing a more equitable form of release than simple bail.

The expansion of the Manhattan Bail Project led to the development of a broader form of ROR program. **Supervised pretrial release (SPTR) programs** were subsequently developed to enable individuals who were considered poor risks for ROR to be released under community supervision prior to trial. In the 1980s, the SPTR programs began to serve a second purpose. They provided a means to respond to growing public safety concerns by monitoring pretrial releases in the community. In the 1984 Federal Bail Reform Act, the safety of other people was included as a criterion to determine the pretrial release decision. The pretrial services report addresses this factor and weighs community risk as well as appearance at trial.

For offenders determined to pose no risk of nonappearance or danger, there is simple release on recognizance. For those who pose some risk, many jurisdictions have created SPTR programs to supervise offenders. Under pretrial supervision, offenders must follow certain conditions (no criminal activity, no drug use, and steady employment), must report to a pretrial supervision officer, and can be violated (returned to jail) if they do not follow the conditions.[9] ROR and SPTR programs are considered successful and usually result in only a small percentage of releasees being arrested while on pretrial release status. Although severity of arrest and defendant's criminal history are most important, pretrial detention also influences the likelihood of conviction, in that cases in which a defendant was detained had a conviction rate of 92 percent compared to 50 percent for those released prior to conviction.[10]

Pretrial services are continually growing as more jurisdictions look for safe and effective ways to reduce jail overcrowding, and so there is a growing need for pretrial services staff. The "Your Career in Corrections" box explains the role and responsibilities of these jobs.

Your Career in Corrections

Pretrial Services Officers

Pretrial services officers are officers of the court, serving the court system in most states, most large cities, and thirty-six federal districts. Their job is twofold: investigation and supervision. In most situations, newly arrested offenders are investigated, and recommendations are made to the court regarding their release or detention. The investigation is completed through the creation of a social history regarding the person's life, including family ties, health, mental health status, employment history, financial assets, and other community relationships. The purpose of this history is to determine the strength of the offender's ties to the community, which is critical in the assessment of risk of flight and failure to appear at future court hearings. The social history is created through interviewing the individual, calling family members or other significant parties, doing a credit check, and searching official records. Pretrial services officers also examine the individual's prior criminal history, using computer networks to check prior offenses, gang affiliations, other court histories, and other confinement records. The report usually must be done very quickly, because the hearing to determine bail occurs early in the criminal justice process. In fact, in the federal court system, officers must do the report and make a recommendation within about two hours. The recommendation usually focuses on whether the person should be released or detained. The officer may also address any need for alternatives to detention, such as the use of a halfway house, an inpatient or outpatient drug or mental health treatment center, or electronic monitoring.

If the individual is released, specific conditions are placed on his or her release, and a pretrial services officer supervises the person in a similar way to probation. Many jurisdictions use a "least restrictive" model of supervision, because the individual has a presumption of innocence. This means that supervision conditions are placed according to the individual case, with the fewest conditions possible to ensure that the offender will show up for court and is not a danger to others. Supervision is similar to probation and each case has a separate plan covering the requirements for supervision, including the frequency of contact and other conditions. Almost always, the officer must visit the residence and walk through every room to ensure that the home is an acceptable placement and that there is no evidence of any criminal activity. After this initial home inspection, the supervision begins, and offenders are reminded of court dates and requirements of supervision.

Supervision typically lasts three to six months, until a trial or plea agreement. It can be extended if the conviction is appealed and the person is granted release status. Some individuals are seen daily, whereas others must only make a monthly telephone report. Many contacts are in the field rather than in the office. Officers who do community contacts are usually allowed to carry a weapon, receive special training in personal protection, and wear bulletproof vests for their personal safety. They also make contacts with treatment providers, such as for drug abuse, sex offenders, and mental health. The supervision usually includes urine testing for drug use.

If there is a violation of supervision, the officer reports to the court with a recommendation to either continue supervision as is, change the supervision conditions, or violate and revoke the release status. A detention hearing is held, and the court must show that there are no conditions that can be supervised in community and still ensure that the person will show up at court. For the hearing, the officer presents a report detailing evidence of the violations and may have to testify.

The Role of Plea Bargaining and Sentencing

More than 90 percent of felony cases result in a guilty plea by the defendant instead of a trial to determine guilt or innocence. **Plea bargaining** is an agreement in which the defendant enters a plea of guilty in exchange for a reduced sentence in comparison to the sentence allowable for the charged offense. In practical

plea bargaining
an agreement in which the defendant enters a plea of guilty in exchange for a reduced sentence in comparison to the sentence allowable for the charged offense

terms, offenders usually plead guilty to an offense less serious than indicted by the prosecution. For example, instead of first-degree murder, the offender may plead guilty to second-degree murder; instead of armed robbery, he or she may plead guilty to theft. Prosecutors are willing to accept a plea in exchange for a lesser sentence for many reasons. Trials are time consuming and costly, and if fewer offenders pleaded guilty, the court resources would be overwhelmed. In addition, even if the prosecution believes it has a sound case against the offender, there is a risk in trying it before a jury, as the jury must be convinced of the offender's guilt "beyond a reasonable doubt." Offenders often plead guilty if they know they are guilty and believe that the evidence against them is overwhelming, and they wish to get a lighter sentence than is possible for the crime they committed.

Plea bargaining is primarily a function of the prosecution and the court system, yet it has many implications for corrections and the sentencing process. Upon a plea of guilty, the court (if accepting the plea agreement) moves immediately to the sentencing process and sentences the offender to the agreed-on sentence. Usually the court, once the plea is negotiated, will ask the probation office to conduct a presentence investigation in order to have more information to ensure that the agreement is within realistic expectations for an offender with this type of background and criminal involvement. Upon sentencing, the offender is then turned over to correctional authorities to carry out the sentence, whether it be probation with certain conditions or a period of imprisonment.

Presentencing Correctional Activities

Following a finding or plea of guilt, criminal courts must determine sentences that will be imposed on criminal offenders. A critical tool used by judges during the sentencing process is the **presentence investigation (PSI)**. The PSI is a report detailing the background of a convicted offender, including criminal history, social background, education, employment, mental and physical health, and other factors valuable to consider in the sentencing process. The PSI often also provides judges the range of sanctions allowable for the crime and recommendations for sentencing based on the risk of the offender and the chance for success if he or she is granted probation and remains in the community.

Most states require a PSI to be completed for felony cases that allow the possibility of probation. When judges have discretion regarding the sentence they will grant offenders, the recommendation within the PSI is followed 80 to 90 percent of the time. The PSI is usually prepared by probation officers working for the court. Probation departments usually have a dual responsibility of investigation (preparation of the PSI) and supervision of offenders placed on probation. Some departments have separate groups of probation officers that do only PSIs or only supervision. Others mix officer responsibilities to do some of both these tasks.

Purposes of the PSI

Although the purpose of the PSI is to assist courts in the sentencing decision, it is valuable in many other ways, including the following:

1. *For use in sentencing by the court.* As noted, the information provided by the PSI is critical in the sentencing decision. The PSI provides judges specific factors about the offender that are considered to determine his or her risk to the

---

mycrimekit

Media—Video: The Sentencing Process.

presentence investigation

a report used during the sentencing process that details the background of a convicted offender, to include criminal, social, education, employment, mental and physical health, and other significant factors

community and mitigating and aggravating circumstances regarding the offense.

2. *For use in determining supervision needs during probation.* If the offender is granted probation, the information in the PSI is helpful in determining the type of supervision needed and the types of programs that could help the offender succeed in the community. Similarly, if the offender is sentenced to prison with a period of supervision after release, the PSI is valuable in determining postincarceration community supervision needs.

3. *For use by prison officials in classifying offenders and determining program needs.* For offenders given prison sentences, the PSI is very valuable to prison officials in determining the level of prison security (minimum, medium, or maximum) required and the types of programs that should be available to the inmate.

4. *For use by the parole board in making release decisions.* In states that still use indeterminate sentences (described shortly) with release by a parole board, information regarding the current offense, past history of crime, and personal background is critical in deciding when an inmate is to be released from prison and put in the community.

5. *For research purposes.* Research studies of the effectiveness of correctional sanctions or programs usually measure outcome as recidivism or return to criminal activity. This outcome variable is much more valuable if it can be correlated with specific factors relative to offenders, such as problems of drug abuse or mental illness, lack of education, or a history of violence.

Throughout the correctional process, officials continually use the PSI to assess the dual needs of offenders for security and supervision and for rehabilitative treatment. Offenders must be placed in a level of supervision (whether in the community or in prison) that is commensurate to their risk of violence or escape. Furthermore, offenders must have the opportunity to participate in programs that can be beneficial in dealing with their problems and treatment needs. Information critical to both of these categories of decisions is collected and included in the PSI.

Collecting Information for the PSI

Shortly after a finding or plea of guilt, the judge sets a date for sentencing of the offender. In addition, the probation office will assign a probation officer to conduct the PSI for presentation to the court to consider for the sentencing decision. The first step in collecting information begins with an interview of the offender. Most states and the federal government provide a worksheet used by probation officers to collect preliminary information during the initial interview. The worksheet includes several questions regarding offenders' criminal history, family situation including marital status and children, physical and mental condition, substance abuse, education and vocational background, and employment record.

Information from the interview is then verified by checking the sources provided by the offender. For instance, all past employers named by offenders are contacted to verify the accuracy of the information. In addition, the investigating officer often interviews other people who can provide additional information or corroborate information provided by the offender. Offenders' spouses or parents are usually interviewed to determine their perspective of the offender and identify other problems not mentioned by the offender. Finally, investigating officers search for official records, such as a copy of the offender's birth certificate, social security card, military records, or verification of high school graduation.

An important part of the creation of a PSI occurs when the officer visits the family and interviews them regarding the offender. Photo by Richard P. Seiter.

Although the types of information necessary to complete the PSI are generally clear, the detailed information required is not. As noted earlier, correctional officials continually try to balance the goal of risk management with the need for rehabilitation. The investigating officer must keep this balance and the end use of the PSI in mind while collecting information. For example, the officer may note that the offender has a poor employment history and a record of constantly changing jobs. These facts are important, yet are much more valuable if the officer continues to pursue the reasons for the job changes. Did they result from the offender being fired for failure to get along with co-workers, for stealing from employers, or for drug use on the job? Or does the offender simply lack responsibility in finding and maintaining employment? The more detailed the PSI regarding the reasons behind the facts, the more useful the PSI is to correctional officials.

Contents of the PSI

The categories of information noted previously have historically been included in a PSI. However, the approach to writing the PSI has changed significantly. Historically, the PSI was a lengthy narrative of these categories, including many subjective conclusions by the investigating officer. The advantage of this type of report was that it often told a story about the offender, in a way that the reader almost got to know the offender and the types of issues and problems that contributed to his or her involvement in crime. PSIs, with their many subjective statements, were considered the property of the court, and offenders were not allowed to see them. This lack of disclosure was supported in the 1949 case of *Williams v. New York*, in which the U.S. Supreme Court upheld a decision to deny the defense access to the PSI, even though the sentencing judge used evidence in the confidential PSI to give a death penalty over the recommendation of a life sentence by the jury.[11] Since the *Williams case*, many courts have modified their decisions and disclose the PSI, and many state legislatures have passed laws requiring full disclosure of the PSI to the defendants' lawyers.

With these changes, PSIs have undergone an expected change in the style in which they are written. Many PSIs are now much shorter, factual without opinion,

Face Sheet
- Pedigree information
- Court information
- Offense information
- Release status
    1. Personal recognizance
    2. Unsecured bond
    3. Percentage bond
    4. Surety bond
    5. Collateral
    6. Third-person custody
- Detainers
- Co-defendants
- Related cases

The Offense
- Charges
- Plea or verdict
- Plea agreement
- Motion for substantial assistance
- Co-defendants
- Related cases
- Pretrial adjustments

Victim Impact
- Financial
- Social
- Psychological
- Medical
- Costs

Adjustment/Obstruction of Justice
- Any attempt to impede prosecution

Acceptance of Responsibility
- Does the offender accept responsibility?

Criminal History
- Arrests
- Convictions
- Pending charges
- Other law enforcement contacts
- Juvenile adjudications

Offender Characteristics
- Personal and family data
- Physical condition
- Mental and emotional health
- Substance abuse
- Educational and vocational skills
- Employment history

Financial Ability to Pay
- Assets
- Unsecured debt
- Net worth
- Income
- Necessary expenses
- Net monthly cash flow
- Analysis

Sentencing Options
- Impact of plea agreement
- Custody options
- Probation options—necessary conditions
- Fines
- Restitution

Recommendations

FIGURE 2.1   Format for Presentence Investigation in U.S. Courts

and designed to avoid legal challenges by the defense. In federal courts, the PSI is provided to the defense attorney before sentencing so that any defense objections to facts or statements in the PSI can be noted to the judge. The defense may even point out inaccuracies or provide new information that results in the PSI being changed before it is sent to the judge. Figure 2.1 illustrates the current format suggested for use by federal courts.

Most of the sections in the PSI are fairly clear. However, two important areas that need further explanation are the victim impact statement and the recommendation. As a result of the recent emphasis of including the victims in the criminal justice process and of emphasizing restitution for the victim as a goal of sentencing, victim impact statements have been added to many states' and to federal presentence investigations. Victim impact information provides the sentencing judge details regarding both the financial loss and emotional trauma that resulted to the victim of the crime. This information then helps the judge set a required amount of money as a fine or for the offender to pay as victim compensation, when the offender has the potential to pay these costs. Victim statements also sometimes reflect the victims' desire for the type of sentences offenders should receive. Initially, there was concern that including statements of the victims' preferences during sentencing would unduly influence judges in their sentencing decision or assignment of monetary payments to the victim. However, studies have indicated that these statements do not overstate victim losses or result in harsher sentencing.[12]

Another key component of the PSI is the recommendation of a sentence by the investigating officer. Because of the recent disclosure of PSIs, some states no longer have the officer make a sentencing recommendation in the PSI. However, it is still believed that a recommended sentence is valuable to the sentencing process. First, the recommendation section often identifies the range of sanctions available to the judge. Second, the officer's recommendation is based on fact and offender background and is seen as both professionally developed and without any biases that may have come about during the trial or other court hearings. Third, judges respect these recommendations and follow them in 80 to 90 percent of cases in which recommendations are made. However, with the high level of concurrence by the judge, it can be argued that allowing a probation officer to make a sentencing recommendation gives the officer authority to make a sentence via the judge. Finally, the recommendation is useful during the judicial consideration of the plea bargain agreement. When the defense and prosecution negotiate a specific sentence in exchange for a guilty plea, the judge can compare that sentence to the recommendation by the probation officer to determine whether the agreement is reasonable based on the risk and treatment needs of the offender.

The Sentencing Decision

mycrimekit

Media—Video: Making the Sentencing Decision.

economic sanction
a requirement that an offender pay a fine or restitution to the victim as a part of his or her sentence

community service
an economic sanction used when offenders do not have funds from which to pay a fine or make restitution; referred to as a "fine on their time," so that indigent offenders do not have to serve prison or jail time merely because they lack the fiscal ability to pay a fine

probation
a prison sentence that is suspended on the condition that the offender follows certain prescribed rules and commits no further crimes

intermediate sanctions
midrange dispositions that fall between probation and imprisonment

At this point in the correctional and sentencing process, offenders have either pleaded or been found guilty, a presentence investigation has been provided to the court, and it is time for the sentencing decision. The judge assigned to preside over each criminal case determines the sentence. The range of sentences that can be used by a judge for any criminal case is identified in the state penal code, a statute passed by the legislature. In the following sections, various sentencing options, models of sentences, and discretion provided to judges are described.

Sentencing Options

Six general categories of sentencing options are authorized in state penal codes and therefore are available to judges. They are as follows:

1. **Economic sanctions:** a requirement that an offender pay a fine or restitution to the victim as a part of his or her sentence, or do **community service** (a requirement that an offender provide personal time to do some public good). In most cases, economic sanctions are a condition of probation; however, in some instances, these are stand-alone sentences without probation.
2. **Probation:** a prison sentence that is suspended on the condition that the offender is supervised in the community, follows certain prescribed rules, and commits no further crimes. If offenders who receive probation meet all the requirements of probation and complete the time they are to be supervised in the community, the suspended sentence is never invoked. Standard conditions of probation include avoiding further crime, maintaining employment, and reporting as required to the probation officer. Additional conditions to have more intensive monitoring or respond to a certain need of the offender (such as substance abuse or mental illness) may be added to standard conditions. Conditions that add monitoring or treatment requirements are sometimes referred to as intermediate sanctions.
3. **Intermediate sanctions:** midrange dispositions that fall between probation and imprisonment. Intermediate sanctions (such as intensive probation

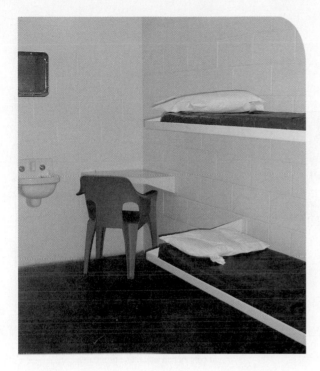

If offenders receive a sentence of short-term confinement, they serve the sentence in a jail and spend much of their time idle in a small cell usually holding two inmates. Photo by Richard P. Seiter.

supervision or house arrest with electronic monitoring) provide more supervision and monitoring than standard probation, yet are less than a sentence of confinement to a jail or prison.

4. **Short-term confinement:** a sentence in a jail for one year or less. Minor offenders (those who have committed misdemeanors or less serious felonies) may receive a sentence of less than one year. With sentences of this length, offenders are often sentenced to stay in the local community jail, rather than being transferred to a state prison.

5. **Imprisonment:** a sentence in a prison for one year or more to a life sentence. Offenders receiving sentences of more than one year are usually ordered into the custody of the state (or federal) department of corrections for placement in a suitable prison.

6. **Capital punishment:** for the most serious crimes (generally first-degree murder), most states and the federal government provide for the death penalty.

Over the past two decades, there has been an emphasis on creating a broad array of sentencing options to meet the varying needs and requirements of different types of crimes and different types of criminals. Figure 2.2 is an example of the sentencing options available for crimes committed in the state of Missouri. These options illustrate how increasing levels of supervision are provided for more serious criminals.

Even with the "tough on crime" approaches resulting in more prison sentences for longer periods of time for many offenders, the largest proportion of offenders remain on probation or are supervised in the community. As indicated in Table 2.1, the estimated number of people under correctional supervision increased from 1.84 million in 1980 to 7.33 million by 2007. Of these, 4.23 million (58 percent) were on probation, 780,500 (10.6 percent) were in jail, 1.51 million (20.6 percent) were in prison, and 824,000 (11.2 percent) were on parole.

One important consideration during sentencing comes in the sequencing of sentences. In a large percentage of criminal cases, offenders are charged with more than one crime or with several counts of the same crime. Penal codes allow

short-term confinement
a sentence in a jail for one year or less

imprisonment
a sentence in a prison of a year or more

capital punishment
punishment for the most serious crimes (generally first-degree murder); most states and the federal government provide for the death penalty

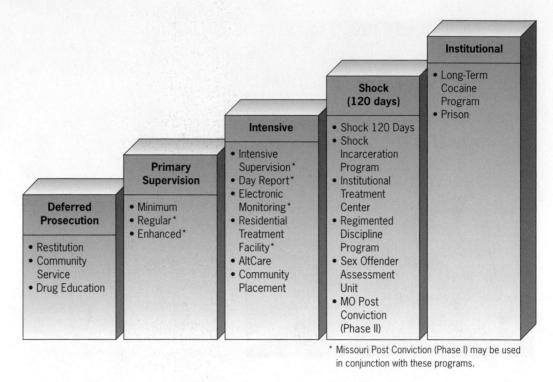

Source: Missouri Department of Corrections, 2000.

* Missouri Post Conviction (Phase I) may be used in conjunction with these programs.

FIGURE 2.2   Supervision Continuum Sentencing Options in Missouri

concurrent sentences

sentences that run at the same time

the sentences for each crime or count to be aggregated separately. As a result, sentences can be either concurrent or consecutive. **Concurrent sentences** are assigned to run at the same time. For example, if an offender is found guilty of three counts of larceny and each count carries a sentence of three years, the total time of the sentences could be nine years. Concurrent sentences would have all three counts begin at the same time, and the offender in the example would then complete the three sentences in three years. However, **consecutive sentences** run one after the other. If sentenced to the three counts in the example to be served consecutively, the offender would have to finish each three-year sentence before beginning the next and would complete the sentences in nine years (3 + 3 + 3 = 9 years). The use of concurrent and consecutive sentencing options is usually a consideration during plea bargain negotiations.

consecutive sentences

sentences that run one after the other

Sentencing Models

As noted earlier, nonincarceration sentences include economic sanctions, probation, and intermediate sanctions; incarceration sentences include both short-term and long-term confinement. As described in the next two chapters, short sentences are sometimes linked with an intermediate sanction, so offenders spend part of their sentence in jail or prison and part of their sentence under supervision in the community. Finally, there are sentences of death. For sentences of incarceration, indeterminate and determinate sentences are the two primary models used throughout the United States, although there are many variations for each of these.

indeterminate sentences

sentences that have a minimum and maximum time to serve; a decision by a release authority determines the actual time served within that range

Indeterminate sentences blend the decision by the sentencing judge and a later decision by a release authority to determine the actual time served. At the time of sentencing, judges sentence offenders to indeterminate sentences, with a minimum and maximum amount of time to be served (for example, two to five years or ten to twenty years). After serving the minimum term, offenders are eligible to be released and their cases are reviewed by a parole board. The parole

TABLE 2.1	**Number of Persons under Correctional Supervision, 1980–2007**				
	Probation	**Jail**	**Prison**	**Parole**	**Total[a]**
1980	1,118,097	183,988	319,598	220,438	1,842,100
1981	1,225,934	196,785	360,029	225,539	2,008,300
1982	1,357,264	209,582	402,914	224,604	2,194,400
1983	1,582,947	223,551	423,898	246,440	2,476,800
1984	1,740,948	234,500	448,264	266,992	2,690,700
1985	1,968,712	256,615	487,593	300,203	3,013,100
1986	2,114,621	274,444	526,436	325,638	3,241,100
1987	2,247,158	295,873	562,814	355,505	3,461,400
1988	2,356,483	343,569	607,766	407,977	3,715,800
1989	2,522,125	395,553	683,367	456,803	4,057,800
1990	2,670,234	405,320	743,382	531,407	4,350,300
1991	2,728,472	426,479	792,535	590,442	4,537,900
1992	2,811,611	444,584	850,566	658,601	4,765,400
1993	2,903,061	459,804	909,381	676,100	4,948,300
1994	2,981,022	486,474	990,147	690,371	5,148,000
1995	3,077,861	507,044	1,078,542	679,421	5,342,900
1996	3,164,996	518,492	1,127,528	679,733	5,490,700
1997	3,296,513	567,079	1,176,564	694,787	5,734,900
1998	3,670,441	592,462	1,224,469	696,385	6,134,200
1999	3,779,922	605,943	1,287,172	714,457	6,340,800
2000	3,826,209	621,149	1,316,333	723,898	6,445,100
2001	3,931,731	631,240	1,330,007	732,333	6,581,700
2002	4,024,067	665,475	1,367,547	750,934	6,758,800
2003[b]	4,120,012	691,301	1,390,279	769,925	6,924,500
2004	4,143,792	713,990	1,421,345	771,852	6,995,000
2005	4,166,757	747,529	1,448,344	780,616	7,051,900
2006[c]	4,215,361	766,010	1,492,973	799,058	7,181,500
2007[d]	4,293,163	780,581	1,512,576	824,365	7,328,200

[a]Because some offenders may have multiple statuses (i.e., held in a prison or jail but remain under the jurisdiction of a probation or parole authority) totals in 2000–04 exclude probationers held in jail or prison; totals in 2005–06 exclude probationers and parolees held in jail or prison; and the total in 2007 excludes probationers and parolees held in jail or prison, probationers who were also under parole supervision, and parolees who were also under probation supervision. For these reasons, details do not sum to total.

[b]The 2003 probation and parole counts were estimated and may differ from previously published numbers.

[c]Illinois did not provide prison or parole data for 2006; therefore, all prison and parole data for Illinois were estimated. See *Methodology* in **Prisoners in 2006** (PDF file 308K) and **Probation and Parole in the United States, 2006** (PDF file 400K)

[d]Illinois, Maine, and Nevada did not provide prison data for 2007; therefore, all prison data for these states were estimated. See *Methodology* in **Prisoners in 2007** (PDF file 195K). Oklahoma did not provide probation or parole data for 2007; therefore, all probation and parole data for Oklahoma were estimated. See *Methodology* in **Probation and Parole in the United States, 2007–Statistical Tables** (PDF file 355K)

Source: Bureau of Justice Statistics, "Correctional Populations," *Key Facts at a Glance*. http://www.ojp.usdoj.gov/bjs/glance/tables/corr2tab.htm (accessed April 12, 2009).

board determines the release date any time between the minimum and maximum sentence. If a parole board never grants parole, the offender serves the maximum sentence and then must be released. The parole decision and postrelease supervision in the community are described in Chapter 6.

As the Reformatory Era of prison operations was initiated in the United States around 1870, many states and prisons began to implement the concepts of rehabilitation and preparing inmates for return to the community. By the beginning of the twentieth century, preparation for release was considered an important part of the prison experience, and correctional systems were organized to provide programs to prepare inmates for the community transition. During the mid-twentieth century, all states used indeterminate sentences with release by parole boards, and by 1977 release on parole reached its peak, as 72 percent of all prisoners were released on parole.[13]

For almost twenty years preceding this high-water mark, the focus of incarceration was rehabilitation, as parole boards reviewed inmates' cases and determined their release dates based on the best judgment of their readiness for successfully returning to the community. Emphasizing rehabilitation made it almost impossible for judges to make a good decision about when offenders should be released at the time of sentencing. Critical to the release decision were efforts by offenders to improve themselves, as demonstrated by their personal status after they had served their minimum sentence. When believed "reformed" and ready to face life in free society, prisoners were released from prison.

The "Case Study" box illustrates some of the costs and other issues that result from changes in sentencing without a thoughtful investigation of the impact of changes.

determinate sentences
sentences of fixed terms

Determinate sentences are sentences of fixed terms. Offenders are eligible for release following the completion of the time to be served (for example, five years). Determinate sentences are not reviewed by any body and offenders are not

A Case Study

Minor Changes Can Have Major Budget Implications

A state experiencing a rapid increase in the number of offenders in prison examined the impact of several suggestions to reduce overcrowding in the prison system. The state used indeterminate sentences, but had greatly increased the minimum time to be served before inmates were eligible for parole. These sentences were often increased from one to two years, from five to seven years, or from ten to fifteen years. It is interesting that when sentences are increased it is usually by some increment of years, rather than months or even days. It is easy to decide to extend the minimum sentence for some crime, especially if the decision to lengthen the sentence comes shortly after a serious crime has occurred that received a lot of media attention, and there is too much emotion and anger involved in the decision.

One argument for stopping the increase by annual increments is that there is not much consideration of the cost of such jumps. In a study in the state of the cost of such increases, it was determined that if every inmate in the state were serving a sentence that was only ninety days shorter, it would save the state $500 million over thirty years! Legislators were shocked by these figures. The state held approximately 20,000 inmates, and reducing the sentence served by each by three months would over time reduce the population by five hundred inmates. To build a five-hundred-bed prison cost approximately $50 million, and it is estimated that construction costs represent only 10 percent of the overall operating costs of a prison over thirty years, or a total of $500 million. This represents how minor adjustments in time served can save state governments massive amounts of money.

subject to release by parole boards. When offenders complete their sentence terms, they are released. Determinate sentences were used throughout the eighteenth century in the United States. Sentencing judges were believed to have the most informed knowledge of offenders and the amount of time needed to punish them and deter them from further crimes. Therefore, judges were granted considerable discretion in determining the prescribed sentence.

An early reform in determinate sentences was the use of **good time.** The concept of good time was initiated first by Captain Alexander Maconochie, who created a system of marks when he was superintendent of the British penal colony on Norfolk Island in the 1840s. By earning marks, inmates could earn time off their sentence through good behavior and efforts toward personal reform. Good time is now the number of days subtracted from the required time to be served due to good behavior and following prison rules. Good time is used in both determinate and indeterminate sentences and affords inmates the opportunity to reduce the time until their eligibility for release. Good time is seen as a critical tool for prison staff to maintain order, because it is a valued reward that can be granted to inmates who behave or not awarded to those who fail to follow the rules of the prison.

good time
affords inmates the opportunity to reduce their eligibility for release by good behavior in prison

A form of determinate sentences that has gained popularity over the past decade is **truth in sentencing.** Recent enactments by Congress have encouraged states to adopt truth-in-sentencing (TIS) statutes and allowed states enacting such laws to qualify for federal funds to aid in prison construction. TIS statutes are determinate sentences, and also limit to 15 percent of the sentence the amount of good time that prison officials may grant inmates as incentives for good behavior or program participation.[14] Inmates under TIS statutes must complete 85 percent of the sentence before they are eligible for release. By the end of 2000, twenty-nine states and the District of Columbia had adopted TIS statutes.[15] From 1980 to 1996, the number of prisoners in state and federal prisons grew from 330,000 to 1,054,000, a more than threefold increase,[16] and reached 1,610,584 by June 30, 2008.[17]

truth in sentencing
requires completion of 85 percent of the sentence before prisoners are eligible for release

The reduction in good time—so that offenders do not get out of prison sooner than the public expects and are held accountable for their crimes—seems warranted. However, the "An Insider's Experience" box in *MyCrimeKit* illustrates how important the discretion to award good time can be for correctional administrators attempting to keep prisons from becoming too overcrowded and to save their agency money.

mycrimekit
Insider's Experience:
Increasing Good Time
Opportunities.

Judicial Discretion in Sentencing

In addition to the return to determinate sentencing over the past twenty years, there has also been a move to reduce the amount of discretion granted to sentencing judges and administrative bodies. As noted, early in the history of U.S. sentencing practices, judges were granted considerable discretion in determining the length and severity of criminal sentences. However, reforms to indeterminate sentencing and a "tough on crime" movement also brought about efforts to reduce discretion by judges and parole boards in modifying sentences. There are three forms of sentencing, based on where discretion resides within the system.

The first is the **judicial form of sentencing,** in which judges are granted considerable discretion in sentencing decisions. Under this form, penal codes create broad ranges of allowable sentences for each crime; allow judges to decide whether to grant a sentence of probation or incarceration; and, if sending the offender to prison, define a broad range of the length of time to be served. The second is the

judicial form of sentencing
judges have primary discretion in creating the sentence

administrative form of sentencing

administrative bodies (correctional officials and parole/release boards) have primary discretion in granting good time and determining the release time of offenders

legislative form of sentencing

legislative bodies create very structured sentencing codes, and therefore have primary discretion in the length of time served by offenders

mandatory minimum sentences

a requirement that for certain crimes or for certain types of offenders, there must be a sentence to prison for at least a minimum term

administrative form of sentencing, which grants considerable discretion to officials of the executive branch of government. This includes prison officials in the award of good time and parole board members in determining when inmates will be released. More recently, the **legislative form of sentencing** has come to dominate sentencing across many states and the federal government. This approach grants most of the discretion to the legislative branch of government; legislative bodies create penal codes with determinate sentences and little (or no) discretion available to judges. Legislative forms of sentencing include mandatory minimum sentences, presumptive sentencing, and the use of sentencing guidelines.

Mandatory Minimum Sentences

During the 1980s there was a concern that certain categories of offenders should be sentenced to prison without the opportunity for probation. Since that time, mandatory minimum sentences were adopted by forty-eight states and the federal government. **Mandatory minimum sentences** require that for certain crimes (violent crimes, crimes using a gun, distribution of narcotics) or for certain types of offenders (habitual criminals, sexual predators) there must be a sentence to prison for a set minimum term. The sentencing judge may not impose a sentence of probation, assess a fine, or suspend the prison sentence.

As with many criminal justice policy reforms, although the theory behind mandatory minimum sentences makes sense, the practical application results in many unintended consequences. The lack of discretion provided to judges often results in their sentencing offenders to prison that they believe warrant only being supervised in the community. Mandatory minimum sentences for drug crimes are particularly telling in this regard. Twenty years ago, 22 percent of the federal prison population were drug offenders, and today drug offenders make up 53 percent of federal inmates.[18] New York has also enacted mandatory prison sentences for drug offenders and, as a result, the percentage of violent offenders in New York prisons decreased from 63 percent in 1982 to 34 percent in 1992.[19] Many experts are questioning the value of incarcerating large numbers of drug offenders, many with no prior history, thereby requiring the construction and operation of hundreds of new prisons to hold this population.

Three-Strikes Laws

three-strikes laws

a legislative mandate that judges sentence third-time felons to extremely long or life prison sentences

Another form of mandatory minimum sentence is called **three-strikes laws,** which require judges to sentence third-time felons to extremely long prison sentences (often twenty years, thirty years, or life). These laws were intended to incapacitate habitual and dangerous law violators who commit three felonies so that they could not continue to prey on law-abiding citizens. The initial passage of such a law by the state of Washington in 1993 was intended to target repeat violent offenders. In 1994, California expanded the definition of those who come under the law and allowed some second-felony offenders to be included. At this time, twenty-six states have passed three-strikes laws. As with other mandatory minimum sentences, three-strikes laws are often an overreaction to crime-control efforts.[20]

An often-cited case of overreach of mandatory prison terms was the 1995 sentencing under the California three-strikes law of Jerry Williams. Williams had a record of two prior felony convictions involving violence when he stole a piece of pizza (without a weapon) from four children. The judge, under the mandatory California law, had to sentence Williams to twenty-five years in prison. The cost to the state for his incarceration for stealing a piece of pizza is estimated to be $500,000. An unintended problem resulting from the California three-strikes law is that offenders with two prior convictions are refusing to plea bargain. For

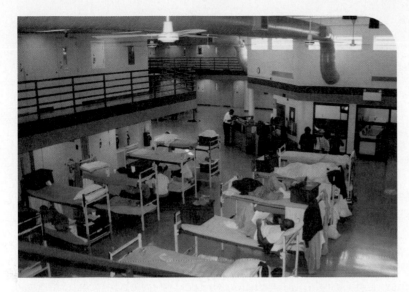

Three-strikes laws and other mandatory minimum sentences have resulted in prisons becoming extremely overcrowded.
Photo by Richard P. Seiter.

offenders with two prior convictions, any new felony results in their receiving either a twenty-five-year sentence or a life sentence, eliminating the likelihood of a plea and resulting in a demand for a trial. The court systems are being engulfed in trials for relatively simple cases. Cases like the Williams sentence and the overall impact on cost and court delays resulting from the California three-strikes law have raised considerable questions about the value of such laws.

There has been much debate about the effectiveness of three-strikes laws and the impact of such laws on crime rates and costs to the correctional system. Since California has one of the oldest of such laws in effect and has used the law more extensively than many other states, it has been the most studied.[21] The most important issue is whether three-strikes laws reduce crime. California's crime rates have decreased since the three-strikes law was adopted. However, the impact of three-strikes laws on this decline is questionable. In one of the most thorough analyses of the California law, Zimring, Kamin, and Hawkins concluded that "declines in crime observed after the effective date of the three-strikes law were not the results of the deterrent impacts of the (three-strikes) statute."[22]

Presumptive Sentencing

Presumptive sentencing is a predetermined range of a minimum, average, and maximum term for a specific crime. Judges are directed to sentence the "typical" offender committing a crime to the presumptive term. The sentencing judge is then granted limited discretion in determining whether there are *mitigating* circumstances (those that indicate reasons for leniency) that should be considered and used to reduce the sentence to below the presumptive term, or *aggravating* circumstances (those that indicate that the offender deserves more than the average), resulting in a sentence of more than the presumptive term. Most presumptive sentences include a minimum and maximum sentence, with very limited ranges of discretion. For example, in one presumptive sentencing model, the presumptive sentence is fifty-four months, the minimum sentence is fifty months, and the maximum sentence is fifty-eight months.

Sentencing Guidelines

Sentencing guidelines combine both minimum mandatory and presumptive sentencing approaches. **Sentencing guidelines** are structured sentences, based on measures of offense severity and criminal history, to determine the length of the term of imprisonment. Figure 2.3 is the Minnesota sentencing guideline grid. It

presumptive sentencing
a predetermined range of a minimum, average, and maximum term for a specific crime for a "typical" offender, with allowances for mitigating and aggravating circumstances to be considered

sentencing guidelines
structured sentences, based on measures of offense severity and criminal history, to determine the length of the term of imprisonment

mycrimekit
Media—Video: Sentencing Guidelines.

A. SENTENCING GUIDELINES GRID
Presumptive Sentence Lengths in Months

Italicized numbers within the grid denote the range within which a judge may sentence without the sentence being deemed a departure. Offenders with non-imprisonment felony sentences are subject to jail time according to law.

CRIMINAL HISTORY SCORE

SEVERITY LEVEL OF CONVICTION OFFENSE (common offenses listed in italics)		0	1	2	3	4	5	6 or more
Murder, 2nd Degree (intentional murder, drive-by-shootings)	XI	**306** 261–367	**326** 278–391	**346** 295–415	**366** 312–439	**386** 329–463	**406** 346–480[2]	**426** 363–480[2]
Murder, 3rd Degree Murder, 2nd Degree (unintentional murder)	X	**150** 128–180	**165** 141–198	**180** 153–216	**195** 166–234	**210** 179–252	**225** 192–270	**240** 204–288
Assault, 1st Degree Controlled Substance Crime, 1st Degree	IX	**86** 74–103	**98** 84–117	**110** 94–132	**122** 104–146	**134** 114–160	**146** 125–175	**158** 135–189
Aggravated Robbery, 1st Degree Controlled Substance Crime, 2nd Degree	VIII	**48** 41–57	**58** 50–69	**68** 58–81	**78** 67–93	**88** 75–105	**98** 84–117	**108** 92–129
Felony DWI	VII	**36**	**42**	**48**	**54** 46–64	**60** 51–72	**66** 57–79	**72** 62–86
Assault, 2nd Degree Felon in Possession of a Firearm	VI	**21**	**27**	**33**	**39** 34–46	**45** 39–54	**51** 44–61	**57** 49–68
Residential Burglary Simple Robbery	V	**18**	**23**	**28**	**33** 29–39	**38** 33–45	**43** 37–51	**48** 41–57
Nonresidential Burglary	IV	**12**[1]	**15**	**18**	**21**	**24** 21–28	**27** 23–32	**30** 26–36
Theft Crimes (over $2,500)	III	**12**[1]	**13**	**15**	**17**	**19** 17–22	**21** 18–25	**23** 20–27
Theft Crimes ($2,500 or less) Check Forgery ($200–$2,500)	II	**12**[1]	**12**[1]	**13**	**15**	**17**	**19**	**21** 18–25
Sale of Simulated Controlled Substance	I	**12**[1]	**12**[1]	**12**[1]	**13**	**15**	**17**	**19** 17–22

☐ Presumptive commitment to state imprisonment. First Degree Murder is excluded from the guidelines by law and continues to have a mandatory life sentence. See section II.E. Mandatory Sentences for policy regarding those sentences controlled by law.

▨ Presumptive stayed sentence; at the discretion of the judge, up to a year in jail and/or other non-jail sanctions can be imposed as conditions of probation. However, certain offenses in this section of the grid always carry a presumptive commitment to state prison. See sections II.C. Presumptive Sentence and II. E. Mandatory Sentences.

1 One year and one day

2 M.S § 244.09 requires the Sentencing Guidelines to provide a range of 15% downward and 20% upward from the presumptive sentence. However, because the statutory maximum sentence for these offenses is no more than 40 years, the range is capped at that number.

Effective August 1, 2006

Source: Minnesota Sentencing Guidelines Commission, *Report to the Legislature* (St. Paul: Minnesota Sentencing Guidelines Commission, 2006), p. 24.

FIGURE 2.3 Minnesota Sentencing Guideline Grid

was one of the earliest enacted sentencing guidelines, adopted in 1983. The left side of the grid is a list of crime categories in order of increasing severity. Across the top, offenders' criminal histories are scored on factors such as the number of prior offenses, age at first offense, history of violence, or escape from a prison or absconding from community supervision.

States have adopted sentencing guidelines for several reasons. First, it was believed that judges might not be harsh enough on certain criminals and required guidelines to ensure that dangerous criminals are sent to prison. Second, sentencing guidelines provide uniformity, ensuring that offenders who commit similar crimes receive similar sentences. Sentencing guidelines provide planners (using projections of crime rates) with a better idea of what future sentences may mean to the number of inmates in prison or offenders under probation supervision. Most important, sentencing guidelines (by combining factors of offense severity and criminal history) provide a rational approach to determining a sentence.[23] In some states, judges have very little discretion and cannot vary from the guidelines. In other states, the guidelines are just "guidelines," and judges are not required to follow them. Finally, some jurisdictions allow judges to sentence above or below the sentencing guidelines if the judge includes a written explanation as to the reason for the deviation.

The "An Interview With" box provides a good indication of the types of decisions and the process used in sentencing and the struggles that judges face in trying to fit a criminal sentence for a particular individual into fairly limited sentencing options.

An Interview With...

A Sentencing Judge

The following is an interview with Robert H. Dierker, Jr., Circuit Judge of the 22nd Judicial Circuit of Missouri (St. Louis). The Circuit Court in Missouri is the sentencing court for adult felons and misdemeanants. Judge Dierker, who received his law degree from the University of Missouri at Kansas City and an LL.M. from Harvard University, has been a judge since 1986. He has presided over numerous civil and criminal trials, including nine capital murder trials.

Question: Thank you, Judge Dierker, for agreeing to be interviewed regarding criminal sentencing. Can you briefly describe your career as a judge?

Judge Dierker: I was appointed a circuit judge in 1986. The circuit court handles all types of criminal and civil cases. I have served in all divisions of the circuit court except probate and juvenile. I have been in the criminal trial division, holding criminal trials, for five years, and also served as the assignment judge to assign criminal cases to courts and judges for four years. I have also sat by designation on the Missouri Court of Appeals and Supreme Court.

Question: Can you describe the sentencing model and process in Missouri?

Judge Dierker: In criminal trials in which the defendant has no prior convictions, the initial punishment is "assessed" by the jury, which means that the jury decides on the sentence ceiling and the judge can use that sentence or depart downward from that sentence. When the defendant has prior convictions or there is a plea, the judge determines the sentence. The sentence, however, must be within

...continued

the statutory sentencing code. The Missouri code classifies felonies into level A, B, C, or D. Each of these levels has a range of sentencing options. There is also first-degree murder, which carries a penalty of death or life without parole. There are also some mandatory sentences for career criminals or consistent offenders. Offenders that have previously been committed to the custody of the department of corrections must serve a mandatory minimum portion of their sentence prior to release. Certain dangerous felonies also carry a mandatory minimum term of imprisonment. The sentencing judge has discretion to determine the sentence within prescribed ranges. There are advisory sentencing guidelines that judges can consider, but they are not mandated to use them.

Question: How has the role of a judge changed regarding the sentencing process over the past several years?

Judge Dierker: Without doubt, the most significant change has been the mandatory minimum sentences for dangerous felons, persistent offenders, or those previously committed to prison.

Question: How do judges feel about these changes and the mandatory sentence requirement?

Judge Dierker: Many judges feel these mandatory minimum sentences simplify the sentencing task, and most are sympathetic to the policy need of the legislature to provide "truth in sentencing." Previously, the parole board had the authority to release an offender after serving considerably less time than the full sentence, and the public often questioned the credibility of such sentences. The Missouri legislature has discussed the adoption of a sentencing model similar to the federal sentencing guidelines, thus making the "advisory" guidelines mandatory, with no discretion for the judge to attempt to individualize a sentence to make the punishment best fit the crime and the offender. I personally testified against this change, and very few judges support this total lack of sentencing discretion.

Question: What are the key issues or circumstances that you consider when deciding on a criminal sentence?

Judge Dierker: The paramount consideration is the nature of the crime. The next most important is the defendant's criminal history. Of some importance is the offender's social history. It is also valuable to consider the consequences, impact, and opinions of the victim.

Question: Is it usual to have a wide disagreement between the prosecutor and the defense attorney on what the sentence should be? Or are most cases plea bargained?

Judge Dierker: There is considerable difference between Missouri and the federal model of sentencing in this regard. In Missouri, there is considerable bargaining over the sentence between the prosecution and the defense. In federal court, the only bargaining is in regard to the charges to be filed by the prosecutor, since the sentencing guidelines dictate the sentence once a plea is reached. Therefore, when there is a plea bargain, the Missouri trial judge has a limited range of options and may either accept or reject the plea and the agreed-upon sentence. In that sense, most plea bargaining sentences are not decisions as much as agreements.

Question: What is the most difficult thing, or the thing you struggle most with, in deciding a criminal sentence?

Judge Dierker: It is interesting that as I grow older the sentencing process seems to become more difficult for me. As I have more experience in sentencing and the people involved, I see or am more conscious of the impact of a specific sentence on the offender and victims and their family members. While it seems easy to invoke a sentence, it really is difficult to consider all these individual aspects and make the punishment fit the crime and the sentence make sense from the standpoint of what the criminal justice system is trying to accomplish. Many cases are not all that difficult, and I have no problem sentencing someone to a severe sentence or even death when the crime warrants it. But there are times when the options available in the statutory sentencing code just do not seem to fit the crime or meet the needs of the individuals involved.

Question: What other general comments would you make about the sentencing process?

Judge Dierker: I have great concern about the efficacy of the sentencing structure for narcotics offenses. I believe we have made progress on sentencing for drug offenses, as the treatment aspects have become much more prominent. Yet we need to continue to be thinking of creative ways to deal with drug offenders and looking for sentencing alternatives, such as a greater range in treatment options for drug offenders. While the drug courts receive much attention, I am not yet persuaded that they are the best approach.

Creative Sentencing Options

As noted, there are many inmates that are deferred from prosecution or diverted from the criminal justice system. In an effort to look at offenders who could be successfully diverted and managed in a nontraditional manner from typical criminal courts, problem-solving courts have developed. The most often used are drug courts and mental health courts.

Drug Courts

One promising innovation regarding sentencing is the use of drug courts. **Drug courts** are an alternative to traditional court models in many ways. First, the overall philosophy is not to punish but to change behavior. Drug courts deal with offenders experiencing a drug problem as the basis of their criminality. Offenders are held accountable and must accept responsibility. Drug courts still oversee the criminal processing, yet all the court players (judges, prosecutors, defense counsel, probation officers, and treatment professionals) acknowledge the need for drug treatment (usually in the community), and therefore the adversarial nature of most criminal court proceedings is replaced with a much more collaborative one. The intent is to quickly and nonbureaucratically get the offender into drug treatment. Identification of the offender as needing intervention immediately after arrest is believed to improve the offender's motivation for change.[24]

Drug courts are usually a unit within the court system, and drug-addicted offenders are diverted from traditional criminal processing. Courts sentence offenders to treatment programs, recognizing that sanctions that merely increase in punitiveness for repeat offenses do not work for drug addicts.[25] The judge continues to oversee the sentence and holds regular status review hearings with the offender to determine progress and compliance with conditions of the sentence.

drug courts
an alternative to traditional court models to deal with the underlying drug problem as the basis of the offenders' criminality

Drug courts have received positive preliminary evaluations for diverting substance abusers from prisons and getting them involved in treatment to deal with underlying problems that are often the cause of their criminality.
Courtesy of Richard Hutchings/PhotoEdit Inc.

Drug courts have proved very promising. From 1998 to December 31, 2004, the number of drug courts in operation in the United States grew from 347 to 1,621, and by December 31, 2007, there were 2,147 drug courts in operation, a 32 percent increase from 2004.[26] "More than 226,000 defendants participated in these programs."[27] A recent review of recidivism of drug court graduates for 1999 and 2000 found that 16.4 percent were arrested and charged with a serious offense within one year of graduation, and 27.5 percent within two years of graduation.[28] These rates, however, have not been compared with a similar group of drug offenders who did not go through a drug court.

Although it is too early in the existence of drug courts to make total claims of success, preliminary evaluations have shown some success in reducing drug use and future criminal activity. An evaluation of one of the first drug courts initiated in Dade County, Florida, in 1989 indicates that drug court offenders experienced lower incarceration rates, longer time to rearrest, and less frequent rearrest.[29] A 2000 evaluation found that graduates of drug court programs are less likely to be rearrested than a comparison group of those who do not graduate from the program.[30] And the Government Accounting Office reviewed data for twenty-three drug court programs and in 2005 concluded that lower percentages of drug court participants than those going through traditional criminal justice courts were rearrested or reconvicted and drug court participants had fewer recidivism events.[31] Although drug courts are still in their relative infancy in the criminal justice system, they have proven very popular and serve as a model for alternative sentencing approaches.[32]

Mental Health Courts

In addition to drug courts, courts to deal with the recycling of mentally ill offenders through the criminal justice system have developed over the past decade. As established, mental health courts are not merely drug courts handling the mentally ill. The principal role of mental health courts is to treat mental illness, which unlike drug use, is not a crime. Therefore, the changes included within the purview of mental health courts are very broad, and the operation of mental health courts varies widely. The standard definition of a mental health court is "a specialized court docket for certain defendants with mental illness that substitutes a problem-solving model for traditional criminal court processing."[33] Although only a few existed in 1999, over 150 courts were operating by 2007.[34]

Even though there is much variation in how they operate, there are some common features of mental health courts. First, they identify individuals who have committed crimes but are mentally ill. The courts screen defendants from any time immediately after arrest to a few weeks later. They look for individuals who are not necessarily criminal in nature, but their mental illness seems to be the key reason they get wrapped up in the criminal justice process. With a priority for community safety, however, most participants are misdemeanor or low-level offenders with no history of serious violence. The courts then attempt to prevent the jailing and detention of these individuals, fearing they will deteriorate even more and end up with greater criminal sanctions as a result of their detention status. The courts use a team approach (judicial officers, treatment providers, prosecutor, defense attorney, and court supervision officer) to identify and recommend candidates for mental health court diversion. The participants must volunteer and agree to participate in treatment. If the individual successfully completes treatment, he or she can avoid a criminal record and continue to seek treatment outside the criminal justice process.

The goals of mental health courts include the following:

- Increase public safety by reducing criminal activity by mentally ill individuals
- Increase treatment to mentally ill individuals
- Improve the quality of life for participants
- More effectively use the resources of communities to treat mentally ill individuals, partly through reducing the repetition of contacts with the criminal justice system[35]

It is still too early to have conclusive data on the success of mental health courts, but preliminary findings are positive. Some studies have found that participants in mental health courts had fewer new bookings into jail compared with a similar period prior to their program participation,[36] and other studies found that participants were less likely to have new charges or to be arrested than a comparison group of non-mental-health courts participants.[37] These positive outcomes lead one to expect that the number of mental health courts will continue to expand.

As we conclude our study of sentencing, you must decide what type of sentencing model you prefer. In the "You Make the Decision" box, you are asked to choose between determinate and indeterminate sentencing for your state.

Summary

Criminal sentencing is one of the most complicated, yet obviously one of the most critical, components of the criminal justice process. Sentencing attempts to meet several distinct yet often overlapping goals and must take into account a variety of factors, laws, and situations. Some consider sentencing the linchpin of the criminal justice system, in that all the presentence activities are designed to lead up to the sentencing decision, and all postsentence activities are designed to carry out the sentence.

As described in this chapter, the functions of corrections no longer just begin after sentencing. Many critical pretrial functions are now considered a part of the correctional process. Correctional personnel help identify offenders who are good risks for release on recognizance. They may also conduct community supervision of offenders not detained while waiting for their trial dates. Probation officers investigate the background of offenders, conduct a presentence investigation that is extremely valuable for the sentencing decision, and provide information throughout the correctional system to classify and assign offenders to prisons or programs.

Sentencing models and forms have changed significantly over the past several decades. During the nineteenth century, judges had significant discretion in sentencing offenders. During most of the twentieth century, parole boards made decisions regarding offenders' readiness and time of release. Over the past two decades, however, legislatures have taken discretion away from most correctional and court personnel and replaced it with mandatory minimum sentencing, three-strikes laws, truth in sentencing, and sentencing guidelines. Some argue that this provides for uniformity and fairness, but others suggest that this "cookie cutter" form of sentencing, in which all offenders committing similar crimes are treated in a "one size fits all" approach, is not a reform, but a step backward into an overly excessive and inefficient system of justice.

CHAPTER REVIEW

Following this chapter describing sentencing are four chapters that describe the theoretical approaches, operations, and issues surrounding the various sentencing alternatives. The use of jails and detention facilities is described in Chapter 3, probation and intermediate sentencing options are described in Chapter 4, the rapidly expanding use of prison sentences and the operation of prisons is discussed in Chapter 5, and the release on parole for offenders serving indeterminate sentences and the difficult transition from prison to the community are presented in Chapter 6. By the end of Part 2 of this text, students will have an understanding of the major components that make up the correctional systems of the United States.

Key Terms

sentencing

felony

misdemeanor

pretrial diversion

preventive detention

bail

surety

release on recognizance (ROR)

Manhattan Bail Project (MBP)

supervised pretrial release programs (SPTR)

plea bargaining

presentence investigation (PSI)

economic sanction

community service

probation

intermediate sanction

short-term confinement

imprisonment

capital punishment

concurrent sentences

consecutive sentences

indeterminate sentences

determinate sentences

good time

truth in sentencing

judicial form of sentencing

administrative form of sentencing

legislative form of sentencing

mandatory minimum sentences

three-strikes laws

presumptive sentencing

sentencing guidelines

drug courts

Review Questions

1. Differentiate between a felony and misdemeanor.

2. Describe the types of diversion programs currently used.

3. List some of the problems with using bail as a requirement for release from jail pending prosecution.

4. Describe the Manhattan Bail Project and how it has expanded and influenced current detention practices.

5. List the pros and cons of plea bargaining.

6. List the five purposes of the presentence investigation.

7. What are economic sanctions and community service?

8. Differentiate between concurrent and consecutive sentences.

9. Describe how truth-in-sentencing legislation works.

10. Differentiate between judicial, administrative, and legislative forms of sentencing.

11. What are mandatory minimum sentences?

12. List the pros and cons of three-strikes laws.

13. Describe how sentencing guidelines work.

14. How do drug courts operate, and what are their advantages?

15. How do mental health courts operate, and what are their advantages?

You Make the Decision...

Determinate or Indeterminate Sentences

As noted, the history of sentencing for criminal offenses has been a combination of determinate and indeterminate sentences. Determinate sentences were used throughout the 1800s, and indeterminate sentences for most of the 1900s. Over the past twenty years, disillusionment with the concept of rehabilitation, the medical model, and parole prompted a "tough-on-crime" philosophy that resulted in an apparent swing back to determinate sentencing and limited discretion with the imposition of mandatory sentencing and truth in sentencing. However, states have more recently become concerned about the increasing costs and prison overcrowding that has resulted from abandoning indeterminate sentences. As a result, some states have reversed themselves and returned to using an indeterminate sentencing structure. It has even been questioned whether the use of determinate sentences reduces public safety. Determinate sentences eliminate the role parole boards play as gatekeepers, keeping inmates who are high risk to repeat their crimes in prison.

In this "You Make the Decision," you must decide which of these two sentencing models you think is best and want implemented in your home state. List the pros and cons for each sentencing model. Consider the benefits of each model you think are most important, and then decide which model you favor. If you are changing from the sentencing model currently used in your state, think of all the potential consequences likely to occur and the possible negative outcomes. You must make a choice: should your state use determinate or indeterminate sentencing?

Chapter Resources on mycrimekit™

Go to http://mycrimekit.com to explore the following study tools and resources specific to this chapter:

- **Practice Quiz:** multiple-choice, true/false, short-answer, and essay questions to help students test their knowledge
- **WebQuests:** learning activities built around Web searches
  - **Restorative Justice:** http://www.restorativejustice.org

- **Insider's Experiences:** "Increasing Good Time Opportunities"
- **Seiter Videos:**
  - See experts discuss sentencing processes
  - See experts discuss making the sentencing decision
  - See experts discuss sentencing guidelines
- **Flashcards:** Thirty-three flashcards to test knowledge of the chapter's key terms

Jails

After reading this chapter, you should be able to:

1. Describe the historical development of jails, their design, and their operations.

2. List the categories of offenders that are housed in jails.

3. Define regional jails and explain their role.

4. Explain the reasons for the increased incarceration rate in jails over the past two decades.

5. Discuss the daily operations of a jail.

6. Identify the staff roles and functions in a modern jail.

7. Compare the various jail designs and explain the positive benefits of direct supervision.

8. Describe efforts to reduce jail crowding.

9. Discuss the challenges jails face with mentally ill offenders.

10. Explain the approaches that jails take to reduce the likelihood of inmate suicides.

Introduction

Probably no major segment of the criminal justice system is less studied, evaluated, or understood than the nation's jails. Yet no segment of the criminal justice system touches more people's lives. Jails hold only about one-tenth of all offenders under correctional supervision, yet admit approximately four times as many offenders each year as all other correctional components combined.[1] Jails are often misunderstood, as the general public regularly confuses prisons and jails. We have all heard someone say something like, "For that crime, I hope the criminal spends years in jail," although jails are not used to hold sentenced offenders for long terms of confinement.

Jails are the watershed of the correctional system. The U.S. jail is the oldest of the correctional components, initiated well before prisons, probation, parole, or halfway houses. Yet the jail still has a diverse and difficult mission and role. Few offenders won't pass through a jail as they enter the correctional system. Jails hold a variety of offenders (those who have been arrested, have been detained pending trial, have been sentenced to short terms of confinement for minor crimes, are awaiting transfer to another facility, and are being held administratively for a criminal justice agency). They may hold offenders arrested for public drunkenness or for multiple murders.

Some jail systems are larger than all but a few state prison systems, and some are extremely small (four or five beds). Jails face unique issues, such as dealing with unknown offenders, managing detoxification and medical problems, and serving the court with security and prisoner transportation. Jails can have budgets in the hundreds of millions of dollars per year, or they may have budgets of only a few hundred thousand dollars. Jails may have sophisticated management and professional training of staff, or they may have poor management with patrol deputies with no specialized training assigned to watch prisoners.

This chapter provides an overview of the nation's jail systems, to include their historical development, current operations with the makeup and characteristics of offenders, their organization and physical design, and current issues such as over-crowding, legal issues, dealing with mentally ill offenders, and preventing sui-cides. Students will find how the diverse makeup of jail clients makes the job of jail staff complex and difficult. Jail inmates may be incarcerated from only a few hours to several months. They hold inmates charged with drunkenness to serial murder, and many offenders are violent and impulsive. These multifaceted challenges of the nation's jails can make other components of the criminal justice system seem simple in their operation and management. By the end of the chapter, students will understand the approaches that jail officials take to deal with these issues and the continuing problems they will face into the next several years.

The History of Jails

gaol
an early English term for a jail

The first jails were created in England. The first **gaol,** as jails were then called, was ordered built by King Henry II in 1166. Originally for use in detaining offenders awaiting trial, as vagrancy became a problem between the fourteenth and eigh-teenth centuries, the jails were used to house displaced persons, the poor, and sometimes even the mentally ill. These early jails had deplorable conditions of filth, violence, poor food, and little medical care. These conditions came to the attention of John Howard, who was appointed sheriff of Bedfordshire in 1773. While inspecting the local jails, Howard was shocked by the conditions of disease, lack of discipline, and lack of sanitation that he discovered. He visited prisons in other European countries to find models that could be replicated in England and worked with members of the English House of Commons to draft the Penitentiary Act of 1779. This act created four requirements for English prisons and jails: (1) secure and sanitary structures, (2) systematic inspections, (3) abolition of fees charged to inmates, and (4) a reformatory regime in which inmates were confined in solitary cells but worked in common rooms during the day. The act also detailed the requirements for diet, uniforms, and hygiene for prisoners.

Early jails in the U.S. colonies followed the English model and were primarily used to house those awaiting trial. Instead of cells, they often had as many as thirty inmates housed in one large room.[2] As punishment for crimes, offenders were often fined. Those too poor to pay their fines were confined until they worked off their debts. *Workhouses* and jails were sometimes different facilities, and sometimes jails held both populations. It was not until the end of the eighteenth century that the concept of confinement for punishment and rehabilitation of convicted offenders came to America. The first prison for this purpose was established in 1790 in a wing of the Walnut Street Jail in Philadelphia, and the function of confining sentenced criminals was established in penitentiaries that were built in most states over the next fifty years. Jails continued their role of housing primarily pretrial inmates, and by the end of the nineteenth century, almost every U.S. city had constructed and operated a jail for this purpose.

Current Jail Operations

Role and Functions of Jails

Jails are locally operated correctional facilities that confine people before or after adjudication. Jails serve a variety of functions and hold a variety of categories of offenders, including the following:

jails
locally operated correctional facilities that confine persons before or after adjudication

- Individuals pending arraignment and awaiting trial, conviction, or sentencing
- Probation, parole, and bail bond violators and absconders
- Juveniles, pending transfer to juvenile authorities
- Mentally ill people, pending their movement to appropriate mental health facilities
- Individuals held for the military, for protective custody, for contempt, and for the courts as witnesses
- Inmates pending transfer to federal, state, or other criminal justice authorities
- Inmates held for federal, state, or other authorities because of crowding of their facilities
- Offenders assigned to community-based programs, such as day reporting, home detention, or electronic monitoring
- Inmates sentenced to short terms (generally less than one year)

This multiple mission makes the operation of contemporary jails very complex and requires systems, staff, and facilities that are flexible enough to meet these various demands. Although several different terms are now used to describe facilities that carry out these functions (*correctional center, house of correction, detention facility,and even prison*), the role is similar. Jails are full-service facilities that offer security, food service, medical care, and offender programs and are therefore different from **lockups,** which are commonly located in police stations and hold people only for a short time, usually no more than forty-eight hours.

lockup
refers to a small jail with only a few cells and no accommodations for food services, medical care, or recreation

Most police departments and even some court buildings have a few cells that are called a *lockup.* However, these are not full-service jails and cannot be used to hold offenders for more than a few hours. Photo by Richard P. Seiter.

The Organization of Jails

The county government almost always operates jails, and almost every county has a jail. It is estimated that there are approximately 3,376 jails in the United States. In some counties in which there is a large metropolitan area, the county and city may combine the jail function and possibly jointly contribute to the jail budget and management. In rural counties, jails are the responsibility of the **sheriff,** the elected official who oversees both policing activities within the county and the operation of the jail. In some metropolitan areas, the sheriff only supervises the jail and a county police force takes care of typical law enforcement activities.

A fairly new development is that of **regional jails.** As the operation of jails became increasingly complex and interventions by the courts required a full range of security and services for all jails, some small counties found it increasingly difficult to provide adequate funding for their jail operation. As a solution, sometimes several small counties form coalitions to jointly fund, build, and operate a regional jail that serves all the counties and results in economies of scale that make its operation more financially reasonable. A regional jail commission oversees these regional jails, with each county having one representative to serve on the commission. The commission hires a jail administrator to supervise the jail, approves the budget and the proportionate contribution of funds from each

sheriff

the elected official who oversees both policing activities within the county and the operation of the jail

regional jail

a jail that serves more than one county and is overseen by a regional jail commission

Regional jails are more efficient for small counties that cannot afford the high cost of modern jail-operating requirements. Photo by Richard P. Seiter.

county, and approves the general policies and operating practices for the facility. In some cases, the management (and sometimes the construction and ownership) of the regional jail is contracted to the private sector. In 2008, there were 312 privately operated prisons and jails in the United States.[3] The role of the private sector in prison and jail operations is discussed in Chapters 5 and 15.

Jail Populations

At midyear 2008, the nation's 3,376[4] local jails held 785,556 inmates, up from 765,819 at midyear 2006 and 780,174 at midyear 2007.[5] As noted in Table 3.1, the annual increase was only 0.7 percent from midyear 2007 to midyear 2008, much less than the average annual increase of 3.3 percent from 2000 to 2007.

The number of people in the nation's jails has clearly risen significantly over the past twenty years. The **incarceration rate** is defined as the number of people per 100,000 U.S. residents who are incarcerated in either a jail or a prison. Figure 3.1 shows that the jail incarceration rate more than doubled between 1983 and 2008. The incarceration rate in jails has continued to steadily increase; on June 30, 2008, the jail incarceration rate rose to 258 per 100,000 U.S. residents compared to 193 in 1995 and 231 in 2002.[6]

The incarceration rate is significantly different by race and ethnicity. Table 3.2 shows that the jail incarceration rate in 1990 for white non-Hispanics was only

incarceration rates
the number of persons per 100,000 that are in jail or prison

TABLE 3.1	Inmates Confined in Local Jails at Midyear, Average Daily Jail Population, and Incarceration Rates, 2000–2008				
	Inmates Confined at Midyear		**Average Daily Population**[a]		
Year	**Number**	**Percent**	**Number**	**Percent**	**Incarceration Rate**[b]
2000	621,149	2.5%	618,319	1.7%	226
2001	631,240	1.6	625,966	1.2	222
2002	665,475	5.4	652,082	4.2	231
2003	691,301	3.0	680,760	4.4	238
2004	713,990	3.3	706,242	3.7	243
2005	747,529	4.7	733,442	3.9	252
2006[c]	765,819	2.4	755,320	3.0	256
2007[d]	780,174	1.9	773,138	2.4	259
2008	785,556	0.7	776,573	0.4	258
Average annual increase					
2000–2007		3.3%		3.2%	
2007–2008		0.7		0.4	

[a]Average daily population is the sum of the number of inmates in jail each day for a year, divided by the number of days in the year.

[b]Number of inmates confined at midyear per 100,000 U.S. residents.

[c]Based on revised data from selected jail jurisdictions for the number of inmates confined at midyear 2006. See *Methodology* for a description of revised data.

[d]Based on revised data from selected jail jurisdictions for the number of inmates confined at midyear 2007 and the average daily population in 2007. See *Methodology* for a description of revised data.

Source: Todd D. Minton and William J. Sabol, *Jail Inmates at Midyear 2008–Statistical Tables* (Washington, D.C.: U.S. Department of Justice, March 2009), p. 2.

Number of jail inmates per 100,000 residents

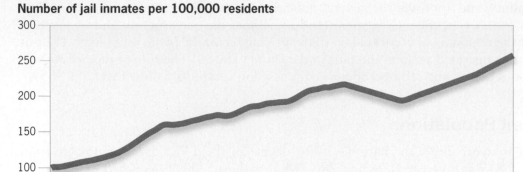

Source: Bureau of Justice Statistics, *Key Facts at a Glance.* http://www.ojp.usdoj.gov/bjs/glance/tables/corr2tab.htm (accessed December 22, 2008); and Todd D. Minton and William J. Sabol, *Jail Inmates at Midyear 2008–Statistical Tables* (Washington, D.C.: U.S. Department of Justice, Bureau of Justice Statistics, March 2009), p. 2.

FIGURE 3.1   Number of Jail Inmates per 100,000 Residents

TABLE 3.2	Jail Incarceration Rates by Race and Ethnicity, 1990–2008		

| | Number of Jail Inmates per 100,000 U.S. Residents | | |
Year	White non-Hispanic	Black non-Hispanic	Hispanic of any Race
1990	89	560	245
1991	92	594	247
1992	93	618	251
1993	94	633	262
1994	98	656	274
1995	104	670	263
1996	111	640	276
1997	117	706	293
1998	125	716	292
1999	127	730	288
2000	132	736	280
2001	138	703	263
2002	147	740	256
2003	151	748	269
2004	160	765	262
2005	166	800	268
2006	170	815	283
2007	170	815	276
2008	167	831	274

Note: U.S. resident population estimates for race and Hispanic origin were made using a U.S. Census Bureau internet release with adjustments for census undercount. Estimates for 2000–2008 are based on the 2000 Census and then estimated for July 1 each year.

Source: Bureau of Justice Statistics, "Demographic Trends in Jail Populations," *Key Facts at a Glance.*//www.ojp.usdoj.gov/bjs/glance/tables/jailrairtab.htm (accessed April 26, 2009).

half that of Hispanics of any race and was less than one-fifth that of black non-Hispanics. At midyear 2004, of all jail inmates, 44.4 percent were white, 38.6 percent were black, 15.2 percent were Hispanic, and 1.8 percent were other.[7] This compares with the 2008 figures of 42.5 percent white, 39.2 percent black, 16.4 percent Hispanic, and 1.8 percent other.[8] It is interesting to examine the makeup of the jail population in the United States. The U.S. Department of Justice, Bureau of Justice Statistics, does a complete survey of the nation's jails approximately every five years. As a part of this survey, a sample of inmates is interviewed. The survey represents a snapshot examination of inmates in jails on a specific day. The 2007 survey resulted in interviews with more than 936 jails in 874 jurisdictions and created a description of jail inmates. This report was updated one year later in June of 2008 and rendered the following information:

- Since midyear 2000, the percentages of men and women in local jails has remained relatively stable.
- The number of women in local jails reached 99,673 in 2008, up from 70,414 in 2000.
- Nearly 56 percent of offenders in local jails were racial or ethnic minorities at midyear 2008. As estimated, 308,000 were black and 128,500 were Hispanic or Latino.
- The percentages of whites and blacks confined in jail experienced a slight increase since midyear 2006; the Hispanic or Latino population grew from 15.6 percent at midyear 2006 to 16.4 percent of all inmates midyear 2008.
- At midyear 2008, 63 percent of inmates had not been convicted or were awaiting trial, up from 56 percent in 2000.
- At midyear 2008, the jail incarceration rate was 258 inmates per 100,000 U.S. residents, up from 226 per 100,000 in 2000.[9]

This description does not paint a pretty picture of the jail population. Inmates in jail are a troubled lot and experience many problems (poverty, substance abuse, mental illness) that contribute to their criminal behavior and must be managed by jail staff. It is also troubling to note that such a high percentage are sitting in jails having been charged with or convicted of a nonviolent crime. This is borne out by a study of Texas jail inmates, which found that of the state's jail population more than half of the jail inmates were there for drug offenses (37.8 percent for possession of a controlled substance and 15.2 percent for delivery of a controlled substance) and almost another 30 percent for other property crimes (14.6 percent for theft/larceny, 8.3 percent for unauthorized use of a motor vehicle, 9.1 percent for forgery, 7.6 percent for burglary of a building, and 3.9 percent for other property offenses).[10]

The Increasing Use of Jails

Although there is no question that the jail population and incarceration rate have been increasing, several theories suggest reasons for the increase. In reality, several factors may underlie this growth. First, the "tough on crime" mentality of the public affects the percentage of offenders who receive bail or release on recognizance. Judges do not want to put potentially dangerous offenders back on the streets and are more likely to set higher bail amounts and less likely to grant release without bond requirements. One review of those arrested for crimes and their release on bail indicated that 61.6 percent of people arrested and jailed for violent offenses were released pending disposition of charges in 1990; this dropped to 57 percent in 1992 and 53.9 percent in 1994.[11] The number of jail inmates who were awaiting trial (not yet convicted of the charged offense) increased from 228,900 in 1993 to 331,000 in 1999, an increase of 40 percent.[12] This resulted in an increase from 50 to 54 percent of all jail inmates (from 1993 to 1999) awaiting trial rather than serving a sentence. By 2008, 63 percent of jail inmates were awaiting court action on the current charge.[13]

Second, the number of arrests increased 20 percent from 1983 to 1993.[14] Since that time, the arrest rate has consistently deceased. There were 14,209,365 estimated arrests in 2007 in the United States, of which the largest percent (13 percent) were for drug abuse violations.[15] Much of this increase is the result of the war on drugs and an emphasis by law enforcement agencies on targeting drug crimes, the increase in the number of police officers, and the subsequent increase of a large number of drug offenders. In 1983, only 9 percent of jail inmates had been arrested for drug offenses; this increased to 22 percent in 1996,[16] and 30 percent in 2007.[17] In Tennessee, there were 48,205 arrests for drug violations for 13.4 percent of all arrests in 2007.[18]

Third, with extensive overcrowding of state and federal prisons over the past decade, more jail inmates are being held by jails as they await transfer to prison. At year-end 2007, state and federal prisons were operating at capacities of between 115 and 136 percent, respectively.[19] In 2000, only 62,884 offenders were held in local jails for state or federal jurisdictions. This figure rose to 80,371 or 5 percent of all prisoners by December 31, 2007.[20]

Finally, there has been increasing use of a split sentence, or the sentencing of adult felons to a short stay in jail in addition to release to probation. The percentage of felons receiving a jail sentence increased from 25 to 30 percent from 1988 to 2004.[21] These reasons influenced the increase in the jail populations over the past decade. However, although the nation's jail populations continue to increase, the growth has been slowing, increasing only 3.3 percent from 2000 to 2008. It is projected that the growth of jails will continue to slow over the next five to ten years.

Admissions and Length of Stay

One factor that truly differentiates jails from prisons is in the number of admissions and length of stay. During 2007, 751,593 inmates were admitted to state and federal prisons, 725,402 inmates were released, and the average length of stay for released inmates was 36 months.[22] These figures are decidedly different for jails. Jails do not report all admissions and releases every year, but estimates are that the 3,376 jails process between 12 and 13 million admissions each year.

In each year between the full censuses of jails, the Bureau of Justice Statistics does a sample survey of jails to estimate baseline characteristics of the jails and the inmates housed in the jails. From 2006 to 2007, it was estimated that there were more than 13 million new admissions to jails or about 17 times the size of the jail inmate population.[23] In addition, 250,950 offenders were admitted to the nation's jails during the week ending June 29, 2007.[24] These figures can include fewer individuals admitted to jail multiple times. A recent study found that approximately 25 percent of the bookings into the Cook County (Illinois) jail were multiple admissions of the same person.[25] Therefore, the 13 million admissions noted earlier probably represent between 9 and 10.5 million different offenders.

length of stay
the time served in a jail or prison by any inmate

The average **length of stay** for a jail is fifteen to twenty days, much less than the average thirty-six month length of stay within a prison. This average length of stay for jails is misleading, however, as a very large percentage of arrested and jailed offenders make bond and are released within forty-eight hours. Those who do not make bail are likely to spend seventy-five to ninety days in jail awaiting trial, whereas sentenced offenders can serve up to one year in jail. O'Toole, in pointing out the difficulty in looking at average length of stay as it pertains to jail populations, notes the following:

> In fact the reality of jail population dynamics is that the vast majority of inmates are released within a few days, and those who are not released early tend to remain in custody throughout the adjudication process. This tends to create two trends in inmate average length of stay (ALOS) figures. One is considerably less than the arithmetically calculated ALOS and the other considerably longer.[26]

The fact that so many jail inmates are released shortly after arrest creates a logistical nightmare for jail operations in terms of bookings and releases. The sheer volume of these admissions and releases often results in mistakes. Unfortunately, it is not uncommon for jails to be plagued with releasing the wrong person or making errors in identification of offenders.[27] These problems seem to continue, no matter what steps are taken by jails to improve their booking and release processes and their record keeping. And mistaken releases of offenders undermine the public confidence in the ability of jail staff to do a professional job.

The Jail Process and Daily Operations

A number of activities and functions are a part of the daily jail routine. The first major function is admissions and releases. Jails have a central area for booking, admitting, and releasing inmates. Police officers or county sheriff deputies bring arrested offenders to the jail, where they are identified and fingerprinted and their property is inventoried and stored. They receive a brief physical and mental health screening and usually talk to a social worker about the process and how potential release on bail or personal recognizance works. If they are there for a minor offense, they may be quickly released on bond. Offenders sit in a relatively unsecured part of

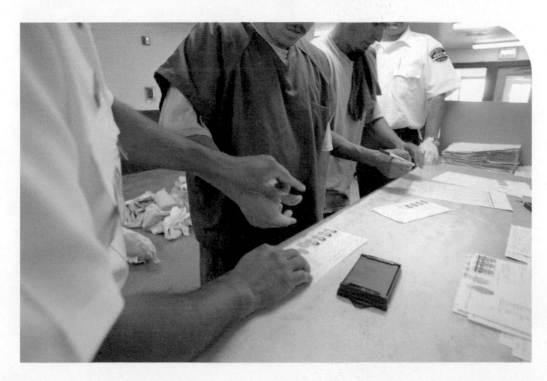

After arrest, offenders are fingerprinted and booked into the jail. Photo courtesy of Corrections Corporation of America.

the jail booking area until someone comes to the jail to post their bond. If they are arrested for a felony, they will have to wait until their initial appearance before a magistrate (usually within twenty-four hours) to see if they are granted bail. During this time, they are placed in a general holding area within the jail, in which they are housed with several other newly arrived offenders.

Offenders not released on bail or personal recognizance are moved to more permanent housing within the jail. They are first placed in a very secure housing unit, often in cells holding only one person, until they can be further interviewed and some preliminary information can be collected regarding their crime and past criminal history. This classification process (described below) identifies the dangerousness and risk of the offender and determines whether there are other offenders from whom they should be separated. In addition, any major problems, such as a need for detoxification, potential for suicide, or potential threats by other jail inmates, are identified and considered in the classification and assignment of housing. Once classified, inmates are moved to the housing unit that holds inmates of similar risk of violence or escape.

In their housing unit, inmates begin the normal routine of the jail. Days are filled with boredom, as there is usually little to do. Depending on the jail design, inmates may be let out of their cells and into a common area in which they can talk to other inmates or watch television. Prepared food is delivered to the common area, where inmates eat their meals. If inmates receive visits, they go to the visiting area, which is often adjacent to the housing unit. Visits with family or friends are usually *noncontact,* meaning that inmates and their visitors talk on a telephone or through sound ports between secure glass to prevent the passing of items that are not allowed in the jail. If visited by their attorney, a probation or parole officer, or some other law enforcement official, inmates usually are provided a small, yet secure area, with direct contact with their visitor, so they can talk in private and sign any necessary papers.

Jails have limited programs, such as education, substance abuse counseling, or work. However, these types of programs and activities are usually welcomed by

Jail inmates have noncontact visiting and have to talk to their visitors through sound ports in the secure glass. Photo by Richard P. Seiter.

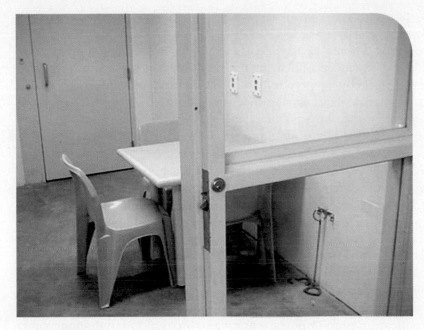

Jail inmates can have contact visiting with their attorneys, so they can review and sign papers. Note, however, the handcuffs attached to the wall to prevent inmates from attacking attorneys or trying to escape out the visitors' entrance. Photo by Richard P. Seiter.

inmates, as the boredom of a regular day is extremely difficult for most offenders. Some programs are provided in the common areas of the housing units, but inmates generally are transported to another location in the jail for these programs. Inmates who are awaiting trial and not yet sentenced may volunteer, but are not required to work. Work opportunities include cleaning the areas of the jail or assisting in food preparation and service. Even for the few inmates who work, there is normally only enough to do to keep them busy a few hours per day.

mycrimekit
Media—Video: The Operations of a Jail.

Jail Classification

An important aspect of the operation of jails is the classification of inmates. Sophisticated classification systems for jails are a relatively recent phenomenon, having been used extensively only over the past two decades. During the early history of jails, all inmates were mixed together. There was later some segregation of inmates, as "separation by sex came first, then separation by age, followed by separation by problem."[28] Brennan notes that "Before 1870, . . . classification was based primarily on type of offense. . . . In the latter part of the 19th century, . . . classification . . . emphasized offenders' personal pathologies."[29] More recently, **objective classification systems** have superceded these subjective classification processes. Objective systems identify offenders' criminal history and personal characteristics (number of violent offenses, history of violence, age, marital status) that have been found to be statistically linked to dangerousness or escape potential; they result in an actuarial assessment of risk that is used in assigning inmates to a type of housing unit or recommending certain mental health or substance abuse programs.

Jail classification systems are plagued with problems not inherent in prison classification systems. First, there is often little information available for jail inmates. Jail social service staff interview inmates to collect information, but usually do not have time to confirm the accuracy of the information. Second, the short stay complicates the process for most inmates, and there is no time for thorough medical or psychological assessments that could aid in the classification process. Finally, Brennan notes that jail classification has "suffered from benign neglect," in that jail administrators have "not accorded classification a central role in management."[30]

objective classification systems
statistical approaches to consider the risk of escape and violence by inmates

However, effective jail classification systems are important for three reasons:

1. They provide a guide for separating violent, predatory inmates from potential inmate victims. One of the most challenging problems for jails is to protect inmates who could be preyed on by dangerous inmates. With little prior information and many housing arrangements in which numerous inmates live together, it is critical to try to separate inmates by risk of assault against one another.
2. They provide a guide for identifying and managing differently inmates with special needs, such as the emotionally disturbed or those at risk for suicide.
3. They provide a guide for identifying inmates with a high risk of escape and housing them in more secure settings than those with a low risk of escape. Such systems allow jails to have a variety of housing assignments, rather than all maximum-security areas that are very expensive to build and operate.

Jail staff use classification systems to make decisions on the housing assignment for inmates, the types of programs they should participate in, the number of staff assigned to various housing areas, the type of supervision to provide inmates, and whether inmates should be allowed to work or participate in diversion programs. In this regard, classification is an important and valuable tool in jail management.

Jail Staffing

One way in which jails and prisons are extremely similar is the importance of professional staff. In both types of correctional facilities, staff are more important than any other element in the operations and policies—more important than the facility, the physical security, the services provided, and the programs offered. Poor-quality or poorly performing staff undermine all these other factors, whereas professional and well-trained staff can overcome other problems in the jail or its operations.

The *Sourcebook of Criminal Justice Statistics, 2003* reported an estimated 250,944 total staff employed by jails in 2005.[31] As indicated in Table 3.3, a 1999 census of jails reported that the largest proportion of jail staff (151,200 of the total staff, or 72 percent) is correctional officers. Most jail correctional officers are assigned to housing units, but others act as transportation officers and move inmates from the jail to the courthouse to attend hearings. The percentage of correctional officers of the total jail staff is higher than in prisons because jails do not offer extensive programs or services, and their primary function is to hold inmates in a secure setting. The next largest categories of staff are clerical and maintenance (12 percent), administrative (6.9 percent), and professional and technicians (5.4 percent).

Jail staff are always extremely outnumbered by the inmates in any correctional setting. There is no way to "rule" a correctional facility through force; jails must be managed through clear procedures, a consistent routine of operations, and professional staff. In 1999, the number of inmates per correctional officer was 4.3.[32] However, this number is misleading, as all correctional officers are not employed at the jail at any single time. Since correctional officers must supervise the jail twenty-four hours per day, seven days per week, only about one-sixth of the total officer work force is likely to be on duty at any one time. Therefore, on a typical day, there would be one correctional officer for more than twenty-five (4.3 times 6) inmates. Yet correctional officers are assigned throughout the jail, and a typical jail housing unit has approximately seventy-five inmates with one correctional officer. Although the number of inmates in jails increased significantly over the past twenty years, the number of jail employees grew at an even faster rate. In 1983, the average number of inmates per all jail staff (not just correctional officers) was 3.5, but this number remained steady as it was 3.6 in 2005.[33]

TABLE 3.3 Jail Staff by Occupational Category, June 30, 1999

Region and Jurisdiction	Total Staff	Administrative	Correctional Officers	Clerical and Maintenance	Educational	Professional and Technical[a]	Other
National estimate[b]	210,600	14,600	151,200	25,400	2,100	11,500	5,800
State estimate[b]	207,600	14,400	149,600	25,300	2,100	10,700	5,500
U.S. total	197,375	13,722	141,663	23,772	1,969	10,764	5,485
Federal	3,110	253	1,685	93	30	715	334
State	194,265	13,469	139,978	23,679	1,939	10,049	5,151
Northeast	40,899	1,819	31,269	3,995	579	2,270	967
Midwest	32,821	2,741	23,190	4,281	320	1,585	704
South	82,245	5,019	62,227	8,878	507	3,398	2,216
West	38,300	3,890	23,292	6,525	533	2,796	1,264

Note: A total of 228 reporting units were unable to provide data on staff by gender or occupation. Total staff includes full-time, part-time, payroll, and nonpayroll staff and excludes contract staff and community volunteers.

[a]Includes psychiatrists, psychologists, social workers, counselors, medical doctors, nurses, paramedics, chaplains, and legal specialists.

[b]National estimates were obtained by summing the item values from reporting units and then multiplying by a nonresponse adjustment factor. All estimates for type of staff were rounded to the nearest 100.

Source: James J. Stephan, *Census of Jails, 1999*, NCJ 186633 (Washington, D.C.: U.S. Department of Justice, Bureau of Justice Statistics, August 2000), p. 25.

Staff who work in jails include jail officers, counselors, and transportation officers who move inmates from the jail to the courthouse for hearings. Photo by Richard P. Seiter.

Another change in jail staff has come in the diversity of employees. In the 1999 *Census of Jails*, women constituted approximately 34 percent (up from 30 percent in 1993) of all jail employees and 28 percent (up from 24 percent in 1993) of all jail correctional officers.[34] In addition, the percentage of white jail staff decreased to 66 percent in 1999 from 71 percent in 1993, while during the same period black employees increased from 22 to 24 percent and Hispanic employees from 6 to 8 percent.[35]

Your Career in Corrections

Jail Officers

As noted in this chapter, there is much less attention, much less research, and much less interest by the public regarding the staffing and operation of county jails than of prisons. Although there are almost three times as many jails as prisons, the nation's jails employ less than half as many staff as state and federal prisons. In 2005, there were an estimated 250,944 correctional employees of local governments.[36] According to the *Census of Jails, 1999* (only completed once every decade), the largest percentage of jail staff (about seven out of ten) are jail correctional officers, who supervise inmates or provide facility security.[37] Other occupational categories in jails include administrators, clerical and maintenance workers, professional and technical employees, and educational employees. Jails have few inmate programs, but most jails offer limited education, counseling, vocational training, religious programming, and health services for inmates.

Jail officers (in some locations called detention officers) do much of the same work as prison correctional officers. Their primary responsibilities are supervising inmates to maintain order and compliance with rules and performing security procedures such as searching for contraband. However, with most of the staff being officers, and with most inmate programs (visiting, education) and services (food, medical) coming to the inmates in housing units, rather than inmates going to the program or service, the function of officers often extends into the provision or supervision of these functions. Food service staff bring meals to the housing area, but the cell block officer supervises the meal service. In addition, visitors come to visiting rooms adjacent to the housing unit, and the cell block officer moves the inmates to a noncontact visiting area and maintains some surveillance over the visit.

Similar to prison staff, jail staff work in stressful and sometimes dangerous environments. Between July 1, 1998, and June 30, 1999, there were 9,276 inmate physical or sexual assaults on jail employees in 848 jail jurisdictions. The total number of assaults compared to the average daily population translated into 17.8 assaults per 1,000 inmates or 48.8 assaults per 1,000 staff during the twelve-month period.[38] Despite this fact, many individuals find work as jail correctional officers challenging and rewarding. Just as in prisons, an officer position is usually the entry-level job, and staff later have the opportunity for advancement and other types of jobs.

This increase in minority employees is important to the management of jails because, in 2007, 39 percent of all jail inmates were black and 16 percent Hispanic. It is commonly acknowledged that management of a correctional facility is benefited when the facility has a like proportion of minority employees to the proportion of minority inmates. See the "Your Career in Corrections" box for a discussion of the opportunities for jobs as jail officers.

Design and Supervision in Jails

Contemporary jails are very different from the earliest jails in the United States. As most can recall from watching old television westerns, every small town had a sheriff's office with a few jail cells to hold those arrested for committing serious crimes or getting drunk in the local saloon. This idea of combining the sheriff's office with the local jail continued into the twentieth century. In many rural counties, the sheriff and his family lived in the second floor of a county-owned house, the main floor was the sheriff's office, and the basement included cells for housing inmates. Most of these jails have now been replaced with more modern facilities. In major metropolitan areas, it is desirable to locate the jail next to the county court building, creating problems for both architectural and security concerns.

Urban leaders do not want a jail to "look like a jail" and ruin the aesthetics of the area in which it is located. Yet jails must be very secure and as escape-proof as possible. They must take into account requirements for lighting and airflow, for offering inmate programs, and for movement of inmates within the jail and between the jail and the courthouse. Architects take great pride in meeting these sometimes conflicting demands of a jail being secure, yet fitting into the current landscape of

This sheriff's office from the 1950s was the standard in most county seats, in which the sheriff's family lived upstairs, the administrative office was on the main floor, and the jail was in the basement. Courtesy of the Ohio Department of Rehabilitation and Correction.

The St. Louis City Jail is a good example of modern jail architecture, in which the jail is conveniently located next to the courthouse, yet fits into the urban look of the other buildings. Photo by Richard P. Seiter.

mycrimekit™

Insider's Experience: Siting an Urban Correctional Facility.

first-generation jails

a linear design was used for housing inmates, in which cells are aligned in long, straight rows, with walkways in the front of the cells for jail correctional officers to walk intermittently to observe what is going on in the cells

podular designs

a design of prisoner housing that provides common day room areas in the center of the unit to allow inmates to watch television or play table games, thereby getting out of their cells and reducing idleness and tension; podular designs make it easier for officers to view inmate activities in the cells and the dayrooms from one central location

the urban environment. The new St. Louis city jail, which opened in early 2003, illustrates this effort. A jury of the American Institute of Architects Committee on Architecture for Justice reviewed the design and appearance and stated, "We found this multi-level solution to be sensitive to its urban context and the fabric of the façade while providing good operational solutions."[39] The *MyCrimeKit* that accompanies this textbook includes "An Insider's Experience" that describes a challenge by the author to find an urban site for a correctional institution.

Creating a Secure Setting Inside the Jail

Designers of jails must not only make the facility attractive to fit into the city skyline, but also make it functional and secure. Jail functionality begins with the fact that inmates are kept in their housing areas most of the time and are seldom moved to other locations in the jail. Therefore, services (food, laundry, medical), programs (education, counseling), and even visitors must be brought to the inmate housing area. The design of the housing areas has evolved and changed significantly over the past several decades.

Historically, **first-generation jails** housed inmates using a linear design, in which cells are aligned in long, straight rows, with walkways in the front of the cells for jail correctional officers to walk intermittently to observe what is going on in the cells. As illustrated in Figure 3.2, this linear approach did not allow officers to observe and supervise inmates from a single location and resulted in little if any communication between officers and inmates as officers patrolled the corridors and looked into cells. The design of the cells and furnishings was very secure. Cell fronts were open bars (allowing no privacy and increasing the noise level), beds and other furniture were solid metal, and toilets and sinks were often stainless steel and difficult to destroy. There was little space for recreation or programs, and therefore inmates remained in their cells and grew restless and irritated. Food had to be delivered to each cell, taking extensive staff time and making it difficult to maintain quality in food service.

To improve the supervision and resolve some of the program and service issues, jail designers introduced a new style of housing in the 1970s. These **podular designs,**

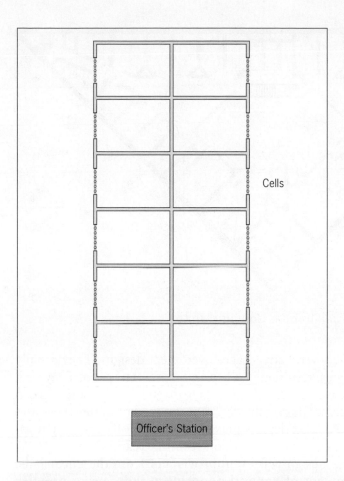

Cells

Officer's Station

FIGURE 3.2   Linear Design of Jail Housing Units

First-generation jails had long rows of cells, and jail personnel saw inmates only as they walked the tier and looked into cells. Courtesy of the Federal Bureau of Prisons.

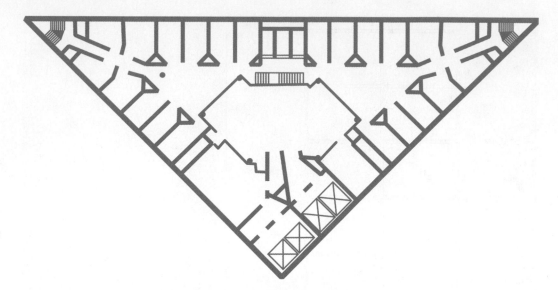

Source: National Institute of Corrections, *Direct Supervision Jails Informational Packet* (Washington, D.C.: U.S. Department of Justice, 1993).

FIGURE 3.3 Podular Design of Jail Inmate Housing Units

second-generation jails
jails using podular housing designs and remote supervision; officers are located in a secure control room overlooking the cells and day room, with electronic controls to open and close individual cell doors

as illustrated in Figure 3.3, have several advantages over linear designs. They usually house smaller numbers of inmates, resulting in a better inmate–staff ratio. They provide common areas in the center of the unit (called dayrooms) in which inmates can watch television or play table games during the day, thus getting out of their cells and reducing idleness and tension. Podular designs make it easier for officers to view inmate activities in the cells and the dayrooms from one central location.

The creation of the podular design was an improvement from the linear jails. They resulted in the development of **second-generation jails,** using podular designs with remote supervision. Remote supervision placed officers in a secure

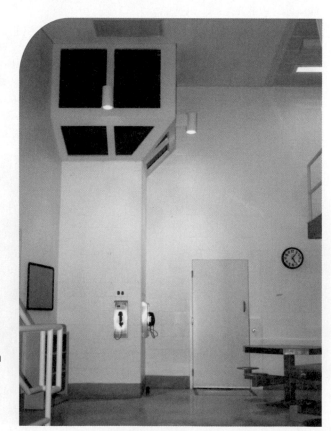

In second-generation jails, officers have no direct contact with inmates, as they oversee activities in the cellhouse from a remote location, similar to a perimeter tower within the building. Photo by Richard P. Seiter.

From their remote location in second-generation jails, officers can open and close cell doors electronically simply by pushing a button. Photo Courtesy of Corrections Corporation of America.

control room overlooking the cells and dayroom, with electronic controls to open and close individual cell doors. There was extensive use of secure glass instead of bars to improve visibility. Although second-generation jails had several advantages over first-generation jails, the disadvantage was that with indirect supervision jail staff had limited contact with inmates; thus there was no communication or ability to talk to inmates, find out issues that were developing, and respond to them in a proactive manner.

To improve the problems resulting from the indirect supervision in second-generation jails, jail officials began to design **third-generation jails,** with the remote control center for staff removed and correctional officers placed in the housing unit in direct contact with inmates. This **direct supervision** approach requires staff to continuously supervise and communicate with inmates, thus reducing tension and avoiding the development of conflicts among inmates or between inmates and staff. The design also allows food to be brought to and served in the common area, and there are often laundry facilities in the unit, allowing inmates to take responsibility for these functions rather than staff having to do it for them.

Officials initially feared for staff safety, but direct supervision of jails was found to provide better control, lessen violence, and be safer for staff and inmates. A study of the behavior of inmates that covered many new direct-supervision jails

third-generation jails
jail designs without remote control centers, in which correctional officers are located in the housing unit in direct contact with inmates

direct supervision
a style of inmate supervision with staff located in direct contact with inmates; requires staff to continuously supervise and communicate with inmates, reducing tension and avoiding the development of conflicts between inmates or inmates and staff

Podular jail designs allow for dayrooms in the center, in which officers can easily view inmates allowed out of their cells and into the dayrooms. Photo by Richard P. Seiter.

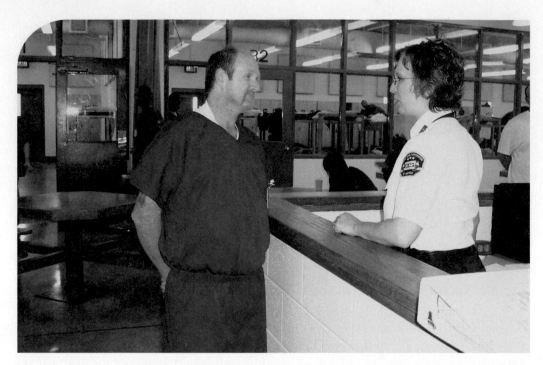

In a third-generation jail with direct supervision, officers work in the housing units and interact continuously with inmates.
Photo by Riffi O'Brien.

mycrimekit

Media—Video: Direct Supervision.

that replaced old indirect-supervision facilities found a reduction in fifty-one of seventy categories of negative conduct by inmates when the direct-supervision jails opened.[40] Since the first podular direct-supervision jail was constructed in 1981 in Contra Costa County, California, more than one hundred jails across the country use direct supervision, and most new jails are constructed and managed on this concept.

Issues in Jails

The nation's jails face many significant challenges. With the increased reliance on jails described previously, jails have become increasingly overcrowded, and many new jails have been constructed to accommodate the increasing numbers of inmates. Some jurisdictions have opted to contract with the private, for-profit sector to build and manage a new jail. Jails also receive and hold people with many problems that can require immediate identification and attention. Detained offenders may suffer from mental illness or drug or alcohol addictions or be suicidal. Jails are also increasingly called on to house juvenile offenders who, because of the severity or nature of their crimes, will be processed through the adult court and correctional systems. These issues will be addressed after the following "An Interview With" box.

Responding to Jail Crowding

The jail incarceration rate has more than doubled, and the population of the nation's jails has almost tripled over the past twenty years. Much of the growth has resulted from the increased numbers of minority inmates. As indicated in Figure 3.4, between 1990 and 2008, the number of white and Hispanic jail inmates increased at a faster annual rate than that of black inmates.[41]

Although some jail officials attempted to deal with the increasing number of offenders by increasing the pretrial release and diversion programs, the problem

Number of jail inmates (one-day count)

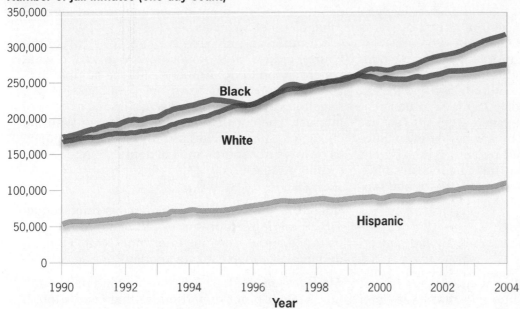

Additions:
White: 2005-331,000; 2006-336,500; 2007-338,200; 2008-333,300
Black: 2005-290,500; 2006-295,900; 2007-301,700; 2008-308,000
Hispanic: 2005-111,900; 2006-119,200; 2007-125,500; 2008-128,500

Source: Bureau of Justice Statistics Correctional Surveys, *Correctional Populations in the United States* and *Prison and Jail Inmates at Midyear* (Washington, D.C.: U.S. Department of Justice, various years).

FIGURE 3.4 Jail Population by Race and Ethnicity, 1990–2008

An Interview With...

A Jail Administrator

Administrators of large urban jails face many serious challenges in trying to manage their facilities. Herbert L. Bernsen, assistant director of the St. Louis County Department of Justice Services and former administrator of the St. Louis County Jail, has a national reputation as a knowledgeable and professional jail administrator, and his thoughts on issues facing jail administrators are valuable for students.

Question: What are the major challenges facing you as a jail administrator?

Mr. Bernsen: There are many, but include (1) hiring competent staff and training them in the multiple competencies required of individuals in this field; (2) communicating the philosophy of our agency and the criminal justice field in general in terms of what we are trying to do as far as our mission; and (3) to bring the community into our mission by contacting social service as well as law enforcement agencies, and integrating them into not just how we intake and hold prisoners, but what we do with them to prepare for release.

Question: What are the characteristics essential for staff to work successfully in a large jail?

Mr. Bernsen: It is not necessary that they have prior criminal justice experience, but valuable to have a combination of education and work experience that lends itself to the qualities that are needed in this facility. These include dependability, discipline, and the ability to communicate and work with others. Most importantly, individuals must have good skills in communicating with individuals from a variety of backgrounds, and the ability to not only work under supervision, but also independently, being able to think on their feet and make decisions in line with the mission and philosophy we want to achieve.

Question: How do you find people with the abilities to perform well in a jail setting?

Mr. Bernsen: You have to put the jail out there, in a variety of places where those individuals that are apt to become interested may see or hear about

...continued

you. You have to do more than just advertise; you have to explain the organization, how it operates professionally, and the critical skills you are looking for. We are looking for more than what the public perceives as a correctional officer, and you emphasize the talent and skill required and the career opportunities that exist. You look at universities, the military, and even use Internet sites so that your message is received by a wide variety of people. Also critical is that your personnel department and administrators that may talk to applicants have a good understanding of what to look for and represent the agency well.

Question: What is the mission of a jail and how do you implement it?

Mr. Bernsen: As a correctional agency, we have a mandate to hold (detain) people that have been assigned to us because of violating a statute or ordinance, and we have to provide a safe, secure, and humane environment for them. Our goal is to provide an environment where staff, inmates, and visitors are free from emotional or physical danger. Inmates must have the opportunity to participate in programs and improve themselves while they are here. This environment should also foster a well-trained staff, capable of direct supervision management. Direct supervision is the philosophy that we use to manage our jail; we believe it creates a better environment for staff, improves our ability to manage inmates, and increases their chances of successful return to the community.

It is important to get others to understand this mission, and the media can play an important role in this. With a jail setting, negative things can always occur, and the media will want to know why these things happen. Even when mistakes or omissions occur, it is an opportunity to get the message of your mission before the public. You may have a tragic incident such as a suicide, but you can also discuss the type of suicide prevention program you have and the plans you have to improve it. It is important to develop a rapport with the media and invite them to learn about the successful programs within the jail. We need to get agencies to be partners in what we do. An example is the mental health court, in which the community was brought into the facility as a partner with us to get other phases of the community mental health groups to determine how best to handle and provide services to offenders with mental health problems. These

can develop into grant opportunities and involvement by other agencies.

Another part of what we can do is to get the courts, judges, and prosecutors involved in what we are trying to do. Any one of these components can block programs from being successful. We have regular meetings to discuss issues of mutual interest. The courts want to be partners with the jail, and through discussions of issues as mundane as how we transport inmates, doors are opened for further discussions.

Question: Tight budget times always force reducing or ending programs or services you see as valuable. How do you determine what you are going to cut when cuts are needed?

Mr. Bernsen: We look for other funding opportunities, such as grant opportunities that can be found through universities or social service agencies. There may be a source of getting funds to develop a program we would otherwise not be able to afford. Another way is to have contacts to begin doing things in house you did not realize you could do, such as using intern students, which provides assistance and recruits staff. Social service agencies may decide they should be providing services at the jail, such as our local school board determining they have a responsibility to offer education classes to our population. It is very important that we have an environment that welcomes outside participation, because even though it takes more time and work, the potential payoff is tremendous. As a result of an active use of volunteers, we have more programs and have a calmer institution.

Question: Looking to the future, do you foresee a "new paradigm" for jails?

Mr. Bernsen: I do, because hopefully organizations like the American Jail Association, the National Institute of Corrections, and the American Correctional Association are getting the word out to national and state decision makers that jails are areas that need assistance and are worth investing in. When you look at the number of individuals that come through jails and go out into the community, jails touch many more offenders than prison or community supervision, and many of the individuals they touch have mental, medical, and emotional problems in need of intervention.

TABLE 3.4	Rated Capacity of Local Jails and Percentage of Capacity Occupied, 1990 and 1995–2008

Year	Rated Capacity[a]	Amount of Capacity Added[b]	Percentage of Capacity Occupied[c]
2008	828,413	14,911	94.8%
2007	810,543	15,863	96.3
2006	794,984	8,638	96.3
2005	786,954	33,398	95
2004	755,603	19,132	94
2003	736,471	22,572	94
2002	713,899	14,590	93
2001	699,309	21,522	90
2000	677,787	25,466	92
1999	652,321	39,541	93
1998	612,780	26,216	97
1997	586,564	23,593	97
1996	562,971	17,208	92
1995	545,763	41,439	93
1990	389,171		104

Note: Capacity data for 1990, 1995–1998, and 2000–2004 are survey estimates subject to sampling error.

[a]Rated capacity is the number of beds or inmates assigned by a rating official to facilities within each jurisdiction.

[b]The number of beds added during the 12 months ending June 30 of each year.

[c]The number of inmates divided by the rated capacity times 100.

Source: Paige M. Harrison and Allen J. Beck, *Prison and Jail Inmates at Midyear 2004,* (Washington, D.C.: U.S. Department of Justice, Bureau of Justice Statistics, April 2005) and Todd D. Minton and William J. Sabol, "Jail Inmates at Midyear 2008 Statistical Tables, (Washington, D.C.. U.S. Department of Justice, March 2009), p. 3.

usually resulted in the need to construct new jails or add onto the existing jail to increase capacity. During the 1990s, approximately 150 additional jails were built (not including new jails constructed to replace old jails), and the capacity of the nation's jails increased from approximately 350,000 to more than 600,000.[42] As of midyear 2008, jail capacity was 828,413.[43]

Table 3.4 illustrates the rated capacity of jails, the amount of capacity that was added each year, and the percentage of the overall capacity of jails that was occupied. Since the major construction boom in the last decade, U.S. jails have been able to add enough capacity to stay ahead of the increasing population, and the population has not been higher than 97 percent of capacity in the last ten years.[44] However, in 2006, twenty of the fifty largest jail jurisdictions operated over their rated capacity and then slightly dropped to nineteen in 2008.[45] The ten most overcrowded jurisdictions are indicated in Table 3.5.

Another approach for dealing with jail overcrowding has been to contract out for the detention of jail inmates with a private correctional company. A *private correctional facility* is any correctional facility operated by a nongovernmental agency and usually in a for-profit manner that contracts with a governmental entity to provide security, housing, and programs for offenders. According to most reports, the first jail contract with a private company was in 1984, for a 250-bed facility operated by Corrections Corporation of America under contract with Hamilton County, Tennessee. Privatizing the operation of prisons or jails has been

| TABLE 3.5 | Large Jail Jurisdictions Overcapacity, Midyear 2008 |

Jurisdiction	Percentage of Capacity Occupied
Denver County, CO	128
Polk County, FL	131
Maricopa County, NM	102
Bernalillo County, NM	116
Jacksonville City, FL	121
Santa Clara County, CA	122
Clark County, NV	106
Riverside County, CA	115
San Diego County, CA	109
Milwaukee County, WI	101

Source: Adapted from Todd D. Minton and William J. Sabol, *Jail Inmates at Midyear 2008–Statistical Tables,* (Washington, D.C.: U.S. Department of Justice, Bureau of Justice Statistics, March 2009), p. 7.

very controversial, and arguments surround the issues of benefits and costs, ethics and corruption, quality of service, security and public protection, and liability.[46]

Today, there are dozens of privately operated jails across the country, and privatization of jail construction or management is seen as a viable option for counties that need a new jail and do not have the funds available to build one. Between 1993 and 1999, the number of private jails in the United States increased from seventeen to forty-seven, and capacity grew from 3,229 to 16,659. Even with this increase, private jails held only 6.6 percent of jail inmates in 1999.[47] Many of the concerns about privatization can be dealt with through the contracting process between the government and the private entity. The county can agree on a contract with a private company, which will build a jail to meet the county needs and charge the county on a per day basis for each inmate the private jail holds. Many of these contracts require the private company to meet established professional standards for jail operations, to provide certain specified programs, and to ensure that the cost per day does not exceed the average cost per day for jail inmates held by the publicly operated jail.

Legal Issues for Jails

One of the primary reasons for increased capacity through new jail construction over the past decade has been the increase in the number of successful legal challenges by jail inmates against jails for either overcrowding or other conditions of confinement. Jail inmates file lawsuits over a variety of things: lack of privacy, privileges (or lack thereof), food, brutality by staff, access to their attorneys, or general conditions of overcrowding. Most lawsuits are not successful, but the courts recognize that most jail inmates are not yet convicted, and afford them more privileges than the typical prison inmate.

Jails are expected to provide a constitutionally acceptable environment, which means they must meet all the requirements of health and safety codes, adequately control violence, provide an acceptable level of privacy as allowed by security concerns, and meet basic inmate needs such as medical care and a nutritious diet. When a jail does not meet the expected level and an inmate files a legal action in federal court, the court can impose requirements for action by the jail to remedy the concerns and bring the jail environment up to constitutional standards.

One of the first major cases in which the U.S. Supreme Court addressed jail conditions was the 1979 case of **Bell v. Wolfish,** in which the Court established the "punitive intent standard."[48] The case dealt with conditions and practices at a federal jail in New York City. The jail, although newly constructed, was already overcrowded and "double-bunked," housing two inmates in cells designed for one. The lawsuit by inmates challenged the crowded conditions as well as practices at the jail of not allowing inmates to observe searches of their cells and of requiring them to submit to visual searches of body cavities after visits with family members or friends. The lawsuit alleged violations of the Eighth Amendment of the Constitution, which states: "Excessive bail shall not be required, nor excessive fines imposed, nor cruel and unusual punishment inflicted."

The Supreme Court ruled that the case should turn only on whether the practices in question violated jail inmates' right to be free from punishment (since they were not yet convicted of a crime), using a standard of whether the individual restrictions were punitive or merely regulatory restraints, whether the practices were reasonably related to a legitimate goal other than punishment, and whether the practices appeared excessive in relation to that alternative purpose. This decision is guidance for jails in what is expected by the courts in operating in a safe and secure manner, yet one that does not overly infringe on the rights of yet-to-be-convicted offenders.

Since the *Bell* decision, courts regularly have ruled against the operating conditions at a jail and required jail administrators to make changes or even build a new jail. In a 1999 survey, approximately 15 percent of the reporting jurisdictions

Bell v. Wolfish
a 1979 U.S. Supreme Court case in which the punitive intent standard was adopted for considering violations of the Eighth Amendment regarding jail operations

The Metropolitan Correctional Center in New York City, operated by the U.S. Bureau of Prisons, was the location of one of the major inmate lawsuits regarding jail operations. Courtesy of the Federal Bureau of Prisons.

reported that they were under a court order or consent decree for crowding or other confinement conditions, and 11 percent were under a court order to limit their population so that it would not be overcrowded.[49] These numbers, however, are lower than in 1993, as many new jails have been constructed and procedures have been improved to avoid the likelihood of inmate suits.

Dealing with Mentally Ill Offenders

Over the last thirty years, the number of criminal offenders with mental illness has been rising. In the 1960s, new antipsychotropic drugs were created and prescribed for people with mental illness, allowing many mentally ill individuals to remain in the community rather than be placed in mental hospitals. As a result, states closed their hospitals, and the number of mentally ill patients went from a high of 559,000 in 1955 to 69,000 in 1995.[50] When these community patients stop taking their medication, the symptoms of the mental illness return; many commit crimes and become clients of the criminal justice system. A report by the National Coalition for the Mentally Ill in Criminal Justice indicates that there are 33 percent more mentally ill people in jails than in mental hospitals.[51]

In another report issued by the U.S. Department of Justice, the Bureau of Justice Statistics estimated that 1,264,300 mentally ill offenders were being held in state and federal prisons and local jails at midyear 2005. The report further estimated that 16 percent of all jail inmates have a mental illness.[52]

Upon arrival in a jail, offenders are usually screened to detect mental illness or the potential for suicide. These assessment instruments are very short, but can accurately indicate a problem that requires immediate attention. The assessment instruments rely on the offenders' honesty and ask them about histories of mental illness, taking of psychotropic medication, and thoughts of suicide. Although most jails (78 percent) do an initial screening, very few offer intensive mental health programs. Of the jails surveyed in 2004 that housed inmates with mental health problems, an estimated 23 percent had received mental health treatment during the year before their arrest, 17 percent had used medication, and about 7 percent had an overnight stay in a hospital as a result of a mental disorder. Further, inmates in 2002 recorded a 5 percent increase in mental health treatment from 1996.[53] Table 3.6 illustrates the number of jail inmates receiving these services by state and region.

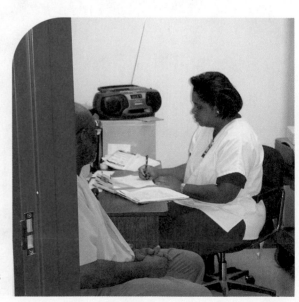

Mental health staff do assessments of inmates as they enter jails to determine whether they are a serious suicide risk. Photo by Richard P. Seiter.

TABLE 3.6 Jail Inmates Receiving Mental Health Services, June 30, 1999

Region and Jurisdiction	Number of Inmates in Jurisdictions Reporting Data	Number of Inmates Who Were Receiving:		
		24-hour Mental Health Care[a]	Mental Health Therapy or Counseling	Psychotropic Medication[b]
U.S. total	490,710	11,323	41,029	44,337
Federal	—	0	—	—
State	490,710	11,323	41,029	44,337
Northeast	84,869	2,395	11,057	9,937
Midwest	68,134	1,078	4,552	5,914
South	223,580	4,175	16,477	19,944
West	114,127	3,675	8,943	8,542

Note: Five states (Connecticut, Delaware, Hawaii, Rhode Island, and Vermont) had combined jail–prison systems and were excluded from the report.

—Not calculated.

The District of Columbia's jail population declined between 1983 and 1993 because the Occoquan complex was reclassified from a jail to a prison and between 1983 and 1993 because an increasing number of inmates were housed in facilities outside the District of Columbia. Except for 15 locally operated jails, Alaska has a combined jail–prison system.

[a] In special housing or a psychiatric unit on or off jail grounds.

[b] Drugs having a mind-altering effect, such as antidepressants, stimulants, sedatives, tranquilizers, and other antipsychotic drugs.

Source: James J. Stephan, *Census of Jails, 1999*, NCJ 186633 (Washington, D.C.: U.S. Department of Justice, Bureau of Justice Statistics, August 2001), p. 40.

Preventing Suicides

Jails do a preliminary screening upon an offender's entry to the jail to determine whether there are immediate concerns about an attempted suicide. Of the total number of inmate deaths (978) while in jail reported in 2002, 32 percent of them (314) were a result of suicide.[54] This is approximately the same proportion as in the previous national jail census in 1993. This is by far the greatest cause of death for inmates in jail other than deaths resulting from illness or natural causes (41.8 percent). Homicides accounted for only 3 percent of jail deaths, and AIDS accounted for 8.5 percent of jail deaths.

suicide prevention programs

jail and prison programs that include early detection of suicide risks, staff education to recognize signs of potential suicide, and procedures for managing inmates that are now suicidal

Since suicide represents a significant concern for jail administrators, most jails have **suicide prevention programs.** As indicated in Table 3.7, less than 3 percent of jails reported that they did not have specific procedures for suicide prevention (84 of 2,866 jails). Suicide prevention programs include risk assessment at admission, special staff training, counseling for inmates, and monitoring and special watches of high-risk inmates. An assessment of offenders upon entering jail is critical, as 48 percent of all jail suicides occur during the first week following admission.[55] Inmates who indicate some risk during the assessment are noted and receive specific counseling from mental health professionals regarding their thoughts of suicide. All staff receive training on the signs of potential suicide among inmates. These include sleeping a lot, depression, staying by oneself, giving away property to other inmates, or confiding their thoughts to family or friends.

suicide watch

management of suicidal inmates who are placed in a specially designed cell and have constant supervision

If inmates are deemed a high risk for suicide as a result of the assessment or staff observations, they may be specially monitored. Some of the monitoring may include **suicide watch** programs, in which inmates are placed in a specially equipped cell without materials that could be used for a suicide attempt (blankets, sheets, belts, shoestrings, places in the cell to hang something from). Some suicide watch cells then have constant supervision by either a camera or a person so that staff can quickly react if the inmate begins any dangerous activity. Others require

Suicide prevention cells have little that inmates can use to harm themselves and are monitored continuously through cameras or personal supervision.
Photo by Richard P. Seiter.

TABLE 3.7   Jail Procedures for Suicide Prevention

| Region and Jurisdiction | Jail Jurisdictions Have Specific Procedures for Suicide Prevention* | | Jail Jurisdictions with Suicide Prevention Procedures Involving: | | | | | | |
	No	Yes	Suicide Risk Assessment at Admission	Staff Training in Suicide Prevention	Counseling or Psychiatric Services	Monitoring of High-Risk Inmates	Suicide Watch Cell or Special Location	Inmate Suicide Prevention Teams	Other Procedures
U.S. total	84	2,782	2,499	1,997	1,764	2,085	2,403	215	151
Federal	0	1	1	1	1	1	1	1	0
State	84	2,781	2,498	1,996	1,763	2,084	2,402	214	151
Northeast	2	180	176	171	173	155	169	24	11
Midwest	36	854	786	635	554	680	742	54	35
South	41	1,347	1,161	892	762	939	1,161	110	72
West	5	400	375	298	274	310	330	26	33

*A total of 218 jail jurisdictions did not indicate whether specific procedures were followed for suicide prevention.

Source: Adapted from James J. Stephan, *Census of Jails, 1999,* NCJ 186633 (Washington, D.C.: U.S. Department of Justice, Bureau of Justice Statistics, August 2001), p. 41.

A Look Into...

Preventing Jail Suicides

The risk of suicide is high in jails. Lindsay M. Hayes is a nationally recognized expert on suicides in correctional facilities. He regularly consults and advises with correctional agencies around the country on actions to take to prevent suicides. He offers the following background and steps to reduce the likelihood of jail suicides.

The suicide rate in jails is much higher than in prison or in the community. A 2005 report by the Bureau of Justice Statistics reported that the 2002 suicide rate in jails was 47 per 100,000 inmates, which was three times the rate in state prisons (14 per 100,000 inmates) and much higher than the rate of suicide in the community (10 per 100,000 people).[56] Even though high, the jail and prison rates have come down substantially since the 1980s. In 1988, the jail suicide rate was 107 per 100,000 inmates. This drop illustrates that suicides can be reduced within a correctional environment.

The primary reason for the drop is the increase in the awareness of suicide risks and potential ways to reduce the risks have increased. Correctional administrators have become more concerned about it, not accepting that suicides just happen, and have become more proactive in their approach. The current philosophy is more likely to be a question of whether we understand what is going on, how we take a broader look at the picture, see if a suicide was an aberration, or if there is a systemic problem that needs to be addressed. In addition, we are better able to hire and train mental health staff to work in jail facilities and are doing a better job of intake screening and assessing the risk of suicide by new admissions.

Once aware, the important question is how we prevent suicides. The most important thing is to have a written suicide prevention policy. The policy must be comprehensive and include the eight most important prevention activities.

1. *Training of both correctional and mental health staff.* All staff should receive eight hours of suicide prevention training in their preservice training so that they understand the risk of suicide. Annually, staff should receive a refresher of two hours as a constant reminder that suicide prevention is an important issue to the jail and its management. It also serves as a reminder that every inmate is potentially suicidal.

2. *Intake screening and assessment.* Specific questions should be asked of every new admission to jail that address the risk of suicide. Are you thinking about committing suicide now? Have you considered it in the past? Have you recently experienced a serious loss? Is there any history of suicide in your family? Do you have a history of mental illness? Arresting or transporting officers should be asked if the inmate mentioned anything or showed any unusual behavior that might be a red flag for suicide.

3. *Communication.* The first level is between the arresting or transporting officer and the jail staff. The second level is among staff in the jail so that everyone knows if an inmate is likely suicidal and how he or she should be managed. The third level is between the staff and the suicidal inmate, watching and teaching the inmate how to deal with the urge.

4. *Housing.* Jails must provide a suicide-resistant housing situation for inmates identified as suicidal. It is usually not practical for all jail cells to be suicide resistant, so jailers must identify and create cells that are protrusion free, that is, without things that inmates can use to hang themselves (95 percent of inmates commit suicide by hanging using clothing or sheets attached to a protrusion).

5. *Levels of observation provided to suicidal inmates.* Most standards recommend at least two levels. The most extreme is constant observation of an inmate that is acutely suicidal, who if not constantly watched will make an effort to commit suicide. The second level of observation is close supervision that results in observation at staggered fifteen-minute intervals (not so routine that inmates can anticipate how frequently the jailer will make the check). This level is appropriate for inmates who are low to medium risk of committing suicide. They may be feeling distraught or suffering from mental illness or depression, or they may have made a suicide attempt in the past.

6. *Intervention in a suicide attempt.* This is similar to a medical emergency response and includes making sure the responding officer is trained in first aid, has a suicide prevention kit that includes a special knife to cut down a hanging victim, and follows a protocol detailing the role

of every staff member when responding to a suicide attempt. There should also be regular mock exercises for staff to practice an emergency situation.

7. *Reporting.* This is straightforward and includes writing a report by everyone involved in finding a suicide or anyone who had contact with the victim.

8. *Morbidity and mortality review process.* After any serious suicide attempt (requiring medical attention at the jail clinic or outside hospital), there should be a morbidity or mortality review. Both include a multidisciplinary approach with

both mental health and correctional staff involved. They look at the total event and not just how staff responded to it. They examine a time line of when the inmate arrived at the facility and look for any issues of mental health or medical issues that went undiscovered. This is not an investigation or internal affairs review, but a systemic review to address what happened and what we can learn to reduce the opportunity for suicides in the future. The review may result in a revision of policy, training, revision of screening forms, improvement of emergency response, or physical plan issues.

officers to check on the offender every thirty minutes to ensure his or her safety. Even with all these programs, it is difficult to prevent suicides of inmates truly committed to ending their lives. "A Look Into" describes a best practice approach to preventing suicides in jails.

In 2003, Maury Travis, an alleged serial killer, was arrested and jailed in the St. Louis County Jail for the brutal rape and murder of multiple victims. Because of the nature of the crimes, he was housed in the jail isolation block and placed on a suicide watch, with trained inmates assigned to sit outside his cell and watch him to prevent the possibility of a suicide attempt. The jail had a policy that inmates housed in the isolation block would be allowed to come out of their cells and walk on the short range immediately outside their cell for one hour per day. Therefore, the inmate watcher had to move back behind another wall, from which he did not have a direct view of the entire cell. Within thirty minutes after the inmate watcher moved from the cell front, Travis tied his bed sheet around his neck and a ventilation grill in the cell and hanged himself to death. The suicide resulted in the county jail hiring several more staff just to conduct the suicide watch, instead of using inmates.

In the "You Make the Decision" box, students consider several factors in a suicide prevention program and decide how they want to structure a prevention policy.

Summary

Jails today represent one of the most challenging operations in the nation's criminal justice process. Jails not only hold more than 700,000 inmates at any one time, but they also admit more than ten times that number per year, hold a wide variety of categories of offenders, house inmates with several unique problems and needs, and must maintain constitutional standards and protect the rights of offenders charged with, yet not convicted of a crime.

As a result of this multitasked mission, jails are extremely difficult to administer and operate. With the high turnover of offenders, jails sometimes make a mistake by releasing the wrong inmate. With many inmates having mental health, drug abuse, and physical problems, there are regularly cases of suicide, assault,

CHAPTER REVIEW

and alleged mistreatment. Located in the center of cities and rural communities, jails get much more public attention than most prisons or other correctional facilities. In many counties, jails are operated by an elected official (the sheriff); sometimes hiring decisions result from political connections or campaign contributions, rather than from the professional or technical skills or knowledge of the applicant.

Through all of these challenges, jails continue to operate almost nine hundred years after the first jail was opened in medieval England. The jail serves a critical role as an offender intake point to the criminal justice system. Even with major efforts to reform, improve, and reinvent the way jails are operated, few major changes have been made in the basic system of operating jails. And while efforts continue to improve and professionalize the nation's jails, it is not expected that the public's perceptions of how jails run will change.

Jails primarily hold offenders before trial, in addition to some offenders serving short terms of confinement. For more serious inmates who are sentenced to longer periods of incarceration, early U.S. colonists invented the prison. Chapter 5 describes the current status of prisons in the United States, how they operate, the types of jurisdictions that oversee them, and the assignment of inmates to various security levels. After reading Chapter 5, students will have a clear understanding of the differences in the policies and practices between jails and prisons.

Key Terms

gaol

jail

lockup

sheriff

regional jail

incarceration rate

length of stay

objective classification systems

first-generation jails

podular design

second-generation jails

third-generation jails

direct supervision

Bell v. Wolfish

suicide prevention programs

suicide watch

Review Questions

1. What role did John Howard play in the early development of jails?

2. Name five categories of jail offenders.

3. What are the advantages of a regional jail?

4. List potential reasons for the increase in the jail incarceration rate over the past decade.

5. Compare the average length of stay in a jail to that in a prison.

6. Describe the normal booking process in a jail.

7. Describe the problems associated with the use of classification systems in jails.

8. How are podular jail designs an improvement over linear jail designs?

9. Describe direct supervision.

10. How widely used are private correctional companies to operate jails?

11. Describe the impact of the *Bell v. Wolfish* decision on modern jail operations.

12. Why are there so many mentally ill offenders in jail?

13. What steps do jails take to reduce the likelihood of suicide by inmates?

14. What is a suicide watch?

You Make the Decision...

Preventing Jail Suicides

The story of Maury Travis is troubling for many reasons. First, a life was lost, even though there was significant evidence of his guilt in kidnapping and brutally murdering several women in the St. Louis metropolitan region. Second, with his death, there are still missing women that fit the description of other Travis victims, and law enforcement personnel are disappointed that they could not question him for information regarding those disappearances. And finally, the county jail failed in its responsibility to safely house Travis and prevent him from harming himself during the investigation and pending prosecution for his alleged acts.

It seems that preventing jail suicides would be easy. After all, the inmates are locked in cells. But if someone really wants to commit suicide, it takes only a few seconds, and almost any piece of clothing, sheet, or shoestring can be used to hang oneself. Suicide prevention screenings upon admission are only as good as the information provided by the offender. And, as in the Travis case, even when an inmate is identified as a risk and placed on suicide watch, weaknesses in the procedures can still result in a suicide.

The issues to consider when developing a suicide prevention policy include: (1) who to place on suicide watch, (2) what clothing and bedding are allowed, and (3) whether to use inmate watchers. Keep in mind that it is expensive to place someone on suicide watch, and there are always limited funds for operation. It is easy to decide to place an offender on suicide watch if he or she admits consideration of suicide. But if someone has a minor history or no history yet faces a long sentence or the death penalty, such as Travis, should he or she be on suicide watch? If the person is placed on the watch, do you strip the inmate and not allow any clothing or bedding? This seems harsh, but keep in mind that almost any item can be used as a noose to hang oneself. Finally, many jurisdictions do use inmates trained as suicide watchers. They cost nothing and have proved to be good companions to suicidal inmates. Through their communications, inmates often end their suicidal thoughts quicker than if a correctional officer is watching them. But if something goes wrong, as in the Travis case, it is difficult to justify the use of inmates as watchers to the public. Consider all these issues and develop your own suicide prevention program.

Chapter Resources on mycrimekit™

Go to mycrimekit.com to explore the following study tools and resources specific to this chapter:

- **Practice Quiz:** multiple-choice, true/false, short-answer, and essay questions to help students test their knowledge
- **WebQuests:** learning activities built around Web searches
  - American Jail Association: www.corrections.com/aja/
- **Insider's Experiences:** "Siting an Urban Correctional Facility"

- **Seiter Videos:**
  - See experts discuss jail operations
  - See experts discuss career opportunities in jails
  - See experts discuss direct supervision in jails
- **Career Center:** A Career as a Detention Officer
- **Flashcards:** Sixteen flashcards to test knowledge of the chapter's key terms

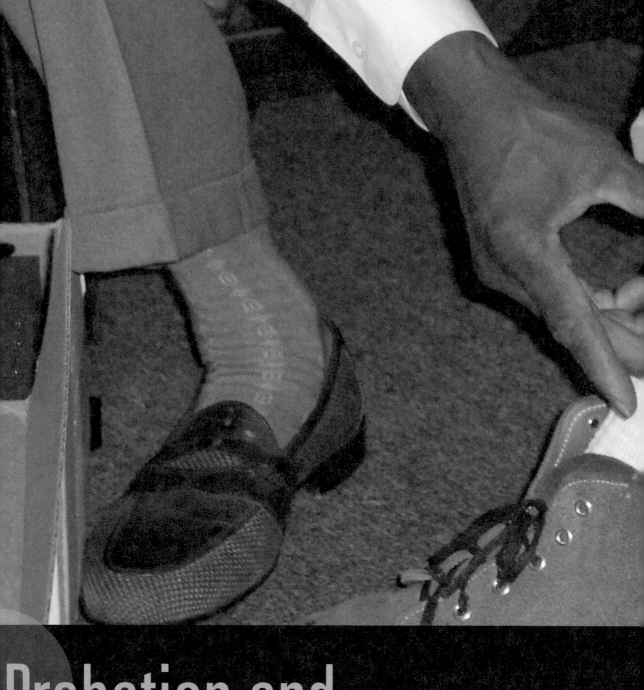

Probation and
Intermediate Sanctions

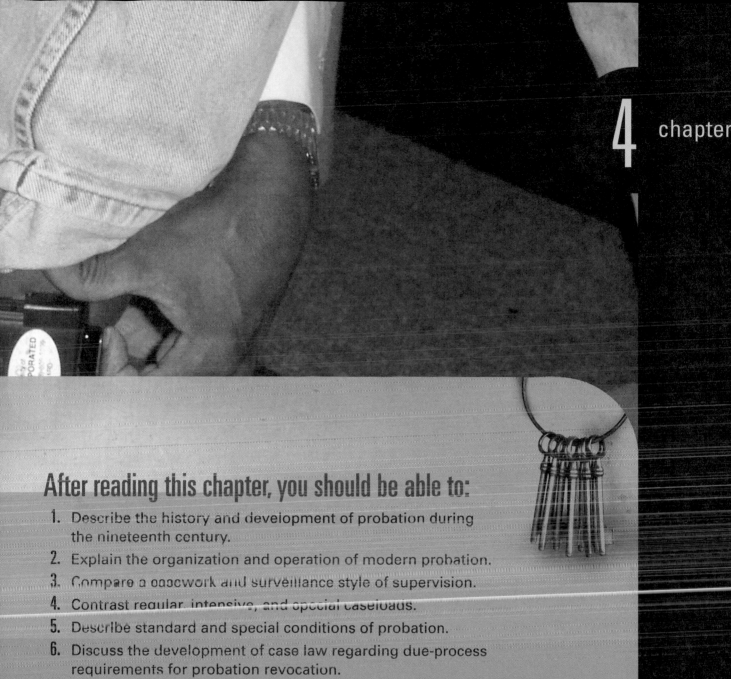

After reading this chapter, you should be able to:

1. Describe the history and development of probation during the nineteenth century.

2. Explain the organization and operation of modern probation.

3. Compare a casework and surveillance style of supervision.

4. Contrast regular, intensive, and special caseloads.

5. Describe standard and special conditions of probation.

6. Discuss the development of case law regarding due-process requirements for probation revocation.

7. Outline the results of evaluations regarding the effectiveness of felony probation.

8. Define *broken windows* probation strategies.

9. Define intermediate sanctions and describe how they are used for criminal sentencing.

10. Describe how intensive supervised probation operates.

11. Explain how house arrest works and contrast active and passive electronic monitoring systems.

12. Discuss the role of community residential centers as an intermediate sanction.

13. Describe the operation and effectiveness of shock incarceration or boot camp programs.

14. Compare shock probation to regular probation.

15. Explain the concept of *net widening* and the problem it creates in the efficient use of intermediate sanctions.

Introduction

community corrections

those criminal sanctions that involve community supervision of offenders, make use of correctional and program resources available in the community, and require offenders to abide by specified conditions to remain in the community

Historically, felony offenders were sentenced to either probation or prison. Over the past fifty years, however, the sentencing options available to judges have increased, with the addition of many other sanctions—some that supervise offenders in the community and some that supervise offenders in some type of institutional confinement. In the 1960s, many alternative sanctions to incarceration were developed, and the term **community corrections** was initiated. Community corrections or community-based corrections are criminal sanctions that involve community supervision of offenders, use correctional and program resources available in the community, and require offenders to abide by specified conditions to remain in the community.

Community corrections gained prominence as an adaptation of the Rehabilitative Era of corrections. During this period, offender problems were identified that required treatment to improve and prepare them for a productive and crime-free lifestyle. Most of the treatment was within institutional settings (prisons). However, it was soon recognized that for these treatments to maximize their effectiveness the community must be a part of the provision of treatment. In the restrictive prison environment, offenders could not test their readiness to return to the community or build relationships with community programs that could be continued as they lived in society. Therefore the Reintegrative Era developed, with the distinct provision that the community be an essential part of the correctional process.

Today, even as corrections becomes more retributive, there is still an emphasis on community corrections. However, the current emphasis on community corrections has changed from the 1960s and 1970s in that the focus is not on the offender and his or her rehabilitation or reintegration, but on public safety. Driving this trend is the realization that we cannot afford to continue to increase the number of offenders in prisons, and therefore safe and cost-effective community alternatives to incarceration must be developed.

This chapter describes the history, evolution, and current operations of community sanctions. Probation has been a part of community corrections for more than 150 years. In many ways, probation has changed little from its original philosophies and practices. In many other ways, however, probation has changed significantly, and some experts even describe a "new paradigm" for probation supervision. However, over the past thirty years, dissatisfaction with standard probation as a sanction for criminal offenders, combined with recognition of the need for alternatives to incarceration, has led to an expansion of intermediate sanctions to provide greater supervision than regular probation, while still monitoring offenders in the community.

The History of Probation

John Augustus

the Boston shoemaker who became the "father" of probation

The earliest history of probation in the United States began in Boston in 1841, when a shoemaker named **John Augustus** posted bail for a man charged with public drunkenness. Augustus had become very interested in the court system and concerned about the dire situation of people charged with crimes who had to spend time in poor jail conditions. While visiting a court hearing, Augustus heard a defendant state than he would drink no more if saved from a sentence in the house of correction, and Augustus asked the judge to defer sentencing and release the man into his custody. In doing so, he became the nation's first probation officer.[1]

Augustus began to help others in the same way, bailing them out, helping them find work and a residence, and keeping the court appraised of their progress. By the time of his death in 1859, Augustus had bailed out more than 1,800 offenders. His records on the first 1,100 offenders whom he bailed out revealed that only one forfeited bond.[2] Augustus's work had a great impact on how many jurisdictions handled criminal offenders, and he became known as the father of probation. Unfortunately, while he was alive, he received little recognition for his efforts; he died destitute, having used all his funds to help others.

As the successes of Augustus became known, jurisdictions began to recognize that not every offender needs to be sentenced to jail or prison. In 1878, Massachusetts passed the first probation statute for juveniles, and probation was officially recognized. Not until 1901, however, did New York pass the first statute authorizing the use of probation for adult felons. Other states quickly followed New York's lead, and by 1938 thirty-seven states, the District of Columbia, and the federal government had passed juvenile and adult probation laws.[3] By 1907, the first directory of probation officers in the United States listed 795 juvenile and adult probation officers.

Augustus's acts of supervising offenders slowly crept into the formalization of the role of probation officers. Augustus himself came up with the term *probation* (based on the Latin term *probatio* meaning "a period of proving oneself"), as well as ideas for requiring offenders to meet conditions of supervision, reporting to the courts, and revoking probation when the conditions were not met.[4] In addition, Augustus's idea of investigating offenders' situations prior to sentencing resulted in the concept of presentence investigations being assigned to probation officers. Although probation has become much more sophisticated in its operation over the years, most of the original concepts created by Augustus continue to this day.

Modern Probation Operations

Probation is a prison sentence that is suspended on the condition that the offender follow certain prescribed rules and commit no further crimes. Even though probation currently suffers from a perception of being "soft on crime," the public and elected officials recognize that not every offender can be sent to prison, and probation is still a sanction regularly used in the United States. In fact, since 1975 the number of offenders under community supervision has risen from less than 1 million to nearly 5.1 million by 2007.[5] However, since that time, the operations of probation have changed significantly. In 1976, a U.S. Comptroller General's Office report criticized probation operations, calling probation a failure due to a lack of adequate resources and recommending a total reevaluation of its operations and practices.[6] As a result, several probation programs, such as intensive probation supervision, house arrest, boot camps, and shock probation, have been created to enhance supervision, increase effectiveness, and increasingly limit offenders' freedom.

Today, probation in the United States is a federal, state, and local activity administered by more than two thousand separate agencies; there is considerable diversity of operations and no uniform structure. Although probation began as a service to the judiciary and an arm of the court, today, in all but eleven of the states, adult probation is located in the executive branch of government. In more than half of the states, probation operations are centralized in the state department of corrections. This move to the executive branch and toward centralization stems from the need for training, professionalism, and uniformity of standards, which can be better accomplished in larger administrative systems; there can also be better coordination with other correctional services. In approximately eight states and the federal government, probation and parole services are provided by the same state agency, which supervises both probationers and parolees.

Even though prisons and issues focusing on incarceration receive much of the attention and most of the resources, probation operations have a tremendous impact on the correctional systems in the United States. In 2007, the Bureau of Justice Statistics reported a total of 7,328,200 adults under correctional supervision. Of these, 4,215,361 were on probation, 799,058 were on parole, and 2,293,200 were in prison or jail.[7] Even with a "tough on crime" mentality gripping the country, probation remains an important component of the correctional process, and the number of people on probation has remained relatively steady for the past several years.

Supervision

Once offenders are granted probation, it is the responsibility of probation officers to supervise them and get them to comply with conditions of their probation. Officers have a dual, and sometimes conflicting, responsibility. The primary purpose of **probation supervision** is to maintain surveillance, enforce conditions of probation, and guide offenders into treatment to protect the public from further crimes. To fulfill this purpose, officers first monitor probationers' activities through a combination of office visits (probationers report to the officer at the probation office), verification of probationers' activities by visiting their homes and contacting their employers or program providers, and monitoring activities such as drug testing of probationers. Second, officers help offenders succeed by determining program or treatment needs and placing probationers in social service programs that address their needs for education, mental health counseling, vocational training, or substance abuse programming.

It has been suggested that officers develop a supervision style that falls into either a casework or a surveillance approach. A **casework style of supervision** emphasizes helping the offender with problems, providing counseling, and ensuring that the offender completes supervision. A **surveillance style of supervision** emphasizes monitoring and enforcing compliance with the rules or supervision and the detection of violations leading to revocation and return to custody. In a survey of probation and parole officers in St. Louis, Missouri, officers were asked what they considered the most important roles for probation officers and how they spent their time in supervising offenders in the community.

probation supervision

the role of a probation or parole officer in monitoring an offender's behavior through office visits; contacts with family, friends, bosses, or treatment providers; and visits to their home or place of work

casework style of supervision

a style of supervising community offenders that places emphasis on assisting the offender with problems, counseling, and working to make sure the offender successfully completes supervision

surveillance style of supervision

a style of supervising community offenders that places emphasis on monitoring and enforcing compliance with the rules or supervision and the detection of violations leading to revocation and return to custody

Part of supervision of offenders in the community is through office visits in which probation and parole officers get updates on the activities of their clients.
Photo by Richard P. Seiter.

Officers responded that the primary role of probation and parole officers is to ensure public safety, to supervise and offer resources to help the client readjust to society, to prevent recidivism, to steer offenders in the right direction, to monitor offenders, and to hold offenders highly accountable for their actions and responsibilities.

Results indicated that officers spend an average of 55.9 percent of their time on casework activities during supervision and 41.4 percent of their time on surveillance activities.[8] These results indicate that officers must do both surveillance (monitoring compliance with conditions) and casework (helping offenders with their problems) in order to enforce conditions of probation and guide offenders to a status that improves their likelihood of success in the community. The types of services that most probation and parole agencies provide include referral services, individual counseling, substance abuse counseling, job development, and family counseling.[9]

Probation agencies generally organize caseloads into three types: regular, intensive, and special. **Regular caseloads** are those for standard probationers who may have a significant risk of reoffending or several program needs but do not warrant assignment to one of the other two types of caseloads. **Intensive-supervision caseloads** (described in more detail later in this chapter) are for offenders with too high a risk or a need to be on regular supervision and were created as an alternative to sending these offenders to prison. Intensive-supervision caseloads are significantly less in number, and the required contacts between officers and probationers are significantly higher. Most jurisdictions also use **special caseloads,** whereby an officer's entire caseload is made up of probationers with a specific type of problem, such as substance abuse, mental illness, or a history of sex offenses. Such specialization allows the officer to become knowledgeable and proficient in dealing with this particular problem. In a 2002 survey, it was reported that 89.5 percent of probationers were on regular caseloads, 15.68 percent were on special caseloads, 4.2 percent were on intensive caseloads, and 0.7 percent were on a caseload using electronic monitoring.[10] The "A Look Into" box gives a good idea of the challenges of managing a special caseload.

mycrimekit

Media—Video:
Probation Officer Jobs.

regular caseload
caseload made up of standard probationers, requiring no special program or supervision

intensive-supervision caseload
caseload for offenders with too high a risk or need to be on regular supervision; created as an alternative to sending these offenders to prison

special caseload
caseload is made up of offenders with a particular type of problem, such as substance abuse, mental illness, or a history of sex offenses

A Look Into...

Dealing with the mentally Ill Probationer

In a ten-year-old report, the Bureau of Justice Statistics found that 13 percent of all probationers had a condition requiring mental health treatment, and there have been no more recent studies to update this estimate. Of those probationers with mental health problems, only 43 percent of those required to participate in such treatment had done so.[11] Historically, mentally ill offenders in the community were spread out among standard caseloads of non-mentally ill offenders. Recently, most probation and parole agencies have created special caseloads for managing the mentally ill offender. These caseloads are usually smaller than standard caseloads, averaging between fifty and fifty-five offenders. Most offenders are placed on a special caseload by an order of the court as a condition of their probation. Otherwise, probation officers may identify an offender as possibly having a mental illness and request his or her placement on a special caseload. A survey published in 2008 found that probation officers supervising offenders with mental health problems who treated them as special offenders

...continued

and met with them more often and used mental health community services more than with traditional case management practices were more successful and less punitive in dealing with violations.[12] The following is a description by a probation officer of his approach to dealing with mentally ill probationers.

The supervision philosophy of this probation officer is to build trust with clients, particularly because he is concerned about the client's risk of suicide or violence to others. The officer notes that he would not know these things unless offenders tell him, and they must believe that they can share sensitive information with their probation officer without fear of immediate violation (return to prison). The officer states that after a few crises with offenders this trust often develops.

Mentally ill probationers report more frequently than standard probationers; weekly contact is not unusual. This frequency of contact often continues even when offenders' behavior is good and they are eligible for less intensive supervision. This is because these probationers may become unstable at any time. Every time the officer sees his probationers, he asks them if they are taking their psychotropic medication, if they are having any thoughts of harming themselves or others, and if they know the date and time of their next psychiatric appointment. He notes that it is very important not just to ask them these questions and accept their answers, but to "pry and push" them. He gave an example of an offender under his supervision that had a history of serious suicide attempts through overdoses of psychotropic drugs. The offender called the probation officer (PO) one day and said his roommate was using drugs, and he was afraid he would get caught up in it. The PO advised him to move as soon as possible, but as they continued to talk, it became clear that something else was bothering him. After some prodding, the probationer finally admitted that he was thinking of harming himself. In fact, he then admitted that he had already begun to take his medicine in a suicide attempt and had called the PO in hopes that the PO would get him to admit what he was doing without his volunteering the information. When asked why someone attempting suicide would not admit it, the PO noted that this is not unusual, as the person planning suicide is often embarrassed and sometimes even concerned about upsetting the PO. Some of his clients become very apologetic about the trouble they cause the PO. In this situation, the PO called emergency medical services (EMS) and continued to talk to the probationer on the phone until the paramedics arrived. He then directed the probationer to go out to meet the EMS workers when they drove up. However, the probationer had kept some pills in his hand, and on the way to the hospital, he took some more pills. The EMS workers were able to treat and save him, and the probationer is now doing very well, both physically and psychologically.

The PO noted that an important part of his job is to be just one part of the mental health treatment team, with the probationer's psychiatrist, the case manager (who acts as community support to help the person keep track of appointments and monitor medication), the probationer's family (although most mentally ill probationers do not have significant family support), and other treatment providers.

One thing that is very different for a PO who specializes in managing mentally ill offenders is the number of hospital visits. The PO indicated that seven probationers out of his caseload of fifty-three were in a mental institution or a psychiatric wing of a hospital. He noted that he also has to work much more closely with the court and judges to educate them regarding the special circumstances of mentally ill offenders. Sometimes he has to be an advocate for the needs of these offenders and suggest that the court show more tolerance for minor violations of probation. Other times, the PO must act in an unconventional manner and have good relationships with court officials in order to get them to act beyond their normal operations. He gave the example of a female probationer who had stopped taking her psychotropic medication, had just had a baby, and was psychotic and delusional. During an evening telephone conversation with the PO in which he was urging her to go to a hospital for inpatient care, the woman threatened to kill her mother and stated that she did not want to go to the hospital. The PO asked her to hold for a minute, called the probation duty officer, obtained an immediate arrest warrant from the court, and asked the police to arrest the probationer immediately. Within half an hour, the police were at her front door to arrest her.

In closing, the PO indicated that to manage a caseload of mentally ill probationers a person must have a strong desire to do it and must be compassionate and understanding, as these probationers do not respond in the typical manner to threats of a probation violation. If they want to die and are planning to commit suicide, the PO cannot simply demand compliance. He noted that even for most compassionate individuals, this work could lead to a great deal of frustration.

TABLE 4.1	Supervision Caseload Approach	
Case Priority	**Hours per Month**	**Total Caseload**
High	4 hours	30 cases
Medium	2 hours	60 cases
Low	1 hour	120 cases*

*Based on a 120 work hour per officer per month.
Source: Matthew T. DeMichele, *Probation and Parole's Growing Caseloads and Workload Allocations: Strategies for Managerial Decision Making* (Lexington, KY: May 2007), p. 16.

Average caseload sizes vary considerably from jurisdiction to jurisdiction. *The 2002 Corrections Yearbook* reports that the average size of probation officer caseloads is very large, as the regular supervision average caseload size was 127, ranging from 314 cases per officer in Rhode Island to 15 cases per officer in Pennsylvania.[13] These large caseloads illustrate that although governments recognize the need for probation, they fail to financially support it at a more reasonable level. Large caseload sizes make it very difficult for probation to be an effective sanction in providing services to offenders, monitoring their behavior, and reducing recidivism. And, high caseloads were reported as one of the primary causes of stress among probation and parole officers.[14]

A report by the American Probation and Parole Association in 2007 recommended the caseload approach described in Table 4.1.

Conditions of Probation

The fundamental premise of probation is that offenders must meet certain conditions to successfully complete their probation and avoid having their supervision suspended and being sent to prison. Jurisdictions have **standard conditions of**

mycrimekit™
Media—Video: Offenders Discuss Supervision.

standard conditions of probation
conditions that must be followed by every probationer

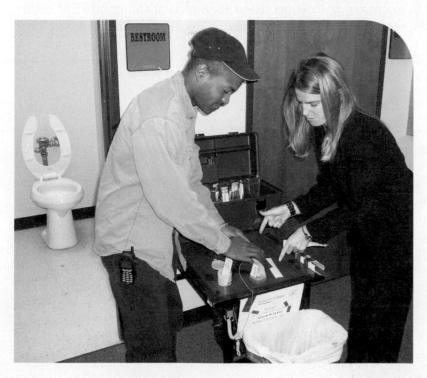

One way to monitor compliance with conditions of no illegal drug use is through random drug testing. Inmates submit urine samples that are sent to a lab for testing.
Photo by Richard P. Seiter.

special conditions of probation

conditions of probation tailored to meet the needs for a particular offender; they can be imposed to meet the specific risks or needs of an individual offender

probation that must be followed by every probationer, and judges usually have the authority to impose **special conditions of probation**. These special conditions are tailored to meet the program needs for an offender, or can be imposed to address an offender's specific risk to the community. During probation, judges may modify conditions as they determine that offenders are performing satisfactorily and no longer need certain conditions or are performing poorly and require added conditions as a part of their supervision.

Standard conditions of probation usually include the following:

1. The probationer shall not leave the judicial district without permission of the probation officer or the court.
2. The probationer shall report to the probation officer as directed and shall submit truthful and complete reports.
3. The probationer shall answer truthfully all inquiries by the probation officer and follow his or her instructions.
4. The probationer shall maintain employment.
5. The probationer shall notify the probation officer of all changes of address within seventy-two hours.
6. The probationer shall refrain from the excessive use of alcohol and is prohibited from the use of controlled substances.
7. The probationer shall not associate with criminals.
8. The probationer shall not commit any crimes.

Examples of special conditions of probation include requiring drug or alcohol counseling, drug testing, mental health counseling, or vocational training; avoiding a particular person or group; or staying out of bars or poolrooms. Judges may also impose any of the intermediate sanctions described below. Judges have considerable discretion in imposing special conditions of probation. If offenders meet the conditions of their probation, the supervising probation agency may recommend that the sentencing court end the period of probation, terminate supervision, and close the case. In 2006, of the 2.2 million offenders exiting probation, 57 percent were successful terminations, meaning that probationers satisfied the requirements of their supervision (completing the number of visits, passing drug tests, receiving counseling, or meeting other conditions required of their supervision).[15]

mycrimekit

Media—Video:
Probation Supervision.

Revocation of Probation

technical violations

violations of conditions of community supervision, without commission of a new crime

new-crime violations

violation of the condition of probation prohibiting the commission of any additional crimes

If probationers violate or fail to meet any conditions of their probation, they are subject to having their probation revoked and their original prison sentence imposed. Probationers can have their probation revoked for either **technical violations** (not meeting all the conditions of their supervision) or **new-crime violations** (violating the condition of not committing additional crimes). For minor violations of technical conditions, it is unlikely that probation will be revoked, but for continued violations, serious technical violations, or commission of a new crime, probation most likely will be revoked. One exception resulted from a 1983 U.S. Supreme Court ruling in *Bearden v. Georgia* in which the Court decided that failure to make restitution payments due to unemployment is not sufficient reason to revoke probation.[16]

For minor technical violations, probation officers usually have the discretion to determine how they will handle the infraction. They may warn probationers or intensify their own supervision of the case by making more community visits or

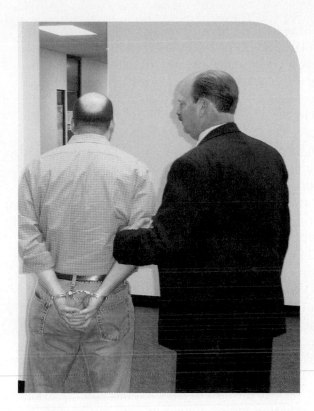

When a probationer commits a serious technical violation or a new crime, the probation office usually issues an arrest warrant and the offender is taken into custody. Photo by Richard P. Seiter.

increasing the reporting requirements. In most jurisdictions, officers cannot impose new conditions without requesting modification by the court. If these actions do not change behaviors or if the violation is serious, probation officers begin the formal probation revocation process.

The revocation process begins with a report of the violation and a recommendation for action by the supervising probation officer. The report goes to the sentencing court, and the probationer is given a copy of the alleged violations and directed to appear for a preliminary hearing. The probationer may be arrested and detained in jail until the preliminary hearing. The preliminary hearing is to determine whether there is probable cause to believe that the probationer has committed the violations. If so, a full revocation hearing is scheduled. The probationer may be taken into custody or released on bail or personal recognizance. The probationer may waive the full hearing and plead guilty to the violation at the preliminary hearing, and the judge will decide how to handle the violation at that time. If the case proceeds to a full revocation hearing, the probation officer bringing the charges and presenting evidence of the violation prepares a full report, and the probationer is given a copy. At the revocation hearing, the officer presents the violation report; the probationer may be represented by legal counsel and have the opportunity to testify and present evidence of his or her innocence of the violations.

In the 1970 case of *United States v. Birnbaum*, the U.S. Supreme Court determined that probation is a privilege and not a right.[17] Once probation is granted, however, the probationer has a liberty interest in avoiding incarceration, and probation cannot be revoked without limited due process requirements. In *Mempa v. Rhay* (1967), probationers were granted the right to legal counsel during the revocation hearing.[18] In 1972, the U.S. Supreme Court decided *Morrissey v. Brewer*, which spelled out the due process rights for parole violations hearings.[19] The next year, the Court decided **Gagnon v. Scarpelli,** which extended the *Morrissey* due

Gagnon v. Scarpelli
a 1973 U.S. Supreme Court decision that created the due process requirements for revoking probation

process rights to probationers.[20] These include the following rights: (1) to be informed in writing of the alleged violations, (2) to have written notice in advance of the revocation process, (3) to have a preliminary hearing to determine whether there is probable cause, (4) to have a revocation hearing prior to the final decision, (5) to attend the hearings and present witnesses on their behalf, (6) to confront and cross-examine adverse witnesses, and (6) to receive a written decision noting the reasons for the decision.

If there is a finding of a violation, the court has three options: (1) reprimand and restore to supervision, (2) add conditions and restore to probation, (3) or revoke probation and order imprisonment under the original sentence. A serious concern is the increase in the number of violations of probation and parole over the past decade. In 1974, the percentage of the U.S. prison population admitted for probation or parole violations was 17 percent, but by 1991 that figure had increased to 45 percent.[21] In 2006, of the 396,324 offenders terminated from probation and incarcerated (18 percent of all exits from probation), 88,072 (22 percent) were for a new crime and 198,162 (50 percent) were for technical violations of the same sentence, and for the rest, the reason for the return was not known.[22] The "tough on crime" attitude and interest in public safety and avoiding risk of further criminality encourages probation officers to report more violations to the court than previously and encourages the courts to violate probationers and send them to prison at a higher level than in past years.

In the "You Make the Decision" box at the end of the chapter, you are asked to consider whether to revoke the probation of an offender who is not complying with all the conditions of his probation.

mycrimekit™

Careers: Careers in Correction as a probation officer.

Issues Regarding Probation

Many issues are discussed when describing the current system of probation operations and determining how the system should be changed or improved. First, does probation work? Many studies have resulted in serious questions as to whether probation is effective. The true answer depends on what probation is expected to do and what is determined to be success. How are offenders supervised in the community, and what is the role of the probation officer? Probation officers' roles have changed over the past few years, yet there is still little understanding of what they do and how they should do it. Finally, how do you allocate resources for probation supervision? Most jurisdictions use some method of classifying offenders by risk and need to both create supervision guidelines and expectations and to determine how many offenders a probation officer will supervise.

Effectiveness

Studies of regular probation (without some type of enhanced supervision) have demonstrated mixed results in probation's effectiveness in protecting society from future crimes. A 1986 review of 79,000 felons sentenced to probation in thirty-two counties across seventeen states revealed that within three years of sentencing, while still on probation, 43 percent were rearrested for a felony.[23] A 1985 RAND study followed California adult felons on probation in Los Angeles and Alameda counties over a forty-month period. Of the sample of 1,672 probationers in 1980, 65 percent were rearrested, 51 percent were reconvicted, and 34 percent were reincarcerated.[24] In the most recent report of probation in the United States,

57 percent of offenders exiting probation during 2006 were successful completions, and 18 percent were incarcerated.[25] Although these studies question the effectiveness of probation, other studies show some success of probation in reducing recidivism, depending on the seriousness of the offender population, the length of the follow-up, and the type of surveillance provided.

One review of probation outcomes gives conflicting data. Clear and Braga examined the success of a group of both felony and misdemeanor probationers and found that 80 percent completed their terms without a new arrest.[26] However, Langan and Cunniff examined the same data, but only for felony probationers, and found that 43 percent were rearrested within three years.[27] A review of seventeen evaluations of felony probation found rearrest rates as low as 12 percent and as high as 65 percent.[28] This review concluded that probation without adequate surveillance and treatment is not effective. However, well-managed and adequately funded probation programs do reduce recidivism.

All of the preceding evaluations only cite success rates, with no comparison of alternative sentencing outcomes. In some evaluations, probation success rates are compared to the success of ex-inmates. Probationers' recidivism is consistently lower, but that is expected because offenders who receive probation are a less serious group than those who are sentenced to prison. However, in a study with groups of 511 probationers and 511 parolees matched to have an equal likelihood of recidivism, the results over a two-year follow-up indicated that probationers were more successful; 72 percent of parolees and 63 percent of probationers were rearrested, 53 percent of parolees and 38 percent of probationers had new charges filed, and 47 percent of parolees and 31 percent of probationers were incarcerated in jail or prison.[29] This finding suggests that, although probationers have high rates of recidivism, prison parolees do even worse.

Some studies also cite the low cost of probation compared to other sanctions. Estimates of the cost of constructing a maximum-security prison are approximately $78,000[30] per bed, and the annual cost of maintaining and housing an inmate is approximately $28,817 or $78.95 per day.[31] Costs for regular probation were reported to be an average of only $3.42 per day in 2008.[32] Therefore, particularly during tight budget times, elected officials and correctional administrators continue to support the use of probation, even while looking for ways to increase its effectiveness to protect society and deter crime.

A Changing Style of Supervision

Even while the public recognizes that not every criminal offender can be sent to prison, there has been an increasing public dissatisfaction with the use of probation, spurred by a belief that those under probation received minimal supervision, and therefore society was not protected against the likelihood of repeat crimes by those who were allowed to remain in the community. However, the manner in which a parolee or probationer is supervised receives relatively little attention, even though its importance was recognized almost forty years ago. In the classic review of prisons and parole, Glaser notes, "The principal functions of parole supervision have been procurement of information on the parolee . . . and facilitating and graduating the transition between imprisonment and complete freedom . . . these functions presumably are oriented to the goals of protecting the public and rehabilitating the offender."[33] Soon thereafter, Alberty analyzed the comparison between styles of parole supervision and violation rates and defined supervision as "the means used to accomplish the goals of protecting society and rehabilitating the offender."[34]

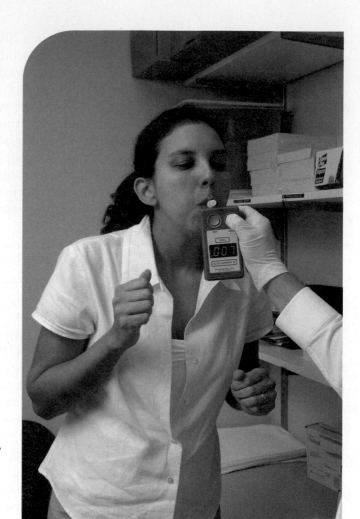

Under the surveillance style of supervision, officers closely monitor probationers' behavior, such as administering frequent Breathalyzer tests. Courtesy of Bob Daemmrich Photography, Inc.

Until the late 1960s, probation and parole supervision focused on the case-work style of supervision, or restoring offenders to the community.[35] However, over the past twenty years, there has been an increasing reliance on surveillance, or closely monitoring offenders to catch them when they fail to meet all required conditions. Rhine, in describing this change in supervision style, suggests that it brings about a new paradigm in the supervision of offenders in the community:

> *Despite their importance to public safety, the past 20 years have witnessed a marked devaluation of traditional probation and parole supervision. Acknowledging this trend, many administrators in the field have adopted a set of practices and a discourse that represent a discernible shift toward risk management and surveillance. This shift in the mission and conduct of supervision reflects a new narrative, the plausibility of which has yet to be established.*[36]

The transition from casework to the surveillance style of supervision could be less of a philosophical than a pragmatic change, as caseload sizes have been increasing, and with less time to provide individual attention to probationers, officers must resort to surveillance tactics. As an example, caseloads in California over the last few decades of the twentieth century increased dramatically; in the early 1990s they reached 500 per officer, and "some 60 percent of Los Angeles probationers were tracked solely by computer and had no face-to-face contact with a probation officer."[37]

The difficult economic times of 2008 moving forward has caused a renewed interest on how we supervise offenders in the community and the result it has on probation and parole revocations. In a pure surveillance style, community officers focus on supervising offenders closely enough to catch them when they fail, but many jurisdictions are revamping their supervision to help offenders be successful and reduce the costly return to prison. An example is in Kansas, which is closing three correctional facilities to save money, and targeting a 20 percent reduction in probationers violated and sent to prison. Kansas has implemented behavior modification as a part of probation supervision. A correctional official noted, "It used to be that it was more about waiting for them [probationers] to mess up and send them back to prison. In this time and this economy, you can't afford to keep doing that. There is a better way to do business."[38]

Perhaps the most promising reform of probation has been a concept called *broken-windows* probation. This concept mimics the philosophy of community policing, in that all broken windows in a neighborhood are to be promptly repaired, as this small indication of a lack of community concern leads to a larger instability and criminal activity in the community. As such, probation supervision follows the lead of community policing by partnering with citizen groups, churches, and other neighborhood organizations to take joint responsibility for supervising offenders. Emphasizing public safety first, broken-windows probation also allocates resources according to risk and need assessments, locates probation officers in the probationers' neighborhoods, and uses graduated sanctions such as house arrest, electronic monitoring, and mandatory substance abuse treatment.[39]

One important function of community supervision officers is to visit offenders' residences or places of employment. These visits lead to concerns about the

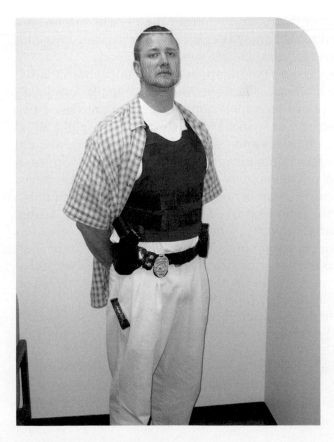

Officers going into the field to conduct home visits usually are armed, wear a protective vest, and carry other equipment similar to a police officer. Photo by Richard P. Seiter.

safety of officers. Therefore, most agencies allow officers to carry a weapon when doing a home visit, and some require them to go with a partner. The safety of officers is a serious and real concern, but there is also a concern that the arming of officers moves supervision even further away from a casework model to more of a policing or surveillance model.

Probation Classification Systems

One important issue in supervising offenders in the community is classifying them in terms of risk to the community and need for treatment programs. Such classification identifies offender risks and provides appropriate supervision to maximize the distribution of resources and focus on public safety. Models of risk assessment were first developed for probation in the mid-1970s and quickly gained support. In 1976, the U.S. Comptroller General tested the predictive power of community risk-prediction models and concluded that "probation prediction models could improve probation systems operations by allocating resources to offenders who most need help. . . . Model sources appeared to be useful in determining supervision levels and more successfully selected probationers for early release."[40] A National Institute of Corrections report titled *Directions for Community Corrections in the 1990s* noted, "In general, one effective way to increase decision reliability is to make visible the criteria for decisions. For that reason, we advocate the use of statistically based devices to classify offenders according to relative risk."[41]

community classification systems

risk assessments that predict the chance of new crimes being committed; they are used to determine the level of supervision an offender will receive in the community

Community classification systems score offenders based on their offense background and personal characteristics. Figures 4.1 and 4.2 illustrate the current Missouri model used to determine levels of community supervision. Probation and parole officers initially complete the Client Analysis Scale-Risk for the offender (Figure 4.1). Each case is scored on the number of prior convictions, employment status, age, present offense, and whether the present offense is a felony. The scores are combined to determine the permanent risk score, which is used to determine the classification of risk and the supervision level.

The highest risk level, *intensive supervision*, applies to offenders posing a significant risk of committing a new offense. They are assigned to smaller caseloads, must report at least once per week to the supervising officer, and are visited two to three times per month at home or at work. Most probationers are placed on *regular supervision*, with larger caseloads and fewer reporting requirements. For offenders who pose little risk to the community, *minimum supervision*, with caseloads as high as three hundred offenders, may be satisfactory. These offenders often have contact with their probation officer only every few months and are basically responsible themselves for following the conditions of their supervision. Some jurisdictions also have *administrative supervision* under which offenders have no contact with a parole or probation officer. However, they still must meet their conditions and commit no further crimes or their original parole or probation will be revoked. Administrative supervision is used only after low-risk offenders demonstrate a good adjustment to supervision.

After the initial classification of risk, each offender is scored on the Monthly Supervision Report (Figure 4.2) to review the status of the supervision and determine the need for changes.

In Missouri, offenders with a risk score of 10 or more and a need score of 11 or more are automatically assigned to participate in intensive supervision or another special-supervision caseload. If the review indicates that considerable supervision time has passed without a violation, a lower level of supervision will likely

STATE OF MISSOURI
DEPARTMENT OF CORRECTIONS
CLIENT ANALYSIS SCALE-RISK

OFFICER CODE

NAME	NUMBER	DATE

PRIOR CONVICTIONS (ADULT-FELONY, MISDEMEANOR, CRIMINAL ORDINANCE INCLUDING SIS)

☐ 1	☐ 2	☐ 3
NONE	1 OR 2 PRIORS	3 OR MORE

EMPLOYMENT/VOCATION

☐ 0	☐ 1	☐ 2
FULL TIME WORK	PART TIME WORK	UNEMPLOYED

AGE (AT ASSIGNMENT)

☐ 0	☐ 1	☐ 2
30 YEARS OR OVER	22 TO 29 YEARS	21 YEARS OR YOUNGER

PRESENT OFFENSE (CHARGE FOR WHICH CONVICTED) (ROBBERY, BURGLARY, STEALING, FORGERY, SEXUAL ASSAULT AS PER RSMo 589.015)

☐ 0	☐ 1
NO	YES

PRESENT OFFENSE A FELONY (OFFICIAL CHARGE)

☐ 0	☐ 1
NO	YES

RISK SCORE

FIGURE 4.1   Missouri Client Analysis Scale-Risk, for Use with Probationers and Parolees

Source: Missouri Department of Corrections.

STATE OF MISSOURI
DEPARTMENT OF CORRECTIONS
BOARD OF PROBATION AND PAROLE
MONTHLY SUPERVISION REPORT

OFFICE USE ONLY
☐ INITIAL SCALE
☐ ENTER

OFFICER NAME AND NUMBER

SUPERVISION NUMBER

NAME

PHONE NUMBER

ADDRESS   (CITY)   (STATE)   (ZIP CODE)

WITH WHOM DO YOU LIVE? (NAME AND RELATIONSHIP)

YOUR SOCIAL SECURITY NUMBER

NAME OF PRESENT EMPLOYER, ADDRESS, CITY, ZIP CODE

EMPLOYER'S PHONE NUMBER

NAME OF SUPERVISOR

IS EMPLOYER AWARE OF PROBATION/PAROLE?
☐ YES ☐ NO

TOTAL INCOME FOR PAST 30 DAYS

DO YOU OWN A VEHICLE? ☐ YES ☐ NO

MODEL   YEAR   MAKE

DESCRIPTION/COLOR

LICENSE NUMBER

HAVE YOU BEEN ARRESTED DURING PAST 30 DAYS? ☐ YES ☐ NO IF YES, DATE OF ARREST _____

ARRESTING DEPARTMENT   CHARGE

SIGNATURE	ACCEPTED BY	DATE	TIME	☐ A.M. ☐ P.M.

DO NOT WRITE BELOW THIS LINE

____ **EMPLOYMENT/EDUCATIONAL VOCATIONAL**
0 - FULL-TIME FOR PAST 3 MONTHS
1 - PART-TIME; SCHOOL; TRAINING; FULL-TIME LESS
     THAN 3 MONTHS; UNEMPLOYMENT COMPENSATION
2 - UNEMPLOYED
     DATE EMPLOYED _____

____ **LEGAL (EXCLUDES PRESENT OFFENSE)**
1 - NO ARRESTS IN THE PAST 3 MONTHS
2 - NO CONVICTIONS, 1 ARREST IN PAST 3 MONTHS
3 - 2 OR MORE ARRESTS, PENDING CHARGE, OR
     CONVICTION IN PAST 3 MONTHS
     DATE OF ARREST/CONVICTION _____

____ **TECHNICAL VIOLATIONS**
1 - NO TECHNICAL VIOLATION REPORT IN PAST 6 MONTHS
2 - TECHNICAL VIOLATION REPORT IN PAST 6 MONTHS
3 - TECHNICAL VIOLATION IN PAST 3 MONTHS OR
     PENDING REVOCATION
     DATE OF LAST TECHNICAL VLTN. RPT. _____
     CONDITIONS CITED _____

____ **SUBSTANCE ABUSE**
1 - NO DRUG USE/ALCOHOL ABUSE WITHIN 6 MONTHS
2 - DRUG USE/ALCOHOL ABUSE IN PAST 4-6 MONTHS
3 - DRUG USE/ALCOHOL ABUSE IN PAST 3 MONTHS
     DATE OF LAST USE/PROBLEM _____

PROBLEM CODES: 1 = NO PROBLEM 2 = IDENTIFIED HISTORY
3 = PROBLEM PAST 4–6 MONTHS 4 = PROBLEM PAST 3 MOS

____ **SOCIAL**
0 - NO PROBLEM
1 - PROBLEM NOT REQUIRING INTERVENTION
2 - PROBLEM REQUIRING INTERVENTION
     DATE OF LAST OCCURRENCE _____

SUBSTANCE ABUSE   ____ # UA'S ____ # POSITIVE
____ ALCOHOL
____ MARIJ/HASHISH   ____ STIM/COCAINE   ____ INHALENTS/SOLVENTS
____ OPIATES   ____ DEPRESSANTS   ____ HALLUCINOGENS
SOCIAL
____ MENTAL PROBLEMS   ____ FINANCIAL   ____ PHYSICAL
____ FAMILY PROBLEMS   ____ ASSAULT/AGGRESSIVE ____ REPORTING

RISK SCORE _____ NEED SCORE _____

_____

ISP/EMP/RF SCREEN FOR PLACEMENT IF RISK
IS 10 OR NEED IS 11 OR MORE

SCORE OVER-RIDES (If scored minimum; check only most serious one)

SPECIAL CONDITIONS
_____ SEXUAL OFFENDER _____ FINANCIAL _____ COMMUNITY SERVICE

LEVEL OF SUPERVISION

MONTHLY ACTIVITIES
_____
_____
_____
_____

MO 931-3698 (2-96)

FIGURE 4.2 Missouri Probation and Parole Monthly Supervision Report

Source: Board of Probation and Parole, Missouri Department of Corrections, 1991

be assigned. Classification processes are extremely valuable to match resources to offenders' risk and needs and help officers make decisions regarding supervision level, revocation, or successful termination of supervision.

Intermediate Sanctions

Defining Intermediate Sanctions

Intermediate sanctions are midrange dispositions that fall between probation and imprisonment. Until the past few decades in many U.S. jurisdictions, judges imposing sentences for any but the most trivial of crimes had to choose between what seemed to be "doing something" (imprisonment) and "doing nothing" (probation). However, the problems of prison and jail crowding forced policymakers to develop punishments that fall between these two sanctions. Intermediate sanctions are commonly referred to as *midlevel punishments* and are designed to fill the gap that is widely perceived to exist between probation and prison.

Several factors have been cited in support of intermediate sanctions:

1. Unhappiness with regular probation supervision
2. An increase in the number in prisons and prison overcrowding
3. Tightening of budgets by states and an inability to continue to fund high numbers of offenders sentenced to prison
4. A belief that intermediate sanctions are more effective in providing effective rehabilitative programs
5. A realization that solid ties in the community are critical to the success of offenders and the knowledge that keeping offenders in the community helps them maintain these ties
6. Proportionality of sentencing, in that with a continuum of sanctions the sentence can be crafted to better fit the crime and offender

During the recession that began in 2008, states have been examining the options for use of community sanctions to save money and not undermine public safety. A March 2009 publication by the Pew Center on the States noted that the cost of probation supervision in fiscal 2008 was $3.42 per day, whereas the average daily cost of imprisoning an offender was $78.95. The report suggested that U.S. policy for the past quarter century has been to expand prison capacity, but "one unmistakable policy truth has emerged: We cannot build our way to public safety."[42] The current use of intermediate sanctions includes economic sanctions, community service, intensive supervised probation, house arrest, community residential centers, split sentences, shock incarceration (boot camps), and shock probation. Electronic monitoring often accompanies some of these midrange punishments.

Types of Intermediate Sanctions

Economic Sanctions

Economic sanctions use money as the means of carrying out criminal sanctions, such as fines, restitution, or forfeiture of assets. In most cases, economic sanctions are attached as a condition of probation; however, for minor offenses they may stand alone as punishments for crimes. When people think of economic sanctions, they usually consider small fines for minor offenses. However, fines and forfeiture of assets can be of very large amounts. For instance, during the 1980s, junk bond king Michael

Fines are a common condition of probation and are paid through the court cashier.

Photo by Richard P. Seiter.

Milken defrauded investors of what was estimated to be hundreds of millions of dollars. As a result, in addition to a short prison term, Milken was fined $600 million, although it was believed to be far less than he made from his illegal trading.

fines
a requirement that offenders pay some dollar amount to the court as punishment for committing the offense

   Fines are a requirement that offenders pay some dollar amount to the court as punishment for committing the offense. Fines can be a set amount for each type of crime or can be more creative and reflect the individual situation of each offense and offender. Courts usually consider both the seriousness of the offense and the economic gain by the offender to determine the amount of a fine. For instance, fines may be appropriate for white-collar offenders, who have a minimal risk of future criminality and perhaps no need for any rehabilitative programs; the sanction focuses on pure punishment, deterrence, and opportunity to repay the victims or society for the wrong done by the offense.

offender restitution
a requirement that offenders repay society for the harm created by the offense

victim compensation
offenders repay their victims directly for their losses and harm caused by the offense

   Although fines are usually paid to the court, a second type of economic sanction is **offender restitution,** which requires offenders to repay society for the harm created by the offense. Restitution can take several forms. One type of offender restitution is **victim compensation,** in which offenders repay their victims directly for their losses and harm caused by the offense. As noted in the discussion of presentence investigations, federal and many state courts allow victims to submit victimization statements to detail the amount of loss they incurred from the crime. Sentencing judges take this into account when sentencing offenders, and often use the submitted amount for assigning a level of victim compensation. Offenders can also pay restitution through *community service.* Community service can include cleaning up trash in a public area or counseling teenagers about the negative results of drug use. Community service is included here as an economic sanction, as it is often used when offenders do not have funds from which to pay a fine or make restitution. It is then referred to as a "fine on their time," so that indigent offenders do not have to serve prison or jail time merely because they lack the fiscal ability to pay a fine. Offenders may also be required to pay for their **cost of supervision** by paying to the court the costs affiliated with their supervision, such as drug testing, counseling, or electronic monitoring, reducing the cost to the taxpayers.

cost of supervision
offenders have to pay for some costs associated with their supervision in the community, such as drug testing or electronic monitoring

Another extremely effective economic sanction is **asset forfeiture,** the authorized seizure by the government of money, negotiable instruments, securities, or other things of value that were obtained through illegal activities. Created over the past thirty years, asset forfeiture enables courts to punish offenders by taking away assets they accumulated as a result of their criminal activity, ensuring that "crime doesn't pay." Asset forfeiture was first authorized in the RICO (Racketeer Influenced and Corrupt Organization) statute, a part of the federal Organized Crime Control Act of 1970. RICO statutes were created to aid law enforcement in investigating and prosecuting organized crime figures by making it unlawful for anyone involved in a pattern of racketeering to derive any income or proceeds from that activity and allowing the government to seize anything of value that can be shown to have been acquired through the racketeering activity.

Asset forfeiture is also regularly used in the prosecution and punishment of drug offenders. When the federal government expanded its powers and more aggressively targeted the arrest and prosecution of drug offenders during the 1980s, asset forfeiture became a valuable strategy. As property assets are seized, they are auctioned off and the proceeds are divided among the federal and local law enforcement agencies that participated in the criminal investigation. Local law enforcement agencies use these funds to enhance their own capabilities to target drug crimes, leading to more arrests and prosecution.

asset forfeiture
the authorized seizure by the government of money, negotiable instruments, securities, or other things of value that were obtained through illegal activities

Intensive Supervised Probation

When regular probation supervision is not considered satisfactory monitoring of offenders who either are high risk or have high treatment needs, yet still do not require incarceration, intensive supervised probation is a viable alternative. **Intensive supervised probation (ISP)** was initiated in Georgia in 1974 to increase the amount of supervision provided to selected felony probationers. ISP programs are now actively used in every state, and more than 50,000 probationers were on intensive caseloads on January 1, 2002.[43] The intent of ISP is to identify offenders who need supervision greater than that available through regular probation, yet are not such a risk to the community that they should be in prison.

Offenders placed in an ISP program are supervised by probation officers who have smaller caseloads (an average of 29 per officer in 2001),[44] and provide more frequent contacts through a combination of office reporting by offenders and home and work visits by the officer. The intensity of supervision allows for enhancing the goal of incapacitation, since the additional contacts reduce the opportunity for slipping into criminal behavior. Also, ISP is more of a punishment and deterrence because the number of contacts required disrupts the daily lives of offenders. Equally, it can enhance rehabilitation, because officers with smaller caseloads can provide counseling or follow-up on treatment plans for the offenders they supervise.

In a review of the effectiveness of intensive supervision for both probationers and parolees, the findings were mixed in terms of the positive results from ISP programs. In a review of fourteen counties in nine states, Petersilia and Turner found that judges placed high-risk probationers in the programs rather than diverting offenders from prison. The ISP participants were watched more closely (having more contacts with their supervising officers) and, while this did not result in more arrests, there were significantly more technical violations (70 percent for the ISP group and 40 percent for regular probationers), which resulted in 27 percent of the ISP participants being returned to prison or jail compared to only 19 percent of regular probationers at the end of one year.[45] However, if the ISP supervision combined drug treatment, community service, and employment programs with surveillance, recidivism rates were 10 to 20 percent lower than for those who did not participate in

intensive supervised probation
supervision of community offenders with higher than average risk, through smaller caseloads and very close monitoring of activities

such activities. Another analysis of 175 evaluations of ISP programs also found that combining surveillance with treatment resulted in reduced recidivism.[46]

House Arrest

house arrest

offenders live at home and must be at home except for times they are to be at work or participating in other activities approved by their probation officer

An even greater level of supervision, even while sanctioned offenders remain in the community, results from house arrest, sometimes referred to as community control. With **house arrest,** offenders are allowed to avoid a prison sentence, yet must be detained or incapacitated in their own homes, while they may remain employed, earn an income, support their families, and pay for their own upkeep and usually the cost of supervision for their house arrest. Offenders under house arrest live at home and must be at home except for times they are to be at work or participating in other activities previously approved by their probation officer. House arrest has the potential benefits of being economical, imposing severe restrictions on the offender's freedom and opportunity to commit crimes, and allowing for participation in community-based treatment programs.

electronic monitoring

the use of technology to monitor an offender's location

Although not always necessary, house arrest is commonly used in conjunction with **electronic monitoring,** or the use of technology to monitor an offender's location. Electronic monitoring requires offenders to wear a tamperproof bracelet around their ankle. The bracelet acts as a receiver for a radio wave sent by a transmitter that is placed in the offender's home. There are two types of systems, active and passive, both of which are monitored from a central location. With active systems, the central location maintains a computerized schedule of when offenders should be in their homes and automatically "alarms" or sends a notice when the signal is not communicated between the transmitter and receiver during those times. This indicates to the monitor or probation officer that the offender has violated the conditions of his or her house arrest, and someone will be dispatched to check on or arrest the offender. The passive system requires random telephone calls during times the offender should be in the home. When a monitoring telephone call is received, offenders have a certain amount of time to place the receiver against the transmitter, proving that they are in the home as required.

Electronic monitoring is not a criminal sanction; it is a method of supervision. The use of electronic monitoring has increased greatly throughout the United

Electronic monitoring involves placing a bracelet around an offender's ankle. The bracelet acts as a receiver and notifies surveillance officers if the offender is not at home at designated times. Photo by Richard P. Seiter.

States; the first systems were activated in 1986, more than 40,000 units were in use by 1992, and their use continued to grow.[47] The use of electronic monitoring is also believed to be cost effective, particularly as many states require offenders using the monitors to pay for the cost of supervision. Although almost every large probation department has the potential for electronic monitoring, on January 1, 2001, less than 1 percent of probationers were reported to be under electronic monitoring, at an average cost per day of $6.47.[48]

Generally, house arrest using electronic monitoring is considered effective. Evaluations of programs in Illinois[49] and several other states[50] indicated good results, and a 1989 survey on telemonitoring of offenders noted, "There were no significant differences in successful terminations among probationers, offenders on parole, or those in community corrections. All had successful terminations rates ranging between 74 and 86 percent."[51]

Community Residential Centers

Community residential centers (CRCs) have been commonly known as halfway houses, which began as programs to help ex-inmates make the transition between prison and the community. Today, CRCs play a much broader role than simply helping in the postprison transition. As an intermediate sanction, CRCs provide a combination of supervision, structure, accountability, and programming to aid in the community supervision of probationers who require more than standard probation in response to their risk of reoffending and program needs. Twenty-five years ago, Governor Pierre du Pont of Delaware identified the role of CRCs as an adjunct to traditional community supervision, while providing an increase in supervision leading to enhanced public safety in the management of offenders.[52] CRCs are less expensive than the operation of a prison. In 2008, the average cost per inmate per day was $78.95[53] considerably more than the 2001 average cost of $46.15 per day for a halfway house operated by the department of corrections and the cost of $43.11 for contracted halfway houses.[54] In most halfway houses or CRCs, residents must pay a portion of the cost of their stay through wages they earn while in the community.

The use of CRCs as an intermediate sanction can occur in two different ways. First, at the time of sentencing, judges can determine that offenders need the services of a residential center and can require probationers to live in a CRC as a condition of their probation. However, CRC placement more commonly occurs later in the period of probation supervision, after probationers are failing under their current

mycrimekit

Media – Investigate: Electronic Monitoring.

community residential centers
houses in which offenders live in the community that provide supervision, room and board, and some treatment as an alternative to prison

mycrimekit

Halfway House Operations.

Halfway houses are usually large, older homes located in an area close to the central city so that public transportation and other services are readily available. Photo by Richard P. Seiter.

supervision requirement. Probation officers may determine that offenders have violated minor conditions of supervision and require more structure and accountability or need a place to live or additional program assistance. The officer then recommends that the court add a CRC requirement as a condition of probation. The following "An Interview With" illustrates some of the operational issues for halfway houses or CRCs.

CRCs are usually an old boarding house, a YMCA, or some other large residential structure in an urban area. They range in size from thirty to two hundred residents. Resident rooms often hold two people, although some rooms are large enough to accommodate six or eight residents in a dormitory-style environment. The CRCs operate their own kitchen and provide meals to residents. Although CRCs have limited physical security to keep residents from leaving (usually standard residential locks, with cameras throughout the center to assist in supervision), residents are not free to come and go as they please. Residents must stay at the center unless they are approved to go to work or attend an authorized program. If they are complying with center rules, they may receive a weekend pass to visit family or friends.

An Interview With...

A Halfway House Director

James J. Lawrence is the president and CEO of Oriana House, a community corrections and chemical-dependency treatment program. Oriana House has facilities in Cleveland, Tiffin, and Akron, Ohio, with 950 offenders in residential beds and another approximately 1,000 in nonresidential programs. Mr. Lawrence has thirty-three years experience in corrections, has been at Oriana House for twenty-five years, and has been in his current position since 1981. He is recognized as one of the most knowledgeable and capable community corrections managers and is very active in professional organizations.

Question: What is the specific role of a halfway house as an alternative to incarceration?

Mr. Lawrence: Most halfway houses serve clients both as an alternative to prison (while on probation) and as postrelease from prison. As an alternative to prison, the role of a halfway house is to supervise and maintain an appropriate offender in the community. Appropriate usually means those that are nonviolent, often drug users or those who commit property offenses. The focus is to keep them in the community while meeting their needs to help make them successful. If they complete the halfway house program, they are likely to be successful and not have to go to prison.

Question: What type of inmates do you get as a diversion from prison?

Mr. Lawrence: We primarily receive nonviolent offenders without a severe mental illness or a history of dangerousness. Most do have serious adjustment problems. There are really no absolutes, as we may take some offenders with crimes of violence if the particular crime and history do not lead us to believe they would be a serious threat to community.

Question: What types of programs does the halfway house offer?

Mr. Lawrence: The halfway house program at Oriana House includes four areas: treatment for chemical dependency, with approximately 70 to 80 percent having a drug or alcohol problem. Second, we offer education programs. Research shows that those who have a GED are more likely to be successful in the community, so we try to increase their educational level. We strongly encourage our clients to take the GED test before they complete the program, and 89 percent of our clients who take the test pass the first time. Third, we focus on employment assistance. We look at both job readiness and job placement. Some offenders want to participate in job training or attend college; for those, we use community resources and help them find and enroll in an appropriate program. Before they can successfully complete the halfway house program, they must have either a full-time job or be enrolled full time in an education program. If they just need a job, we provide assistance in job referral. We also teach them how to determine if a job is right for them and how to be interviewed. We target getting a job at better than minimum wage with benefits. Finally, we try to change the way offenders think about their behavior and reduce their risk to reoffend. We target their criminogenic needs, or the issues and behaviors that result in their return to crime. As an example, if you hang out with criminals, you are more likely to get involved in crime. If you make bad decisions, you are likely to return to crime. We get them to look at their problem solving and how they think through issues to avoid problems. For instance, we had a guy who was doing well, had completed his education plan, had a good job, and was reunited with his family. Some other guy in the halfway house owed him $50 and wasn't paying as they agreed. His solution was to beat him up, thereby ruining all that he had accomplished. Fortunately, he made the decision to forget about the $50, completed the halfway house program, and did well.

Question: Can you describe the process or steps offenders must take to successfully complete the program?

Mr. Lawrence: First, most offenders do successfully complete the program. For those here as an alternative to prison, there is approximately a 65 to 70 percent rate of success, defined as fully completing the halfway house program. We have several phases. The first is orientation, lasting from seven to fourteen days. During this time, they cannot leave the house, get accustomed to the rules, and look for a job or education assignment. Once they complete orientation and get a job, they move to phase 2, during which they can leave the house for treatment or a job. They must successfully meet the phase 2 requirements for at least forty-five days before they can go to phase 3, when they get weekend passes to go home. During phases 2 and 3, they are expected to meet their goals for education (such as get a GED), complete treatment, or maintain employment. The first three phases average approximately ninety days, and if they are successful, they can go to phase 4, during which they live at home and participate in aftercare for thirty to sixty days. In aftercare, we continue to make contact with them, they return to the house, and we monitor their continuation of treatment, working in their job, or other requirements.

We find that too often offenders who left the house and got their own place would fail. The aftercare with drug screening and follow-up has improved the phase 4 success rate.

Question: Of those who fail, what are the general circumstances under which they fail?

Mr. Lawrence: Almost all fail with technical violations, not the commission of new crimes. They fail a drug test or do not return to the facility. They may break the rules of the house. We have very little inmate-on-staff or inmate-on-inmate violence.

Question: What are the three biggest issues and challenges in operating a halfway house for these offenders?

Mr. Lawrence: We are always looking for new or additional resources to provide the best services we can. Our focus is to provide treatment that has been shown to reduce recidivism. We do programs that work, not what is nice to do. That is cost efficient.

It is also critical to have a good relationship with the community in which the halfway house is located. Oriana House stays actively involved in every community in which we are located; we attend ward and other community meetings, and we educate our neighbors so there is no question as to what we do and what the community thinks of us. We spend a lot of time talking to neighbors and even survey them to get their feedback. We explain how we operate, provide them factual information, and tell them that offenders are more like than unlike other citizens; being a criminal is not their only defining characteristic. They have made mistakes, but many do not have to be locked away to do well and improve their likelihood of success.

Question: What is the potential for students to find jobs in a halfway house?

Mr. Lawrence: There are jobs available to work in halfway houses. I think a halfway house is a great place to work. You get to see your clients on a regular basis (twenty-four hours a day, seven days a week). You know what they are doing and whether they are making progress. The best thing is the positive impact you can have on the offender and the community. If we only turn around the lives of 20 percent of our clients, that is huge in terms of the good to society and the individual.

A bedroom of a halfway house is dormitory style, typically shared by three to six residents. Photo by Richard P. Seiter.

The stay at CRCs is usually only a few months and may be as short as thirty days. There are sometimes emergency placements to provide room and board for probationers who do not have a place to stay, and they stay at the center only until they find another place to live. Other probationers may need supervision or programs that require a longer stay, perhaps up to six months. During this time, many CRCs have stages of privileges, and residents earn the opportunity for more time away from the center as they follow rules and appear successful in their adjustment. In general, CRCs are only for temporary placement when either the need arises for housing or the probationer exhibits less than responsible behavior that requires a period of additional supervision.

There is no or very minimal physical security at halfway houses. The security relies on offenders taking responsibility for being at the house when they are required to be and staff ensuring that they are accounted for when they come and go from the house. The "Your Career in Corrections" box illustrates some of the roles of halfway house staff in this regard.

Split Sentences

split sentence
a combination of a short jail sentence and then return to the community on probation

Split sentences are a combination of a short jail sentence and then supervision in the community on probation. The jail sentence can be anywhere from 30 to 180 days. The purpose of a split sentence is to provide a clear combination of

The main security of a halfway house is the role of desk monitor, in which staff check residents in and out of the house. Photo by Richard P. Seiter.

Your Career in Corrections

Halfway House Staff

Most students do not think of working in a halfway house or CRC as they begin a career in corrections. However, in 2005, there were 221 community-based correctional facilities (halfway houses) in the United States.[55] So there are many job opportunities in these facilities. Historically, since most of the contracted houses were operated by church-affiliated or other not-for-profit agencies, the program mission of helping offenders was the primary emphasis, salaries were quite low, and staff turnover was high. To a great extent, that is still the case. Yet halfway houses have improved their professionalism in the management of these programs, salaries have improved somewhat, and there is less turnover, at least in the higher management of the houses. However, the lack of a career track or promotional opportunities still makes this more likely to be a short-term entry-level job than a career.

Most individuals enter one of two positions when beginning work at a halfway house. The first is a paraprofessional position often called *desk monitor*. Desk monitors control access into and out of the facility. Most houses have a nonsecure control point at the front door, and residents must sign a logbook when they go in or out. The monitor ensures that residents sign in and are in the house when required. In many ways, it is equivalent to the role of a correctional officer in a prison. If someone leaves when not permitted or fails to return when required, desk monitors notify management and the police and probation or parole officers are likely to be called. When not watching the desk, monitors do room checks to make sure there is no contraband (items not allowed in the possession of residents) or activities such as drinking or drug use. They also search for contraband in rooms or other locations throughout the house. These positions are often paid between $8 and $12 per hour and have limited benefits. However, they are very good part-time positions for students preparing for a corrections career and good entry-level jobs to get experience

working in a criminal justice agency and with offenders. This experience is very good preparation for work as a police officer, probation or parole officer, or correctional officer.

The second category of halfway house jobs is professional positions, such as counselor, case manager, or substance abuse specialist. Counselors and case managers are assigned a caseload of residents and are responsible for guiding them through their stay by suggesting (or requiring) participation in certain programs, initiating disciplinary action for violation of probation or parole when required, and overseeing the collection of fines or costs for staying at the house. A college degree in criminal justice, social work, psychology, or one of the other social sciences is usually required. These jobs are very interesting and very challenging. These staff must be directive with residents and hold them accountable for following the rules. They must be knowledgeable of programs and job-finding resources to assist residents. And they must deal with the difficult situation of offenders being restricted in their activities and movements, yet in a nonsecure facility in which they go into the community on almost a daily basis.

The overall organization of a halfway house for approximately seventy-five residents would include a director, an assistant director, two to three professional staff, and ten to fifteen desk monitors. Therefore, there is limited opportunity for advancement, and most staff who want a career in corrections must go to another agency for a promotion. Yet students are encouraged to consider these jobs to get experience and help them decide what type of future jobs they would like. Halfway house staff interact with several categories of criminal justice and social service professionals and get the opportunity to see what they do and network to develop contacts who can help them in future job-finding efforts. Although the pay is low and career opportunities limited, the work is challenging and provides a great training opportunity.

punishment and rehabilitation for offenders who have not committed crimes serious enough to require a sentence of imprisonment. However, when offenders' behavior is seen as particularly irresponsible, judges may use a short jail term to get their attention and expose them to the uncomfortable environment of jail to encourage a change of attitude. The jail sentence is simply to add punishment to a sentence of standard probation and, once completed, the offender returns to the community under probation supervision—hence the term *split sentence*, because the sentence is divided between a term in jail and a period of probation.

The jail part of a split sentence is sometimes served on weekends. This lessens the negative impact of serving time in jail, and offenders are able to keep their jobs and maintain ties to family. They must check into the jail on Friday evenings and are released Sunday nights until the total number of days of their sentence has been met. Split sentences have become more common over the past twenty years, as the "tough on crime" mentality has emphasized punishment as well as rehabilitation for even minor offenders. Data from the Bureau of Justice Statistics show that percentages for persons under correctional supervision by type of sentence in 2007 included 12 percent prison, 59 percent probation, and 78 percent local jail and probation.[56] A split sentence was the most frequently imposed sentence for felony offenders in California in 2001.[57]

Shock Incarceration or Boot Camp

An interesting correctional sanction that has developed since the mid-1980s is **shock incarceration** or **boot camp**. The first boot camps were initiated in Georgia in 1983 and Oklahoma in 1984. Quickly gaining in popularity, boot camps were implemented in many other states over the next ten years. This development is interesting in regard to the accomplishment of correctional goals, as boot camps were created with the purpose of holding offenders accountable for their crimes with a harsh punishment and deterrent effect. Correctional boot camps are operated similarly to a military boot camp; offenders are required to have short hair, shine their shoes, wear uniforms, do extensive physical exercise, and perform hard physical labor. At times, these activities are complemented with education or drug programming, but the major components of boot camps remain military regimentation, discipline, exercise, and hard work. Boot camps appeal to both liberals and conservatives because they focus on being tough on crime and tough on the offender, but are also a community alternative to traditional imprisonment. If offenders complete boot camp, they receive a shorter sentence than if they had received a traditional prison sentence.

Boot camps are usually reserved for young, first-time prisoners who are deemed likely to benefit from structure and discipline while gaining self-control with the rigorous daily routine. Evaluations in some states have indicated that offenders who complete boot camp programs leave with more positive attitudes.[58] However, boot camps have been criticized as expensive and less than effective.

shock incarceration/ boot camp

alternatives to traditional incarceration that are operated similar to a military boot camp; offenders are required to have short hair, shine their shoes, wear uniforms, do extensive physical exercise, and perform hard physical labor; at times, these are complemented with education or drug programming, but the major components of boot camps are military regimentation, discipline, exercise, and hard work

Graduation from the boot camp illustrates the regimentation and discipline gained by participants over their stay.
Courtesy of the Georgia Department of Correction.

Boot camps are more expensive to operate than probation and many prisons because they require a high staff to inmate ratio, and they are especially expensive compared to minimum-security prisons, where most of the boot camp offenders would otherwise be incarcerated. In fact, daily per-inmate costs for operating boot camps in thirty-one states and the federal system in 2000 were $67.85, even higher than the average cost for all prisons during 2001 of $62.22.[59]

Several recent findings have been very critical of the impact of boot camps on reducing recidivism.[60] A review by the U.S. General Accounting Office (GAO) reported that boot camps only marginally reduce recidivism, and the differences between boot camp and non-boot camp offenders diminish over time.[61] Although the GAO study found an improvement in attitudes, it determined the impact on recidivism to be "at best negligible."[62] As a result of the negative findings, several states are questioning their efficacy and reconsidering the concept, and New Hampshire, Connecticut, and Arizona have all closed their boot camp operations.

Shock Probation

A final intermediate sanction is **shock probation,** a short period of imprisonment to "shock" the offender, with a return to the community within a few weeks to continue supervision on probation. The concept originated in Ohio when 1965 legislation authorized the sentencing judge to reconsider a sentence of imprisonment within 90 to 130 days after incarceration of the offender. If the offender meets the criteria (a nonviolent offense with no prior offense history) and the judge believes that the punitive and deterrent value of the sentence has already been met, the sentence can be modified and the offender released to regular probation. Shock probation is based on a specific deterrence model; with a belief that the shock of the sentence and admission to prison shows offenders the punishment they will receive if they continue to commit crimes. The theory is that, as a result of placement in prison for a short period of time, offenders granted shock probation will be deterred from commission of further crimes.

In an evaluation of the effectiveness of shock probation, this theory proved to be true, as Vito concluded:

1. The shock experience should not be limited to first-time offenders; eligibility should properly include those with prior records, as deemed eligible by the judge.
2. The length of incarceration necessary to secure the deterrent effect could be much shorter, probably thirty days or less.
3. Reincarceration rates have never exceeded 26 percent and, in Ohio, have been as low as 10 percent. The level of these rates clearly indicates that the program has potential for reintegration.
4. Shock probation has considerable potential to reduce institutional overcrowding characteristics of contemporary corrections.[63]

Shock probation is generally believed to be a low-cost and effective intermediate sanction for less serious felons, and many states have implemented shock probation as a part of their sentencing structure.

The Effectiveness of Intermediate Sanctions

The use of intermediate sanctions has increased significantly over the past two decades, and with recent budget crises in many jurisdictions, may play a more important role in the next decade. However, there are still a fairly limited number of research studies from which to evaluate the effectiveness of these programs

shock probation
a short period of imprisonment to "shock" the offender, with a return to the community within a few weeks to continue supervision on probation

against their desired outcomes. The following list suggests some reasons for the limited number of studies of effectiveness and the lack of use of these evaluations for correctional policymaking:

1. Political, ethical, and programmatic reasons may not permit random assignment of clients to either the treatment or control group.
2. Treatment or program effects "bleed over" to the control group, or the intended treatment is inappropriately or unevenly applied.
3. It is rare to have only one treatment in operation at a time, thus contaminating the impact of the measure of outcome.
4. Varying measures of success and failure make it difficult to generalize across studies and program results.[64]

In the preceding descriptions of the intermediate sanctions, some outcome studies were identified, with mixed conclusions as to their overall effectiveness. To fully evaluate their success, intermediate sanctions should be analyzed against their desired goals. Examples of such analyses follow.

net widening

the overlapping of criminal sanctions and added supervision for community-placed offenders, rather than diversion of offenders from prison

mycrimekit

Insider's Experience: Implementing Intermediate Sanctions.

Goal 1: Intermediate sanctions should be used to divert offenders from prison. Most experts would agree that one goal of intermediate sanctions is to manage more offenders in the community who would (without intermediate sanctions) have to be sentenced to prison. However, it is generally concluded that intermediate sanctions are not always used with high-risk probationers and therefore add to the supervision of probationers who would not have been sent to prison even if the intermediate sanction did not exist. This phenomenon is called **net widening,** the overlapping of criminal sanctions and added supervision for community-placed offenders, rather than diversion of offenders from prison.

Goal 2: Intermediate sanctions should reduce the cost of corrections. Common sense would seem to indicate that it would be less expensive to maintain offenders in the community rather than sentence them to prison. However, most offenders who are assigned to intermediate sanctions would, if sentenced to prison, be assigned to minimum-security prisons and sentenced to short terms of confinement. If offenders are maintained in the community and net widening occurs, the overall cost of supervision could end up being more than if they are sent to a minimum-security prison. For instance, placement in a boot camp or community residential center costs more per day than placement in a minimum-security prison.

Goal 3: Intermediate sanctions should reduce the level of recidivism for offenders. The studies noted earlier provide mixed indications of the effectiveness of intermediate sanctions in reducing recidivism. However, the most consistent conclusion is that recidivism is not significantly affected by mere community surveillance unless it is combined with participation in treatment programs. Petersilia, in reviewing studies of intermediate sanctions, concluded, "The empirical evidence regarding intermediate sanctions is decisive: without a rehabilitation component, reductions in recidivism are elusive."[65] When these two components are combined in a quality fashion, intermediate sanctions have proved effective in reducing recidivism.

In the past decade, there has been more emphasis on identifying programs that show evidence of success in reducing recidivism and funding those for intermediate sanctions. In 2003, the Oregon legislature mandated that all treatment programs that will receive state funds were to be evidence based. Oregon has targeted improving services so that drug addicts would not constantly go through treatment only to fail and return to drug use. As an example, they have used motivational interviews to harden clients' commitment to treatment, as upon entering treatment addicts must explain why their drug problem exists. One addict noted that "You can get through a lot of programs just by faking it."[66] Almost 54 percent of Oregon's addiction treatment budget of $94 million funds programs that are evidence based. Before the 2003 legislative mandate, only 25 to 30 percent of programs were evidence based.[67] Although Oregon has taken the lead, many states are now following suit and focusing attention and funding on evidence-based programs.

Summary

CHAPTER REVIEW

This chapter has described the first set of sentencing sanctions in the correctional process: probation and intermediate sanctions. The least intrusive and least intensive sentencing option is probation. Probation has the advantages of maintaining offenders in the community so that family and employment ties are maintained, of being less costly than imprisonment, and of focusing on offender rehabilitation to a greater extent than does imprisonment. For many minor offenders who have a low risk of reoffending and little or no history of violence, probation is a viable sanction.

For offenders who have a greater risk of reoffending or treatment needs that cannot be met through regular probation, intermediate sanctions can provide additional supervision and program opportunities. When they are used for offenders who (without their availability) would be sent to prison, intermediate sanctions have all the benefits of probation and are generally less expensive than imprisonment. Intermediate sanctions add proportionality to the sentencing process, in that they provide a wide range of alternative supervision and treatment options and can be more appropriately matched to the crime committed and to the offenders' risks and needs. Research has also determined that if surveillance is combined with treatment, intermediate sanctions can effectively reduce recidivism.

Probation and intermediate sanctions represent community-based alternatives to institutional-based sentences. The next chapter continues the discussion of modern correctional operations by moving further into the continuum of correctional sanctions and describing the theories and operational approaches of U.S. prisons. We will then complete our overview of correctional operations by describing the postprison programs of supervision and reentry to the community. At the end of Part II of this textbook, students will have a thorough understanding of the major correctional components used today, and we can move into a more detailed examination of correctional perspectives, issues, and challenges.

Key Terms

community corrections

John Augustus

probation supervision

casework style of supervision

surveillance style of supervision

regular caseloads

intensive-supervision caseloads

special caseloads

standard conditions of probation

special conditions of probationer

technical violations

new-crime violations

Gagnon v. Scarpelli

community classification systems

fines

offender restitution

victim compensation

cost of supervision

asset forfeiture

intensive supervised probation (ISP)

house arrest

electronic monitoring

community residential centers (CRCs)

split sentences

shock incarceration

boot camp

shock probation

net widening

Review Questions

1. What contributions to modern probation did John Augustus make that continue today?

2. Approximately how many people were on probation in the United States in 2006?

3. What are the primary emphases of probation supervision?

4. Differentiate between the casework and surveillance styles of probation supervision.

5. What is the difference between standard and special conditions of probation?

6. List five standard conditions of probation.

7. Name three types of probation caseloads.

8. What are the two types of probation violations?

9. What were the important findings in the *Gagnon v. Scarpelli* decision regarding revocation of probation?

10. Describe the philosophy of the broken-windows approach to the operation of probation.

11. How do community classification systems work, and what is their impact on probation supervision?

12. What is an economic sanction?

13. Differentiate between offender restitution and victim compensation programs.

14. What is asset forfeiture and why can it be called an economic sanction?

15. Describe the results of evaluations regarding intensive supervised probation.

16. How is electronic monitoring used to enforce the requirements of house arrest?

17. Differentiate passive and active electronic monitoring systems.

18. What are the two ways that community residential centers are used as intermediate sanctions?

19. What is a split sentence?

20. Describe the operation of a boot camp.

21. How long does an offender usually stay in prison under shock probation?

22. How can net widening reduce the effectiveness of an intermediate-sanctions program?

You Make the Decision...

Should I Revoke Him?

One of the most difficult challenges for a probation officer is deciding whether to initiate a revocation process for a probationer. To some, it may seem very clear-cut. If probationers violate the conditions of their supervision, their probation should be revoked. Most probation agency policies require that violations be brought to the attention of the court for action to either revoke or modify probation conditions. Yet courts do not want to see every technical violation of a probationer, and officers have considerable

discretion in how to handle most minor infractions. For instance, a probationer may be required to report several times per month to the officer and is usually very responsible in doing so. If the offender misses one appointment, agencies do not want officers reporting it as a violation to the court. However, all criminal activities should be reported.

The officer must decide whether to initiate a revocation process for several situations that fall between these two obvious extremes. It is easy for officers to take a hard line and report almost any violation. They can never be criticized if the offender later commits a serious crime. However, research findings indicate that recidivism is not reduced by only surveillance techniques of probation, but by a combination of casework and surveillance and by the officer's getting offenders to take responsibility for their crimes and the behaviors that lead to criminal acts. The best officers use this discretion wisely and counsel offenders or issue agreements to modify supervision conditions as intermediate actions. Many probation agencies now give officers limited authority to add requirements to be better able to hold the offender accountable, such as drug testing, additional reporting to the officer, or even (in a few situations) residence in a halfway house or electronic monitoring. The following scenario is for students to consider and then decide how to handle the case.

You are the probation officer for John Smith. Smith is a 32-year-old offender with a history of serious drug use, three misdemeanor theft offenses, and one prior felony conviction for breaking and entering. The current offense is auto theft and possession of cocaine. He received a sentence of two years of probation with standard conditions and a requirement to participate in drug abuse counseling and random drug testing. Smith did rather well the first eight months of supervision, but his behavior then began to deteriorate. In month nine, he missed two

of his four appointments with you, with excuses that his car broke down and that there was a family emergency. He also lost his job and has yet to find another. His sister called and told you that Smith was again using drugs. You had him come in immediately for a random drug test, which proved negative.

In month ten, he missed two of his drug counseling sessions, claiming that he was not using drugs and the sessions were a waste of time. He said he would rather spend his time trying to find a job. In month eleven, he tested positive for cocaine use. You had not notified the court before this time, but had counseled Smith repeatedly and told him that continued failure to meet the conditions of his probation could result in revocation and a prison sentence. You believe that Smith is not a dangerous person, as he does not have a violent history. You also believe that if he could stay in the community and conquer his drug use, he could stay out of trouble. Yet he has not been honest with you and seems to not respond to your more intensive counseling (and threats). You now must report the violations to the court and recommend how to deal with Smith. You can recommend continuation of probation with current conditions, added conditions as an intermediate sanction, or revocation and implementation of Smith's eighteen-month prison sentence. What do you recommend, and why?

Chapter Resources on mycrimekit

Go to mycrimekit.com to explore the following study tools and resources specific to this chapter:

- **Practice Quiz:** multiple-choice, true/false, short-answer, and essay questions to help students test their knowledge
- **WebQuests:** learning activities built around Web searches
  - American Probation and Parole Association: www.appa-net.org
  - Bureau of Justice Statistics: www.ojp.usdoj .gov/bjs/
  - Center for Community Corrections: www.communitycorrectionsworks.org
- **Insider's Experiences:** "Implementing Intermediate Sanctions"

- **Seiter Videos:**
  - See a probation officer talk about her job
  - See a judge and probationer discuss probation
  - See offenders discuss probation supervision
  - See information regarding electronic monitoring
  - See experts discuss halfway house operations
- **Career Center:** A Career as a Probation Officer
- **Flashcards:** Twenty-eight flashcards to test knowledge of the chapter's key terms

Prison Systems

After reading this chapter, you should be able to:

1. Describe how the role and prevailing philosophies of prison operations have changed significantly over the past century.

2. Explain the mission of a prison.

3. Explain the reasons for the dramatic increase in the number of prisoners since 1980.

4. Discuss how the construction of new prisons paralleled the growth of the inmate population.

5. Explain the changing makeup of the inmate population regarding age, gender, race, and ethnicity.

6. Describe the creation and development of the federal prison system.

7. Compare and contrast the federal with state prison systems.

8. Describe the characteristics of state prison inmates and how they receive a security classification.

9. List the other public correctional systems.

10. Suggest the reasons for the development of private prisons, and speculate regarding their role in the future.

Introduction

prisons

institutions designed to house convicted, adult felons, serving a sentence of one year or more

We now turn our study of corrections to **prisons,** institutions designed to house convicted, adult felons serving a sentence of one year or more. Prisons are a relatively new phenomenon in criminal justice and corrections. As described in Chapter 1, the early sanctions for convicted offenders were primarily corporal and capital punishment, mixed with public humiliation. It was not until the end of the eighteenth century that the Quakers of Pennsylvania decided that a more humane and efficient way to punish and reform criminals was needed, and the penitentiary was first established in Philadelphia.

Over the next two hundred years, prisons evolved with a variety of theoretical foundations influencing policies and practice. Over the past twenty-five years, a toughening public attitude toward crime and criminals has helped prisons emerge as the sanction believed to most effectively meet the correctional goals of punishment, deterrence, and incapacitation. Unfortunately and inaccurately, the public has come to believe that probation and intermediate sanctions do not successfully meet their concern for public safety, and increasingly more offenders are sentenced to prisons, many for extremely long periods of time.

This change in philosophy and practice has resulted in an unprecedented level of prison construction, a burgeoning industry of prison operations, and a significant percentage of federal and state budgets going toward construction and operation of prisons. In 1980, almost two hundred years after prisons were first used as a criminal sanction, there were only 316,000 sentenced prisoners under state or federal jurisdiction. In only twenty-eight years, from 1980 to 2008, the number of prisoners increased by almost 500 percent, to more than 1.6 million inmates. This chapter describes recent trends in the makeup of the prison population in the United States, the construction of prisons to keep up with the increase in inmate numbers, the types of prison systems in the United States, and the way in which prisons are organized by security levels to manage the different levels of offender risk.

Current Status of Prisons in the United States

There has been tremendous growth in the role of prisons in the U.S. criminal justice system over the past twenty-five years. As an example of the difference in philosophy regarding the operation of prisons, the 1967 report by the President's Commission on Law Enforcement and Administration of Justice, Corrections Section, recommended the following:

1. Long sentences are self-defeating in regard to rehabilitation.
2. Most offenders do not need to be incarcerated and could function in the community under supervision.
3. Most inmates derive maximum benefit from their incarceration during the first two years.
4. Community-based corrections are less expensive than and at least as effective as incarceration.
5. Corrections must encompass all aspects of rehabilitative service, including mental health, employment services, education, and social services.
6. Because of their dangerousness, some offenders will require extensive incarceration in secure institutions.

7. Most inmates are not mentally ill but suffer from a variety of educational, medical, maturational, economic, and interpersonal handicaps that are seldom reduced or resolved in prison.
8. Inmates must be given the opportunity and capability to earn a living wage to compensate their victims and support their families.
9. The pay for inmates is too low. The rates of pay should be at least the minimum wage for similar labor.
10. The private sector should be used to provide training and work programs that are realistic to develop employable workers at the end of their sentence.[1]

As is obvious, public opinion and the purpose of prisons in the criminal justice system have changed significantly since this report was written. In 1967, state and federal prisons held less than 300,000 inmates.[2] The medical model, with an emphasis on rehabilitating offenders, was the prevailing philosophy. Shichor noted that rehabilitation was strongly emphasized as the goal of prisons until the 1970s, when this emphasis began to diminish as the United States experienced large increases in crime rates, resulting in rising numbers of prison commitments.[3] Before that time, however, prisons were reserved for the most violent and dangerous offenders, and property offenders were usually granted probation and supervision in the community. Also, prisons held a generally homogeneous group of offenders, with very similar histories of criminality, sentences, age, and treatment needs.

Today, the role and prevailing philosophies of prison operations have changed significantly. The "tough on crime" mentality of the public and elected officials has forced prisons to become a catchall for all types of offenders, as punishment became favored over rehabilitation.[4] Property offenders are now as likely to be imprisoned as violent offenders. Drug offenders, even those with no prior involvement in crime, often receive mandatory prison sentences of five to ten years. The prison population is much more heterogeneous in terms of prior criminal history, sentence, age, and treatment needs. By the middle of 2008, the number of prisoners under the jurisdiction of federal or state adult correctional authorities had risen dramatically to 1,610,584.[5]

Inmates are now very diverse in terms of age, race, gender, and ethnicity.
Courtesy of A. Ramey/PhotoEdit.

The Role and Mission of Prisons

The primary function of prisons is to hold convicted felons, usually serving a sentence of one year or more, whereas convicted felons serving shorter sentences usually serve their time in local jails. Inmates consider jail sentences very "hard time," since jails do not have the full range of education, vocational training, work, recreational, or other treatment programs that are available in prisons. Therefore, jail inmates spend most of their time just sitting in their cells, watching television, or playing cards with other inmates. Since prisons are designed to hold inmates for longer terms, they need to provide a full range of programs, both for rehabilitative purposes and to keep inmates productively busy.

Many people perceive that prison inmates just sit in cells. This could not be further from the truth. For both management and legal reasons, prison administrators develop activities to keep inmates out of their cells and busy as much of the day as possible. During the period of transition of prisons described in Chapter 1, prison administrators discovered how difficult it was to operate prisons without the ability to let inmates out of their cells and keep them busy. When Congress passed laws in the 1930s restricting the sale of inmate-made goods on the open market, prisons constructed with large factory operations emphasizing production had to find another way to manage large prison inmate populations (many prisons during that time housed 3,000 to 4,000 inmates). Fearful of violence and tension erupting from the forced idleness, prison administrators tightened security and kept inmates locked in their cells for much of the day. This resulted in even more tension and, after a series of prison riots, officials were forced to find better methods to operate modern prisons.

Prison administrators now understand the problems that can result if inmates are confined to housing units for long periods of time. Although not specifically stating that inmates had to be out of cells and involved in work and program activities for any particular number of hours, the federal courts have also encouraged this type of operation through their decisions regarding prison operations. In ***Rhodes v. Chapman*** (1981), the U.S. Supreme Court decided that overcrowded conditions resulting from two inmates housed in cells designed for one person at the Southern Ohio Correctional Facility (SOCF) was not a violation of the Eighth Amendment right of protection from cruel and unusual punishment.[6] Very important in the decision was the Court's consideration of the "totality of conditions" at SOCF, finding that inmates were out of their cells for much of the day, and no other problems, such as poor medical care or food service, resulted from the crowded conditions. If prison officials attempted to keep inmates locked in their cells without adequate programs and work activities, the Court would likely reconsider the *Rhodes* decision.

The federal courts have allowed inmates to be locked in cells for all but five hours per week in the case of *Bruscino v. Carlson*.[7] However, this case did not involve the operations of a traditional prison. Bruscino is based on a lockdown of a U.S. penitentiary (USP) in Marion, Illinois, and the elimination of inmate programs outside cells resulting from continued violent acts by inmates that culminated in the murder of two correctional officers in the same day. The Court considered the fact that inmates were placed in USP-Marion because they were unmanageable and had violated rules at other prisons. There was a process for reviewing their assignment to and their removal from USP-Marion. A federal judge, in denying a motion by inmates to stop the lockdown, stated that "the Court is of the firm conviction that this litigation was conceived by a small group of hardcore inmates who are bent on the disruption of the prison system in general and of USP-Marion in particular."[8] However, it is unlikely that the federal courts

Rhodes v. Chapman
a 1981 U.S. Supreme Court decision that overcrowded conditions resulting in two inmates housed in cells designed for one person was not a violation of the Eighth Amendment right of protection from cruel and unusual punishment

would accept this type of lockdown for a standard prison not designated for the most violent and dangerous inmates.

Currently, prison officials keep inmates locked in cells (or confined to their housing areas in dormitory-style facilities) for only about eight hours per day, generally from 11:00 P.M. to 7:00 A.M. During the day, inmates work or participate in educational or vocational programs. In the evening (from dinner until lockdown time), inmates participate in recreational activities or other treatment programs, such as substance abuse programs, religious activities, or counseling. The key to a successfully operated prison is to keep inmates productively occupied and under the supervision of staff for the sixteen hours per day that inmates are not confined to their housing units.

A **mission** is a statement of what an organization is to accomplish, or a "statement of its basic purposes, often in terms of broad outcomes that it is committed to achieving or the major function it carries out."[9] In many cases, the mission is the statement of why an agency exists. For most state prison systems, the mission is legislatively created. State legislatures, in creating the agencies that operate prisons, often include the purpose or function of the agency in the authorizing legislation. A common mission statement for a prison is "to supervise criminal offenders during the period of their sentence, protect the public, and offer programs that assist in the rehabilitation of criminals." When a mission statement is not created by the legislative body, agencies regularly generate their own mission statement. The mission statement for the Federal Bureau of Prisons (BOP) appears on its website: "The mission of the Federal Bureau of Prisons is to maintain secure, safe, and humane correctional institutions for individuals placed in the custody of the U.S. Attorney General; to develop and operate correctional programs that seek a balanced application of the concepts of punishment, deterrence, incapacitation and rehabilitation; and provide, primarily through the National Institute of Corrections, assistance to state and local correctional agencies."[10]

As is clear from both the example of a legislatively created mission and the BOP mission, most prisons have a dual-purpose mission statement. First, prisons are to be safe and secure, protecting inmates and staff from harm while they live and work in the prison environment and protecting the public from further criminality by not allowing inmates to escape and further prey on society. Second, prisons provide programs that assist in the management of prisons by keeping inmates busy, but more important, prepare offenders for release and the transition to the community. By concentrating on the rehabilitation of offenders in addition to simple incapacitation, prisons further protect society by improving the chance of inmates' successful return to society and reduction of the long-term likelihood of further criminal activity.

Creating a safe and secure prison environment, and one that encourages inmates to participate in meaningful treatment programs, is a difficult balance. This balancing act usually falls on the shoulders of the warden, who must set the tone and ensure that both security and treatment get the appropriate level of attention. Not many students go through college studying to be a warden. Yet the warden's job is one of the most challenging and interesting in the public management arena. The "Your Career in Corrections" box illustrates some of these challenges.

Growth of the Prison Population

Currently, the U.S. public believes that confinement facilities are the most effective sanction to protect the public, punish criminals, and deter them from committing further crimes after release. We continue to increase the number of

mission
a statement of an organization's major function and what it is to accomplish, or its basic purposes, to include general outcomes that it is committed to achieving

mycrimekit
Media—Video: The Role of Prisons.

mycrimekit
Careers: Career in Corrections as a warden.

Your Career in Corrections

Wardens

The author of this textbook is a career correctional administrator and was warden of two federal prisons. He thoroughly enjoyed these jobs and often described a warden's job as similar to that of a city manager, in that wardens are responsible for many service functions (food service, health care, sanitation and maintenance, policing, construction, human resources, and budget management), as well as the correctional aspects of security, inmate programs, and legal issues.

As of December 30, 2005, there were 1,821 state and federal prisons, each having a warden as the chief executive of the prison. On January 1, 2002, it was reported that a warden's pay ranged from $34,680 to $122,281,[11] with the average approximately $70,000. The average time that wardens had worked for their correctional agency was 15.2 years,[12] indicating that they are experienced when taking a position as warden. In most states, there is no minimum educational level, although most wardens have a college degree. There is also no specific requirement for education or experience, as wardens can begin their correctional careers in almost any discipline, including security, counseling, or any other area of corrections.

College students do not usually plan a career toward the job of warden. In fact, most college students do not plan to go to work in a prison. Many who end up in institutional corrections often plan to be a social worker or counselor and later find opportunities to work in prisons both exciting and challenging. Warden is a job that takes many years of training and experience. As noted previously, the average correctional job experience for wardens was more than fifteen years. No matter how much education, how much experience in management, or how much willingness to work a person has, nothing is more important to prepare someone to be a warden than working in a prison at a variety of levels. Most decisions that come to a warden's desk are not simple, and there are no easy or obvious solutions. Many have multiple problems and risks, and the difficulty lies in selecting a solution that has the least likelihood of dire consequences. There are always so many varying impacts from what a warden does (if it helps security, it may hurt treatment; if it is something positive for inmates, it may be problematic for staff; if it has great potential for a positive outcome, it may not be affordable within the budget) that each decision must be thoughtfully considered as to how it affects different groups or other prison functions.

Some of these problems are what makes a job as a warden rewarding for most. Surveys have indicated that prison wardens have much greater job satisfaction than all but a few other professions. There is never a boring day, and each day brings something different. It takes skills in every different area of management (budget, human resources, security and treatment, and facility maintenance). But most important, being a warden is a very people-oriented job. Wardens get things done by dealing with people—staff and inmates—and must enjoy and be good at getting others to implement and follow what has been decided.

offenders sentenced to correctional institutions. By the middle of 2008, there were 2,310,984 offenders incarcerated in prisons and other detention facilities. Table 5.1 illustrates the makeup of offenders housed in the various types of correctional facilities. Whenever criminal justice policymakers have a concern about the risk of placing offenders in the community, they shift to a policy of increased use of confinement. Although this option undoubtedly maximizes community safety, in many cases it does so marginally and comes at a great expense to taxpayers.

It is interesting that from the invention of the prison in 1790 until about 1980 (almost two hundred years) the state and federal prison population rose from zero to only about 300,000. In just twenty-eight more years, the prison population grew by 500 percent, to approximately 1.5 million. In one-tenth the time, the population multiplied five times over. This growth illustrates a remarkable shift in the policies that

TABLE 5.1	Number of Offenders Housed in U.S. Correctional Facilities, December 31, 2007	
Federal and state prisons		1,512,576
Territorial prisons		14,678
Local jails		780,581
Immigration and Customs Enforcement facilities		9,720
Military facilities		1,794
Jails in Native American country		2,163
Total		2,413,112

Source: Heather C. West and William J. Sabol, *Prisoners in 2007* (Washington, D.C.: U.S. Department of Justice, Bureau of Justice Statistics, December 2008), p. 7.

had previously influenced the use of prisons as a criminal sanction throughout our history. Why the tremendous increase? Several factors have predisposed the increase.

First, since 1980, the public has become more fearful of crime, less tolerant of criminals, and more demanding of tougher sentencing laws. This was understandable during the 1980s, when crime rates (particularly for violent crime) were increasing. According to Gallup polls, in 1989, 84 percent of citizens polled felt there was more crime in the United States than the year before. Since that time, crime rates have been declining and have gone down in almost every category of felonies every year since 1993. However, a 2008 Gallup poll indicated a concern, as 44 percent of citizens polled still believed that there was more crime now than the year before.[13] As a result of this belief and the resulting fear of crime, the public demands that criminals be sentenced for longer periods of time and wants punishment and offender accountability to be the primary focuses of such sentences.

Elected officials have responded and continually lengthened sentences. With every high-visibility, heinous crime, elected officials respond by proposing an increase in criminal sanctions for that crime or type of criminal. As a result, the average length of incarceration has increased significantly since 1990. The average length of stay for inmates released during 1990 was 23.7 months. By 1996, the average time served for inmates released was 30.0 months (an increase of more than 25 percent). Since then, the average time served has leveled off and was 29.2 months for inmates released in 2001.[14]

Unfortunately, elected officials do not have many crime policy alternatives that they believe will have a short-term impact, while demonstrating to voters that they are serious about the crime problem. Therefore, these officials continue to emphasize an increased use of incarceration, rather than alternative sanctions or preventive approaches. Crime has now become a partisan political issue, and both Republicans and Democrats try to show they are tough on crime by using "sound bites" that fit into thirty-second commercials, rather than thoughtfully debating the substance and effectiveness of crime policy alternatives. Tonry, in analyzing reasons for the increase in incarceration rates in the United States, suggests that the partisan political approach to crime policy results in "widespread adoption of broadly defined three-strikes laws, mandatory minimum-sentence laws, sexual psychopath laws, and the federal sentencing guidelines. . . . [These laws] are too rigid and often result in unjustly harsh penalties. . . ."[15]

Sentencing practices have also changed. During the mid-1900s, all states used indeterminate sentences, and release on parole peaked in 1977, as 72 percent of all prisoners were released on parole.[16] But with the demise of the medical model, the "tough on crime" attitude of the public and elected officials, and the belief that rehabilitation did not work, fifteen states and the federal government moved to the use of determinate sentences, and only 28 percent of offenders were released on parole in 1997.[17] By the end of 1999, twenty-nine states had adopted truth-in-sentencing (TIS) statutes, requiring inmates to serve 85 percent of a determinate sentence before release.[18] These sentencing changes have resulted in an unprecedented level of the prison population.

This toughening of philosophical approaches has influenced not only sentencing decisions, but also supervision in the community. For most of the 1990s, community supervision (probation and parole) underwent a transition from helping and counseling offenders to risk management and surveillance. This resulted in the allocation of resources for increased monitoring, rather than for counseling and rehabilitative programs for offenders on probation and parole. In this **new penology** perspective, Rhine writes, "The traditional corrections objectives of rehabilitation and the reduction of offender recidivism give way to the rational and efficient deployment of control strategies for managing (and confining) high-risk criminal populations."[19]

As a result, there is more strident parole and probation monitoring with little tolerance for risk of crime by offenders, and increasing numbers of offenders are sent to prison as community supervision violators. During 2007, of the 697,975 state prison admissions, 248,923 were from parole or other conditional release supervision violations.[20] Even more alarming is that, for states reporting reasons for which individuals were returned to custody, 190,677 of 279,421 (68 percent) were returned for technical violations without commission of a new crime.[21] Courts and parole boards do not want to risk keeping uncertain offenders in the community. If minor violators later commit a serious crime, those deciding to allow them to continue in the community face criticism or even legal action. This

new penology

an emphasis on the rational and efficient deployment of control strategies for managing and confining high-risk criminal populations

The federalization of drug laws has had the greatest impact on the increase in the number of drug offenders in prisons. Courtesy of AP/Wide World Photos.

risk-free approach has a tremendous impact on prison populations and the commitment of taxpayer dollars to the prison systems of the United States.

In addition, since the 1980s, society has operated on the premise that illicit drug use and trafficking create a serious danger to our society and way of life, and we have declared a **war on drugs.** The U.S. Department of Justice reports that "there is extensive evidence of the strong relationship between drug use and crime,"[22] noting that drug users report more involvement in crime, people with criminal records are more likely than those without criminal records to report being drug users, and crime rises as drug use increases.

In 2004, the office of National Drug Control Policy's Operations budget was $27.8 billion, consisting of $9.5 billion for interdiction or investigations, $11.4 billion for prevention or treatment, $1.3 billion for research and development, and $5.6 billion for state and local assistance.[23] With the continued increase in the dollars directed toward law enforcement efforts to find and arrest drug dealers and users, the increased federalization of drug crimes, and the enactment of federal criminal statutes requiring either five- or ten-year mandatory sentences for drug offenders, more than two-thirds of Federal Bureau of Prisons inmates are currently serving sentences for drug crimes. These statutory and policy or operational changes have resulted not only in an increase in the total number of prisoners, but also in a continuous and dramatic rise in the incarceration rate of the United States. In 1980, the United States incarcerated 139 individuals per 100,000 population; by 2008, the rate had reached 762 people per 100,000 population.[24]

> **war on Drugs**
> a Reagan initiative to reduce the availability and dependence on illicit drugs through interdiction, criminal sanctions, and treatment

Likelihood of Going to Prison

A 1997 report by the Bureau of Justice Statistics (BJS) indicated that an estimated 5.1 percent of all people in the United States would be confined in a state or federal prison during their lifetime.[25] However, this estimate was made on the assumption that 1997 incarceration rates would remain unchanged since 1991 (the base year for estimates). However, since 2000, incarceration rates have increased from 684 to 762 per 100,000 population in 2008.[26] Therefore, the estimated percentage of the population likely to go to prison has also increased. A report of 2004 statistics indicates that men (0.9 percent) are much more likely to go to prison than women (0.06 percent). The prison population of men and women with a sentence of more than one year included the following racial components: 34 percent white, 41 percent black, and 19 percent Hispanic.[27]

Lifetime chances of incarceration are very different from the basic incarceration rates. The BJS report also notes that at year-end 2004, about half of 1 percent of the nation's adult population was confined in a state or federal prison—approximately 1.4 million adults.[28] Lifetime incarceration rates summarize the chances of going to prison over an entire lifetime, rather than just looking at a snapshot of those in prison at any one time. The chance of going to prison at some time was about ten times that of the snapshot percentage of the population. These lifetime numbers bring another reality to most individuals. Many people do not know anyone who has gone to prison. But this report estimates that one in every twenty Americans will go to prison at some time during their life and makes the use of incarceration as a response to crime seem much bigger than snapshot numbers indicating "only" about 1.3 million people in state or federal prison.

Meeting Growth Demands

To respond to the major increase in prison population over the past two decades, most jurisdictions have expanded capacity by building new prisons. As the inmate population increased, state legislatures and the U.S. Congress responded

Over the past two decades, billions of dollars have been spent to construct new prisons to keep up with the increase in the number of inmates.
Courtesy of the Federal Bureau of Prisons.

mycrimekit™

Insider's Experience: Throwing Out a $2 million Prison Design

with financial support to construct hundreds of thousands of new prison beds. From 1993 to 2000, there were 288 new prisons constructed and opened,[29] and from June 30, 2000 to December 30, 2005, 153 new state and federal prisons and 151 new private prisons were constructed and opened.[30] When building new prisons, there are many options for designs, and the way a prison is built will influence the style of management for years to come. The "An Insider's Experience" box in *MyCrimeKit* tells of how I was faced with one of these decisions.

This tremendous increase in the number of inmates and new prisons has also required constant increases in the operating budget of state and federal correctional agencies. As illustrated in Figure 5.1, the budgets for all three areas of the criminal justice system (police, courts, and corrections) have increased dramatically. However, neither police nor court budgets have increased as much as corrections budgets, with a 660 percent increase in direct expenditures between 1982 and 2006. Most of this is due to the increasing number of prisons, and not increased use of community supervision. State and federal and local adult correctional agencies alone increased their total budgets from $41 billion in 1996 to $68.7 billion in 2006.[31]

Adult Prison Systems in the United States

Most people think that only the federal and state governments operate prisons for adult offenders, but there are actually several other correctional systems and agencies in the United States. These include private companies that contract to house offenders for other jurisdictions, immigration facilities that hold noncitizens subject to deportation to their home country, and military prisons that house violators of the military justice system. However, by far the largest numbers of prisoners are housed in state and federal prisons. On December 30, 2005, there were 1,821 state and federal prisons in the United States, with a capacity of housing (without overcrowding) 1,430,208 prisoners.[32] However, the Bureau of Justice Statistics reported that state and federal prisons confined 1,512,576 inmates in 2007, operating at 113 percent of capacity.[33]

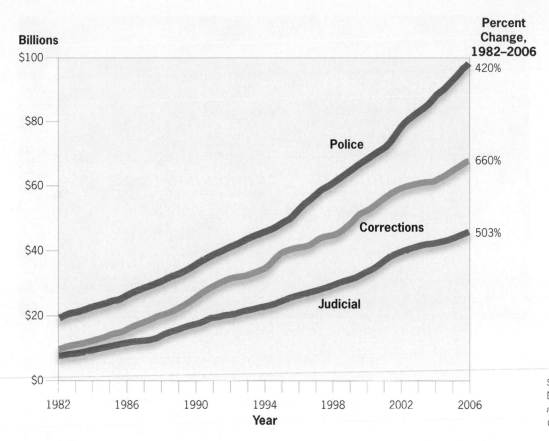

Billions

Percent Change, 1982–2006

FIGURE 5.1   Direct Expenditure by Criminal Justice Function, 1982–2006

Source: U.S. Department of Justice, Bureau of Justice Statistics, Key Facts at a Glance, *Direct Expenditures by Criminal Justice Function*, 1982–2006.

Historically, there has been a significant difference between federal and state prison systems. Each holds offenders convicted under the jurisdiction's specific criminal statutes. State penal codes usually include the standard **street crimes,** such as murder, robbery, burglary, assault, and theft. In the past, federal crimes included fraud and other white-collar offenses, movement of criminal activity across state or national boundaries, and crimes specific to the federal government, such as postal fraud or treason. However, over the past several decades, Congress has continually **federalized** crimes such as bank robbery, kidnapping, murder of public officials, drug distribution, and certain crimes using a weapon. As a result, there is now less distinction between the types of inmates in state and federal prisons than in the past.

The Federal Prison System

Until the late 1800s, offenders convicted of federal crimes were housed in state prisons if their sentence was for more than one year and in local jails if they were to serve less than one year. After the establishment of the U.S. Department of Justice in 1870, an official of the department was charged with the responsibility for the "care and custody" of all federal prisoners. However, as state prisons became more overcrowded, the states became reluctant to house federal offenders and pressured the Department of Justice to create facilities to maintain federal inmates.

As a result, Congress passed the **Three Penitentiary Act** on March 3, 1891, authorizing the construction of three penitentiaries to house federal offenders.[34] The act included the construction and operation of federal prisons in Leavenworth, Kansas (construction beginning in 1896),[35] McNeil Island,

street crimes
traditional reference to crimes with little sophistication required, such as murder, robbery, burglary, assault, and theft

federalized
the making of a crime a federal rather than a state offense; results when the U.S. Congress decides that it desires federal law enforcement and prosecution of certain offenses

mycrimekit
Media—Video: A Prison Tour.

Three Penitentiary Act
the 1891 act of Congress that authorized the construction of the first three federal prisons

The U.S. Penitentiary in Leavenworth, Kansas, was one of the first three federal prisons authorized and built under the Three Penitentiary Act of 1891.
Courtesy of the Federal Bureau of Prisons.

Washington (constructed from 1892 to 1895), and Atlanta, Georgia (construction completed in 1899). These three prisons served the needs of the federal government and housed almost all federal inmates for several decades. As these facilities became more crowded, however, the Department of Justice sought the authority to construct additional prisons. As a result, Congress in 1925 authorized the construction of a reformatory for male prisoners between ages 17 and 30 at Chillicothe, Ohio, and a federal prison for women was opened in Alderson, West Virginia, in 1927.

Establishment of the Federal Bureau of Prisons

By the end of the 1920s, officials in the Department of Justice determined that a separate agency within the department was needed to oversee the operation of the growing number of prisons. The Congressional Special Committee on Federal Penal and Reformatory Institutions agreed and recommended the establishment of a central agency to administer federal prisons. In 1930, Congress passed an act to establish the **Federal Bureau of Prisons (BOP)** to "provide more progressive and humane care for Federal inmates, to professionalize the prison service, and to ensure consistent and centralized administration of the 11 Federal prisons in operation at that time."[36] President Herbert Hoover signed the act into law on May 14, 1930, and **Sanford Bates** was appointed the first director of the Bureau of Prisons. Bates had been chief of the Massachusetts prison system, and his appointment began a trend (that continues today) of the director of the BOP being an experienced correctional administrator, rather than a political appointment. Since its origination, the BOP has had only seven directors:

Federal Bureau of Prisons

an agency within the U.S. Department of Justice charged with housing and managing federal law offenders

Sanford Bates

the first director of the Federal Bureau of Prisons

Sanford Bates	1930–1937
James V. Bennett	1937–1964
Myrl E. Alexander	1964–1970
Norman A. Carlson	1970–1987
J. Michael Quinlan	1987–1992
Kathleen Hawk Sawyer	1992–2003
Harley G. Lappin	2003–present

The U.S. Bureau of Prisons has been fortunate to have had only seven directors since its creation in 1930. The first three Bureau directors are shown here. Courtesy of the Federal Bureau of Prisons.

Growth of the Bureau of Prisons

It is interesting to examine the growth of the BOP over its history. Since federal offenders are those who commit crimes that Congress has placed under federal jurisdiction, growth comes primarily as a result of such acts of Congress. The growth of the federal prison population, from the establishment of the BOP to current times, resulted from passage of criminal statutes extending the authority of the federal government to prosecute new crimes that were difficult for local law enforcement agencies to handle. Early examples of these acts include the following:

- The *White Slave Act* in 1910 (interstate commerce of prostitution)
- The *Harrison Narcotic Act* in 1914 (taxing and records must be kept on controlled substances)
- The *Volstead Act* in 1918 (prohibition of the sale and consumption of alcohol)
- The *Dyer Act* of 1919 (interstate transportation of stolen vehicles)[37]

By the end of the year the bureau was established (1930), there were fourteen federal prisons housing just over 13,000 inmates. By 1940, the bureau had grown to twenty-four institutions with 24,360 inmates. This total population did not change significantly between 1940 and 1980. However, the bureau decided that large institutions (averaging more than 1,000 inmates) were difficult to manage, and several new prisons were opened to reduce the average prison size. By 1980, there were forty-four federal prisons, just over 24,500 inmates, and approximately 10,000 employees.

During the 1980s, the bureau experienced the beginning of a tremendous population growth, the result of the **Sentencing Reform Act of 1984,** which abolished parole, established determinate sentencing, and reduced the amount of good time available to federal offenders. Other acts of Congress in 1986, 1988, and 1990 created mandatory minimum sentences for various crimes. Between 1980 and 2008, the inmate population increased dramatically from just over 24,000 to over 200,000.[38]

Sentencing Reform Act of 1984

the act of Congress that abolished parole, established determinate sentencing, and reduced the amount of good time available to federal offenders

At the end of the 1980s, the federal government acted again, declaring the war on drugs and passing several new laws to prosecute drug offenders under federal statutes. These included federalizing drug possession and distribution (the federal role had previously been limited to the prosecution of importers of illegal drugs), imposing mandatory minimum sentences of five and ten years for any offenders distributing illegal drugs, and lengthening other drug crime sentences. About the same time, federal government efforts to crack down on illegal immigration resulted in placement of more illegal aliens in federal prisons. As a result, the federal prison population again more than doubled, reaching approximately 136,000 at the end of 1999.[39] During the late 1990s, Congress ordered the District of Columbia to close its prison system, and the Bureau of Prisons was directed to house District of Columbia felons. This transfer was completed in 2001, and on December 31, 2001, the federal prison system held 6,930 District of Columbia inmates.[40]

During the early 2000s, some state prison systems actually reduced their prison populations, and the growth of state prisoners averaged only 1.7 percent between 2000 and 2007.[41] However, with the federalization of many offenses and increased BOP responsibility for housing District of Columbia and immigration offenders, the federal prison population has continued to grow at an average rate of 4.6 percent for the same time period.[42] For the week of August 6, 2009, the Bureau of Prisons website reported more than 35,000 staff and 207,424 offenders in BOP custody.[43] Table 5.2 breaks this population into categories in terms of the type of facilities in which they are held.

The Bureau of Prisons Today

security levels

levels such as minimum, low, medium, high, or maximum are distinct by such features such as the presence of towers and other perimeter security barriers (fences or walls) with detection devices, the type of housing for prisoners (cells or dormitory), and the staff-to-inmate ratio

The federal prison system is a nationwide system of prisons and detention facilities for the incarceration of inmates sentenced for federal crimes and for the detention of individuals awaiting trial or sentencing in federal court. In April 2009, the BOP consisted of 118 prisons.[44] Institutions are classified as one of five different **security levels** (minimum, low, medium, high, or administrative), with each level holding inmates with similar risks of violence and escape. Security levels are distinguished by such security features as towers and other perimeter security barriers (fences or walls) with detection devices, the type of housing for prisoners (cells or dormitory), and the staff-to-inmate ratio.

TABLE 5.2 U.S. Bureau of Prisons Population on March 28, 2009

Type of Facility	Number of Inmates
BOP-operated prisons	171,293
Long-term contract facilities	22,146
Community correctional centers	8,756
Home confinement	1,901
Jails/short-term detention	3,034
Contract juvenile facilities	142
Long-term boarders	152
Total	207,424

Source: Federal Bureau of Prisons website http://www.bop.gov (accessed August 9, 2009).

Dormitory housing, in which beds are lined up next to one another and inmates are not locked into cells, is used for minimum-security prisons. Photo by Richard P. Seiter.

Minimum-security institutions (federal prison camps) have dormitory housing, a relatively low staff-to-inmate ratio, and limited or no perimeter fencing. Low-security prisons (federal correctional institutions) have double-fenced perimeters, mostly dormitory housing, strong work and program components, and a staff-to-inmate ratio higher than in minimum-security facilities. Medium-security prisons (also called federal correctional institutions) have double fences with electronic detection systems, mostly cells for housing, and an even higher staff-to-inmate ratio than low-security prisons.

High-security institutions (U.S. penitentiaries) have highly secure perimeters (featuring walls or reinforced fences), cell housing, high staff-to-inmate ratios, and close control of inmate movement within the prison. The fifth category of federal prisons, administrative facilities, comprises institutions with special missions, such as detention of pretrial offenders, treatment of inmates with serious or chronic medical problems, or containment of extremely dangerous, violent, or escape-prone inmates. The BOP also houses prisoners under the jurisdiction of the U.S. Marshals Service and therefore must build and operate detention facilities (jails) to house these inmates in several cities across the country. The Administrative Maximum (ADX) U.S. Penitentiary in Florence, Colorado, is an example of a BOP administrative facility; it is a "supermax" prison designed to hold federal inmates who have proved unmanageable by being violent or attempting escape at other secure prisons.

The BOP also operates three intensive confinement centers (boot camps) for minimum-security, nonviolent offenders with no significant history of prior incarceration. These facilities feature physical training, labor-intensive work assignments, education, vocational training, and treatment programs in a highly structured and disciplined, no-frills environment. Figure 5.2 illustrates the location of current BOP facilities. As noted in Table 5.2, the BOP makes extensive use of community correctional centers (halfway houses), placing many inmates in these facilities thirty days to six months prior to their release from prison to help them adjust to life in the community. Some of these offenders are then placed in home confinement at the end of their halfway house terms. The number of offenders in community correctional centers grew from 6,143 at the end of 2000 to 8,930 in March 2009, an increase of about 45 percent. For fiscal year 2007, there were 39,379 inmates referred to residential reentry centers from institutions and about 90 percent successfully completed the program.[45]

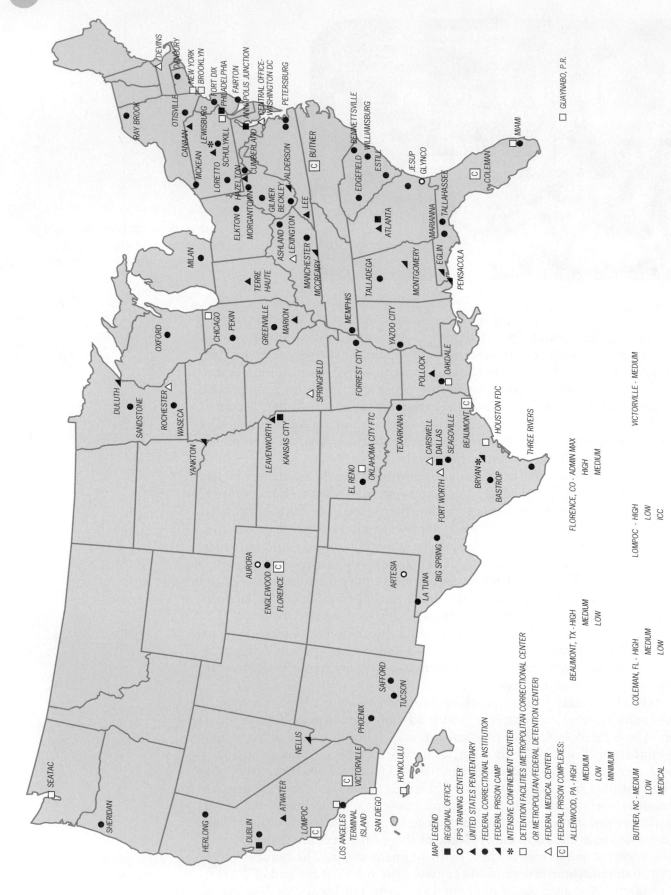

FIGURE 5.2 Current Locations of Prisons in the Federal Prison System

Source: http://www.bop.gov/locations/maps/jsp (accessed August 8, 2009).

An Interview With...

The Director of the Federal Bureau of Prisons

In 2003, Harley G. Lappin became the seventh director of the Federal Bureau of Prisons (BOP) since its establishment in 1930. He is a career public administrator, who began his career with the BOP in 1985 as a case manager at a prison in Texarkana, Texas. Since that time, he has worked in four other prisons, serving as camp administrator, associate warden, and warden of two facilities. He was promoted to regional director in July 2001 and sworn in as director on April 4, 2003.

Question: What makes the Bureau of Prisons a successful correctional organization?

Director Lappin: It is really a combination of several important factors. The first and most significant one is our employees; our staff are our single most important resource. They facilitate the accomplishment of our mission and the outcomes we strive for every day. In that regard, quality training, on-the-job development, and an experienced cadre of employees who assist new employees in understanding the culture and expectations are critical to our success. The fact that our experienced staff have a commitment to our new employees certainly contributes to the success of this agency.

A second is leadership. Last week at our national wardens' training we had a panel of past directors who discussed leadership and the importance of selecting leaders at every level of the organization. It was fascinating to hear how each of the former directors understood the critical role leadership plays in continuing the success of the BOP. It was quite clear that one of the most important decisions we make as leaders is selecting future leaders like wardens, associate wardens, and other senior and middle-level managers who will lead the agency into the future.

And finally, I would have to say the availability and consistent application of policy and oversight. The BOP is a policy-driven agency. While we encourage staff to be innovative, we recognize that we have many tried and true methods that have been developed through years of experience that are consistently carried out at all BOP facilities through our written policy and procedures.

Question: How has the BOP been successful in creating a culture of professionalism?

Director Lappin: Again, leadership and experienced employees who continue this spirit of professionalism are critical. We establish high standards in terms of how our prisons look and are managed, as well as how employees approach their jobs and their personal and professional responsibilities. Another important consideration is our emphasis on communication among employees and between staff and inmates. We constantly reinforce the importance of communication and how it is essential to proactive and effective prison management.

Question: What are the key challenges facing the BOP in the future?

Director Lappin: The key to our continued success is the recruitment and development of good people for our work-force. Predictions are that the work-force of the future will vary in skill level and there will more than likely be a smaller pool of candidates than in years past. Our challenge is to recruit and retain staff with skill levels consistent with our needs or deploy a training program that enhances the skill level of the candidate pool to meet our needs. For example, for us to be successful we must have staff that communicate effectively and are problem solvers. With greater competition for this group, we must ensure that if we hire less skilled people, we provide them with training opportunities to acquire the level of skill necessary in these areas to succeed as correctional professionals.

A second challenge is the continued expansion of the federal prison system. We see that even while the prison population of some states is declining, some of that decline is due to the federalization of crimes and leads to continued growth for the BOP. In addition, the post-9-11 focus on terrorism and the immigration/border initiatives will result in an increase in the federal inmate population.

...continued

Question: What advice would you give to college students thinking about a career in corrections or a career with the Bureau?

Director Lappin: I would encourage them to consider public service of any kind. Serving your country in this manner is not only personally rewarding, but also critically important to the future of our country. Specifically, corrections provides a wealth of opportunities and experiences that may not be found in many other occupations. I encourage our high school and college students to prepare themselves for entrance into the work-force of the future. It is critically important they be effective, skilled communicators. I suggest they take advantage of every opportunity to improve writing and public speaking skills, whether they intend to work in the public or private sector.

As noted previously, the Federal Bureau of Prisons has had a stable leadership over its more than seventy-five-year history. Harley G. Lappin is the current director of the Bureau. An interview with him is presented above.

State Prison Systems

Most adult prisoners serving more than one year are housed in facilities operated by the fifty states. As of June 30, 2008, the states operated almost 1,250 prisons holding approximately 1.41 million inmates.[46] Just as the states are very different in terms of the size and demographics of their populations, the state prison systems vary dramatically as well. Prison populations in 2008 ranged from Texas with 173,232 inmates to North Dakota with 1,450,[47] and in 2005, the number of prisons ranged from five in Washington D.C. to 132 in Texas.[48] Each state adopts its own penal code, specifying what acts are considered felonies, what range of sentences is available for each category of crime, and what type of sentencing structure it will have. As noted in earlier chapters, this results in considerable differences in the incarceration rates and therefore in the prison populations among states.

The Organization of State Prison Systems

Over the past decades, state correctional agencies have gone through a slow but deliberate transformation. The early eras of state prison operations were similar to the pre-1930s for the federal prison system, with no central control of prisons and legislatures allocating budgets and personnel directly to each individual prison. State prison wardens were often said to have their own individual "fiefdoms," with complete control over the hiring and firing of staff and the management and discipline of inmates.

Even as late as the first half of the twentieth century, many wardens of state prisons were appointed by governors, with no cabinet-level agency to oversee prison operations. However, as prison systems became larger, as their missions became more complex resulting from the increasing intervention of courts defining expected constitutional standards, and as prisons became more visible and accountable to the public, many states formed cabinet-level departments specifically to oversee the state prisons. Riveland writes, "Thirty-two states are organized with separate Departments of Corrections reporting to the Executive; 11 as separate departments reporting to boards or commissions; 5 under a Department of Public Safety umbrella, and 1 under a social services umbrella. Twenty-four of the separate departments have been so organized since 1979."[49] These state correctional agencies have become very large and very complex. Of the fifty state adult correctional systems, nine are also responsible for juvenile corrections, twenty-seven

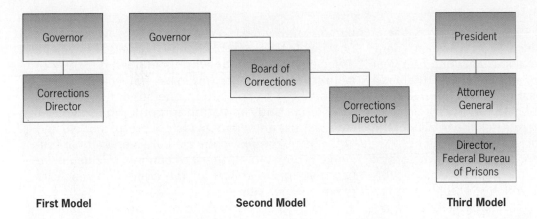

First Model   Second Model   Third Model

FIGURE 5.3 Three Models of Correctional Agency Relationship to the Chief Executive

have some probation responsibility, thirty-three supervise parole functions, and twenty-nine manage community corrections programs.[50]

The most common organizational model (twenty-four states) has the director, commissioner, or secretary of corrections as a cabinet-level officer, appointed by and reporting directly to the governor. In eleven other state correctional agencies, the corrections chief reports to a board or commission. The purpose behind this type of organizational model is to have some separation between politics and correctional policy.

The members of the corrections boards or commissions are appointed by the governor and usually must be made up of individuals from different political parties (often a like number of Republicans and Democrats) and serve overlapping terms. Therefore, governors are not able to immediately replace the board or commission with their own appointees, having to wait until terms end to replace members. The boards and commissions are relatively stable as a result, maintaining consistency of policy and leadership in the correctional agency. Figure 5.3 illustrates three models of reporting by correctional agencies. In the first, the corrections director reports directly to a governor. In the second, the director reports to a board or commission. The third is the federal model, in which the BOP director is appointed by and reports to the attorney general of the United States. An interesting trend in the appointment of correctional directors is described in the "A Case Study" box.

A Case Study

Appointing Correctional Directors

A very important issue is how directors of state and federal prison systems are appointed. As noted previously, there are three types of organizational structures for departments of corrections: reporting to a governor, a state board of corrections, or the U.S. attorney general. The most relevant factor is the stability of the director in the position, how often there is a change of leadership, and the continuity of leadership that results. As noted in the discussion of the U.S. Bureau of Prisons (BOP), the agency has had

...continued

only seven directors since 1930. In Ohio, I was one of only five state directors since 1970. However, many states have governors that serve only one four-year term, and with each turnover of governors, there is a new director of corrections. Such rapid turnover usually results in a lack of continuity of programs, operations, and leadership that reduces the quality of the overall operation of the correctional agency.

There are three scenarios in which directors of corrections are appointed. The first is the career correctional professional, in which the politics of the governor or the attorney general have little impact on the selection of the corrections chief. With the federal prison system, there has never been a "political" change of directors, even though there have been dozens of attorneys general and changes in political parties throughout the seven decades of the BOP. A few states are similar in that the corrections director survives changes in governors and political parties, as the professionalism and competence of the leader are considered more important than being of the same political party or the person that the governor wants in the position. This, in most people's opinions, is the best situation, allowing for competent leadership and a long-term shaping of the department's culture and organization to best accomplish its mission. As well, staff see the agency as a career and strive to work to the top of the agency, without fear that promotion will at some point lead to dismissal.

The second scenario is that in which a professional correctional person is appointed as director of a state correctional agency, but the leadership turns over with every new governor. Most states unfortunately fall into this category, although a few state directors prove themselves so accomplished at their jobs that the governor decides to keep that person rather than replace him or her with someone new just for the sake of change. I have several close associates and friends who have been directors of state correctional agencies in several states, moving on as they are replaced in one state, but with the knowledge and reputation to get a job in another state almost immediately (as governors are elected at the same time in many states). Even with professional leadership, this lack of continuity is usually a negative in the ability for the agency to reach its maximum potential.

The third scenario is, in most professional correctional administrators' minds, the worst. As correctional agencies become more of a political concern to elected officials, they sometimes decide not to appoint a correctional professional, but instead to appoint someone with a strong political background. This occurs when governors believe there is more danger to their reelection from making political than correctional management mistakes. These governors sometimes look to the state legislature to select someone who they know supports their criminal justice policies, or sometimes select a sheriff who may have some correctional background in running a jail but has also stood for election for the office of sheriff. One of the worst examples of this scenario occurred in a state in which the governor had originally appointed a professional correctional administrator who was extremely well respected throughout the country. However, after some disagreement between the governor and director regarding some issues of correctional policy (such as whether to have a chain gang), the director was fired. The governor appointed a funeral director as head of corrections, whose only experience was as a member of the state legislature.

Inmates in State Prison Systems

On June 30, 2008, the makeup of prison inmates was predominantly male (89.1 percent);[51] for 2007, the racial breakdown was 34.1 percent white, 38.2 percent black, 20.8 percent Hispanic, and 6.9 percent other minority);[52] and violent offenders served an average sentence of 7.5 years.[53] A large percentage of state prison inmates are serving time for violent offenses. Table 5.3 illustrates the percentage of sentenced state inmates by type of crime in 1990, 2000, and 2005. The Bureau of Justice Statistics reports that in 2005 the estimated percentage of state prisoners incarcerated for violent offenses was 53 percent, for property offenses it was 19.2 percent, and for drug offenses it was 19.5 percent. Murder accounted for 12.9 percent, rape accounted for 4.7 percent, and other assault offenses accounted for 10 percent.[54]

The largest growth of state prison inmates at the end of 2005 was among violent offenders. This is very different from the growth by offense category

TABLE 5.3	Percentage of Sentenced State Inmates by Type of Crime, 1990, 2000, and 2005		
Type of Crime	**1990**	**2000**	**2005**
Violent	46%	49%	53%
Property	25	20	19
Drug	22	21	20
Public order/other	7	10	8

Source: Heather C. West and William J. Sabol, *Prisoners in 2007* (Washington, D.C.: U.S. Department of Justice, Bureau of Justice Statistics, December 2008), p. 22.

(predominantly drug offenses) within federal prisons. As many drug crimes were federalized, the federal prison population grew, resulting in more than two-thirds of all federal prison inmates serving sentences for drug offenses. In 1980, in both state and federal prisons, drug offenders made up less than 10 percent of the nation's prisoners and violent offenders, almost 60 percent. By 1993, the number of drug offenders had risen to 26 percent of the total, and the number of violent offenders had dropped to 45 percent of the total.[55] By 1995, there were 52,782 drug offenders in federal prisons, and by 2007, 95,446 federal prisoners were drug offenders.[56] Therefore, the growth of violent offenders in state prisons comes about from two phenomena. First, violent offenders are receiving much longer sentences than in the past and therefore, as more are admitted to prison without others being released, the overall number increases. Second, the percentage of the total inmates that is serving sentences for violent offences increases as many drug offenders are diverted to federal prisons.

A recent phenomenon among state prison systems is the decline in the growth of inmates. After almost two decades of dramatic increases, the growth has begun to slow and the level of overcrowding in state prisons has decreased. Table 5.4 illustrates the growth in the number of state inmates over the past seven years. State prison populations grew only 1.7 percent from 2000 to 2007.[57] However, state prisons have become more overcrowded, as from 2000 to 2005, the states went from operating at 100 percent to 108 percent of rated capacity.[58]

There is debate over what issues have most influenced the declining increase in the number of state prison inmates, and several possible reasons exist for the drop. The first possibility is that demographics have changed; fewer Americans are in the high-crime age group and have enough criminal history to be sent to prison. Second, crime rates have been dropping. But the most likely reason is that more crimes are being prosecuted at the federal level, and offenders who would have otherwise been in state prisons are now in federal prisons (the federal prison population grew 4.6 percent during the period the state prison population only increased 1.7 percent).[59]

Classification within State Prison Systems

State prison systems use security-level classifications similar to the federal prison system. One major difference, however, is that many states have central reception centers at which all inmates are initially placed until they are classified. Upon their arrival at the reception center, state inmates receive a **security classification** to determine to which prison they will be assigned. The purpose

security classification
to match offenders to institutions that have the physical security and staff resources to prevent escapes and control their behavior

TABLE 5.4	Persons Held in State Prisons, December 31, 2000–2007, and June 2007 and 2008
Year	**State**
2000	1,245,845
2001	1,247,039
2002	1,276,616
2003	1,295,542
2004	1,316,772
2005	1,340,311
2006	1,376,899
2007	
June 30	1,395,493
December 31	1,398,624
2008	
June 30	1,409,442
Annual change	
Average annual change, 12/31/2000–12/31/2007	1.7%
Percent change, 06/30/2007–06/30/2008	1.0
Six-month change	
12/31/2006–06/30/2007	1.4%
12/31/2007–06/30/2008	0.8

Source: Adapted from Heath C. West and William J. Sabol, *Prison Inmates at Midyear 2008–Statistical Tables* (Washington, D.C.: U.S. Department of Justice, March 2009), p. 2.

of a security classification is to match offenders to institutions that have the physical security and staff resources to prevent escapes and control their behavior. However, also important for the assignment to a prison is the need for specific programs for the inmate. Both security and program need determinations are the result of several factors. Inmates go through psychological, educational, or vocational testing, and their past records are reviewed. The presentence investigation (PSI) provides much of the information regarding criminal history, family and social history, education and vocational achievement, and employment history.

Objective classification systems, or actuarial methods to score past criminal behavior and program needs and predict offenders' risk of violence and escape, are used in most states to determine security classification. Points are assigned based on offenders' history, and the point totals indicate the level of security (minimum, medium, maximum) that is required for each inmate. In addition to security classification, inmates' program needs and home are also considered in the decision of prison assignment. Most states have many similar-security-level prisons (for instance, Michigan has twenty-five medium-security prisons), and inmates are assigned both geographically (as close to home as possible) and to meet specific program needs (some prisons may have specialized mental health or substance abuse programs).

The states use somewhat different terminologies for security classifications. In 2005, slightly more than a third of inmates were classified as maximum security, two-fifths as medium security, and one-fifth as minimum security.[60] The following illustrates the number of state prisons by security level at the end of 2005:

Maximum security	355
Medium security	438
Minimum security	926

The number of facilities by security classifications has shifted a little from 2000 to 2005, as the number of maximum-security prisons has increased by 12 percent, the number of medium-security facilities has declined by 8 percent, and the number of minimum-security facilities has increased by 19 percent. Objective classification systems put much weight on the length of time to be served before release. Part of the reason for the growth of maximum-security facilities is because as sentences lengthen, an inmate with the same criminal history and background may be increased in security level, only because he or she is serving a longer sentence. Minimum-security numbers have increased as many more offenders who used to get probation for such crimes as drunk driving or low-level drug sales are now serving short prison terms.

After classification at the reception center, inmates are transferred to the prison at which they begin serving their sentence. At their assigned prison, inmates go through an orientation regarding rules and regulations, policies and procedures, and processes such as adding people to their visiting or telephone list. Inmates then go through another classification process to determine what type of prison job they will have and what type of programs they will be assigned. This classification and assignment process uses the results of the education, vocational and mental health tests, and assessments that were completed in the reception center. These are discussed with inmates, who state their preference for work and program assignments. In most states, all inmates must have a job unless they receive a full-time program assignment. Most programs (education and substance abuse) are voluntary, although in some states and under certain sentences, education (up to the level of basic literacy) and substance abuse programs may be mandatory. Table 5.5 illustrates the types of assignments inmates receive in prisons.

Prisons are classified by the physical security features, primarily focused on preventing escapes. Reprinted with permission of the Corrections Corporation of America.

TABLE 5.5	Inmate Prison Assignments as of January 1, 2002	
Assignment	**Number of Inmates**	**Percent of Total**[a]
Prison industry	78,881	7.8%
Prison farm	34,180	3.6
Other work	550,583	47.0
Full-time education or vocational	129,049	13.9
Part-time education or vocational[b]	129,683	14.5

[a]The total will not be 100 percent because some inmates are unassigned and some states have other assignments not included in these categories.

[b]Part-time includes release preparation, adult continuing education, parenting, and fitness and wellness programs.

Source: Adapted from Camille Graham Camp and George M. Camp, *The 2002 Corrections Yearbook: Adult Systems* (Middletown, Conn.: Criminal Justice Institute, 2003), p. 82.

After assignment, inmates begin the daily routine that they will carry out throughout their sentence. These routines and inmate activities are described in Chapters 12 and 13.

Other Public Correctional Systems

Immigration and Customs Enforcement (ICE)

formerly the U.S. Immigration and Naturalization Service (INS), responsible for housing illegal aliens pending a hearing or deportation back to their home country

State and federal prisons by far hold most of the adult prisoners housed in correctional facilities in the United States. However, there are almost 10,000 inmates in immigration facilities, almost 1,800 inmates in military facilities, and nearly 15,000 inmates in territorial facilities at year-end 2007. The U.S. **Immigration and Customs Enforcement (ICE),** formerly the U.S. Immigration and Naturalization Service (INS), is responsible for housing illegal aliens pending a hearing or deportation back to their home country. Offenders are usually detained in two ways: first, if caught while attempting to illegally enter the United States, and second, if they commit a crime and are arrested while not a citizen of the United States and are subject to potential deportation. The number of ICE detainees has been increasing over the past few years (see Table 5.6) as enforcement efforts to catch and detain individuals attempting to enter the United States illegally have increased. By the end of 2007, there were 30,431 detainees held under ICE jurisdiction, up from 8,177 in 1995. With the war on terrorism and increasing efforts to protect the U.S. borders and detain more people caught entering the United States illegally, the number of ICE detainees is expected to continue to increase.

As illustrated in Table 5.6, ICE detains only about a third of its total detainees. The remainder are housed by the Federal Bureau of Prisons or other federal facilities, under contract to private facilities, or under intergovernmental agreements in state prisons or local jails. Among the ICE detainees at year-end 2007, just over 42 percent (12,889) had been convicted of a criminal offense, and 45 percent were being held for only an immigration law violation.[61]

brig

a military term meaning a correctional facility

The U.S. military services also operate prisons or **brigs** to house offenders convicted of violating the military justice codes. In 2004, the Army operated six, the Navy operated eleven, the Marine Corps operated six, and the Air Force operated

TABLE 5.6	Number of Detainees Held by the U.S. Immigration and Customs Enforcement (ICE), by Type of Facility, December 31, 1995, 2002, 2006, and 2007			
Facility Type	**2007**	**2006**	**2002**	**1995**
Total	30,431	27,368	21,065	8,177
Intergovernmental Service Agreement and Bureau of Prisons	20,711	17,753	14,042	3,749
ICE owned and contract	9,720	9,615	7,023	4,428

Source: Adapted from Paige M. Harrison and Allen J. Beck, "Prisoners in 2002," *Bureau of Justice Statistics Bulletin*, July 2000 (revised August 27, 2003), p. 8; and Heather C. West and William J. Sabol, "Prisoners in 2007," *Bureau of Justice Statistics Bulletin* (Washington, D.C.: U.S. Department of Justice, December 2008), p. 26.

thirty-four correctional facilities. The total capacity of these fifty-seven facilities was 3,290.[62] Table 5.7 illustrates that the military branches held 1,794 detainees in 2007, with 61 percent serving sentences of one year or more.

The final category of public correctional institutions described is that of territorial prisons. The five U.S. territories and commonwealths operate correctional facilities that serve as jails and prisons for these jurisdictions. Each has a court and correctional system similar to those of a state, and these correctional populations are also growing. From 2006 to 2007, the number of sentenced prisoners in U.S. territories had decreased by 2.4 percent, and three-fourths of the territorial prison population (11,465) was serving a sentence of more than one year.[63] Table 5.8 illustrates the number of inmates in custody in the five territories.

TABLE 5.7	Prisoners under Military Jurisdiction by Branch of Service, Year-End 2006 and 2007				
		Total		**Sentenced to More than 1 Year**	
Branch of Service	**2006**	**2007**	**Percent Change, 2006–2007**	**2006**	**2007**
Total	1,944	1,794	−7.7%	1,135	1,089
To which prisoners belong					
Air Force	328	280	−14.6	215	185
Army	880	829	−5.8	542	555
Marine Corps	407	396	−2.7	167	164
Navy	315	268	−14.9	201	173
Coast Guard	14	21	50.0	10	12
Holding prisoners					
Air Force	92	61	−33.7	20	9
Army	996	912	−8.4	711	721
Marine Corps	329	338	2.7	98	97
Navy	527	483	−8.3	306	262

Source: Heather C. West and William J. Sabol, "Prisoners in 2007," *Bureau of Justice Statistics Bulletin,* December 2008, p. 26.

TABLE 5.8	**Prisoners in Custody of Correctional Authorities, in the U.S. Territories and Commonwealths, Year-End 2006 and 2007**						
	Total			**Sentenced to More than 1 Year**			
Jurisdiction	**2006**	**2007**	**Percent Change, 2006–2007**	**2006**	**2007**	**Percent Change, 2006–2007**	**Incarceration Rate, 2007***
Total	15,205	14,678	−3.5%	11,743	11,465	−2.4%	261
American Samoa	210	236	12.4	113	122	8.0	188
Guam	495	535	8.1	337	320	−5.0	182
Commonwealth of the Northem Mariana Islands	126	137	8.7	76	78	2.6	90
Commonwealth of Puerto Rico	13,788	13,215	−4.2	10,789	10,553	−2.2	267
U.S Virgin Islands	586	555	−5.3	428	392	−8.4	357

*The number of prisoners with a sentence of more than 1 year per 100,000 persons in the resident population. July 1, 2007 population estimates were provided by the U.S. Census Bureau, International Data Base.

Source: Heather C. West and William J. Sabol, "Prisoners in 2007," *Bureau of Justice Statistics Bulletin,* December 2008, p. 26.

Private Correctional Systems

Although the use of private facilities to house prisoners is a recent phenomenon, the private sector has been involved in the administration of various correctional aspects almost since the origination of penal codes. During the 1960s, the use of halfway houses as a transition from prison to the community grew rapidly. Most of the halfway houses were privately operated, although most were owned by faith-based or not-for-profit charitable organizations such as the Salvation Army. By the 1980s, almost every state had contracts with privately operated halfway houses to provide residential services, supervision, and transitional programs for inmates leaving prison and returning to the community.[64] Also, many states with very small juvenile offender populations have often found it cost effective to contract with privately operated facilities, rather than to open state-run juvenile facilities. In 1984, it was reported that 65 percent of all juvenile facilities were private, housing approximately 32,000 offenders.[65]

Although these uses of the private sector in corrections have not been found controversial, contracting to house adult prisoners in private for-profit prisons raised serious ethical and practical questions, resulting in a slow beginning to the use and role of private prisons. A **private prison** is any secure correctional facility, operated by an organization other than a governmental agency and usually in a for-profit manner that contracts with the government to provide security, housing, and programs for adult offenders. In a private prison, staff are not public employees, but are employees of the company that owns and operates the prison. Such prisons can be administered without cumbersome governmental purchasing and personnel policies, although they are still held to the same constitutional standard for treatment of inmates as a public prison.

The first private contract to house adult offenders was in 1984, for a small, 250-bed facility operated by Corrections Corporation of America under contract with Hamilton County, Tennessee. Soon thereafter, additional contracts

private prison
any secure correctional facility, operated by other than a governmental agency and usually in a for-profit manner, which contracts with a governmental entity, to provide security, housing, and programs for adult offenders

with the private sector to house illegal aliens (contracted with the U.S. Immigration and Naturalization Service) and youthful offenders (with the Federal Bureau of Prisons) were established. The growth over the next few decades in the privatization of correctional facilities was spurred by the increasing number of inmates and the rapid need to build new prisons, the budgetary challenges required to fund these new prisons, and the Reagan-era support of using the private sector to help downsize the scope of government. Welch notes,

> *At that time, the prevailing political and economic philosophy encouraged government officials to turn to the private sector to administer public services, such as sanitation, health care, security, fire protection, and education. As a result of the introduction of free-market principles into the administration of public services, . . . the privatization of corrections appeared to be a new and novel approach to some old problems (i.e., overcrowding and mounting costs).*[66]

By 1990, Logan reported that private prisons held just over 9,000 adult inmates,[67] but by June 30, 2008, there were 126,249 state and federal prisoners held in private prisons, accounting for 7.8 percent of all prisoners.[68] Table 5.9 illustrates the numbers and percentage of all state and federal inmates held in private prisons.

TABLE 5.9 — **Number of Prisoners Held in Private Facilities, December 31, 2000–2007, and June 30, 2007 and 2008**

Year	Number of Prisoners			Percent of all Prisoners
	Total	Federal	State	
2000	90,542	15,524	75,018	6.5%
2001	91,053	19,251	72,702	6.5
2002	93,912	20,274	73,638	6.5
2003	95,707	21,865	73,842	6.5
2004	98,628	24,768	73,860	6.6
2005	107,940	27,046	80,894	7.1
2006	113,697	27,726	85,971	7.2
2007				
June 30	118,239	30,379	87,860	7.4%
December 31	125,997	31,310	94,687	7.9
2008		32,712	93,537	7.8%
June 30	126,249			
Anual change				
Average annual change, 12/31/2000–12/31/2007	4.8%	10.5%	3.4%	:
Percent change, 06/30/2007–06/30/2008	6.8	7.7	6.5	:

Note: Includes estimates for Illinois for 2006, 2007, and 2008 and Nevada for December 31, 2007.

: Not Calculated

Source: Heather C. West and William J. Sabol, *Prison Inmates at Midyear 2008-Statistical Tables* (Washington, D.C.: U.S. Department of Justice, Bureau of Justice Statistics, March 2009), p. 12.

This private prison owned by the Corrections Corporation of America is one of many private prisons now operated throughout the United States. Courtesy of the Corrections Corporation of America.

Corrections Corporation of America

the largest of the private prison corporations that opened the first private, for-profit correctional facility in 1984 in Tennessee; currently operates seventy correctional facilities

The GEO Group, Inc.

a private correctional company headquartered in Florida that operates fifty-one correctional facilities in the United States.

Cornell Correctional Companies

a private correctional company headquartered in Texas that operates sixty-nine correctional facilities in the United States.

Private Correctional Companies

The use of private prisons has continued to expand, and on January 30, 2005, there were 107 privately operated secure prisons contracting to hold adult criminal offenders.[69]

Several companies contract with government agencies to house adult offenders, but only three have a significant market share. There are three publicly traded private prison companies, with their size and approximate revenues listed in Table 5.10. These companies include **Corrections Corporation of America, The GEO Group, Inc.,** and **Cornell Correctional Companies.** There are at least five other private prison companies with significant contracts and revenues to hold federal, state, or county inmates.

The operation of private prisons is a fairly accepted practice, and more than one-half of the states use private facilities. The issue of private prisons in more fully addressed in Chapter 15. However, it is expected that private correctional operations will continue to remain strong, due to a number of factors. Although the growth in the number of state and federal prisoners has slowed over the past two to three years, there is still expected to be significant increases in the number of inmates, and with state and federal revenues down due to the 2008/9 recession continuing,

TABLE 5.10	Major Private Correctional Companies	
Company	**Number of Facilities**	**Revenues for 2008**
Corrections Corporation of America	62	$1,594 million
The GEO Group, Inc.	49	$711 million
Cornell Correctional Companies	71	$387 million

Source: Each company's website accessed March 15, 2009. Corrections Corporation of America website, www.correctionscorp.com; The GEO Group, Inc., website, http://thegeogroupinc.com; Cornell Companies website, www.cornellcompanies.com.

very few jurisdictions are constructing new prisons. Tightening government budgets force public officials to increasingly look for alternatives to the traditional approaches. And the continued lack of public confidence in the public sector leads many citizens to support giving the private sector a chance. Gowdy notes:

> Nonetheless, the public's unsatisfactory view of today's penal system in terms of its costs and high recidivism rates are two factors that are likely to encourage further expansion of the private sector's role.[70]

A Question of Policy

The increase in the number of inmates of the past two decades and the resultant cost to construct new prisons to keep up with this growth lead to an important question of policy. In the "You Make the Decision" box at the end of this chapter, students are to consider the policy of construction and cost implications of this option to respond to the constant expansion of the prison population and the increasing resources necessary to operate new prisons.

Summary

Although prisons have been an important component in the criminal justice system since shortly after the creation of the U.S. Constitution and the formation of our current system of justice, they have changed in scope and role only minimally during their first two hundred years of operation. However, over the past two decades, there have been major changes in their role, mission, and scope; the attributes of inmates; and the length of time that inmates serve. This chapter has described these trends and discussed our nation's current approach of constructing new prisons to avoid severe overcrowding of correctional facilities. This policy decision, however, has been at great cost to the taxpayers; direct expenditures to correctional agencies are now greater than $68 billion per year.

This chapter has also presented the different correctional agencies that operate prisons, including states, the Federal Bureau of Prisons, the U.S. Immigration and Customs Enforcement, the military, U.S. territories, and private correctional companies. Major changes in policies and populations within the public agencies were described, specifically how changes in federal laws regarding crimes affect the federal and state prison systems. Also, the controversial issues surrounding for-profit private companies operating correctional institutions were described.

Much of the challenge in operating prisons under today's approach of construction of new facilities to keep up with the increasing number of inmates has to do with finding the budgetary resources to continue to operate correctional agencies. In the final two chapters of this textbook, this challenge and the future approaches and alternatives to our current overreliance on prisons are addressed. It is critical to examine and consider alternative methods of managing offenders and to search for preventive approaches to offenders becoming involved in crime. We must also consider diversion from the criminal justice system for minor, first-time offenders and juveniles and using alternatives to incarceration that do not seriously endanger public safety as reasonable sanctions for minor property and drug

CHAPTER REVIEW

offenses. Our society cannot continue to fund the growth of imprisonment to the detriment of other important government functions.

The next chapter examines what happens to inmates as they get out of prison. The declining use of parole and indeterminate sentences and the changing issues that confront prisoners as they leave prison and return to the community are reviewed. The past two decades have witnessed not only a change in the prison population, but also a change in the makeup of those being released. These changes require a renewed examination of how we prepare inmates for release and the ability of the community to readily accept them upon their return.

Key Terms

prisons
Rhodes v. Chapman
mission
new penology
war on drugs
street crimes
federalize
Three Penitentiary Act
Federal Bureau of Prisons (BOP)
Sanford Bates

Sentencing Reform Act of 1984
security levels
security classification
Immigration and Customs Enforcement (ICE)
brig
private prison
Corrections Corporation of America
The GEO Group, Inc.
Cornell Correctional Companies

Review Questions

1. How did *Rhodes v. Chapman* change the operations of prisons?

2. What is the general mission of most correctional agencies?

3. How many inmates are there in U.S. correctional facilities?

4. Describe recent trends in terms of the inmate population, commission of violent crimes, and length of sentence.

5. Describe the increase in the number of prisons over the past decade.

6. What three prisons were included in the Three Penitentiary Act of 1891?

7. What was the result of the Sentencing Reform Act of 1984, and what impact did it have on the Bureau of Prisons?

8. What factors influenced the continued significant growth of the Bureau of Prisons into the 2000s?

9. Describe the physical security factors that go with prison security levels (minimum, medium, maximum).

10. Why do some inmates go to state and others federal prisons?

11. What factors have influenced a recent decline in the number of prison inmates in some states?

12. What state prison security level has the highest percentage of inmates?

13. What is the role of the U.S. Immigration and Customs Enforcement?

14. When and where was the first private prison opened under contract to house adult offenders?

15. Describe the most controversial issues in the use of for-profit private companies to house inmates.

You Make the Decision...

Is Incarceration Worth the Cost?

The question to consider is whether the changes in laws resulting in an increase in the number of inmates, construction of new prisons, renovation of existing facilities, and spending tens of billions of dollars to house prisoners are good public policy. As noted previously, the absolute number of violent and dangerous offenders in prison has not increased significantly. The largest portion of the growth has come from the incarceration of drug offenders. Whether our nation can withstand another decade of a policy to try to build our way out of prison crowding is a question that must be addressed in a thoughtful and pragmatic manner by corrections and elected officials.

The dramatic differences in the incarceration rates among various states require the review of perhaps the most important policy issue regarding corrections in the United States: Does the increase in the use of incarceration reduce the risk to citizens of being victimized and, if so, is that reduction of risk worth the additional cost of such incarceration? This is an important issue for students of corrections to confront. Look at the states with the highest

incarceration rates (Louisiana, Oklahoma, Alabama, and Mississippi). Compare these states with those having the lowest incarceration rates (Minnesota, Maine, North Dakota, Massachusetts, and New Hampshire). Do trends in crime rates provide any parallels to increases in rates of incarceration?

Students should examine many factors and then come to their own conclusion as to whether the increased use of incarceration is worth the cost. Factors that should be considered include the trends in crime rates (particularly violent crime), the cost of building and operating new prisons, the available alternatives to incarceration, the mission and goals of corrections, and the effectiveness of both imprisonment and community correctional programs. Students should weigh the cost of incarceration against the impact it has on crime, while considering the need for these tight funds for other uses. Unfortunately, this policy deliberation does not occur in the public policy debate among legislative bodies or most elected officials. It is a critical public policy dilemma that deserves a thorough debate.

Chapter Resources on mycrimekit

Go to mycrimekit.com to explore the following study tools and resources specific to this chapter:

- **Practice Quiz:** multiple-choice, true/false, short-answer, and essay questions to help students test their knowledge
- **WebQuests:** learning activities built around Web searches
  - Federal Bureau of Prisons: www.bop.gov
  - United Nations Crime and Justice Information Network: www.uncjin.org

- Association of Private Correctional and Treatment Organizations: www.apcto.org
- **Insider's Experiences:** "Throwing Out a $2 Million Prison Design"
- **Seiter Videos:**
  - See experts discuss the role of prisons
  - See the author provide a tour of a prison
- Career Center: A Career as a Warden
- Flashcards: Twenty-eight flashcards to test knowledge of the chapter's key terms

Parole and Prisoner Reentry

After reading this chapter, you should be able to:

1. Describe the historical development of parole in the United States, and specify the role played by Maconochie and Crofton.

2. Explain the importance of the Elmira Reformatory in the early development of parole in the United States.

3. Discuss the operation of the medical model as it relates to the use of rehabilitation, indeterminate sentences, and parole in the United States.

4. Describe alternatives proposed to the use of parole and indeterminate sentences during the 1970s.

5. Compare and contrast the ways inmates can be released from prison, including parole, supervised mandatory release, and unconditional mandatory release.

6. Outline the use of parole guidelines using salient factor scores to determine parole readiness.

7. Describe the process of parole revocation and list the due process rights for offenders during this process.

8. Identify how the process of prisoner reentry is different today from twenty years ago.

9. List the collateral consequences of imprisonment and discuss how they affect successful prisoner reentry.

Introduction

Throughout the history of the United States, prisons have held criminal offenders sentenced to their authority under many different sentencing structures. During the 1800s, prisoners served set amounts of time in crowded prisons, with little emphasis on rehabilitation or preparation for release. During the first half of the twentieth century, criminals continued to be confined in prisons under determinate sentences; however, there was a developing emphasis on work and some rehabilitative programs. By the middle of the twentieth century, prison sentences began to be for indeterminate terms, prisons accentuated rehabilitation programs, and parole board experts decided when prisoners would be released based on their readiness for returning to the community. This move to the use of parole was a major change in philosophy, as well as sentence structure, and affected not only prison operations, but also the type of supervision that offenders received after release. This approach continued until the last two decades of the twentieth century.

Over the past twenty years, parole and indeterminate sentences have been abandoned in many states, and there has been a return to set, determinate sentences. Offenders are often limited in the amount of good time they can earn during their sentences, as truth-in-sentencing laws requiring the completion of 85 percent of the sentence before prisoners are released have been enacted and implemented in many states. This emphasis on holding offenders accountable through tough sentencing laws results in a focus on punishment, incapacitation, and deterrence. Prison rehabilitation programs are often reduced in importance, both to save money and to avoid making prisons too soft a punishment for crime. Many offenders are now released without the review of a parole board to determine readiness or consider the soundness of their release plans.

These changes make the status of prisoner reentry to the community very different from that of only a few decades ago. The number of releasees is greater, the majority is not released through parole, and the prisoners serve longer sentences. They are also less prepared to return to their communities, and their communities are less able to accommodate them. A large number of releasees are subsequently returned to prison, many for violating the technical conditions of their parole or release supervision rather than for the commission of a new crime.

This chapter reviews the development of parole in the United States and how it is administered for those states in which it is still in use. The release decision, supervision on parole, the violation process when offenders fail to meet their parole conditions, and the overall effectiveness of parole and indeterminate sentences are discussed. The challenge of reentry to the community is also described, and the types of challenges faced by returning prisoners are illustrated. There is also a review of the types of programs that help prisoners reenter the community and examples of the types of programs that are used to both supervise and aid offenders as they leave prison and return to the community.

The History of Parole

parole
the conditional release of inmates by a parole board prior to the expiration of their sentence

The term *parole* is from the French word *parol*, meaning "word of honor." It was first used in the 1700s as a means of releasing prisoners of war upon their promise not to resume arms in the current conflict. This evolved to the modern meaning of **parole** as a conditional release of inmates by a parole board prior to the expiration of their sentence. It is often thought that parole had no history in U.S. prisons until the mid-1900s, but a much earlier use of conditional release influenced the development of parole as currently used. In colonial America, there was a shortage of labor, leading to the transportation of children and pardoned criminals from England to the American colonies to provide a ready workforce. As the pardoned criminals returned to England after serving their indentured time, specific conditions for their freedom had to be created. Even with the end of the transportation of children and convicts to the United States after the Revolutionary War, the idea of a period of punishment and work followed by a requirement to meet conditions of freedom was established.

Maconochie and the Mark System

The more formal use of conditional release from prison most likely had its roots in 1840, when **Alexander Maconochie** became superintendent of the British penal colony on Norfolk Island, about one thousand miles off the coast of Australia. Maconochie had been captured by the French while serving as a British naval officer and was sensitive to the brutal way prisoners were often treated. Upon his appointment as superintendent, he decided to initiate a revolutionary philosophy of reforming the prisoner by instilling self-discipline with an emphasis on "punish for the past, and train for the future."

Since the amount of time necessary to instill self-discipline could not be estimated in advance, Maconochie advocated open-ended (indeterminate) sentences and a **mark system**. Instead of sentences for a specific amount of time, Maconochie required offenders to earn a specific number of marks based on the severity of the crime, and they would be released once they earned the required level of marks through work and good behavior. His system consisted of four stages on the way to release, each providing more personal liberty to the prisoner.[1] The *penal stage* emphasized punishment and included solitary confinement and a diet of bread and water. The *associated stage* allowed inmates to associate and begin to earn marks through work, program participation, and good behavior. Poor behavior resulted in

Alexander Maconochie
the superintendent of the British penal colony on Norfolk Island from 1841 to 1844 who created a system of marks for good behavior that could lead to a graduated release from prison

mark system
credits against a sentence that allowed for inmates to be released once they earned the required level of marks through work and good behavior

The concepts of indeterminate sentences and parole were developed while Alexander Maconochie served as superintendent of the British penal colony on Norfolk Island between 1840 and 1844. Courtesy of Hulton Archive/Getty Images.

ticket of leave

a form of release used by
Maconochie; once prisoners
earning the required level of
marks, they received a
conditional pardon and were
released to the community

an increase in the number of marks required for release. The third stage was the *social stage*, in which inmates were grouped and held jointly responsible for the conduct of each other, as a way to begin the process of living responsibly in society. The final stage was a **ticket of leave**, in which prisoners earning the required level of marks received a conditional pardon and were released to the community.

Norfolk Island had deplorable conditions prior to the arrival of Maconochie. Hughes described conditions as so bad that "convicts would choose two men by drawing straws: one to die, the other to kill him . . . the killer and witnesses would have to be sent to Sydney for trial . . . a boon to the prisoners, who yearned for the meager relief of getting away from the ocean of hell."[2] The mark system worked well on Norfolk Island and brought tranquility to what had been a violent prison with regular riots. Unfortunately, his English overseers saw Maconochie's approach as "coddling" criminals, and he was relieved of his duty in 1844. After his return to England, Maconochie continued to write and encourage prison reform. In a review of some of Maconochie's writings, Morris noted that Maconochie desired to maintain a sanitary prison with adequate diet and decent treatment for prisoners. In his view, "punishment, allowing for and facilitating redemption, dignifies society, makes prison service a constructive occupation, and enhances public safety. By contrast, vengeance-based punishment, posing as effective deterrence, demeans society, makes torturers of prison guards, and lessens public safety."[3] Word of Maconochie's approach and system became widely known even after his dismissal and influenced others, particularly Sir Walter Crofton.

Walter Crofton and the Irish System

Sir Walter Crofton

the director of Irish prison
system in 1854, who began
to implement many of the
ideas of Maconochie's work

Even though Maconochie was dismissed as superintendent of Norfolk Island, some of his ideas were later accepted, and the Penal Servitude Act, enacted by the British Parliament in 1853, enabled prisoners to be released on a ticket of leave and supervised by the police. In 1854, **Sir Walter Crofton** was appointed director of the Irish prison system and began to implement many of the ideas of Maconochie's work. He created the following four-stage system of graduated release from prison and return to the community:[4]

1. *Solitary confinement* of approximately nine months. Much like Maconochie's first stage, it included an emphasis on punishment, little interaction with other prisoners, silence, chapel, and work.
2. *Special prison* in which the offender worked with other inmates and earned marks to gain privileges and move further toward release. Inmates also had to complete three conduct classes, taking up to twelve months.
3. *Open institution,* a transitional stage to society, with training on the freedoms and requirements of release and continued earning of marks to reach the fourth stage.
4. *Ticket of leave,* a conditional release for the remainder of the sentence, and the first use of parole as it is known today. The police supervised offenders in rural Ireland, but Dublin had a civilian employee who worked with the police, but also secured employment for the released prisoners, visited their homes, and had them report to him. If they disobeyed the rules, the ticket of leave could be revoked.

These ideas and stages worked well. A report regarding 557 prisoners released during the 1850s noted that only seventeen had their tickets of leave revoked.[5] These stages of release and subsequent supervision in the community are the forerunners of the modern indeterminate sentence, parole officer supervision, and focus on finding employment as a key criterion for success. The Irish system was well received internationally, and many U.S. penologists were soon campaigning to bring these ideas and procedures to the United States.

Parole Begins in the United States

With parole and indeterminate sentences still decades away, the idea of rewarding good behavior with reductions in the time served was initiated in 1817 when the New York legislature authored the first "good time" statute, allowing up to a 25 percent reduction in time served for good behavior and industrious work. Over the next fifty years, twenty-three states passed similar statutes authorizing the use of good time, which was seen as important in encouraging good behavior and preparing for successful release.[6]

In 1869, New York passed an act to build a reformatory in Elmira for youthful offenders, which would use indeterminate sentences and hold offenders until "reformed." In 1870, the American Prison Association was formed and held its first meeting in Cincinnati, Ohio. The major discussion was about the use of indeterminate sentences and the Irish parole system. One of the leading U.S. penologists, **Zebulon R. Brockway** of Michigan, presented a paper on the Irish system. The association adopted a Declaration of Principles, promoting the use of the Irish system, parole, good time, and assistance to released prisoners in the United States. These reforms, when made public, were well received across the country. When the **Elmira Reformatory** opened in 1876, Brockway was appointed its superintendent. A system of classification allowing inmates to earn privileges for their work and behavior was implemented, and the reformatory was organized so that inmates spent much of their day in education programs and learning trades. Once inmates demonstrated reformation, prison administrators had the authority to conditionally release them to be supervised by state agents in the community.[7]

Zebulon R. Brockway
a leading U.S. penologist in the mid-1800s who was a proponent of adopting the Irish system in the United States and who became the first superintendent of the Elmira Reformatory

Elmira Reformatory
the first reformatory in the United States; it opened in 1876 and used the principles of the Irish system, indeterminate sentences, and parole

Rehabilitative programs with conditional release were a key element of the operation of the Elmira Reformatory under superintendent Zebulon Brockway. Courtesy of Corbis/Bettmann.

As reformatories were opened, they stressed education of youthful offenders. Courtesy of the Ohio Department of Rehabilitation and Correction.

Over the next several decades, the use of parole increased, with many states adopting prison programs similar to those of the Elmira Reformatory. By 1900, twenty states had begun to use indeterminate sentences and to have correctional officials determine dates of inmate release by parole. In 1930, New York was the first state to develop an independent parole authority to make release decisions separate from the state department of corrections.[8] Even though the idea was solidly supported, the Great Depression was the real impetus for expansion of parole, as unemployment and Prohibition created a crime wave resulting in an increasing number of people being sent to prison. As prison populations grew and prisons became more overcrowded, states could not afford their operation and looked to parole as a less expensive way to manage offenders. The number of offenders released annually on parole increased from 21,632 in 1923 to 37,794 in 1936.[9] By 1944, all states had adopted the use of parole and indeterminate sentences.[10]

Parole and the Medical Model

As indicated in Chapter 1, after World War II, the country began to recognize the value of the scientific approach to solving problems and incorporated this model into dealing with crime and criminals. The medical model of corrections was adopted as the dominant theory influencing prison practices. The medical model assumed that offenders were inflicted with an environmental or psychosocial condition that was the underlying reason for their criminality. Under the belief that offenders were sick, when they were sentenced to prison, their problems were diagnosed and a treatment plan was developed by prison officials who were experts in a variety of areas, such as education, vocational training, and mental health issues. The prison treatment continued until another group of experts (the parole board) determined that the "patient" could no longer benefit from institutional treatment and was ready for release and return to the community.

The medical model perfectly fit the use of indeterminate sentences and parole. Offenders were sentenced to open-ended sentences, with the minimum term determined to meet society's need for punishment, deterrence, and incapacitation. After they met this threshold level of the sentence term, their release depended on how well their treatment plan worked to remedy their deficiencies and prepare

With the medical model of corrections, classification of inmates involved many professionals to evaluate the inmate and plan a treatment program. Courtesy of the Federal Bureau of Prisons.

them for successful return to the community. A parole board of rehabilitative experts was believed well suited to determine when inmates' treatments were complete and what would be optimal times for release from prison and supervision in the community. In most cases, treatment continued in the community under the supervision of parole officers.

Under this indeterminate sentencing structure, parole served many positive functions. First, dangerous inmates could be incarcerated for longer periods of time than if they had a determinate sentence, which would usually be shorter than the maximum time allowable under an indeterminate sentence. Parole boards regularly require dangerous, high-risk inmates to serve the maximum sentence. Colorado abolished parole as a release mechanism in 1979, but reinstated it after finding out that the length of prison sentences served was decreasing, particularly for high-risk offenders. Second, parole boards act as gatekeepers to ensure that inmates have sound release plans for their return to the community. For inmates to be released they must have a place to live and must address their possibilities of finding a job. If they have no community contacts, inmates are often released to a halfway house or given more time to develop a release plan. However, when a determinate sentence ends, there is usually no way to delay a release due to an insufficient plan.

Third, the fact that a parole board will review inmates is an incentive for good behavior and program participation by inmates. Opponents of parole criticize program participation that is done to impress the parole board and suggest that program participation with no implied coercion will be more effective. Halleck argued that it was almost impossible to distinguish between fully voluntary and coercive treatment participation, especially in a correctional setting in which decisions affecting offenders' parole considered such participation.[11] Morris, in *The Future of Imprisonment*, asserted that rehabilitation is a valuable correctional goal, yet it could not be effective if seen as coercive by offenders, or if they saw it as an element of the punishment they were receiving for their criminal offenses.[12] And Irwin argued that inmates viewed decisions of the parole board as arbitrary, capricious, prejudicial, unpredictable, and not subject to review by an external body.[13] However, there has been no evidence that nonvoluntary program participation was less effective than participation with some coercion.

A final positive function of parole is that consideration for release begins the process and creates guidelines for supervision and treatment needs in the community. Parole boards consider inmates' levels of risk and chances for success and create conditions for supervision and treatment to respond to these risks and needs. Without parole, even with mandatory supervision following determinate sentencing release, supervision is often less individualized and based primarily on risk rather than need. Abadinsky suggests that the medical model is based on two questionable assumptions:

- Criminals are "sick" and can thus benefit from treatment/therapy.
- The behavioral sciences can provide the necessary treatment/therapeutic methods.[14] Unfortunately, these two premises were seriously questioned during the 1970s.

Attacks on the Medical Model and Parole

The medical model came under attack during the early 1970s, partly precipitated after Robert Martinson and his colleagues attempted to determine what worked in correctional treatment. They reviewed 231 studies of correctional treatment programs and, although they found a few isolated correlations between a treatment program and a reduction in recidivism, there were no consistent findings of the effect of any single treatment program significantly reducing recidivism.[15] Therefore, the Martinson review concluded, "nothing works," which was just the support that opponents of the medical model and parole were looking for. For public officials desiring to reduce costs and make corrections more punitive, this study provided statistical support, and their arguments for a return to determinate sentences gained momentum.

New models for sentencing and release to replace parole began to be proposed by a variety of individuals with varied philosophical rationales. In 1975, David Fogel, a liberal former correctional official, argued that treatment in prison was a myth, and parole board discretion was unpredictable and unfair to inmates. He proposed the **justice model** as an alternative, in which he suggested the following:

justice model
the model for sentencing proposed by Fogel that would use flat, determinate sentences, eliminate parole boards, and make all treatment voluntary

- A return to flat, determinate sentences, with procedural rules to limit sentencing discretion
- The elimination of parole boards and parole agencies
- Making all treatment programs strictly voluntary[16]

just deserts model
a model for sentencing proposed by von Hirsch that had fixed sentences for each crime so that the punishment fit the crime

In 1976, conservative Andrew von Hirsch proposed the **just deserts model**, with a return to the classical model of criminology, letting the punishment fit the seriousness of the crime.[17] In this model, indeterminate sentences would be replaced with fixed sentences based solely on the severity of the crime and not on any individual offender characteristics. Also in 1976, the Twentieth Century Task Force on Sentencing proposed presumptive sentencing.[18] A presumptive sentencing system provides a sentence for each category of crime that would be imposed for a typical first-time offender (similar to the just deserts model). However, with this model, the sentencing judge has limited discretion to consider mitigating and aggravating circumstances that would reduce or increase the presumptive sentence.

The "nothing works" findings of Martinson and the criticism of parole by both the political right (for being too soft on crime) and left (for unpredictability and unfairness) created momentum toward abolishing parole and indeterminate sentences. In 1977, the use of parole reached its peak as more than 70 percent of prisoners were released on discretionary parole.[19] Over the next two

TABLE 6.1	Abolition of Discretionary Parole

Jurisdiction Abolishing Parole	Year Abolished
Maine	1975
Indiana	1977
Illinois	1978
Minnesota	1980
Florida	1983
Washington	1984
Federal government	1984
Oregon	1989
Delaware	1990
Kansas	1993
Arizona	1994
North Carolina	1994
Mississippi	1995
Virginia	1995
Ohio	1996
Wisconsin	1999

decades, fifteen states and the federal government ended the use of indeterminate sentencing and **discretionary parole,** in which the decision to release the offender is made by a parole board (see Table 6.1). Twenty other states severely limited the parole-eligible population. Only fifteen states still have full discretionary parole for inmates. The move to determinate sentences was a primary reason why the prison population grew more rapidly than in any other period in the history of prisons.[20] From 1980 to 1996, the number of prisoners in state and federal prisons went from 330,000 to 1,054,000, a threefold increase,[21] and reached 1.6 million on June 30, 2008.[22]

Parole has gone through several changes and transitions in its support, operations, and processes. Today there are at least three major methods (or statuses) in which inmates are released from prison. No consistent terminology is used to describe the three release statuses from jurisdiction to jurisdiction. The first is the use of discretionary parole, or release from prison to community supervision by the decision of a parole board, after completing the minimum portion of an indeterminate sentence. Parolees are required to meet certain conditions as a stipulation of their release and are subject to being returned to prison if they violate the conditions or commit another offense. A second status of inmate release is **supervised mandatory release** (also referred to as mandatory parole), the release of inmates after they have served a determinate sentence, but with a period of supervision in the community. Supervised mandatory release is a conditional release, as there are still requirements and conditions that must be met or fulfilled or offenders can be returned to prison. Finally, inmates can serve the full portion of their sentence, pay their full "debt to society," and have no supervision after release from prison. This status is often referred to as **unconditional mandatory release** or expiration of sentence.

The Bureau of Justice Statistics reports that the percentage of releases from state prisons on discretionary parole has continued to decline since 1980, as mandatory

discretionary parole
Release of inmates in which the decision to release is made by a parole board

supervised mandatory release
a type of release in which inmates serve a determinate sentence and are then released, but with a period of supervision to follow

unconditional mandatory release
a type of release in which inmates serve the full portion of their sentence and have no supervision after release from prison

Percentage of releases

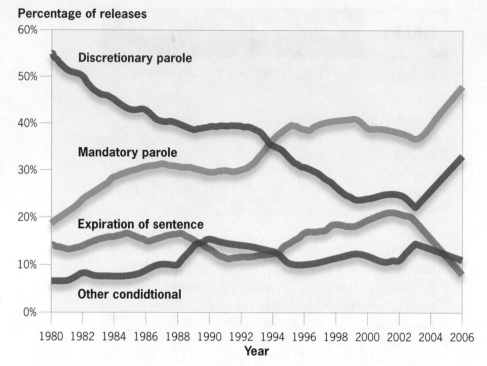

Source: Lauren E. Glaze and Thomas P. Bonczar, *Probation and Parole in the United States, 2006* (Washington, D.C.: U.S. Department of Justice, Bureau of Justice Statistics, December 2007), p. 6.

FIGURE 6.1   Releases from State Prison, by Method of Release, 1980–2006

parole and expiration of sentence releases increased (see Figure 6.1). In 2006, only 33 percent of inmates were released on discretionary parole, another 48 percent were released on mandatory parole with supervision, 9 percent were reinstated on parole after a brief prison stay, and 11 percent were released under other parole arrangements.[23]

Alternatives to Indeterminate Sentencing

The major emphasis of the move away from parole and indeterminate sentencing has been to limit discretion and to focus sentences more on offender accountability than on rehabilitation. Many of the states maintaining parole created mechanisms to ensure the consideration of community safety in parole board decisions. **Parole guidelines** were created as a means to reduce disparity and make decision making more understandable to the public and inmates. Parole guidelines, like sentencing guidelines, use predictive factors to determine the offenders' risk to the community and chance for success. Guidelines are then used to prescribe a presumptive time to be served based on the seriousness of the crime and the factors predictive of success for each inmate. The guidelines suggest a projected parole date after the inmate has served a set number of months, assuming good behavior during the prison term. Since guidelines are based on the severity of the sentence as well as factors predicting success, they focus on the "just deserts" form of sentencing.

The U.S. Parole Commission was the first to investigate the possibility of using guidelines during the mid-1970s and was required to use guidelines beginning in 1976 by the Parole Commission and Reorganization Act (Public Law 94–233). To develop the guidelines, the commission hired a group of researchers to identify the factors available to parole board members that are most salient to success on parole. The researchers found several factors regarding the past

parole guidelines
similar to sentencing guidelines, these use predictive factors to determine the offenders' risk to the community and chance for success; guidelines prescribe a presumptive time to be served based on the seriousness of the crime and the factors predictive of success for each inmate

SALIENT FACTOR SCORE (SFS 98)

Item A. PRIOR CONVICTIONS/ADJUDICATIONS *(ADULT OR JUVENILE)* . . . .

None = 3; One = 2; Two or three = 1; Four or more = 0

Item B. PRIOR COMMITMENT(S) OF MORE THAN 30 DAYS *(ADULT/JUVENILE)* . . . .

None = 2; One or two = 1; Three or more = 0

Item C. AGE AT CURRENT OFFENSE/PRIOR COMMITMENTS . . . .

26 years or more	Three or fewer prior commitments	= 3
	Four prior commitments	= 2
	Five or more commitments	= 1
22–25 years	Three or fewer prior commitments	= 2
	Four prior commitments	= 1
	Five or more commitments	= 0
20–21 years	Three or fewer prior commitments	= 1
	Four prior commitments	= 0
19 years or less	Any number of prior commitments	= 0

Item D. RECENT COMMITMENT FREE PERIOD *(THREE YEARS)* . . . .

No prior commitment of more than 30 days (adult or juvenile) or released to the community from last such commitment at least 3 years prior to the commencement of the current offense = 1; Otherwise = 0

Item E. PROBATION/PAROLE/CONFINEMENT/ESCAPE STATUS VIOLATOR THIS TIME . . .

Neither on probation, parole, confinement, or escape status at the time of the current offense; nor committed as a probation, parole, confinement, or escape status violator this time = 1; Otherwise = 0

Item F. OLDER OFFENDERS . . . .

If the offender was 41 years of age or more at the commencement of the current offense (and the total score from Items A–E above is 9 or less) = 1; Otherwise = 0

TOTAL SCORE . . . .

Source: U.S. Parole Commission, *Rules and Procedures Manual* (Washington, D.C.: U.S. Parole Commission 1998).

FIGURE 6.2 U.S. Parole Commission Salient Factor Score Sheet

history of offenses that are most predictive of success (or failure) after release. These factors are combined to find the **salient factor score** for inmates. The salient factors have been continually reviewed and validated. Figure 6.2 illustrates the most recent (1998) listing of six elements used to predict success. Each inmate is scored on the list of salient factors. The sum of the six factors is the score predicting success, with higher scores indicating a lower probability of recidivism.

The salient factor score is then inserted into the guidelines table (Figure 6.3). The categories of offenses are based on the severity of the crime. The combination of the offense severity and parole prognosis (salient factor score) then gives a guideline range for the number of months that should be served before release. As an example, for an offender in Category Five (which includes bank robbery and intent to sell hard drugs) who had a salient factor score of 6, the guidelines suggest a range of 36 to 48 months served before release. The parole board can consider other mitigating or aggravating circumstances of the offense or offender to set the release date within the guideline range.

After the federal government developed and began using guidelines, many states adopted similar guidelines for their parole decision making. Guidelines continually focus on the risk of the offender and make it more difficult to release offenders on parole. This overprediction of dangerousness results in the buildup of prison populations by increasing the amount of time that inmates serve prior to release.[24]

salient factor score
a point determination for each inmate for use with parole guidelines; the score is based on factors predictive of success on parole

GUIDELINES FOR DECISION MAKING
[Guidelines for Decision Making, Customary Total Time
to Be Served Before Release (Including Jail Time)]

OFFENSE CHARACTERISTICS	OFFENDER CHARACTERISTICS: Parole Prognosis (Salient Factor Score 1998)			
Severity of Offense Behavior	Very Good (10–8)	Good (7–6)	Fair (5–4)	Poor (3–0)
Category One	Guideline Range			
	<=4 months	<=8 months	8–12 months	12–16 months
Category Two	Guideline Range			
	<=6 months	<=10 months	12–16 months	16–22 months
Category Three	Guideline Range			
	<=10 months	12–16 months	18–24 months	24–32 months
Category Four	Guideline Range			
	12–18 months	20–26 months	26–34 months	34–44 months
Category Five	Guideline Range			
	24–36 months	36–48 months	48–60 months	60–72 months
Category Six	Guideline Range			
	40–52 months	52–64 months	64–78 months	78–100 months
Category Seven	Guideline Range			
	52–80 months	64–92 months	78–110 months	100–148 months
Category Eight*	Guideline Range			
	100+ months	120+ months	150+ months	180+ months

*Note: For Category Eight, no upper limits are specified due to the extreme variability of the cases within this category.

Source: U.S. Parole Commission, *Rules and Procedures Manual* (Washington, D.C.: U.S. Parole Commission, 1998).

FIGURE 6.3 U.S. Parole Commission Guidelines for Decision Making

Problems with Moving Away from Indeterminate Sentences

Although there are some valid reasons to adopt determinate sentences, there are also many problems with moving away from parole and indeterminate sentences, and often a poor fit between theory and practice in regards to "getting tough on criminals." These include the following:

1. With determinate sentences, inmates often serve shorter sentences and smaller portions of the sentence than with parole. Parole boards consider the dangerousness of offenders and often hold them in prison well beyond their minimum eligibility for parole.
2. Without parole, there are few ways to hold inmates accountable for misconduct in prison. Prison administrators miss the control and emphasis on prison discipline that resulted from inmates trying to have a good record to take before the parole board.
3. Elimination of parole does reduce discretionary release decisions, but prosecutorial discretion is just substituted for correctional discretion. One problem with prosecutorial discretion is that it is exercised in private, and there is no review or public consideration of the use of plea bargaining.
4. One advantage of the use of parole boards is that they can reduce disparity in sentencing decisions by individual judges if there are no sentencing guidelines.
5. Parole boards, although they do not admit to consciously trying to do so, can act as a safety valve for prison overcrowding. In more formal ways, parole boards have been used to identify the most deserving inmates for release when there is a need to do so due to prison crowding.[25]
6. In some states (such as Maine), abolishing parole has also included abolishing supervision after release.

Current Status of Parole in the United States

Parole and community supervision are still very important functions in several states. In fact, the number of offenders under state parole or mandatory release supervision at year-end 2007 was 731,692, which was almost a fourfold increase in the number of parolees or other postrelease supervision offenders in 1980 and a 3 percent increase over the year-end 2006 total.[26] Nearly all these offenders (96 percent) had been convicted of a felony and sentenced to incarceration of more than one year. Similar to the makeup of the adult prison population, a high percentage of minorities are under community supervision, with approximately 42 percent of parolees white, 37 percent black, and 19 percent Hispanic at the end of 2007. As of December 31, 2007, 12 percent of the parole population was female, an increase from 10 percent in 1995.[27]

This 2.3 percent growth during 2006 is greater than the average annual growth (1.5 percent) in the number of parolees from 1995 to 2006 (see Table 6.2). For the year ending December 31, 2007, eight states reported an increase of 10 percent or more in their parole populations, led by Rhode Island with a 39 percent increase, followed by Indiana (26 percent), West Virginia (20 percent), and Colorado (16 percent). Fourteen states reported a decrease in their adult parole populations during 2007. Connecticut decreased by 15 percent, South Carolina by 12 percent, and all others were less than 10 percent. In general, the states with significant positive and negative deviations change from year to year.[28]

Table 6.3 illustrates the number of adults on parole, the entries and exits, the percent change during 2007, and the number of parolees per 100,000 population in state and federal jurisdictions during 2007.

TABLE 6.2 Change in the Number of Adults on Parole, 1995–2006

Year	Annual Increase	
	Number	**Percent Change**
1995	−10,950	−1.6%
1996	312	0.0
1997	15,054	2.2
1998	1,598	0.2
1999	18,072	2.6
2000	9,441	1.3
2001	8,435	1.2
2002	18,601	2.5
2003	23,654	3.1
2004	20,230	2.7
2005	8,764	1.1
2006	17,586	2.2
Total increase, 1995–2006	85,934	12.6%
Average annual increase, 1995–2006	9,548	1.5%

Source: Lauren E. Glaze and Thomas Bonczar, *Probation and Parole in the United States, 2006* (Washington, D.C.: U.S. Department of Justice, Bureau of Justice Statistics, December 2007), p. 2.

TABLE 6.3 Adults on Parole, 2007

Region and Jurisdiction	Parole Population, 1/1/2007	2007				Parole Population, 12/31/2007	Percent Change, 2007	Number on Parole per 100,000 Adult Residents, 12/31/2007
		Entries		Exits				
		Reported	Imputed[a]	Reported	Imputed[a]			
U.S. total[b,c]	799,058	505,965	555,900	482,180	531,400	824,365	3.2%	360
Federal	88,993	43,077	43,077	39,397	39,397	92,673	4.1%	40
State[b,c]	710,065	462,888	512,800	442,783	492,000	731,692	3.0	319
Northeast	152,744	55,405	70,000	54,210	67,500	155,288	1.7%	367
Connecticut	2,567	2,319	2,319	2,709	2,709	2,177	−15.2	81
Maine	31	2	2	1	1	32	3.2	3
Massachusetts[d]	3,435	4,952	4,952	5,178	5,178	3,209	−6.6	64
New Hampshire	1,621	709	709	677	677	1,653	2.0	162
New Jersey	14,405	9,505	9,505	8,867	8,867	15,043	4.4	226
New York	53,001	25,467	25,467	24,799	24,799	53,699	1.3	360
Pennsylvania[e]	76,386	11,432	26,000	11,060	24,300	78,107	2.3	807
Rhode Island	332	515	515	385	385	462	39.2	56
Vermont[d,f]	966	504	504	534	534	936	−3.1	190

TABLE 6.3　Continued

Region and Jurisdiction	Parole Population, 1/1/2007	2007 Entries Reported	2007 Entries Imputed[a]	2007 Exits Reported	2007 Exits Imputed[a]	Parole Population, 12/31/2007	Percent Change, 2007	Number on Parole per 100,000 Adult Residents, 12/31/2007
Mideast[b]	130,821	71,105	105,400	64,837	99,800	136,343	4.2%	270
Illinois[d]	/	/	34,300	/	35,000	33,354	:	344
Indiana	8,205	9,217	9,217	7,060	7,060	10,362	26.3	217
Iowa	3,578	2,500	2,500	2,532	2,532	3,546	−0.9	155
Kansas[f]	4,886	5,278	5,278	5,322	5,322	4,842	−0.9	232
Michigan	18,486	13,373	13,373	10,528	10,528	21,131	14.3	277
Minnesota	4,445	5,715	5,715	5,416	5,416	4,744	6.7	120
Missouri	18,815	14,114	14,114	13,080	13,080	19,849	5.5	443
Nebraska	797	1,015	1,015	1,012	1,012	800	0.4	60
North Dakota	372	784	784	814	814	342	−8.1	69
Ohio	17,603	10,007	10,007	10,035	10,035	17,575	−0.2	201
South Dakota	2,767	1,845	1,845	1,800	1,800	2,812	1.6	466
Wisconsin	16,767	7,457	7,457	7,238	7,238	16,986	1.3	395
South[c]	238,484	106,989	108,000	101,793	102,800	243,512	2.1%	291
Alabama[d,g]	7,508	2,464	2,464	2,182	2,182	7,790	3.8	221
Arkansas	18,057	9,082	9,082	7,751	7,751	19,388	7.4	904
Delaware	544	366	366	375	375	535	−1.7	81
District of Coloumbia	5,341	2,468	2,468	2,240	2,240	5,569	4.3	1,169
Florida[d]	4,790	7,036	7,036	7,172	7,172	4,654	−2.8	33
Georgia	22,958	11,935	11,935	11,782	11,782	23,111	0.7	326
Kentucky	11,755	5,945	5,945	4,959	4,959	12,741	8.4	392
Louisiana	23,832	13,052	13,652	13,399	13,399	24,085	1.1	746
Maryland	14,351	7,122	7,122	7,617	7,617	13,856	−3.4	324
Mississippi	1,899	1,021	1,021	905	905	2,015	6.1	93
North Carolina[d]	3,326	3,552	3,552	3,477	3,477	3,311	2.3	48
Oklahoma[d]	/	/	1,000	/	1,000	/	:	:
South Carolina	2,766	599	599	932	932	2,433	−12.0	72
Tennessee	9,570	4,568	4,568	3,474	3,474	10,496	9.7	222
Texas[d]	100,053	33,897	33,897	32,202	32,202	101,748	1.7	582
Virginia[g]	7,201	1,845	1,845	2,196	2,196	6,850	−4.9	116
West Virginia	1,523	1,437	1,437	1,130	1,130	1,830	20.2	128

...continued

| TABLE 6.3 | Continued |

Region and Jurisdiction	Parole Population, 1/1/2007	2007 Entries Reported	2007 Entries Imputed[a]	2007 Exits Reported	2007 Exits Imputed[a]	Parole Population, 12/31/2007	Percent Change, 2007	Number on Parole per 100,000 Adult Residents, 12/31/2007
West	188,016	229,389	229,389	221,943	221,943	196,549	4.5%	373
Alaska[g]	1,527	709	709	692	692	1,544	1.1	305
Arizona[d]	6,463	14,862	14,862	14,518	14,518	6,807	5.3	144
California[f]	118,592	178,161	178,161	174,076	174,076	123,764	4.4	453
Colorado	9,551	9,089	9,089	7,554	7,554	11,086	16.1	299
Hawaii	2,308	694	694	892	892	2,110	−8.6	210
Idaho	2,732	1,689	1,689	1,307	1,307	3,114	14.0	282
Montana	844	769	769	647	647	966	14.5	130
Nevada	3,824	3,653	3,653	3,824	3,824	3,653	−4.5	189
New Mexico[d,f,g]	3,517	2,013	2,013	2,003	2,003	3,527	0.3	238
Oregon	22,031	9,210	9,210	8,583	8,583	22,658	2.8	779
Utah	3,342	2,524	2,524	2,269	2,269	3,597	7.6	194
Washington	12,611	5,708	5,708	5,302	5,302	13,017	3.2	262
Wyoming	674	308	308	276	276	706	4.7	176

Note: Because of nonresponse or incomplete data, the parole population for some jurisdictions on December 31, 2007, does not equal the population on January 1, plus entries, minus exits. Rates were computed using the estimated adult resident population in each state on January 1, 2008

/Not reported.

:Not calculated.

[a]Reflects reported data except for jurisdictions in which data were not available. see *Methodology*. Details may not sum to totals because of rounding.

[b]Includes an estimated 34,100 parolees under supervision in Illinois on January 1, 2007. See *Methodology*.

[c]Includes an estimated 3,100 parolees under supervision in Oklahoma on January 1 and December 31, 2007 See *Methodology*.

[d]Some or all data were estimated.

[e]Data for entries and exits were estimated for nonreporting county agencies. See *Methodology*. The December, 31, 2007, population includes 25,475 parolees under state parole supervision. Reported entries are parolees who entered state parole supervision through a discretionary release from prison.

[f]Excludes parolees in one of the following categories: absconder, out of state, inactive, or only have financial conditions remaining.

[g]Due to a change in recordkeeping procedures, data are not comparable to previous reports.

Source: Lauren E. Glaze and Thomas P. Bonczar, *Probation and Parole in the United States, 2007 Statistical Tables* (Washington, D.C.: U.S. Department of Justice, Bureau of Justice Statistics, December 2008), pp. 4, 5.

Operations of Parole

The sentencing and release process for discretionary parole includes three major steps: (1) an indeterminate sentence with a minimum time to serve before parole eligibility and a maximum term to be served if not paroled, (2) consideration of release by a parole board authorized to conditionally release offenders, and (3) supervision in the community under specific conditions. When inmates complete their minimum term, there is no guarantee that they will be released from prison. In fact, in the 1979 case of *Greenholtz v. Inmates of the Nebraska Penal and Correctional Complex*, the U.S. Supreme Court determined that parole was legally considered a privilege and not a right, and full due process rights need not be afforded.[29] If offenders are not granted parole at their first eligibility, the parole board continues them until a later time, when they will again receive a hearing and consideration of release. This process can be repeated until an inmate either is paroled or reaches the maximum sentence term.

The Organization of Parole Boards

Parole authorities can cover either or both of the two major parole functions: the release decision and postrelease supervision. In some states, two separate agencies are responsible for each of these parole functions. In others, the state department of corrections assumes responsibility for both functions. A third model is a separate parole decision-making authority, with parolees supervised by the state department of corrections. An important feature in the organization of parole decision making is that the parole board is independent from the administrators of the prisons. This can create problems if parole board members do not understand the programs provided within the prisons and what certain actions by prison officials may mean regarding an inmate's behavior and readiness for release. However, it would be a much greater problem if the parole board were overly influenced by prison staff opinions of the inmate. Boards are to independently consider the seriousness of the crime, the risk to the community, the chance for success, and institutional conduct and program participation as elements of their decisions.

For the past several decades, almost all parole boards consist of full-time employees of the state, and in most states the governor appoints parole board members. The size of the parole board can vary from two members in Minnesota to nineteen in New York.[30] Historically, governors appointed experts in criminology, social work, or community reintegration to best determine when offenders were rehabilitated and able to return to the community. In fact, the 1967 report of the President's Crime Commission recommended the appointment of parole board members on merit, including qualifications for prospective members of "broad academic background, especially in the behavioral sciences."[31] However, with the era of "tough on crime" attitudes and offender accountability, this has changed, and over the past twenty years the appointment of parole board members has become much more of a political decision.

As a result of parolees committing highly publicized crimes in the community, governors became very concerned about the impression of being soft on crime and letting dangerous criminals out of prison too early. Therefore, they often began to appoint less qualified (in terms of having a background in corrections or rehabilitation), yet politically connected individuals who can represent the governor's views on crime and community safety, rather than focusing on inmate preparation for release. Although this may be perceived as very reasonable, the practical problem is that there is no guarantee that any offender will be successful and avoid further criminality, and therefore every parole decision represents a political and community safety risk. As a result of the change in philosophy by parole boards, they are less likely to approve offenders for parole, and the average sentence served has increased as a result. During the 1990s the average time served before a parole decision to release increased from twenty-nine months in 1990 to thirty-five months in 1999.[32] The "An Insider's Experience" box illustrates the unique situation in Ohio regarding parole board appointments.

The Parole Hearing

In some states, the actual parole board members hold parole hearings in the prisons, whereas in other states **hearing officers** conduct the hearings and recommend decisions to the parole board, which confirms or modifies the decision. A few weeks after the hearing, the parole decision is communicated to the inmate

mycrimekit

Insider's Experience:
Appointing Parole
Board Members

hearing officers
Officials who are not appointed parole board members, yet they hold parole hearings and make recommendations to the parole board regarding inmates' release

Inmates appear before a parole board, and board members question them to determine whether they are ready to be released to the community. Courtesy of the Ohio Department of Rehabilitation and Correction.

in writing through the prison staff. It is unusual to have the final decision made and announced to the inmate at the hearing, but some procedures allow the hearing officers or board members conducting the hearing to immediately inform the inmate of their recommendation.

The hearing procedures vary by state. Although inmates are not provided full due process during a parole hearing, a few states allow inmates to have legal representation. At the beginning of the hearing, the board members or hearing officers review the file or records regarding the inmate and complete the parole guidelines if they are used in the jurisdiction. The prison staff usually provides a summary report of the inmate's background, criminal history, and performance while in prison. In most states, they do not make a recommendation regarding parole. The board also considers outside opinions from the inmate's family, law enforcement professionals, or victims regarding the inmate's parole. Some states allow victims to appear at the hearing, and others provide victims the chance to provide input in writing or through a personal meeting with board members prior to the parole hearing.

During hearings, inmates are asked to provide some background as to why they committed the crime, what they have done while in prison, and why they believe they are now ready to return to the community as productive and law-abiding citizens. The board also reviews and questions inmates regarding their release plans. The board is primarily interested in the inmates' plans for housing, employment, and continued participation in necessary treatment programs. Prior to the hearing, prison staff assist inmates in developing release plans, and these plans are forwarded to field parole offices for investigation into the validity of the plan.

After reviewing all material, hearing from the inmate, and receiving any outside input, parole boards decide whether to grant inmates parole at that time or to "continue" them (to serve a longer period of time) until a later date. Some parole boards give presumptive parole dates at the first hearing in many states; they hold the first hearing shortly after the inmate's incarceration, even before parole eligibility. A **presumptive parole date** is a date the inmate can expect to be released on parole, even if it is several years later than the hearing. The presumption is that if inmates have good institutional conduct and program participation they will be granted parole at that date. As the date nears, the prison staff provide the parole board a report as to the inmate's conduct and program participation. If the behavior and programming are as expected, the board confirms the date in writing without another hearing. If the board has some concerns regarding the inmate's prison performance, it may schedule a hearing and thereafter make a decision as to whether to parole or continue the inmate. If performance has been poor, the board

mycrimekit™

Media—Video: The Parole Decision

presumptive parole date

a date the inmate can expect to be released on parole, even if it is five or ten years later than the hearing

may do a continuance without a hearing and either reset another presumptive date or set a date for a later hearing.

Decisions regarding parole are seldom simple. The "You Make the Decision" box illustrates this point.

Supervision and Conditions of Parole

If the board grants parole (or if the inmate is granted supervised mandatory release), the inmate will also receive a list of conditions that must be followed during the period of supervision in the community. The list of conditions is similar to a contract between the parole board and the inmate. Inmates meeting the conditions can expect to be released from supervision successfully. However, if they violate conditions of supervision, they can expect to receive additional conditions or be returned to prison to serve more time on their sentence. There are two general types of parole conditions: *standard conditions* that are applicable to all parolees and *special conditions* pertaining to a particular parolee. Standard conditions of parole are usually the same as the standard conditions for probation described in Chapter 4, including reporting to their parole officers and keeping them informed of any changes in employment, residence, or other status. Figure 6.4 represents the conditions for community supervision for the state of Ohio for offenders released after serving a term in prison. After the statement of conditions, there is a brief statement of the supervision plan or activities required during the period of supervision. At the bottom of the form, releasees sign the conditions, indicating that they have received and understand the expectations of their supervision.

Special conditions of parole are again similar to special conditions of probation, such as a requirement for drug or alcohol counseling and testing, vocational training, mental health counseling, or other treatment programs; avoiding a particular person or group of people; residing in a halfway house; or being placed under electronic monitoring. The parole board considers the specific characteristics of each inmate when imposing special conditions that can add to the monitoring of the parolee, improve his or her rehabilitation and chance for success, or increase community safety.

Offenders on parole are supervised by a parole officer who monitors their compliance with the conditions of parole.

Photo courtesy of Bob Daemmrich Photography, Inc.

STATE OF OHIO
Department of Rehabilitation and Correction
Adult Parole Authority
CONDITIONS OF SUPERVISION

In consideration of having been granted supervision on ____ / ____ / ____ , I agree to report to my supervising officer according to the instructions I have received and the following conditions:

1. I will obey federal, state and local laws and ordinances, including Chapter 2923 of the Revised Code relating to conduct involving firearms and other deadly weapons, and all orders, rules and regulations of _____ County Common Pleas Court or the Department of Rehabilitation and Correction. I agree to conduct myself as a responsible law abiding citizen. I understand that if I am convicted of a new felony offense while under Post Release Control, the Court may impose an additional prison term consecutive to any prison sentence imposed for the new felony offense.

2. I will always keep my supervising officer informed of my residence and place of employment. I will obtain permission from my supervising officer before changing my residence or my employment. I understand that if I am a releasee and abscond supervision, I may be prosecuted for the crime of escape, under section 2921.34 of the Revised Code.

3. I will not leave the State of Ohio without written permission of the Adult Parole Authority.

4. I will not enter the grounds of any correctional facility nor attempt to visit any prisoner without the written permission of my supervising officer. I will not communicate with any prisoner in any manner without obtaining permission from my supervising officer.

5. I will follow all orders verbal or written given to me by my supervising officer or other authorized representatives of the Court or the Department of Rehabilitation and Correction.

6. I will not purchase, possess, own, use or have under my control, any firearms, ammunition, dangerous ordinance or weapons, including chemical agents, electronic devices used to immobilize, pyrotechnics and/or explosive devices.

7. I will not purchase, possess, use or have under my control any narcotic drug or other controlled substance or illegal drugs, including any instrument, device or other object used to administer drugs or to prepare them for administration, unless it is lawfully prescribed for me by a licensed physician. I agree to inform my supervising officer promptly of any such prescription and I agree to submit to drug testing if required by the Adult Parole Authority.

8. I will report any arrest, citation of a violation of the law, conviction or any other contact with a law enforcement officer to my supervising officer no later than the next business day. I will not enter into any agreement or other arrangement with any law enforcement agency which might place me in the position of violating any law or condition of my supervision, unless I have obtained permission in writing from the Adult Parole Authority, or from the Court.

9. I agree to a search, without warrant, of my person, my motor vehicle, or my place of residence by a supervising officer or other authorized representative of the Department of Rehabilitation and Correction at any time. *Notice: Pursuant to section 2967.131 of the Revised Code, Officers of the Adult Parole Authority may conduct warrantless searches of your person, your place of residence, your personal property, or any property which you have been given permission to use if they have reasonable grounds to believe that you are not abiding by the law or terms and conditions of your supervision.*

10. I agree to sign a release of confidential information from any public or private agency if requested to do so by a supervising officer.

11. I agree not to associate with persons having a criminal background and/or persons who may have gang affiliation, or who could influence me to engage in criminal activity, without the prior permission of my supervising officer.

12. I agree to comply with all financial obligations, including child support and/or supervision fees as ordered by any court and/or the Department of Rehabilitation and Correction.

13. I agree to give all information regarding my financial status to assist in determining my ability to pay specific financial obligations, to my supervising officer.

DRC 3019 (Rev 02/03)

FIGURE 6.4 Conditions of Supervision, Ohio Department of Rehabilitation and Correction

Source: Ohio Department of Rehabilitation and Correction, Policy Manual 3019, revised August 2003.

14. I agree to follow all rules and regulations of treatment facilities or programs of any type in which I am placed or ordered to attend while under the jurisdiction of the Court, and/or Department of Rehabilitation and Correction.

15. I agree to fully participate in, and successfully complete, the following indicated Sanctions/Special conditions:

16. I agree and understand that if I am arrested in any other state or territory of the United States or in any foreign country, my signature as witnessed at the end of the page will be deemed to be a waiver of extradition and that no other formalities will be required for an authorized agent of the State of Ohio to bring about my return to this state.

I understand that I am required to pay the Financial Obligations listed. Failure to do so will negate any eligibility for an early termination of supervision and result in civil suit by the Attorney General's Office.

Financial Obligations

Type	Supervision Fees	Fines	Restitution	Court Costs	Child Support	Other
Amount						
Payment Frequency						
Completion Date						

I understand that I have a grievance process available to me and may request a grievance form from my supervising officer at any time, *However,* I also understand that I may not grieve Parole Board or Court Ordered Special Conditions and/or Sanctions, being arrested for supervision violations, failure to follow directions/instructions of my supervising officer, the final decision of previous grievances, complaints unrelated to supervision, e.g., legislative action, judicial proceedings and sentencing, or any matter exclusively within the jurisdiction of the courts or other agencies, e.g. Human Services. The grievance procedure has been read and/or explained to me and I am indicating by my signature that I understand this process.

I have read or had read to me the conditions of my _____ . I fully understand these conditions and I agree to follow them. I understand that a violation of any of these conditions may result in the revocation of my _____ which may result in additional imposed sanctions, including imprisonment.

In addition, I understand that I must follow these conditions until notified by my supervising officer. By my signature I acknowledge that I have received a copy of these conditions of supervision. I further understand that I may request a meeting with my supervising officer or his/her supervisor if I feel any of the conditions or instructions are causing problems. I shall make this request in writing if at all possible.

I further acknowledge I understand that I am under the supervision of the Adult Parole Authority until I receive a certificate or journal entry terminating my period of supervision. Be advised, ORC 2967.16 (B) establishes the categories for final release from post release control as "favorable" or "unfavorable." If you receive an *unfavorable* final release from your post release control, this could result in an enhancement of any future felony sentence.

Witness:	Date:	Offender Signature:	Date:

FIGURE 6.4 Continued

Once offenders begin their terms of supervision, they are classified to determine their risk and needed frequency of contacts with their parole officer, the types of programs in which they should be involved, and any specific monitoring (such as intensive caseload or electronic monitoring) requirements. The purpose of classification is to assess the risk of the offender to commit further crimes and the need for treatment programs to improve the offender's chance for success. Most states and the federal government use some type of objective classification instrument as a guide for supervision strategies. Figure 6.5 is an example of risk assessment for community supervision and the variety of characteristics regarding history of crime, employment, and alcohol or drug use that affects classification. Each characteristic is scored, and the total score then determines the classification level. A serious history of substance abuse, mental illness, or some other treatment need may result in an immediate designation to an intensive caseload.[33] Otherwise, the supervision level is based on the assessment score as follows:

Basic high	Risk score of 28 and above
Basic medium	Risk score of 11 to 27
Basic low	Risk score of 10 or below

Based on the classification level, supervision policy often requires a certain minimum frequency of contacts, but additional contacts can be required if they are deemed necessary to meet the supervision needs of the individual offender:

Intensive: Five contacts per month, with at least one positive contact. For substance abusers, there should also be four drug tests per month.

Basic High: Three contacts per month with at least one positive contact. Substance abusers should be tested three times per month.

Basic Medium: One contact per month. Substance abusers should be tested twice per month.

Basic Low: No contacts required, but the offender completes and submits a form listing his or her activities related to jobs, residences, and so on. For substance abusers, there is one drug test per month.[34]

positive contact
Face to face contact between a parole officer and an offender

A **positive contact** is a face-to-face contact with the offender by the officer, and other contacts are those in which significant information is collected (from the offender or an ancillary service such as a treatment provider or employer). Currently, however, many parole agencies no longer specify a set number of contacts per risk level. Instead, the parole officer develops a supervision plan unique to the individual needs of the offender. In 2007, agencies reported that 84 percent of parolees were on active supervision, with weekly or monthly face-to-face contact with their supervision officer.[35]

Similar to probation, parolees are placed on a special caseload, regular caseload, or intensive caseload. Special caseloads are for offenders with a special treatment need, such as mental health, substance abuse, or sex offenses. Intensive caseloads are also for offenders with a special treatment need; however, they are more commonly used for offenders with a high level of risk for reoffending. In addition, some states use electronic monitoring for a small portion of their parolees. In most jurisdictions, those under electronic monitoring are placed on a caseload with others under electronic monitoring. On January 1, 2002, 87.0 percent of parolees were on regular caseloads, 5.3 percent on intensive caseloads, 5.0 percent on special caseloads, and 0.8 percent on electronic monitoring.[36]

ASSESSMENT OF OFFENDER RISK

Offender Name:		Offender #:
Date:	F.U. Date:	Unit Location:
Officer (Last, First):		

Select the appropriate answer and enter the associated weight in the score column. Total all scores to arrive at the risk assessment score.

<u>SCORE</u>

Number of Prior Felony Convictions: . . . .
(or Juvenile Adjudications)

  0 None
  2 One
  4 Two or more   _____

Arrested Within Five (5) Years Prior to Arrest . . . .
for Current Offense (Exclude Traffic):

  0 None
  4 Yes   _____

Age at Arrest Leading to First Felony Conviction: . . . .
(or Juvenile Adjudications)

  0 24 and over
  2 20–23
  4 19 and under   _____

Amount of Time Employed in the Last 12 Months:
(Prior to Incarceration for Parolees/PRC Offenders) . . . . .

  0 More than 7 months
  1 5 to 7 months
  2 Less than 5 months
  0 Not applicable   _____

Alcohol Usage Problems (Prior to Incarceration
for Parolees/PRC Offenders): . . . .

  0 No interference
    with functioning
  2 Occasional abuse;
    some disruption
    of functioning
  4 Frequent abuse;
    serious disruption;
    needs treatment   _____

Other Drug Usage Problems (Prior to Incarceration
for Parolees/PRC Offenders): . . . .

  0 No interference
    with functioning
  2 Occasional abuse;
    some disruption
    of functioning
  4 Frequent abuse;
    serious disruption;
    needs treatment   _____

Number of Prior Adult Incarcerations in a State
or Federal Institution: . . . .

  0 0
  3 1–2
  6 3 and above   _____

Age at Admission to Institution or Probation/Community
Control for Current Offense: . . . .

  0 30 and over
  3 18–29
  6 17 and under   _____

Number of Prior *Adult* Supervisions: . . . .

  0 None
  4 One or more   _____

Number of Prior Probation/Community Control/Parole/
PRC Revocations Resulting in Imprisonment
(Adult or Juvenile): . . . .

  0 None
  4 One or more   _____

TOTAL: _____

CLASSIFICATION CODE:

_____

1 INTENSIVE
2 BASIC HIGH (28 & above)
3 BASIC MEDIUM (11–27)
4 BASIC LOW (10 & below)
5 MONITORED TIME

OVERRIDE CODE:

_____

1 HIGHER
2 LOWER
3 NONE

IF OVERRIDE, SUPERVISOR'S
INITIALS:

_____

DRC 3001 (7/97)　　DISTRIBUTION:　WHITE–Central Records　　CANARY–District File

FIGURE 6.5　Assessment of Offender Risk

Source: Ohio Department of Rehabilitation and Correction, Policy Manual 3019, revised July 1997.

TABLE 6.4	Average Caseload per Officer during 2001 by Type of Caseload

Type of Caseload	Average Size of Caseload
Regular	63
Intensive	18
Special	35
Electronic	28

Source: Adapted from Camille Graham Camp and George M. Camp, *The 2002 Corrections Yearbook: Adult Systems* (Middletown, Conn.: Criminal Justice Institute, 2003), p. 195.

Table 6.4 lists the average size for each of these four types of caseloads. The average size of intensive, special, and electronic monitoring parole caseloads is almost equal to the same caseload types for probation. However, there is a significant difference between the average regular caseload size for parole (63) and that for probation (133) during 2001. It seems reasonable that parole caseloads be smaller, since they are made up of more serious offenders who received a sentence of prison rather than probation. "Your Career in Corrections" box describes the job of parole officers.

mycrimekit

Media—Video: Release from Prison

Terminating Parole Supervision

The length of parole supervision following release from prison can vary from six months to several years. Parolees can either successfully or unsuccessfully terminate their period of supervision. A Bureau of Justice Bulletin reveals that 44 percent of parolees in 2006 successfully terminated from supervision, whereas 39 percent were returned to incarceration for various reasons.[37] Most states allow for release from supervision before the end of the supervision period and before the date that ends the full maximum term of the inmate's sentence. For this to occur, the parole officer must write a recommendation detailing why the

Your Career in Corrections

Parole Officers

Parole officers are the line-level employees responsible for supervising parolees in the community from the time of their release until they either successfully leave supervision or have their parole revoked. Even though many states have abolished parole, almost all states still provide supervision after release. If not on parole, supervised offenders are often called mandatory releasees, and the supervision (by whatever the supervising officer is called) is the same as if on parole. The only difference is that the authority over the offender during supervision is usually held by the sentencing court, rather than by the parole board.

Officers usually have two primary tasks, supervision and investigations, with supervision making up approximately 80 percent of their responsibilities. Investigations determine the adequacy of the proposed release plans. A prison staff member transmits the proposed plan (including residence, job possibilities, program needs) to the officer, who interviews the person the inmate proposes to live with, prospective employers, and potential program providers. A report on the plan is then sent to the parole board. If the plan is not satisfactory, the parole officer usually suggests an alternative plan (such as living at a halfway house) to allow the inmate to have an adequate plan upon release.

In many jurisdictions, supervision of both parolees and probationers is done jointly by the same agency and many times by the same officers. Supervision entails scheduling offenders for office visits, visiting them in the community at their residence or job/program site, and interviewing significant individuals regarding offenders' progress and conduct. Officers may also place offenders into needed programs, such as substance abuse, parenting classes, or vocational training, and some officers run counseling groups. If offenders violate the conditions of their supervision, the officer must begin the revocation process by preparing a report of the violation and possibly an arrest warrant. Later in the process, the officer may have to testify at a revocation hearing regarding offenders' behavior during supervision.

On June 30, 2006, there were an estimated 14,00 full-time parole officers supervising nearly 528,000 parolees, which resulted in an average caseload of about 38 persons on active parole supervision.[38] Although a forty-hour week is standard, almost all officers (80.5 percent) report receiving overtime pay or compensatory time for hours in excess of the normal workweek.[39] Most states require a college degree, but no specific major is usually designated. In a survey of states in 2001, the average starting salary for parole officers was $31,652,[40] and a college career website reported that in 2004 the median salary for all parole officers was $39,600 per year, with the highest ten percent earning $66,660 per year.[41]

Parole officer jobs are challenging, yet can be very rewarding. There is considerable flexibility in hours worked and significant autonomy on how the job is done. Officers can have a major impact on the success of a parolee in the community. Many officers enjoy their jobs and maintain them throughout their working career, but others see their jobs as great work experience and use them to move into other criminal justice career tracks.

supervision should be terminated; the report is considered by the full board, which can agree and terminate supervision or disagree and continue the parolee's supervision. Unsuccessful terminations of parole result from revocation as a result of offenders violating the conditions of their supervision.

Table 6.5 illustrates the percentage of successful parole discharges by various characteristics of the parolees. Overall, the rate of successful discharges has remained steady from 2000 to 2006 with a successful rate of completion of 44 percent. As would be expected, parolees granted parole at first consideration are more successful than those released at later consideration, and the longer time they

mycrimekit

Careers in Corrections as a parole agent.

TABLE 6.5	Characteristics of Adults on Parole, 2000 and 2006	
	Percent of Adults Exiting Parole	
Type of Exit	**2000**	**2006**
Completions	43%	44%
Returned to incarceration	42	39
With new sentence	11	11
With revocation	30	26
Other/Unknown	1	2
Absconder	9	11
Other unsatisfactory	2	2
Transferred	1	1
Death	1	1
Other	2	3
Total estimated exits	459,400	519,200

Source: Lauren E. Glaze and Thomas P. Bonczar, *Probation and Parole in the United States, 2006* (Washington, D.C.: U.S. Department of Justice, Bureau of Justice Statistics, December 2007, NCJ 210676), p. 7.

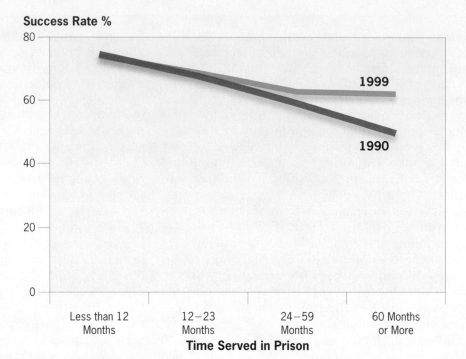

*First Releases only

Source: Adapted from Timothy A. Hughes, Doris James Wilson, and Allen J. Beck, *Trends in State Parole, 1990–2000* (Washington, D.C.: U.S. Department of Justice, Bureau of Justice Statistics, October 2001), p. 12.

FIGURE 6.6 Percent of Successful State Parole Discharges by Length of Time Served in Prison, 1990 and 1999.*

serve in prison, the less their success rate following release. As illustrated in Figure 6.6, in both 1990 and 1999, for first-time parole releases, the less time served, the higher the percent of successful parole completions. Very interesting, and discussed shortly, is the fact that inmates released under discretionary parole have a significantly higher success rate than those under mandatory parole.

Revoking Parole

If offenders do not meet the required conditions of their parole or mandatory release supervision, the violations will be reported to the parole board, which will consider what action to take. For released prisoners under mandatory release supervision, some states have created an authority similar to a parole board to review success during supervision; in other states the sentencing court continues to have jurisdiction during postprison supervision. There are two types of parole violations: technical violations of a standard or special condition of parole and new-crime violations when a conviction of a new crime occurs. When offenders commit a new crime, they can be prosecuted and sentenced for the crime, it is considered a violation of their original conditional release, and they can be processed as a parole violator in addition to the prosecution for the new offense.

When either type of violation occurs, a formal revocation process begins, which includes several steps: (1) determining that there is a violation, (2) a possible stipulated agreement, (3) notice of violation, (4) possible warrant for arrest and custody, (5) preliminary revocation hearing, (6) full revocation hearing, and (7) either reprimand/modification of conditions with return to supervision or violation and return to prison. Obviously, the first step is for the parole officer to determine that there is a **violation,** or failure to follow conditions of supervision. If the offender has committed a new crime, the officer usually receives a notice of arrest and charges from the local police and prosecutor. For technical violations, the officer must make the *determination of a violation.* Violations may be obvious, in that the offender fails a drug test or does not report to the officer as required; the officer may also determine

violation

Failure to follow conditions of parole supervision

In many jurisdictions, parole officers and parolees can agree on a stipulated agreement to modify conditions, as a way to respond to minor violations by the parolee. Photo by Richard P. Seiter.

a violation through his or her own investigation, such as if the offender has failed to maintain employment or has moved without notifying the officer.

The second step is authorized in most jurisdictions. If the violation is considered minor, yet does deem that action be taken, the parole officer may discuss the violation with the offender and propose a modification of the conditions of supervision with a continuation of parole. If the offender agrees, the officer writes a report that is referred to as a *stipulated agreement* in many states. In the federal system, it is referred to as an *action with consent and waiver*. In either case, since the offender agrees to the modification, the officer merely files the report with the parole board or supervising court. If the offender does not agree, the officer requests a hearing by the board or the court with a recommendation to modify the conditions.

When a violation occurs and the offender does not cooperate or absconds from supervision and cannot be found, the officer writes a *notice of violation* to the supervising authority and may request a *warrant for arrest and custody* if the officer believes that the offender should be taken into custody. The authority then schedules a preliminary hearing. The offender receives a notice of the violation, with a listing of the alleged violations and date of the preliminary hearing (usually required within fifteen days of notice of violation or arrest warrant). The purpose of the preliminary hearing is to determine whether *probable cause* exists to believe that the offender has committed the violation. This is particularly important if offenders have been taken into custody, as the preliminary hearing allows a timely determination of whether they should continue to be held pending the full revocation hearing. Offenders may waive the preliminary hearing and proceed to the revocation hearing. If they choose to have the hearing, the officer presents the evidence of the violation before a hearing officer, usually an attorney employed full time by the authority to conduct such hearings. At the hearing, offenders have limited due process rights to have legal representation, challenge the evidence, confront witnesses, and present evidence on their behalf. If the hearing officer determines that there is probable cause, the parolee is held in custody until the full revocation hearing.

The *full revocation hearing* is similar to the preliminary hearing, except that it is more comprehensive. It is held within ninety days of the preliminary hearing, and its purpose is to determine whether a violation of parole is serious enough to warrant a return to prison. The hearing is presided over by parole board members or the sentencing court for mandatory release violators. All activities during the supervision of the offender are reviewed, to include positive adjustment as well as the violation. The board or court can take one of three actions if they determine that the offender violated conditions of release. First, they can return the offender to supervision with no modification of conditions. This is unlikely; if the violation was serious enough to warrant a revocation hearing, there is probably the need to modify the conditions. Second, the offender can be returned to supervision with a modification of conditions. Finally, the offender's conditional release can be revoked and the offender returned to prison to serve additional time.

Legal Issues Regarding Revocation

Morrissey v. Brewer

A 1972 U.S. Supreme Court decision that once parole is granted, a liberty interest is created and offenders must have certain dur process to revoke that liberty

The principal case regarding parole revocation was the 1972 U.S. Supreme Court decision ***Morrissey v. Brewer***.[42] While recognizing the Greenholtz decision that parole is a privilege and not a right and that full due process is not required, the Court noted that once parole is granted a liberty interest is created, and offenders must have certain due process rights in actions to revoke that liberty. The limited due process that must be followed in the revocation process includes the following:

- The parolee is provided advance written notice of the alleged violation and the evidence of the violation.
- The parolee must have the opportunity to attend the hearing and present witnesses and documentary evidence.
- The parolee has the right to confront and cross-examine adverse witnesses.
- A neutral and detached body must hold the hearing.
- The parolee must receive a written decision of the hearing body, as well as the evidence relied upon to revoke the parole.

The *Morrissey* case did not, however, establish the right to counsel during the revocation process. In 1973, in *Gagnon v. Scarpelli*, the U.S. Supreme Court did extend the *Morrissey* due process rights to probationers during revocation proceedings and established that parolees have a limited right to counsel and that the hearing body must determine whether counsel shall be provided to the offender.[43] These two cases are the primary ones that influenced the required process for parole revocations described previously.

Effectiveness of Parole

Views on the effectiveness of parole vary. Parole is often criticized for the wrong reasons, primarily because the public believes that parole is a lenient approach to incarceration and lets dangerous criminals out of prison early. In reality (or at least by design), when indeterminate sentences are created in the penal codes by state legislatures, the minimum time is the term determined to hold offenders accountable for their crimes and satisfy the sentencing goals of punishment, deterrence, and incapacitation. Release at any time after the minimum then considers the individual characteristics of offenders, such as any aggravating circumstances of their crime, dangerousness, and potential for rehabilitation.

To examine the effectiveness of parole, a definition of effectiveness must first be agreed on, although several definitions are often used. First, effectiveness can be defined in terms of how many (or what percentage of) offenders successfully complete their terms of supervision. The U.S. Department of Justice reports that, of the more than 519,200 parolees discharged from supervision in 2006, 44 percent had successfully met the conditions of their supervision, and 39 percent had been returned to incarceration because of either a rule violation or a new offense.

An additional 11 percent had absconded and 2 percent failed to successfully meet the conditions of supervision but were discharged without incarceration. The success rate among those discharged from parole dropped from 50 percent in 1990.[44]

During 2006, 179,259 parole violators were admitted to adult prisons in the United States. It is interesting to note, however, that about 5 percent were returned to incarceration as a result of a new offense, a figure unchanged since 1998.[45] Over the past decade, there has been less tolerance for technical violations of parole, offenders are more likely to be returned for violations that do not include committing a new felony, and parole failures now constitute a growing proportion of all new prison admissions. In 2000 there were a reported 203,569 parole violators being admitted into prison or about 35 percent of the new admissions. This figure increased to 248,923, or about 36 percent by 2007.[46] Parole agencies are hesitant to take the risk of continuing offenders on parole who are not following the conditions of the release, in case they later commit a crime and the parole agency is blamed for not violating them for the technical violation.

A second definition of effectiveness considers the percentage of offenders who do (or do not) recidivate by committing new crimes or being returned to prison. A thorough review of recidivism among released inmates was a study completed by Langan and Levin for the Bureau of Justice Statistics in 2004. The report states, "Of the two-thirds persons released from prisons in 15 states in 1994, an estimated 67.5% were rearrested for a felony or serious misdemeanor within 3 years, 46.9% were reconvicted, and 51.8% returned to prison or jail."[47] The findings also indicate that rearrest rates were the highest during the first year (see Table 6.6). Although not all the released inmates were on parole, most states still used parole as a release mechanism in 1983. These numbers are obviously not a strong endorsement that parole works, yet the figures must be considered both in terms of the size of parole caseloads and how much supervision parolees received, as well as whether they would have recidivated at the same rate if not conditionally released on parole.

Therefore, the third and perhaps the most valid measure of effectiveness is how parole and the supervision following discretionary release compare to unconditional mandatory release without parole or supervision. In a study by Sacks and Logan to determine the effect of supervision after release, parolees who received supervision

TABLE 6.6	Recidivism Rates of Prisoners Released in 1994 from Prisons in 15 States, by Time after Release		
	Cumulative Percent of Released Prisoners Who Were:		
Time after Release	**Rearrested**	**Reconvicted**[a]	**Returned to Prison with New Sentence**[b]
6 months	29.9%	10.6%	5.0%
1 year	44.1	21.5	10.4
2 years	59.2	36.4	18.8
3 years	67.5	46.9	25.4

[a]Because of missing data, prisoners released in Ohio were excluded from the calculation of percent reconvicted.

[b]"New sentence" includes sentence to state or federal prisons, but not to local jails. Because of missing data, prisoners released in Ohio and Virginia were excluded from the calculation of "Percent returned to prison with a new prison sentence."

Source: Patrick A. Langan and David J. Levin, *Recidivism of Prisoners Released in 1994* (Washington, D.C.: U.S. Department of Justice, Bureau of Justice Statistics, 2002), p. 3.

TABLE 6.7	Percentage of Successful State Parole Discharges, by Method of Release		
		Method of Release	
Year	**All Discharges**	**Discretionary Parole**	**Mandatory Parole**
1990	44.6%	51.6%	23.8%
1991	46.8	52.6	24.9
1992	48.6	50.7	29.8
1993	46.9	54.8	33.5
1994	44.3	52.2	30.4
1995	44.3	54.3	28.0
1996	45.2	55.9	30.2
1997	43.4	55.8	30.8
1998	43.8	55.3	32.2
1999	41.9	54.1	33.1

Source: Timothy A. Hughes, Doris James Wilson, and Allen J. Beck, *Trends in State Parole, 1990–2000* (Washington, D.C.: U.S. Department of Justice, Bureau of Justice Statistics, October 2001), p. 11.

were compared to a group of court-ordered prison releasees who received no supervision, in terms of recidivism defined as conviction of a new felony or misdemeanor. After three years, the parole group recidivated at a rate of 77 percent, whereas the group receiving no supervision recidivated at a rate of 85 percent.[48] In addition, a federal study compared prison releasees who received supervision with those receiving no supervision after release. In a review of those who recidivated and were returned to prison, the average time remaining in the community before return to prison was seventeen months for those receiving supervision and only thirteen months for those without supervision.[49] Finally, the Bureau of Justice Statistics compares the percentage of successful discharges from parole by method of release (see Table 6.7). In each year from 1990 to 1999, inmates released under discretionary parole (by the decision of a parole board)were more successful than those under mandatory parole (those released after serving a determinate sentence with supervision to follow).

In the "A Question of Policy" box, consider the issue of the future of parole.

A Question of Policy

Should Parole Be Saved?

Parole has been commonly acknowledged to aid prisoner reentry in several ways, and with the indeterminate sentencing structure, parole served many positive functions. First, extremely dangerous inmates were often detained in prisons longer than they would have been under a determinate sentence structure. Determinate sentences are usually shorter than indeterminate sentences, and parole boards regularly require dangerous, high-risk

inmates to serve the maximum sentence. The state of Colorado abolished parole as a release mechanism in 1979, but reinstated it after finding out that the length of prison sentences served was decreasing, particularly for high-risk offenders.

Second, parole boards do act as a gatekeeper to ensure that inmates have solid release plans when they return to the community. Parole boards always ask inmates questions such as, "Where will you live when you get out of prison?" and "What job opportunities are available to you?" The boards also have reports available to them from parole officers who have investigated the inmates' release plans. Third, the existence of parole is an incentive for good behavior by inmates and an incentive for program participation that can be beneficial, even if not truly voluntary. There is no evidence that nonvoluntary program participation is less effective than participation with some coercion, and recent data indicate the benefit of participation in a variety of prison programs (cognitive skills training, drug treatment programs, education and work programs, and treatment of sex offenders) on reducing recidivism.[50]

Finally, parole consideration sets the framework for supervision and treatment needs following release. Parole boards create conditions under which parolees must be supervised and attend treatment programs from which they would benefit. Without parole, supervision is less individualized and based on risk rather than need, setting supervision levels based primarily on offenders' history of criminal behavior.

With these issues in mind, students should struggle with the policy question of whether parole should be continued in the states that still have it or reestablished in states that have abolished it. There is no question that the abolition of indeterminate sentences and parole has affected the increase in the number of prisoners. Yet there are many valid reasons why determinate sentences are seen as advantageous. List the pros and cons of parole, and decide whether you think it should be saved.

Prisoner Reentry: A Changing Phenomenon

The prison population in the United States has grown tremendously, with 1.6 million prisoners currently in federal and state prisons. With so much attention on the number of offenders in prison, until recently little attention has been paid to the fact that many more offenders are also leaving prison and returning to the community than at any prior time in history. During 2007, 725,402 prisoners were released by adult prisons, an increase from 120,544 in 2000.[51] In the state of California, 178,161 prisoners left prisons after completing their sentences in 2007, more than ten times the number of releases only twenty years earlier.[52]

This high number of offenders returning to their communities, many without parole supervision and some with no supervision, has created new issues regarding **prisoner reentry**. The issues of finding housing, lack of ties with family and friends, finding a job, alcohol and drug abuse, continued involvement in crime, and the impact of parole supervision were described in a study by the Vera Institute of Justice.[53] In addition, Petersilia identified six collateral consequences of imprisonment: (1) community cohesion; (2) employment and economic well-being; (3) democratic participation and political alienation; (4) family stabilization and childhood development; (5) mental and physical health; and (6) homelessness. These are the result of recycling parolees in and out of families and communities.[54] These issues and consequences make it difficult for ex-inmates to avoid a return to crime, and therefore it is critical that prisons have programs to prepare inmates for what they will face upon release and return to the communities.

The world of prisons is very different from the world inmates face when they are released, and the transition from prison to the community often seems surreal to offenders. One ex-offender characterized his experience in leaving prison and returning to the community as "like entering Disneyland" and further describes his release:

> Leaving prison after all those years was like entering a strange new world. Inside I was a respected convict. I knew where I stood with others, how to act, and what to expect. Once outside in the "free world," everything changed. Moreover, my self-concept and orientation got flipped on its head.[55]

prisoner reentry
the process of an inmate leaving prison and returning to the community

Prisoners have been released from prison for more than two hundred years, yet reentry is currently very different from only a few decades ago. These differences include the following:

1. Many more offenders are released from prisons than in the past.
2. Many prisoners are released after serving a determinate sentence, and some have no supervision requirements after release.
3. Prisoners are serving significantly longer prison terms.
4. Only a small percentage of inmates receive the benefit of extensive rehabilitation or prerelease programs.
5. The communities to which prisoners return are more disorganized, their families are less likely to be supportive, and they find fewer social services available to them in the community.
6. With reduced tolerance for risk, a larger number of releasees are returned to prison for commission of new crimes or for violating the technical conditions of their parole or release supervision.

These differences result from many factors, including a "tough on crime" attitude, reduced funding for prison programs and community social services, a weakening of the traditional support structures within communities and neighborhoods, and less (sometimes zero) tolerance for lapses by prison releasees under official supervision. The changing nature of prisoner reentry has made successful transitions from prison to community more difficult. For much of the twentieth century, preparation for release was considered an important part of the prison experience, and all states used indeterminate sentences with release by parole boards to assist in determining offenders' release preparation. The medical model emphasized that prisons should provide programs to prepare inmates for release. Educational and vocational programs, substance abuse and other counseling programs, therapeutic communities and other residential programs, and prison industry work programs were important parts of prison operations.

When prisoners were nearing release, extensive efforts were made to ease their transition to the community. Parole boards closely reviewed inmates' release plans in consideration of parole, and community parole officers investigated the

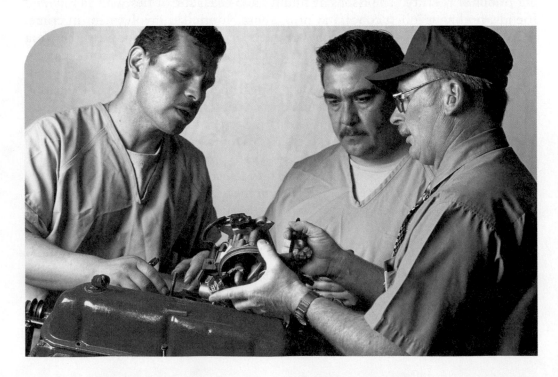

Learning a skill and developing good work habits is part of an effective program for successful reentry to the community from prison.

Photo reprinted with permission of the Corrections Corporation of America.

plans and reported on their acceptability to the parole board. If there were not acceptable plans, inmates were usually released through a halfway house so they could be assisted with issues of housing, employment, family relationships, and mental health or substance abuse counseling. Correctional officials recognized the difficulty in the prison-to-community transition, and reintegrative programs were expanded and developed to ease the transition. There was experimentation with specialized caseloads, the use of volunteers in parole, and even ex-offenders as parole officer aides. Inmates' return to the community was intensely supervised. Parole officers' primary responsibility was to guide offenders to programs and services and supervise their successful completion of parole.

Changes Over the Past Two Decades

Over the past two decades, however, this traditional process began to deteriorate. The demise of the medical model, the "tough on crime" attitude of the public and elected officials, the belief that rehabilitation did not work, the reduced funding for prison and transitional programs, and the change in parole supervision from casework to surveillance changed the model of release used until the 1980s. The current model of prison operations and prisoner reentry focuses less on inmate rehabilitation and preparation for release than on punishment, deterrence, and incapacitation. Most offenders serve a determinate sentence that is much longer than in the past. Inmates are seen as making a conscious decision to commit crimes, and punishment is believed important to produce a proper deterrent effect. Prison programs are considered valuable to keep inmates busy and maintain order, more than for release preparation. Without parole boards in many states, there is no gatekeeper to review the inmate's preparation and release plans. After release, if the offender is under supervision, there is little tolerance for drug use, technical violations, and minor criminal behavior, and offenders are quickly returned to prison for even minor violations.

Most inmates face serious problems, and there are not enough programs within prison to deal with them. Many inmates have long histories of criminal involvement and substance abuse, are gang members, and have few marketable skills. With the decline of support for mental illness by states, a greater number of mentally ill people are being admitted to prisons and jails, as a recent survey revealed that nearly one in five U.S. prisoners report having a mental illness.[56] In 1997, only about one of six prisoners who had used alcohol or drugs in the month before the offense for which they were incarcerated received substance abuse treatment while in prison.[57]

Programs that are effective in improving prisoner reentry, such as work and prison industry programs, substance abuse counseling, sex offender programs, and release from prison through a halfway house, are available only to small numbers of inmates. However, as of December 30, 2005, only 31 percent of all prisons offered prison industries, 28 percent offered work release, 36 percent offered sex offender programs, and 74 percent offered drug or alcohol dependency counseling.[58] And on January 1, 2002, state and federal prisons reported only 117,945 inmates (12.9 percent) in drug treatment programs, a decline of more than 50,000 inmates since 2000.[59] On the same date, only 78,881 inmates (7.8 percent) were assigned to prison industries, which have been found extremely successful in improving work skills and reducing recidivism.[60] Only 12,192 inmates (2.6 percent) were enrolled in sex offender programs on January 1, 2002.[61] Only 31,390 inmates were placed in halfway houses during 2004, yet this represented only 4.7 percent of the 669,132 inmates released from state and federal prisons that year.[62] And, during 2001, only 59,180 inmates were placed in work or study release.[63]

Petersilia reports that parole and release officers also have a difficult challenge. In the 1970s, parole officers handled an average caseload of approximately forty-five parolees, but the average caseload is now more than seventy. Approximately 80 percent of all parolees are supervised on these large regular caseloads and result in an average of less than two 15-minute face-to-face contacts with the parole officer each month.[64] And in 2004 nearly 19 percent left prison under expiration of sentence and had no postrelease supervision.[65]

Issues Faced by Offenders Returning to the Community

Many obvious issues face offenders after they serve long sentences in prison and then try to return to their communities, find jobs, support their families, and have a crime-free lifestyle. Simply finding a suitable place to live is difficult. Most ex-offenders have few financial resources when they leave prison, cannot afford high monthly rents or the required deposits of first and last months' rent, and therefore must look for public housing. Unfortunately, some public laws allow providers of federally assisted housing to exclude individuals with a criminal record from receiving public housing.[66]

Incarceration also disrupts relationships with offenders and their families. In a three-year study of the incarceration of males in the District of Columbia (of which 10 percent of African American men between ages 18 and 35 were imprisoned), findings indicate that a result of the extensive use of incarceration was "injuring the families of prisoners often as much as and sometimes more than criminal offenders themselves."[67] The incarceration not only affected the ability of the offender to support the family and provide child care, but also diminished the relationship between husband and wife and father and children. Most males in prison are fathers and maintain monthly contact with their children.[68] However, these men fail to offer support as a parent or serve as a positive role model for their children. Incarceration further strains these relationships and makes it difficult for families to stay together even after the prisoner is released.

mycrimekit

Media—Video: The Transition from Prison

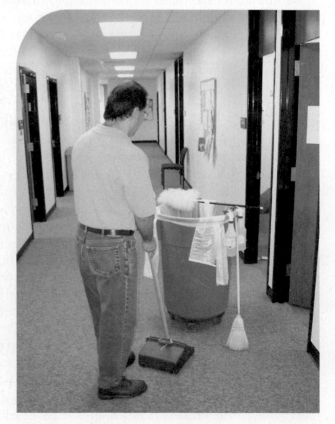

Many former offenders can find only low-paying, entry-level jobs during these difficult economic times. Employment is key to successful reentry. Photo by Richard P. Seiter.

Finally, it is not easy for ex-inmates to find suitable employment, particularly in difficult economic times. In these conditions, employers are less likely to hire ex-offenders, and a larger percentage of former prisoners are unable to find and keep jobs. In the "get tough on criminals" movement, legislatures place more statutory restrictions on ex-offenders. In many states, ex-prisoners are restricted from working in the professions of law, real estate, medicine, nursing, physical therapy, education, dentistry, engineering, and pharmacology. Suitable employment for ex-offenders is difficult to find, yet we continue to recognize that employment is one of the most important vehicles for improving offender reintegration and increasing desistance from crime.[69] Uggen and Staff consider work a turning point for offenders, noting the research indicating a relationship between work and crime and that the quality of employment is important for reducing recidivism.[70] The potentials for obtaining quality work, finding suitable housing, and maintaining strong family relationships are all negatively affected by long terms of imprisonment. A 2008

An Interview With...

An Ex-Offender

Reentry of prisoners is extremely difficult and many ex-offenders fail and go back to prison. The following interview regarding prisoner reentry was with Dr. Charles Terry, a professor of criminal justice who served four terms of imprisonment (a total of approximately twelve years during the 1970s and 1980s) and was in and out of local jails several more times.

Question: Dr. Terry, can you provide a brief history of your criminal life and incarceration?

Dr. Terry: I was first sent to prison at the California Rehabilitation Center (CRC) in 1975. I served fifteen months, was released, but committed another burglary to buy drugs and was returned to prison within two months. I was sent to the California Correctional Center (CCC) at Susanville for sixteen months, released, and again out for two months. I committed another crime to buy drugs and was put in jail. Somehow I beat the case and was released. I tried to get jobs, but no one would hire me. I finally got a job as a dishwasher. I continued to use drugs, and even though I had eight dirty UAs (positive urine tests indicating the use of drugs), my parole officer believed I was not doing crimes, so she let me stay out. Finally, after the eighth dirty UA, she told me either she had to violate me, or I had to go on methadone maintenance, which was a substitute for heroin. After one and a half years on methadone and doing pretty well, I decided to get off the methadone. But as I gradually reduced the dosage of methadone, I got sick, and decided I might as well use heroin to feel better. I started

to just use enough to not be sick, but it just got worse and worse. Soon, I ran out of money to buy heroin, committed another burglary, and got caught.

California by then had determinate sentencing, and I got a three year sentence. I was sent to the California Correctional Institution (CCI) at Tehachapi, but manipulated a transfer to the Sierra Conservation Center (SCC) in Jamestown. In 1981, I was released after serving two years. I went home to Santa Barbara, but moved to Oregon to try to stay out of trouble. I stayed out three years, had a job, and was doing OK. Parole supervision in Oregon was minimal. I just had to report in; they did not do UAs. I started using heroin again, got busted, and was sent to the Oregon State Penitentiary (OSP) for six and a half years for burglaries. I got out in 1990, and have been out since.

Question: What made the difference the last time that allowed you to stay out?

Dr. Terry: I started taking some education classes at OSP, did pretty well, and found that I liked to read and learn. The teachers were competent and caring people who treated us like human beings. After two years of school, I began to make a radical shift in self-concept. About ninety days before I was to be paroled, I injected a good dose of heroin: and remember wondering why I wasted so much of my life for this feeling. I then believed I could go straight without the use of heroin. My parole plans were vague, but I wanted to go to college. I knew I

...continued

was institutionalized, but knew school was an institution, so I would just switch college with prison. School became a substitute for using drugs. I really don't think I would have changed if I hadn't become interested in school.

Question: What do you think is the biggest detriment to prisoners making a successful transition from prison to the community?

Dr. Terry: Prisonization. It is totally assimilation into the prison culture. This means you see the world through the eyes of someone adapted to the prison culture. It is not a reflection of the individual, but of the culture. The attributes of prisonization that are important for living in prison (don't tell on anyone, don't show weakness, mind your own business) are not those of the streets, and continuing to live the prison culture makes it more difficult to move to the street. The more time I did inside prison, the more alienated I felt around nonconvicts. Because in this culture, you are able to live with self-respect, dignity, others respect you. One central effect of prisonization is resistance; you learn to resist everything (pains of imprisonment, authority). This is counter to the norms of a successful life on the street. For instance, you get this "I don't give a damn" attitude, and you have tattoos all over you. A convict in prison has respect, knows the system, what to expect. He knows and enjoys the routine. You leave your cell, go to work, go work out, know there will be certain food for certain meals. Once you get out, the comfortable familiarity is gone. The convict status you had in prison is seen as something strange in the community. Therefore, you experience more alienation. To me, that is the biggest obstacle to a successful transition.

Question: How did you decide to become a "convict," in prison, and adopt the culture of the prison?

Dr. Terry: I did not just decide to be a convict rather than square john. When I first went to prison I thought these inmates or convicts were really strange people, and I did not want to be like them. But over time, I moved more and more in this direction. I saw these guys that had adapted to the prison life, with tattoos, working out and getting big, laughing and joking, and seemed to not be having a bad time. This seemed like a magnet to me. I also wanted to not have a bad time, so I gradually started to move in that direction in terms of my behavior, appearance, and attitude. Becoming a convict took years for me, because I came from a middle-class background. If you come from the inner city, you adjust to the prison life pretty quick. I just used all the information I collected and the lessons I learned from the guys I hung out with. I think the younger a person is when they go into prison, the more likely they are to become prisonized. You see people go in one way, and come out very different.

Question: How do inmates overcome prisonization to be successful once they get out?

Dr. Terry: The more social support you have, the better your chances of staying out. If you have a support system, you feel safe. You know you have people that will take you as you are and provide you the support you need as you try to find work and, as my goal always was, "to do good." I did not know what "doing good" meant, but I always had that intention.

But regardless of what support you have, it is hard. You get a job, maybe a girlfriend, and at first it seems like things will be fine, as you are just glad to get out. But soon you realize you don't like your job, you don't like the "old lady," and gradually the excitement of getting out is not enough, and you begin to feel more and more like there is something missing. You may actually miss being with the guys in prison, working out, hanging out, and laughing and joking around. The gap between the two worlds narrows as you learn to do OK in the community or stay off drugs. I was involved in NA and hanging out with other NA guys, most of whom were also convicts. We were learning together, found out how to ask for help, and how to change the effects of prisonization.

Question: What is the most important change we can make to improve the likelihood of successful reentry for prisoners?

Dr. Terry: The most important thing we can do is to keep time spent in prison to the least possible time, thereby reducing the likelihood and impact of prisonization.

In addition, the focus taken by most criminologists is that the support outside is very important. That is true, but beyond that, we need a different reference group. When I go into a grocery store, I look around, and everything seems so strange. There are no guards to tell me where to go and what to do, food is everywhere, but I am always surprised that they expect me to pay for this stuff. The norms and values associated with the world outside prison are just too different from the world inside.

survey illustrated the critical nature of release planning and identified seven basic needs that should be addressed for inmates before they leave prison. These include transportation, clothing and food, financial resources, housing, employment and education, health care, and support systems.[71] Reentry programs must address these collateral consequences to improve offenders' chances for successful and crime-free lives. The following "An Interview With" box illustrates many of the issues facing offenders as they come out of prison.

Recent Progress in Prisoner Reentry

Over the past few years, there has been considerable progress in the understanding of reentry issues and the development of programs to improve successful reentry. The Urban Institute launched a "policy conversation" by hosting an ongoing forum of academics, correctional practitioners, community leaders, policymakers, advocates, and former prisoners, and published several reports as a result of these discussions. Soon thereafter, the Re-Entry Policy Council—a bipartisan collection of nearly one hundred elected officials, policymakers, and practitioners— was formed. In 2005, they released a comprehensive set of recommendations to reduce recidivism and help ex-offenders succeed in their communities.[72]

These recommendations received strong support and were the impetus for President Bush including the issue of prisoner reentry in his 2005 State of the Union. In the address, he proposed a four-year $300 million prisoner reentry initiative to expand job training and placement services, to provide transitional housing, and to help newly released prisoners get mentoring. In 2007, the Second Chance Act (H.R. 1593 / S. 1060) was introduced in Congress with 92 cosponsors in the House and 33 cosponsors in the Senate.[73] The act was passed in both houses and signed into law by President Bush in 2008. The act as passed will ease the reentry process for individuals leaving prison by providing funding for prisoner mentoring programs, job training, and rehabilitative treatment designed to protect public safety and reduce recidivism rates. The bill's provisions authorize $362 million to expand assistance for people currently incarcerated, those returning to their communities after incarceration, and children with parents in prison. The services to be funded under the bill include:

- mentoring programs for adults and juveniles leaving prison;
- drug treatment during and after incarceration, including family-based treatment for incarcerated parents;
- education and job training in prison;
- alternatives to incarceration for parents convicted of nonviolent drug offenses;
- supportive programming for children of incarcerated parents; and
- early release for certain elderly prisoners convicted of nonviolent offenses.

Another example of progress in prisoner reentry is the development of specialized reentry courts. These courts function similarly to drug courts in that their purpose is to oversee a prisoner's reentry to the community, review their plans and progress, order (when necessary) participation in treatment and reintegration programs, use drug and alcohol testing to monitor compliance, and provide graduated sanctions in lieu of a violation and return to prison. To test reentry courts, the U.S. Department of Justice Office of Justice Programs awarded grants to nine states to set up courts and track their success. The research is still inconclusive and has to date produced mixed results,[74] but continues to be studied and modified to improve operations.[75]

The focus on work as critical for reentry success is also commonly accepted. Surveys show that about one-third of prison inmates were jobless at their time of incarcerations,[76] and upon release from prison, they are out of work about half the time and earn on average only around $9,000 per year.[77] Therefore, there have been efforts to improve employment among ex-offenders to include transitional employment programs. The transitional employment programs provide subsidized work to former prisoners with close supervision, mentoring, and on-the-job training. Evaluations of these programs have shown improved employment records and reductions in recidivism.[78]

It is critical that continued focus and innovation continue in prisoner reentry. We cannot afford to simply recycle criminals through prison to the community and back to prison. We must invest in successful programs that have proven to work in prisoner reentry. The following section presents a guideline on what can be done to improve prisoner reentry.

What Else Can Be Done To Improve Prisoner Reentry?

One of the most important elements to improving the success of prisoner reentry is to build on what we know works. In a review of research regarding prisoner reentry programs, Seiter and Kadela identified several programs that work to reduce the recidivism of released prisoners.[79] The authors first created the following definition of prisoner reentry programs:

- All correctional programs that focus on the transition from prison to community (prerelease, work release, halfway houses, or specific reentry programs), or
- Programs that have initiated treatment (substance abuse, life skills, education, cognitive/behavioral, sex/violent offender) in a prison setting and have linked with a community program to provide continuity of care.

The method to then identify whether a category of program was successful used the Maryland *Scale of Scientific Methods* (MSSM), developed by Sherman and colleagues in 1998 for the National Institute of Justice, to identify crime prevention programs that work. This scale ranks research studies from 1 (weakest) to 5 (strongest) on overall internal validity. Seiter and Kadela identified thirty-two studies that fit the definition of prisoner reentry. Each study was placed into an MSSM level, and evaluations of similar programs have been grouped into (1) vocational training and work, (2) drug rehabilitation, (3) educational programs, (4) sex/violent offender programs, (5) halfway house programs, and (6) prison prerelease programs.

The next step was to determine whether any of these six categories of prison reentry programs were effective, using the Sherman framework definitions. For a program to be considered to be working, at least two level 3 evaluations with statistical significance tests must indicate that the intervention was effective and the preponderance of the remaining evidence must support that conclusion. For a program to be coded as *not working*, at least two level 3 evaluations with statistical significance must indicate the ineffectiveness of the program and the preponderance of the remaining evidence must support the same conclusion. Programs for which the level of certainty from available evidence is too low to support generalizable conclusions were defined as *promising*. Any program not classified in one of these three categories is defined as having unknown effects.

Results indicate a positive result for vocational training and work release programs (found effective in reducing recidivism rates as well as improving job readiness skills for ex-offenders), for drug rehabilitation (graduates of treatment programs were less likely than other parolees and noncompleters to have been arrested, commit a drug-related offense, continue drug use, or have a parole violation), to some extent for education programs (only to increase educational

Idleness in prison makes prison management more difficult and does nothing to prepare inmates for release to the community. Photo by Richard P. Seiter.

achievement scores, but not to decrease recidivism), for halfway house programs (found effective in reducing the frequency and severity of future crimes), and for prerelease programs (effective in reducing recidivism rates of ex-offenders). In addition, there are promising results for sex and violent offender programs.

Even with the problems resulting from the changes over the past two decades, this analysis of prisoner reentry programs has identified several categories of programs in which there is evidence of success. Public officials should take note of these programs; implement or expand the use of vocational training and/or work release programs, drug rehabilitation programs, education programs, halfway house programs, and prerelease programs that have proved successful; and expand the use of sex and violent offender programs that show promise. These programs can be expanded significantly with only a small portion of funding that is currently used for imprisoning offenders.

The nation has invested billions of dollars in locking up offenders. Policies concerning reentry have become increasingly an avoidance of risk. As a result, we have created a revolving door of offenders who will be committed to prison again and again as they fail in the community. This is not only a failure by the inmate; it is a failure of release and reentry policies. This analysis has pointed out that certain programs can improve prisoner reentry and reduce the revolving-door syndrome. With billions of dollars focused on imprisonment, it is only fitting that a few million more be focused on their return to the community.

A Systems Approach to Prisoner Reentry

In the review of prisoner reentry discussed above, you have seen the changes over the past two decades (longer sentences, fewer community ties, inmates with more serious problems) that have caused more problems for inmates attempting to leave prison and successfully reenter society. You have seen the types of prison programs that have been identified as contributing to successful reentry, yet the low percentage of inmates that participate in these programs. And you have seen the issues in postincarceration community supervision in terms of large caseloads and a surveillance style of supervising offenders that often results in technical violations and return to prison. What you have not seen is a model for addressing these challenges in a systemic and comprehensive manner.

This section presents the State of Washington Department of Corrections plan for a reentry-focused correctional system.[80] This plan, implemented in late 2006, created a total focus toward successful return of inmates to the community. This plan begins with the question of whether a reentry-focused correctional system is necessary (see Figure 6.7) and is significant for several reasons. It addresses what experts believe is key to successful reentry: that the reentry process begins at reception. It highlights the many needs that offenders have when they enter a prison that must be addressed while they are serving their sentence. It recognizes the important link between prison programming and the transition to community-based services for continuity of care. It focuses on the reduction of recidivism. And by reducing recidivism, it has a goal of reducing the need for prison beds and the long-term costs to the correctional system. From this review, Washington decided that it needed to refocus its entire correctional system on improving the reentry of inmates to the community.

The next chart (Figure 6.8) is the result of their planning efforts. This comprehensive restructure and alignment of activities is extremely unusual, and the Washington Department of Corrections is to be commended for it. The plan begins with an assessment of inmates at the reception center to determine their needs and

---

Department of Corrections
OFFENDER RE-ENTRY

Does Washington need a re-entry focused correctional system?

A re-entry focused correctional system is designed to:

- **Reduce offender deficits correlating to criminal behavior:**
  - 83% of females and 71% of males enter DOC with less than a 9th grade level education
  - 75% of prison offenders have previously been in a country juvenile system
  - 50% of male children whose parents have been incarcerated will end up incarcerated
  - 73% of females and 55% of males in prison have mental health problems
  - 62% of females and 56% of males in prison reported using drugs the month before their offense

- **Increase community participation in supporting offender re-entry**
  - 97% of prison inmates re-enter communities
  - DOC has on average only 21 months to work with each offender
  - Offenders are community members before and after they are with DOC

- **Reduce recidivism**
  - Washington's rate has climbed from 31% to 37% over the last 10 years
  - Estimating over 3,500 offenders releasing in 2006 will commit new crimes by 2011

- **Reduce demand for prison beds**
  - 2006 demand exceeds supply by about 1,600 beds
  - 2017 demand is estimated to exceed supply by about 4,000 beds

A public safety focused Washington needs:

- DOC's re=entry focused correctional system

      AND

- A systemic and collaborative approach from state and local agencies
  - to reduce deficits that precede crime
  - to increase community capacity for successful offender re-entry

FIGURE 6.7 Does Washington Need a Reentry-Focused Correctional System?

Source: Washington Department of Corrections, *A Re-Entry Focused Correctional System* (Olympia, Wash: Government Management, Accountability, and Performance Forum, November 2006).

Department of Corrections
OFFENDER RE-ENTRY

A Re-entry Focused Correctional System

ASSESS ▸ PLAN ▸ MANAGE ▸ MONITOR ▸ RESPOND ▸ IMPROVE ▸

Increased Public Safety

DOC's Contribution to Reducing Re-Offense Behavior

Assess and Plan

<u>Reception Diagnostic Center</u>
- Reception and Orientation
- Assessments
- Diagnosis
- Personalized Plan

<u>From Jail to Community Supervision</u>
- Assessments
- Personalized Plan

Manage and Monitor

<u>Prisons</u>
- Focusing on Behavior and being held accountable for their actions
- Step Down through programs and custody levels
- Targeted Programs based on Individual needs identified in their Personalized Plan
- Focused Reentry Programming Facilities

<u>Community Participation</u>
- Collaborative Partnerships with other Agencies, Communities and Stakeholders
- Enhanced Family Connections

Respond and Improve

<u>Community Corrections</u>
- Targeted Programs based on Personalized Plan
- Focused Reentry Programs in Community Justice Centers
- Increased investments in Work Releases

<u>Community Participation</u>
- Collaborative Partnerships with other Agencies, Communities and Stakeholders
- Enhanced Family Connections

Personalized Plan

Accountable Behavior

Responsibility/Community

Assessment Components

Initial Interview, Personality Assessment Inventory, Educational Assessment, Vocational Assessment, Sex Offender Risk/Treatment Assessment, Chemical Dependency Screening, Risk/Needs, Self Reported Information, Custody Designation, Criminal History, Medical, Mental Health, and Dental Assessment.

Targeted Programs

Basic Education, English as a 2nd Language, Long-term Vocational Technology Life Skills, Anger Stress Management, Violence Reduction, Cognitive Behavioral Therapy, Correctional Industries, Off-site Work Crews, Department of Natural Resources, Primary Work Programs supporting facility operations, Work Release, Sex Offender Treatment, Long-term Chemical Dependency Treatment, Therapeutic Community, Family Connections, Mental Health Services

Targeted Programs

Long-term Chemical Dependency Treatment, Cognitive Behavioral Therapy, Sex Offender Treatment, Employment and Job Training, Vocational Programming, Work Crews, Work Release, Therapeutic Community, Family Connections, Mental Health Services

---

FIGURE 6.8   A Reentry-Focused Correctional System

Source: Washington Department of Corrections, *A Re-Entry Focused Correctional System* (Olympia, Wash.: Government Management, Accountability, and Performance Forum, November 2006).

create a personalized plan for addressing these needs. The next stage has programs provided within prisons that target the individual needs, while expecting good behavior and rewarding inmates with a step down of security levels for positive behaviors and program completions. There is also a focus on inmates rebuilding their ties with their families and building relationships with community agencies and other stakeholders. And finally, there is the move to the community using Community Justice Centers and work release, and managing the personalized plan for offenders to complete their programs and live a crime-free and productive lifestyle.

Summary

During much of the history of corrections, indeterminate sentences and discretionary parole were a cornerstone of both theory and practice. The minimum term of an indeterminate sentence satisfied the punishment, deterrence, and incapacitation sentencing goals, and a parole board of experts then examined the individual offender characteristics to determine when the goal of rehabilitation was maximized and the offender was best prepared for release to the community. However, this model came under attack and was completely abandoned in a third of the states and seriously compromised in another third. The use of determinate sentences that were longer than the minimum indeterminate sentence term developed in its place in an effort to make the punishment fit the crime and to hold offenders accountable for their criminal acts. Unfortunately, punishment, deterrence, and incapacitation became so predominant that rehabilitation was often ignored or seriously reduced in emphasis.

Several problems have resulted from these changes in philosophy, policy, and practice. There has been a fivefold increase in the number of prison inmates, at a tremendous cost to society and, many argue, with little benefit in the reduction of crime or successful return of offenders to the community. With criminal offenders now predominantly receiving determinate sentences, there is no parole board to act as gatekeepers between the prison and community. Some high-risk offenders actually serve shorter sentences than when a parole board could deny parole and continue them even until their maximum sentence term was met. Without a parole board, there is no review of release plans, and there is very little incentive for good behavior while in prison. Almost 80 percent of inmates were released on discretionary parole only twenty-five years ago, yet just over 20 percent are now similarly released. Most prison releasees still receive supervision as a postprison requirement, and violation of conditions results in the possibility of returning to prison. However, approximately 18 percent of prison releasees go into the community with no requirement for supervision.

Prisoner reentry has become a much more significant issue than it was twenty years ago. As pointed out by Jeremy Travis, former director of the National Institute of Justice, in referring to the recent interest and problem of prisoner reentry, "they all come back."[81] Inmates are serving longer periods of time, are older when released, are more prisonized from serving longer times in prison, are less likely to participate in prison rehabilitative programs, and enter communities that are more disorganized and unable to provide them services and assistance. Fortunately, some reentry programs have been found to help prisoners return to the community. It is critical that public policymakers build on these findings and fund and expand those programs proved successful, while hopefully ending the negative cycle of crime–prison–release–crime.

CHAPTER REVIEW

Key Terms

parole	Elmira Reformatory
Alexander Maconochie	justice model
mark system	just deserts model
ticket of leave	discretionary parole
Sir Walter Crofton	supervised mandatory release
Zebulon R. Brockway	unconditional mandatory release

parole guidelines
salient factor score
hearing officers
presumptive parole date

positive contact
violation
Morrissey v. Brewer
prisoner reentry

Review Questions

1. Describe the four stages of the system of release implemented by Alexander Maconochie on the Norfolk Island penal colony.

2. Describe the four stages of release implemented by Sir Walter Crofton in the Irish system.

3. How did the Elmira Reformatory move toward the implementation of a system of parole in the United States?

4. How did the Martinson findings of "nothing works" influence the use of parole and the medical model?

5. Describe some of the suggested models to replace the medical model of corrections.

6. Compare and contrast parole, supervised mandatory release, and unconditional mandatory release.

7. What two factors do parole guidelines attempt to predict?

8. Name and describe the two types of parole conditions.

9. What are the two types of parole violations?

10. Describe the process for revoking parole.

11. List the due process rights prescribed by the *Morrissey v. Brewer* decision.

12. List some of the ways in which issues facing prisoners reentering the community are different than they were in the past.

13. Describe Seiter and Kadela's findings regarding the effectiveness of prisoner reentry programs.

You Make the Decision...

Parole or Not?

The following scenarios represent the types of cases that can come before a parole board. Students should consider the situation in each case and determine what decision they would make regarding the individual's parole.[82]

Inmate A was convicted of vehicular manslaughter and received a sentence of seven years. He killed two teenagers in a head-on collision. He had been drinking, but his blood-alcohol content was below the limit. The inmate has never been arrested for any other offenses. He is 21 years old and was a senior in college when the offense occurred. He has been an excellent inmate and is a tutor in school. The victims' families are opposing parole. He has served ten months on the sentence. The minimum time he must serve is thirteen months. His conditional release date is fifty-six months. How much time should he serve?

Inmate B is a 31-year-old male who committed two burglaries and received two ten-year sentences running concurrently. He has two prior prison incarcerations. One is for stealing and the other is first-degree burglary. He is a severe drug addict who has strong family ties. He has received his GED while incarcerated. His minimum mandatory prison term is five years, and he has served three years. His conditional release date is at seven years. How much time should he serve in all?

Inmate C is a 19-year-old female who has sold a large quantity of cocaine with no prior incarcerations. She has a prior probation for possession of drugs and is pregnant. She indicated that she is not a drug user but sold drugs because she needed money. She has a ninth-grade education and is going to school to get her GED. She has a five-year sentence with a minimum eligibility of twenty months. The conditional release date is at forty

...continued

months and she has served six months. How much time should she serve in all?

Inmate D has a five-year sentence for felony DWI. He has two prior convictions and served time in jail for one of the offenses. He was on probation for DWI and this probation was revoked for the commission of this present DWI. He is 35 years old, married with two children. He works steadily when he is in the community. He has been in an inpatient alcohol treatment program before and also attends AA in prison. He states that he had been sober for one year when this present DWI occurred. He is illiterate, is attending school, but is having a difficult time grasping the work. He has served six months and his minimum eligibility is nine months. The conditional release date is at forty months. How much time should he serve in all?

Inmate E has a ten-year sentence for rape after being found guilty by a jury. He has never been in trouble before, and the victim of the offense was a woman that he took out on a date and then raped. He denies it was rape and indicated that she consented. He is divorced with two children. He has never been in trouble before and is in business for himself. His family is taking care of his business. He has had difficulty adjusting in prison and has had a few minor violations. He has a tenth-grade education. He refuses to go to school. He has served six years and has a minimum eligibility of eight and a half years. How much time should he serve?

Inmate F has a thirty-year sentence for killing her husband. She states that her husband had beaten her during their fifteen-year marriage, and there was some evidence that she had called the police and stated her husband had hit her, but denied the accusations when the police came. She is 34 years old and has three children, who are being cared for by relatives. She has a college education. She has no prior arrests and no indication of prior assaultive behavior. She has served eight years and the minimum eligibility is ten years. There is opposition by the victim's family. Her conditional release date is at twenty-five years. How much time should she serve in all?

Inmate G has a twenty-five-year sentence for first-degree robbery. He was 16 years old when the offense occurred and was certified as an adult. He has a juvenile record and was in a juvenile institution for assaultive behavior for six months. He does not use drugs and there is family support. He has received his GED while incarcerated and is working in the furniture factory. He has had some minor violations and two major violations for assault. He has served ten years and his minimum eligibility has passed. His conditional release date is at twenty years. How much time should he serve in all?

Inmate H has a ten-year sentence for child molestation and the victim was his son. He was on probation for this offense, which he violated when he failed to obtain treatment. He is married and has the support of his wife, who is not the mother of his son. He is a high school graduate and is working in food service. He has served three years and his conditional release date is at seven years. How much time should he serve?

Chapter Resources on mycrimekit™

Go to mycrimekit.com to explore the following study tools and resources specific to this chapter:

- **Practice Quiz:** multiple-choice, true/false, short-answer, and essay questions to help students test their knowledge
- **WebQuests:** learning activities built around Web searches
  - Bureau of Justice Statistics—Probation and Parole: www.ojp.usdoj.gov/bjs/
  - Urban Institute—Reenty: www.urban.org/pressroom/prisonerreentry.cfm
  - Reentry activities: www.reentry.gov

- **Insider's Experiences:** "Appointing Parole Board Members"
- **Seiter Videos:**
  - See experts discuss the parole decision
  - See offenders discuss release from prison
  - See offenders discuss the transition from prison
- **Career Center:** A Career as a Parole Agent
- **Flashcards:** Twenty-one flashcards to test knowledge of the chapter's key terms

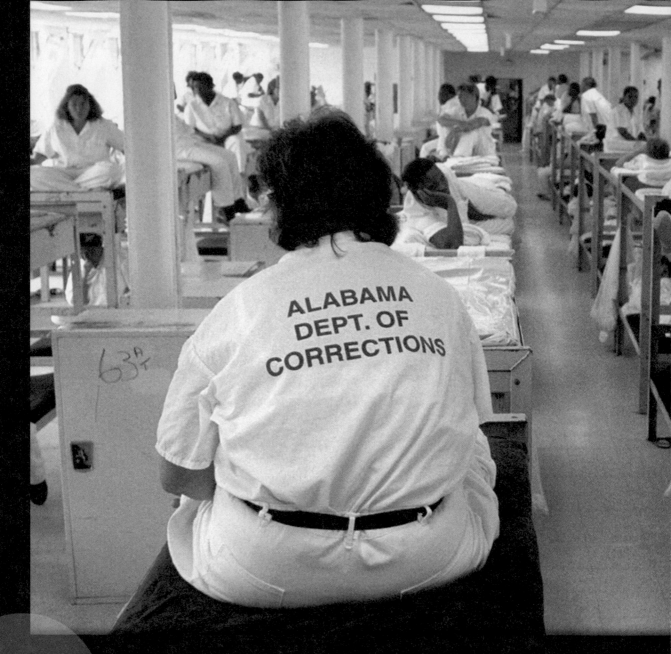

The Clients of Adult Correctional Agencies

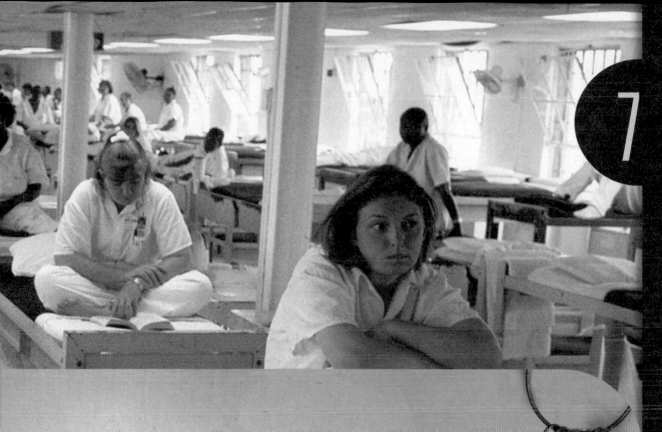

After reading this chapter, you should be able to:

1. Identify the trend in the number of offenders under correctional supervision since the early 1980s.

2. Understand the use of incarceration rates to compare numbers of offenders over various time frames.

3. Explain the issue of racial disparity with regard to offenders under correctional supervision.

4. Identify the link of male offenders and violent crimes.

5. Describe how male offenders are assigned to various security levels of prisons and how their daily routine operates.

6. Specify the growth of female offenders under supervision and in prison and suggest reasons for the growth.

7. Identify the special needs of women inmates and how correctional agencies have responded to their needs.

8. Describe the challenge facing women prisoners as mothers.

9. Compare the classification of female prisoners with that of male prisoners.

10. Understand the impact that the *Barefield v. Leach* and *Pargo v. Elliott* court cases had on programming for female inmates.

Introduction

In Chapters 3 through 6, we covered the scope of the correctional process, including pretrial services, sentencing, probation and intermediate sanctions, imprisonment, and release and reentry to the community. Each of these process descriptions included historical developments, theoretical basis for the evolution of policy and practice, and an explanation of how the process currently operates. Now we will cover correctional perspectives and address topics such as the clients of correctional agencies, distinctions of the operations of the juvenile justice system as separate from the criminal justice system, and special offender groups.

In this chapter we identify and provide a basic understanding of the clients of adult correctional systems. Questions asked include the following: What categories of clients do correctional agencies serve? What theoretical underpinnings are the bases of past and current operations? What are the backgrounds and characteristics of the different categories of correctional clients? What might make them unique and require special processing, handling, or management? Has anything in their background contributed to their criminality? For each group, characteristics that make them distinctive and influence how they are handled and managed are described. The chapter begins with an overview of offenders who make up the adult correctional system, including the numbers under supervision and their makeup by gender, offense category, and race and ethnicity. Particular note is made of the increasing number of offenders under correctional supervision and especially the significant increase in the number in state and federal prisons over the past two decades.

The prison population today is very large and more diverse than in the past. Much of the prison growth resulted from the incarceration of many property and drug offenders who previously did not get sent to prison. The makeup of the prison population is increasingly black and brown, as white offenders make up a continually smaller proportion of the prison population. And the prison population is no longer "middle crime age" (age 25 to 35) and physically and emotionally healthy. Many juveniles are now tried as adults and sentenced to adult prisons, the percentage of elderly offenders is increasing, mental illness among inmates is a difficult problem, and inmates experience a variety of severe health problems. This chapter identifies characteristics of the unique groups of offenders and some of the activities, policies, and programs that are used to respond to their special situations.

The clients of corrections are what corrections is all about. Corrections is not a manufacturing operation with products. Corrections is not information technology, with hardware and software to make work more efficient. Corrections is about people and about dealing with correctional clients. All too often, students of corrections study, analyze, and consider the strengths and weaknesses of the *process* rather than the *people* the process is designed to manage. This chapter provides many facts and figures that may seem impersonal and inconsistent with this admonishment to consider the people. However, using these facts and figures as a beginning point, students can then work to understand the issues that must be considered as government and correctional officials develop policies and operations to meet public safety, offender rehabilitation, and inmate security goals for various criminal sanctions and the variety of criminal offenders. It is important for students to have a clear understanding of the situations and issues that face correctional clients and therefore how specific policies and operations will affect them similarly or differently. With this perspective, students will have both the background and sensitivity to better understand and critically assess issues described in later chapters detailing security, inmate programs, the prison environment, and management of special offenders.

Overview of Adult Offenders

The number of adults under correctional supervision (individuals on probation, in jail, in prison, or on parole) has grown dramatically over the past two decades. As indicated in Table 7.1, only 1.8 million adults were on probation and parole and in jail and prison in 1980. This number had doubled in only eight years by 1988, and by 2007, there were more than 7.3 million adults under the supervision of correctional agencies in the United States. Most private companies and even public agencies would welcome an increase in clients, as there is no group, business, or clients served by government agencies that have grown at anywhere near this rate over the same period of time.

As illustrated in Table 7.1, a significant part of the growth in the number of adults under correctional supervision comes from growth in the prison population. The use of incarceration as a criminal sanction has skyrocketed over the past two decades. In 1980, the rate of sentenced inmates incarcerated per 100,000 population was only 139. By 2008, the rate of sentenced adults incarcerated per 100,000 population had reached 762.[1] Although the incarceration rate increased every year during the period and more than doubled between 1980 and 1990, the rate of increase has continued to grow from 2000 to 2008. Figure 7.1 illustrates the continued growth since 1980. Note that the rate remained relatively stable from 2000 to 2001, declined slightly during 2001, and showed a slow, steady increase in subsequent years. On June 30, 2008, the states reporting the highest incarceration rates per 100,000 population were Louisiana (858), Mississippi (749), Texas (668), and Oklahoma (668). Those reporting the lowest incarceration rates were Maine (133), Minnesota (191), and New Hampshire (221).[2]

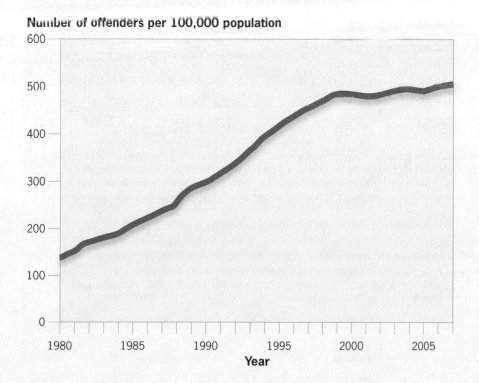

Number of offenders per 100,000 population

Note: Number of sentenced inmates incarcerated under state and federal jurisdiction per 100,000, 1980–2007.

Source: Heather C. West and William J. Sabol, *Prisoners in 2007* (Washington, D.C.: U.S. Department of Justice, Bureau of Justice Statistics, December 2008), p. 4.

FIGURE 7.1   Incarceration Rate for Adult Offenders, 1980–2007

TABLE 7.1 **Number of Persons Under Correctional Supervision 1980 to 2007**

	Probation	Jail	Prison	Parole	Total[a]
1980	1,118,097	183,988	319,598	220,438	1,842,100
1981	1,225,934	196,785	360,029	225,539	2,008,300
1982	1,357,264	209,582	402,914	224,604	2,194,400
1983	1,582,947	223,551	423,898	246,440	2,476,800
1984	1,740,948	234,500	448,264	266,992	2,690,700
1985	1,968,712	256,615	487,593	300,203	3,013,100
1986	2,114,621	274,444	526,436	325,638	3,241,100
1987	2,247,158	295,873	562,814	355,505	3,461,400
1988	2,356,483	343,569	607,766	407,977	3,715,800
1989	2,522,125	395,553	683,367	456,803	4,057,800
1990	2,670,234	405,320	743,382	531,407	4,350,300
1991	2,728,472	426,479	792,535	590,442	4,537,900
1992	2,811,611	444,584	850,566	658,601	4,765,400
1993	2,903,061	459,804	909,381	676,100	4,948,300
1994	2,981,022	486,474	990,147	690,371	5,148,000
1995	3,077,861	507,044	1,078,542	679,421	5,342,900
1996	3,164,996	518,492	1,127,528	679,733	5,490,700
1997	3,296,513	567,079	1,176,564	694,787	5,734,900
1998	3,670,441	592,462	1,224,469	696,385	6,134,200
1999	3,779,922	605,943	1,287,172	714,457	6,340,800
2000	3,826,209	621,149	1,316,333	723,898	6,445,100
2001	3,931,731	631,240	1,330,007	732,333	6,581,700
2002	4,024,067	665,475	1,367,547	750,934	6,758,800
2003[b]	4,120,012	691,301	1,390,279	769,925	6,924,500
2004	4,143,792	713,990	1,421,345	771,852	6,995,000
2005	4,166,757	747,529	1,448,344	780,616	7,051,900
2006[c]	4,215,361	766,010	1,492,973	799,058	7,181,500
2007[d]	4,293,163	780,581	1,512,576	824,365	7,328,200

[a]Because some offenders may have multiple statuses (i.e., held in a prison or jail but remain under the jurisdiction of a probation or parole authority) totals in 2000–04 exclude probationers held in jail or prison; totals in 2005–06 exclude probationers and parolees held in jail or prison; and the total in 2007 excludes probationers and parolees held in jail or prison, probationers who were also under parole supervision, and parolees who were also under probation supervision. For these reasons, details do not sum to total.

[b]The 2003 probation and parole counts were estimated and may differ from previously published numbers.

[c]Illinois did not provide prison or parole data for 2006; therefore, all prison and parole data for Illinois were estimated. See *Methodology* in Prisoners in 2006 (PDF file 308K) and Probation and Parole in the United States, 2006 (PDF file 400K)

[d]Illinois, Maine, and Nevada did not provide prison data for 2007; therefore, all prison data for these states were estimated. See *Methodology* in Prisoners in 2007 (PDF file 195K). Oklahoma did not provide probation or parole data for 2007; therefore, all probation and parole data for Oklahoma were estimated. See *Methodology* in Probation and Parole in the United States, 2007–Statistical Tables (PDF file 335K)

Source: Bureau of Justice Statistics, Correctional Populations, *Key Facts at a Glance*, http://www.ojp.usdoj.gov/bjs/glance/tables/corr2tab.htm (accessed April 12, 2009).

Gender, Race, and Ethnicity

In addition to the tremendous growth in the number of individuals in prison, there has been a change in the makeup of this population by gender, race, and ethnicity. First, the rate for females under all types of correctional supervision has grown more rapidly than the number of males under supervision. The Bureau of Justice Statistics reported in 1999, "Women represent about 21% of those on probation, 11% of those in local jails, just under 6% of those in prisons, and 12% of those on parole."[3] By midyear 2008, females were 7.2 percent of the prison population and the average growth from 2000 to 2006 was 3.4 percent compared to an annual growth of 2.1 percent for male inmates.[4] In 2007, 12 percent of the 799,058 parolees in the United States were females, and of the 4.2 million U.S. probationers, 23 percent were females.[5]

The gender makeup of the U.S. prison population is perhaps experiencing the greatest change. From 2000 to 2008, the number of males increased 15 percent (from 1,298,027 to 1,494,805), whereas the number of females increased 24 percent (from 93,234 to 115,779).[6] At midyear 2008, the 115,779 women incarcerated in state and federal prisons made up 7.2 percent of the total prison population.[7] Although the proportion of the prison population that is female is still relatively small, the average annual rate of growth of state and federal prisoners has increased more rapidly for females (3.0 percent per year) than for males (2.0 percent per year) from 2000 to 2008.[8] Table 7.2 illustrates the number of women in prison from 2000 to 2008 by state. Three of the largest jurisdictions (Texas, the federal system, and California) hold more than one-third of all the female prisoners.[9]

Similarly, there has been a shift in the racial makeup of adults under correctional supervision. Whites made up a majority (65 percent) of the correctional population in 1986. However, by 1997, whites represented only 60 percent of all adult offenders under supervision.[10] A majority of the prison population are minorities. At midyear 2008, the population of state and federal prisons was 34.9 percent white, 39.5 percent black, 19.9 percent Hispanic, and 6 percent other races.[11] Of the 1,262,000 individuals under probation supervision in 2007, 56 percent were white, 30 percent were black, and 12 percent were Hispanic.[12] The fact that white offenders make up 56 percent of probationers, yet only 36.6 percent

The rate of growth in the number of female offenders is even greater than that of males. Photo by Richard P. Seiter.

TABLE 7.2 Sentenced Female Prisoners Under the Jurisdiction of State or Federal Correctional Authorities by Jurisdiction

Region and Jurisdiction	Number of Prisoners					6-Month Change	
	12/31/2000	12/31/2006	6/30/2007	12/31/2007	6/30/2008	12/31/2006–6/30/2007	12/31/2007–6/30/2008
U.S Total[a]	93,234	112,459	115,314	114,407	115,779	2.5%	1.2%
Federal	10,245	12,975	13,572	13,338	13,482	4.6	1.1
State[a]	82,989	99,484	101,742	101,069	102,297	2.3	1.2
Northeast	9,082	9,730	9,852	9,694	9,920	1.3%	2.3%
Connecticut[b]	1,406	1,594	1,610	1,496	1,578	1.0	5.5
Maine	66	145	135	139	168	−6.9	20.9
Massachusetts	663	846	851	790	850	0.6	7.6
New Hampshire	120	172	194	202	208	12.8	3.0
New Jersey	1,650	1,428	1,395	1,410	1,377	−2.3	−2.3
New York	3,280	2,859	2,837	2,754	2,691	−0.8	−2.3
Pennsylvania	1,579	2,249	2,403	2,463	2,592	6.8	5.2
Rhode Island[b]	238	280	278	282	305	−0.7	8.2
Vermont[b]	80	157	149	158	151	−5.1	−4.4
Midwest[a]	14,598	17,670	18,064	17,832	17,892	2.2%	0.3%
Illinois[a]	2,849	2,720	2,778	2,727	2,754	:	:
Indiana	1,452	2,167	2,269	2,295	2,332	4.7	1.6
Iowa[c]	592	789	763	717	757	−3.3	5.6
Kansas	504	638	653	625	582	2.4	−6.9
Michigan	2,131	2,170	2,101	2,080	2,098	−3.2	0.9
Minnesota	368	562	648	602	666	15.3	10.6
Missouri	1,993	2,579	2,535	2,522	2,471	−1.7	−2.0
Nebraska	266	413	415	399	381	0.5	−4.5
North Dakota	68	157	144	147	161	−8.3	9.5
Ohia	2,808	3,701	3,891	3,822	3,905	5.1	2.2
South Dakota	200	350	396	369	346	13.1	−6.2
Wisconsin	1,367	1,424	1,471	1,527	1,439	3.3	−5.8
South	39,652	47,086	48,453	48,503	49,599	2.9%	2.3%
Alabama	1,826	2,050	2,171	2,158	2,167	5.9	0.4
Arkansas	772	1,042	1,067	1,066	1,068	2.4	0.2
Delaware[b]	597	571	639	577	605	11.9	4.9
District of columbia	356	~	~	~	~	:	:
Florida	4,105	6,489	6,691	6,854	6,965	3.1	1.6
Georgia[c]	2,758	3,557	3,530	3,545	3,559	−0.8	0.4
Kentucky	1,061	2,058	2,378	2,441	2,326	15.5	−4.7
Louisiana	2,219	2,389	2,399	2,458	2,536	0.4	3.2
Maryland	1,219	1,081	1,169	1,184	1,149	8.1	−3.0
Mississippi	1,669	1,789	1,882	1,962	2,001	5.2	2.0
North Carolina	1,903	2,686	2,710	2,626	2,794	0.9	6.4
Oklahoma	2,394	2,547	2,618	2,607	2,616	2.8	0.3
South Carolina	1,420	1,603	1,651	1,604	1,760	3.0	9.7
Tennessee	1,369	1,958	1,989	1,923	2,114	1.6	9.9
Texas	13,622	13,799	13,957	13,931	14,282	1.1	2.5
Virginia	2,059	2,893	2,986	2,933	3,024	3.2	3.1
West Virginia	303	574	616	634	633	7.3	−0.2
West	19,657	24,998	25,373	25,040	24,886	1.5%	−0.6%
Alaska[b]	284	518	621	564	606	19.9	7.4
Arizona[c]	1,964	3,151	3,279	3,460	3,645	4.1	5.3
California	11,161	11,977	12,117	11,628	11,607	1.2%	−0.2%
Colorado	1,333	2,302	2,327	2,335	2,288	1.1	−2.0
Hawaii[b]	561	734	755	746	758	2.9	1.6
Idaho	493	777	798	800	797	2.7	−0.4
Montana	306	354	302	301	336	−14.7	11.6
Nevada[a]	846	1,136	1,155	1,179	975	1.7	:
New Mexico	511	667	620	576	576	−7.0	0.0
Oregon	596	1,020	1,044	1,060	1,097	2.4	3.5
Utah	381	623	643	631	602	3.2	−4.6
Washington	1,065	1,496	1,474	1,514	1,363	−1.5	−10.0
Wyoming	156	243	238	246	236	−2.1	−4.1

~Not applicable. As of December 31, 2001, sentenced felons from the District of Columbia were the responsibility of the Federal Bureau of Prisons.

:Not calculated.

[a]Includes estimates for Illinois for 2006, 2007, and 2008 and Nevada for December 31, 2007. See *Methodology*.

[b]Prisons and jails form one integrated system. Data include total jail and prison populations.

[c]Prison population based on custody counts.

Source: Heather C. West and William J. Sabol, *Prison Inmates at Midyear 2008–Statistical Tables* (Washington, D.C.: U.S. Department of Justice, Bureau of Justice Statistics, March 2009), p. 10.

Current correctional populations are made up of a large percentage of minorities. Less than 50 percent of the current prison population is white. Courtesy of AP/Wide World Photos.

of prisoners, raises further concern. And the state and federal prison, or local jail populations on June 30, 2008, included more black males (846,000) than white males (712,500) and Hispanic males (427,000), and one in every 9 black men and one in every 103 white men aged 20 to 24 were behind bars.[13]

This issue of the vast **racial disparity** within the makeup of the U.S. correctional population merits an examination of whether criminal justice and correctional policies are in some way discriminatory. It is important to examine how race (separate from social class, level of poverty, drug use, and other issues) affects discretionary decisions by police, prosecutors, judges, prison officials, and parole board members. The National Urban League reports in 2009 that, "Ironically, even as an African American man holds the highest office in the country, African Americans remain twice as likely as whites to be unemployed, three times more likely to live in poverty and more than six times as likely to be incarcerated."[14]

But why are these numbers disproportionate to the racial and ethnic makeup of the U.S. population? Wilbanks, in *The Myth of a Racist Criminal Justice System*, proposed that the "perception of the criminal justice system as racist is a myth," in that while there are incidents of individual racism, most studies do not show sufficient evidence of racism; he concludes that prejudice and racism are not systematic.[15] In turn, many researchers argue that the disproportion results from the fact that minorities are disproportionately involved in crime, especially violent crime, both as the perpetrators and also as the victims. Minorities in poverty-stricken, urban neighborhoods are most likely to be victims of violent crime. In 2007, the Uniform Crime Report noted that the homicide and nonnegligent manslaughter arrest rates were, 47.6, 50.4, and 2.0 percent for white, black, or "other" races, respectively.[16]

Crime is also closely linked to poverty, drug use, and lack of opportunity for legitimate approaches to economic success. With crime more prevalent in neighborhoods where African Americans and Hispanics reside, it is not surprising that they are arrested at a higher rate than whites. Law enforcement efforts are always more intense in urban areas with high crime rates and high drug use. A study of how the police responded to the war on drugs noted that arrests for drug use and possession usually occur in the city rather than the suburbs and "have had a disproportionate effect on African Americans."[17] Although it appears that the disproportionate numbers of minorities under correctional supervision

racial disparity
the fact that minorities make up a greater percentage of those under correctional supervision than their makeup in the U.S. population

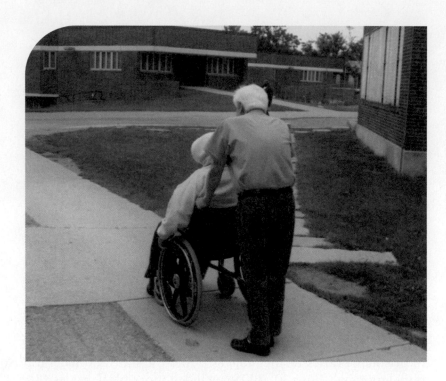

Prisons are now housing a much larger number of elderly offenders, many with serious health problems. Photo by Richard P. Seiter.

have less to do with racism within the criminal justice system than with social factors influencing crime, race, and social class, these high numbers of minorities in correctional systems still create a phenomenon that can cause the perception of racism and challenges to the management of correctional agencies.

Age of Offenders

Another factor that has changed significantly is the age of the typical prisoner in the United States. Historically, criminals often began their criminal behavior between ages 18 and 21 and were first incarcerated between ages 25 and 30. Most prisoners were age 30 to 35, with very few young or old inmates. However, the bell-shaped age curve of the prison population is leveling out (see Figure 7.2). On December 31,

Number of inmates

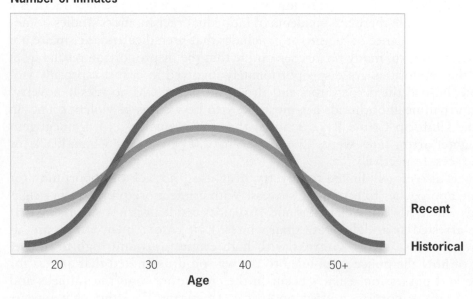

Recent

Historical

20   30   40   50+

Age

FIGURE 7.2 The Leveling Out of Prison Population by Age

2007, 10.2 percent of the nation's inmates were age 50 or older.[18] This is an increase from 8.0 percent in 1995,[19] and 8.6 percent reported in 2000. Three phenomena contribute to the aging of the prison population. First, the overall U.S. population is aging, as Americans over age 50 constituted only 26 percent of the population in 1992, but this figure is estimated to reach 33 percent by 2010.[20] Second, inmates are serving longer sentences and therefore stay in prison until they are older. Finally, mandatory sentences and sentencing guidelines take away the discretion of judges who may have kept older offenders in the community on probation rather than sending them to prison, as they are not believed to be a risk to the community. Current sentencing approaches are "age blind," and offenders who may have been allowed to remain in the community because of their advanced age are now sent to prison if their crime severity warrants it.

There has also been an increasing number of offenders under age 18 in state and federal prisons. Over the past decade, many high-publicity and serious crimes have been committed by juveniles. As a result, many states enacted legislation to prosecute serious juvenile offenders as adults, with a sanction of imprisonment in adult rather than juvenile correctional facilities. On December 31, 1997, only 5,400 offenders in state prisons (less than 1 percent of the total prison population) were under age 18. However, the number of juvenile offenders admitted to prison each year more than doubled, from 3,400 in 1985 to 7,400 in 1997.[21] Since 1997, however, the number of juveniles under age 18 in adult correctional facilities has declined. As of June 30, 2006, there were 2,364 juveniles in state prisons and none in federal prisons.[22] Demographics suggest that the proportion of the nation's population age 18 and younger will increase during the first decade of the twenty-first century. With the increase in commission of violent crimes by youthful offenders, it is expected that a higher number of juveniles will be committed to adult institutions over the next ten years.

Types of Offenses and Lengths of Confinements

In addition to the preceding changes in offender populations, the types of offenses for which individuals are under correctional supervision have changed. As Table 7.3 indicates, there has been a growth in the relative number of offenders who have

TABLE 7.3	Number of People in Custody of State Correctional Authorities by Most Serious Offense, 1980–2005			
Year	**Violent**	**Property**	**Drug**	**Public Order**
1980	173,300	89,300	19,000	12,400
1985	246,200	140,100	38,900	23,000
1990	313,600	173,700	148,600	45,500
1995	459,600	226,600	212,800	86,500
2000	589,100	238,500	251,100	124,600
2005	687,700	248,900	253,300	98,700

Source: *Correctional Populations in the United States, 1997* (Washington, D.C.: U.S. Department of Justice, 1998); *Prisoners in 2004* (Washington, D.C.: U.S. Department of Justice, 2005); *Prisoners in 2002* (Washington, D.C.: U.S. Department of Justice, 2003), p. 10; and *Prisoners in 2007* (Washington, D.C.: U.S. Department of Justice, 2008), p. 21.

The use and sale of drugs represent the primary increase in crimes during the 1990s, and the principal reason for an increase in the number of inmates in prison. Courtesy of Corbis Royalty Free.

drug offenders

those convicted of crimes regarding the possession or sale of drugs

committed the most serious crimes from 1980 to 2005. The number of people in custody for committing violent offenses increased 397 percent (from 173,300 to 687,700), and the number of those committing property offenses increased by 279 percent (from 89,300 to 248,900). Overall, the percentage of sentenced state inmates incarcerated for violent crimes increased from 46 to 53 percent from 1990 to 2005, whereas the percentage of those convicted of property crimes decreased from 25 to 19 percent during the same period.[23]

The most significant increases in the number of prison inmates were for those sentenced for committing drug and public-order offenses, both of which increased nearly thirteen times during the past two decades. Both of these categories were very small parts of the total population under custody in 1980, with drug offenses making up only 6.5 percent and public-order offenses 4.2 percent. However, by 2005, violent offenders comprised 53 percent, **drug offenders** made up 19.5 percent, and public-order offenders 7.6 percent of the total population under custody.[24]

Sentence length has also been increasing. The average length of incarceration (determined by the number of months served by all prison releasees during any specific year) was 23.7 months for 1990 releases from prison and increased by more than 25 percent to 30.0 months in 1996[25] and to 29.2 months in 2001.[26] More than 300,000 inmates were serving sentences of twenty years or more or life on January 1, 2002.[27] Sentences increased through many "tough on crime" statutes that were passed since 1980. In an effort to alleviate public fear of crime, elected officials have vowed to "lock 'em up and throw away the key" for any criminal that commits serious crimes or continues a pattern of criminality. With many prisoners having no possibility for release in the distant future, prison administrators fear continuously increasing tension and violence in the nation's prisons. Order within prison does not result from physical control, numerical superiority, or intimidation by correctional staff. It results from clear and consistent enforcement of rules and inmates perceiving they "have something to lose" if they misbehave.

Male Offenders

As is well known, males commit the largest proportion of crimes and make up the largest proportion of the correctional population under supervision. During 2001, males made up 78 percent of all arrests by law enforcement agencies,[28] yet

Violent victimizations per 1,000 population age 12 or over

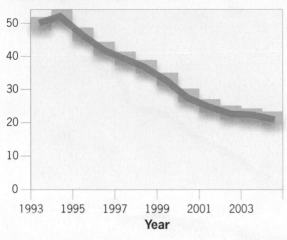

Property victimizations per 1,000 households

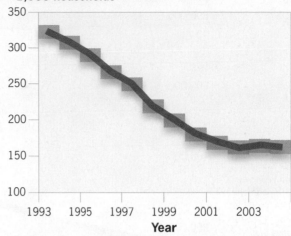

FIGURE 7.3   The Crime Rate has been Dropping

by midyear 2008, males made up 92.8 percent and females only 7.2 percent of the population of state and federal prisons.[29] When the general public thinks of criminals or inmates in prisons, they have a picture in mind of a large, tough-looking male, not a small female. Even though crime rates have been decreasing over the past few years (see Figure 7.3), the role and scope of corrections in managing **male offenders** continues to increase. Some pertinent facts include the following:

- 1,483,896 male inmates were under the jurisdiction of state and federal departments of corrections on December 31, 2007.

- Males represented 77 percent of all probationers and 88 percent of all parolees under active supervision status on December 31, 2007.[30]

male offenders
men who are convicted and sentenced; they constitute over 93 percent of all prison inmates

mycrimekit
Media—Video: Offenders and Crime

Male Offenders and Violence

Male offenders are much more linked to violence than are female offenders. In 2007, males represented 75.5 percent of felony arrests in the United States and 81.7 percent of arrests for violent crime. From 1995 to 2004, male arrests decreased by 8.9 percent for all crimes and declined by 20 percent for violent crime. Yet, from 1998 to 2007, male arrests for all crimes have decreased by 6.1 percent and decreased by 10.5 percent for violent crimes. Female arrests for all crimes increased by 9 percent and increased by 3.1 percent for violent crimes from 1995 to 2004, and increased for all crimes by 6.6 percent and decreased for violent crimes by 1.1 percent from 1998 to 2007.[31] As indicated in Figure 7.4, over half of the increase in state prison populations since 1995 is due to an increase in the prisoners convicted of violent offenses.

Even with violent crime seemingly on the decline for males and on the incline for females, males are still predominantly involved in the commission (illustrated by the arrest totals) of violent crimes. Table 7.4 illustrates the number of violent crimes committed by adult males (over age 18) as a percentage of the total of such crimes by both male and female adults. Even though they are a minority of the population of the United States, adult males represented 89.3 percent of the murder and nonnegligent manslaughter arrests and 88.5 percent of all robbery

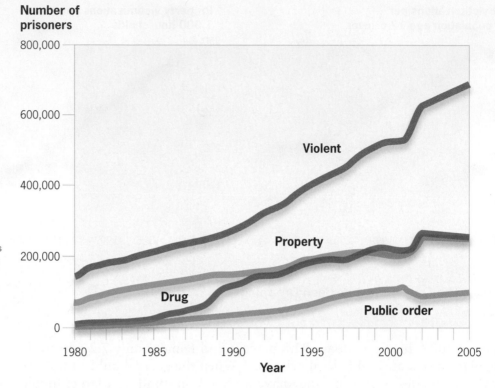

Source: Bureau of Justice Statistics, *National Crime Victimization Survey* (Washington, D.C.: U.S. Department of Justice, 2003), p. 4; Heather C. West and William J. Sabol, "Prisoners in 2007," *Bureau of Justice Statistics Bulletin* (Washington, D.C.: U.S. Department of Justice, December 2008), p. 21; and Paige M. Harrison and Allen J. Beck, "Prisoners in 2004," *Bureau of Justice Statistics Bulletin* (Washington, D.C.: U.S. Department of Justice, October 2005), p. 9.

FIGURE 7.4 State Prison Population by Offense Type, 1980–2005

TABLE 7.4	Total Arrests of Adult Males in 2007 for All Index Crimes		
	Number of Persons Arrested		
Offense Charged	**Total**	**Male**	**Percent Male**
Total	**8,814,016**	**6,656,579**	**75.5**
Murder and nonnegligent manslaughter	7,623	6,805	89.3
Forcible rape	13,699	13,552	98.9
Robbery	70,536	62,432	88.5
Aggravated assault	269,706	212,486	78.8
Burglary	192,743	163,537	84.8
Larceny-theft	735,272	439,829	59.8
Motor vehicle theft	67,316	55,010	81.7
Arson	9,792	8,309	84.9
All violent crimes[a]	361,564	295,275	81.7
All property crimes[b]	700,523	666,685	95.2

[a]Violent crimes are offenses of murder, forcible rape, robbery, and aggravated assault.
[b]Property crimes are offenses of burglary, larceny-theft, motor vehicle theft, and arson.
Source: Adapted from Federal Bureau of Investigation, *Crime in the United States, 2007*, Table 35 (Washington, D.C.: U.S. Department of Justice, 2007).

Males are much more involved in violent crimes than females and represent more than 80 percent of the arrests for violent crimes. Courtesy of Jerome Sessini/In Visu/Corbis/Bettmann.

arrests. Only for larceny-theft are a relatively high proportion of the arrests for females, as males make up 59.8 percent of arrests for that crime.

With the violent background of so many male offenders, violence is much more likely in male prisons than in female prisons. In 2005, 53 percent of adults sentenced to state prisons were committed for violent offenses, 19.2 percent for property offenses, 19.5 percent for drug offenses, and 7.6 percent for public-order offenses.[32] Table 7.5 illustrates the percentages of sentenced prisoners under state jurisdiction by offense and gender in 2005. More than 156,800 male inmates were convicted of murder, more than 162,600 were convicted of rape or other sexual assault, more than 170,300 were convicted of robbery, and more than 121,400 were convicted of assault. Within all state prisons, 656,400 male inmates are serving time for violent offenses.

With so many violent inmates in prisons, there is no question that staff must work in situations that can result in assault or even death. In MyCrimeKit, I share with you in the "An Insider's Experience" box one of my most frustrating times as a correctional administrator: how helpless I felt when an inmate killed one of the staff members who worked for me.

Male Prisoners

Prison systems are predominantly planned and administered around the management of male inmates. The state and federal prison systems have subcomponents of groups of offenders, including women, juveniles serving time in adult prisons, mentally ill inmates, substance abusers, and other groups that are housed and managed separately. However, the majority of adult prisons hold normal, male inmates (often referred to as the **general population**) without a particular designation requiring special housing or management. Male inmates in the general population are received into the prison systems, assessed, and classified to one of the various security level prisons to serve their sentence. Security levels of prisons are designed to match physical security, staff resources, programs, and prison operations with the risk of violence and escape by male inmates assigned to each level.

mycrimekit

Insider's Experience: The Murder of a Prison Worker.

general population
inmates in prison who do not have any specific designation as a special type of offender

| TABLE 7.5 | Estimated Number of Sentenced Prisoners under State Jurisdiction, by Offense and Gender, Year-End 2005 |

Offense	All Inmates	Male	Female
Total	1,296,700	1,208,500	88,200
Violent offenses	687,700	656,400	31,200
Murder[a]	166,700	156,800	9,800
Manslaughter	16,700	15,100	1,700
Rape	60,800	60,300	500
Other sexual assault	103,800	102,300	1,500
Robbery	177,900	170,300	7,600
Assault	129,200	121,400	7,700
Other violent	32,500	30,200	2,400
Property offenses	248,900	223,700	25,200
Burglary	124,900	118,800	5,600
Larceny	45,200	38,200	7,100
Motor vehicle theft	22,400	21,100	1,300
Fraud	32,100	22,800	9,200
Other property	24,800	22,800	2,100
Drug offenses	253,300	228,000	25,300
Public-order offenses[b]	98,700	93,400	5,300
Other/unspecified[c]	8,100	7,100	1,100

Note: Data are for inmates with a sentence of more than one year under the jurisdiction of state correctional authorities. The numbers of inmates by gender were based on jurisdiction counts at year-end (NPS-1B).

Numbers within each category by offense were estimated using the National Corrections Reporting Program, 2005.

All estimates were rounded to the nearest 100.

[a]Includes negligent manslaughter.

[b]Includes weapons, drunk driving, court offenses, commercialized vice, morals and decency charges, liquor law violations, and other public-order offenses.

[c]Includes juvenile offenses and unspecified felonies.

Source: Adapted from Heather C. West and William J. Sabol, "Prisoners in 2007," *Bureau of Justice Statistics Bulletin* (December 2008), Table 10, p. 21.

The various states and federal government uses differing titles and definitions of prison security level, such as intake, community, minimum, medium, high/close, maximum, or multiple custody. Table 7.6 illustrates the numbers and percentage of all prisons in each category in 2002. The 1,821 state and federal prisons on December 30, 2005 held 1,427,316 inmates. Of these, 21.6 percent were classified as minimum security (to include minimum or low), 42.4 percent were medium security, and 35.9 percent were maximum (includes close and high) security.[33] Each increasing level of security has more physical security to reduce the potential for escapes, a higher staff-to-inmate ratio, more restrictions on inmate movement, more emphasis on security, and less emphasis on inmate programs. The overall goal of inmate security classification is to maintain homogeneity of inmates by risk of violence and escape and therefore ensure that they are placed in prisons that are physically designed to meet these risks. Housing high-security inmates in a facility that is low or minimum security creates the danger of escape, predatory behavior, or violence against staff or other inmates.

TABLE 7.6	The Makeup of Prisons by Security Level	
Institution Security Level	**Number of Prisons**	**Percent of Total**
Intake	43	3.2%
Community	210	15.4
Minimum	300	22.0
Medium	330	24.2
High/close	85	6.2
Maximum	98	7.2
Multiple	298	21.8
Total	1,384	100

Source: Camille Graham Camp and George M. Camp, *The 2002 Corrections Yearbook, Adult Systems* (Middletown, Conn.: Criminal Justice Institute, 2003), p. 75.

To ensure that inmates are in the proper security level and to plan for their participation in work and programs, prison caseworkers and counselors oversee the classification and program process. The "Your Career in Corrections" box describes the role of these staff members.

Your Career in Corrections

Caseworkers and Counselors

A common entry-level job for recent college or community college graduates is that of counselor or caseworker (sometimes called a social worker in some agencies). These professionals work directly with inmates, with the primary responsibility of classifying offenders and creating and monitoring plans for program and work participation. The plans continue throughout the period of confinement and build to the preparation for release.

A key component of the caseworker's job is security and treatment classification of an inmate. When inmates are sent to prison, they must first be classified to determine the security level of the prison in which they will be placed. The caseworker reviews the presentence investigation and any other informational documents to determine criminal and social history, sentence information, medical and psychological needs, education and work history, and other relevant preincarceration information. From this review, the caseworker usually completes an objective classification form to determine whether the inmate will be minimum, medium, or maximum security. The caseworker must continue to update the classification instrument with new information (such as prison behavior and time left to serve) to see if the security classification changes. The classification plan also assists with the assignment of work and program participation to meet identified inmate needs.

In describing the role played by these staff persons, Carlson suggests:

> Case management staffers maintain the official classification documents. . . . These staff members are not only responsible for determining the prisoner's custody and security needs, but charged with helping the inmates plan their institution-based work and program assignments.[34]

Caseworkers often perform as a team with prison educators, mental health professionals, and substance abuse counselors to create treatment plans and monitor inmates' progress toward their goals. Some caseworkers actually perform counseling, but in most state and federal prisons, their

...continued

principal role is to guide inmates through all aspects of their prison sentence, including the legal sanction and expectation for release, an understanding of their individual treatment needs, and the availability of prison programs to meet these needs. Caseworkers can also assist inmates with services outside the prison (job assistance, family counseling, or halfway house agencies) that will aid in their transition from prison to community.

Jobs as a caseworker require good interpersonal, decision-making, and writing skills. Most states require that applicants for these jobs have a college degree (often in the social sciences), but a few states do not require a degree if the person has experience. The type of college degree may vary with the specific job requirements of the position.

Williamson writes, "The primary determinants of educational requirements are the specific job description and the states in which they are located."[35] If caseworkers perform therapeutic treatment themselves, they may be required to possess a clinical degree in mental health or social work. While the salary for most state or federal caseworker jobs is usually 15 to 20 percent higher than the starting pay for a correctional officer, caseworkers usually have less opportunity to earn additional overtime pay, and the annual earnings may actually end up being about the same. However, these are excellent jobs, providing the broad experience, the challenge of interaction with inmates, the need for planning ahead, and the ability to have an important impact on the future lives of criminal offenders.

Female Offenders

mycrimekit

Careers—Correctional Treatment Specialist

female offenders

women who are convicted and sentenced; just over 7 percent of prison inmates are females

In 2007, women made up about 24.5 percent of all arrests by law enforcement agencies, an increase from 8.3 percent in 2003.[36] As women's involvement in crime has increased, the growth in the number of **female offenders** under correctional supervision has grown rapidly. Most of the detailed information available regarding female offenders is from Greenfeld and Snell's 1999 publication, *Women Offenders*. This study indicated that the number of women under correctional supervision increased at a greater rate (118 percent) than the number of males (70 percent) under supervision between 1986 and 1997, and in 1998, women constituted approximately 16 percent of the total correctional population, including 21 percent of the probation population, 11 percent of those in jails, 6 percent of prisoners, and 12 percent of parolees.[37] As indicated in Table 7.7, in 2007 women made up 3.2 percent of all arrests for violent offenses, 15.8 percent of arrests for property offenses, and 10.1 percent of arrests for drug offenses.[38] A recent review by the Illinois Criminal Justice Information Authority examined cases of 2,438 adult probationers and found that female probationers were much more likely than males to have been convicted of drug or property offenses.[39]

The growth of women under correctional supervision during the early 1990s can be seen from the increase in the felony convictions in state courts from 1990 to 1996 (see Table 7.8). The growth in the number of females convicted of felonies increased at two and a half times the rate of the growth in the number of male convictions between 1990 and 1996.[40] This trend continued into the 2000s, and by 2005, women accounted for about 6.8 percent of all prison sentences, including 4.5 percent of all convictions for violent crimes, 10 percent for property crimes, and 10 percent for drug offenses.[41]

Once sentenced, women have historically been given lesser sentences than men. However, as a result of sentencing guidelines and mandatory prison sentences, judges have less discretion and are now treating women more similarly to men than in the past. A 1993 study in Pennsylvania reported that similar sentences were received by men and women charged with similar offenses.[42] Chesney-Lind reports, "Twenty years ago, nearly two-thirds of the women convicted of federal felonies were granted probation, but in 1991, only 28 percent were given straight probation."[43] Female offenders under correctional supervision have similar traits to male

TABLE 7.7   Arrests of Females, 2007

	Arrests of Females	
	2007	Percent of All Arrests
Total arrests	2,576,284	24.2%
Violent offenses	81,962	3.2%
Murder	1,031	0.1%
Robbery	11,176	0.4%
Aggravated assault	69,569	2.7%
Property offenses	409,587	15.8%
Burglary	33,296	1.3%
Larceny	358,704	13.9%
Motor vehicle theft	15,781	0.6%
Drug offenses	261,256	10.1%
Driving under the Influence	219,310	8.5%

Note: Violent offenses, which include rape, and property offenses are the Part I offenses in the *FBI Uniform Crime Reports. Total arrests* includes Part I and Part II offenses.

Source: Federal Bureau of Investigation, *Crime in the United States, 2007* (Washington, D.C.: U.S. Department of Justice, 2007), Table 42, *Arrests*, http://www.fbi.gov/ucr/cius2007/data/table_42.html (accessed April 2, 2009).

TABLE 7.8   Felony Convictions of Women in State Courts, 1990–1996

	Estimated Number of Women Convicted of Felonies in State Courts				
	1990	1992	1994	1996	Percent Change, 1990–1996
Total	112,800	120,550	131,404	160,470	42%
Violent felonies	10,428	12,313	13,936	13,509	30
Murder	1,051	1,205	1,289	1,005	−4
Rape/sexual assault	202	375	630	442	119
Robbery	3,047	3,142	2,854	2,920	−4
Aggravated assault	5,043	6,152	6,906	7,786	54
Other violent	1,085	1,440	2,256	1,356	25
Property felonies	48,206	52,230	53,649	69,536	44
Burglary	5,593	5,830	6,603	6,847	22
Larceny	20,728	22,179	22,136	28,786	39
Fraud	21,885	24,221	24,910	33,902	55
Drug felonies	43,000	42,047	46,468	59,027	37
Trafficking	24,562	23,529	25,561	33,005	34
Possession	18,438	18,518	20,907	26,022	41
Other felonies	11,166	13,959	17,351	18,399	65

Note: Murder includes nonnegligent manslaughter, larceny includes motor vehicle theft, and fraud includes forgery and embezzlement. Details may not equal totals because of rounding.

Source: Lawrence A. Greenfeld and Tracy L. Snell, *Women Offenders* (Washington, D.C.: U.S. Department of Justice, Bureau of Justice Statistics, December 1999), p. 5.

Females are committing more crimes and are being sent to prison rather than receiving probation. Reprinted with permission of the Corrections Corporation of America.

offenders. As illustrated in Table 7.9, although nearly two-thirds of women on probation are white, almost two-thirds of women in jail or prison are minorities. Women in prison are older than those on probation or in jail. This simply indicates the factoring of criminal history in sentencing decisions. As offenders grow older and accumulate a more extensive offense history, they are more likely to receive a prison sentence. Women under correctional supervision are more likely than the general population to have never been married, and the majority of female offenders have completed high school.

In terms of recidivism, rates for female offenders are high, yet are thought to be less than recidivism rates for comparable male offenders. In a 1983 study of 6,400 women (and more than 100,000 men) released from prison in eleven states, 52 percent of the women were rearrested, 39 percent were reconvicted, and 33 percent were returned to prison during a three-year follow-up.[44]

The most important factor in predicting recidivism for women is prior arrest history; the greater the number of prior arrests, the higher the rate of rearrest among women released from prison over a three-year follow-up. A national study reports the following:

> [A]mong women with only the one arrest for which they had been imprisoned, 21% were rearrested within 3 years. Among women with 2–3 prior arrests, 33% were rearrested; those with 4–6 prior arrests had a 47% rearrest rate; among those with 7–10 priors, 69% were rearrested; and, nearly 8 out of 10 women with 11 or more priors were rearrested.[45]

Women in Prison

In 1925, only 3,438 women were in prison, representing 3.7 percent of the national prison population. This percentage of women in the overall prison population remained relatively stable until the 1980s, when it began to rise as many states

TABLE 7.9	Characteristics of Adult Women under Correctional Supervision			
Characteristics of Women	**Probation**	**Local Jails**	**State Prisons**	**Federal Prisons**
Race/Hispanic origin				
White	62%	36%	33%	29%
Black	27	44	48	35
Hispanic	10	15	15	32
Other	1	5	4	4
Age				
24 or younger	20%	21%	12%	9%
25–34	39	46	43	35
35–44	30	27	34	32
45–54	10	5	9	18
55 or older	1	1	2	6
Median age	32 years	31 years	33 years	36 years
Marital status				
Married	26%	15%	17%	29%
Widowed	2	4	6	6
Separated	10	13	10	21
Divorced	20	20	20	10
Never married	42	48	47	34
Education				
8th grade or less	5%	12%	7%	8%
Some high school	35	33	37	19
High school graduate/GED	39	39	39	44
Some college or more	21	16	17	29

Source: Lawrence A. Greenfeld and Tracy L. Snell, *Women Offenders* (Washington, D.C.: U.S. Department of Justice, Bureau of Justice Statistics, December 1999), p. 7.

implemented sentencing guidelines and mandatory prison sentences. The percentage of women in the prison population increased to 5.7 percent by 1990.[46] On June 30, 2008, there were 1,610,584 prisoners in state and federal prisons, of which 115,779 (7.2 percent) were women.[47] As with male offenders, much of the increase in the number of women incarcerated resulted from the war on drugs and expansion of arrests and prosecutions for drug offenses. In 2007, 29 percent of all women in prison had been convicted of drug offenses.[48]

The average length of prison sentence served by women is considerably less than that served by men. On January 1, 2002, men in prison were serving an average sentence of 5.3 years, whereas women in prison were serving an average of 3.7 years.[49] Some would argue that this indicates that women still receive less severe sentences than men. However, it is more likely the result of the fact that men in prison have more extensive criminal careers than women and commit a greater proportion of violent and serious crimes. A report by the Bureau of Justice Statistics in 1999 indicated that about 65 percent of women in state prisons had prior convictions compared to 77 percent of men in state prisons, and that "Based on self reports of victims of violence, women account for about 14 percent of violent offenders."[50] In addition, the same report noted that the consequences of male violence were more serious for the victim, in the sense of weapon use (15 percent of women used a firearm, knife, or blunt object compared to 28 percent of men), injury to the victim (5 percent of victims of women were seriously injured compared to 8 percent of victims of men), and average loss to the victim ($595 for victims of women and $943 for victims of men). Even though they still make up a small percentage of all prisoners in the United States, when women go to prison, they have many issues and needs that are different from those of male offenders and create challenges for correctional administrators.

Special Issues and Needs of Female Inmates

Some issues facing female inmates that are different from those of male inmates include health care, vocational training and work opportunities, potential of sexual abuse from staff, alcohol and drug use, and problems relating to their children. Approximately 60 percent of women in state prisons experienced physical or sexual abuses prior to their incarceration.[51] A 2007 report by the Bureau of Justice Statistics estimated that 60 percent of incarcerated women are mothers,[52] and the Bureau of Justice Statistics lists 65,600 female inmates (approximately 60 percent) in 2007 as having minor children.[53] Approximately one-fourth of the women who enter prison are either pregnant or have given birth within the past twelve months.[54] As mothers, female inmates often feel guilt for abandoning their children and must ask other family members to care for their children during incarceration. Because a small percentage of inmates are women, there are fewer female than male prisons. Therefore, the distance from home for female offenders is usually greater than for males, making it more difficult for family and the children to visit.

Many states have created innovative programs that they believe are particularly effective in responding to the special needs of female inmates. A survey of these programs in several states identified the following innovations. The number of programs that are operational in each category in all states is shown in parentheses.

Psychological programs (90): substance abuse, mental health counseling, and domestic violence counseling
Work programs (48): work training, prison industry programs, and other work-related programs
Parenting programs (42): child visitation, parent education, and other parenting programs
Other programs (62): transition and aftercare programs, education programs, health programs (including HIV/AIDS education), and life skills programs[55]

In addition to establishing these programs, administrators of women's correctional facilities noted specific program elements that are key to making the programs successful (see Figure 7.5). The most important elements for success are staff characteristics, comprehensiveness of approach, and pertinence to women's own interests. Of secondary importance is that these programs involve female staff, and female offenders have the opportunity to identify with this staff. Some of the specific issues that confront incarcerated women are described below. As a prelude to these issues, the following "An Interview With" illustrates the many challenges faced by women who become a part of the correctional system.

Separation from Family and Children

In a way very different than male inmates, women inmates suffer from the separation from their family and children and feel helpless in their child-raising role. Approximately 62 percent of women held in state prisons have children under age

mycrimekit
Media—Video: Issues for Female Offenders

Program Staff

- Staff are dedicated/caring/qualified.
- Ex-addicts or ex-offenders are on staff.
- Women staff members serve as role models.

Meeting of Specific and Multiple Needs

- Program has a comprehensive or multifaceted focus.
- Program addresses rudimentary or basic needs.
- Program establishes a continuum of care.

Program Participation

- Participants like the program.
- Inmate participation is high or self-initiated.
- Participants help run the program.

Peer Influence

- Other participants provide positive peer influence.
- Other participants provide pressure (e.g., to be a good mother).
- Other participants provide support.

Individualized, Structured

- Clear, measurable goals are established.
- Treatment plans and programming are individualized.
- Program is intensive and of appropriate duration.
- Appropriate screening and assessment are provided.

Technology, Resources

- Equipment, money, and other resources are available.
- Adequate space is available.

Acquisition of Skills

- Marketable job skills can be acquired.
- Parenting and life skills are taught.
- Education addresses thinking and reasoning.
- Anger management is taught.

Program Environment

- Atmosphere is "homey"; climate is conducive to visits.
- Communications are open; confidentiality is kept.
- Rapport with other participants is good.
- Participants are separated from the general population.
- Program enrollment is small.

Victimization Issues

- Program addresses self-esteem.
- Women are treated like human beings.
- Program addresses domestic violence.
- Program addresses empowerment and self-sufficiency.

Administrative and Staff Interaction

- Administrative support and communication are good.
- Management style is nonaggressive.
- Security staff are understanding and supportive.

Assistance from Outside the Facility

- Outside private-public partnerships exist.
- Interagency coordination exists.
- Some staff come from outside the department of corrections.

Source: Merry Morash, Timothy S. Bynum, and Barbara A. Koons, "Women Offenders: Programming Needs and Promising Approaches," *National Institute of Justice: Research in Brief* (August 1998): 7.

FIGURE 7.5 Elements Related to Successful Programs for Women

18 and report an average of 2.38 children per inmate. About two-thirds of these women (compared to 42 percent of male inmates) lived with their young children before entering prison.[56] Most children of female offenders end up with their maternal grandmothers, and the remainder are placed in foster homes. This is because the husband and father of the children is usually also incarcerated. In contrast, almost 90 percent of children of male inmates live with the children's mothers. This placement seems to be the most acceptable to female inmates and gives them the most peace of mind about how their children are being treated and the ease of getting their children back after release.[57] Female offenders know that their criminal involvement has caused a hardship for and separation from their children and feel shame and guilt for their own actions, as well as anger and bitterness with the criminal justice system for their situation.

With such a large proportion of women inmates having children, visiting in prison is particularly important. However, elderly parents of inmates caring for children often have a difficult time making the trip to visit regularly. Visits are also problematic due to the long distance between the inmates' homes and the prisons in which they are incarcerated. Female prisoners make up a relatively small portion of the nation's prison population, and most states have several male

mycrimekit

Media—Video: The Children of Inmates

An Interview With...

A Female Offender

Christine Wideman is a 42-year-old woman, originally from Detroit. At age 19, she moved to Texas to get away from home and be far enough away that she couldn't "go running home" to Daddy. She was doing pretty well, got a job, and had an apartment. She met her ex-husband and her troubles started. She had five children and is an epileptic. This interview was held in the fast-food restaurant where Christine has worked for several months. Before sitting down, Christine went to the regulars, greeted them, and gave many of them hugs. During the interview, two others came by the table to say hello. The following interview illustrates some of her challenges, which are often typical of the lives of women offenders.

Question: Christine, how did you begin to get in trouble and involved in drugs and crime?

Christine: When I moved to Texas, I met and married my husband. He was one of those "bad boys," working in construction, who moved around a lot. We lived in several cities in the Southwest looking for work. My husband got hooked on crack, and to get money for his drugs, he prostituted me. He was abusive and beat me regularly. He would beat me if I was gone for too long or didn't come home from prostituting with enough money. Many beatings were so bad that I had seizures.

I also got involved in drugs and became an addict. He would give me some of his drugs as my reward for bringing home money. That became the only thing I looked forward to. By that time, I had three children; they were in foster care. We were homeless, living off what I earned. I got pregnant again and tried to wean myself off drugs. Eventually, I decided to hide from my husband. People on the street saw what was happening. Other prostitutes and my drug dealer helped me hide when my husband started looking for me. My husband threatened to kill me and my family if I left with the kids. And he said if he couldn't find me, he would find and kill my family.

I was arrested several times for prostitution and later was arrested for neglect and prostitution and was sentenced to jail for six and a half months. At that time, I was pregnant with my youngest child. The day I was arrested, it was the only day I didn't cry as I had every other time. I just hated my life. I realized God had answered my prayers, and prison would keep me safe and cured

of drugs. I knew my children were safe in foster care, my husband couldn't hurt me or the kids, and I would have access to treatment. Overall, I was in and out of jail several times.

In jail, I wasn't diagnosed and was denied medication for epilepsy until I had a dozen grand mal seizures and was hospitalized. While in jail, I had my fourth baby, and I participated in a drug recovery program. I put my fourth child in temporary custody with a couple, with the agreement that when I got out of jail and was back on my feet, I would get her back. When I was released from jail, I tried to contact them to see her and found out that the couple had already started the paperwork to adopt her. After an almost two-year court battle, I agreed to let them adopt my child.

Question: What type of drug abuse programs did you participate in while in jail?

Christine: "Chances" was the name of the drug program that helped me while in jail. I credit this program with helping me develop a strong desire to recover from drugs. After completing the program, I had the option to transfer out of the drug program or stay there and counsel others as a "big sister." I stayed in the program and was so good at counseling them, I was assigned five little sisters when we were only supposed to have two.

While I was in jail, a caseworker with the Magdalene program came to visit and told me about their two-year recovery program. It sounded good, so I enrolled. When I got out of jail that time, I waited tables to earn a living. I became pregnant with my fifth child, but the strain of pregnancy increased the frequency of my seizures. I had to quit working and continued to live at Magdalene House until the birth of my daughter.

For about a year, I went to the "John" school to talk to other addicts. It's a weeklong program that men, who have been arrested for soliciting, pay $250 (which went to Magdalene House) to attend in order to avoid arrest. I told them about the dangers of soliciting, such as "tag teaming," when one prostitute would go with a man and another would come over and beat and rob the man.

Now, I attend AA, which is a requirement of Dr. Hazel's program. Dr. Hazel runs the recovery program at Magdalene.

Question: You have had a tough life. What are some of the concerns of other female inmates?

Christine: Quite frankly, many seemed concerned with their kids but not "that" concerned. They seemed to be more concerned about getting out of jail. Some of their families took care of their kids; others were in foster care. I had three boys and one girl from my first marriage. At the beginning of my stay in prison, a social worker brought my three boys to see me. The oldest, which refused to be adopted, was placed in guardianship. The next two boys were adopted by different families in a different cities. Like I've already said, my daughter was adopted by a couple.

I was actually lucky. My family was normal, my parents were married, I had five siblings, and there was no abuse or alcoholism in our history. My parents tried to obtain custody of my children while I was incarcerated, but they couldn't do it, even though I would have granted it.

Question: What was it like to get visits from your kids while incarcerated?

Christine: It was horrible. I remember the only time the boys came to visit about a month after I went to prison. The oldest understood a little about what was going on, but the others didn't understand why I was there. I told them I was sick and was staying there to get better. My daughter, who was born while I was in jail, was the only one who visited on a somewhat regular basis.

The next time they visited was after I was released. I continued to see them in foster care throughout that period and was fighting for their custody. I went for scheduled visits at DCS (Department of Children's Services) after I was released from jail and was fighting for their custody.

Question: Is there a lot of drug use in prison?

Christine: If you want it, you can get it. I was in minimum security, and it was easy to recognize when people were on drugs because they were dazed and acted very secretive.

Question: How was your medical care in prison?

Christine: It was pretty good after they recognized I was an epileptic. I received the medication I needed. I also had a baby in Meharry (Metro General) Hospital under a physician's care. They treated me well there.

Question: How is your life coming now?

Christine: Pretty good. I have been in a relationship with a man for seven years, with whom I have another daughter. My oldest child is twenty-one and he lives with us, as does our daughter.

But, I will always have a place in my life for all my kids. Even the ones who were adopted. I want to be ready in case they come home. On their birthdays, I always prepare each one's favorite meal so that if they come home, they will know I remembered them. I try to put all this behind me, but there are some things I never will forget.

Words of wisdom (my take on life): One day, when my son and I had the same day off, we decided to make the most of it by walking around and window shopping. During our travels, he started telling me how, when every time life starts looking up for him, something happens and things go downhill. His question: "Mom, why is this always happening to me?" My reply was simple: "Some people like to think that God puts the 'downhill' times in your life so you'll appreciate the ups." My son, at the "ripe old age" of twenty-one, still looked confused and unsatisfied with my response. I elaborated. Chris, you are young, and life is a rollercoaster ride. When you're born, you start out at the top. The ups and downs are your learning experiences, some downs are deeper than others, but you have to keep in mind that the rollercoaster will go up again, and the ride will be exhilarating! No matter how many "downs" you have on this rollercoaster ride called life, the ride ALWAYS lets you off at the top.

prisons, but only one or two female prisons. Therefore, women are often placed farther from their homes than men. It is interesting that wives of male inmates regularly bring children to visit their fathers. However, when mothers end up in prison, they receive fewer visits with children due to the distances and the logistical problems those giving child care have in making visits.

Unfortunately, when women receive visits from their children, prison visiting room conditions are not conducive to fostering a parent-child relationship. Prison visiting areas usually provide seating similar to that in an airport waiting area, although many now provide a small room or area of the larger visiting room for

Most female inmates are mothers, and separation from their children is a difficult consequence of their imprisonment.

parenting programs
prison programs to assist inmates to improve their parenting skills, even while in prison

Girl Scouts Behind Bars
Girl Scout troops that have their chapter based in a prison so inmates with children can participate as Scout parents

small children with a television, videos, and books or toys for children to play with. To improve the parental relationship between women inmates and their children, many prisons have established **parenting programs**. These programs often include training classes to improve parenting skills and suggest methods to "parent" from prison. One example is how to play the role of mother as teacher, by emphasizing the mother reading to children (sometimes on audiotape) and helping children with their school homework during visits. A few programs include special visiting situations where children may be able to spend extended time or even overnight with their mothers and may include special use (separate from other inmates) of the prison recreation or dining areas. A great example of an outstanding program is "PS, I Love You," a family literacy program in the New Mexico Women's Correctional Facility. This program videotapes inmates who are mothers reading a book that is then sent to her children.

Another unique program to assist inmate mothers in staying connected to their children is **Girl Scouts Behind Bars**. Some female prisons have established Girl Scout chapters, have meetings with female inmates and their daughters in the visiting room, and get the inmate mothers involved in "den mother" activities, such as planning meetings or providing snacks. The Girl Scout chapters are usually linked to a chapter in the community so that the children can also be involved in normal Girl Scouts activities. This program also encourages the continued involvement of mothers and daughters in Girl Scouts after the mothers' release from prison.[58]

Alcohol and Substance Abuse

Many women offenders have a serious history and problem with alcohol and substance abuse, often even more serious and more involved in their criminality than men. Fifty-nine percent of female state prisoners in 2004 were using drugs within the month before their offense, 17 percent of females inmates (compared to 10 percent of men) used methamphetamines in the month before their offense,[59] and 40 percent of women (compared to 32 percent of men) were under the influence of drugs at the time of their crime.[60] Also, "[n]early 1 in 3 women serving time in State prisons said they had committed the offense which brought them to prison in order to obtain

Many prisons have added a room for children to play in or for parents to read to them so that there is some semblance of normalcy as children visit their parents in prison.
Courtesy of the Ohio Department of Rehabilitation and Correction.

money to support their need for drugs."[61] The Center for Substance Abuse Treatment reports that almost 80 percent of the women in state prisons have "severe, long-standing substance abuse problems."[62] Unquestionably, women offenders are in need of programs and services to reduce their dependence on alcohol and drugs.

Unfortunately, the need for substance abuse treatment in prison is generally not satisfactorily met. Although 74 percent of all prisons offered drug or alcohol counseling in 2005,[63] in 2002, only 12.9 percent of the prison populations participated in drug treatment programs. Of these, 63,960 were in either individual or group treatment and the remainder were in separate drug treatment units.[64] Twenty percent of women offenders report receiving drug or alcohol treatment during the period of their incarceration.[65] Another Bureau of Justice Statistics report noted that one in four inmates participate in drug treatment programs, most of which are self-help groups, and only 4 percent receive professional counseling for their abuse.[66]

It is important to increase the overall number of **substance abuse programs** and particularly the number of those for female inmates. Also, the women's programs should focus on the specific issues around the reasons for female drug abuse and special circumstances around their postincarceration needs. Chesney-Lind suggests:

> *Women's programs must, first and foremost, give participants strategies to deal with their profound substance abuse problems. They must also be gender-sensitive in additional ways: they must understand that most women take drugs as a form of self-medication, and they must be sensitive to women's unique circumstances (by providing such services as child care and transportation).*[67]

substance abuse programs
programs for offenders to reduce their likelihood of further abuse of alcohol or drugs

Need for Medical Care

Medical care is very difficult to provide in a quality fashion within a prison. Moore suggests, "Problems in providing care to the incarcerated fall into two broad categories: health status of the inmate population and deficiencies in the delivery of medical care,"[68] and identifies six factors inherent in correctional settings that hamper the provision of health services:

1. not a priority of the correctional institution;
2. limited financial resources;
3. difficulties in staff recruitment;
4. absence of a current manual of health care policies and procedures;
5. isolation of the institution from community health care; and
6. lack of a constituency for inmate health services.[69]

Although all inmate medical care is difficult to provide, one issue without question is that female inmates have more serious health problems than male inmates. This results not only from the need for gynecological care, but from a history of poverty, drug and alcohol abuse, poor diet and nutrition, and past neglect and lack of health care.[70] Women, of course, also have medical issues around pregnancy. Greenfeld and Snell report that 5 percent of women admitted to state prisons are pregnant, and although 90 percent of these had received a gynecological exam since their admission, only 4 percent had received prenatal care since their admission.[71] Another survey of pregnant prisoners noted that only half were provided prenatal care, 15 percent were provided a special diet or nutrition education, 15 percent received counseling regarding placement of their child after birth, and 11 percent were provided postnatal counseling.[72]

The delivery of correctional health care has improved over the past two decades. However, there is a serious need for correctional administrators to continue to make improvements and, specifically, to address the challenges in providing health care for women prisoners. In describing these challenges for correctional administrators, Seiter notes,

> [T]here are unanswered philosophical questions about the quality and quantity of medical care that should be provided incarcerated felons. Costs of inmate health care continue to rise, and there is constant pressure on administrators to reduce medical spending. Prisons have never been an attractive recruiting ground for medical personnel, and competition for providers has intensified over the past decade. All of these issues require prison administrators to look for new ways to solve serious problems. Yet, there are few states that would suggest they have found the answers, and are comfortable with the cost and quality of the medical care provided in their prisons.[73]

Classification Systems for Female Offenders

One concern that has recently come to light is that objective classification systems developed for male offenders often tend to "overclassify" female offenders. In a 2001 review of all fifty states, the National Institute of Corrections examined the current classification practices used for female offenders and discovered that, although many states recognized the differences by gender regarding needs and risks, few had incorporated these differences into their objective classification systems.[74] Overclassification is the placement of offenders in prisons more secure than needed for their level of risk and results from using risk factors (such as seriousness of the offense) that were developed using predominantly male offender examples and did not take into account the specific variables that reduced the risk posed by women.

In the early 1990s, the Federal Bureau of Prisons (BOP) reviewed its classification system based on these gender issues. The BOP found that it was placing female offenders at a higher level of physical security prisons than their risk to escape or tendency for violence warranted. In most cases, women's criminal involvement was as accomplices to men, and if the crime included the use of a weapon or violence, male offenders actually handled the weapon or resorted to violence. Also, a previously unconsidered factor was that female inmates often had children and close ties in the community, and these were important factors in predicting escape. Therefore, the BOP administratively reduced the number of points assigned for certain types of crimes (such as crimes of violence or use of a weapon during the offense) committed by women and was able to move a large percentage of the female inmate population to less secure prisons.

The "A Look Into" box describes the issues and challenges that prison staff have in dealing with female inmates.

A Look Into...

Working with Female Inmates

One interesting point regarding female offenders is the differences in them as inmates from their male counterparts. I have worked as a case manager and a unit manager for female inmates and in three other prisons that held male inmates. To develop this case study, I talked to someone who has recently been a case manager for a male and a female caseload. It is interesting to see the differences he describes in working with the two populations.

- Females need more contact with agencies outside of the prison. More women are filing for divorce and need contact with the family courts. More have children issues and must contact the division of family services. These types of contacts often require telephone calls, as they cannot be completed only through the mail.
- Sentences for women overall are less than for men, so the turnaround is greater. More women are referred to halfway houses, and staff have to move more quickly to get referrals completed.
- Medical and mental health issues are different and more intense. Female inmates are sometimes pregnant while in prison and need prenatal care. Mental health issues seem more pronounced for female inmates, they need more psychological services, and a higher percentage seem to be on antidepressants.
- Women stay much more attached to the community than men, who seem to divorce themselves from their families and community ties. Female inmates take more responsibility with regard to their children and family, especially

their parents, and are continually more stressed out about their problems in the community.
- Female inmates are very different in regard to their relationships with staff and other inmates. Women seem to need someone to talk to and will talk more freely than men to staff about their problems. They are also much more with open about their sexual relationships (in prison) than men. They may have a girlfriend; they may have a breakup; and there is more fighting about these sexual relationships. A higher percentage of women seem to participate in homosexuality, or they hide it less. Men get involved in homosexual activity more for the sexual gratification, whereas women get involved for the emotional relationship.
- Women are more interested in being involved in programs. There is a high demand for drug programs, and they are more willing to confront their drug use as a problem that needs attention. They work better with staff and are more willing to take orders and follow instructions.
- One interesting issue concerns property. Men want food or snacks, but women try to accumulate hobby or craft items, to create more of a "homey" atmosphere in their cell or dormitory area than men. They try to get jewelry and often have visitors bring them things that are not allowed. They have different demands of the commissary; they desire hair dye, skin care products, and other personal cosmetic items.
- Race is not as much of an issue as with men. Female inmates seem less concerned about

...continued

race and do not self-segregate nearly as much. In male dining rooms, inmates often sit at tables with only their race, whereas women are much less concerned about this.

- Women have fewer disciplinary issues than men. They just seem to accept their incarceration without breaking the rules as much.
- Female inmates, however, are far more manipulative with staff than male inmates. They are more likely to exaggerate or outright lie about a problem at home that requires immediate attention or a crisis phone call home.

- In general, women have many more demands and take much more staff time than men. They realistically have more issues, particularly related to home, and desire immediate attention from staff. When case managers need to talk to male inmates to prepare a progress report, they almost have to order them to come in to talk and discuss their community plans. Women are lined up at the door to talk about issues at home.

Legal Issues Regarding Parity for Female Inmates

Barefield v. Leach

a 1974 federal court decision that a disparity of programs for female inmates could not be justified because the smaller number of female inmates made it more costly to provide program parity

Over the past ten years, correctional agencies have made many improvements in responding to the specific needs of women in prison. Many of these developments have resulted from the intervention of federal courts, noting the disparate treatment received and conditions faced by female offenders. As early as 1974, a federal court in the case of **Barefield v. Leach** found that the state of New Mexico was not providing parity in vocational training and work opportunity for female inmates and ruled that such disparity could not be justified just because the smaller number of female inmates made it more costly to provide parity in these programs.[75] In *Butler v. Reno*, female plaintiffs who were federal inmates claimed gender discrimination due to denial of access to facilities, programs, and services available to similarly situated male federal inmates. The U.S. District Court for the District of Columbia agreed with the plaintiffs, and the parties entered into a

Female offenders have developed some of the same habits as male offenders (such as adding tattoos), and the courts have declared that they deserve parity with male offenders in programs and services. Photo by Richard P. Seiter.

stipulated order of settlement in 1995. In the order, the Bureau of Prisons agreed to provide programs, services, and facilities for female inmates that were comparable to those offered to male inmates. This included placing minimum-security female inmates in camps with limited physical security; maintaining similar staff-inmate ratios; providing work, education, parent-child, and recreation program opportunities; and providing health care comparable to that in male prisons.

In the 1995 case of ***Pargo v. Elliott,*** the Eighth Circuit Court found that just the fact that there are differences in programs between male and female prisons is not necessarily a violation of the equal protection clause of the Constitution. The Court suggested that five criteria should be used to examine whether differences in prison programs are discriminatory: the number of inmates in a prison, the prison security level, the crimes committed by inmates, the length of sentences being served by inmates, and any other special characteristics that could be identified by the prison as reasons for program differences.[76] It is recognized that women will look for different types of jobs after release from prison and that many need training in parenting and child-care issues that are not as critical for men.

The solution to the problem of parity has been lessened with the growth in the number of female inmates. Rafter reports that, although only two to three new female prisons were opened every decade between 1930 and 1950, during the 1980s more than 34 new women's prisons were opened, by 1990 there were 71 women's prisons, and in 1995 there were 104 prisons designated for female offenders.[77] With 115,779 women in state and federal prisons on June 30, 2008, many new prisons have opened for women and most have been expanded. This allows for greater economies of scale to provide additional categories of vocational training or other treatment programs for women inmates. New prisons also provide the opportunity to begin new types of educational, vocational, and work programs, focusing on the nontraditional roles of women offenders and providing parity with male programs. Finally, additional prisons scattered across states enable women to be more likely housed closer to their homes than when a state had only one female prison.

Pargo v. Elliott
the 1995 Eighth Circuit Court case that allowed that differences in programs between male and female prisons does not necessarily violate the equal protection clause of the Constitution

The Franklin County Prerelease Center in Ohio is a facility to which women inmates move in their last few months of incarceration to prepare for release to the community.
Courtesy of the Ohio Department of Rehabilitation and Correction.

Alternatives to Prison for Women Offenders

Many experts believe that the most effective way to prepare female offenders for success in the community is to maximize the use of alternative programs to incarceration. Even though the public has taken a "tough on crime" approach for male offenders, most people are willing to recognize that women present less risk (or at least are perceived to present less risk) of further victimization and therefore are good candidates to be supervised and managed in the community.

With this in mind, nine out of ten state correctional administrators reported that they use some type of alternative to prison for women, even after they are committed to prison. Some of these programs shorten the prison stay and move female inmates into the community more quickly, whereas others target successful reentry of women from prison to community. Figure 7.6 illustrates the types of

Alternative program

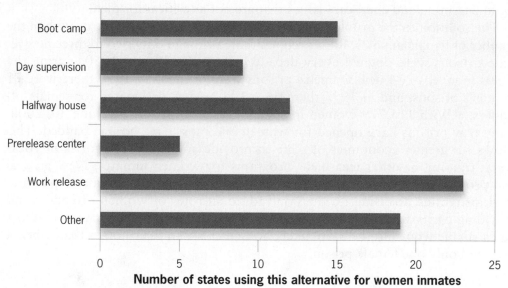

Alternative program

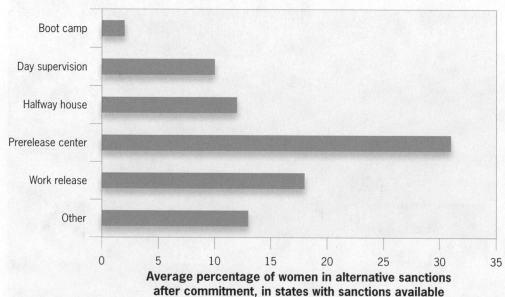

Source: Merry Morash, Timothy S. Bynum, and Barbara A. Koons, "Women Offenders: Programming Needs and Promising Approaches," *National Institute of Justice: Research in Brief* (August 1998): 7.

FIGURE 7.6   Alternative Sanctions for Women Offenders after Commitment to Prison

alternative programs that are used by states in this regard, both by number of states and by percentage of women in the alternative sanctions. The alternative used by most states is work release, in which inmates either leave the prison during the day and go into the community and work or are moved to community residential centers (halfway houses) to find jobs and work in the community. The highest percentage of female inmates is involved in prerelease centers. An example of a state prerelease center is the Franklin County (Ohio) Prerelease Center, to which inmates are moved in their last three to six months in prison in order to participate in programs focusing on release preparation. At the center they receive training in life skills (finding a residence, opening a checking account, applying for credit) and preparation for entering the world of work (writing a résumé, interviewing for a job, and responding to the issue of their criminality and incarceration). Women also learn how to deal with the day-to-day issues in the workplace, such as the importance of quality, taking responsibility, and getting along with supervisors and peers.

Now that students have learned the issues that face women convicted of a crime and have considered the potential for alternatives to incarceration, it is time to struggle with the challenging question of whether women should face justice for their crimes just as men do. Consider this issue in the "You Make the Decision" box at the end of the chapter.

Summary

In the last twenty years, the number of adults under correctional supervision has increased from just over 1.3 million to almost 6.6 million, and the number of prison inmates grew from just over 300,000 to more than 1.6 million offenders. These increases have resulted from several factors, including the war on drugs and a tremendous increase in the number of arrests for drug offenses; toughened sentencing statutes that lengthened the time offenders serve in prison, on probation, and on postprison supervision; sentencing guidelines and mandatory minimum sentences that took discretion away from judges and resulted in more female offenders being sent to prison; and a lower tolerance for risk, resulting in an increased number of parole and probation revocations.

Even though the gender makeup of offenders throughout the criminal justice system is still predominantly male, female offenders are "catching up" in that their rate of growth in most areas is greater than that of male offenders. Women now make up 24.5 percent of all arrests by law enforcement agencies, 18 percent of all felony convictions, and 7.1 percent of the state and federal prison population. Much of the attention and study of the criminal justice system, offenders, and their characteristics have been historically directed toward male criminals. However, with the increasing number of women offenders, the impact of gender differences on the correctional system is now an important area of study.

Although much of the increase in women's criminal involvement has been linked to drug crimes, it is estimated that women commit 10 percent of violent offenses. Women in prison face a variety of different problems and therefore have different needs for programs and services. Their family ties and separation from their children make visiting and parenting programs even more critical for female than male prisoners. Many women suffer from long-term and serious substance

CHAPTER REVIEW

abuse histories, which are unfortunately not being addressed in prison. Their medical needs are much greater than those of men. And the recent implementations of objective classification systems have tended to overclassify them to prisons with a higher emphasis on security than is necessary.

This chapter has set the groundwork for a further and more detailed examination of the makeup of the correctional population in the United States. The next chapter examines the handling of juvenile offenders; following that, the many special groups of offenders who require handling or management are described. As noted in the introduction to this chapter, offenders are what corrections is all about. Corrections is not simply policy, operations, or laws. It is the management of people and the various considerations that must be taken into account as we attempt to manage a diverse group of people in an environment that is safe and secure and contributes to the long-term safety of the public.

Key Terms

racial disparity

drug offenders

male offenders

general population

female offenders

parenting programs

Girl Scouts Behind Bars

substance abuse programs

Barefield v. Leach

Pargo v. Elliott

Review Questions

1. What has been the primary factor in the growth in the number of individuals under correctional supervision over the past twenty years?

2. Compare the increase in females versus males in terms of the number under correctional supervision.

3. What does Wilbanks say about the presence of racism in the criminal justice system and what do most researchers believe is the reason for the disproportionate number of minorities under correctional supervision?

4. How has the age of offenders changed?

5. What percentage of people arrested for violent felonies are male?

6. What is the "general population" within a prison?

7. What is the overall goal of a prison classification system?

8. Why are women now sentenced similarly to male offenders?

9. How does the recidivism rate for women offenders compare to that for men?

10. What percentage of the prison population is female?

11. List the special problems faced by female inmates.

12. What programs do prisons have to deal with the parenting needs of female prisoners?

13. How do female inmate classification systems differ from those for men?

14. Describe the impact that the case *Barefield v. Leach* has had on the operation of female prisons.

You Make the Decision...

Should Women Go to Prison Just Like Men?

In 1925 women represented only 3.7 percent of the national prison population, but in the 1980s this percentage began to climb. By 1990, it had increased to 5.7 percent, and by January 1, 2007, 7.1 percent of the 1,598,316 prisoners in state and federal prisons were women. Historically, judges gave female offenders a break by often granting them probation instead of incarceration, thinking that they were not a risk to society and most of their crimes were as accomplices to men. With the war on drugs, the imposition of mandatory prison sentences, and the use of sentencing guidelines, women now receive a prison sentence in almost equal proportion to men. However, the average sentence served by women is still significantly less than that served by men (in 2001, men in prison were serving an average sentence of 5.22 years, whereas women in prison were serving an average of 3.63 years).

As noted in this chapter, women face different issues than men do when they go to prison. Eighty percent of incarcerated women are mothers, one-fourth of the women who enter prison are either pregnant or have given birth within the past twelve months, and 65 percent of women held in state prisons have children under age 18. About two-thirds of these women (compared to 44 percent of male inmates) lived with their young children before entering prison. More female inmates have a link between their criminality and substance abuse than male inmates. Approximately one-third of women inmates committed the offense that brought them to prison to obtain money to support their need for drugs.

It is not difficult to argue that female offenders are not as dangerous or as serious a risk as their male counterparts. In terms of recidivism, rates for female offenders are high, yet thought to be less than recidivism rates for comparable male offenders. Female offenders are less likely to be involved in violent crimes, and the consequences of male violence are usually more serious for the victim. The facts that there is a significant increase in the number of women in prison, they have many collateral consequences associated with their incarceration, and they are less dangerous to society suggest the need to reconsider the "one size fits all" sentencing approach. Consider all these issues and decide whether women should be sentenced differently than men, or whether there should be more discretion for judges to consider individual factors and sentence women to community alternatives instead of prison.

Chapter Resources on mycrimekit™

Go to mycrimekit.com to explore the following study tools and resources specific to this chapter:

- **Practice Quiz:** multiple-choice, true/false, short-answer, and essay questions to help students test their knowledge
- **WebQuests:** learning activities built around Web searches
  - Bureau of Justice Statistics—Offenders: www.ojp.usdoj.gov/bjs/
  - FBI-Sex Offenders: www.fbi.gov/cid/cac/registry.htm
- **Insider's Experiences:** "The Murder of a Correctional Worker"

- **Seiter Videos:**
  - See offenders discuss crime
  - See female inmates discuss issues they face
  - See a female inmate discuss separation from her children
- **Career Center:** A Career as a Correctional Treatment Specialist
- **Flashcards:** Ten flashcards to test knowledge of the chapter's key terms

The Juvenile Correctional System

After reading this chapter, you should be able to:

1. Describe the problem of juvenile crime and identify any trends in such crimes.

2. Explain the development of the juvenile justice system and the concept of *parens patriae*.

3. Discuss the reasons why juveniles are waived to adult courts and the concerns about this process.

4. List and define the three categories of offenders referred to the juvenile justice system.

5. Outline the steps in the juvenile justice process and compare them with similar steps in the adult justice process.

6. Describe the operations of juvenile residential facilities.

7. Identify and specify the result of key federal court cases affecting the rights of juvenile offenders.

8. Describe the problems regarding juvenile gangs and juvenile drug use.

Introduction

When I was director of adult corrections for Ohio, I used to tell my colleague who was director of the juvenile correctional system, "I am glad I do not have your job." Our mission was much clearer in dealing with adult sanctions. We supervised and incarcerated adult felons so that society is protected. We built secure prisons and knew how to manage inmates. But my colleague's mission was far less clear. Some people want to treat serious juvenile offenders just as we treat adults. Others argue that these offenders are still children and should not be punished as criminals, but treated as delinquents who need to be led back on the right path to becoming mature and responsible adults. In the juvenile system, no one can decide whether correctional institutions are prisons or training schools, whether offenders are inmates or students, or whether clients and society are better off with them in institutions or maintained in the community. Unfortunately, these statements are still accurate. The juvenile justice system was originally created to deal with delinquent acts committed by individuals under age 18 (in most states), in a separate system designed to deal differently with juveniles than with adults. Over the years, however, the juvenile justice system has suffered from a lack of consistency and agreement on the mission and approach.

This chapter describes the problem of juvenile crime, the history and creation of the juvenile justice system, and recent developments to ensure that the system can respond to modern challenges of criminal and delinquent behavior by youth. Issues regarding developing case law, drug crimes by youth, and juvenile gang membership are also described. To introduce some of the problems, the "An Insider's Experience" in *MyCrimeKit* illustrates some of the mission confusion faced by juvenile correctional agencies.

mycrimekit

Insider's Experience: Defining the Role of Juvenile Institutions.

The Problem of Juvenile Crime

Similar to adult crimes, juvenile crime rates and trends fluctuate over time, yet there is often a disconnect between actual crime data and public perception and justice policies. It often appears that media coverage of crimes and criminal activity by juveniles has more influence on policy than actual trends in the data. The Federal Bureau of Investigation (FBI) collects both juvenile and adult crime data in the annual *Uniform Crime Reports* (UCR). Serious and violent crime trends are reviewed by monitoring four crimes in the UCR (murder and nonnegligent manslaughter, forcible rape, robbery, and aggravated assault) and the Violent Crime Index.

Over the past few years, the high number of juveniles arrested for crimes has been a serious concern. In 2006, 2.2 million juveniles were arrested. This is level with 2003, although 24 percent lower than 1997. Table 8.1 illustrates the overall numbers of juveniles arrested for all categories of offenses during 2006.

Although the volume of these numbers is alarming, they actually represent some good news. The 1,310 arrests of juveniles for murder in 2006 is a reduction of 42 percent since 1997 and 3 percent since 2002. Since 1997, juvenile arrests for motor vehicle theft declined by 53 percent, and burglary arrests declined by 37 percent. The only significant increase in juvenile arrests from 1997 to 2006 is for prostitution (15 percent).[1] However, these increases may not necessarily indicate an increase in the volume of this type of crime, as much as law enforcement efforts targeting this type of activity. Interesting is the large number of arrests for runaway. Runaway is an example of a **status offense,** an act that is determined a violation of law for juveniles but not for adults.

status offense

an activity that is considered a crime only because the offender is under the age of 18 and would not be a crime if committed by an adult; includes acts such as running away from home, ungovernability, truancy, or underage drinking

TABLE 8.1   Arrests of Juveniles in 2006

Most Serious Offense	2006 Estimated Number of Juvenile Arrests	Percent of Total Juvenile Arrests		Percent Change		
		Female	Under Age 15	1997–2006	2002–2006	2005–2006
Total	2,219,600	29%	29%	−24%	−3%	1%
Violent Crime Index	100,700	17	29	−20	8	4
Murder and nonegligent manslaughter	1,310	5	8	−42	18	3
Focible rape	3,610	2	36	−31	−20	−10
Robbery	35,040	9	23	−16	34	19
Aggravated assault	60,770	23	32	−21	−1	−2
Property Crime Index	404,700	32	33	−44	−17	−5
Burglary	83,900	11	32	−37	−6	5
Larceny-theft	278,100	41	34	−45	−19	−8
Motor vehicle theft	34,600	17	23	−53	−28	−8
Arson	8,100	14	58	−22	−5	0
Nonindex						
Other assaults	249,400	34	39	2	5	−1
Forgery and counterfeiting	3,500	33	11	−59	−34	−20
Fraud	8,100	34	15	−31	−14	−5
Embezzlement	1,400	45	4	3	−3	20
Stolen property (buying, receiving, possessing)	21,300	15	25	−45	12	1
Vandalism	117,500	13	41	−14	10	11
Weapons (carrying, possessing, etc.)	47,200	10	33	−10	31	2
Prostitution and commercialized vice	1,600	74	14	15	16	9
Sex offense (except forcible rape and prostitution)	15,900	10	47	−16	−18	−9
Drug abuse violations	190,700	16	15	−11	1	2
Gambling	2,200	3	15	−43	20	−14
Offenses against the family and children	5,200	37	31	−48	−40	−6
Driving under the influence	20,100	23	3	1	−8	9
Liquor laws	141,400	36	9	−15	−5	9
Drunkenness	16,300	25	11	−30	−7	12
Disorderly conduct	207,700	33	39	7	8	0
Vagrancy	5,000	30	33	−36	4	10
All other offenses (except traffic)	386,000	27	25	−19	−3	2
Suspicion (not included in totals)	500	22	22	−74	−72	−15
Curfew and loitering	152,900	31	27	−31	6	4
Runaways	114,200	57	33	−45	−11	−2

- In 2006, there were an estimated 60,770 Juvenile arrests for aggravated assault. Between 1997 and 2006, the annual number of such arrests fell 21%.
- Between 1995 and 2004, juvenile robbery and aggravated assault arrests declined substantially (down 44% and 23%, respectively). However, in the next two years, while juvenile aggravated assault arrests continued to fall (slightly), juvenile arrests for robbery increased (11% in 2005 and 19% in 2006).
- In 2006, females accounted for 17% of juvenile Violent Crime Index arrests, 32% of juvenile Property Crime Index arrests, and 16% of juvenile drug abuse arrests.
- In 2006, youth under the age of 15 accounted for about one-third of all violent (29%) and property crime (33%) arrests.

Note: Detail may not add to totals because of rounding.

Source: Howard N. Snyder, "Juvenile Arrests in 2006," *Juvenile Justice Bulletin* (Washington, D.C.: U.S. Department of Justice, November 2008), p. 3.

Arrests per 100,000 juveniles ages 10–17

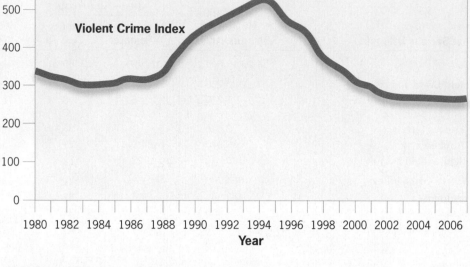

Source: Analysis of arrest data from unpublished FBI reports for 1980 through 2007 and from *Crime in the United States, 2007* (Washington, D.C.: U.S. Government Printing Office, 2008).

FIGURE 8.1   The Juvenile Violent Crime Index Rate, 1980–2007

Over the past several decades, the number of juvenile arrests has been relatively stable except for increases in juvenile violent crime, as murder arrests for juvenile offenders increased by 93 percent during the 1980s and arrests for aggravated assault increased by 72 percent.[2] As illustrated in Figure 8.1, between 1988 and 1994 there was a dramatic increase in the arrest rates for juvenile serious violent crimes, and public attention and concern regarding the problem of juvenile violent crime increased. Since 1997, however, these arrest rates have dropped 20 percent and reached the lowest levels since 1987.

Public concern is about not only juveniles' violent crimes, but also all crime that is being committed by juveniles. The proportion of violent crimes cleared by juvenile arrests averaged about 9 percent of all violent crimes during the late 1980s, but climbed to 14 percent of all violent crimes in 1994. From 1997 to 2006, the percentage of violent crimes committed by juveniles declined by 20 percent.[3] Table 8.2 compares the change in the number of violent crime arrests for juveniles and adults between 1997 and 2006, indicating that the decline was actually greater for juveniles than adults.

TABLE 8.2	Percent Change in Arrests of Juveniles and Adults, 1997–2006	
	Percent Change in Arrests, 1997–2006	
Most Serious Offense	**Juvenile**	**Adult**
Violent Crime Index	−20%	−11%
Murder	−42	−12
Forcible rape	−31	−8
Robbery	−16	−3
Aggravated assault	−21	−12

Source: *Crime in the United States 2006,* Table 32.

Juveniles involved in gangs contributed to the increases in violent and other crimes during the past two decades. Courtesy A. Ramey/PhotoEdit.

The FBI *Uniform Crime Reports* also include trends in the volume of property crimes committed by juveniles, using the four property index crimes of burglary, larceny-theft, motor vehicle theft, and arson. During the increase in juvenile violent crime from 1988 to 1994, arrest rates of juvenile property crime remained relatively constant and then began to fall after 1994, as did violent crimes. From 1997 to 2006, the juvenile Property Crime Index arrest rate dropped 44 percent to its lowest level since at least the 1970s.[4]

Several theories suggest the reasons for the increase in juvenile violent crime from 1988 to 1994. The first is that, as in crime statistics regarding adults, the emergence of crack cocaine and the violence around its use and sale caused an increase in juvenile violent crime. Crack cocaine is an extremely addictive drug and can result in violent behavior by those using it. Crack cocaine is also considerably less expensive than powder cocaine, and its emergence created a new drug of choice in urban, poverty-ridden areas. Violent confrontations between various

Juvenile and adult gangs like to "mark" their territory, warning other gangs to stay away and informing local residents that the gang is in control of the area. Photo by Jeffrey J. Rojek.

factions of drug sellers occurred as groups attempted to control areas of drug sales for their own group or individual profit.

Second, the expansion of juvenile gang membership during this period resulted in expanded juvenile violence. Gangs lead to violence in a variety of ways. Gangs use violence to get attention, show their toughness, and recruit new members. Violence is also a way that gangs show that they are in control of an area, other gangs should stay out, and nongang youths should join them to be a member of the dominant group and avoid becoming victims themselves. Gang violence also occurs between gangs. Gangs will fight rather than let any other gang gain members or take control of their area. The proliferation of weapons in the possession of juveniles also led to an increase in violence. The number of juvenile arrests for weapons charges increased 103 percent from 1985 to 1994; eleven large cities reported that approximately 40 percent of their juvenile males were in possession of a weapon at some time,[5] and there has been a noted increase in the use of guns by juveniles who participate in the illegal drug market.[6] However, from 1997 to 2006, the percentage of juvenile arrests for weapons charges has declined by 10 percent.[7]

Development of the Juvenile Justice System

Refuge Period

a period from 1824 to 1899 when delinquent or neglected children were placed in a home for training and discipline

In the late eighteenth century, as the American colonies were establishing systems of government and courts, juveniles under age 7 were seen as below the age of reason and thereby incapable of the formation of criminal intent. However, those over age 7 were handled in the criminal justice system, the same as adults. Soon thereafter, recognition of the need to deal separately with delinquent or neglected children developed. As a result, between 1824 and 1899, the **Refuge Period** developed. Houses of Refuge were created to house, train, educate, and provide good habits for these wayward children through strict discipline.[8] These houses were usually operated by charitable or religious organizations, they had few controls or standards, and the attempt to change the behavior of delinquents often resulted in harsh and brutal conditions. As the need for reform of the entire approach to managing juveniles was recognized, the Society for the Prevention of Juvenile Delinquency began to advocate for reforms to include a separation of juveniles from the adult system as early as 1825.

During the 1800s, Houses of Refuge were operated to house wayward youths and provide them with structure and discipline. Courtesy T. A. Carlson/CORBIS-NY.

When John Augustus, the Boston shoemaker regarded as the "father of probation," began to bail criminals out of jail in the middle 1800s, he also persuaded judges to place wayward youth under his supervision, and he brought the distinctions between juvenile and adult offenders to the courts' attention. However, the **juvenile justice system** was not created until Illinois passed the Juvenile Court Act, and the first juvenile court was established in Cook County (Chicago) in 1899. By creating a separate juvenile court, the concept of ***parens patriae*** was recognized as the basis for giving the court the authority to take over supervision of children when their parents failed to provide proper care and guidance. The concept of *parens patriae* means "parents of the nation" and was first established in England with the 1601 Elizabethan Poor Laws, which allowed officials to take charge of delinquent children and place them in poorhouses or orphanages to gain control of them. In more modern times, this doctrine was expanded as the basis for juvenile court and correctional systems to take responsibility for educating and nurturing delinquents, with an emphasis on reform and rehabilitation.

The use of a separate juvenile court, initiated in Cook County, proved to be popular, and by 1925 all but two states had established juvenile courts or probation departments separate from their adult systems.[9] Even though the concept of *parens patriae* is no longer fully applicable in juvenile courts, the theory of nurturing and reforming juveniles continued, and mission statements for most juvenile courts still stress the benevolent nature of the system and emphasize rehabilitating rather than punishing youthful offenders. With this underlying concept, the juvenile system was much less formal and less reliant on legal precedent and due process than the adult system. Hearings were not adversarial proceedings but attempts by the court to determine what actions were in the best interest of the juvenile and society.

By 1960, these philosophies and processes began to be questioned because of concern for the impact they had on the juvenile offender. There was apprehension that the juvenile system's emphasis on treatment could result in the indefinite institutionalization of delinquents until treatment was deemed complete. There was a belief that juveniles, even for benevolent reasons, were often pulled into the system, removed from their family and community, and put into juvenile institutions without a clear ability to treat and return them in a better state. Therefore, there was a move to formalize the court processes, include more due process, and use the criminal standard of proof *beyond a reasonable doubt*, rather than *by a preponderance of evidence*.

There were also efforts to remove status offenders not charged with criminal conduct from the juvenile court system. In the Juvenile Justice and Delinquency Prevention Act of 1974, the U.S. Congress required assessments of the juvenile justice system to identify youth who were victimized, rather than helped, by placement in juvenile facilities.[10] The juvenile institutions, which had been considered a positive environment for youths while emphasizing education and training, began to be seen as an overly aggressive sanction. Advocates for juveniles believed that they should be diverted from the justice system and could better be treated in the community. The highlight of the movement to **deinstitutionalize** juvenile correctional facilities came when Jerome Miller, commissioner of the Massachusetts Department of Youth Services, closed most of that state's juvenile institutions and placed the youths in community programs. Miller believed that institutions were more damaging to juveniles than helpful and that they could be better treated in the community.

Since the early 1980s, however, another reform of the juvenile justice system has prevailed. This reform was prompted by concern not for the juvenile offender, but for community safety. Just as public sentiment regarding adult offenders supported punishment and offender accountability over treatment and rehabilitation, there was a similar swing in attitudes regarding juveniles. The increases in juvenile violent

juvenile justice system
a system to handle juveniles separate from adult offenders, based on the concept of *parens patriae*, which was used as the basis for giving the court the authority to take over supervision of children when their parents failed to provide proper care and guidance

parens patriae
means "parents of the nation," established in 1601 to allow officials to take change of delinquent children and place them in poorhouses or orphanages to gain control of them; in more modern times, this doctrine was expanded as the basis for juvenile court and correctional systems to take responsibility for educating and nurturing delinquents, with an emphasis on reform and rehabilitation

deinstitutionalize
the move to remove juveniles from correctional institutions and place them in community alternatives

superpredator

a term created by Dilulio to describe a generation of violent youths who practiced almost indiscriminant violence on the streets

waiver to adult courts

because of the serious nature of a juvenile offender's crime, statutory exceptions were granted to allow the movement from juvenile to adult courts for criminal processing

crime created a fear by the public of dangerous, marauding gangs of juveniles creating havoc and violence throughout the urban landscape. During the early 1990s, Dilulio even coined the term **superpredator** in warning of a coming generation of violent youths who practiced almost indiscriminate violence on the streets.[11]

As a result, state legislatures enacted laws to respond in a more punitive and public safety–conscious manner, re-creating some juvenile court processes to parallel the adult courts, establishing mandatory prison sentences for some juvenile offenses, and waiving serious juvenile offenders from the juvenile to the adult court systems. By the end of the twentieth century, nearly all states had passed laws to permit **waiver to adult courts** of serious juvenile offenders. These waivers allow the movement of serious juvenile offenders to adult courts for criminal processing. States use other terms for this process, including *certification, remand,* or *bind over,* for criminal prosecution. In Kansas and Vermont, juveniles as young as age 10 can be tried as adults, and often prosecutors, rather than judges, have the authority to waive the case and have it transferred to an adult court.

Waiver of Juvenile Offenders

Transferring juveniles to adult criminal courts is not a new phenomenon, and provisions for such transfer were available in some states even before the 1920s; many other states have permitted transfers since the 1940s.[12] However, state transfer provisions changed extensively between 1992 and 1999, as forty-nine states and the District of Columbia modified their transfer provisions. Many of these modifications instituted *mandatory waiver,* or direct assignment of specific crimes committed by juveniles to be handled in adult courts.

In *discretionary waivers* from juvenile to adult courts, juvenile courts usually decide on a case-by-case basis whether the court will waive the processing of the juvenile and allow prosecution as an adult in the criminal justice system. In this situation, the juvenile court must first find probable cause to believe that the juvenile committed the alleged act and, if so, must also find that it is in the court's best interest to waive its right to handle the case and give jurisdiction to the adult court. The process and how juvenile offenders are managed in adult prisons are described in Chapter 9.

Many correctional professionals question the efficacy of serious juvenile offenders being tried and sentenced in adult courts. The American Correctional Association (ACA) standards distinguish the juvenile justice system as having significantly different processes, procedures, and objectives from adult corrections.

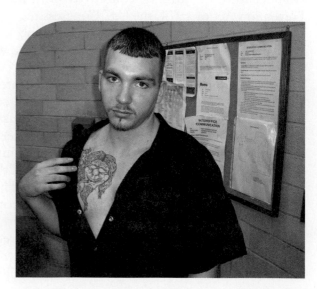

The waiver of juvenile offenders has resulted in many juveniles now serving their time in adult prisons.
Photo by Richard P. Seiter.

James A. Gondles, executive director of the ACA, adds, "We will never, in my view, solve our problems on the back end with punishments. . . . Treating kids as adults solves very little; it's another quick-fix solution to a complex problem that took years to reach and will take years to resolve."[13] In the "You Make the Decision" box at the end of this chapter, you must take a position on this issue.

Categories of Juvenile Offenders

The juvenile justice system defines three categories of offenders: dependent, neglected, and delinquent. **Dependent children** have committed no legal offense but may be without a family (parent or guardian) or without support, possibly because the parent is physically or mentally unable to act in that capacity. **Neglected children** have a family or guardian but are not receiving proper care, or the situation in the home is harmful to them and their upbringing. **Delinquent children** have committed an act that would be considered criminal if committed by an adult. In many jurisdictions, a fourth category is *status offenders*, children who have committed acts that are law violations only if committed by a person of juvenile status.

Status offenses include running away from home, ungovernability (being beyond the control of parents or guardians), truancy, status liquor law violations (such as underage drinking, which also applies to young adults up to age 21), and other miscellaneous offenses that apply only to minors (such as curfew violations and tobacco offenses).[14] When status offenses do not constitute a separate category of juvenile offenders, states classify them in two other ways. In some states, status offenders are an "incorrigible" subcategory of delinquent children. Other states have moved status offenses from acts of delinquency to the category of dependent children, thereby removing them from the juvenile courts and placing them in a family court or child welfare agency. If the status offense behavior continues, however, the juvenile will be referred to the juvenile court.

dependent children
children who, although committing no legal offense, may be without a parent or guardian, possibly because the parent is physically or mentally unable to act in that capacity

neglected children
children who have a family or guardian, but are not receiving proper care or the situation in the home is harmful to them and their upbringing

delinquent children
children who have committed an act that would be considered criminal if committed by an adult

Even with most juvenile crime decreasing, many status offenses such as runaway increased between 1988 and 1997. Courtesy of Cleo Photography/PhotoEdit.

TABLE 8.3	Offense Profile of Petitioned Status Offense Cases, 1995 and 2004		

Most Serious Offense	1995	2004
Total	100%	100%
Running away	17	13
Truancy	29	35
Curfew violations	10	10
Ungovernability	14	14
Liquor law violations	23	19
Miscellaneous offenses	7	9

Detail may not total 100% because of rounding

Source: Ann L. Stahl, Petitioned *Status Offense Cases in Juvenile Courts, 2004,* OJJDP Fact Sheet #02 (Washington, D.C.: U.S. Department of Justice, Office of Justice Programs, February 2008), p. 1.

In 2005 (the most recent data available), juvenile courts in the United States processed approximately 150,600 status offense cases, including the following:

- 14% runaway cases
- 35% truancy cases
- 15% ungovernability cases
- 19% status liquor law violation cases
- 8% other miscellaneous status offense cases[15]

Table 8.3 indicates a general increase in the number of status offense cases handled by juvenile courts in the United States. From 1995 to 2004, the number of truancy cases resulting in adjudication by the juvenile courts increased from 29 percent to 35 percent, runaways dropped from 17 percent to 13 percent, liquor law violations decreased from 23 percent to 19 percent, ungovernability remained steady at 14 percent, and miscellaneous offenses increased about 2 percent.

age of original jurisdiction

the upper or oldest age that a juvenile court will have jurisdiction over categories of offenders

One important factor for each of these offender categories is the **age of original jurisdiction,** the upper or oldest age at which a juvenile court has jurisdiction over categories of offenders (see Table 8.4). Each state defines juveniles by age for

TABLE 8.4	Age of Original Juvenile Court Jurisdiction

Age	State
15	Connecticut, New York, North Carolina
16	Georgia, Illinois, Louisiana, Massachusetts, Michigan, Missouri, New Hampshire, South Carolina, Texas, Wisconsin
17	Alabama, Alaska, Arizona, Arkansas, California, Colorado, Delaware, District of Columbia, Florida, Hawaii, Idaho, Indiana, Iowa, Kansas, Kentucky, Maine, Maryland, Minnesota, Mississippi, Montana, Nebraska, Nevada, New Jersey, New Mexico, North Dakota, Ohio, Oklahoma, Oregon, Pennsylvania, Rhode Island, South Dakota, Tennessee, Utah, Vermont, Virginia, Washington, West Virginia, Wyoming

Source: Howard H. Snyder and Melissa Sickmund, Office of Juvenile Justice and Delinquency Prevention, *Juvenile Offenders and Victims: 2006 National Report* (Washington, D.C.: U.S. Department of Justice, 2006).

Age	State
TABLE 8.5	**Youngest Age for Juvenile Court Jurisdiction over Delinquency Matters**

Age	State
6	North Carolina
7	Maryland, Massachusetts, New York
8	Arizona
10	Arkansas, Colorado, Kansas, Louisiana, Minnesota, Mississippi. Pennsylvania, South Dakota, Texas, Vermont, Wisconsin

Source: Howard N. Snyder and Melissa Sickmund, Office of Juvenile Justice and Delinquency Prevention, *Juvenile Offenders and Victims: 2006 National Report* (Washington, D.C.: U.S Department of Justice, 2006), p. 103.

the various categories. For status offenses, abuse, neglect, or dependency, the age of original jurisdiction varies and may often go through age 20.[16] In almost every state, the age of delinquency (for the delinquent category) is under age 18 at the time of the offense, arrest, or referral to court. However, many states have statutory exceptions to this age criterion and allow exceptions related to the youth's age, alleged offense, and prior court history. These exceptions (called *statutory exclusions*) can place a youth under the original jurisdiction of the adult criminal court. In other states, these exceptions can place the youth under the original jurisdiction of both the juvenile and criminal courts (called *concurrent jurisdiction*). In concurrent jurisdiction, the prosecutor is given the authority to decide which court will initially handle the case.

In 2000, sixteen states set an age as the lowest level at which there can be juvenile court jurisdiction over acts of delinquency, because children below that age are presumed incapable of criminal intent. Table 8.5 illustrates these age levels.

The Juvenile Justice Process

In many ways, the juvenile justice process is similar to the adult criminal justice process described in Chapter 1. However, as noted in the history of the juvenile justice system, the goals and philosophies in the juvenile justice system differ from those of the criminal justice system. A good example of the differences in the two systems is a comparison of the mission statements of the adult and juvenile correctional agencies in Missouri. The Missouri Department of Corrections states its mission as follows:

> *The Department of Corrections is an agency dedicated to public safety through the successful management and supervision of offenders on probation, in prison, and on parole. The Department's responsibility is to administer the sentence set by the court—ranging from probation to capital punishment—in ways that promote the longest lasting public safety at the lowest cost to taxpayers. Offenders assigned to the Department are successfully managed by ensuring they are supervised at the correct custody or supervision level.*[17]

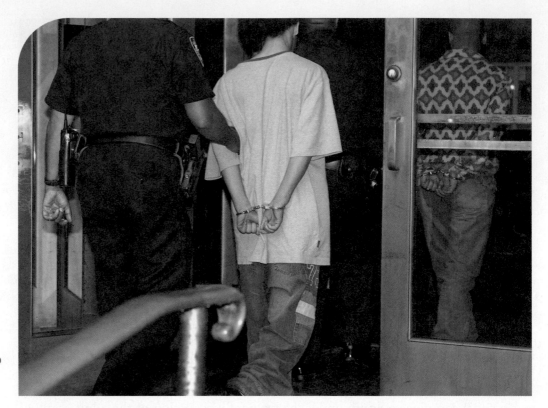

Juvenile offenders go through a process similar to the adult criminal process.
© Chet Gordon/The Image Works.

The Missouri Department of Social Services, Division of Youth Services lists the following mission statement:

> *The mission of the Division of Youth Services is to enable youth to fulfill their needs in a responsible manner with respect for the needs of their families and their communities. DYS programs are established to provide the mandated services enumerated, . . . to include assessment, care and treatment, and education of all youth committed to its care.*[18]

mycrimekit

Media—Video: Juvenile Justice Issues

The adult system emphasizes public safety through managing offenders; it mentions administering sentences imposed by the court, including capital punishment; and promotes carrying out responsibilities at the lowest cost to taxpayers. This mission gives readers a sense of punishment and cost effectiveness. The juvenile agency, on the other hand, focuses on enabling youth to fulfill their needs within the context of the family and community. Assessment, care and treatment, and education of youth are seen as the most important functions. This example illustrates how most states differentiate their role in dealing with adult criminals versus juvenile delinquents. The language, processes, and steps in each justice process reiterate these differences.

The juvenile justice process usually begins, just like the adult criminal justice process, with a complaint to the police and a contact between a law enforcement officer and the offender. Table 8.6 illustrates a comparison of the juvenile and the adult criminal justice systems, while highlighting the common ground that exists between them.

TABLE 8.6	Comparison of the Juvenile and Criminal Justice Systems	
Juvenile Justice System	**Common Ground**	**Criminal Justice System**
Operating Assumptions		
• Youth behavior is malleable. • Rehabilitation is usually a viable goal. • Youth are in families and not independent.	• Community protection is a primary goal. • Law violators must be held accountable. • Constitutional rights apply.	• Sanctions should be proportional to the offense. • General deterrence works. • Rehabilitation is not a primary goal.
Prevention		
• Many specific delinquency prevention activities (e.g., school, church, recreation) are used. • Prevention is intended to change individual behavior and is often focused on reducing risk factors and increasing protective factors in the individual, family, and community.	• Educational approaches are taken to specific behaviors (drunk driving, drug use).	• Prevention activities are generalized and are aimed at deterrence (e.g., Crime Watch).
Law Enforcement		
• Specialized "juvenile" units are used. • Some additional behaviors are prohibited (truancy, running away, curfew violations). • Some limitations are placed on public access to information. • A significant number of youth are diverted away from the juvenile justice system, often into alternative programs.	• Jurisdiction involves the full range of criminal behavior. • Constitutional and procedural safeguards exist. • Both reactive and proactive approaches (targeted at offense types, neighborhoods, etc.) are used. • Community policing strategies are employed.	• Open public access to all information is required. • Law enforcement exercises discretion to divert offenders out of the criminal justice system.
Intake–Prosecution		
• In many instances, juvenile court intake, not the prosecutor, decides what cases to file. • The decision to file a petition for court action is based on both social and legal factors. • A significant portion of cases is diverted from formal case processing. • Intake or the prosecutor diverts cases from formal processing to services operated by the juvenile court, prosecutor's office, or outside agencies.	• Probable cause must be established. • The prosecutor acts on behalf of the state.	• Plea bargaining is common. • The prosecution decision is based largely on legal facts. • Prosecution is valuable in building history for subsequent offenses. • Prosecution exercises discretion to withhold charges or divert offenders out of the criminal justice system.

...continued

TABLE 8.6   **Continued**

Juvenile Justice System	Common Ground	Criminal Justice System
Detention–Jail/lockup		
• Juveniles may be detained for their own protection or the community's protection. • Juveniles may not be confined with adults unless there is "sight and sound separation."	• Accused offenders may be held in custody to ensure their appearance in court. • Detention alternatives of home or electronic detention are used.	• Accused individuals have the right to apply for bond/bail release.
Adjudication–Conviction		
• Juvenile court proceedings are "quasi-civil" (not criminal) and may be confidential. • If guilt is established, the youth is adjudicated delinquent regardless of offense. • Right to jury trial is not afforded in all states.	• Standard of "proof beyond a reasonable doubt" is required. • Rights to be represented by an attorney, to confront witnesses, and to remain silent are afforded. • Appeals to a higher court are allowed. • Experimentation with specialized courts (i.e., drug courts, gun).	• Defendants have a constitutional right to a jury trial. • Guilt must be established on individual offenses charged for conviction. • All proceedings are open.
Disposition–Sentencing		
• Disposition decisions are based on individual and social factors, offense severity, and youth's offense history. • Dispositional philosophy includes a significant rehabilitation component. • Many dispositional alternatives are operated by the juvenile court. • Dispositions cover a wide range of community-based and residential services. • Disposition orders may be directed to people other than the offender (e.g., parents). • Disposition may be indeterminate, based on progress demonstrated by the youth.	• Decisions are influenced by current offense, offending history, and social factors. • Decisions hold offenders accountable. • Decisions may give consideration to victims (e.g., restitution and "no contact" orders). • Decisions may not be cruel or unusual.	• Sentencing decisions are bound primarily by the severity of the current offense and by the offender's criminal history. • Sentencing philosophy is based largely on proportionality and punishment. • Sentence is often determinate, based on offense.
Aftercare–Parole		
• Function combines surveillance and reintegration activities (e.g., family, school, work).	• The behavior of individuals released from correctional settings is monitored. • Violation of conditions can result in reincarceration.	• Function is primarily surveillance and reporting to monitor illicit behavior.

Source: Howard N. Snyder and Melissa Sickmund, *Juvenile Offenders and Victims: 1999 National Report* (Washington, D.C.: U.S. Department of Justice, National Center for Juvenile Justice, September 1999), pp. 94–96.

Steps in the Juvenile Justice Process

As with adults, juveniles begin their entry into or contact with the justice system with a contact with law enforcement, an investigation after a complaint has been filed that leads to a juvenile as a suspect of a crime, or through police witnessing activity that they believe to be a crime or act of delinquency. However, juveniles can also come into contact with the justice system through referrals by parents, school officials, or other citizens. In 2005, law enforcement personnel were the source of 81 percent of delinquency referrals to juvenile court.[19] Currently, the police are more likely to divert juvenile offenders or handle them informally than to do so with an adult. It is estimated that approximately one-quarter of juveniles arrested are handled informally and released by the police, and nearly seven out of ten are referred to juvenile court.[20] Figure 8.2 is a simplified diagram of the process by which a case travels through the juvenile justice system, although the steps vary from state to state.

Once a juvenile comes in contact with the police, he or she may be detained for a short time to contact a parent or guardian or while awaiting transfer to a juvenile facility. Approximately one-fifth of arrested juveniles are detained. **Juvenile detention,** as defined by the National Council of Crime and Delinquency, is the temporary care of children in physically restricted facilities pending court disposition or transfer to another jurisdiction or agency.[21] In general, juveniles will be detained if they are believed to be a threat to the community, are at risk in the community, or may fail to appear for future processing. Juveniles detained must

juvenile detention
the temporary care of children in physically restricted facilities pending court disposition or transfer to another jurisdiction or agency

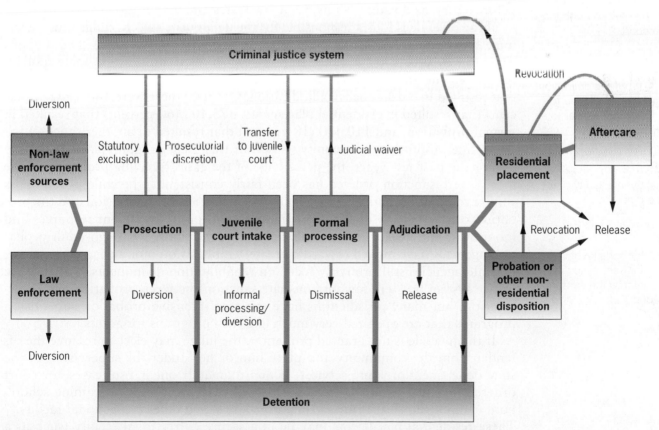

Note: This chart gives a simplified view of case flow through the juvenile justice system. Procedures vary among jurisdictions.

FIGURE 8.2   Stages in the Juvenile Justice Process

Source: Office of Juvenile Justice and Delinquency Prevention, *Juveniles in Court* (Washington, D.C.: U.S. Department of Justice, June 2003), p. 5.

be separated from adult offenders and must have a detention hearing within a few days (usually within twenty-four hours).

intake

determination if a juvenile case should be dismissed, handled informally, or referred to the juvenile court

The next step in the juvenile justice process is **intake,** carried out by the juvenile probation department or prosecutor's office to determine whether the case should be dismissed, handled informally, or referred to the juvenile court. The purpose of this step is to determine whether sufficient evidence exists to formally process the allegation. At this point, approximately 40 percent of cases are diverted, dismissed, or otherwise handled informally; the other 60 percent continue in a formal manner. With informal handling, the case is often concluded with a **consent decree,** whereby the delinquent juvenile must admit to wrongdoing and agree to specific conditions of behavior (similar to pretrial diversion for adult offenders). This stage is sometimes referred to as *informal probation*. If the juvenile meets all the conditions of the consent decree, the case is dismissed and there is no formal record of delinquent action.

consent decree

an informal handling of a juvenile justice case, in which the delinquent juvenile admits to wrongdoing and agrees to specific conditions of behavior; sometimes called informal probation

If during intake the determination is to handle the case formally, or the case was originally handled informally and the juvenile does not meet the consent decree conditions, it will be formally handled and a **referral** will be made to the juvenile court. The referral is similar to charging an adult offender with a crime. In the referral, a **delinquency petition** (similar to an indictment for adults) states the delinquent acts the juvenile is alleged to have committed and asks the juvenile court to **adjudicate** (or find the juvenile guilty of the delinquent act) and make the juvenile a ward of the court. A hearing is then scheduled, facts are presented, witnesses may be called, and the court determines whether the juvenile is responsible for the delinquent act. Juveniles do not universally have a right to a hearing before a jury, as do adult felons, yet a few states allow a jury to hear the case.

mycrimekit

Media—Video: Managing Juvenile Offenders

referral

the formal processing of a juvenile offense through the juvenile court

If the juvenile is found responsible for the delinquent act, the judge must determine what sanction or **order** (similar to the sentence for an adult) should apply. The primary orders for juveniles are for either probation or out-of-home residential placement. In 2005, there were a total of 623,900 cases in the United States that resulted in a delinquency adjudication. Of these, there were 140,100 (22 percent) that resulted in residential placements, 373,400 (60 percent) that resulted in formal probation, and 110,400 (18 percent) that resulted in another sanction (either a fine, restitution, community service, or treatment program participation).[22]

delinquency petition

a statement of the delinquent acts a juvenile is alleged to have committed; similar to an indictment for adults

For the past few years, the percentage of the cases receiving probation as the most severe sanction ordered has been fairly consistent.[23] Juvenile probation is similar to adult probation in that there are conditions of supervision and the probation officer plays a dual role of finding appropriate treatment resources and monitoring the juvenile for compliance with conditions. Although adult probation agencies have moved toward a greater emphasis on monitoring compliance, juvenile agencies still primarily focus on rehabilitating delinquents. The juvenile justice system has very few intermediate sanctions between probation and incarceration, but many jurisdictions have initiated intensive probation supervision programs that are operated very much like such programs for adults.

adjudicate

to find a juvenile guilty of a delinquent act

order

the sanction for a juvenile found delinquent by juvenile court; similar to the sentence for an adult

If the juvenile is not granted probation, the judge may elect to remove the offender from the community and place him or her under the supervision of the state department of youth services. In approximately one in four cases, the court ordered juveniles to out-of-home residential placement such as training school, boot camp, drug treatment, a group home, or some other correctional facility.[24] These residential placements may be in a secure correctional facility (such as a training school or reform school) or a nonsecure group home, depending on the severity of the act and the background of the juvenile. In some states, the sanction is for an open-ended period of time (indeterminate sentence), and the decision to release is the responsibility of the department of youth services. In other states,

TABLE 8.7	Terminology in the Juvenile and Adult Justice Systems	
Juvenile Justice System	**Activity**	**Adult Justice System**
Delinquent	Violator of laws	Offender
Detention	Holding offenders by police	Arrest
Intake	Determination to handle case	Preliminary hearing
Consent decree	Informal handling with conditions	Pretrial diversion
Referred to court	Formal processing by the court	Charges filed
Delinquency petition	Statement of the allegations	Indictment
Respondent	Individual alleged guilty	Defendant
Adjudicate	Find responsible for act	Convict
Hearing	Review of factual issues	Trial
Responsible	Committed the act	Guilty
Order	Court determination of sanction	Sentence
Probation	Supervision in the community	Probation
Commitment	Placed in a correctional facility	Incarcerated
Resident	Institutionalized individual	Inmate
Residential Placement	Correctional facility	Prison
Aftercare	Supervision after release	Parole

the judge sanctions the juvenile for a set period of time (determinate sentence) until release back to the community. After release, the juvenile is on **aftercare** supervision, much like adult parole, with specific conditions that must be followed. If these conditions are not met, the juvenile may be returned to the residential placement or placed in a more secure facility to serve additional time.

aftercare
supervision of a juvenile in the community after serving time in a juvenile correctional institution; similar to parole for adults

The process for juveniles is similar to the adult criminal justice system. However, the terminology is distinct. Table 8.7 compares the terminology used in the juvenile and adult justice systems.

The juvenile justice process provides the opportunity for many career opportunities, including detention staff, juvenile court workers, probation and aftercare staff, and social service staff who work in juvenile correctional institutions. The "Your Career in Corrections" box describes the work of juvenile social service workers.

Your Career in Corrections

Juvenile Social Service Workers

Juvenile social service workers are staff who work in juvenile correctional institutions. Interestingly, these individuals fill a dual role of case managers and correctional officers in adult prisons. They usually supervise delinquents, develop treatment plans, and help them prepare for release. Until the 1950s, most juvenile institutions had "house parents" who lived in the institution housing complex with the delinquents and acted as parents would in counseling, guiding, rewarding, and punishing the residents under their care. Today, the role is much more professional, usually requiring a two- or four-year college degree, some training in counseling, and much more adherence to policy rather than individual discretion.

...continued

Juvenile social service workers have challenging yet rewarding jobs. First, they have to play the role of correctional officers, as they are usually the only person supervising juvenile residents (a term used similarly to adult prison inmates) and therefore must be sensitive to security issues and maintain control and order of residents. However, they also are often responsible for counseling and program planning for residents and therefore have to play a dual role of case manager. Much of their work in this regard consists of creating a responsible living environment with the other residents of the housing unit. An important part of the management of juvenile correctional facilities is the "governing" of the housing unit. Social service workers direct and mentor residents in how to get along with one another and how to work together to reach the unit's goals of sanitation, positive program participation, and good behavior on the part of all residents. Many juvenile facilities use some type of group behavior modification program in which the housing unit as a group receives or loses privileges based on the group's performance.

Juvenile social service worker jobs can be stressful as well. It is difficult to work with 16- to 18-year-old offenders who do not have a history of responsible behavior or self-control and may resort to violence as a way to get what they want. These positions are entry level and the pay is usually fairly low. However, these are excellent positions in which to learn how to deal with youthful offenders and use personal communication skills to gain compliance and positively influence behavior. From these positions, there are also opportunities for promotion to midlevel management positions throughout the juvenile justice system.

Juvenile Residential Facilities

Juvenile residential facilities are similar to prisons for adult offenders, holding mainly those youths found delinquent and receiving an order of commitment. When juvenile offenders are placed under the residential supervision of a state department of youth services, they usually are temporarily sent to a reception and diagnostic center. At these centers, juveniles receive psychological, educational, and risk assessments to determine the type of facility to which they should be assigned. After a few months at the reception centers, they are placed in a long-term confinement facility, often called a training or reform school. Sickmund reported that in 2003, there were 109,225 juveniles confined in 2,861 facilities across the United States.[25] These facilities can be public or private, and while 62 percent of juvenile offenders are held in one of the 1,170 public facilities, there are actually more (1,682) private facilities under contract to state agencies[26]

The number of youths committed to residential care is decreasing. Between 1997 and 2003, the number of adjudicated youths ordered to residential placement decreased 6.4 percent.[27] Most (78 percent) juvenile offenders in long-term confinement are held for juvenile delinquency offenses that would be criminal law violations for adults.[28] Status offenders account for only 5 percent of all residents. Although the number of facilities has increased from 2,842 to 2,861 from 1997 to 2003,[29] there has been an increase in crowding. Austin and colleagues suggest that crowding results in dangerous conditions that make facility management difficult, can be detrimental to rehabilitation and treatment of youth, and creates logistical problems such as how to feed, deliver health care, and find places for youth to sleep.[30]

Juvenile facilities are similar to adult prisons in that security must be the primary emphasis in the medium- and higher-security facilities. Programs are very important, especially education, as most juveniles have not completed their high school diploma and therefore participate in the general educational development (GED) programs. Vocational training is also important, and most facilities offer extensive programs in a variety of skills that can lead to employment after release. Drug and substance abuse programs are also provided in almost every facility, and recreation and religious instruction are also available on a voluntary basis.

Although the rate of incarceration for juvenile offenders is much lower than that for adults, the institutions are similar.
© Muhammed Muheisen/APR Wide World Photos.

Placing delinquents in a residential facility is usually the last resort, because juvenile court judges believe that the most effective interventions come about in the local community. In 1993, the Ohio Department of Youth Services (DYS) created the RECLAIM Ohio (Reasoned and Equitable Community and Local Alternative to the Incarceration of Minors) program, a funding initiative to encourage juvenile courts to develop or contract for a range of community-based options for juvenile offenders that would keep them in the community and avoid incarceration in state juvenile facilities. The following interview with the then-director of DYS explains the program.

An Interview With...

The Creator of the RECLAIM Ohio Plan

Geno Natalucci-Persichetti had a long history in corrections, beginning his career as a social worker in Lebanon Correctional Institution in 1967, working from 1970 to 1973 as a parole officer and supervisor, becoming the director of a halfway house for twelve years, heading up parole and community services for an adult correctional system, and serving as director of the Ohio Department of Youth Services from 1987 to 2005. Director Geno (he preferred this informal title) is credited with starting a program for diverting youthful offenders from juvenile institutions that has been copied in several states.

Question: What was the impetus for starting RECLAIM Ohio?

Director Geno: Overcrowding was the impetus for us to look at creating a new incentive program. We (DYS) were a "free good" in an economic sense for the juvenile courts. There was no incentive or disincentive for the courts to not send kids convicted of a felony delinquency to DYS. By the summer of 2003, DYS had over 2,600 youth in facilities that had rated bed capacity of around 1,400. Creating RECLAIM gave the courts an incentive (a subsidy

...continued

for keeping kids in the local community and money to create programs to divert these delinquent youth to local programs).

We began by researching what types of subsidy programs have worked in the past. We went as far back as the first "probation subsidy program" that started in California in the 1970s. We tried to develop incentives for local counties to create programs to monitor and treat offenders in the community, rather than sentencing them to a state facility. We used a formula based on the number of adjudications counties had for the total state courts. Counties would get a percent of the local subsidy budget based on the overall share of the total percent of juveniles adjudicated for felony offenses. After the county got its share of the money, it would go into a checking account they held. For each juvenile sent to a state institution, 75 percent of the per diem cost of the state facility was deducted from the checking account. In this way, the counties could send as many juveniles as they felt necessary, and they had money to create diversion programs they thought were right for their community.

One component of RECLAIM that we learned of by looking at other subsidy programs was the "public safety bed" concept. To ensure that a court would not waive a juvenile to the adult court because the nature of the offense was a public safety risk (for example, robbery, rape, or manslaughter) and required lengthy incarceration, RECLAIM legislation allowed the court to send the youth to DYS at no cost or no deduction of their subsidy funding.

Question: What are some examples of how the counties set up their diversion programs?

Director Geno: They did everything from developing alternative schools, expanding drug treatment programs, creating mental health programs, and using intensive probation programs, electronic monitoring, and day treatment programs. They could use their money for almost anything other than construction of new beds. We encouraged them to look at the "what works" literature and implement programs that have proved most effective in reducing future criminal behavior among youthful offenders.

Question: How were these programs received by the local counties?

Director Geno: When we first started, the judges were very skeptical. Lt. Governor Mike DeWine invited many of the juvenile court judges to the statehouse, where we all met in the governor's cabinet room. Lt. Governor DeWine encouraged them to trust the process and give it a try. Before RECLAIM, every time I went before a legislative budget committee, it was always "DYS against the judges." They wanted money to fund their pet programs, but with no accountability for how it was spent. I would give my budget presentation, and then the judges followed me and made their own budget presentation. The Ohio General Assembly, being fellow elected officials, made a big show of the judges being there. After RE-CLAIM, however, the judges and DYS had the best relationship of any state in the country. The judges and department met monthly, they were involved in our strategic planning, and they helped redesign the formula for RECLAIM funding as money got tight and we had to reduce the overall funding for the juvenile justice system. By then, the judges joined me for a budget presentation, and they supported our budget and the RECLAIM portion. In 2004, we were going through another round of budget cuts. I called some of the judges and told them I needed their help, because I believed these cuts would go too deep. Approximately twenty judges joined me at a Senate hearing, and we told them that some of the money the House cut had to be restored because it would seriously hamper our operation. It was somewhat funny, because when the hearing first started, the vice-chair was chairing the committee. One of the judges had each of the other nineteen judges stand up and introduce themselves. The vice-chair sent word to the chair and all others members to get up to the hearing because of all the judges there. Once they all arrived, there was another round of introductions, the judges received a standing ovation, and all the money originally cut was restored.

Question: How has the program affected the juvenile facilities in Ohio?

Director Geno: When we kicked it off in 1993, there were 2,600 juveniles incarcerated in facilities terribly overcrowded with a rated capacity of 1,400. We were out of bed space and needed a way to avoid building more institutions. As a result of RECLAIM, there are only about 1,700 juveniles now confined in state facilities. This is in a state that has a population of 11.3 million people. We had been second to California in the rate of incarceration of juvenile offenders, and now Ohio is sixth in the rate of incarceration.

Question: Have there been any studies of the effectiveness of RECLAIM Ohio?

Director Geno: The University of Cincinnati has done two studies and confirmed there has been a reduction in the number of commitments to state facilities. Also, findings were that youth sent to DYS facilities had a lower success rate than comparable offenders maintained in the community under RECLAIM programs.

Question: Has there been interest from other states?

Director Geno: Yes, there has, and we received a Ford Foundation grant to train twenty other states. Each state has done something a little different, but the principle of subsidizing the counties for diverting and keeping juvenile delinquents locally is the basis of most. At this point, RECLAIM Ohio is the longest running subsidy program in the nation. Students can go to the DYS website at www.dys.ohio.gov to find out more about it.

Legal Issues Affecting the Juvenile Justice System

As in adult correctional systems, federal courts had little involvement in the operation of juvenile correctional agencies until the 1960s. The first major case reviewed by the U.S. Supreme Court was *Kent v. United States* in 1966. In this case, a 16-year-old was charged with rape and robbery and the juvenile court waived jurisdiction to the adult court. The juvenile received a sentence of thirty to ninety years in prison as an adult. The Supreme Court acceptance of the case was the first challenge to the *parens patriae* foundation of the juvenile justice system, in that juveniles charged with offenses should not receive less due process just because the system has a greater concern for juveniles and provides a "compensating benefit." The Court ruled that juveniles must have "the essentials of due process," including the right to notice of the charges in time to prepare for trial, the right to counsel, the right to confront and cross-examine accusers, and the privilege against self-incrimination.[31]

The next year (1967), the Court accepted and decided **In re Gault**. Gerald Gault, a 16-year-old on probation, called a neighbor and made some obscene remarks. Gault did not attend the adjudication hearing and was committed to a juvenile training school for the period of his minority (to age 18). If he had been an adult, this act would have been a misdemeanor punishable by a small fine and a two-month jail sentence. The Court rejected the doctrine of parens patriae as giving the juvenile court unbridled discretion and required that, in hearings in which juveniles may be committed to an institution, they must have the right to counsel, to notice of the charges against them, to question witnesses, and to protection against self-incrimination.[32]

In the 1970 case of *In re Winship*, the 1971 case of *McKeiver v. Pennsylvania*, and the 1975 case of *Breed v. Jones*, the U.S. Supreme Court further clarified the due process rights of juveniles. In *Winship*, the Court determined that a finding of guilt for juveniles required more than just a preponderance of the evidence, but had to meet the adult standard of *beyond a reasonable doubt*.[33] In *McKeiver*, the Court did not further expand due process provided to juveniles, deciding that jury trials are not a requirement in juvenile courts.[34] In *Breed*, the Court found that waiver to an adult court after an adjudication hearing in juvenile court constitutes double jeopardy.[35]

In re Gault
a 1967 U.S. Supreme Court case requiring that, in hearings in which a juvenile may be committed to an institution, they must have the right to counsel, to notice of the charges against them, to question witnesses, and to protection against self-incrimination

In two later cases, the U.S. Supreme Court indicated that it had perhaps taken the expansion of due process rights for juveniles to a conclusion. In *Fare v. Michael C.* (1979), the Court affirmed the conviction of murder of a juvenile who claimed he had asserted his right to remain silent. Michael C. was arrested for murder and, when advised of his *Miranda* rights, he asked to see his probation officer. The police said the officer would be contacted later, and Michael could talk to the officer then if he desired. The Court ruled that asking for a probation officer is not the same as asking for a lawyer or asserting the right to remain silent.[36] In *Schall v. Martin* (1984), the Supreme Court upheld the use of preventive detention pending trial for juveniles, stating that the protection of both the juvenile and society from pretrial crimes is not intended to punish the juvenile.[37] In addition, the Court did not rule out the importance of *parens patriae* and reasserted the interest of the state in promoting the welfare of children.

In addition to addressing the due process rights of juveniles, the Supreme Court has also addressed the use of the death penalty for juvenile offenders. In 1982, the Court decided *Eddings v. Oklahoma*, declaring that the youthful age of a defendant should be considered a mitigating factor in deciding whether to apply the death penalty during the penalty phase of a capital punishment trial.[38] In *Sanford v. Kentucky* (1989), the Court determined that the minimum age at which a juvenile could receive the death penalty is 16.[39] In 2002, the Court refused to accept and hear the case of *In re Stanford*, which asked the Court to again address the issue of capital punishment juveniles.[40] On January 27, 2003, the Court again declined to accept a case to reconsider the death penalty for Scott Allen Hain, an Oklahoma offender who was 17 at the time of his crime. Four justices believed that executing juveniles for murder was unconstitutional, as Justices Stevens, Souter, Ginsburg, and Breyer issued a statement that "the practice of executing such offenders is a relic of the past and is inconsistent with evolving standards of decency."[41]

In October 2004, the U.S. Supreme Court heard the case of *Roper v. Simmons*, and on March 1, 2005, the Court, by a 5–4 vote, held "the Eighth and Fourteenth Amendments forbid the imposition of the death penalty on offenders who are under the age of 18 when their crimes were committed."[42] The Court believed that, because of a lack of maturity and an underdeveloped sense of responsibility, juveniles are vulnerable and susceptible to negative influences and outside pressures, and their character is not as well formed as that of an adult. With this ruling, the Court removed seventy-two juveniles in twelve states from death row, substituted life in prison for execution, and disallowed the death penalty for juvenile offenders.

As a result of the active role the Supreme Court played in defining the due process rights of juveniles, there is now little difference in the procedural due process requirements between the juvenile and adult justice systems. Juveniles have the right to notice of charges against them, the right to counsel, the right to confront and cross-examine witnesses, the right to avoid self-incrimination, the right to a judicial hearing with full consideration of their individual case before transfer to adult court, and the right to the standard of *beyond a reasonable doubt* to be found responsible for a delinquent act. While *parens patriae* as a foundation of the juvenile court is not applicable as open discretion for actions by the court, the recognition that the court is to act in the best interests of the juvenile is still acknowledged.

Issues in Juvenile Corrections

Many aspects of the juvenile justice system are similar to the adult criminal justice system. These include the role played by juvenile gangs in street crime and the continued influence of these gangs within juvenile correctional institutions. Additionally, a major concern within the juvenile justice system is how to break the cycle of juvenile substance abuse and involvement in drug crimes. Juvenile justice administrators and policymakers attempt to look into the future to determine what new issues will confront juvenile corrections and create new approaches to effectively deal with these issues.

Juvenile Gangs and Juvenile Crime

Over the past twenty-five years there has been a proliferation of juvenile gangs in most large inner cities, and research indicates that gang membership intensifies delinquent behavior. From the earliest to the most recent investigations, criminologists have consistently found that, when compared to youth who do not belong to gangs, gang members are far more involved in delinquency, especially serious and violent delinquency.[43] Gang activities create a fear and perception of danger among most citizens regarding inner-city youth, make neighborhoods unsafe, and prompt a reaction by police to intensify patrolling and arrests of juveniles not only for delinquent acts, but also for loitering and other status offenses.

Juvenile gangs are defined as groups of adolescents or young adults who see themselves as a group and have been involved in enough crime to be of considerable concern to law enforcement and the community.[44] Since 1995, the National Youth Gang Center has gathered annual data from law enforcement agencies from all states about youth gangs. The 2006 survey results show that there were approximately 785,000 gang members from 26,500 active gangs in the United States. There is no reason to believe that the number has done anything but increase since that time.[45] Most gangs are formed within racial or ethnic groups; law enforcement reported gang membership in 2001 as approximately 33 percent African American and 49 percent Hispanic.[46] Gangs are about 92 percent male, and male members commit most gang crime. Gangs are very chauvinistic, and although many male gangs have female auxiliaries, only a few allow female members. Interestingly, new gangs are forming in smaller, more rural communities.[47]

Gangs get involved in criminal activities to make money, to intimidate others and protect their turf, and as a part of the structure and role of members. Law enforcement officials believe that much gang violence results from their involvement in drug sales, but gangs are regularly involved in all types of index crimes. Gangs have a definite organizational structure. Individuals involved with gangs on a continued and long-term basis are *core members* and are the gang members most regularly involved in crime and violent acts. Some core members are regular or associate members who actively participate in the gang, and others are fringe members who are less involved in the gang activities and its criminal acts. The average age of arrested gang members is 17 or 18. The younger individuals who want to join the gang are called "wannabe's," or those being recruited for membership.

Law enforcement officials attempt to control gang activity through suppression and social programs. They collect intelligence regarding gang members, their

juvenile gangs
groups of adolescents or young adults who see themselves as a group and have been involved in enough crime to be of considerable concern to law enforcement and the community

activities, their areas of operation, and their historical activities. Police then target their areas of operation and attempt to disrupt the gang's activities by patrolling and arresting gang members for loitering, curfew violations, or any crime that can get them off the streets. In addition, some cities have passed ordinances against ganglike activities, and gang members can be arrested and imprisoned for simply hanging out with the gang and violating the ordinances.[48]

Another approach to reduce gang activities is through social programs. In-school education programs inform students of the dangers of gang involvement and how to avoid being forced to enter a gang. Parents are provided information regarding gang activities and what to watch for to determine whether their child is getting involved in gang activities. Recreational, educational, and vocational programs target potential or even current gang members and get them working or using their leisure time in a noncriminal manner. Although there is some evidence that suppression tactics reduce gang criminal activity, it is more difficult to determine whether social programs reduce gang membership or juvenile crimes.

Responding to Juvenile Drug Crime

A serious concern regarding juveniles is substance abuse that leads to health problems, undermines family relationships, creates problems in school, and results in delinquency that often continues into adult criminality. The juvenile justice system struggles with how to break this cycle and redirect juveniles into productive and law-abiding patterns of behavior. In the early history of the juvenile justice system, the focus was on the individual juvenile and how he or she could be rehabilitated. Over the past two decades, more emphasis has gone to protecting society and victims while holding delinquents accountable for their behavior, and there is an increased use of incarceration and out-of-the-home placements. With neither rehabilitation nor juvenile accountability proving to be effective in dealing with juvenile drug crime, a blending of both into a balanced and restorative justice (BARJ) perspective has emerged. In a 2001 National Institute of Justice document encouraging the use of a balanced approach, the authors note:

> *Specifically, the model strikes a balance among offender accountability (making amends to the victim and community), competency development (changing behaviors and improving functional skills), and community safety (protecting the community by carefully monitoring the juvenile's behavior).*[49]

As indicated in Figure 8.3, BARJ integrates the goals of public safety and rehabilitation, using graduated sanctions to reward good behavior and increased punishments for improper behavior, collaboration with the juvenile justice system and other community resources such as substance abuse treatment providers, and a case management approach identifying and using community services to build on each juvenile's strengths and talents. Figure 8.3 illustrates the continuous process of entry, assessment, judicial decision making, supervision and treatment, and continuing care to move delinquents from substance abuse to successful community reintegration.

In many ways, the BARJ approach is similar to that used in adult drug courts. BARJ emphasizes collaborative (rather than adversarial) efforts by all parties within the juvenile justice system to focus on the outcome of reducing juveniles'

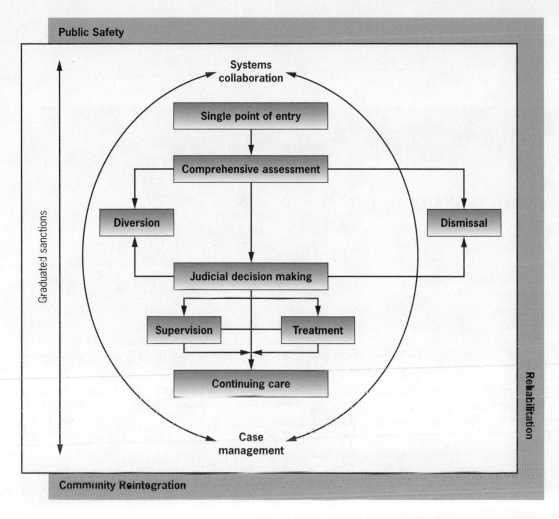

Public Safety

Source: Curtis C. VanderWaal, Duane C. McBride, Yvonne M. Terry-McElrath, and Holly VanBuren, *Breaking the Juvenile Drug-Crime Cycle: A Guide for Practitioners and Policymakers* (Washington, D.C.: U.S. Department of Justice, National Institute of Justice, May 2001), p. 5.

FIGURE 8.3   The Balanced and Restorative Justice Perspective

substance abuse and criminal involvement. The model is multidimensional, in that it uses treatment, punishment, and psychological, social, and cultural factors to work toward freedom from drugs for juveniles. Although the system must continue to deal with criminal and delinquent activity by juveniles, the model focuses on the underlying problem of substance abuse as a cause, more than as an effect (involvement in illegal behavior).

The approach of the BARJ model is also consistent with the overall vision of what is needed in the future for the juvenile justice system. In a 1998 publication, the director of the Office of Juvenile Justice and Delinquency Prevention, addressing the needs of the juvenile justice system for the twenty-first century, concluded that an effective justice system must meet three objectives: holding juvenile offenders accountable; enabling the juvenile to become a capable, productive, and responsible citizen; and ensuring the safety of the community. The author concludes that

these objectives are best met when a community's key leaders, including representatives from the juvenile justice system, health and mental health systems, schools, law enforcement, social services, and other systems, are jointly engaged in the planning, development, and operation of the juvenile justice system.[50]

The following "A Case Study" box is an illustration of how many cases in the juvenile justice system seem to result in an unsatisfactory outcome for all involved parties.

A Case Study

Is the Juvenile Justice System "Just"?

A recent case handled in the juvenile justice system is a good example of the challenges faced by either juvenile or criminal justice systems regarding their ability to create a "just" outcome for some cases. A group of teenagers was at a church picnic, horsing around as teenagers do. A 13-year-old was bragging about how tough he was and how he could take a blow to the head. He had his skateboard with him and hit himself over the head with it, laughingly telling his friends that it did not hurt. He then challenged any of them to hit him over the head with it to show how tough he was.

Another 13-year-old, but one who was much bigger and stronger than the first youth, took up the challenge. He took the skateboard and walloped his friend over the head with it. The youth fell to the ground, began to convulse, and was rushed to the hospital, where he subsequently died. The friend who hit him was taken into custody and charged in juvenile court with murder. A few months later, he pleaded guilty to involuntary manslaughter and received a sentence of one year in a juvenile detention center. There was no indication that this juvenile was a bully or had ever before been violent, and all information was that he had grown up in a typical middle-class family with no serious problems.

The case received considerable media attention, and debate raged about whether justice was served for either party. The victim had been tragically killed, and nothing could bring him back to life or provide his parents any comfort regarding their loss. The youth who hit him had to live with the fact he had killed his friend. Taking him out of his home and away from his family was going to do nothing and would probably make it more difficult for him to deal with the result of his actions. Placing him in a juvenile correctional institution illustrated that he had to be responsible and be held accountable for his act of stupidity. Even those who argued for a strong punishment had to admit that incarceration was probably going to make it even more difficult, if not impossible, to get his own life back together. This event and the subsequent sentence will probably result in the loss of two promising lives.

Some argue that if the boy had been in adult court, with the opportunity to go before a jury and the prosecutor required to prove guilt beyond a reasonable doubt, he might have been able to argue for a lesser sentence. Some also suggested that he was too accepting of responsibility for the act, and that he should have fought the sentence more, trying to get probation, the opportunity to stay in his parents' home, and counseling and treatment regarding his own psychological issues around this event. The one thing most people agreed on is that there seemed to be no "good" sentence for the individual in this case, and they questioned the ability of the juvenile justice system to provide a just outcome.

Summary

The juvenile justice system has a long and distinguished history. Formed to protect children who needed society's assistance and to keep juvenile delinquents separate from adult criminals, the juvenile justice system has played a valuable role in the treatment and rehabilitation of generations of the nation's youth. However, during the past two decades, this "kinder and gentler" approach has come under attack, and fear of dangerous and violent juvenile offenders has forced the U.S. Congress and state legislatures to push for reforms and make the juvenile court similar to adult courts in terms of its goals, processes, and punishments. Although it is difficult to argue with the point that victims don't much care whether their vicious assailant is 17 or 19 and that the increase in violent crime does require new methods, it is only normal to think that perhaps we have thrown out the baby with the bathwater and lost some of the rational reasons for the original creation and organization of the juvenile justice system.

The juvenile justice system has had these mixed missions and inconsistent approaches for several decades, and the issues seem to get more confused rather than clearer. Crimes committed by offenders under age 18 are getting more serious. Some juvenile offenders are now bound over to adult courts and correctional systems for incarceration. Urban youths are joining gangs that encourage violence and a life of crime. Some experts think there should not be a juvenile justice system at all—that all criminals should be treated the same, regardless of their age. Yet others recognize that immaturity leads to mistakes of judgment that require considerations of age, and most people do not want to give up on youthful offenders and accept that they cannot be reformed and made into productive and law-abiding citizens.

The next decade will be an interesting time for the juvenile justice system. Will it continue in the trend toward adversarial judicial processes, waiver from juvenile to adult courts for a growing number of delinquents, and more harsh punishments to include incarceration of juveniles with adult offenders? Or will there be a realization that intervention with rehabilitation and treatment approaches is still the best opportunity society has to correct delinquent behavior and push juveniles back to an acceptable lifestyle? Most likely, the BARJ model, emphasizing a balance between a punitive and restorative approach, will be accepted and implemented in many local and state jurisdictions.

Key Terms

status offense

Refuge Period

juvenile justice system

parens patriae

deinstitutionalize

superpredator

waiver to adult courts

dependent children

neglected children

delinquent children

age of original jurisdiction

juvenile detention

intake

consent decree

referral

delinquency petition

adjudicate

order

aftercare

In re Gault

juvenile gangs

Review Questions

1. What trends have resulted from the rates of juvenile crime over the past decade?

2. What is a status offense and how are delinquents with status offenses handled?

3. What was the Refuge Period?

4. Define the concept of *parens patriae*.

5. How did the term *superpredator* develop, and what does it mean for the future of juvenile violent crime?

6. What is a waiver to adult courts, and why are some juvenile offenders handled in adult criminal courts rather than juvenile courts?

7. What are the four categories of juvenile offenders and how is each managed in the juvenile justice system?

8. How does the typical mission of a juvenile justice agency differ from the mission of an adult correctional agency?

9. Describe the process followed as a juvenile moves through the juvenile justice system and compare it to the adult criminal justice system.

10. What are the two primary court orders (sentences) for juvenile offenders, and approximately what percentage of juveniles receives each?

11. What has been the trend in the numbers of juveniles receiving an order of commitment to a residential facility?

12. What was the most significant outcome of the U.S. Supreme Court decision in *In re Gault*?

13. Describe and list the most important court decisions regarding sentencing juveniles to the death penalty. What is the current legal position on this issue?

14. How do juvenile street gangs contribute to street crime and what two approaches are taken to control gang behavior?

15. What is the BARJ model for juvenile justice and how does it work?

You Make the Decision...

Should Juveniles Be Tried as Adults?

More juveniles arrested for serious crimes are being bound over to adult courts to be tried as adults and, if convicted, will serve an adult sentence. Since serious crimes are those handled in the criminal justice system, the sanctions usually include imprisonment. Three models of incarceration of juveniles tried and convicted as adults are used. Most states place these juvenile offenders in adult prisons with adult inmates. A few states house juveniles with adults, but require them to be housed and programmed separately. And some states place juveniles in juvenile institutions until they reach age 18, and they then are transferred to adult prisons.

In 1997, there were 5,400 juveniles in adult prisons; 92 percent were male, 61 percent were committed for violent crimes, and the average maximum sentence was 82 months. Fifty-eight percent were black, another 15 percent were Hispanic, and 2 percent were of other races. However, by 2007, the number of juveniles in adult prisons declined to 2,639 (almost all males). The original punitive attitude of the late 1990s has lessened, and many people are reconsidering the prosecution of juvenile offenders as adults.

You are to decide whether it is good public policy to try and punish juvenile offenders as adults. Either individually or in a small group, list the pros and cons for juveniles being waived to adult courts. Be sure to address issues such as cost, long-term impact on the juveniles, impact on the various sentencing goals, and protection of the public. You will find this is not an easy issue to agree on, and there are many good arguments on both sides. Once you list and discuss the pros and cons, decide if this is good public policy.

Chapter Resources on mycrimekit™

Go to mycrimekit.com to explore the following study tools and resources specific to this chapter:

- **Practice Quiz:** multiple-choice, true/false, short-answer, and essay questions to help students test their knowledge
- **WebQuests:** learning activities built around Web searches
  - Office of Juvenile Justice and Delinquency Prevention: http://ojjdp.ncjrs.org/

- **Insider's Experiences:** "Defining the Role of Juvenile Institutions"
- **Seiter Videos:**
  - See a judge discuss juvenile justice issues
  - See experts discuss managing juvenile offenders
- **Flashcards:** Twenty-one flashcards to test knowledge of the chapter's key terms

Special Offenders

After reading this chapter, you should be able to:

1. Define special offenders and describe how they require special handling under correctional supervision.

2. List and describe the three ways in which juveniles can be transferred to adult courts.

3. Identify the three approaches for incarcerating juveniles in adult correctional facilities.

4. Explain the scope and trends regarding drug offenders' involvement in the criminal justice system.

5. Identify the types of substance abuse programs provided in prisons for inmates.

6. Specify the reason why so many mentally ill individuals were able to remain in the community rather than being institutionalized over the past fifty years.

7. Describe the impact of the deinstitutionalization of the mentally ill on the criminal justice system.

8. Identify changing trends in the age of offenders and prisoners.

9. Discuss the concerns about violence in prisons by inmates.

10. Describe the operation of supermax prisons and suggest reasons for and against their use.

11. Define the types of sex offenders and outline the problems facing the treatment of sex offenders under correctional supervision.

12. Identify types of infectious diseases common with criminal offenders and the issues facing them while under correctional supervision.

Introduction

Correctional agencies, unfortunately, have become "all things to all people." The typical offender was historically young, was in good mental and physical health, was convicted of property crimes, and did not require unusual handling or management. There were only "standard" caseloads for probation and parole agencies until the 1960s, because all inmates under supervision in the community were handled similarly. Prisons built during the early 1900s were extremely large, with extensive factory space, in order to house prisoners inexpensively, while they produced goods that the prison could sell to help support itself. These standard approaches were fine until the makeup of the offender population began to change and the need for special management of certain offenders was recognized.

This change in the management of smaller groups of the correctional population based on their characteristics and needs is referred to as differential handling of special offenders. **Special offenders** are those offenders whose circumstances, conditions, or behaviors require management or treatment outside the normal approach to supervision. This may be the result of some physical problem or infectious disease, a mental disorder, a tendency for violence, a history of sexual assaults, age (juvenile or elderly), or serious substance abuse. All these circumstances required correctional officials to create special methods of managing, handling, or treating these offenders.

This chapter describes the circumstances and management approaches that result from the individual needs of a variety of special offenders. Included are offenders under age 18 who are waived from jurisdiction of the juvenile court to adult court and correctional systems, as well as offenders who have serious drug problems or a mental illness. In addition, the chapter includes descriptions of the needs and management of aging offenders (older than 50), offenders who exhibit violent and dangerous tendencies, and those convicted and sentenced for a sexual offense. Finally, the particular management and treatment of offenders with infectious diseases such as HIV/AIDS and tuberculosis are described. This chapter provides students with an understanding of the challenges and difficulties in attempting to manage all these special populations within a correctional environment.

special offenders

offenders whose circumstances, conditions, or behaviors require management or treatment outside of the normal approach to supervision

Juvenile Offenders in Adult Criminal Courts

As noted in Chapter 8, the past twenty years have seen an increase in the number of waivers of jurisdiction from juvenile to adult court for juveniles who commit what would be serious felony offenses if they were over 18. States had historically limited the opportunities for such waivers and protected the authority of the juvenile court to determine whether to waive jurisdiction to allow a delinquent to be prosecuted as an adult, thereby continuing to emphasize the juvenile court philosophy of rehabilitation and providing young offenders the chance to make positive changes in their lives. However, during the 1990s, all states but one expanded their statutory provisions to ease the transfer of juveniles to criminal court.[1] States have added statutory exclusions, expanded the list of offenses for which transfer is allowable, or lowered the minimum age for which a juvenile may be transferred to adult court.

Currently, all states allow juveniles who commit offenses to be waived from the jurisdiction of the juvenile court and be prosecuted in the adult criminal court system. The legal process for transferring juveniles to the adult court system varies from state to state, primarily focusing on who has the discretion to make the transfer or waiver decision. An Office of Juvenile Justice and Delinquency Prevention report outlines the three variations of how this can occur.

1. *Waiver.* The juvenile court judge is the decision maker and determines whether the offender is waived from the juvenile justice system to adult criminal court. Waivers are usually limited by age (must be above a certain age) and by offense criteria. Some states provide juvenile court judges with guidelines on the types of criteria to consider (such as the juvenile's potential for rehabilitation), whereas others reduce judicial discretion by presuming that the juvenile will be waived for certain types of cases.

2. *Direct file.* Fifteen states have concurrent original jurisdiction, in that the prosecutor has the discretion to file charges in either the juvenile justice or criminal justice system. In these states, the prosecutors' discretion is limited by specific age and offense criteria.

3. *Statutory exclusion.* Twenty-eight states have mandatory waiver to adult courts for specific age and offense criteria. If a juvenile is above the minimum age specified and commits a serious offense designated by statute, judges and prosecutors have no discretion; the case must be prosecuted in adult criminal court.[2]

In addition, twenty-two states allow **blended sentencing,** whereby the courts can impose juvenile or adult sentences on certain juvenile offenders.[3] In some states, the authority to blend sentences lies with the juvenile court; in other states, it lies with the adult court. Blended sentences are a middle ground between juvenile and adult sentences in that judges can choose from a broad array of both juvenile and adult sanctions. At times these offenders are given a juvenile sentence as a last chance to avoid an adult sanction.

Even with the concern for dealing with serious juvenile offenders in a punitive and public safety-oriented approach and with the expansion of authority to move juveniles into the adult court and correctional process, there has not been an overwhelming number of cases transferred to criminal courts. Figure 9.1 illustrates the increase in the number of cases judicially waived to adult crime court from 1985 to 2005. The number of delinquency cases judicially waived to criminal court peaked in 1994 with 12,100 cases, a 51 percent increase over the number of cases waived in 1989 (8,000). However, by 2005, the number of cases waived to criminal court has declined to 7,000 cases.[4] The decline in the number of cases waived may be the result of many states passed legislation excluding certain types of serious offenses from juvenile court jurisdiction, and therefore they go directly to adult criminal court. Cases most likely (almost 50 percent) to be waived to adult court in 2005 were crimes against persons.[5]

Over the past several years, the number of people under 18 held in state prisons has increased, yet remained relatively constant as a proportion of the overall prison population. From 1985 to 1997, the number increased from 2,300 to 5,400,[6] yet by midyear 2008, there were only 3,650 inmates under age eighteen held in state prisons. Of these, 3,531 were male and only 119 were female.[7] Nine states had more than a hundred juvenile prisoners, six states had fewer than ten, and nine states and the Federal Bureau of Prisons had no inmates under 18 at midyear 2008.[8]

There are three approaches for housing offenders under age 18 in state correctional systems. **Straight adult incarceration** places juveniles in adult prisons, with no separate housing or differentiation in programming or job assignment. Although all but six states allow juvenile inmates to be housed in prisons with adult inmates, most separate them from adults to some extent, most often in separate housing units or in separate program assignments. **Graduated incarceration,** used in twelve

blended sentencing
a middle ground between juvenile and adult sentences that allows judges to choose from a broad array of both juvenile and adult sanctions

mycrimekit
Media—Investigate: The Waiver of Juveniles to Adult Courts

straight adult incarceration
a form of incarceration in which juveniles handled by adult courts are placed in adult prisons with no separate housing or differentiation in programming or job assignments

graduated incarceration
a system in which juveniles handled by adult courts are placed in juvenile facilities until they reach the age of 18; they are then transferred to an adult prison to complete the sentence

Cases judicially waived to criminal court

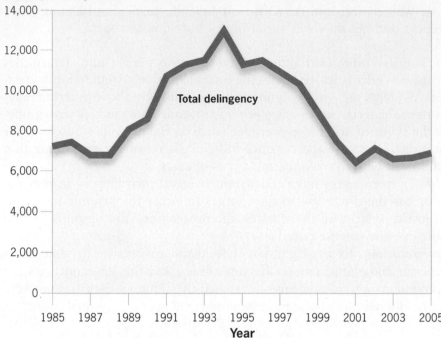

FIGURE 9.1 The Number of Cases Judicially Waived to Criminal Court Peaked in 1994

Source: Charles M. Puzzanchera and Melissa Sickmund, *Juvenile Court Statistics 2005* (Washington, D.C.: U.S. Department of Justice, National Center for Juvenile Justice, July 2008), p. 40.

segregated incarceration

a form of incarceration in which juveniles handled by adult courts are assigned to an adult prison, yet they are housed separately and placed in specialized educational, vocational, life skills training, and substance abuse programs that meet their age and needs

states, initially places inmates under age 18 in juvenile facilities. Once they reach a certain age (usually 18), they are then transferred to an adult prison to complete their sentence. Finally, eight states use **segregated incarceration,** in which inmates under age 18 are constantly separated from adults, even though they are housed in the same facility. The juvenile prisoners are housed separately and placed in specialized educational, vocational, life skills training, and substance abuse programs that cater to their age and needs.[9]

The waiver of juveniles to adult systems and incarceration in adult prisons causes difficult problems for correctional administrators who try to provide proper programs while maintaining the juveniles' safety. Photo by Richard P. Seiter.

Many correctional officials are opposed to housing offenders under age 18 in prisons with older adult felons, and even most states that allow integration of juvenile prisoners with adults prefer to maintain some type of separation. This is sometimes difficult, especially in states that have only a handful of juvenile offenders. With small numbers, it is almost impossible to keep juveniles separate from adults, yet provide a full range of program offerings. In states with large numbers of juveniles in adult prisons, the administrative problems are less burdensome, as an entire prison can be dedicated to the youthful offenders and specialized programs developed to meet their needs. Unfortunately, there does not appear to be an approach fully supportive for housing juvenile offenders in adult facilities, and there is evidence that this may not be working satisfactorily. A recent study found that the prevalence and frequency of misconduct and violence among juveniles housed in adult prisons was higher than comparison groups. The study further found that age was the most consistent and strongest determinant of prison violence, as the juveniles are far more likely than adult offenders to be involved in prison violence and misconduct.[10]

Drug Offenders

One commonly held belief is that drug use leads to criminality. With the initiation of the war on drugs in the late 1980s, the U.S. criminal justice system is targeting and increasing the number of people arrested and punished for selling or using illegal drugs. In fact, the war on drugs has provided substantial dollars for stopping drugs from entering the United States, prosecuting and punishing those who commit drug offenses, and treating drug addicts. From fiscal year 2007 to 2009, the federal drug control budget was $13.7 billion, of which 36.5 percent was for demand reduction, 27.8 percent was for domestic law enforcement, 12.2 percent was for international supply reduction, and 23.5 percent was for interdiction.[11] These budget figures do not include the cost to local and state governments for prosecuting and incarcerating drug offenders.

The U.S. Department of Justice reports a strong relationship between drug use and crime. In **drug use forecasting** studies of incarcerated populations, it was discovered that in eighteen of twenty-three cities included in the study, more than 50 percent of those booked on criminal charges tested positive for some illicit drug.[12] According to a report by Jennifer C. Karberg and Doris J. James with the Bureau of Justice Statistics in 2002, more than two-thirds of jail inmates were determined to be dependent on or to abuse alcohol or drugs. In 2004, 32 percent of state and 26 percent of federal prisoners reported drug use at the time of their offense.[13] In addition, 17 percent of state prisoners and 18 percent of federal inmates in 2004 said they committed their current offense to obtain money for drugs.[14] Table 9.1 illustrates the high percentage of offenders who committed a variety of crimes who indicated that they committed their offense to get money to buy drugs for their own use. Although the overall drug use by state prisoners has changed little over the past decade, there has been an increase in the reported use of stimulants, as use in the month before the offense increased from 9 percent in 1997 to 12 percent in 2004. This increase is primarily attributed to the rising use of methamphetamines.[15]

Not all drug offenders are drug addicts, or even drug users. Some offenders commit drug crimes simply to make money and avoid serious drug use because they know it will hurt their business and increase their chance for arrest. An estimated 21 percent of probationers without a mental health problem reported that

drug use forecasting
surveys of jailed inmates by the U.S. Department of Justice to determine the extent of drug use related to criminality

| TABLE 9.1 | Percentage of Prisoners Who Committed Offense to Get Money for Drugs | |

Most Serious Offense	State	Federal
Total*	16.6%	18.4%
Violent	9.8	14.8
Property	30.3	10.6
Drug	26.4	25.3
Public-order	6.9	6.8

*Includes offenses not shown.

Source: Christopher J. Mumola and Jennifer C. Karberg, Drug Use and Dependence, State and Federal Prisoners, 2004, *Bureau of Justice Statistics Special Report* (Washington, D.C.: U.S. Department of Justice, October 2006), p. 6.

their current offense was a drug offense.[16] Approximately 109,200 (about 22 percent) of all 1996 jail inmates were held for a drug offense, a growth of over five-fold since 1983.[17]

There is also a large proportion of state and federal prisoners serving a sentence for a drug offense. From 1990 to 2005 the number of drug offenders in state prisons increased by 70 percent from 148,600 to 253,300.[18] In federal prisons, drug offenses constituted the largest group of inmates, as approximately 53 percent of federal prisoners were serving a sentence for a drug offense in 2007.[19] Revisions in the federal criminal code over the past decade have resulted in mandatory sentences of either five or ten years for offenders convicted of trafficking or sale of drugs, resulting in the Federal Bureau of Prisons prison population rapidly climbing and becoming increasingly a population of drug offenders.

Although the United States is targeting a tremendous amount of resources toward the arrest, prosecution, and punishment of drug offenders, the relationship between drug and alcohol use and crime is complex and lacks a cohesive conclusion. The *National Household Survey on Drug Abuse* (NHSDA) has tracked patterns of licit and illicit drug use among the general U.S. population since 1971. Findings indicate that illegal drug use, as measured by the number of people using an illicit drug in the previous month, steadily declined from 1979 to 1992, and although there has been a leveling off of the decline since that time, data on the use of illicit drugs demonstrate a downward trend.[20] This seems to indicate that drug abuse is substantially less of a problem than it was two decades ago, but there is no question that substance abuse remains a serious problem among criminal offenders. Many experts believe that a more general theory of deviance applies, in that individuals who commit one deviant act (substance abuse) are likely to commit another (criminal behavior). The mixed theories are perhaps the underlying reason that public opinion on drug users is divided. In a 2001 poll, 47 percent agreed with jailing people for possessing drugs, and 47 percent disagreed.[21] When asked to rate the effectiveness of selected approaches to drug use, 36 percent of Americans rate "provide drug treatment" as very effective (with only 19 percent rating it as not very effective); and 30 percent rate "arrest drug users" as very effective, while 34 percent rate it as not very effective.[22]

Without question, it is critical that prisons offer drug abuse programs. In 2004, it was estimated that 686,700 state prisoners and 64,900 federal prisoners

TABLE 9.2	Drug Treatment or Program Participation since Admission among State and Federal Prisoners who Met Drug Dependence or Abuse Criteria, 2004

Type of Drug Treatment or Program Since Admission	Percent of Prisoners Meeting Criteria for Drug Dependence or Abuse —	
	State	Federal
Any drug treatment or programs	40.3%	48.6%
Treatment	14.8%	17.4%
Residential facility or unit	9.5	9.2
Counseling by a professional	6.5	8.7
Detoxification unit	0.8	0.9
Maintenance drug	0.3	0.4
Other programs	34.8%	41.0%
Self-help group/peer counseling	28.0	22.1
Education program	17.8	30.2

Source: Christopher J. Mumola and Jennifer C. Karberg, Drug Use and Dependence, State and Federal Prisoners, 2004, *Bureau of Justice Statistics Special Report* (Washington, D.C.: U.S. Department of Justice, October 2006), p. 9.

reported drug use in the month before their offense.[23] Table 9.2 illustrates the percentage of state and federal inmates who were involved in various types of drug treatment programs in 2004. These programs include residential units with a total environment directed toward dealing with the addictions. Evidence has shown these types of programs effective in both reducing drug use and recidivism.[24]

As an example of how a residential drug program operates within prisons, the Federal Bureau of Prisons' drug abuse program (DAP) has separate units in several prisons with the same staffing, structure, length of treatment, and programs provided. All inmate participants in the 500-hour program reside in a treatment unit separate from the prison general inmate population. The program requires offenders to assume responsibility for their behavior and to make a conscious decision to avoid engaging in drug taking and criminal behavior. The treatment model is "bio-psycho-social," emphasizing a comprehensive lifestyle change, with issues of physical well-being, family relationships, and criminality all targeted for change while participants acquire positive life skills as a vehicle to avoid future drug use.[25]

The BOP program has a five-part treatment strategy: (1) orientation screening and referral, (2) drug abuse education, (3) nonresidential drug abuse treatment services, (4) residential drug abuse treatment, and (5) transitional services. Specific unit-based drug treatment is typically delivered no less than four hours a day, five days a week, supplemented by other complementary programs such as education, work skills training, recreation, disease prevention, and health promotion instruction. The BOP, in conjunction with the National Institute of Drug Abuse, is conducting an ongoing evaluation of the effectiveness of the program. In an early review of outcomes, findings indicate that in high-security prisons, misconduct among inmates who completed the residential drug abuse treatment program was reduced by 50 percent. For the first six months after release from custody, inmates who completed the residential drug abuse treatment program were 73 percent less likely to be rearrested for a new offense than those who did

mycrimekit

Media—Video: Drug Use by Offenders

These female inmates are participating in a residential drug program and are having a full-unit meeting regarding the program objectives and their personal commitments. Photo by Richard P. Seiter.

not participate in a residential drug abuse treatment program and were 44 percent less likely to use drugs or alcohol than those who did not participate in a residential drug abuse treatment program.[26]

Although it is critical to offer drug abuse programs to inmates, it may be even more important to provide drug treatment to offenders on probation and hope that through treatment they can avoid further criminality resulting in a prison sentence. In New York City, the Department of Probation manages probationers with a history of drug abuse through a combination of specialized supervision caseloads and contracts for outpatient treatment programs. The specialized units have smaller than normal caseloads, supervising about 65 probationers, compared with the approximately 175 probationers in regular caseloads. The department contracts with an outside provider for a twelve-month outpatient treatment program that provides counseling services while working closely with offenders and reporting their progress to probation staff. Probationers receive a mandatory urinalysis within the first two weeks of entry to the program, a second urinalysis within two weeks after the first, and then random monthly testing thereafter.

Research indicates that the program is effective because probationers who receive the drug treatment have significant reductions in recidivism, "with the greatest reduction in recidivism among those clients who were appropriately matched to outpatient drug treatment on the basis of the severity of their drug use."[27] Recidivism rates were also significantly lower for probationers who stayed in the program more than ninety days than for those who dropped out earlier, as "about half of the probationers who stayed in treatment less than 3 months were rearrested, while only about one-quarter of those who stayed longer were rearrested."[28]

Many types of drug treatment programs are delivered to correctional clients, and not every type of program has been found effective with all types of abusers. However, there is positive evidence that drug abuse programs reduce levels of rearrest and other measures of recidivism. In a recent meta-analysis of a variety of drug abuse programs, the evaluators found that therapeutic communities are effective in reducing recidivism, whereas boot camp and group-counseling programs did not show consistently good results.[29] Therefore, the National Task Force on Corrections Substance Abuse Strategies recommends that correctional agencies "provide a range of quality programs to meet offenders' control, supervision, and treatment needs."[30] With the high level of correctional clients that do have substance abuse problems, it is critical that correctional agencies provide substantial opportunities for involvement in drug abuse programs.

Mentally Ill Offenders

During the past half century, the United States has made tremendous progress in the treatment and management of the mentally ill. Unfortunately, reforms and improvements in the mental health field have also caused issues and problems for corrections. **Antipsychotic drugs** were invented in the 1960s, and they helped many people with mental illness remain in the community rather than be placed in mental hospitals. These drugs provided a humane alternative to the deleterious placement of patients in the old state mental hospitals, where patients often had little to do and received minimal treatment. Taking antipsychotic drugs can help most mental health patients stay in the community, and many state mental hospitals closed during the latter half of the twentieth century. In fact, the number of patients in state mental institutions went from a high of 559,000 in 1955 to 69,000 in 1995.[31]

However, with minimal monitoring, some patients in the community stop taking their medication, as they may not like the uncomfortable side effects, think they are doing better, or just decide to stop taking the medicine. Or they may lose their insurance coverage and cannot afford to buy the medicine. Without their medication, the symptoms of the mental illness return, and many such mentally ill people do not receive treatment, their behavior deteriorates, they end up committing crimes, and they become clients of the criminal justice system rather than patients of the mental health system. It is estimated that at midyear 2005, there were 1,255,700 offenders in state and federal prisons and local jails representing 56 percent of state prisoners, 45 percent of federal prisoners, and 64 percent of local jail offenders which had a mental health problem.[32]

When inmates are sent to prison, they are initially screened for mental illness. The screening is primarily a self-report by inmates as to whether they have ever experienced a mental health problem. Drawing from inmate surveys conducted as

antipsychotic drugs
drugs administered to mentally ill individuals to counteract the symptoms of their mental illness, often allowing them to live successfully in the community rather than needing to be institutionalized

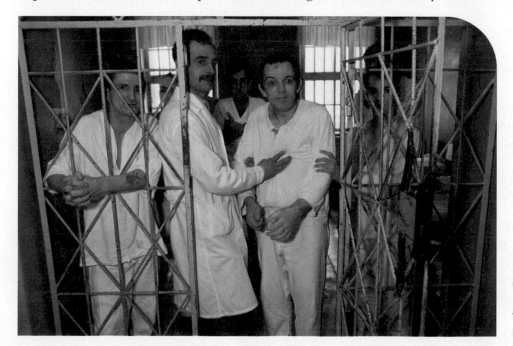

State mental institutions in the early 1900s were places of misery that provided little treatment for most patients.

Photo by Peter Turnley/CORBIS-NY.

Your Career in Corrections

Correctional Psychologists

Correctional psychologists do all the things associated with clinical psychology, only they do them in a correctional setting. Correctional psychology has some subspecialties, such as forensic psychology (conducting evaluations to establish competency and responsibility for crimes or doing judicial evaluations that may influence sentencing), or specialty programming, such as drug or sex offender treatment. The first thing that staff psychologists working in a prison do with new inmates is conduct an intake screening to look for past histories of mental health treatment, determine current mental health status, and make program recommendations. They then conduct both individual or group counseling, advise managers on how to best manage inmates, and may be involved in the employee assistance program. They sometimes must respond to and assist with emergency situations and may have special duties such as hostage negotiations, confrontation avoidance (trying to talk an inmate out of an action to avoid a calculated use of force), crisis interventions for inmates or staff (such as an inmate finding out that he or she has an unfaithful spouse), and working closely with medical staff to monitor inmates' compliance in taking medications.

Not everyone is suited for working as a correctional psychologist. Those considering such jobs should be able to work in a paramilitary situation in which psychology and mental health evaluations may not be the primary factor in action taken. They must also recognize that they will work in what could become an unsafe environment with the potential for violence. However, training that psychologists receive and use in a nonprison clinical practice is very similar for correctional psychologists. The correctional psychologist will treat a greater number of individuals with depression and anxiety and will see more cases of serious mental illnesses such as schizophrenia.

For most states and the federal government, a doctoral degree is required, although some states require only a master's degree in psychology. On an individual basis, a correctional psychologist must have emotional security to work in a prison and be able to work within the structure of an organization focused on security and order. Pay, benefits, and working conditions for correctional psychologists are similar to those of other institutional settings (such as Veterans Administration hospitals or state mental hospitals). On the other hand, many individuals find that career opportunities for correctional psychologists are greater than for an outside clinical psychological practice, since working for a large organization provides not only a more extensive career ladder but also opportunities outside psychology.

a part of the BJS report cited previously, "An estimated 15% of State prisoners and 24% of jail inmates reported symptoms that met the criteria for a psychotic disorder."[33] Treatment for the mentally ill in prisons generally falls into three categories: (1) screening inmates at intake for mental health conditions, (2) therapy or counseling, and (3) psychotropic medications. As of June 30, 2005, 3.1 percent of state prison inmates had received residential care, 12.7 percent were receiving therapy or counseling, and 15.1 percent were on psychotropic medication.[34] Overall, most inmates with identified mental health needs are receiving some level of care. Table 9.3 illustrates the level of mental health screening and treatment provided by each state prison system.

In prisons, the responsibility of assessing and treating mentally ill inmates falls to correctional psychologists. The "Your Career in Corrections" box illustrates the types of jobs available to psychologists in a prison setting.

In jails and prisons, mentally ill inmates create a dual problem of control and treatment. Since they have committed a criminal act and often are violent, they may require a high-security institutional placement, resulting in their often being

TABLE 9.3	Mental Health Screening and Treatment in State Correctional Facilities, June 30, 2000

	Number of Facilities, by Type of Policy								
Region and State	Total*	Screen Inmates at Intake	Conduct Psychiatric Assessments	Provide 24-Hour Mental Health Care	Provide Therapy/ Counseling	Distribute Psychotropic Medications	Help Released Inmates Obtain Services	No Services Provided	No Data Reported
Total	1,558	1,055	990	776	1,073	1,115	1,006	125	39
Northeast	233	154	163	152	173	178	167	5	3
Midwest	301	190	167	140	207	210	196	25	1
South	730	527	497	338	514	535	471	59	17
West	294	184	163	146	179	192	172	36	18

*Includes 1,295 state-operated facilities, 22 facilities under joint state and local authority, 3 facilities operated by the District of Columbia, and 238 private facilities with more than 50% of their inmates held for state authorities.

Source: Allen J. Beck and Laura M. Maruschak, *Mental Health Treatment in State Prisons, 2000*, Bureau of Justice Statistics Special Report (Washington, D.C.: U.S. Department of Justice, July 2001), p. 5.

housed with non–mentally ill offenders who have also committed serious offenses and are serving equally long sentences. While they must be controlled, they must also receive treatment for their mental illness and be protected from other violent and dangerous inmates.

Mentally ill inmates are more likely than other inmates to have disciplinary problems while in prison. A recent survey found that 36 percent of mentally ill state prison inmates, compared to 27 percent of non-mentally ill inmates, were involved in fights. Twenty percent of mentally ill state prison inmates were involved in a fight since admission, whereas 10 percent reported involvement in a fight. Among jail inmates, 9 percent of the mentally ill were involved in a fight, compared to 3 percent of those who were not mentally ill. Other disciplinary problems were also more common among mentally ill inmates. About 60 percent of state prison inmates with mental illness had been formally charged with breaking prison rules since admission.[35]

While on probation or postprison community supervision, the mentally ill have similar problems. As a condition of their community supervision, offenders must often maintain employment, submit to drug testing, or participate in treatment. Managing offenders in the community creates unique problems, and only recently have most probation and parole agencies created special caseloads for managing the mentally ill. These caseloads require patience, treatment expertise, and control by the officers in charge. Offenders must have a treatment program developed, must receive counseling for their mental illness, must be encouraged to continue to take their medication, and require much more time and patience in supervising than the typical criminal offender. Probation officers responsible for such caseloads require specialized training to be able to address the difficult dilemma created by the overlap of criminality and mental illness.

Mentally ill offenders are not only a problem to manage while in prison or under community supervision; they are also more likely to recidivate than are other offenders. The Bureau of Justice Statistics reports the following:

Among repeat offenders, 53% of mentally ill State inmates had a current or past sentence for a violent offense, compared to 45% of other inmates. Forty-six percent of mentally ill jail inmates and 32% of other jail inmates with a criminal history had a current or past sentence or a current charge for a violent crime. Among Federal prisoners with a prior sentence, the mentally ill (44%) were twice as likely as other inmates (22%) to have a current or prior sentence for a violent offense. Although offenders on probation had shorter criminal histories, nearly 3 in 10 of the mentally ill were recidivists with a current or past sentence for violence.[36]

Managing mentally ill offenders in the community and in prison is a difficult challenge. These offenders are not deterred by typical punishment. They may understand that they have received a long prison sentence for their crimes, yet may not be able to use that punishment as an incentive to discontinue criminal activities. While they are supervised in the community, their commission of crimes is not the result of a simple decision to recidivate, but is more likely a result of their inability to manage themselves, to maintain the use of their psychotropic medication, and to deal responsibly with problems regarding housing, employment, or relationships.

Aging Offenders

The prison population in the United States is getting older. Part of the reason for this is that the general population of the United States is also aging. Individuals age 65 and older represent the fastest growing age group in the United States; their numbers reached 38 million in 2007.[37] Americans over age 50 constituted only 26 percent of the population in 1992, but it is estimated that the proportion of this age group will reach 33 percent by 2010.[38] Changes in the models of sentencing are a second reason why more elderly offenders are imprisoned, as sentencing guidelines and mandatory sentencing take away sentencing judges' discretion to consider age, health issues, and risk to the community. Previously, judges would consider these factors and often grant older offenders probation for crimes and criminal backgrounds that would result in a prison sentence for younger offenders.

Finally, with the statutory lengthening of prison sentences for almost every crime over the past two decades, once someone is sentenced to prison he or she stays a longer time. Also, three-strikes and habitual-offender laws often require offenders to go to prison for life without parole. These prisoners naturally age while serving their sentence and end up dying while in prison. These factors increase the average age of the U.S. prison population. In 1995, only 6.1 percent of the inmates in state and federal prisons were age 50 or older,[39] and on December 31, 2007, there were 156,600 inmates older than age 50, representing 10.2 percent of the prison population.[40]

This increase in the average age and number of older offenders creates many management, resource, and programmatic issues for correctional administrators. Perhaps the most critical, expensive, and difficult issue is increased health care needs. A *Time* magazine article notes, "Because elderly people require more medical care, it costs nearly three times as much to incarcerate them, or about $65,000 a year per inmate."[41] Many illnesses and general health problems result from the aging process and years of risky lifestyle choices, such as tobacco use, extensive drug and alcohol use, and high-risk sexual behavior. The health problems of the elderly are not only more severe than, but very different from, those of younger offenders, and prison medical clinics are usually not prepared to deal with the depression, sexually transmitted diseases, tuberculosis and other infectious diseases, heart problems, and reduced circulation that occur in older inmates. There are also security, work opportunity, and program issues. Prisons were designed and operational processes created to hold young and physically active inmates. Prison architecture, recreation facilities, and types of housing were all designed without consideration for older inmates. Simple problems, such as difficulty in getting around in wheelchairs or inability to walk long distances, result from the campus-style prison architecture emphasizing space to spread out inmates over as much area as possible. Prison recreation programs such as basketball, jogging, and weight lifting do not meet the needs or interests of the elderly. Few work opportunities can be assigned to older inmates.

Prison housing and bed arrangements often cause problems for older inmates. Prisons usually have bunk beds. Many older inmates cannot get into upper bunks, and assignment to lower bunks due to age causes morale problems among younger inmates who believe they deserve these beds due to their good behavior and time served in prison (the criteria usually considered for preferred assignments). Most prisons have two inmates assigned to each cell. Many older and younger inmates do not want to share a cell because they have different habits and interests in radio or television stations. Younger inmates may have little tolerance for older inmates getting up to go to the bathroom several times per night, resulting in tension and requests for prison managers to change housing and bed assignments. Finally, prison administrators may need to protect older inmates from being victimized by younger and stronger predators, who find older inmates easy victims from whom to steal or extort money. Prison officials are constantly challenged with finding solutions to these problems, which have no easy or clear answers.

To remedy these problems, most prisons make allowances in standard policies for cell and bed assignments, or even for inmate movement, and let older inmates begin moving from one building to another before younger inmates. Some correctional agencies even use entire prisons or housing units to house older inmates and create counseling programs and recreation that meet their needs. Prisons also try to identify specific jobs that can be done by older inmates and have recreation departments create leisure activities such as stretching classes or table-game tournaments to occupy these inmates and meet their special needs. The "A Case Study" box illustrates issues that result as older inmates are sentenced to prison.

A Case Study

Senior Citizen Inmates

The discussion about current issues in corrections that includes the aging of the prison population creates a question of whether all these inmates should come to prison and whether they should stay for their full sentence if their health puts them in danger of dying in prison. An interesting case involved the sentence received by a male offender in his sixties. This person had been a law enforcement officer for more than thirty years, rising to the executive level of two different law enforcement departments. He was respected in his community and spent several hours a week serving his community.

Surprisingly, this person had another life. He had been sexually molesting his grandchildren for the past several years. As the story became public,

...continued

most people who knew him were shocked, because he did not seem like someone who would do this, and they knew the good he did for the community. However, all his built-up goodwill was not enough to keep him from getting a lengthy prison sentence for his offenses. Even his closest allies and friends could not argue against his receiving a term in prison for molesting his grandchildren.

After the sentence, his life became very difficult. He had a double problem as an inmate. Although inmates do not usually physically abuse child molesters, as had been the case in the past, molesters are held in contempt and are subject to continual harassment by the inmate population. Also, as a past and well-known law enforcement officer, this person had personally arrested many offenders and put them in prison. Prison administrators had to make intense efforts to protect his safety, including placing him in a prison far away from his home with a population that was less likely to assault him. At times, he had to be placed in administrative detention for his own protection.

His punishment of imprisonment was much greater than that of a "normal" inmate.

As time went on, the inmate's health worsened, and it became apparent that he was going to die in the next few years, even though he still had several years to serve on his sentence. The state in which he was incarcerated had a policy that allowed emergency release of a dying inmate. However, due to the nature of his crime, there was little sentiment by anyone that he should be released. So, in effect, his sentence became a life sentence rather than a multiyear sentence.

The issue that surfaces in this situation is how a regular sentence for older offenders can become a life (some may say death) sentence for aging inmates. Yet with mandatory sentences and sentencing guidelines, a judge often cannot consider the age or medical condition of an offender. The other side of the issue is whether someone should receive a lesser sentence for the same crime due to age or infirmity. Unfortunately, there is no easy solution to this dilemma, and aging offenders cause unique problems for correctional administrators.

Violent Offenders

Many violent individuals are under correctional supervision and particularly in prison. At year-end 2005, 53 percent of all adults sentenced to state prisons were committed for violent offenses.[42] However, a much smaller number and percentage of inmates are truly violent and predatory and continue violent acts even while in prison. These violent and predatory inmates think nothing of assaulting, raping, or killing other inmates, and correctional officials must take extraordinary actions to protect both staff and other inmates. The standard inmate disciplinary process described later in Chapters 13 and 14 is the procedure used to respond to inmate violence. However, some inmates who exhibit extremely violent behavior in prison are not deterred by standard inmate discipline and cannot be allowed to remain in even high- or maximum-security prisons without being a threat to security.

supermax prisons
either freestanding or distinct units within other prisons that provide for the management and secure control of inmates designated as violent or seriously disruptive in other prisons

For these inmates, many states and the Federal Bureau of Prisons have developed **supermax prisons.** Supermax prisons had their historical beginning with Alcatraz, the most famous prison in the world. During the crime wave that swept across the United States during the Great Depression of the 1930s, correctional administrators were first challenged with how to handle offenders with serious criminal histories of violence. As a result, in 1934 the federal government opened Alcatraz Island as the most supermaximum prison ever created in the United States. Alcatraz was designated to handle the most notorious and dangerous criminals of the era, using strict regimens of control and tight security. However, Alcatraz was very expensive to operate, with no freshwater wells and all supplies needing to be ferried across the water from San Francisco. As a result of cost, Alcatraz closed in 1963, and was replaced with the United States Penitentiary (USP) in Marion, Illinois.

Alcatraz. Perhaps the most famous and mysterious prison in the history of corrections. Courtesy of the Federal Bureau of Prisons.

USP Marion had problems adjusting to this mission to control the nation's most dangerous offenders. As a result of continuously tightening security, inmates in 1980 staged a work strike, and the Bureau of Prisons permanently closed Marion's prison factory and terminated all classes. Tensions increased between prison officials and inmates, and on October 22, 1983, two inmates separately killed two correctional officers. Four days later, a prisoner was found murdered in his cell. Marion was placed on emergency status and implemented a twenty-four-hour lockdown of prisoners in solitary cells.[43] Inmates were allowed out of their cells only five hours per week for recreation, showers, and visits with family members. Inmate programs were eliminated, except those provided over video on in-cell television sets or by program staff (such as chaplains) coming to the inmates in their cells. In 1985, inmates filed suit against the lockdown. In the case of **Bruscino v. Carlson,** a federal judge denied their motion, stating, "the Court is of the firm conviction that this litigation was conceived by a small group of hard-core inmates who are bent on the disruption of the prison system in general and of USP Marion in particular."[44] The U.S. Court of Appeals upheld that decision in 1988, claiming that the conditions were not a violation of the Constitution, and in 1989 the U.S. Supreme Court let that decision stand. Marion

Bruscino v. Carlson
a 1985 federal court decision that the lockdown of inmates at the U.S. Penitentiary in Marion, Illinois, was not a violation of the Constitution

Warden James A. Johnson served as the first warden of Alcatraz. Courtesy of the Federal Bureau of Prisons.

was then free to continue the lockdown and became the model for supermax prisons that has since been copied by more than thirty states.

A supermax prison is defined as follows:

> A freestanding facility, or distinct unit within a facility, that provides for the management and secure control of inmates who have been officially designated as exhibiting violent or seriously disruptive behavior while incarcerated. Such inmates have been determined to be a threat to safety and security in traditional high-security facilities, and their behavior can be controlled by separation, restricted movement, and limited access to staff and other inmates.[45]

The following "An Interview With" is with the warden of USP Marion during the *Bruscino v. Carlson* trial that opened the door to allowing all the supermax prisons across the United States.

An Interview With...

A Supermax Prison Warden

Jerry T. Williford had a very distinguished career in corrections. He worked for over twenty years for the Federal Bureau of Prisons, was the warden of three prisons, and was a regional director in charge of fifteen prisons. He later became the chief federal probation officer in Atlanta, Georgia. Mr. Williford was warden of the United States Penitentiary (USP) in Marion, Illinois, then labeled the "toughest prison in America." Marion represented the first supermax prison in the United States, and during the time he was warden the federal courts decided the case of *Brucino v. Carlson*. In a decision in favor of Marion and the Federal Bureau of Prisons, the door was opened to other supermax prisons, and several states soon opened their own version of USP Marion.

Question: Could you describe the federal prison in Marion, Illinois, at the time you were warden.

Warden Williford: USP Marion housed about 300 maximum-security inmates and about 120 inmates in a minimum-security camp. The maximum-security inmates were seldom allowed out of their cells, so the minimum-security inmates did the work to maintain the outside grounds and the front of the prison, but came in no contact with the max inmates. I came to the prison as warden shortly after inmates murdered two correctional officers on the same day, and we started a lockdown that ended up as the model for future supermax prisons.

Question: What was the philosophy under which Marion operated as a supermax?

Warden Williford: The overall philosophy was one of total security and control. Inmates sent to Marion were the worst in the federal prison system. They were sent there based on their misconduct in other maximum-security prisons or they were considered extremely high escape risks because of previous escape attempts or a belief that they were serious escape risks. The inmates sent there for misbehavior almost always were sent for serious violence. In many cases, they had a history of several serious assaults or multiple murders at other prisons. Just being a murderer on the street would not get you sent to Marion. We had two inmates that had both murdered four people while in prison. These inmates were violent and dangerous and had to be in a controlled setting. A study by the University of Minnesota found that inmates at Marion were seven times more dangerous than inmates at Alcatraz.

Question: What were the cells like at Marion?

Warden Williford: The cells at Marion were approximately 7 by 10, and housed one inmate. The walls were concrete and the front was open bars. Originally, inmates had metal beds, but they began to use the metal to make weapons, so we took out the metal beds and poured concrete a foot high with a 30-inch-wide mattress on it. The cell had a toilet and wash basin, but nothing else.

Question: What was the procedure for controlling inmate behavior?

Warden Williford: When inmates first arrived at Marion, they were in a total lockdown status. They were in their cells all the time except an hour per day for recreation time and once every other day for a shower. They were allowed to participate in minimal in-cell programs. They had televisions in their cells on which they could watch regular programming or religious or education programming created by our religious and education departments. If inmates desired, a chaplain would go to their cells to talk to them. They were brought books from the library. Most of their time was spent just lying in bed with the opportunity to contemplate their wrongdoing. They may stay in this first phase at least a year. If during the year, they had no misconduct reports, they could be considered for movement to the second phase. However, we had some extremely violent inmates and gang leaders that were never allowed to move to the second phase, even if they did not misbehave.

The second phase was pretty much like the first phase, but inmates were allowed out of their cells into the center of the cellblock to eat their meals with a small group of other inmates (no more than fifteen). They could also come out of their cells for recreation in these same small groups. We tried to separate known enemies and gang members from gangs that were at war and would kill each other if given the opportunity.

The final phase was called the honor unit. Inmates were out of their cells most of the day and got to work in the prison industries program. They went to the prison dining room to eat their meals. They had to keep at least a year of good conduct in this unit to be considered for release from Marion. If they had misconduct, they were sent back and had to start their control program at the beginning. Those released from Marion were sent to a regular maximum-security federal prison.

Question: What was Marion like when you first arrived as warden?

Warden Williford: I arrived in Marion just months after the two correctional officers were murdered on the same day. As warden, my first focus was to rebuild the confidence of staff and show them that they could be safe in their work. In the early days, I think staff were scared, and some responded by overreaction to inmate violence and with too much

bravado. As they felt safer, they realized they could still control inmates and the facility through sound security procedures, rather than to respond to violence with violence. As staff became more confident and calm, the inmates also seemed to relax some as well.

For a long time, the media was very critical of our staff and portrayed them as the aggressors and the inmates as the victims. I tried to open the prison more to the media so that they would see the professionalism of our staff.

About six months after I arrived, the trial for *Bruscino v. Carlson* started, with court held in a prison courtroom. This was so inmates could testify without having to be taken to the federal courthouse. I think the inmates believed they would win the lawsuit and be released from Marion, or at least the lockdown would have to end. There was much tension and hostility between inmates and staff during this time. Whenever I walked the prison, inmates would make catcalls and were extremely disrespectful of staff and myself. After a three-month trial, we won the lawsuit and were allowed to continue to operate Marion on a lockdown status. Once we won, the inmates realized the only way to get out of Marion was to behave, and they started treating staff with respect and worked to try to get out of Marion the right way.

Question: Can you tell us some of the things that went on while you were at Marion?

Warden Williford: While I was there, we had two murders of inmates by other inmates. In both, the murder did not include the use of a weapon and occurred during a one-on-one fight. In one case, an inmate beat the other inmate's head on the concrete floor. In the other, one inmate got the other inmate down on the ground and kicked him in the head until he died.

I spend a lot of time walking the cellblocks, talking to staff, and being accessible to inmates. I would often talk to inmates at the front of their cells. However, an inmate I had known for a while told me there was a "hit" on my life and I should step back from the cell fronts. I took him at his word and, while I still walked the tiers and talked to inmates, I stood back an arm length and protected myself.

Question: Who were some of the more notorious inmates at Marion?

Warden Williford: One of the best-known inmates there was Christopher Boyce, who was convicted of treason and had escaped from another federal

...continued

maximum-security prison. There was a movie called *The Falcon and the Snowman*, the nicknames for Boyce and his codefendant. Timothy Hutton played the Falcon, based on the Christopher Boyce character. Hutton came to Marion to view the movie with Boyce. Boyce first said he would not see Hutton unless he could do it without being handcuffed. We refused, and Mr. Hutton agreed with our position. So Boyce changed his mind and agreed to watch the movie with Mr. Hutton while handcuffed.

Jack Abbott was another notorious inmate. Norman Mailer helped him get released on parole after he left Marion. Abbot's letters to Mailer were used as the basis for a play called *In the Belly of the Beast*, about being in prison, killing other inmates, and what it took to commit a murder in prison.

Garrett Trapnell was another well-publicized inmate. Dan Rather interviewed him and Trapnell told him he would escape within a year. Trapnell had formed a relationship with a woman who started to correspond with him while in prison. She hijacked a helicopter and tried to use it to help him escape. She forced the pilot at gunpoint to fly from St. Louis to the prison. Just before landing in the prison yard, the pilot was able to wrestle the gun from the woman and shot her dead. During the fight over the gun, the helicopter crash landed on the prison grounds.

Question: It sounds like a fascinating time, yet it had to be a challenging job.

Warden Williford: It was both. I will never forget the courage and professionalism of the Marion staff. Without their hard work, we would have not won the lawsuit, and there might not be any supermax prisons today.

Security is the dominant feature of the supermax prison. All aspects of maintaining the prison, including structure of the building, education and programs, human contact, medical services, food service, property, and policies and procedures, revolve around proper security measures. When inmates do come out of their cells, they are handcuffed, often placed in leg irons, and escorted by at least two correctional officers. Human contact in a supermax prison is very limited, as inmates have minimum (or no) contact with other inmates, and have contact with medical staff, clergy, or counselors only when these staff members visit their cells. Inmates are almost always alone in solitary cells and generally eat, recreate, and participate in programs (via video) by themselves.

USP Marion served as the supermax prison for the U.S. Bureau of Prisons from the closing of Alcatraz in 1963 until 1994, when ADX Florence, Colorado, became the only BOP supermax prison. Courtesy of the Federal Bureau of Prisons.

A supermax cell. All the materials in the cell are built to be indestructible and are not able to be used as weapons. Courtesy of the Ohio Department of Rehabilitation and Correction.

Supermax prisons were created for inmates who exhibited violent and predatory behavior in other prisons. However, the use of supermax prisons has expanded; in some states, to reduce gang activity and related violence in other prisons, identified prison gang members are also removed from general-population prisons and placed in a supermax prison, even if they have not committed a violent act while in prison. Connecticut was one of the first states (beginning in the early 1990s) to move gang members and leaders to a supermax prison. The only way for gang members to get out of the lockdown situation is to refute their membership and debrief or tell correctional officials everything they know about

In a supermax prison, inmates often can recreate out of their cells only in a small caged area with a small number of other inmates. Photo by Richard P. Seiter.

the gang operations and membership. Once they do tell officials about the gang activities, they would not be welcome back into the gang and would probably be assaulted or killed by other gang members if given the chance. Since the first identification of prison gangs, California has had the most gang members and the most problems and now uses a similar strategy: all gang leaders are placed in the supermax prison at Pelican Bay, are kept in a single-person cell, and recreate by themselves.

The purpose of the solitary isolation and extraordinary security within a supermax prison is to prevent extremely violent and dangerous inmates from harming others. Supermax prisons serve two functions in this regard. First, they control very violent and dangerous inmates. With constant diligence, security, and caution, these inmates have very limited opportunity to harm others. As inmates comply with security rules and show less intent to be disruptive, they usually earn small additional privileges, such as added time out of their cells or the opportunity to recreate or eat with a small number of other inmates. Over two or three years, if they continue to behave, supermax inmates can progress in privileges and work their way out of the supermax to a traditional maximum-security prison. The second function of supermax prisons is to discourage violent behavior in general-population prisons. Correctional administrators point out that the presence of supermax prisons is an incentive for good behavior, because inmates want to avoid being sent to this type of lockdown confinement.

The overall emphasis on security has resulted in controversy surrounding supermax prisons. Correctional officials maintain that these prisons are incentives for good behavior in other prisons, as inmates detest the thought of being sent to lockdown confinement. And taking the most violent and predatory inmates out of other prisons keeps general-population institutions more peaceful and orderly. However, opponents of supermax prisons assert that the lack of human contact, the absence of work, and the deficiency of intellectual stimulation are human rights violations and have negative consequences on individuals. The Federal Bureau of Prisons has shown that violence in other federal prisons has gone down since the advent of supermax prisons. A 2004 report by the Urban Institute provided a benefit-cost approach to evaluating supermax prisons, but did not have enough years of outcome data to come to a conclusion of their value.[46] More research is necessary to determine the impact of these facilities on overall inmate behavior. The "You Make the Decision" box at the end of the chapter asks you to decide whether you support the operation of supermax prisons.

Sex Offenders

Over the past twenty-five years, as a result of two major factors, the number of sex offenders under correctional supervision has risen significantly. First, public education regarding sex offenses has led to more victims reporting the sexual offense to police. Victims had previously been very hesitant to make their allegations public, fearing that they would not be believed, would be humiliated, and might suffer reprisal. The criminal justice system is better prepared to respond to the allegations of sex offenses, and DNA testing and other advances in forensic science have made some of them easier to prove. Second, legislatures have passed laws to support and aid victims, to clarify definitions of sex offenses that aid in the prosecution of such crimes, and to toughen sanctions for such offenses.

John Geoghan, a priest who was sentenced to a Massachusetts prison for child molestation, was shortly thereafter murdered by another inmate. Courtesy of AP/Wide World Photos.

Sex offenders are commonly defined as those who commit a legally prohibited sexual act or, in some states, any offender who commits any crime that is "sexually motivated." For instance, an assault that was an unsuccessful rape attempt may still be classified as a sex offense. The term *sex offender* usually includes offenders convicted of rape or sexual assault. Sexual assault includes the crimes of statutory rape, forcible sodomy, lewd acts with children, and other offenses relating to fondling, molestation, or indecent practices. **Pedophile** is the term for someone who is sexually attracted to and molests children.

Females are the primary victims of sexual assaults, although both male and female children are more equally molested by pedophiles. According to the Sourcebook of Criminal Justice Statistics, there were 248,300 rapes or sexual assaults in 2007.[47] Most rapes and sexual assaults were committed against females: Female victims accounted for 95 percent of all completed rapes, 76 percent of all attempted rapes, and 89 percent of all completed and attempted sexual assaults.[48] Table 9.4 illustrates the characteristics of victims of rape and sexual assault, and Table 9.5 illustrates the characteristics of imprisoned sex offenders. Both victims and offenders of sexual assault are more likely to be white. Although 47 percent of all victims of violent crimes are strangers to the offender, only 30 percent of rapes and 15 percent of sexual assaults are strangers to the victims.

Data on conviction and sentencing for rape and sexual assault indicate the following:

- In 1992 an estimated 21,655 felony defendants nationwide were convicted of rape.

- Just over two-thirds of convicted rape defendants received a prison sentence, 19 percent received a jail sentence and probation, and 13 percent were sentenced to probation supervision in the community.

- For rape defendants sentenced to prison, the average term imposed was just under fourteen years. The average jail term for an offender convicted of rape was eight months, and the average probation term was just under six years. An estimated 2 percent of convicted rapists received a term of life imprisonment.

- About a third of rape defendants had one or more additional felony convictions collateral to the conviction for rape.

sex offenders
offenders who have committed a legally prohibited sexual act or in some states any offender who commits any crime that was statutorily defined as sexually motivated

pedophile
someone who is sexually attracted to and molests children

| TABLE 9.4 | Victims of Imprisoned Rape and Sexual Assault Offenders |

Characteristic	Violent Offenders in State Prison Reporting Single Victims		
	All Violent	Rape	Sexual Assault
Sex of victim			
Male	55.8%	5.5%	15.2%
Female	44.2	94.5	84.8
Race of victim			
White	64.5%	67.8%	76.4%
Black	29.8	27.6	20.1
Other	5.7	4.6	3.5
Age of victim			
12 or younger	9.9%	15.2%	44.7%
13–17	8.8	21.8	33.0
18–24	17.5	25.1	9.4
25–34	31.1	25.4	7.7
35–54	26.5	10.2	4.3
55–older	6.3	2.3	0.9
Median age	29 yrs	22 yrs	13 yrs
Relationship to offender			
Family	12.9%	20.3%	37.7%
Spouse	2.5	1.2	0.6
Child/stepchild	6.1	14.0	25.9
Other relative	4.3	5.1	11.2
Intimate	5.5	9.1	6.2
Boyfriend/girlfriend	5.0	8.8	5.4
Ex-spouse	0.5	0.3	0.8
Acquaintance	34.7	40.8	41.2
Stranger	46.9	29.8	14.9

Source: Lawrence A. Greenfeld, *Sex Offenses and Offenders: An Analysis of Data on Rape and Sexual Assault* (Washington, D.C.: U.S. Department of Justice, Bureau of Justice Statistics, February 1997), p. 24.

- Sentences of convicted rape defendants also carried additional penalties, which included a fine (13 percent of convicted defendants), victim restitution (12 percent), required treatment (10 percent), and community service (2 percent).[49]

In 2005, sex offenders constituted approximately 4.7 percent of all offenders under correctional supervision. Most sex offenders are supervised in the community. In 2005, there were 491,720 offenders in state sex offender registries, a 47 percent increase from 1997.[50] However, the number of imprisoned sex offenders is growing. In 1980, only 20,500 sex offenders were in state prisons; by 1994, this number had climbed to 88,100,[51] and by 2005 to 164,600.[52] By 2007, 12.6 percent of all state prisoners were sex offenders.[53] Once in prison, sex offenders are serving longer periods of time. In 1990, offenders convicted of rape were serving an average

TABLE 9.5	Characteristics of Imprisoned Rape and Sexual Assault Offenders		
	Offenders in State Prison		
Characteristic	**All Violent**	**Rape**	**Sexual Assault**
Estimated number of offenders, 1994	429,400	33,800	54,300
Sex			
Male	96.2%	99.6%	98.8%
Female	3.8	0.4	1.2
Race			
White	48.1%	52.2%	73.9%
Black	48.2	43.7	22.8
Other	3.7	4.1	3.3
Age at arrest for current offense			
Less than 18	3.1%	0.6%	1.1%
18–24	38.1	33.7	23.6
25–29	22.1	20.9	17.0
30–34	15.0	17.7	16.3
35–39	8.8	10.9	13.4
40–44	5.0	4.1	10.2
45–49	3.4	4.8	6.6
50–54	1.7	2.9	4.4
55–59	1.5	3.2	4.2
60 or older	1.4	1.3	3.2
Average at arrest	29 yrs	31 yrs	34 yrs
Marital status			
Married	17.1%	22.1%	21.8%
Widowed	2.6	1.2	1.7
Divorced	21.4	28.5	35.0
Separated	5.6	6.2	4.9
Never married	53.3	42.0	36.6

Source: Lawrence A. Greenfeld, *Sex Offenses and Offenders: An Analysis of Data on Rape and Sexual Assault* (Washington, D.C.: U.S. Department of Justice, Bureau of Justice Statistics, February 1997), p. 21.

of 62 months in jail or prison, and those convicted of other sexual offenses were serving 36 months. By 1999, this had increased to 79 months for rape and 47 months for other sexual assaults.[54]

Treatment and Management of Sex Offenders

Sex offenders present a difficult challenge for management in both community and institutional settings. Not all sex offenders share similar characteristics, and the most effective management and treatment comes from creating a program that relates to the individual characteristics of the offender. A National Institute of Justice survey of state supervision of sex offenders in the community identified a five-part containment process that "seeks to hold offenders accountable through the combined use of both offenders' internal controls and external control measures (such as the use of the polygraph and relapse prevention plans)."[55]

containment model

an approach to managing sex offenders that includes treatment to develop internal control over deviant thoughts, supervision and surveillance to control external behaviors, and polygraph examinations to monitor conformance to treatment plans and supervision conditions

The **containment model** is designed to use a "triangle" of supervision: "treatment to teach sex offenders to develop internal control over deviant thoughts; supervision and surveillance to control offenders' external behaviors; and polygraph examinations to help design, and to monitor conformance to, treatment plans and supervision conditions."[56] The five components of the model are as follows:

1. An overall philosophy and goal of community and victim safety
2. An individualized case management system of sex offender–specific containment tailored to the needs of the sex offender
3. A multidisciplinary approach of collaboration among teams of law enforcement, probation and parole, treatment providers, and prison personnel to manage the offender
4. Consistent public policies reflecting the latest knowledge regarding effective management of sex offenders
5. A quality-control component to monitor whether policies are being implemented as intended and that they are producing the desired impact

Sex Offender Recidivism

Although sex offenders are a difficult group to rehabilitate, the recidivism rates generally attributed to sex offenders are not as high as many people think. In examining sex offender inmates in state prisons in 1991 who were recidivists, an estimated 24 percent of those serving time for rape and 19 percent of those serving time for sexual assault had been on probation or parole at the time of the offense for which they were incarcerated.[57] In a study by the Bureau of Justice Statistics of recidivism by probationers, rapists on probation were found to have a lower rate of rearrest for new felonies (19.5 percent) than other violent probationers (41 percent) over the three-year follow-up.[58] Another three-year follow-up of recidivism of offenders discharged from prison during 1994 had similar findings. Table 9.6

TABLE 9.6	Recidivism Rates of Violent, Rape, and Sexual Assault Offenders, 1994			
	Percent of All Inmates			
Offenders	**Rearrested**	**Reconvicted**	**Reincarcerated with New Sentence**	**Reincarcerated without New Sentence**
All violent offenses	61.7%	39.9%	20.4%	49.8%
Rape	46.0	27.4	12.6	43.5
Sexual assault	41.4	22.3	10.5	36.0

Source: Bureau of Justice Statistics, *Sourcebook of Criminal Justice Statistics, 2001* (Washington, D.C.: U.S. Department of Justice, 2003), p. 508.

illustrates the lower rearrest, reconviction, and reincarceration rates for ex-inmates who had served a sentence for rape or sexual assault than for those who served a sentence for all violent offenses.

The management and treatment of sex offenders are difficult and often unsuccessful, even though offenders convicted of rape and sexual assault have lower recidivism rates than other violent offenders. However, there is little tolerance for sexual offenders under community supervision, as almost two of every five offenders are returned to prison, even when not committing a new crime. Intensive treatment and monitoring in the community, including the use of polygraph examinations to confirm compliance with treatment and supervision conditions, often lead to revoking supervision as a preventive approach to avoid further criminality.

Civil Commitment of Sexually Violent Predators

Over the past decade, state legislatures began to take another step in controlling sexual offenders and protecting potential victims (especially children) from them by passing a new type of mental disorder that allows a diagnosis of sex offenders as sexually violent predators. When a person is convicted of a sex offense, he or she receives a specific sentence for that crime. Once the inmate serves his time and is nearing release, the state files a petition to have him involuntarily and indefinitely committed to a mental institution or special correctional setting that is a blend of a prison and a mental institution. The process includes the completion of an evaluation by mental health professionals, and a probable cause hearing is held to determine whether to label the offender a sexually violent predator. Most jurisdictions require that the offender be judged to suffer from a mental abnormality or personality disorder that makes it likely he will continue to commit acts of sexual violence, even though there is no specific professional criteria that can objectively be considered. If so labeled, once finishing his prison sentence, he is confined in the mental health facility until he is judged by mental health professionals to no longer be a danger to the community. By 2006, seventeen states had passed laws to involuntarily commit sexually violent predators. There are variations in the approaches to these civil commitment laws taken by the states. However, all have four common elements that are considered in the screening process: a past history of sexually harmful conduct, a determination of a current mental disorder or abnormality, a finding of risk of future sexually harmful conduct, and a link between the mental abnormality and the risk of future sexual violence.[59]

The civil commitment and confinement of sexually violent predators are a relatively new, evolving process. In 1997, the U.S. Supreme Court in *Kansas v. Hendricks* supported the civil commitment of sexually violent predator (SVP) laws as long as specific requirements are followed and, since that time, have confirmed this decision in *Selling v. Young* (2001) and *Kansas v. Crane* (2002).[60] The courts have recognized that the confinement at issue is civil and not criminal, imposed as punishment. Those identified as sexually violent predators are not housed with a prison population. The confinement model is the same as for other involuntary committed mentally ill clients, and as long as the purpose of confinement is to treat the sex offender, the state may commit the offender for an indefinite period as far as the Constitution is concerned. There is an expectation of the following:

- Comprehensive treatment programs that are geared toward eventual release of the resident are required. The treatment provider performs sex offender risk assessment and discharge planning, which entails recommendations concerning continued commitment or release to the community.

- Confinement is a nonpunitive setting, and residents are civil commitments, not criminals.
- There is extensive, ongoing interaction with the court system in providing frequent mental health status reports. Residents are provided hearings at which judges review the residents' progress toward treatment goals and potential release.

The implementation of civil commitment statutes creates several operational problems for correctional officials that must confine, treat, and recommend release of these offenders. First, the case law is far from settled as to what is adequate treatment. Few standards for providing treatment to sexually violent predators have been shown to work. Second, the indefinite nature of commitment makes it difficult to plan for release. Even after it is determined that an SVP can be released, there is often community opposition to release and, if it is a high-publicity case, communities object to the offender coming to that location. A recent case in California resulted in the Department of Corrections putting a trailer outside a prison on state grounds and housing the offender there, since he could no longer be confined, yet no release plans were acceptable to the local community. Finally, the in-between status of these offenders as part prisoner and part mental patient creates confusion in how to operate a facility. The residents may still be violent and be a danger to staff or other residents, but the confinement restrictions against punishment sometimes make it difficult to house them safely. The next decade should provide additional experience and case law that gives correctional officials additional guidance on the management of this population.

Offenders with Infectious Diseases

Criminal offenders generally come from a high-risk group for infectious diseases. They usually have not had a healthy lifestyle, including poor nutrition, a lack of medical care, high stress, likelihood of involvement in violent acts, shared needles for drug use, and interaction with other high-risk individuals. Reviews have identified that the populations of our nation's jails and prisons account for a higher percentage of the total population who are infected with HIV or AIDS, hepatitis C, and tuberculosis than would be expected.[61] Therefore, the problems of infectious diseases are often greater than in the general U.S. population, and management by correctional officials of infected offenders causes more serious problems in handling offenders and keeping disease from spreading. Infectious diseases most common to and most problematic with correctional populations include HIV/AIDS, tuberculosis, and hepatitis C.

HIV/AIDS

human immunodeficiency virus (HIV)
a virus that attacks the body's immune system, increasing the chance of infection and other diseases

Human immunodeficiency virus (HIV) attacks the body's immune system, increasing the chance of infection and other diseases. The HIV virus can develop into acquired immune deficiency syndrome (AIDS), which usually proves fatal after some period of time. HIV/AIDS is a serious concern for correctional agencies, especially prisons and jails, in which offenders and staff interact regularly; there is the chance of violence and blood spills, and staff and inmates fear the transmittal of the disease, even though it is passed only through body fluids

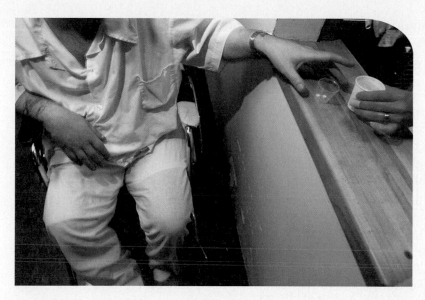

HIV/AIDS-infected inmates represent just over 2 percent of the incarcerated population and receive counseling and medical care while in prison. Photo by Mark Peterson/Corbis/SABA Press Photos, Inc.

(blood, semen, vaginal fluids, and other body fluids) and there is usually little likelihood of individuals contracting the disease through casual or chance contact. HIV is known to be spread by sexual contact with an infected person or by sharing needles or syringes for drug injection with someone who is infected. HIV/AIDS is a disease that is very difficult and expensive to treat and taxes the staff and budgets of correctional agencies.

It is estimated that between 800,000 and 900,000 Americans are infected with the HIV virus. The overall rate of confirmed AIDS cases among the U.S. prison population (0.50 percent) was approximately three times the rate in the general U.S. population. On December 31, 2004, there were 21,336 state prison inmates (1.9 percent of the state prison population) and 1,680 federal inmates (1.1 percent of the population) known to be HIV-positive, and 6,027 were confirmed to have developed AIDS.[62] As indicated in Table 9.7, the percentage of the prison population infected with HIV has declined over the past few years, from 2.3 percent of

TABLE 9.7	Percentage of HIV-Positive Prison Inmates by Year	
Year-end	**Number**	**Percent of Population**
1995	24,256	2.3%
1996	23,881	2.2
1997	23,886	2.1
1998	25,680	2.2
1999	25,801	2.1
2000	25,333	2.0
2001	24,147	1.9
2002	23,864	1.9
2003	23,663	1.9
2004	23,046	1.8

Source: Laura M. Maruschak, *HIV in Prisons, 2004.* Bureau of Justice Statistics Bulletin (Washington, D.C.: U.S. Department of Justice, November 2006), p. 1.

the prison population in 1995 to 1.8 percent in 2004. During 2004, 203 inmates died from HIV-related causes. In 2004, the rate of confirmed AIDS among the prison population was more than three times the rate in the U.S. general population.[63]

HIV/AIDS is not distributed evenly throughout the prison population. A slightly greater proportion of female inmates (2.6 percent of the prison population) as compared to male inmates (1.8 percent) in state prisons on December 31, 2004, were HIV-positive.[64] As indicated in Table 9.8, states in the Northeast had a significantly higher proportion of HIV-infected inmates (4.6 percent) than other regions, with only 2.2 percent in the South, 1.0 percent in the Midwest, and 0.7 percent in the West.

To determine whether inmates have HIV/AIDS, many states require inmates to have an HIV test. In a 2005 survey, 33 percent of state and federal prison systems reported that they conduct mandatory HIV testing of inmates.[65] Every state and the federal prison system provide educational information to inmates to inform them of the potential for inmates in population to have HIV/AIDS, describe the types of behaviors that can lead to infection, and reduce the fear of infection from other inmates. Once inmates are determined to be positive for HIV, prisons take different approaches to the management of this population. In a survey conducted by the Criminal Justice Institute during 2005, 38 states reported that they did not separate inmates testing positive for AIDS, whereas twelve reported that they did separate these inmates from the general inmate population.[66]

Those separated are housed together, some in a medical setting and some in a standard prison housing unit, to reduce concern among other inmates and the potential of transmission to other inmates. Most systems that adopt a nonseparation policy do not divulge the identity of inmates with AIDS to avoid discrimination against them in program and work opportunities and harassment by other inmates and possibly staff. Inmates and staff are told to "take universal precautions," meaning to treat every inmate as HIV-positive by avoiding behavior by which HIV could be transmitted and handling inmates or blood spills in a way that avoids the risk of infection (such as by wearing a surgical mask and using rubber gloves when blood is visible).

A controversial issue is to what extent HIV is transmitted inside of prisons. In a recent study, Krebs found that in a sample of 5,265 male inmates incarcerated as of 1978 and released from prison before 2000, 33 inmates (0.63 percent) contracted HIV while in the sampled state prison system.[67] Another 238 inmates released were positive for HIV, but there was no evidence they contracted HIV while in prison. These findings are consistent with other studies indicating that most inmates who have HIV are probably infected in the community prior to their incarceration.[68] Hammett notes that "although transmission within correctional facilities has been documented, it does not occur often enough to justify the all-too-commonly used metaphor of correctional facilities as 'breeding grounds' for HIV/AIDS."[69]

Inmates who are in advanced stages of AIDS require substantial medical care. They are usually hospitalized during the terminal stage of AIDS to provide them treatment and to avoid possible contagious illnesses from other inmates due to their reduced immunity and ability to fight infections. Some prisons have created hostels to provide a sympathetic and dignified setting for inmates who are near death and beyond the ability of medical care to save. Being in prison is difficult for many inmates, but one can only imagine the suffering by inmates who know they are dying and are unable to spend much time with family or friends.

TABLE 9.8 **Inmates in Custody of State or Federal Prison Authorities Known to Be HIV Positive, Year-end 2002–2004**

Jurisdiction[a]	Total HIV Cases[b]			HIV Cases as a Percent of Total Custody Population[c]		
	2004	2003	2002	2004	2003	2002
U.S. total						
Reported[d]	23,046	23,663	23,866	1.8%	1.9%	1.9%
Comparable reporting[e]	22,961	23,653	23,808			
Federal	1,680	1,631	1,547	1.1%	1.1%	1.1%
State	21,366	22,032	22,319	1.9%	2.0	2.0
Northeast	6,756	7,394	7,620	4.1%	4.5%	4.6%
Connecticut	477	572	666	2.7	3.2	3.6
Maine	11	10	/	0.6	0.5	/
Massachusetts	215	230	290	2.2	2.3	2.9
New Hampshire	31	21	16	1.3	0.9	0.6
New Jersey	655	657	756	2.9	2.8	3.2
New York	4,500	5,000	5,000	7.0	7.6	7.5
Pennsylvania	693	775	800	1.7	1.9	2.0
Rhode Island	161	120	86	5.1	3.4	2.5
Vermont	13	9	6	0.9	0.6	0.4
Midwest	2,025	2,087	2,133	0.9%	1.0%	1.0%
Illinois	488	551	570	1.1	1.3	1.3
Indiana	/	/	/	/	/	/
Iowa	32	31	33	0.4	0.4	0.4
Kansas	41	32	48	0.5	0.3	0.5
Michigan	575	579	591	1.2	1.2	1.2
Minnesota	44	40	37	0.6	0.5	0.5
Missouri	294	268	262	1.0	0.9	0.9
Nebraska	20	21	24	0.5	0.5	0.6
North Dakota	6	2	4	0.5	0.2	0.4
Ohio	387	416	417	0.9	1.0	1.0
South Dakota	9	11	6	0.3	0.4	0.2
Wisconsin	129	136	141	0.6	0.7	0.8
South	10,691	10,740	10,656	2.1%	2.2%	2.2%
Alabama	270	270	276	1.1	1.0	1.1
Arkansas	102	94	100	0.8	0.7	0.8
Delaware	149	105	128	2.2	1.6	1.9
Florida	3,250	3,112	2,848	3.9	3.9	3.8
Georgia	1,109	1,095	1,123	2.2	2.3	2.4
Kentucky	74	/	/	0.6	/	/
Louisiana	487	511	503	2.5	2.6	2.5
Maryland	792	988	967	3.4	4.2	4.0
Mississippi	254	200	224	2.2	1.6	1.9
North Carolina	647	640	602	1.8	1.9	1.8
Oklahoma	133	162	146	0.8	1.0	0.9
South Carolina	489	520	544	2.2	2.3	2.4
Tennessee	215	208	218	1.5	1.5	1.5
Texas	2,405	2,460	2,528	1.7	1.8	1.9
Virginia	302	361	425	1.0	1.2	1.4
West Virginia	13	14	24	0.3	0.4	0.7
West	1,894	1,811	1,910	0.7%	0.7%	0.7%
Alaska	/	/	16	/	/	0.5
Arizona	155	123	130	0.5	0.4	0.4
California[f]	1,212	1,196	1,181	0.7	0.7	0.7
Colorado	185	162	182	1.1	1.0	1.1
Hawaii	15	27	22	0.4	0.7	0.6
Idaho	33	26	20	0.7	0.6	0.5
Montana	5	4	8	0.2	0.2	0.4
Nevada	116	107	113	1.1	1.0	1.2
New Mexico	25	29	30	0.4	0.5	0.5
Oregon	/	/	42	/	/	0.4
Utah	39	37	58	0.8	0.8	1.4
Washington	102	93	101	0.6	0.6	0.6
Wyoming	7	7	7	0.6	0.6	0.6

/Not reported.
[a]At yearend 2001 responsibility for housing District of Columbia sentenced felons was transferred to the Federal Bureau of Prisons.
[b]Counts published in previous reports have been revised.
[c]Percentages are based on custody counts, except for New Mexico for which percentages are based on its jurisdiction count.
[d]Excludes inmates in jurisdictions that did not report data.
[e]Excludes data from Maine, Kentucky, Alaska, and Oregon for all 3 years due to incomplete reporting.
[f]The number of HIV-positive inmates in California was estimated by applying the percentage of inmates known to be HIV positive in 2002 to the 2004 custody population.

Source: Laura M. Maruschak, *HIV in Prisons, 2004,* Bureau of Justice Statistics Bulletin (Washington, D.C.: U.S. Department of Justice, November 2006), p. 2.

Tuberculosis

Tuberculosis (TB) was a serious medical problem during the early 1900s in the United States, declined, and then resurged in the 1980s and 1990s. It is particularly a problem in prisons and jails, as inmates have high rates and risk of TB because of their background of poverty, poor living conditions, substance abuse, and a higher level of HIV/AIDS than the general U.S. population. As well, overcrowded conditions in correctional facilities increase the potential for transmission of TB among inmates. Early in the 1990s, particular concern was raised by various outbreaks of multi-drug-resistant TB in New York State and other jurisdictions. In a 1994 report by the National Institute of Justice regarding tuberculosis in prison and jails, the authors write, "Tuberculosis is an airborne disease, transmitted via droplet nuclei (e.g., the dried residue of droplets from sneezes or coughs) from patients who have pulmonary or laryngeal TB and who cough, laugh, spit, or otherwise emit sputum containing the TB bacteria (called *Mycobacterium tuberculosis)*. TB can be transmitted through repeated exposure in crowded, poorly ventilated environments; it does not require intimate contact.[70] Although many individuals may test positive for TB infection, the infection may not develop into active TB.

To determine whether inmates have TB, all state and federal prison systems screen inmates at intake. During the year 2003, there were a total of 14,355 tuberculosis cases among the noninmate population, and 475 cases (3.8 percent) among the federal, state, and local prisoner population.[71] In a recent survey of inmates and medical concerns, 95 percent of surveyed state inmates and 96 percent of federal inmates reported they had been screened for TB.[72] The screening is accomplished through a purified protein derivative (PPD) skin test. One problem, both for health care and for detection, is that there can be a false-negative skin test for inmates coinfected with TB and HIV, because the skin test may show negative for TB and the individual does not receive treatment when in fact he or she has both TB and HIV.

To avoid the spread of TB in correctional facilities, the Centers for Disease Control recommend the following actions:

- Rapidly identifying, reporting, isolating, and initiating appropriate therapy for active and potentially infectious cases of TB

The Hocking Correctional Facility in Nelsonville, Ohio, was originally a TB hospital. Once TB was able to be treated with medication, those infected were no longer removed from society, and these facilities were available for other uses—such as prisons. Courtesy of the Ohio Department of Rehabilitation and Correction.

- Ensuring the continuity and completion of therapy through direct observation and other adherence-enhancing strategies
- Rapidly identifying and evaluating contacts of infectious TB cases and initiating preventive therapy for infected people
- Identifying people with TB infection at high risk for developing active TB and ensuring that they complete a full course of preventive therapy[73]

An inmate found to have active TB is immediately removed from the rest of the inmate population, and all effort is made to prevent any staff or inmate from breathing the contaminated air around him or her. Most prisons now have negative pressure isolation rooms in their medical areas and prison hospitals, in which the ventilation system for that room is contained and does not flow into the general ventilation system for the prison. Inmates are placed in these rooms and treated with medication until they prove no longer contagious. They will be regularly screened to detect whether they have returned to an active state.

One key element to dealing with TB is multiagency collaboration and a coordinated legislative and regulatory approach. In California, a law was passed requiring notification to health departments of all TB cases, spurring collaboration with various correctional systems in developing reporting procedures. The state board of corrections has the power to regulate local and county jails, and it passed regulations to require each jail to have a communicable-disease control plan created collaboratively by jail and local health officials. A success story of managing the threat of TB occurred in New York State. As reported in a 1998 National Institute of Justice and Centers for Disease Control research brief,

> Since 1988, the New York State DOH (Department of Health) Bureau of TB Control and the DOCS (Department of Correctional Services) have had extensive and . . . exemplary collaborations in screening, treatment, case management, surveillance, outbreak investigation, discharge planning, education and training of staff and inmates, and technical assistance to staff. TB cases in DOCS have declined steadily since reaching a peak in 1993. No TB outbreaks have occurred in DOCS facilities since 1993.[74]

Hepatitis C

Hepatitis C virus (HCV) is the most common blood-borne illness in the United States and is a serious problem among criminal offenders. It is a serious viral disease that attacks the liver and can result in lifelong infections of the liver, cancer, liver failure, or death. The disease is most commonly spread through the bloodstream as a result of drug users sharing needles. In a 2004 publication, a survey with 1,209 prisons responding indicated that almost all facilities test for the disease and of all inmates tested, 17,911 (31 percent) were positive for hepatitis C.[75] It is estimated that 39 percent of all Americans infected with the disease are in prison.

Hepatitis C was not identified until the mid 1990s, and it is widely accepted that 15 to 20 percent of those who contract the disease will require no treatment, but in the remainder, the disease will lead to a chronic infection.[76] Treatment with a combination of drugs requires from 24 to 48 weeks, and many prisoners with relatively short sentences have to defer treatment until they are released to the community. This creates problems upon release both for finding treatment in the community and for community correctional officers who have to work with local medical groups to link offenders to treatment opportunities. State and federal prisons struggle with how to care for inmates with this serious disease, and the Centers for Disease Control in 2003 sponsored a meeting for correctional health care workers to share experiences and improve the delivery of treatment options in a correctional setting.[77]

Hepatitis C, although only recently discovered, has quickly become of epidemic proportions and is a serious problem in correctional systems. The ability to identify, diagnose, and treat has improved, but it is often complicated by the simultaneous problems of drug abuse and mental illness among those infected. The long and costly requirement for treatment challenges both prison and community correctional agencies, and it is believed that if treatment options are successful, it can similarly have a positive impact on recidivism. For that reason, researchers and health care officials are calling for a more comprehensive and systemic approach to dealing with criminal offenders with hepatitis C.[78]

Summary

Most correctional agencies are organized to manage, control, and treat the typical adult offender, who is relatively young, is in good physical and mental health, does not have a serious substance abuse problem, and is not a sex offender. However, it could be argued that when inmates with all these characteristics are removed from the overall group of offenders, very few are left to be deemed "typical." Yet groups of offenders with any of these individual issues or needs are defined as special offenders and require specialized treatment, handling, or management. Most community and institutional correctional agencies have unique units (or individuals) trained to deal with these offenders apart from or with different approaches to the mainstream adult offender.

Correctional agencies today face many serious management problems that they did not have in the past as a result of the increasing proportion of the correctional population that may be termed as special offenders. The increasing number and percentage of the population that are drug offenders, mentally ill offenders, violent offenders, sex offenders, older offenders, or those with an infectious disease create significant problems of control, treatment, and provision of services. Each special group requires additional programs, new policies and procedures, and modified services or even housing arrangements. Such provisions seem difficult enough during times of available budgets and almost impossible during the current times of budgetary constraints.

Another group that is growing in number and in its impact on correctional agencies well beyond the small numbers of prisoners is offenders under age 18 who have been waived into the adult criminal justice system. Once incarcerated (since most juveniles are waived to adult court for a serious offense, most end up sentenced to prison), correctional agencies struggle with the best way to manage these offenders. Most states attempt to keep juvenile prisoners as separate as possible from adults. Yet when a state has small numbers of prisoners, it is difficult to provide the scope of programs and services that these offenders require, and there seems to be no simple solution to this problem.

Special offenders will continue to be a significant problem for adult correctional agencies. They strain the budgetary resources of an agency, as their management is usually much more expensive per inmate than for nonspecial offenders. They strain the organizational makeup of an agency because they require unique units of specially trained staff to manage, and with so many of these units being created, they take attention away from the central mission and role of most correctional agencies. They also put a strain on staff members, who are under more stress and have greater challenges in dealing with these special groups. Unfortunately, it is not expected that the number of special offenders served by correctional agencies will decline. As this chapter indicates, many more offenders in the correctional population are not being treated or specially managed and require continued expansion of the special services described. Special offenders within prison cause staff members and other inmates serious problems. As we close this chapter, I want to share with you in the "An Insider's Experience" box in *MyCrimeKit* a story that illustrates a problem we had in managing mentally ill and violent inmates that almost cost me my job.

mycrimekit

Insider's Experience:
I Thought I Would Get
Fired

Key Terms

special offenders
blended sentencing
straight adult incarceration
graduated incarceration
segregated incarceration
drug use forecasting
antipsychotic drugs

supermax prisons
Bruscino v. Carlson
sex offenders
pedophile
containment model
human immunodeficiency virus (HIV)

Review Questions

1. What is a special offender, and why do they require special handling while under correctional supervision?

2. What forces encouraged the movement toward the waiver of juveniles into adult courts?

3. In what ways do correctional agencies deal with juveniles under confinement?

4. Explain the distinction between drug offenders and drug addicts.

5. What role have antipsychotic drugs played in the deinstitutionalization of mentally ill individuals?

6. What problems do mentally ill inmates cause?

7. List the reasons for the increased proportion of elderly inmates in the prison population.

8. Why have supermax prisons become such an attractive option for the management of violent or seriously disruptive inmates?

9. What issues are cited by opponents of supermax prisons?

10. Why do sex offenders present such a difficult challenge for management in both community and institutional settings?

11. What is the containment model of supervising sex offenders?

12. What is civil commitment and who is it used for?

13. Identify the various categories of offenders with infectious diseases.

14. What is the rate of confirmed cases of HIV among inmates, and how does this compare to the rate of those infected with the virus in the nonprison population?

You Make the Decision...

Implement a Supermax Prison?

Over the past fifteen years, supermax prisons have been "the rage" in corrections, as most states and the federal government have initiated or expanded their use of this type of facility. Prison systems have more inmates and many more inmates with histories of violence and gang involvement. With longer sentences and three-strikes laws, many inmates have little hope of ever being released, and they have few disincentives for acting out violently or attempting escape. As a result, prison officials believe supermax prisons are a way to prevent prison violence. If inmates are locked in their cells all but a few hours per week, if programs and services are brought to them instead of them going to the service, and if when they do come out of cells they are handcuffed and escorted by staff, they have little opportunity to be violent. Prison officials also believe that the existence of supermax prisons keeps other prisons more peaceful, both because the most violent inmates are in the supermax and because the supermax acts as a disincentive for serious rule violations.

However, there are also many critics of supermax prisons. Opponents express concern that the lack of human contact, the absence of work, and the absence of intellectual stimulation have negative consequences on prisoners. They also argue that physical violence toward inmates may be common in such a controlled atmosphere, and question whether staff working in such a rigid and secure facility will experience problems as well. Supermax prisons are also extremely expensive to build and operate. The requirement for high-security building materials and components, elaborate electrical and technical systems, and the overlay of physical security drives construction costs up to almost double that of a normal medium-security prison. The increased staff-to-inmate ratio, the need to take services to inmates in a lockdown status, and the absence of inmate workers to carry out many functions also drive up the day-to-day operational costs.

Either individually or in a small group, consider these pros and cons, and decide whether you support the use of supermax prisons. If you do, specify the types of inmates or the acts committed by inmates that would warrant their assignment to a supermax. If you do not, specify how you would handle violent and dangerous offenders.

Chapter Resources on mycrimekit™

Go to mycrimekit.com to explore the following study tools and resources specific to this chapter:

- **Practice Quiz:** multiple-choice, true/false, short-answer, and essay questions to help students test their knowledge
- **WebQuests:** learning activities built around Web searches
  - National Commission on Correctional Health Care: www.ncchc.org
  - Journal of Correctional Health Care: http://jchc.sagepub.com
- BJS-Medical Problems of Prisoners: www.ojp.usdoj.gov/bjs/
- **Insider's Experiences:** "I Thought I Would Get Fired"
- **Seiter Videos:**
  - See attorneys discuss the waiver of juveniles to adult courts
  - See offenders discuss drug use
  - See a warden discuss supermax prisons
- **Flashcards:** Thirteen flashcards to test knowledge of the chapter's key terms

Prison Life

The Management
of Prisons

After reading this chapter, you should be able to:

1. Explain how prisons are organized to accomplish their mission.
2. Describe the functions that are usually a part of the office of the director of a state correctional agency.
3. Discuss the role the inspector plays for a correctional agency.
4. Describe the functions of custody, treatment, and services in a prison.
5. Define unit management and describe the role it plays in the management of a prison.
6. Identify the methods available to prisons to control inmate behavior.
7. List ways in which the classification of inmates contributes to the management of a prison.
8. Outline the way an inmate disciplinary system operates within a prison.
9. Suggest ways the staff of a correctional agency can help or hinder a prison accomplishing its mission.

Introduction

How are prisons managed? What does it take to accomplish their mission of creating a safe and secure environment and providing inmates the opportunity for program participation that can help them reenter the community? Prisons are complex organizations, based on a tenuous relationship of greatly outnumbered staff controlling potentially violent and dangerous inmates. They must provide all services necessary for their operation in a cost-effective manner and endeavor to change inmates' future behavior through the provision of treatment programs. None of these activities is easy in its own right and trying to accomplish them all can seem like an impossible goal. However, modern prisons do a very good job of meeting these objectives through a combination of organization, methods to control inmate behavior, working through their staff, and taking steps to ensure quality performance of their functions.

The first section in this chapter covers how prisons and their headquarters agencies are organized. The organization of any agency should be designed to enhance the completion of the agency mission. However, in the public sector, the agency must also address many external pressures and interests, which are thus reflected in the agency organization. However, the key components of a headquarters correctional organization are to help the prisons operate effectively and efficiently and to oversee the supervision of offenders in the community. The organizational charts for both a state department of corrections and a state prison are presented to illustrate and explain these functions. Also, the use of unit management as a more efficient method of managing prisons is presented and discussed.

In the second section of this chapter, the methods used to manage inmates and control behavior are addressed. These include the consistent implementation of state of the art policies and procedures, a classification system to match inmate needs and security risks with staff and prison resources, and the use of a fair and equitable system for disciplining inmates who violate rules. There are far fewer prison staff than inmates at any time in a prison. Therefore, the key to effective management of a prison is to have these types of functions in place to create expectations for staff and inmates, to divide inmates into similar groups of risks and needs so that policies and practices can be tailored to each group, and to reward compliance and punish violation of prison rules by inmates.

Finally, the critical role that staff play in the management of prisons is described. No matter how good the physical security of a prison, no matter how thorough the policies, and no matter how well implemented a classification or inmate disciplinary system, if staff are not competent and professional in carrying out their duties, all these other managerial aspects are undermined. In this regard, this chapter also describes the practices used to recruit and hire quality staff, as well as the role that collective bargaining plays in managing a prison.

The Organization of Prisons

Prisons are organized in a manner that leads toward their ability to carry out their mission of creating a safe and secure environment and providing inmates the opportunity for program participation that can help them reenter the community. Although prisons could, most likely, carry out this mission independently, with no guidance or oversight by a state department of corrections, states and the federal government have found it more effective to have an umbrella agency that oversees prisons, is the link between elected officials and the prisons, and can ensure quality and consistency in the operations of all the prisons within that agency. In

Chapter 5, the reasons for and stages of the development of state and the federal correctional agencies were described.

Therefore, to understand the way prisons are organized to carry out their mission, it is also important to understand the role of a state department of corrections and the activities it undertakes to guide and assist in the effective operation of individual prisons. In the following sections, both the organizations of the umbrella agency and individual prisons are presented and described. As of December 30, 2005, the fifty states and the federal government operated 1,821 prisons. The agency with the most prisons on that date was the Federal Bureau of Prisons, which had 102, and the state with the fewest prisons was the District of Columbia, with one.[1] These prisons had a capacity to house 1,430,208 inmates and were operating at 11 percent over capacity.[2]

State Departments of Corrections

The central organization that oversees state and federal prisons is often called the *central office* or *headquarters*. For much of their history, U.S. prisons were operated independently, governors appointed wardens, state legislatures appropriated the budget for each prison, and wardens ran the prison without interference and in whatever manner they saw fit. As noted in Chapter 5, most of these headquarters organizations have been established over the past thirty years, as states did not previously have a separate agency to oversee the operations of prisons and other correctional components. However, the increasing political and public interest in how states ran their prison systems, the increasing litigation by prisoners regarding conditions of confinement, and the need for quality and efficiency caused the creation of central agencies to ensure consistency of standards and guide the administration of prisons.

As the numbers of prisoners and prisons have grown significantly over the past thirty years, the central headquarters of the state and federal correctional agencies have grown in the number of functions and employees required for overseeing large and complicated organizations and maintaining central control and consistency among prisons. As an example, the table of organization of the central office of the Ohio Department of Rehabilitation and Correction (Figure 10.1) is presented. Ohio is the seventh largest correctional agency in the United States in terms of the number of inmates under supervision, with approximately 51,160 offenders in Ohio prisons in 2008.[3] The largest in order of number of inmates as of June 30, 2008, were Federal Bureau of Prisons (201,142), California (173,320), Texas (173,232), Florida (100,494), New York (62,211), and Georgia (54,016).[4]

The Ohio Department of Rehabilitation and Correction has responsibility not only for all the state prisons, but also for the parole board and parole supervision, probation services and supervision in some counties, and assistance to counties for jail inspections and developing and funding community sanctions. This department is similar to most state correctional agencies and illustrates the complexity in the management of an agency that operates thirty-two prisons, has a 2006 budget of $1.7 billion, employs approximately 14,000 staff, and supervises 45,179 inmates and 34,000 offenders in the community. Several key functions deserve note in review of the organizational chart for a state department of corrections.[5]

Functions of the Office of Director

The chief executive of a state department of corrections is usually called the **director** or secretary of the department. Many functions are attached to the office of the director. Most central correctional agencies organizationally locate

director
the chief executive officer of a state or federal department of corrections

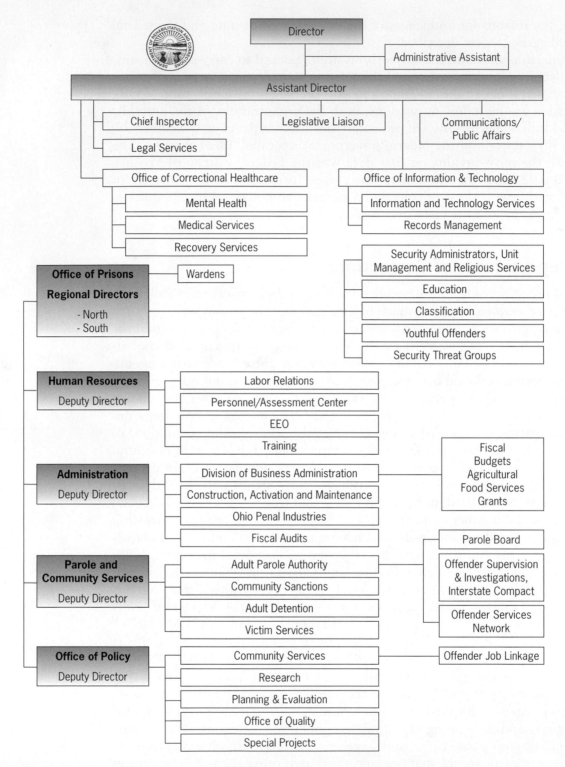

FIGURE 10.1 Table of Organization for the Central Office of the Ohio Department of Rehabilitation and Correction

Source: Ohio Department of Rehabilitation and Correction. Reprinted with permission.

the external management functions (legal services, legislative liaison, public affairs, investigations) close to the director and sometimes reporting to the director. Correctional agencies have found that external management issues are very sensitive and can quickly become political or media crises and, therefore, there should be immediate access to the issue between the staff dealing with it and

The director of a state prison system makes regular visits to the prison, talks to the warden and other staff, and clearly communicates expectations.
Photo by Richard P. Seiter.

the director. The worst thing that can happen to a correctional agency is for an issue that is potentially sensitive to be misrepresented by lower-level staff who have not been provided input from the person in charge of the agency.

Directors of correctional agencies often become like managers of professional baseball teams in that, when things go wrong, they get the blame and are replaced. This is not always because they have done a bad job, but because a change is seen as necessary to appease important groups or individuals outside the agency. Directors of state correctional agencies can lose the confidence of their elected supervisors and therefore most often lose their jobs because of the way agency policies are perceived, rather than from an actual failure in the internal management of the agency. Therefore, directors of corrections do not want "surprises" when it comes to developments around sensitive external communications, and they maintain these organizational functions as components of the director's office.

The organizational entities that often reside in the office of the director include public and media affairs, legislative liaison, legal advisors, and internal affairs. As criminal justice and correctional issues have become of great interest to the public, there is a tremendous demand for information from the media. Minor incidents in one prison with local media interest are usually handled at that local prison. However, an issue of state correctional policy or a major incident will usually result in the headquarters public information section responding to requests from the media.

As state correctional agencies have grown to be one of the largest state departments and use a large percentage of the state budget, legislatures have become much more interested in correctional policy and operations, and legislative members regularly have questions about a prison in their district or an issue regarding a constituent. Therefore, correctional agencies usually have an office of legislative affairs, which responds to legislative requests and builds support for the department regarding resources and programs. Staff of the office of legislative affairs regularly brief staff from legislative offices and committees so that they know the purpose of programs and are not surprised by media reports or bills submitted by the department.

Legal sections within correctional agencies also often report to the director of corrections. Legal offices deal with three general categories of issues: (1) responding to inmate lawsuits, (2) reviewing policy for legal impact, and (3) giving general advice regarding implementation of programs in line with past legal decisions. As described more fully in Chapter 14, with the demise of the hands-off doctrine by federal courts, the floodgates were opened to inmate litigation. Prison petitions from state inmates involved 23,122 in 2006, and legal actions from federal inmates were 1,116.[6] Legal staff of correctional agencies usually do not actually argue the cases in court, as that is the responsibility of the state and federal attorneys general. However, correctional lawyers must often review the lawsuits and initiate investigations to aid in the defense. Also, correctional legal staff usually review new or changed policy to identify any potential legal concerns.

The office of the director also will usually have an **inspector** or internal affairs division as a part of the organization. The ethical behavior by staff of a correctional agency is a very high priority, and the opportunity for unethical or even illegal behavior is great when staff are in daily contact with manipulative inmates. Therefore, complaints of staff misconduct by anyone (inmates, other staff, inmate families, or the general public) are investigated. An objective look by trained investigators is the best defense for staff against untrue allegations, and it is necessary to find cases in which staff have acted unethically or unprofessionally to maintain a credible and effective operation of prisons. In addition, many inmate complaints often end up in a lawsuit, so an early investigation of the complaint also creates a documented record for later use (perhaps months or even years later) when the department needs to respond to a legal suit.

State directors of correctional agencies have the opportunity to influence the lives of many people. The "Your Career in Corrections" box describes their roles and responsibilities.

Administration Functions

The central headquarters of a correctional agency usually carries out two major functions: budget development and accounting and new prison construction. The central budget division collects information from all the prisons, other divisions, and the governor's office to create a budget that represents desired programs, growth, and continued operations. The corrections budget becomes a part of the entire state budget that the governor presents to the state legislature. Once a budget is approved for a correctional agency, the administrative division maintains accountability of funds and keeps current on spending levels so that the agency does not go beyond its allocated amount.

For the past twenty years of tremendous growth in the number of prison inmates, these budget requests have regularly included funds to construct new prisons. In 2001, nine new prisons were opened in the United States at a cost of $387 million; twenty-eight prisons were under construction and fifty-eight existing ones were expanding their capacity at a total cost of $1.5 billion; and funding for capital construction for budget year 2002 was $1.5 billion.[7] From June 30, 2000 to December 30, 2005, 153 new state and federal prisons and 151 new private prisons were constructed and opened.[8] The administration division is usually charged with overseeing the design and construction of these new and renovated facilities, including hiring architects, coordinating their design with the departments' correctional experts, overseeing construction, and preparing to open the new facilities.

Human Resources Functions

In some states, the central headquarters performs all human resources activities. In other states, each prison carries out the personnel functions of recruitment, hiring, evaluations, and retirement, whereas the broad human resources functions

inspector
a person in a department of corrections who investigates allegations by inmates against staff

(labor relations, affirmative action or equal employment opportunity [EEO], and the operation of a central training academy) are carried out by the headquarters human resources division. Most states have a unionized correctional workforce, and negotiating and administering labor contracts are very legalistic and time consuming. Therefore, the central office usually has staff with expertise in labor relations to do the negotiations and advise prison managers on labor contract issues. Although each prison conducts some staff training, almost every state operates a central academy for training new hires and providing specialty training statewide.

Your Career in Corrections

Correctional Administrators

There are only fifty-two jobs of this kind in the United States—in the fifty states, the District of Columbia, and the Federal Bureau of Prisons (BOP): director of a correctional agency. How do directors get this job? They have to be appointed by the governor of a state, the mayor of the District of Columbia, or the attorney general of the United States (for the BOP). The people appointed to do these jobs usually have years of correctional experience, but with more sensitivity by elected officials regarding the political impact of correctional policies, people with no correctional experience (but close to the governor or with extensive political experience) have been appointed to these jobs more frequently.

In 2008, the average correctional administrator had responsibility for over 30,000 prisoners, 8,500 staff, and annual budgets of almost $900 million.[9] They must oversee the operations of twenty-six prisons (the average in each state); create a politically supported agenda; be responsible for the safety and security of staff, offenders, and the general public; and provide rehabilitative programs to improve the chance of offenders becoming productive and law-abiding citizens. When things go well—there are no prison riots or escapes, no horrible crimes are committed by former clients (offenders under their supervision), and there are no union complaints because of low pay or perceived unsafe working conditions—they are merely doing the job they were hired to perform. However, when bad things happen or when elected officials or the public are upset about specific correctional policies, how they are implemented, or how much they cost, directors get the blame. One would wonder why anyone takes such a job.

Staff who work in corrections usually do not do so because they are motivated by power or pay. They desire to make a difference, to serve the public, and to assist offenders. They work in corrections for several years and find that they have an affinity for the discipline and management and leadership talent. They see that the individuals in authority have the opportunity to initiate programs and improvements that can benefit staff, offenders, and the public. So as they move into an executive position and the opportunity comes along to be considered for the top administrator position, they do not think of the downside of the position, but only the opportunities it brings.

Pay is not bad for correctional administrators, although similar levels of responsibility in the private sector would pay considerably more. Although the pay has continued to increase, the average salary for directors of adult correctional agencies as of January 1, 2002, was $106,893; however, the average tenure in office at that time was only 4.4 years.[10] Not too many directors stay in the job much longer than this, because with every change of governor, there is often a change in corrections director. Also, the positions are highly stressful, and when things go wrong, there is often a change in leadership.

However, these are great jobs if you enjoy a challenge and having a lot of responsibility. This responsibility is not to be taken lightly, as it can involve the safety of staff and the potential of life-threatening situations. However, the rewards of satisfaction for a job well done, of serving the public, and of helping offenders get their lives in order make this job one worth striving for.

Community Supervision Functions

For states that still use indeterminate sentences and parole for release decisions, the parole board and postrelease supervision are usually located within the department of corrections. In some states, the probation functions are also operated by the state rather than the counties (see Chapter 3). Statewide parole and probation functions are organized into geographic regions, districts, or city offices to supervise offenders. In addition, many states carry out intermediate sanctions programs (electronic monitoring, house arrest, intensive supervision, or halfway houses) that are also coordinated by central headquarters. Finally, states sometimes provide assistance to county jails. Assistance may be in the form of grant funds to build new jails or to upgrade policies, procedures, or operations. In addition, every state has statewide jail standards, and department of corrections employees are usually responsible for inspecting jails for compliance with these standards.

Field Operations Functions

Finally, central offices have a division (or geographic regions) that directly supervises prisons. The Ohio system is divided into North and South regions that supervise the prisons. The role of the central office is to supervise the prison wardens and general operations, to create policy, and to oversee consistent implementation of policy. The following sections describe the organization of a prison and how the prison implements policies prescribed by the central headquarters of a correctional agency.

An interesting link between the headquarters of a correctional agency and the prisons is the personal role of the leaders of the department in overseeing the work of the prison. Although prisons are led and managed by a warden, the director (correctional administrator) of the department sets the tone and should be a role model for managing the correctional institutions. The "An Interview With" box illustrates this role and some ways that correctional administrators keep in contact with what goes on in a prison under their supervision. This interview is with myself, when I was director of the Ohio Department of Rehabilitation and Correction.

Prison Staff Organization

Prisons are organized in a manner to carry out the mission of operating a safe and secure environment and providing offenders an opportunity for program participation that can help them after release. Figure 10.2 is the table of organization for the Lebanon (Ohio) Correctional Institution. The chief executive officer of a prison is usually called a warden, although in some states, he or she is called a superintendent. Reporting to the warden are deputy (as in Ohio), associate, or assistant wardens. The general functions supervised by these individuals usually fall into three categories:

1. **Custody**—all the functions that come under the security activities within a prison; includes all uniformed employees, such as correctional officers and correctional supervisors
2. **Treatment**—all of the rehabilitative functions focused on keeping inmates productively engaged and preparing them for release, including counseling, religious services, substance abuse programs, or education
3. **Services**—all the functions that are required to operate the prison, such as budget and finance, maintenance of the facility, human resources management, and those that provide basic services to inmates, such as food and health services, work programs, commissary, and laundry operations

---

mycrimekit

Media—Video: Prison Management

custody
the functions within a prison that come under the security activities and includes all "uniformed" employees such as correctional officers and correctional supervisors

treatment
the creation of an environment and provision of rehabilitative programs that encourage inmates to accept responsibility and to address personal disorders that make success in the community more difficult

services
the functions required to operate a prison such as budget and financial, maintenance, human resource management, food and health services, work programs, commissary function, and laundry operations

An Interview With...

A Correctional Administrator

This is an interview with Richard P. Seiter, who served as director of the Ohio Department of Rehabilitation and Correction from 1983 to 1988. He had been previously a warden for the Federal Bureau of Prisons and chief of the National Academy of Corrections. He was 34 years old when he was appointed director, the youngest person ever appointed director of this Ohio department.

Question: I understand that you regularly visit the prisons in the state and that these visits are "from dawn to dusk," covering every area and talking to every staff member in the prison. I also understand that when you are there, you do a thorough sanitation inspection, looking, as I am told, "for dust in every corner and on every ledge, for soap grime in the bathroom sinks, and at every fire extinguisher for the monthly inspection documentation." First of all, why do you make such regular and extensive visits to the prisons?

Director Seiter: Well, the problem with working in a headquarters of an agency is that you get removed from the day-to-day working of the agency and its people. So, I do it so I do not forget what it is like, how hard the jobs are, and to hear from our staff firsthand how they are doing and what issues are on their mind. But, as much as anything, I do it because I enjoy it. This may sound pretty strange, but I really get a kick out of being in the prisons, and interacting with staff and inmates.

Question: Let's discuss that in more detail. Talk more about the danger of getting too far removed from the day-to-day operations of the prisons.

Director Seiter: I see my job as primarily to make the job of the staff working in a prison easier. This means many things. First, I need to stay ahead of the issues that are confronting them so that the problems do not get to a point where they are out of control. Every prison has problems in management. That is just the nature of the beast. Inmates are not used to following rules and complying with authority. So, every day, someone will try to avoid compliance, and staff have to deal with each situation—many will not work out as perfectly as planned. They have to take care of those issues by themselves; I can't help them with each situation.

But I can understand the forces that create situations and make prison management more difficult. For instance, if we are beginning to have a newly developing friction between some competing gangs, it is important to get on top of it as soon as possible. By being in the prisons, I can get a sense for what is happening from those having to deal with it, gather some intelligence they have picked up, and see what urgency there is to create some system-wide response.

Let me stick to that point for a second. I think an extremely underacknowledged skill of administrators is to understand when an issue has urgency, especially when the administrator is removed from the situation (in his or her prison office or in the state headquarters) and does not feel the intensity of the staff that have to react to it. Not all issues or situations (regardless of how serious they may be—for instance a murder of an inmate by another) have the urgency that requires a system-wide response. Some just need to be handled as best staff can deal with them as they come up. Others need a deliberate and thoughtful response, and the proper response can almost "bubble up" from each sequential incident. Administrators must be careful not to do the wrong thing or create the wrong response, just to react to something before they really understand the cause and underlying issues.

Finally, some issues do have real urgency, and staff are crying out for guidance and policy change or new direction. Let me go back to the example I started to reference about developing gang tensions. If I hear staff concern about this issue in one prison, it is worth having our gang staff (often called security threat groups) in headquarters survey other prisons to see if they are having similar situations. The fact that I heard about the issue from prison staff firsthand helped me understand the urgency and my responsibility for action. Otherwise, you may just read reports about a variety of incidents in a variety of prisons, and while you sense a link and ask staff to look into it, you do not do so with the sense that it is critical to the safe management of the prisons. I have talked to my colleagues about issues like this one that have gone on in a state, with staff constantly seeking help on how to deal with it. However, because the

...continued

top administrators are so tied up with their own issues (budget, the legislature, media pressure about an escape), they don't jump on the importance of this to the prisons. I personally get a better sense of the urgency of an issue by being in the prisons and hearing staff talk about it. One final note: Line staff and even wardens tend to downplay certain things when talking to their bosses; they do not want to give the impression that they can't handle it. So they don't "sound an alarm" themselves and don't often communicate a sense of urgency. That is when your own correctional experience and common sense come into play, and you hear a sense of urgency that is not overtly communicated.

The second way I try to make the job of prison staff easier is to show them that I support them, appreciate them, and respect the job they are doing. Correctional administrators can do this in a variety of ways. They can provide an adequate level of funding for employee awards programs to recognize staff that do a good job. They can urge managers to use incentive awards and can create special awards to recognize the behaviors they think are important at any particular time. They can send notes to employees who have done some especially good job or had a significant accomplishment. They can do media interviews and make public statements of support for staff and the jobs they do. However, nothing is more important than giving staff your time, going to them and saying hello, shaking their hands, and showing you care about them personally. I received feedback from a prison in the town in which I grew up. In fact, it was told to my mother, which really made me feel good. She met a staff member of the local prison, a relative of a friend of hers in her church. The staff member told her he thought I was a pretty good guy, that when many "dignitaries" visited the prison where he worked and came into an area he was working, they often acted as if he were invisible and did not talk to him. The dignitaries just talked to the warden or whoever was showing them around. But the staff member told my mother that whenever I entered the area where he worked, I went straight to him, said hello, and shook his hand. This made him feel that I respected him and thought he was important. Line staff make these kinds of judgments about the administrators they work for, and those interactions are more important than creating the most effective policy and getting the most favorable budgets from the legislature. They do tough jobs and have to know and believe that their bosses acknowledge this and acknowledge them.

Another thing I do when I go to the prisons, which I enjoy and I believe that the staff enjoy, is to challenge them. All staff take pride in their work and want it to be recognized. They feel even better if they have to work really hard and are still successful. When I made my first round of visits to all the state prisons, I checked every fire extinguisher for the required monthly inspections. Each has a tag on it showing that it has been inspected every thirty days to ensure that it is ready for action if needed. Every prison probably has two or three hundred extinguishers and it is easy to miss a few. I always found a few that had not been checked, until I went to one prison that had an extremely dedicated fire and safety officer. I found only one or two extinguishers that had been missed in some month over the past few months that were noted on the tag. I was extremely complimentary of the fire and safety officer, and he responded that he would be sure none were missed for my next visit. So I returned the challenge and assured him that I would check. Each time I returned I would look in one new place that I thought he might have missed—in a security tower guarding the fence or on a farm tractor. Our challenge, his attempt to be sure no fire extinguishers were missed, and my attempt to find one that had been missed became almost legendary at the prison. Staff would follow my prison tour route by radio, trying to anticipate where I would look on this visit. If I found one, everyone knew within minutes, and the fire and safety officer had to live with the ribbing of his fellow staff for days. If he won, he could bask in their still ribbing him about trying to please the boss. I would do the same thing with sanitation issues with all staff, looking for dirt or dust in some of the less obvious places, complimenting them when I found none, and poking fun at them when I found some. Seldom would I find much after the first couple of visits to a prison. Staff enjoyed the challenge and the fact that I pushed them to be better and appreciated them when they did.

Finally, I can make their jobs easier by creating a culture with a positive work environment. Prison jobs are tough enough, without administrators second-guessing staff and the decisions they make. I can help with this by not accepting problems or mistakes, but accepting that individuals will make some. I have a saying: "Be tough on the issue, but be soft on the staff." Don't accept that things just happen and that nothing can be done to reduce the likelihood that problems will occur. But don't let it be taken personally by the staff that make the error. If they blatantly disregarded policy, they will be disciplined for that. However, if staff make an error of judgment or don't deal with a situation as well as they should, look for ways to improve the likelihood that they will do better next time. This may mean that a particular type of training should be provided. It may mean that a new policy, procedure, or response to a situation needs to be developed. It may mean that causal factors need to be found and dealt with. But it is wrong not to look for underlying issues, ask tough questions of responsible staff, and try to respond appropriately when possible. And it is wrong to overreact to a staff error with discipline of only that staff member and to do nothing to improve all staff members' ability to be successful the next time.

Question: That was a really interesting overview of the role of an administrator in setting a tone and helping staff do their jobs. But you usually don't think of a director of corrections checking toilets for sanitation, checking fire extinguishers, or looking at farm tractors. Why do you spend so much of your prison tour time on these kinds of activities?

Director Seiter: That's really a good question and one I am not surprised you asked. It can seem odd to do these things. But I do this for a couple of reasons. First, when you enter an area of a prison and want to interact with the staff person working in the area, there are limits to what you can focus on. Many line staff working an area rotate regularly and do not have much control over policy or operational procedures. But they do have control over sanitation. So by checking this so thoroughly you can deal with something under their control, and your few minutes with them will be focused on their work, rather than something they have no control over.

But the most important reason is for the staff and me to pay attention to detail. In corrections, there is a saying that "if you pay attention to detail, the big issues will be worked out." As strange as that seems, it is very true in this environment. Prisons work on routine and consistent following of policy and procedures. Staff and inmates come to expect certain things to happen in certain ways. Inmates also watch staff that shortcut the way they do their jobs, which often results in a security breakdown that observant inmates will take advantage of. If every staff member pays attention to detail and makes sure that each step of a procedure is done the right way every time, there are no security breaches or breaks in routine that can undermine the safe and secure environment you are trying to accomplish. There will be fewer resulting problems and therefore fewer big issues.

When staff see how much attention I pay to detail, they realize the importance of it. I don't just check sanitation, I check the details of the policy. I look at log books to see that they are used as required, I note how staff lock doors behind them, even if they know they are going to have to unlock the door thirty seconds later. I check how we control and keep inventories of syringes in the hospital. Staff expect me to look at the details of how they do their jobs, and they know that these things are important to me. I have seen an improvement in their attention to detail since I have been doing this. I seldom find the same thing twice in a visit to a prison. So I combine a concern for them personally with a challenge for them to do their jobs right every time. Through those two things, I send the messages I want to send and do what I can to help establish the environment in the prisons that I think is necessary.

The organization of modern prisons is almost as complicated as that of the central headquarters. Although the mission of prisons has changed little over the past fifty years, the organizational structure has changed considerably. Organizational entities that internally control and manage staff and inmates are very much the same, but (similar to central headquarters) functional entities have been added to respond to external management needs. Included in the organization of the warden's office in Figure 10.2 are an inspector of institutional services, an institutional investigator, labor relations, and a management analyst supervisor who also serves as EEO (equal employment opportunity) chairperson. None of these functions was part of a prison table of organization a few decades ago, but changing times require changing organizational focus. Inmate complaints against staff must be promptly and thoroughly investigated, and prisons often have inspectors or investigators to carry out this function. Since collective bargaining and labor relations are prevalent in many correctional agencies, there is often a staff person dedicated to managing the local prison

mycrimekit

Careers—Correctional
Facility Administrator

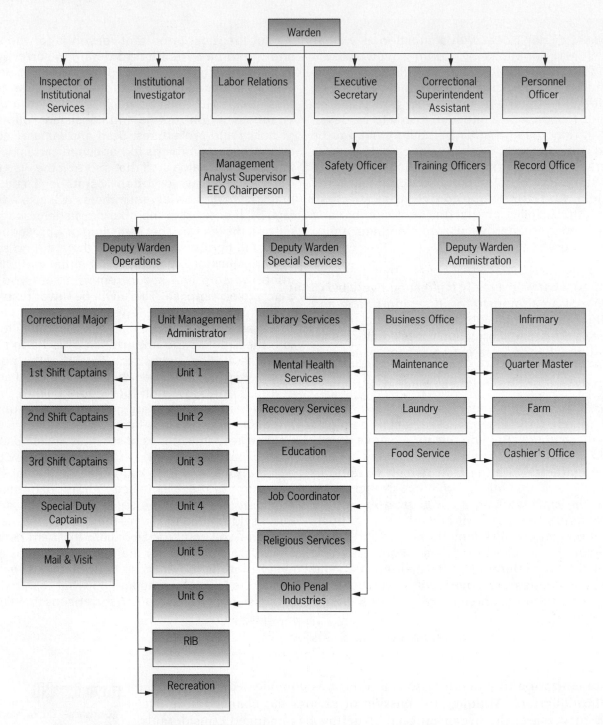

FIGURE 10.2   Table of Organization for the Lebanon (Ohio) Correctional Institution

Source: Ohio Department of Rehabilitation and Correction. Reprinted with permission.

collective-bargaining agreement and dealing with grievances by union members. The general components of a prison organization are presented next.

Custody and Security Functions

The custody and security component is often referred to as *correctional services* and encompasses all the security activities within a prison, including the duties of the security staff, the operations of the special housing unit (SHU), inmate transportation, and the inmate disciplinary process. Correctional services

Correctional officers in most states are organized in a paramilitary fashion, wear uniforms, and have ranks of sergeant, lieutenant, and captain. Photo by Richard P. Seiter.

departments are sometimes also referred to as *uniformed staff;* they are paramilitary in organization, rank, and dress (wearing uniforms that are similar to military dress uniforms). The rank of major is usually the highest-ranking uniformed officer, who supervises the security department. Captains run each eight-hour shift and coordinate security operations during that period. Lieutenants are responsible for an area of the prison, such as recreation or the SHU, and sergeants are supervisory correctional staff who either supervise a smaller area than lieutenants or are senior correctional officers assigned to work the most difficult posts.

Correctional services is the largest department (in number of staff) in a prison, ranging from 50 to almost 70 percent of all staff, depending on the state. In many state and federal prisons, no correctional officers are assigned to certain areas of the prison, such as education or prison industries. The non-uniformed staff who work in those areas (such as teachers and industrial specialists) carry out the security functions, as well as their specialty functions. In other states, correctional officers do more than the pure security functions and may supervise recreation areas such as the gym or yard, oversee inmate leisure-time activities, or even direct inmates who work in prison industries or maintenance departments.

Treatment Functions

The departments within a prison that are labeled as treatment or programs include education and vocational training, recreation, mental health, religious services, and substance abuse or recovery services. These functions serve the second part of the mission of a prison: to provide programs to inmates that can help them prepare for reentry to the community. In other words, they provide the rehabilitative activities within a prison. Staff who work in these departments are sometimes referred to as *professional staff,* because most of the jobs within these disciplines require a college education and specific preparation or certification to perform.

Education departments operate academic teaching, vocational training, library services, and sometimes recreation programs for inmates. These departments are

Teachers are very important to the management of a prison. They provide inmates with counseling and instruction in educational areas that are critical to inmates' future lives. Photo by Richard P. Seiter.

managed similarly to a community elementary or high school. In a few states, the prison system is actually an accredited "school district." Teachers must be certified, but teach a general topic (math, English, or science), rather than a grade. As inmates enter prison, they are tested for academic competence and work toward completion of a GED (general equivalency diploma) at their own pace under the guidance of a teacher, who usually has a class of fifteen to twenty inmates. Vocational programs include carpentry or general building maintenance, landscape or horticulture, food service, and office skills. In many states and the Federal Bureau of Prisons, recreation is also a part of the education department; however, in the Ohio prison organization, recreation is a separate department. Recreation staff are assigned to areas such as the gymnasium or the recreation yard and not only supervise the area, but also plan and schedule leisure-time activities to try to involve the largest possible number of inmates.

Mental health programs are provided in every prison, since (as discussed in Chapter 9) approximately 16 percent of prison and jail inmates are mentally ill. Mental health departments usually employ one or two Ph.D. psychologists to assess and counsel inmates. There may also be counselors with master's degrees to provide counseling programs. Few prisons have a full-time psychiatrist, but usually contract with one for a few hours per week to see the most ill patients who require psychotropic medication. Substance abuse or recovery programs that provide counseling for alcohol and drug abuse are sometimes a part of the mental health department; in other states they are a separate department. Another critical treatment area within a prison is religious services. Prisons usually employ one or two full-time chaplains (often a Catholic priest and a Protestant minister) who hold religious services and coordinate other programs. Since all inmates have a right to practice the true tenets of their religious faith, prisons contract with clergy of other faiths (Muslim, Buddhist, Native American, or Jewish) to provide religious services and counseling to these inmates.

Service Functions

Service functions within a prison are those that deal with staff or facility issues (budget and finance, maintenance, human resources management) and those that provide services to inmates such as food and health services, work programs, commissary, and laundry operations. The functions of operating a business office and human resources department are very similar to those of other government organizations. The budget office has accountants to maintain control and record budget allocations, purchasing agents to buy necessary supplies and equipment, and financial managers to prepare budget needs and do budget projections. The human resources department follows overall government requirements for accepting and scoring applications for employment, going through the hiring process, and training new employees to prepare them for work in the prison. This department also oversees the **employee awards program** to recognize and reward staff who perform well, the evaluation of staff by supervisors each year, and the labor relations program to monitor compliance with collective-bargaining contracts and respond to labor union issues.

The components of the organization that provide services to inmates are also similar to those that would be in place on any military base or Veterans Administration hospital. Whenever there is a relatively isolated group of individuals, basic services of food, health care, laundry, commissary, and maintenance of the facility must be provided. Staff roles in the food and health care areas are described in Chapter 12. Unique in prisons, compared to other public or private agencies, is the work program for inmates. Work programs serve several purposes. They benefit inmates as a rehabilitative tool; inmates learn how to work for a supervisor, follow instructions, and develop positive work habits. Work programs benefit prison administrators by keeping inmates busy and assisting in maintaining control of the prison environment. And work programs benefit the public, by selling prison products and performing other work to reduce the cost of incarceration.

Work programs in a prison are unique in how they are supervised and organized. Each area of work assignment (prison industries, building maintenance, sanitation, food services) has full-time staff who are experts in the area, but instead of doing the work themselves, they supervise inmate crews to perform the tasks. A good example is how a plumbing shop in a prison operates. There will be one or two plumbers who know how to do all the required plumbing tasks. The plumbers will be assigned a crew of approximately ten to fifteen inmates. The plumbers organize work in the shop for inmates to do (such as repairing damaged equipment) and take inmates into areas of the prison to do maintenance and repair work as necessary. These employees seldom are assigned inmates who are experienced or able to perform these duties without training. Therefore, the staff members have to train inmates as well as supervise them in performing these tasks.

employee awards program
a program to recognize and reward staff who perform beyond their expected level

Maintenance workers supervise inmates in several trade areas that both maintain the prison and develop beneficial skills for inmates. Photo by Richard P. Seiter.

Unit Management

Unit management is a way to organize a prison into smaller components, decentralize the authority to manage the inmate population, and make staff more accessible to the inmate population. Unit management was first established in 1966 by the Federal Bureau of Prisons (BOP) at the National Training School for Boys, to decentralize the management of the prison and enhance communication between staff and inmates, and has been implemented at every federal prison since that time.[11] The BOP defines a unit as a "small, self-contained, inmate living and staff office area that operates semi-autonomously within the larger institution."[12] The average prison holds approximately 1,000 inmates, and many prisons have as many as 3,000 inmates. Managing such a large inmate population is difficult, so unit management breaks the prison into more manageable units (between 200 and 300 inmates) based on housing assignments. Casework and other unit staff are assigned and located within the housing unit to be accessible and deal directly with inmates and are given the authority to make decisions and manage the unit.

Unit management enhances staff and inmate communication. The location of staff offices in the housing unit not only makes them more accessible to inmates, but also provides staff the opportunity to monitor inmate activities and see how each inmate behaves on a daily basis. Freeman suggests that accessibility of staff in each unit provides "each [unit] with a sense of group identity, and increases the frequency of employee–staff contacts [with inmates] so that small problems can be addressed before they become large problems."[13] The "A Case Study" box is a good illustration of the practical impact that unit management can have in enhancing prison security.

The unit team reviews each inmate's background, evaluates his or her needs, and determines appropriate program and job assignments. Upon their arrival, new inmates meet with their team to develop a plan for their work and program activities and then meet with their team every six months to review progress and adjust the plan. Figure 10.3 illustrates the organization of a unit team. The team includes staff from a variety of disciplines and departments within the prison. Units are directed by a **unit manager,** and include case managers and correctional counselors. **Case managers** (called *social workers* or *case workers* in some

Unit management offices are located in the inmate housing areas (see window in lower center of picture) so that staff are accessible to inmates. Photo by Richard P. Seiter.

A Case Study

The Effectiveness of Unit Management

When I worked at the U.S. Penitentiary in Leavenworth, Kansas, two incidents occurred that illustrated the positive impact unit management can have on the operations of a prison. When I first arrived at Leavenworth, it was not operated under the unit management concept. There were correctional counselors, but instead of being assigned to housing units, they were assigned to areas of the prison, such as industries, the dining room, the main corridor, the recreation yard, and the segregation building. Their duties were to be accessible to inmates in those areas and help out in the management as necessary.

About a year after I began working there, we had a work strike. Several inmates were upset with a change in the telephone policy (how they were allowed to make telephone calls) and decided to organize a work strike to get the attention of the administration and try to force a change in the policy. Early on a Monday morning, when inmates were on their way to work, groups of inmates blocked them in some of the main work areas, showing knives or other prison made weapons and threatening inmates who did not comply with their demands to go back to their cells and not work.

We quickly discovered what was going on and to avoid putting inmates in danger, we ordered all inmates to return to their cells. We locked down the prison and began to try to identify the organizers of the work strike. We began by interviewing inmates and called all the correctional counselors together to see whether they had an idea of which inmates were behind the work strike. Unfortunately, we discovered the counselors did not really know the inmates and could not put together a credible list of suspects.

About six months later, we implemented unit management at Leavenworth and assigned unit managers, case managers, and correctional counselors to each housing unit. Their offices were in the housing units, and they spent most of their day observing and talking to inmates. A few months after implementation, there was a serious stabbing in one of the cell houses, and the inmate who was assaulted died a few hours later. When he was being carried out of the cell house on a stretcher, a counselor asked him who stabbed him. The inmate did not know the full name of his assailant (the cell house had about 400 inmates living in it); he just said, "Tommy from California."

The unit staff quickly got together to see whether they knew who this might be. They had recently noticed some Aryan Brotherhood inmates who appeared to be talking and planning something together, and they knew that one of its leaders was named Tommy and was from California. They immediately went to his cell, found bloody clothes he had not yet gotten rid of, and found him in the shower washing off blood and evidence. Tommy was charged with and convicted of the inmate's murder. In this case, the fact that the unit staff knew the inmates, their names, and their habits led to the staff's ability to bring justice to a killer, whereas the previous management model for the prison was unsuccessful in identifying the organizers of a work strike.

states) have a caseload of 100 to 150 inmates and are responsible for developing the program of work and rehabilitation for each inmate and writing progress reports that release (parole) authorities or classification staff can use when considering an inmate for a program or transfer to another prison. **Correctional counselors** are promoted from the ranks of correctional officers and still wear officers' uniforms.

correctional counselor
a former correctional officer who works with inmates on prison issues such as creating a visiting or telephone list or getting a prison job assignment

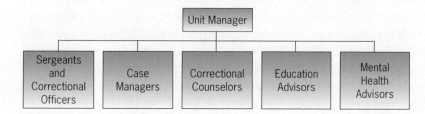

FIGURE 10.3   Table of Organization for a Unit Management Department in a Prison

Correctional counselors work with inmates on the daily issues that confront them while in prison, such as creating a visiting or telephone list, correcting an error on their account of finances held by the prison, or learning how to find a prison job or get along with other inmates. Because these staff members wear officer uniforms, the stereotype that all security personnel do regarding inmates is enforce rules and give them orders is diluted.

There are also correctional staff (sergeants and officers) who work in the housing unit. In some states, these staff report to and are evaluated by the unit manager, whereas in others they report to security supervisors, and the unit manager provides input for their performance evaluations. Also considered a part of the unit team, but usually not reporting to the unit manager, are education and mental health specialists. They evaluate inmate needs and help the unit team create appropriate programs for education, vocational training, substance abuse counseling, and psychological assistance. Although a goal of unit management is to enhance communication between staff and inmates, it has a secondary benefit of enhancing communication between these various groups of staff as they work together on the unit team.

Over the past two decades, most states have decided to implement unit management. Although it is generally recognized as a positive way to manage prisons, when a prison decides to implement it, there are still many questions and concerns from staff members regarding the impact on them and the types of positions that are available. Unit management can also be costly, because there may be additional positions for unit counselors and unit managers that were not in the prison prior to the unit management implementation. In Ohio, we were able to reduce the costs of perimeter security to fund unit management, but making this decision and change was still difficult. The "An Insider's Experience" box in *MyCrimeKit* describes the change process.

mycrimekit

Insider's Experience:
Taking Down the
Towers

Controlling Inmate Behavior

The mission of a correctional institution includes creating a safe and secure environment, yet because inmates tremendously outnumber staff, they cannot control behavior (over the long term) through threats, intimidation, and physical dominance. Many activities are key in the management of prisons, contribute to the ability of staff to control inmate behavior, and move toward accomplishing the mission of safety and security. These activities include the consistent implementation of prison policies and procedures, the use of classification to match inmate risks and needs to the appropriate prison, and an inmate disciplinary system to encourage adherence to prison rules and punish inmates who fail to comply with these rules.

Policies and Procedures

One key to controlling inmates' behavior is to have clearly written, well-communicated, and consistently implemented policies and procedures. Every organization uses fairly detailed policies and procedures to guide staff on how to perform and provide clients an understanding of what to expect from the organization. Such guidance and expectations for performance are especially critical within a prison, in which inmates are likely to sue staff for performing their duties in a way that they believe negatively affects them and in which inmates must be held accountable for following the rules and policies of the prison. Although it is almost impossible to imagine an agency not having written policies and procedures for almost any occurrence or situation, thirty years ago many prisons did not have written policy manuals or consistent implementation of procedures.

At least four conditions are necessary for prison policies and procedures to effectively contribute to the overall prison mission. First, policies must be consistent with professional standards and be written and authorized by the prison administration. The **American Correctional Association** (ACA), the major professional organization for corrections in the United States, publishes standards manuals for all types of correctional practices. These policies and practices were created through a rigorous development, review, and approval process conducted by national correctional experts. Similar to the American Medical Association or the American Bar Association, ACA standards are created by practicing professionals in the field and are used to guide and evaluate acceptable modes of operation.

Second, for policies and procedures to be effective in managing and controlling inmate behavior, they must be clearly communicated to staff and inmates. A few security policies give details of how staff shall respond during a riot or other emergency situations and are not communicated to inmates, but most policies are made available to inmates. Usually, these policies are available for review in the inmate library so that inmates will understand what is expected of both them and staff. The third element of effective policy is to have procedures consistently carried out. If one correctional officer follows all policies in detail, and another officer follows only those that seem most important, it makes enforcement of the policy difficult and can cause confusion and tension among inmates and between inmates and staff. Inmates realize the need for policy and almost welcome it. Their whole life revolves around the activities within the prison. They recognize the importance of routine in a correctional environment and want to know what they and other inmates have to do in each situation. Inmates also recognize that if policies are not consistently implemented or staff are not diligent in their monitoring and enforcement, some inmates will take advantage of the complacency, violate the policy, and compromise the overall safe environment for inmates as well as staff. The fourth component of effective policy is to ensure its consistent implementation in a quality fashion. The next section describes some of the quality-assurance practices used in correctional institutions.

Quality Assurance in the Implementation of Policy

Two activities used to ensure consistent implementation of prison policies are monitoring policy compliance and ACA accreditation. The method most commonly used to monitor policy compliance by staff is an active auditing program to determine the extent to which policy is effectively carried out and contributes to the mission of the prison. Prisons use a variety of auditing procedures to monitor compliance with operational policies. One of these, a **policy audit,** determines whether broad agency policy is in place at the prison. Policy audits match agency required policy with local prison implementation procedures to ensure that procedures are in place at each prison to address each agency policy. In most states, the central headquarters dictates broad policy with which each prison in the state must comply. An example of a statewide policy regarding keeping contraband from entering the prison is that "all vehicles, carts, and boxes or packages must be thoroughly inspected before being allowed to enter or exit a prison." Each prison is required to develop and implement operational procedures to affect the required statewide policy. In this example, the prison describes how it will inspect the vehicles, carts, and boxes or packages, including where it will be done, who will do it, and what equipment will be necessary. A policy audit is valuable to begin an overall review of security operations, but only identifies whether the

American correctional Association
the largest professional organization for corrections in the United States

policy audit
a review to ascertain whether broad agency policy is in place at the prison

required scope of written, authorized, and mandated policies at the prison exists. It does not determine compliance with implementation, consistency in practice, or thoroughness of procedures.

policy implementation audit
a review to identify whether the procedures prescribed by policy are consistently being carried out by staff in their daily duties

Compliance with policy is determined by a **policy implementation audit,** which identifies whether procedures are consistently being carried out by staff in their daily duties. The policy audit is a review of written documents, whereas the policy implementation audit is a review of actual operations. It is completed by a team of knowledgeable staff from outside the prison who observe the methods by which staff carry out their assignments and identify any lack of compliance with established policy. Even though staff members are aware that their behavior is being observed during an audit and will be sure to follow the policy as they know it, the audit still identifies weaknesses in compliance resulting from failure to train staff, improper procedures, or a misunderstanding about the policy requirements. And if staff would normally take shortcuts in following policy, the audit reminds them of the importance of following procedures.

ACA accreditation
a process to promote and recognize improvement in the management of correctional agencies through the administration of voluntary standards

The second method of ensuring compliance with policy is **ACA accreditation.** In the early 1970s, corrections improved its ability to be seen as professional through adopting the acknowledged approaches associated with a profession: (1) a systematic body of theoretical knowledge acquired through lengthy academic study and not possessed by those outside the profession, (2) community interests rather than self-interest as a motivator of professional behavior, (3) self-regulation, and (4) a system of rewards.[14] Corrections made many progressive strides to be recognized as meeting these components, especially creating a body of knowledge (standards) of acceptable performance and a system of self-regulation. The American Correctional Association formed the Commission of Accreditation for Corrections (CAC), and standards identifying state of the art practices were developed. Agencies that implement and meet these standards may then apply for consideration to be accredited by the ACA. According to the ACA, the purpose of this accreditation process is as follows:

> *to promote improvement in the management of correctional agencies through the administration of a voluntary accreditation program and the ongoing development and revision of relevant, useful standards. . . . The recognized benefits from such a process include improved management, a defense against lawsuits through documentation and the demonstration of a "good faith" effort to improve conditions of confinement, increased accountability and enhanced public credibility for administrative and line staff, a safer and more human environment for personnel and offenders, and the establishment of measurable criteria for upgrading programs, personnel, and physical plant on a continuing basis.[15]*

When a prison applies to be accredited, ACA conducts an audit to determine whether it meets the required standards. The audits are completed by a team of objective ACA-trained auditors who spend one week at the prison, review written policy, and observe procedures. If all standards identified as "life safety" and 90 percent of others are met, ACA will accredit the prison, meaning that it meets acknowledged standards of professional operations. Not every correctional administrator supports accreditation, arguing that ACA accreditation means nothing and requires a considerable amount of work to complete. Yet most recognize that it gives a professional credibility to those outside corrections (the courts, the public, elected officials), and the process is an excellent reminder and confirms the importance of consistent implementation of policy by staff.

Inmate Classification

Another essential prison management device for controlling inmate behavior is inmate classification. Prison classification systems help control inmate behavior in three ways. First, classification is used to determine the appropriate prison security level to which an inmate should be assigned. When inmates are initially sentenced, the correctional agency does an assessment to determine their risk of escape and potential for violence. By matching inmates' risk of escape and violence to prison physical security, security policies and procedures, and staff allocations, the potential for escape or violence is reduced. Second, once inmates are assigned to a prison, classification systems are used (in some states) to determine the type of housing assignment within a prison (single cell, multiple-inmate cell, or dormitory) that is most suitable for each inmate. Finally, the reclassification of inmates after they are assigned to a prison acts as a motivator for good behavior. Inmates' behavior is regularly reviewed and can lead to a reassignment to a higher-security prison with tighter restrictions and fewer privileges or to a lower-security prison.

Until the 1970s, most states used a clinical classification process, in which a team of experienced correctional staff interviewed inmates and reviewed their criminal, medical, psychological, and social histories. They would then decide what type of prison housing, work assignment, and treatment programs would be best for the inmate. Currently, most states use an objective classification system—an actuarial risk assessment—to determine an inmate's initial assignment to a prison. This initial classification is based predominantly on offense history and sentence length. In describing the need for these actuarial systems, Dallao writes, "Instead of assigning offenders to certain security levels based on gut reaction and subjective discussion, this new system provided an orderly and objective way of separating violent from nonviolent inmates."[16]

The Federal Bureau of Prisons was the first correctional agency to implement such a system; in the mid-1970s it assigned a team of specialists to design a classification system that was more predictive of behavior than the early clinical approaches. The team initially identified ninety-six factors that were considered important for classification purposes and sought the opinion of correctional professionals across the country on these factors. The original list was pared to forty-seven factors, and later to six: history of escape or attempted escape, detainers, types of prior commitments, history of violence, severity of offense, and length of sentence. These factors focus on public risk by using acts that occurred prior to sentencing. Brennan suggests that these security classifications emphasize "legal variables, history of criminality, seriousness of current offense, and past escape attempts."[17]

To make the initial assignment of an inmate to a prison, a BOP staff member reviews the background of the offender and assigns a score for each of the six areas. Figure 10.4 shows the form used to determine security designations for each inmate. Inmates are assigned the points indicated on the Security Designation form, and the total points are then used to determine the security level of the prison to which the inmate is assigned. The following security point totals result in placement in the corresponding security level of federal prison:

Security point totals	Prison security level
0–7	Minimum
8–11	Low
12–18	Medium
19+	High

INMATE LOAD AND SECURITY DESIGNATION FORM—MALE (BP-337)

INMATE LOAD DATA	1. REG NO		2. LAST NAME	
3. FIRST NAME		4. MIDDLE		5. SUFFIX
6. RACE	7. SEX	8. ETHNIC ORIGIN		9. DATE OF BIRTH

10. OFFENSE/SENTENCE

11. FBI NUMBER	12. SOCIAL SECURITY NUMBER	
13. STATE OF BIRTH	14. OR COUNTRY OF BIRTH	15. CITIZENSHIP
16. ADDRESS-STREET		17. CITY

18. STATE	19. ZIP CODE	20. OR FOREIGN COUNTRY

21. HEIGHT—FT: IN:	22. WEIGHT	23. HAIR	24. EYES

25. ARS ASSIGNMENT

SECURITY DESIGNATION DATA

1. PUBLIC SAFETY FACTORS

A—NONE	F—SEX OFFENDER	I—SENTENCE LENGTH
B—DISRUPTIVE GROUP	G—THREAT GOVT OFFICIAL	L—SERIOUS ESCAPE
C—GREATEST SEVERITY OFFENSE	H—DEPORTABLE ALIEN	M—PRISON DISTURBANCE

2. USM OFFICE	3. JUDGE	4. REC FACILITY	5. REC PROGRAM

6. TYPE OF DETAINER	0—NONE 1—LOWEST/LOW MODERATE	3—MODERATE 7—GREATEST 5—HIGH

7. SEVERITY OF CURRENT OFFENSE	0—LOWEST 1—LOW MODERATE	3—MODERATE 7—GREATEST 5—HIGH

8. MONTHS TO RELEASE _____

9. TYPE OF PRIOR COMMITMENT	0 = NONE	1 = MINOR	3 = SERIOUS

10. HISTORY OF ESCAPE OR ATTEMPTS		NONE	>15 YEARS	10–15 YEARS	5–10 YEARS	<5 YEARS
	MINOR	0	1	1	2	3
	SERIOUS	0	3 (S)	3 (S)	3 (S)	3 (S)

11. HISTORY OF VIOLENCE		NONE	>15 YEARS	10–15 YEARS	5–10 YEARS	<5 YEARS
	MINOR	0	1	1	3	5
	SERIOUS	0	2	4	6	7

12. PRECOMMITMENT STATUS	0 = NOT APPLICABLE −3 (R) = OWN RECOGNIZANCE −3 (V) = VOLUNTARY SURRENDER

13. VOLUNTARY SURRENDER DATE	14. VOLUNTARY SURRENDER LOCATION
15. CRIM HX PTS _____	16. SECURITY POINT TOTAL

17. OMDT REFER (Y/N) _____

18. REMARKS

FIGURE 10.4 Inmate Load and Security Designation Form (BP-337)

Source: Federal Bureau of Prisons, *Security Designation and Custody Classification Manual* (Washington, D.C.: U.S. Department of Justice, 1996), Chapter 5, p. 1.

Since the adoption of this system by the BOP, almost every state has developed objective classification systems to assign the levels of prison security for inmates. As of December 30, 2005, 20.4 percent of all prisons were classified for maximum-security inmates, 26.3 percent of all prisons were classified for medium-security inmates, and 53.2 percent of all prisons were classified for minimum-security inmates.[18] Objective classifications reduce the tendency to overclassify that often resulted from clinical systems. As support for this, in 1978, 51 percent of prisoners were in maximum-security, 38 percent in medium-security, and 11 percent in minimum-security prisons.[19]

The classification process also is useful in determining the type of housing assignment within a prison that is most suitable for each inmate. Many prisons have a variety of housing areas for inmates, which may be either individual or multi-person cells or dormitory-style housing with several (possibly hundreds of) inmates in an open area without any physical security to separate them from each other or from staff. **Internal classification systems** are instruments used to assign inmates to housing or programs after they are placed in a particular prison. However, most prisons still make these decisions based on clinical judgments or make housing assignments only on the availability of space.

The most widely used internal classification system is the Adult Internal Management System (AIMS) developed by Herbert Quay, which classifies inmates on the analysis of life history records and a correctional adjustment checklist. These factors identify inmates who are likely to be violent and aggressive or likely to be victimized and therefore allow staff to separate likely victims from likely aggressors. Another system developed by the state of Illinois uses an internal classification system to make assignments within its maximum-security prisons. The Illinois system makes housing, work, and program assignments by using some past criminal behavior factors from the external classification system and adding prison disciplinary conduct and history of gang activities to predict a level of institutional aggression.

Classification is an incentive for good behavior by inmates because it is used to guide inter-institutional transfers due to security or treatment purposes. Inmates seldom stay at the prison to which they were originally assigned throughout their entire term of incarceration. Their time served and institutional behavior changes their predicted risk of violence and escape. Correctional agencies regularly reclassify and move inmates to higher- or lower-security prisons

internal classification system
instruments used to assign inmates to housing or programs after they are placed in a particular prison

Inmates strive to work their way down to minimum-security prisons, which are often less restrictive of their movements and often have additional programs available. Photo by Richard P. Seiter.

based on these changes. Objective classification systems make it very clear to inmates what they need to do to have their security level reduced or what behavior will result in an increase in security. Most inmates strive to get to lower-security prisons throughout their term of imprisonment and therefore work for good behavior to reduce their level of security and increase their freedom and opportunity for program involvement.

The reclassification review is scheduled at regular intervals (often three or six months). At the reclassification review, an inmate's behavior and the percentage of his or her sentence served are combined into the classification score system. If behavior is good and as the inmate reaches certain stages in his or her sentence (so many months served or a certain percentage of the sentence completed), it may result in a lowered security score and corresponding prison assignment. Serious misbehavior by inmates can also result in reclassification, as it indicates that the inmate cannot be controlled in the current security level. An inmate who commits a serious disciplinary infraction or continues to commit less severe infractions receives extra points on the security instrument and may be upgraded to a higher-security prison.

Figure 10.5 shows the California Department of Corrections Reclassification Score Sheet. Unfavorable and favorable behavior scores are combined to recalculate an inmate's classification score. Unfavorable factors include serious rule violations, escapes, assaults on staff or inmates, drug smuggling, weapon possession, or inciting a disturbance. Favorable behaviors include maintenance of minimum custody, continuous living in dormitory-type housing, no serious rule violations, and good program performance. Inmates are reviewed every six months or whenever there is a serious rule violation.

The goal of initial classification is to have similar-risk inmates assigned to appropriate security-level prisons, and the goal of reclassification is to maintain homogeneity of inmates by security level. Both overclassifying and underclassifying inmates can cause problems: housing high-security inmates in a low- or minimum-security facility increases the potential for escape, predatory behavior, or other types of violence, whereas housing low- or minimum-security inmates in high-security prisons places them in danger of violence and intimidation and wastes correctional resources, because high-security prisons cost three to four times as much to build and operate as do minimum-security prisons.

Inmate Discipline

inmate disciplinary system

a policy that clearly prescribes the process required to find that an inmate committed a proscribed act and identifies allowable punishments for each act; a key to controlling inmate behavior

Another key to controlling inmate behavior is a system of disincentives and punishment for violation of prison rules. Prisons create and use an **inmate disciplinary system** to respond to violation of prison rules by inmates. The disciplinary process includes an accusation of the violation, investigation of the incident, a hearing to determine guilt, and imposition of a sanction if found guilty. Inmate disciplinary systems usually include (1) a written policy documenting prohibited behavior, which is provided to all inmates, (2) a fair and equitable set of corresponding sanctions increasing with the severity of the rule violation and a process to appeal those sanctions, (3) a way to separate inmates accused of rule violations from the general inmate population when the security of the prison could be threatened, and (4) provisions for long-term separation or special security handling for inmates who continuously threaten institutional security or against whom a serious threat of violence exists.

The first component of an inmate disciplinary system is a written policy of specific prohibited behavior. The policy also explains the process used to determine

STATE OF CALIFORNIA   CDC Reclassification Score Sheet   DEPARTMENT OF CORRECTIONS

II. RECALCULATION OF SCORE

A. UNFAVORABLE BEHAVIOR SINCE LAST REVIEW

Last Review Date

[ ][ ] – [ ][ ] – [ ][ ] 24
mo   day   year

1. Number of serious
   disciplinaries
   dates: _____ _____ ____ x 6 = [ ][ ] 30

2. Number of escapes during
   current period
   date: ____ x 8 = [ ][ ] 32

3. Number of physical assaults
   on staff
   date: ____ x 8 = [ ][ ] 34

4. Number of physical assaults
   on inmates
   date: ____ x 4 = [ ][ ] 36

5. Number of smuggling/trafficking
   in drugs
   date: ____ x 4 = [ ][ ] 38

6. Number of deadly
   weapon possessions
   date: ____ x 16 = [ ][ ] 40

7. Number of inciting
   disturbance
   date: ____ x 4 = [ ][ ] 42

8. Number of assaults that caused
   serious injury
   date: ____ x 16 = [ ][ ] 44

9. TOTAL UNFAVORABLE POINTS = + _____

B. FAVORABLE BEHAVIOR SINCE LAST REVIEW

	Number of Six Month Periods	
1. Continuous minimum custody	____ x 4 =	[ ] 46
2. Continuous dorm living	____ x 2 =	[ ] 48
3. No serious 115's	____ x 2 =	[ ] 50
4. Average or above performance in work, school, or vocational program	____ x 2 =	[ ] 52

5. TOTAL FAVORABLE CREDITS = – _____

C. COMPUTATION OF CLASSIFICATION SCORE

1. Prior Classification Score = [ ][ ] 54

2. Net Change in Behavior Score
   (A.9 minus B.5) = [ ][ ] 57
   (+ or –)

3. Change in term points = [ ][ ] 60
   (+ or –)

4. Current Classification Score = [ ][ ] 63

III. PLACEMENT

A. SPECIAL CASE FACTORS

1. Placement Concerns
   a) Hold   b) Restricted   c) Medical Restriction
   (enter A, P, or #) Custody Suffix   (enter FULL, REST,
   Felony   INS   (enter R or *)   UNAS, or *)
   [ ] 66 [ ] 67 [ ] 68 [ ][ ][ ][ ] 69

2. Other Placement Concerns
   a) (*)   b) (*)
   [ ][ ][ ] 73   [ ][ ][ ] 77

3. Caseworkers
   a) Counselor
   [ ][ ][ ][ ][ ][ ][ ][ ][ ] [ ] 81
   Last Name   FI

   b) Supervisor
   [ ][ ][ ][ ][ ][ ][ ][ ][ ] [ ] 90
   Last Name   FI

4. Current Custody
   [ ][ ][ ] – [ ] – [ ][ ][ ] 99

5. Current Institution and Facility
   [ ][ ][ ][ ] – [ ][ ][ ] 107

B. CLASSIFICATION STAFF REPRESENTATIVE ACTION

1. Classification Staff Representative
   [ ][ ][ ][ ][ ][ ][ ][ ][ ] 114
   Last Name

2. Date of CSR Action
   [ ][ ] – [ ][ ] – [ ][ ] 122
   mo   day   year

3. Administrative Determinants
   a) (*)   PRIMARY
   [ ]   [ ][ ][ ] 128

   b) (*)   c) (*)
   [ ][ ][ ] 132   [ ][ ][ ] 136

4. Placement Approved   a) Cat.
                             [ ]
   b) Institution and Facility
   [ ][ ][ ][ ] – [ ][ ][ ] 141

5. Reason for Administrative or Irregular Placement
   [ ][ ][ ] 148

I. IDENTIFYING INFORMATION

A. CDC NUMBER
   [ ][ ][ ][ ][ ][ ] 1

B. INMATE'S LAST NAME
   [ ][ ][ ][ ][ ][ ][ ][ ] 7

C. Date of Current Review
   [ ][ ] – [ ][ ] – [ ][ ] 15 –
   mo   day   year

D. PAROLE VIOLATOR
   ADMISSION TYPE   [ ][ ] 21
   (enter RTC or WNT)

FIGURE 10.5   The California Department of Corrections Reclassification Score Sheet

Source: State of California, *Code of Regulations,* Title 15, Crime Prevention and Corrections, Division 3, updated through December 31, 2004, p. 156.

Inmates may violate prison rules and therefore must be punished using the inmate disciplines. Reprinted with permission of the Corrections Corporation of America.

guilt and the range of punishments that result from rule violations. The purpose and scope of the BOP policy regarding inmate discipline is stated as follows:

> So that inmates may live in a safe and orderly environment, it is necessary for institution authorities to impose discipline on those inmates whose behavior is not in compliance with Bureau of Prisons rules. The provisions of this rule apply to all persons committed to the care, custody, and control (direct or constructive) of the Bureau of Prisons.[20]

Correctional agencies provide a copy of the inmate discipline policy to every inmate upon the inmate's arrival at a prison, and inmates sign that they have received, read, and understand the policy. Informing inmates and ensuring that they understand prohibited acts not only is fair, but also reduces the potential for successful appeals of inmate disciplinary actions before a federal court. Most correctional systems categorize prohibited acts by severity. The BOP policy lists four categories of prohibited acts: greatest, high, moderate, and low moderate,[21] with a specific range of sanctions authorized for each category of prohibited act. The BOP provides for a two-stage disciplinary process, with minor violations handled in a less formal manner than serious infractions, and time frames are associated with each step in the process so that the inmate knows the time available for collecting evidence or seeking assistance. Figure 10.6 illustrates the disciplinary process and time limits for each step in the BOP policy.

According to the BOP policy, once an incident report is issued to an inmate, an initial hearing must occur within three workdays. If the infraction is minor, the hearing panel (referred to as the Unit Disciplinary Committee or UDC) can determine guilt and impose minor sanctions, such as a loss of privileges. If the violation is more serious and could result in loss of good time, disciplinary transfer to another prison, or disciplinary isolation from the general inmate population, the UDC will refer the case to an upper-level hearing panel, a Discipline Hearing Officer (DHO), who is not a staff member of the prison in which the incident

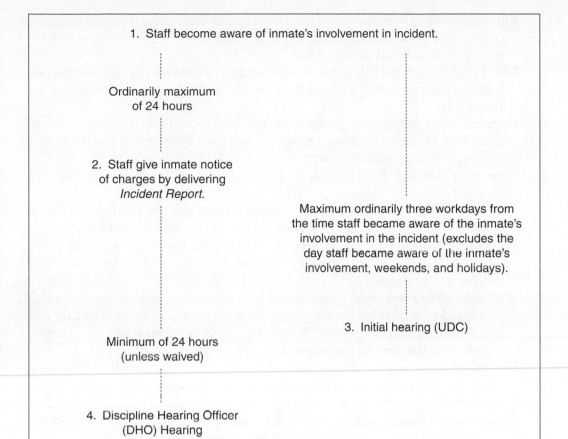

1. Staff become aware of inmate's involvement in incident.

Ordinarily maximum
of 24 hours

2. Staff give inmate notice
of charges by delivering
Incident Report.

Maximum ordinarily three workdays from
the time staff became aware of the inmate's
involvement in the incident (excludes the
day staff became aware of the inmate's
involvement, weekends, and holidays).

3. Initial hearing (UDC)

Minimum of 24 hours
(unless waived)

4. Discipline Hearing Officer
(DHO) Hearing

Note: These time limits are subject to exceptions as provided in the rules. Staff may suspend disciplinary proceedings for a period not to exceed two calendar weeks while informal resolution is undertaken and accomplished. If informal resolution is unsuccessful, staff may reinstitute disciplinary proceedings at the same stage at which suspended. The requirements then begin running again, at the same point at which they were suspended.

Source: Federal Bureau of Prisons, "Inmate Discipline and Special Housing Units," Federal Prison System, Policy Statement #5270.07 (Washington, D.C.: U.S. Department of Justice, December 29, 1987), Chapter 4, p. 8.

FIGURE 10.6   U.S. Bureau of Prisons Disciplinary Process

took place and is therefore seen as impartial.[22] Most states have a similar two-tiered system to handle inmate discipline.

Sanctions for commission of prohibited acts can be minor, such as restriction from privileges, or serious, such as transfer to a supermax prison. The following list describes the types of sanctions in order of severity used by most correctional systems.

Warning: Some jurisdictions allow a temporary suspension of disciplinary action, with an inmate receiving a warning. If there are no further violations during the period of suspension, the rule violation may be expunged from the inmate's record.

Reprimand: A reprimand is a written admonishment against the behavior with no other sanction or punishment.

Assignment of extra duty: Assignment of additional work for an inmate, usually for a specific number of hours.

Restriction to quarters: Restriction to quarters requires the inmate to remain in the housing location for a specific period of time (such as one week) whenever he or she is not at work, meals, or an assigned program.

Impoundment of personal property: Inmates may have their personal property confiscated or impounded, and either it will be held or the inmate will have to pay to send it out of the prison.

Loss of job: When the infraction has something to do with the job assignment, inmates may lose their job and have to find or be assigned another less favored job.

Removal from program or group activity: Similar to the loss of a job, an inmate may be removed from a program or group activity if the infraction is related to a program or activity.

Change of quarters: Inmates may be required to move from one housing unit to another.

Loss of privileges: Inmates may be restricted from specific privileges, such as participation in recreation or loss of the use of the prison commissary.

Monetary restitution: If the infraction included damaging government property or another inmate's property, the violating inmate may be required to pay for the damage.

Withholding of good time: Correctional sentences allow inmates to earn a certain number of days off their sentence for each month of good behavior, and if a violation of prison rules is serious, good time may not be granted, lengthening the term of the sentence.

Disciplinary segregation: Inmates may have to serve a sentence in segregation, in a separate facility from the general inmate population, with little time out of their cell.

Disciplinary transfer: Inmates who continually violate prison rules or commit a serious violation can be transferred to a higher-security prison.

Placement in a supermax prison: Supermax prisons (described in Chapter 9) house the most violent and dangerous inmates, and inmates who have shown an inability to follow rules in a standard prison may be transferred to a supermax prison for an indeterminate period of time.

administrative appeals process

an informal process for inmates to appeal a disciplinary sanction or to seek remedy of any other injustice they feel they have received at the hands of correctional officials

Once there is a finding of guilt and imposition of a sanction, correctional agencies usually provide an **administrative appeals process** to allow inmates to appeal a disciplinary sanction or to seek to remedy any other injustice they believe they have received at the hands of correctional officials. Having an appeals process promotes acceptance by inmates and avoids expensive and burdensome review of disciplinary decisions by federal courts. Administrative appeals usually have at least two levels: first a reconsideration by the warden, and if the inmate is not satisfied with the response, a second level of reconsideration by the agency headquarters. For disciplinary processes, the inmate appeal cannot dispute a finding of fact, but is limited to procedural and due process rights. Inmates usually have thirty days after notice of the decision to appeal. In describing the review process, Cripe writes:

> *The records (the disciplinary offense report, the investigation report, and the written report of the hearing officer or committee) are examined, to be sure that the procedures required by the agency's disciplinary policy have been followed. The facts of the case and the sanction imposed are summarily reviewed. There must be some evidence to support the finding of the disciplinary authority. The reviewer ensures that the sanction imposed is within the range of punishments authorized for that offense. There is a legal requirement that the hearing officer or committee record the evidence relied on to support the conclusion reached, and that the reasons for the sanction(s) imposed be given.*[23]

The Role of Staff in a Prison

Everyone who works for a correctional agency recognizes that the staff is the agency's most valuable resource. Corrections is a business in which people are more important than the bars and fences, prison cells, or available technology. Correctional staff supervise offenders, monitoring and guiding their behavior toward the development of a crime-free and productive lifestyle. In 2006, state and federal correctional agencies employed 507,733 prison staff and approximately 85 percent of a correctional agency budget is spent on staff salaries.[24]

Historically, the role of correctional staff who worked in prisons was very narrowly defined, and there was little effort to recruit, develop, or retain the most educated and professional staff. Line prison staff (such as correctional officers) had minimal discretion or decision-making authority. In 1965, Cressey wrote, "Most guards have nothing to do but stand guard; they do not use inmates productively any more than they themselves are used productively by prison managers."[25] The role of correctional staff in modern prisons has changed considerably, spurred by the emphasis on rehabilitation as a correctional goal during the 1950s and 1960s. As a part of this transformation, new professional staff, including psychologists, educators, and administrators, were brought into prisons, and the importance of the overall prison experience in inmate rehabilitation was recognized.

In addition, with the dramatic increases in the number of prisoners during the 1980s, most prisons became overcrowded, and correctional staff often felt overworked and frustrated and feared losing control. Totally outnumbered, correctional officials recognized that the authoritarian style of inmate supervision was ineffective, and staff skilled in interpersonal communications were better able to gain the compliance of inmates and maintain order. Correctional officials moved aggressively to recruit educated individuals trained in supervising and communicating with others. Many states and the BOP require candidates for correctional officer positions to have either a bachelor's degree or at least two years' experience working in a correctional or law enforcement setting. Corrections began to recognize the critical value of all staff, not just those delivering treatment programs, in accomplishing their mission.

Good correctional staff performing their duties are the key to controlling inmate behavior. Reprinted with permission of the Corrections Corporation of America.

Recruiting and Hiring Correctional Staff

Recruiting for prisons in the past was done very haphazardly or not at all. Prisons usually relied on recruitment through encouragement by relatives or friends who already worked at the prison. There was no plan by which characteristics of successful employees were identified, organizational needs considered, and an aggressive recruitment effort implemented, and correctional agencies usually accepted the hiring of a nondiverse workforce with little experience or academic preparation. Most correctional agency recruitment was all too often like that described here regarding the state of Massachusetts:

> *Massachusetts in the 1970s had a depressed economy with high unemployment. At the same time, the Massachusetts prison system had a high turnover rate among officers and a chronic need for new officers. Yet. . . corrections with its similar salary and benefits (to police and fire departments) was in reality a "walk-in" job. Screening and selection were largely limited to investigation of possible criminal records of applicants. The prison officer recruit was largely self-selected.*[26]

Prompted by high turnover and the challenge of a growing workforce, correctional agencies recruitment is now much more sophisticated and has been very successful in recruiting from a variety of sources, including other criminal justice agencies; individuals leaving the military; public and private social service agencies; and community and four-year colleges. Even with quality recruiting generating a large pool of qualified applicants, there still must be effective hiring practices to screen and select the most qualified individuals from this pool. Correctional agencies identify the areas of competence that they want in prison employees and create a screening process to rate applicants' abilities. Some of the traits and abilities identified to be a successful correctional worker are the following:

- Good interpersonal skills (both oral and written)
- Ability to make sound decisions
- Lack of prejudice toward criminal offenders
- Understanding of the need to treat all clients or inmates in a fair and consistent manner
- Ability to "think on one's feet"
- Ability to supervise others
- Good presentation of oneself

integrity interview
interviews of candidates for correctional employment used to determine if the candidate has issues or conditions that could put them in a compromising situation or make them more likely to accept a bribe to show favored treatment to an inmate

Correctional agencies use several screening and rating mechanisms. Candidates must not only complete a fairly extensive application (including past education, military, and job experience), but also provide examples of how these past experiences are indicative of the identified traits and abilities. After the agency identifies the best group of candidates from the applications, screening usually includes a personal interview, review of a writing sample to determine their ability to communicate in writing, and one of the most important screening mechanisms, the **integrity interview**. During the personal interview, interviewers present candidates with difficult and stressful scenarios, have them describe how they would handle them, and then rate how desirable the candidate's response would be in a correctional environment working with inmates. Since correctional staff are continually confronted with opportunities to personally benefit from giving offenders favored treatment, integrity interviews are used to determine whether candidates have issues such as financial problems, past employment problems, current drug or alcohol abuse, or other conditions that could put them in a compromising situation or make them more likely to accept a bribe to show favored treatment to an inmate.

Line staff such as correctional officers are critical to the success of a prison, but only if they are properly trained, supervised, guided, and managed. Management of prisons in the early 1900s was much simpler than it is today. An autocratic warden cannot just create and enforce rules to maintain control and punish staff who did not follow the leader's directives. Currently, prison order has more to do with fairness and equity, with leadership and empowerment, and with organization and management. As suggested by DiIulio in *Governing Prisons:*

> *The answer to be offered. . .is that the quality of prison life varies according to the quality of prison management. The evidence will lead us to the conclusion that prison management is the strategic variable, one that may be subject to change with predictable and desirable consequences.*[27]

Collective Bargaining within Correctional Agencies

Although a few states (Connecticut in the 1940s and New York and Washington in the 1960s) have had public employee unions for some time, collective bargaining is relatively new to most state correctional agencies. By the 1970s, more than twenty states had formally authorized collective bargaining by public employees, and by the end of the twentieth century, more than half of the states had collective bargaining for at least some correctional employees. Due to the mission of safety and security and the role of supervising felony offenders, collective bargaining is more complex for correctional agencies than for many other public and private organizations.

Collective bargaining is the formal recognition of employee organizations and their right to negotiate with management regarding conditions of the workplace. The purposes of collective bargaining are as follows:

collective bargaining
the formal recognition of employee organizations and their right to negotiate with management regarding workplace issues

- To establish and protect employees' rights
- To improve working conditions and benefits
- To establish and maintain more harmonious employer–employee relationships
- To establish a participative role for employees in management decisions that affect employees[28]

Even though the purposes seem nonconfrontational and in line with the mission of a prison, many correctional administrators have feared that they would diminish their management authority and undermine prison security. The biggest point of debate is the role in which **seniority** of staff is considered in such things as work schedules, post assignment, and promotion. Union officials usually desire seniority to be key in determining employees' work assignments, days off, shift schedules, and even promotions. Correctional management officials want to have as much discretion as possible to place staff with unique abilities in the positions that require their strengths and create schedules to meet security needs. Over the years in which correctional agencies have used collective bargaining, the fears that it would jeopardize an agency mission have not materialized, and input by the unions representing line staff has usually resulted in improved decision making and higher morale.

seniority
the use of the length of employment to determine an employee's assignment, days off, or other job-related functions

Many national labor organizations represent public-sector and correctional employees, including the AFL-CIO, AFSFME (the American Federation of State,

Federal and Municipal Employees), and the International Brotherhood of Teamsters. In some states, several different organizations represent different groups of correctional employees (correctional officers, nurses, professional staff), and in others employees elect a single labor union to represent all of them. The labor organization that represents employees is able to negotiate issues of pay and benefits for public employees and sometimes other issues, such as how staff are selected for overtime, the type of clothing provided to staff by the agency, and the number and areas of coverage by correctional officers. Although collective bargaining is well entrenched in many prisons and correctional agencies and has a major impact on policy and practice, and there is usually a harmonious relationship between management and labor, in some jurisdictions there has been a lack of trust and constant battles for power and influence. Jacobs and Crotty write, "[Collective bargaining] has redefined the prison organization in adversary terms so that wardens are bosses and complaints are grievances."[29]

One historical concern by both parties has been the right to strike. Most public-safety organizations are not allowed to strike, which takes away a major union tactic to get management to accept labor's negotiating demands. Although a crisis could occur if police or correctional officers were allowed to strike, unions representing these groups sometimes sanction informal job actions (the "blue flu") to get the attention of management. In the past, there have also been illegal strikes by correctional officers. In New York State, even with the Taylor Law penalties whereby strikers lose two days' salary for each day they are on strike,[30] a strike of New York state correctional officers occurred in 1979. An analysis of the strike found that collective bargaining was not well suited to resolve the problems in this situation (officers believed they had lost status and authority, and racial tension existed within the officer ranks and between officers and inmates) and may have even aggravated them.[31]

Another concern regarding collective bargaining is its impact on security and correctional efforts toward rehabilitation. During the 1960s and 1970s, the rehabilitative movement created a fear by officers that the interest in helping inmates would lead to a reduction of authority for correctional officers, and unionization gained strength within prisons. However, many labor and correctional officials recognize that interests of prisoners and officers are intertwined, and both groups stand to benefit from the rehabilitative philosophy. As rehabilitative programs improve inmate morale, reduce idleness, and enhance security, the workplace situation improves for prison staff.

Several states still do not authorize collective bargaining for correctional employees, fearing it will undermine security and the authority and flexibility for management to effectively operate prisons. In the "You Make the Decision" box, students are to read through the information, weigh the pros and cons, and decide (if they had the authority) whether they would implement collective bargaining in a state.

Summary

Many questions were asked at the beginning of this chapter regarding how prisons are managed. These include how a prison manages staff and inmates to accomplish its mission, how a greatly outnumbered staff controls potentially violent and dangerous inmates, how prisons ensure quality performance of their functions, and what role staff members play in the accomplishment of the mission. In this chapter, these questions have been addressed and we hope answered

CHAPTER REVIEW

to students' satisfaction. Prisons and their oversight agencies must first organize themselves in a way to manage the staff and resources provided to have a safe and secure environment, while offering programs that help inmates return to their communities as successful and law-abiding citizens. Since prisons have become such big businesses and use such a large percentage of state taxpayer dollars, there is much more interest from the public and elected officials in how they perform than ever before. Therefore, these agencies must organize to manage both internal and external environments in the prisons.

The various methods for managing inmates have also been described. Prisons must begin with professional policies and implementation procedures, communicate these to staff and inmates, and consistently carry them out. Since there is a considerable difference in the methods and expense of handling maximum- and minimum-security inmates, an effective classification instrument to separate inmates by needs and risks is beneficial. Prisons must have a fair and equitable disciplinary process to punish violation of prison rules, control misbehavior, and maintain order.

Finally, this chapter describes how important correctional staff members are to the management of a prison. Prisons are sometimes referred to as a "people business," meaning that they are all about people managing other people. Even though prisons must have sufficient physical security, they must also have well developed and state of the art policies, and they must consistently implement these policies; the accomplishment of their mission is impossible without dedicated and committed professional staff. This chapter has provided information regarding how prisons recruit, hire, and manage staff, including when a collective-bargaining agreement exists between management and labor. Prisons are complex organizations and require the utmost in management and leadership.

Key Terms

director
inspector
custody
treatment
services
employee awards program
unit management
unit manager
case manager
correctional counselor

American Correctional Association
policy audit
policy implementation audit
ACA accreditation
internal classification system
inmate disciplinary system
administrative appeals process
integrity interview
collective bargaining
seniority

Review Questions

1. Why are entities such as public and media affairs, legislative liaison, legal advisors, and internal affairs often organizationally located in the office of the director?

2. What is the role of an inspector in a department of corrections or prison?

3. Describe the three functions of custody, treatment, and services within a prison organization.

4. What is unit management and how does it contribute to the management of a prison?

5. Name the three common staff titles working in unit management.

6. Why is it important to consistently implement policies and procedures within a prison?

7. What processes are used to determine whether policies and procedures within a prison are being consistently applied?

8. What is an objective classification system?

9. What is an internal classification system, and what function does it play in a prison?

10. How can a classification process assist in gaining inmate compliance?

11. Define an inmate disciplinary system.

12. List five sanctions that can be taken against inmates for failure to abide by prison rules.

13. What processes are available for inmates to appeal a disciplinary decision or seek to redress wrongs done them by prison staff?

14. Why are staff so important to the functioning of a prison?

15. Why is staff recruitment and hiring so important to the accomplishment of the mission of a prison?

16. Define collective bargaining and describe its history in corrections.

You Make the Decision...

Implement Collective Bargaining?

When a state or local government authorizes public employees to organize and engage in collective bargaining, the first step is for the employees to select a labor organization to represent them. A key decision in the collective-bargaining process is how to align employee groups for representation. For instance, will all correctional employees be represented by one labor organization, or will employees be clustered into logical groups (all correctional officers, all trade employees, all treatment staff) to be represented by a union. After the employees are grouped for representation, they vote to select the labor organization (such as the AFL-CIO; the American Federation of State, Federal and Municipal Employees; or the International Brotherhood of Teamsters are some that represent correctional workers) that will represent them in negotiations and contract management.

The election process can be extremely highly contested and difficult for both management and employees, as competing unions want to find issues and convince staff that they can best represent their interests. One state director of corrections noted the following:

The organizing and election process was horrible. We are a large state, and our employees would end up being several thousand union members. I thought management had a really good relationship with staff, and I personally spent a lot of time with line staff whenever I visited the prisons. I know they appreciated it and respected me for my concern and leadership. All of a sudden, the three national unions vying to represent them were campaigning and trying to find issues to get employee attention. Since there really were no major issues regarding safety or prison management, they had to make things up. It was a personal affront to me with some of the things they came up with. I couldn't believe some of the nefarious schemes they came up with to suggest why we made certain decisions.

After selection of the union, the parties prepare for negotiations. One of the most important issues is how seniority will be used. It may be used for assignments, promotion, or pay. After the contract is negotiated, the parties must live with it and use it daily. Unfortunately, there are always questions that come into dispute about the true meaning of the contract. When in dispute, management can make a decision, and the union can file a grievance against it. A grievance is a formal complaint that the action taken by management is not within the language or intent of the labor contract, and the grievance then goes through a formal process for resolution. One thing is clear in a collective-bargaining environment: If either or both parties want to be confrontational and argue almost every minor contract issue, they will spend a tremendous amount of time and money to resolve their disputes.

Many people believe that collective bargaining has more positive than negative implications. It certainly can work if both management and labor communicate and listen to each other and are reasonable in their positions. However, when the parties in collective bargaining stop listening, let the issues get personal, and become overly adversarial in the relationship, collective bargaining makes a difficult workplace even more tense and stressful.

You must now decide if you think a state without it should implement collective bargaining. Consider the positives and the negatives, and remember that once the decision is made to implement, it is unlikely it can ever be changed.

Chapter Resources on mycrimekit

Go to mycrimekit.com to explore the following study tools and resources specific to this chapter:

- **Practice Quiz:** multiple-choice, true/false, short-answer, and essay questions to help students test their knowledge
- **WebQuests:** learning activities built around Web searches
  - American Correctional Association: www.aca.org

- **Insider's Experiences:** "Taking Down the Towers"
- **Seiter Videos:**
  - See experts discuss prison management
  - See an expert discuss unit management
- **Career Center:** A Career as a Correctional Facility Administrator
- **Flashcards:** Twenty flashcards to test knowledge of the chapter's key terms

Prison Life for Inmates

After reading this chapter, you should be able to:

1. Describe the activities within total institutions that Goffman suggested make it more difficult for prisoners to successfully return to and adapt to community living.

2. Define the concept of prisonization and explain its impact on inmates both while serving a prison sentence and as they return to the community.

3. Identify many of the common prison slang terms and what they mean within a prison setting.

4. Compare the different types of violent acts that occur within prisons and the forces that increase the likelihood of violence.

5. Explain the history, development, and operation of prison gangs and identify their threat to operating a safe and secure prison.

6. Discuss the methods that prison staff use to identify gang members and control gang activities.

7. Specify the reasons why homosexual activities are disallowed in prisons and suggest activities that can reduce their likelihood.

8. Explain the focus of the Prison Rape Elimination Act and the findings of sexual assault in prisons.

9. Identify the ways that illegal drugs come into prisons and evaluate the potential of various methods to limit their availability within prisons.

10. Describe the development of women's prisons in terms of management and philosophical approaches.

11. Compare the culture of women's prisons to the culture of men's prisons.

12. Define and describe the way pseudofamilies function in women's prisons.

Introduction

Now that we have covered the organization, functions, and models used to manage prisons, we move to a look at life for both inmates and staff within a prison environment. From the next two chapters, students will not only assimilate information and facts, but also get a feel for what it is like to be in the closed environment of a prison; the unique relationships among inmates and between inmates and staff; and matters such as material possessions, routines, privileges, and interpersonal communications that take on much more importance in prison than in normal society. The prison world is a social realm of its own, and although it is difficult to describe to those who have not seen or experienced it, it has some structure and organization that need to be considered and understood.

In Chapter 7, characteristics of the clients of correctional agencies were described, as well as certain activities, policies, and programs related to these characteristics. This chapter addresses the world in which inmates live and the issues of violence, inmate culture, drugs, gang activity, and homosexuality that inmates face. The chapter presents the prison environment for both male and female inmates, because institutions for each have many unique characteristics in terms of the culture, inmate relationships, and potential for violence. The male inmate's world is based more on survival, watching one's back, and getting along without creating problems that can result in assaults or other serious problems. Male inmates adapt to incarceration by isolating themselves; they try to do their time independently and avoid being involved in other inmate problems or issues. However, the existence of prison gangs often requires them to group together and protect themselves or avoid intimidation or coercion for sex or money. However, male inmates (whether in a gang or not) see these groupings only as a value for strength or financial benefit.

Female inmates, on the other hand, adjust to imprisonment by forming close relationships to other inmates, seeking relationships to provide a support structure. With less concern for personal safety than male inmates, women in prison desire a family relationship similar to what they experience outside prison, with specific roles of parent, child, or partner. They also do not mentally separate themselves from their families on the outside as men do, and their lives stay integrated into those of their outside family. The potential for abuse by staff is more of an issue with women inmates, however, and female inmate treatment programs are usually different in terms of their goals and operations than many of those in male institutions. At the end of this chapter, students should understand how inmates adapt to the culture of a prison and how the inmate and staff structures affect their life in prison and influence their life when they return to outside society.

Prison Life for Male Offenders

Prisons strive to provide a balanced approach to accomplishing the multiple goals of corrections. By merely holding offenders against their will and taking away their freedoms, prisons inflict punishment. At the same time, they attempt to create a positive and interactive environment, providing rehabilitative programs to help offenders prepare for release and their return to their communities. However, the somewhat isolated nature of prisons through their location and separation from normal society can easily result in a punitive atmosphere in which inmates lose their identity and ability to make decisions for themselves.

In 1961, Erving Goffman wrote of the impact a prison environment could have on those housed within the institution. Goffman described the concept of a **total institution,** a setting isolating people from the rest of society and unnecessarily manipulating them through the actions of the administrative staff.[1] He suggests that certain characteristics of such institutions result in isolation and inability to act for oneself:

total institution
Goffman's concept of a setting isolating people from the rest of society and unnecessarily manipulating them through the actions of the administrative staff

- Staff members supervise all spheres of daily life, such as where inmates eat, work, and sleep.
- The environment is highly standardized, with one set of activities for everyone.
- Rules and schedules dictate how inmates perform all aspects of their daily routine.

Prisons take on these characteristics for controlling and managing inmates' behavior and, through the use of rewards and punishments, attempt to *resocialize* inmates to a law-abiding lifestyle. However, Goffman warns that, although institutions can bring about the desired change in some inmates, others become confused, hostile, and bitter and that extended periods of institutional living can actually reduce an individual's capacity for independent living.

Goffman argues that institutional activities such as making new inmates publicly strip, wear degrading striped uniforms, and shave their heads fail to resocialize inmates. Most of these actions have been recognized as problematic and have been changed in most prison systems. However, subtler, yet perhaps even more important, is the effect of the prison environment resulting from the tone set by interactions between staff and inmates. Staff are charged with consistent enforcement of rules and maintenance of control. Yet they are not to do so in a punitive or derogatory manner. This balance is sometimes difficult to carry out.

Some aspects of prison life can take away inmates' self-concept and ability to act for themselves, making a successful adjustment back to the community more difficult. Courtesy of Corbis/Bettmann.

The experiment by Zimbardo at Stanford University illustrates how hostility can develop between staff and inmates within a prison setting. Courtesy of Philip G. Zimbardo, Inc.

The challenge in creating and continuing positive interactions between staff and inmates is illustrated in Zimbardo's classic experiment.[2] To test the ways in which prisons change human behavior, Zimbardo constructed a mock prison in the basement of a building at Stanford University and used students in one of his college classes to play the roles of staff and inmates. Twenty-four male students were then randomly assigned to roles as either guards or prisoners. For two weeks, the prisoners were to spend time in the "Stanford County Prison," with the guards responsible for operating the prison. Soon after the experiment began, guards and prisoners became hostile toward each other; guards humiliated and yelled at prisoners, and prisoners resisted and insulted guards. The situation deteriorated to the point that after the first week Zimbardo had to cancel the remaining week of the experiment. Zimbardo wrote that "some boys (guards) treat others as if they were despicable animals, taking pleasure in cruelty, while other boys (prisoners) became servile, dehumanized robots who thought only of escape, of their own individual survival and of their mounting hatred for the guards."[3] This experiment illustrates the type of relationship that can easily develop between staff and prison inmates; constant diligence and strong leadership by prison administrators are needed to avoid such a situation.

Prison Culture and the Inmate Code

To the student of corrections, nothing seems more fascinating than the formation of a separate and unique culture within prisons. For many reasons, and in a way that has changed over time, inmates construct a culture with unique values, traditions, roles, expectations, language, and customs while in prison. This culture is called the **inmate code,** the expected rules and behaviors represented by the model prisoner that reflect the values and norms of prison society. What factors influence the creation of a prison culture and inmate code, the extent to which prisonization (inmates accepting and adapting to the prison culture) occurs, and whether the inmate code still exists are topics of continued study and debate.

More than sixty years ago, Clemmer studied prisons and was one of the first to identify the special adaptation that inmates make as they spend time together in prison. He coined the term **prisonization** to describe the process by which inmates "[take] on in greater or lesser degree the folkways, mores, customs, and general culture of the penitentiary."[4] Clemmer suggested that inmates learn the

inmate code
the expected rules and behaviors represented by the model prisoner and reflecting the values and norms of prison society

prisonization
the process whereby inmates take on the folkways, mores, customs, and general culture of the penitentiary

behaviors of being in prison (dressing, working, new language, dependence on others, degradation of status) and that this process of prisonization leads to an increased identification with criminal lifestyles and more difficulty in successfully returning and adapting to the community after release.

Over the next two decades, others who studied the effects of being in prison identified many aspects of the inmate code. The code is how those who want respect as a "con" act and behave. As a philosophy, it emphasizes loyalty to convicts and distrust of correctional officers (*hacks* or *screws*), being trustworthy, and not getting involved in other inmates' business. From the work of Sykes in the 1950s[5] and Irwin and Cressey in the 1960s,[6] several behaviors have been identified that are elements of the inmate code:

- Do your own time (don't get involved in the business of other inmates)
- Be a stand-up guy (be someone that other inmates can count on)
- Don't rat on other inmates (do not tell staff what other inmates have done or are doing—don't be a "snitch")
- Don't trust the guards (don't become overly friendly with staff, don't show them respect, and talk to them only when you have to)
- Don't exploit other inmates (don't take advantage of others or their problems or steal from them)
- Maintain dignity and respect (don't show staff a weakness and show respect to other inmates)
- Settle conflict between inmates (don't go to staff with problems between inmates, settle it yourself)
- Respect the real "cons" (the inmates who have done a lot of time, know the system, and live the inmate code deserve respect)

There are two theories on how the inmate culture becomes a part of prison life. The first is that the culture is *indigenous* to prisons; Clemmer believed that it develops as a result of the environment in which inmates find themselves. Sykes believed that the norms arise specifically in response to the deprivations and loss of liberty inherent in incarceration. The other theory is that the culture is *imported* or brought in with the values of the inmates from the outside

Younger inmates don't respect the code that was followed by older inmates. Photo by Richard P. Seiter.

The availability of telephones and other ways to communicate with the world outside prison is thought to be one reason why the inmate code is dying. Photo by Richard P. Seiter.

convicts

long-term inmates who become used to the prison society and find a way to live in this environment with a minimal amount of problems and disruptions

thieves

inmates who have adopted a career of crime and are doing their prison time until they can get out and hit the "big score"

square johns

inmates who are usually first-time offenders and have more identification with "straight" society and norms of the noncriminals

world. Irwin and Cressey identified three types of offenders that bring characteristics to the prison setting, and the blending of these characteristics creates the prisoner subculture. **Convicts** are long-term inmates, probably beginning with youths who were in foster homes, reform schools, and then prisons. They become used to the single-sex, masculine society and find a way to live in this environment with a minimal amount of problems and disruptions. **Thieves** have adopted a career of crime and are just doing their time in prison until they can get out and hit the "big score." **Square johns** are probably first-time offenders and have more identification with straight society and the norms of noncriminals.

Today, many people believe that the inmate code is dead, or at least ignored by most inmates. The older inmates talk of "young punks," inmates who are always out to exploit others, don't respect the old-timers, constantly cause trouble that brings greater supervision from staff, and use muscle and not brains to get through their prison experience. The change in adhering to the inmate culture comes from at least several developments. The first is that, with a greater reliance on prison than on probation for many offenders, there are more square johns in prison, and even though they serve short sentences and turn over rapidly, they represent a larger percentage of inmates who do not adhere to the inmate culture. Second, there are many young and impulsive inmates who respect only physical power or intimidation. Finally, the fact that prisons are not as isolated as in the past undermines the solidarity and formation of the inmate code. Today, inmates talk to their family and friends on the telephone on a regular basis, they have visitors several times per week, and they read newspapers and magazines and stay attuned to what is occurring in the outside world. Even though the inmate code has not been seen as a valued commodity by many prison staff, most staff and inmates who have been around for several years regret its demise. They feel that at least the inmate code provided an expected order, organization, and understanding of how the prison would informally work and how inmates would behave toward staff and other inmates.

As with any culture or society, a special language develops. The "A Look Into" box contains a glossary of prison terms and slang.[7]

A Look Into...

A Glossary of Prison Slang

A&P	Inmate store, commissary	Hugging the bars	Refers to someone who wants to get out of prison quickly or doesn't want to get involved in an incident
Bad Mammy Jammy	Good-looking female visitor		
Bird bath	Taking a sponge bath in the sink in the cell	Jamming	Fist fighting
		Joint	Prison or jail
Blow	Cigarette	Joint converted	Inmate who finds religion
To blow	To get mad	Juice	Power; an inmate who can make things happen
Bo-hog	An inmate who bosses other inmates around and preys on weaker inmates		
		Keister stashed	Contraband inserted into the rectum
Bomb	Letter denying parole; also refers to rolled-up toilet paper used for cooking in a cell	Kite	A letter from home, or an informant's tip to the authorities
		Lowlife rouger	Someone who steals other inmates' belongings
Bricks	Life outside prison; a person hits the bricks when he or she leaves prison	The Man	Correctional officer
		Mud water	Cell-brewed coffee
Bull	Correctional officer or police officer	Mule	Free person who transports contraband into and out of the prison for inmates
Bull sisters	A gang of predatory homosexual inmates		
Bust a nut	Relief by masturbation	Off someone	To kill a person
Buzzard	An inmate who looks out for officers on patrol	On the Rio	Not joking, serious
		P.C.	Protective custody
Carry a lunch pail	To hold a routine 9–5 job on the outside; something many inmates despise	Peckerwood	In Georgia, refers to a white correctional officer and is an insult; in California, refers to a high-status inmate and is something to be attained
Cellie	Cellmate		
Convict	A tough prisoner who has proved himself in multiple encounters over the years; also referred to as a *regular, solid,* or *right guy*		
		Pimp slap	Slap across the face
		Pruno	Prison-made booze concocted from yeast, fruit juices, bread, or potatoes; doesn't taste good, but does cause a buzz
Cop out	To confess; inmates claim it is unwise to cop out to anything		
Crib	Inmate's bunk or cell	Pumping iron	Lifting weights
Crow	An inmate who watches out for officers while other inmates violate the rules	Punk	Someone who submits sexually to a stronger inmate
		Put it on ice	Don't give up information
Dirty dog	Sorry, no-good inmate	Rabbit	Escaped inmate
Double trouble	When an inmate borrows something and must pay back twice the amount borrowed	Railroad	To get blamed for something you didn't do
		Reruns	Inmates who return after being released
Fishing line	Bag and rope tied together to reach something under the cell door	Road dog	Inmate who roams the yard looking for trouble
Free worlder	Anyone who is not an inmate		
Front	To pretend to be tough	Screw	Correctional officer
Ghetto penthouse	Top tier in the cellblock	Shank or shiv	Prison-made knife
Goon squad	Officers who dress in riot gear to quell inmate riots or extract resistant inmates from their cells	Silent beef	Crimes suspected but not proved in court; the parole board often considers these offenses in deciding on parole
Hardcastle	Warden or any officer who acts tough		
		Snitch	An inmate who informs on other inmates in return for favors from the prison officials
Hard stuff	Heroin or opium		
Head up	One-on-one fight		
Hold your mud	Not backing down in the prison setting	Speeding ticket	Minor write-up, disciplinary report
		Throw down	Fight
Hole	Isolation cell	Tunk	An inmate card game
Home boy	Inmate from your neighborhood	Went for a rib	Provoked an inmate into doing something
House	Cell		

Violence in Prisons

As noted in Chapter 7, a large percentage of male inmates have a lengthy history of violence. At the end of 2005, 53 percent of adults sentenced to state prisons were committed for violent offenses.[8] With such a large proportion of inmates previously involved in violent acts, it is not surprising, therefore, that violent behavior is a way of life within prisons. Many inmates just resort to violence as their normal reaction to frustration, disagreements, or lack of power. Those who are not prone to violence are constantly watchful to avoid situations that could lead to violent confrontations. A 2008 study of inmate-on-inmate violence in thirty prisons confirmed what is called the "importation" theory, or that violent inmates bring their violent ways into prison with them.[9]

Overcrowded prison conditions;[10] tensions between inmate gangs;[11] the powerlessness, boredom, and sexual frustration of inmates;[12] and the importation of street cultures of "face to face rivalries, retaliation, machismo, disrespect, and drunkenness"[13] are suggested reasons for violent acts in prisons. The simple conclusion as to why there is a high level of violence within prisons is that prisons hold violent people who act out in violent ways, and the prison culture and environment add to the tension and threat of violence by inmates.

Hassine suggests another reason for prison violence: inmate avoidance of the reality of their incarceration. He writes,

> *Violence in Graterford (a state prison in Pennsylvania) had also become a form of escape for many inmates. In creating and maintaining a predatory environment, these men were able to avoid the reality of imprisonment by focusing all their attention on fighting one another. The more hostile the environment, the more they saw themselves as victims and the less responsible they felt for their own action.*[14]

interpersonal violence
prison violence that occurs between two or more individual inmates; the reason for the violence is a personal issue between the individuals

collective violence
prison violence that is between and initiated by groups of inmates and includes prison riots and disturbances; it can be groups of inmates against staff or against one another, as this violence stems from the fundamental difference in values and positions of the two groups

In *Prison Violence in America*, Braswell and colleagues distinguish between interpersonal violence and collective violence.[15] **Interpersonal violence** occurs between two or more individual inmates, and the reason for the violence is a personal issue between the individuals. **Collective violence** is between and initiated by groups of inmates and includes prison riots and disturbances. Although collective violence is usually by inmates against prison staff and administration, large-scale gang conflicts also come under this category. Collective violence stems from the fundamental difference in values and positions of the two groups, rather than an individual conflict.

The threat of interpersonal violence causes the constant fear and tension of individual inmates in a correctional environment. Some inmates are always looking for a reason to violently act out, and others are always worried that they may be that reason. Johnson, in describing life in prison, writes,

> *The convict world is populated by men who doubt their worth as human beings and who feel they must constantly find occasions to "prove" themselves. . . . The convict world is a world of continuing— and generally escalating—conflict. Aggrieved parties cannot afford to back down, for then they are seen as weak and hence vulnerable to more abuse. Violence in the convict world establishes one's competence as a man who can survive in a human jungle.*[16]

mycrimekit™

Media—Video: **Prison Life for Inmates.**

Terry, in *The Fellas: Overcoming Prison and Addiction*, uses interviews with inmates and ex-inmates to paint a similar view of the constant problem of violence in prisons. He notes that violence in prison is rampant and likely to continue for some time. He points out how violence occurs, even though inmates may try to avoid it. He quotes some of the "fellas" as follows:

> *Doing your own time, minding your own business or staying away from trouble while serving a prison sentence. . .may be next to impossible. . .what it comes down to is this—I don't care how much you try to stay out of it—nowadays, as crazy as it is, you're gonna be involved some way, some how.*[17]

After experiencing an increasing level of violence within federal prisons, officials attempted to identify the types of inmates more likely to commit violent acts. Innes and Verdeyen write that there are three general categories of inmates who resort to violence:

1. *Antisocial offenders* have developed the habit of using force and coercion to get what they want. This group has used violence on the streets, and even though they have the competencies and skills to act in prosocial ways, they have found that violence works successfully for them.
2. *Special-needs offenders* are those with physical or mental deficiencies. As a result of their impairments, they are unable to function satisfactorily in a prison environment and often react to situations violently.
3. *Psychopathic offenders* are predatory, cold, and calculating, and usually act violently for no good reason. They do not feel compassion and will be violent simply for their own enjoyment.[18]

Male inmates live in an environment with the constant threat and potential for violence. Not only are many violent people in prison, but the environment and culture create a breeding ground for violence, with the need to act tough and not back down; a prevalence of gang members and gang activities; pressure for homosexual sex from some inmates; and conflicts that result from the sale and use of drugs. Even though homicide rates dropped 93 percent from 1980 to 2002, in 2002, there were forty-eight homicides in state prisons. In addition, violence seems to breed violence, as 61 percent of all homicides in state prisons were themselves violent offenders.[19]

Unfortunately, violence in prisons, especially in high-security prisons, is a common event. There are days without fights or serious assaults, but a prison administrator with his or her eyes open and an understanding of the environment knows that inmates are pressured and extorted every day. Prisons are full of individuals who have lived their lives violently and try to intimidate others to get what they want. It is not possible for prison administrators to stop all this from happening; their focus is (1) to provide a situation that allows inmates to protect themselves (in nonviolent ways and using legitimate means) and (2) to do everything possible to isolate the predators from potential victims.

Gangs in Prisons

Prison gangs not only are disruptive within a prison environment, but also contribute greatly to acts of violence and the resulting tension. A recent report indicated that according to crime victims, 6 percent of violent crimes (or 373,000 per year) were committed by gang members between 1993 and 2003.[20] In addition, the 2009 National Gang Threat Assessment estimates that there are approximately one million gang members belonging to more than twenty thousand gangs active in crimes in the United States.[21] As would be expected, these gang members continue their predatory, violent ways in prison. Gang members stick together to intimidate

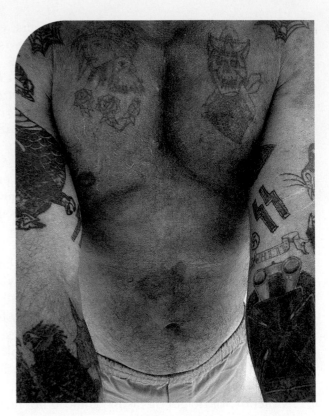

The existence of prison gangs results in intimidation of staff and inmates and leads to tension and violence within prisons. Photo by A. Ramey/PhotoEdit.

other inmates, control drug sales and prostitution, and gain power and influence. In a study of the relationship between gang affiliation and violent acts in federal prisons, researchers found that both specific and generic gang indicators were statistically related to violence and misconduct[22] and concluded that controlling gang activities has great potential to reduce tension and violence within prisons.

Prison gangs were first identified in California in the early 1960s, when prison administrators realized that many of their problems—violence, intimidation of staff and inmates, and introduction of drugs—were being controlled and coordinated by organized groups of inmates. A Department of Justice report on the early development of gangs and their prison activities notes, "Their organization was so firmly entrenched (in California) before authorities understood the danger confronting them that control of the institutions was seriously threatened. This phenomenon has been repeated in numerous jurisdictions as the presence and influence of gangs have spread throughout the country."[23]

Since that time, prison gangs have continued to grow in number and influence in the nations' prisons. A national survey in 1985 identified more than a hundred gangs, with a total membership of approximately 13,000.[24] An American Correctional Association 1993 survey identified thirty-nine different, major gangs in the nation's prisons and estimated that 6 percent of prisoners were members of a gang.[25] In the most recent survey in 2002, state and federal correctional agencies reported a total of 61,353 gang members in prisons, making up 4.9 percent of the prison population.[26]

Gang members in prisons usually have a more extensive history of crime than nongang members, get in more trouble in prison, participate in fewer prison programs, and are more likely to have a substance abuse problem.[27] Several authors suggest that gangs are a natural outgrowth of large groups of criminals placed together in a prison setting. Scott suggests, "The prison gang, as both a process and an organization, facilitates the adaptation of inmates to life in the prison and, more locally, the cell block."[28] Sykes, describing the prison environment in the 1950s,

prison gangs
groups that form in prison and use the threat of violence to intimidate other inmates, control drug sales and prostitution, and gain power and influence

noted that inmates find ways to cope with their confinement and the deprivations they encounter.[29] However, other authors describe gangs as more hedonistic than social phenomena and note that through money and power, gang members can avoid the deprivation of property, freedom, and influence that a prison tries to accomplish. Fleisher and Decker suggest, "Motivated by a desire to make money and be at the top of an institution's inmate power structure, prison gangs exploit the inherent weaknesses resulting from overcrowded, understaffed mega-prisons."[30]

Fortunately, correctional agencies have gained sophistication in understanding prison gangs, and much more is currently known about their operations, membership, and organization. In an issue of *Correctional Management Quarterly* devoted entirely to the threat of prison gangs, Seiter writes, "Correctional administrators can never hesitate, stop gathering intelligence, or fail to stay ahead of the gangs' operations. . . . For the individual correctional staff involved, their will to further the correctional mission—to provide a safe environment for staff and inmates—cannot waiver."[31]

Many prison gangs started as an extension of street gangs. When such groups as Bloods and Crips found that many of their street gang members ended up in prison, it was only natural that they continue their criminal activities while recruiting membership, intimidating other inmates, and attempting to control the drug dealing in prison. Other gangs, such as the Mexican Mafia, Dirty White Boys, and Black Guerilla Family, originated in prison as ethnic and racial groups of inmates began to band together for strength and support. They discovered that such alliances could lead to control over other prisoners, create funds, and provide members power to gain advantages in prison they might otherwise not have. The following list describes some of the current major prison gangs.

- *Aryan Brotherhood (AB):* The Aryan Brotherhood started in 1967 in San Quentin Prison, is limited to Caucasians, and is a Nazi-oriented, antiblack gang that dislikes authority and adheres to violence to gain prestige. They have no hesitancy to kill to keep their membership and organization secure and once had a rule of "making one's bones" to get in, meaning that prospective members had to kill for the gang to show their worth. It was also said that the only way to get out of the gang was to die. The AB has been aligned with many street motorcycle gangs and has extensive prison and street networks for dealing drugs. They also have alliances with other white supremacist gangs to gain numbers and power in prison. They have (from time to time) had an association with the Mexican Mafia to expand their drug dealing and ability to perform contract killings.

- *Mexican Mafia (MM):* The Mexican Mafia is a Hispanic gang that requires members to take an oath of "blood in, blood out," meaning that prospective members must assault someone for the gang to prove themselves and are badly beaten or even killed to get out of the gang. It originated in the Deuel Vocational Institution (California) in 1958; it has since become one of the most powerful prison gangs in the country. Having no underlying political views, the gang is focused on committing crimes to support its members in prison. The leaders organize the entire criminal activity and often rob banks to gain funds to support their prison activities.

- *Black Guerilla Family (BGF):* The Black Guerilla Family also started in San Quentin Prison, and its first leader was George Jackson, the Black Panther who was killed in a 1971 escape attempt. They follow a politically charged revolutionary philosophy intent on destruction of the "white establishment" and overthrow of the government. They hope to coalesce all black inmates so they can "control their own destiny."

- *La Nuestra Familia (NF):* The NF ("our family") was established in the late 1960s in Soledad Prison (California), primarily by Chicano inmates from Northern California, to protect themselves from the Southern California-based Mexican Mafia. They have been at war with the Mexican Mafia (and the Aryan Brotherhood) for most of their existence, but more recently have tried to have a peace agreement. In their battles against these two gangs, they often form an alliance with the Black Guerilla Family. A board of directors, known as *La Mesa*, controls them. Rank in the gang depends on the number of killings accomplished for the gang.

- *Mexikanemi (EME):* This gang, also known as the Texas Mexican Mafia, started in the Texas prison system in 1984. They have spread rapidly in federal prisons across the country and are also in other southwestern states. Gang members are very violent and kill enemies in and outside prison. They usually act alone, but have aligned with the Texas Syndicate to fight the Mexican Mafia. They also are organized in military fashion with generals, lieutenants, sergeants, and soldiers. Members work their way up the organization within the prison they are in and are elected to positions based on their leadership. If transferred to another prison, they lose their rank unless reelected there.

- *Texas Syndicate (TS):* This is another California-originated prison gang; it started by inmates who had migrated to California from Texas. Instead of joining one of the two California Hispanic gangs, they formed their own to maintain their Texas heritage and band together to protect Texas inmates from other gangs. The TS is well organized and has a national president, with appointed chairmen at each prison. There are vice-chairmen, captains, lieutenants, sergeants at arms, and soldiers. When the early gang members were released from California prisons, they returned to Texas and established the TS in Texas and other southwestern prisons. Their primary agenda is drug trafficking and selling protection to other inmates. They have a reputation for violence and are feared by other inmates.

Prison Gang Control Strategies

To control the activities and violence of gangs, correctional staff focus on a variety of strategies. These include early detection of gang activities, identification of leaders and members, surveillance of gang activity, denial of gang turf or wearing of gang colors and symbols, and a variety of gang control tactics. Lesce identifies six measures to control prison gangs:

1. Transferring gang members to maximum-security prisons
2. Limiting inmates' access to money, which often plays a critical role in inmates' underground economy
3. Placing the most violence-prone gang members in special facilities
4. Developing gang intelligence
5. Recruiting informers
6. Observing inmates' daily routine activities to identify patterns of activities and associations of gang members[32]

The most important action that prison staff can take to control gangs is early detection of gang activities. Correctional staff are informed of gangs' organization, activities, and known membership at a prison and are asked to report any intelligence regarding gang member activities. To identify gang leaders and other members, correctional agencies collect and maintain detailed records of gang membership, often divided into leaders, hard-core members, and marginal members.[33] Other terms to identify levels of gang involvement are *member, associate,* or *suspect*. A **gang validation process** requiring several identifiers of gang activity is used to confirm individuals' gang involvement level. Five or six different items are needed to validate an inmate as a *member*, three or four items may substantiate an inmate as an *associate*, and one or two identify an inmate as just a *suspect*. Gang validation identifiers include inmate self-admission that he or she is a gang member; information from a presentence investigation report that the inmate has participated in street gang activities; confiscated gang documents, such as membership lists, photographs, or correspondence from other gang members; violation of prison rules that indicates involvement in gang activities, such as drug trafficking, gambling, extortion, or strong-arming other inmates; involvement with known gang members; or tattoos indicating gang signs.[34]

The next gang control strategy is surveillance of gang activities. After gang members are identified, their activities are closely monitored and recorded. The National Major Gang Task Force of the U.S. Department of Justice recommends the following actions to monitor gang members:

- *Posted picture file:* A centralized photo and data file on significant gang members, suspects, and associates.
- *Confidential reports:* All staff report gang-related grouping activity on the daily confidential reports.
- *Gang communications:* There should be a priority with prison staff to intercept notes passed between gang members.
- *Identify gang visitors:* Visitors of gang members should be identified and their names shared with other prisons. Often visitors of gang inmates at multiple institutions pass along gang information and "hit contracts."
- *Gang control efforts:* Staff should watch for efforts by gangs to dominate any physical area of the institution or access to any inmate program.[35]

Another important activity to control prison gangs is to keep them from showing their power. Gangs like to show their strength to recruit members, tout themselves as controlling activities or areas, and show willingness to be violent against their enemies. To do this, gangs try to flaunt colors, hand signs, and symbols; wear clothing

gang validation process
an identification of the number of identifiers of gang activity used to confirm individuals' gang involvement level

Gang members like to flaunt their power by showing displays of membership and group strength, such as tattoos, hand signs, staking out turf, or wearing clothes a certain way.

Photo by Mark Richards/PhotoEdit.

a certain way; and stake out turf. Prison staff need to be aware of the meaning of the different signs or colors and prohibit inmates from wearing or showing them.

Some jurisdictions, once they identify inmates as gang members, isolate them by moving them either to a high-security prison or to a supermax prison in lockdown status. The Federal Bureau of Prisons policy requires that validated members (not associates or suspects) be assigned to a maximum-security prison. In the early 1990s, Connecticut developed a unique gang control strategy (now used by many other states), in which they moved gang members and leaders to a high-security prison in lockdown status, similar to disciplinary segregation or a supermax prison. The only way for members to get out of the lockdown situation is to renounce their membership and **debrief** or tell correctional officials everything they know about the gang operations and membership. Once inmates debrief, they can never be accepted back into the gang and, in fact, become an enemy of the gang.

debrief
gang members tell correctional officials everything they know about the gang operations and membership; once inmates debrief, they become an enemy of the gang

Recently, the California Department of Corrections (CDC) began to racially segregate prisoners for up to sixty days each time they enter a new correctional facility. The CDC asserted that this prevents violence caused by racial gangs. Most of the gang violence in California prisons comes from gang conflicts based on the racial makeup of the gangs. Johnson, an African American inmate, alleged the policy violated his Fourteenth Amendment right to equal protection. The District Court initially granted the CDC summary judgment on grounds that they were entitled to qualified immunity. This was affirmed by the Ninth Circuit. However, the U.S. Supreme Court in February 2005 reversed and remanded the Ninth Circuit decision and, while not deciding if the policy violates Johnson's right to equal protection, required the district court to rehear the case and use a test that must narrowly tailor any racial segregation and prove it serves a compelling state interest.[36]

Gangs are a danger to staff and other inmates within a prison, and correctional staff spend considerable time and effort to identify gang members and control their activity. If they do not, the gangs gain power, other inmates feel compelled to join a gang for their own protection, and prisons become a "war zone" rather than a secure and safe place in which inmates who desire to participate in self-improvement programs can do so. To break the cycle of crime and have any chance of returning prisoners to their communities as law-abiding citizens, prisons must control gang activities and limit potential violence. The "Your Career in Corrections" box describes the role of gang intelligence officers.

Homosexual Behavior in Male Prisons

A problem that results from the operation of any single-sex prison is homosexual behavior, whether forced or consensual. It is difficult to identify the actual amount of homosexual activity in prisons; inmates are hesitant to admit such involvement and therefore staff are not aware of the full extent of involvement. A well-designed study by the federal prison system in the early 1980s surveyed more than three hundred inmates regarding their sexual activity in prison and found that more than 30 percent admitted some type of homosexual experience.[37] However, less than 1 percent admitted that they were forced into such activities, and 7 percent stated that inmates who were nice to them or gave them gifts later seduced them.

All prisons have a rule against any type of sexual behavior between inmates; if caught, inmates are punished for even consensual homosexual acts. Even though homosexual relationships are accepted in society, they are still not allowed in prisons, because there is no way to ensure that relationships are really consensual. A stronger inmate may actually be forcing a weaker inmate to have sex, while threatening to have him beaten or killed if he tells correctional staff about it. Also, many fights and stabbings in prisons result from **sexual triangles** in which two inmates become

sexual triangles
two inmates become jealous and fight over another one

Your Career in Corrections

Gang Intelligence Officers

For students who like the idea of working in a prison, are fascinated with investigative strategies, and are challenged by the idea of trying to keep ahead of the "bad guys," gang intelligence officer might just be the job to have. Most prisons and large correctional agencies have staff who act as **gang intelligence officers** (the title varies by jurisdiction). These staff members collect intelligence and advise administrators regarding strategies to manage and contain prison gang activity. As prisons have implemented gang control strategies, gangs are increasingly becoming more secret and try to hide their illegal and strong-arm tactics from detection. Prisons do not specifically recruit and hire gang intelligence officers, but select promising individuals from their internal employee ranks and train them for these jobs. The positions are usually midlevel managers in the prison security departments, but act rather independently, as they are not in the traditional chain of command.

The primary function of gang intelligence officers is to collect and organize intelligence regarding gang activities and members. First, officers train prison staff regarding the types of behavior, dress, or other activities that could indicate gang functioning and how to report it to be included as intelligence information. Second, officers organize the information they collect to identify specific gangs and specific individuals who may be involved in the gang. Third, officers use this information to designate individuals as gang members, associates, or suspects. Once gang members are identified, staff can pay particular attention to the activities and associations of these inmates. Finally, gang intelligence officers use this information to anticipate gang activities and proactively move to thwart their implementation.

The second function served by gang intelligence officers is the development of comprehensive gang control strategies. The information they gather can be used for control or discovery of gang activities by individuals or small numbers of gang members. It can also be used to develop broader strategies that may be implemented agency-wide to subvert the formation and illegal behavior of gangs. For instance, states such as Connecticut and California have decided to place all identified gang members in a lockdown situation and not let them off lockdown unless they debrief by telling officers all that they know about the gang, its operations, and its members and leaders. Gang intelligence officers, through their experience and knowledge, are the key staff members who develop such strategies to control gang activities to make prison safe for other inmates and staff.

jealous and fight over another one. Most inmates who admit homosexual relationships while in prison state that they are heterosexual, but due to long periods of sexual deprivation, they get involved in homosexual activity for sexual release.

Prisons do have a problem with forced sex acts or rape. Although some rapes are strictly for sexual gratification, Hassine reports that most sexual assaults (rapes) in prison are committed to "generate fear and to maintain power over the general population."[38] The most likely targets of such assaults are inmates who are young, physically small, and seen as weak and easily intimidated.[39] Inmates often watch for the newly arrived inmates ("fish") to identify likely targets of sexual aggression and then take advantage of them while they are feeling alone and do not yet understand the avenues they can take to protect themselves from assault. These inmates are led to believe that they can later report this sexual pressure and be protected by staff.

On September 4, 2003, President George W. Bush signed the Prison Rape Elimination Act of 2003 into law. The act required the collection of information on the incidence and prevalence of sexual assault within correctional facilities and the development of national standards for the prevention, detection, and reduction of sexual violence in prison. A survey was conducted of jails and prisons to identify the level of sexual violence reported to the correctional agency. The results were an estimated 5,386 alleged incidents of sexual violence during 2004, 6,241 in 2005,

gang intelligence officers
prison staff charged with collecting intelligence and advising administrators regarding strategies to manage and contain prison gang activity

and 6,528 in 2006.[40] Translating these allegations into rates per 1,000 inmates, this would be 2.46 in 2004, 2.83 in 2005, and 2.91 reported allegations per 1,000 inmates in 2006. The increase may have resulted from jurisdictions adopting an expanded definition of rape under PREA and improved reporting by inmates and agencies. Of these allegations, 36 percent were allegations of staff sexual misconduct, 34 percent of inmate-on-inmate nonconsensual sexual acts, 17 percent staff sexual harassment, and 13 percent abusive sexual contact. The report notes that upon investigation, more than half of the allegations (55 percent) were unsubstantiated, 29 percent were determined not to have occurred, and 17 percent were substantiated. These figures have been consistent over the past three years of reporting.

The U.S. Department of Justice also conducted a self-administered and anonymous inmate survey in 2007. Results were that an estimated 60,500 (4.5 percent of all prisoners) experienced one or more incidents of sexual victimization. These fell into one of four categories. About 1.3 percent of inmates (16,800) reported nonconsensual sex with another inmate, and 0.8 percent of inmates (10,600) said they only experienced abusive sexual contact such as unwanted touching by another inmate. About 1.7 percent of inmates (22,700) reported that they had willing sex or sexual contact with a staff member, and another 1.7 percent (22,600) reported sexual contact with staff as a result of physical force, pressure, or offers of special favors or privileges.[41]

In response to PREA and the frequency of reported acts, almost all states formed special task forces or steering committees to implement best practices identified throughout the states to prevent sexual violence.[42] Dimensions that are targeted to impact sexual violence are staff training, inmate education, classification at intake, zero tolerance, reporting procedures, investigative protocols, mandatory separation, and inmate victim aftercare.[43] To try to reduce the number of sexual assaults in prisons, correctional staff use several preventive and reactionary measures. First, they advise inmates during the reception process that sexual assault is a possibility and that they have the option of telling staff and being separated from the aggressors. Second, staff watch for signs of such aggressive acts and question potential targets about such pressure. Finally, staff investigate every allegation of sexual pressure or assault and will separate the inmates from one another as a precautionary measure. Even though most allegations cannot be proved because they become one inmate's word against another's, if staff fail to act to protect victims once an issue is brought to their attention, they could be held legally liable for any injury or psychological trauma that later results.

Prison wardens were recently surveyed to determine their beliefs on the best methods to prevent prison rape and sexual assault. Although they believed that good policies and procedures could be somewhat effective (69 percent) and that good staff training was also somewhat effective (52 percent), the most favored method was that increased and enhanced supervision by staff could be "completely effective" (71 percent).[44] The real key to prevention is changing the culture rather than training staff and implementing procedures after a sexual violent act occurs. Culture change includes positive interaction and communications between staff and inmates along with inmate education, so that inmates feel comfortable reporting any beginning pressure for sex well before it develops into a forced sexual act.[45]

One controversial approach to reducing the degree of homosexual activity in prison is to allow **conjugal visiting,** sometimes referred to as family visiting. Conjugal visiting is private visiting between inmates and their spouses, and it is expected that they will engage in sexual relations. Only six states (California, Connecticut, Mississippi, New Mexico, New York, and Washington) permit conjugal visits.[46] Supporters of conjugal visiting argue that it provides a normal release of

conjugal visiting
sometimes referred to as family visiting, these are private visiting opportunities between inmates and their spouses, and it is expected that they will engage in sexual relations

sexual tension, is an incentive for good behavior as only inmates with good records earn such a visit, and reduces homosexual activity in prison. Opponents believe it can only be provided to a small number of inmates and therefore has little impact on homosexual activity. Also, it creates issues such as discriminating against inmates who are not legally married and degrades women in that the visit becomes more sexually oriented than family- or social-oriented. There are many arguments for and against implementing conjugal visiting. In the "You Make the Decision" box at the end of this chapter, you have to decide regarding its implementation.

Drugs in Prisons

There are thousands of drug offenders in state and federal prisons, and a high proportion of inmates have a history of drug or alcohol abuse. In their report, *Prisoners in 2007*, authors Heather C. West and William J. Sabol stated that an estimated 53 percent of federal inmates and 19.5 percent of state inmates were serving a sentence for a drug offense.[47] In addition, 265,000 prisoners were serving a sentence for which their most serious offense was a drug law violation.[48] Data for 2004 indicated that 32 percent of state inmates and 26 percent of federal inmates were under the influence of drugs at the time of their offense, and (see Table 11.1) 56 percent of state prisoners and 50 percent of federal prisoners reported drug use

TABLE 11.1 — Drug Use in the Month Before the Offense by Selected Characteristics of State and Federal Prisoners, 1997 and 2004

| | Percent of Prisoners Reporting Drug Use in the Month Before the Offense — | | | |
| | State | | Federal | |
Characteristic	2004	1997	2004	1997
All prisoners	56.0%	56.5%	50.2%	44.8%
Gender				
Male	55.7%	56.1%	50.4%	45.4%
Female	59.3	62.4	47.6	36.7
Race/Hispanic origin				
White[a]	57.7%	55.2%	58.2%	49.4%
Black[a]	56.0	58.3	52.7	47.2
Hispanic	53.5	55.0	38.4	37.5
Other[a,b]	52.9	52.7	48.4	38.5
Age				
24 or younger	66.2%	63.2%	62.0%	57.2%
25–34	60.9%	60.0	56.7	48.5
35–44	54.9	56.5	47.9	46.8
45–54	47.4	40.4	44.9	35.2
55 or older	19.2	18.4	20.9	24.3

[a]Excludes persons of Hispanic origin.

[b]Includes Asians, American Indians, Alaska Natives, Native Hawaiians, other Pacific Islanders, and inmates who specified more than one race.

Source: Christopher J. Mumola and Jennifer C. Karberg, *Drug Use and Dependence, State and Federal Prisoners, 2004* (Washington, D.C.: U.S. Department of Justice, October 2006), p. 3.

Random drug tests, in which inmate urine is sent to a lab to be tested, are a good way to deter and detect the use of drugs in prison.
Photo by Richard P. Seiter.

in the month before the offense.[49] Therefore, as expected, drug use is a serious problem in the nation's prisons.

Prison inmates are always scheming to find avenues to bring drugs into prisons. They look for opportunities through the mail, by bribing or paying staff to bring in drugs, by getting their visitors to bring in drugs, and through any other weakness they discover in a prison's security procedures. Once the drugs are inside, inmates sell them at a tremendous profit. The price of drugs depends on their availability, and when prison officials are doing a good job of keeping drugs out of prison, the price gets very high and inmates get much more desperate for ways to bring drugs into prisons. Money is not allowed in prison, so inmate sellers require their buyers to get family or friends to pay the seller's outside contact. If payment is not made, violence usually results. Because of the opportunity for huge profits, prison gangs usually try to control the drug trade. Dealing drugs in prison perfectly fits the gangs' desires to make money, have power, and use violence to enforce payment of debts.

Prisons attempt to reduce the use of drugs in several ways. First, they try to keep drugs from being brought into the prison by visitors or staff. Inmates are stripped and searched when they leave any contact visit, and mail and packages are checked for contraband before they are given to inmates. In addition, 23 percent of the states conduct random "frisking" of staff.[50] Second, prison staff continually search within the prison, especially inmates' cells and other living areas. Finally, the federal prison system and forty-seven states do **random drug testing** of inmates for drug use, and all do testing if an inmate exhibits traits of being under the influence of drugs. On average, agencies test 22 percent of all inmates annually.[51] For the forty-three state and federal jurisdictions reporting on the most recent data on these drug tests, of more than 2 million tests completed, 3.5 percent of the tests were positive for drug use.[52]

Prisons also provide drug and other substance abuse programs. Chapter 13 describes the types of treatment programs provided in prisons. Substance abuse is an important program in light of the high number and percentage of inmates with prior drug use. Table 11.2 indicates the percentage of inmates who have participated in drug treatment and other types of drug abuse programs since their admission to prison. Although the need for drug treatment far exceeds the provision, from 1997 to 2004 the percentage of inmates participating in drug treatment increased from 34.3 percent to 39.2 percent for state offenders and 38.8 percent to 45.3 percent for federal offenders.[53]

random drug testing
randomly selecting a percentage of inmates to urine test to see whether they have used any drug recently; a good deterrent to and source of data about prisoner drug use

TABLE 11.2	**Drug Treatment or Program Participation Since Admission among State and Federal Prisoners Who Used Drugs in the Month Before the Offense, 1997 and 2004**

	Percent of Prisoners Meeting Criteria for Drug Dependence or Abuse —			
	State		**Federal**	
Type of Drug Treatment or Program Since Admission	**2004**	**1997**	**2004**	**1997**
Any drug treatment or programs	39.2%	34.3%	45.3%	38.8%
Treatment	14.1%	14.6%	15.2%	15.4%
Residential facility or unit	9.2	8.8	8.7	10.9
Counseling by a professional	6.0	6.0	6.8	5.5
Detoxification unit	0.9	1.0	0.8	0.3
Maintenance drug	0.3	0.3	0.2	0.4
Other programs	33.7%	28.3%	38.8%	31.7%
Self-help group/peer counseling	26.9	23.1	20.8	15.8
Education program	17.0	14.1	28.1	23.8

Source: Christopher J. Mumola and Jennifer C. Karborg, *Drug Use and Dependence, State and Federal Prisoners, 2004* (Washington, D.C.: U.S. Department of Justice, October 2006), p. 9.

The Function of Humor in Prison

One interesting note regarding prison life for inmates is the function of humor. Charles Terry, who served lengthy prison sentences in both California and Oregon, writes regarding the use of humor by inmates to negotiate the gap between a normal and a convict identity.[54] Sociologists have used humor to study the cultures of various societies for years, yet its importance in the inmate culture has been less a focus of analysis. Other authors have described how humor in prisons is unique to that environment. Goffman has described inmates' use of humorous "sad tales" to account for their problemed past and reasons for failure.[55] Ungar builds on the use of humor in telling sad tales in describing inmates' use of "self-mockery."[56] And Terry suggests that inmates regularly use humor to "denigrate the system" and blame it for the conditions in which inmates find themselves.

Humor in prison serves many purposes. Male inmates live in an environment that makes it difficult to express their true feelings; they constantly have to show masculinity and toughness. Through humor, they have the opportunity to show real human feelings without showing vulnerability. And, oddly enough, humor allows inmates to achieve control. Terry notes that this is accomplished in two ways:

> It is the only social mechanism within the prison environment that allows feelings to be expressed and authorities cannot control its expression. . . . It (humor) acts as proof of their power and their release from domination.[57]

The world in which inmates live is very different from the world of normal society in many ways, yet in a few ways is very similar. Humor in prison, just as in society, lets one convey a sad story in a way that does not show weakness. It allows inmates, just as in society, to put oneself down, both to make others laugh and to make an excuse for certain conditions or lack of success. Yet humor in prison is in some ways a chance to get back at the correctional staff who control inmates' lives in almost every way. By laughing, perhaps much louder and longer than the story or joke deserves, in front of correctional staff, inmates in some ways think that they are annoying staff or showing that their imprisonment won't dampen their spirits. Humor is one legitimate way inmates can show staff that, although their actions are controlled, their emotions are not.

All the activities related to crimes, prison culture, gang membership, and homosexuality are different for male offenders than for female offenders. The next section describes the parallel profiles of women who commit crimes and go to prison. Even though they have several similar issues, there are varying ways that female prisoners group together, look for emotional support, deal with and shape the prison culture, and participate in programs and attempt to prepare for return to the community.

As an illustration of the real world facing prison inmates, the following "An Interview With" is presented.

An Interview With...

A Three-Time Loser

Kevin has been in prison three times, but avoided crime and prison for several years. He served all three sentences in Texas prisons, at times when the Texas Department of Corrections was undergoing massive change after a consent decree in the case of *Ruiz v. Estelle*. Among other things, it required an overhaul of virtually every aspect of prison structure, policies, and life. One key element was that the order forbids the use of "building tenders," who were inmates who acted as guards and kept the other inmates in line. As the department went through a period of upheaval adjusting to the court order, there was a record amount of violence and murder.

Question: How many times have you gone to prison and how many years have you served?

Kevin: I was in prison three times. The first offense, I was convicted for two robberies, but got ten years' probation. After about eighteen months of probation, I was convicted on multiple counts of credit card abuse (identity theft), was sentenced to three 5-year terms, and served slightly less than two years in a medium-security prison. After being released on parole, I again was convicted of ID theft, was sent to a maximum security, but quickly worked my way down to medium and then minimum. I served slightly more than two years that time. The third time, I was convicted of burglary of a motor vehicle with intent to commit theft. People

often say this, but I really didn't do it. I decided to fight it and went to trial. The jury came back with a guilty verdict, and I received a thirty-year sentence. The sentence for that crime was only two to ten years, but because Texas law requires a minimum of twenty-five years for habitual offenders, I was sentenced to thirty years by a jury. Fortunately, I was paroled after four years. I was in maximum security for the first half of this period, and eventually became a trustee and reclassified to minimum. In the first offense, the state made an effort to assign the inmates near their homes if possible, but as a second and third offender, unit assignment was made on the general basis of bed space, rather than a calculation of my risk level.

Question: You experienced a real variety of prisons and fellow inmates. In your opinion, how safe are inmates while in prison?

Kevin: The first time in prison I was assigned to a pretty rough facility, in spite of being medium security. An extended stay in a long-term county jail facility served as a primer for the prison experience. On this unit, the threat was mostly as a result of racial tension because the prison had been integrated for only five years. The risk of violence and assault was primarily cross-racial. The unit classification was for younger first-time offenders. I was fortunate to get a job assignment that allowed a good deal of control in my schedule. This allowed me to avoid the daily schedule of mass movement for showers, work, and exercise and avoid situations that had the highest probability for violence. The initial adjustment presented some tense situations, but my job-related flexibility kept me out of the higher-risk situations. The job assignment also has some status among prisoners, and eventually that status resulted in a reduction in confrontational events. Inmate-on-inmate assault was a regular occurrence inside the building, but most of it could be avoided by adherence to the convict code. There was some confusion and disruption to the daily life as a result of the *Ruiz v. Estelle* court order. The court mandated many new policies and procedures, but the old ways of doing things would persist. It was a time of mixed messages for convicts and staff alike.

The second time, because of a history of satisfactory institutional adjustment and a nonviolent offense, I was assigned to a relatively low-risk prison. This unit had fewer episodes of violence, and I felt pretty safe. I was assigned to a cluster of minimum/medium prison units. Everyone came in as medium and some were reclassified as minimum as personal risk was determined as lower. This was an inmate unit in contrast with a convict unit, and safety was a lower concern. The tone of this unit was more consistent with the consent decree and characterized by new school wardens who had not spent years under the old system.

On my third term I had a thirty-year sentence and was classified a habitual offender. I was sent to an older prison with a large working farm. Every day, a hundred of us were walked outside to work on the farm under armed guards on horseback. This prison was very old school and very "convict" oriented. During the period immediately preceding my arrival, this prison had recorded a very high number of inmate homicides. This was due largely to prison gangs struggling to fill the power vacuum created by the court-ordered dismantling of the previous system. The violence was gang related as they fought over control of prison vices. As a result of this violence, laws and policies were changed to permit extreme consequences for inmate assaults, especially those with weapons. These changes along with segregation of confirmed gang members resulted in a change in the atmosphere from very volatile to reasonably manageable.

Question: The general public perception is that inmates (especially those considered weak) are constantly threatened by stronger and more violent inmates. How safe are inmates, and what do they have to do to reduce the risk of assault?

Kevin: Most every inmate, especially those who were new to the system, would be tested. This testing took many forms, but was always employed to determine if the individual would fight to protect himself, or would be easy prey. Once the person had passed the test by presenting himself as too much trouble to exploit, he would be left alone. However, subsequent events could create problems. If a person had a reputation as weak (snitch, homosexual, paying for protection) from previous prison terms or from the county jails, this could cause new waves of predators testing the situation. Another situation that could lead to violence was getting into debt—gambling, drug use, or borrowing were the most common paths to trouble. My personal way to avoid conflict was to remain clear of these activities and only gambling with cash, not credit. Most inmates knew what led to trouble, but some continued to make poor choices and found themselves being exploited to repay debts.

Question: There are many gang members in prison. How do the gangs act in prison, and what do inmates who are not gang members have to do to avoid getting at odds with gangs?

Kevin: On my first stay, I was unaware of a significant gang presence. During my second sentence, the system had identified many members and responded by segregating them from each other, which diluted gang members' influence. If someone entered the system with known gang connections (gang tattoo), he was automatically segregated. The zero tolerance for gang activity was well known, and it reduced the visibility of much of the gang activity.

When I went back the third time, I was sent to more of a convict unit. By then, the gangs had adapted to prison policies and knew how to work the system to communicate with each other and avoid detection. For convicts, it wasn't too hard to figure out who the gang members were and what the gang business was. They conducted business in a subterranean economy, primarily drugs and prostitution. My only interaction with known gang members was selling materials to make wine. I was in a clerical job that gave me a tremendous amount of latitude in terms of behavior. I had good access to all prison activities and the job permitted mobility. There was no overt pressure to join a gang at that time, because the slightest appearance resulted in segregation and possibly relocation.

...continued

Question: How prevalent are drugs in prison? How do inmates get and hide drugs or avoid detection from officials?

Kevin: Marijuana was very prevalent. If anyone wanted it, he could get it. I heard rumors of other drugs, but I didn't participate. There was also buying and selling of prescription drugs that had been provided by the prison.

Inmates obtain drugs through contact visits or from dirty COs (correctional officers). Visitors would also smuggle in cash so inmates could buy drugs. One smuggling method was for a visitor to flush something down the toilet (like a small rubber ball full of drugs or cash) in the visitor's bathroom. The inmate workers in the wastewater treatment plant would then retrieve the balls from the screening system. They would receive a cut of the balls' contents. Another way was through the craft shops. Inmates could make things (like wooden jewelry boxes with false bottoms) and mail them to people on the outside. The recipient would open the box very carefully, remove the false bottom, fill it with drugs, and retape it so it looked untouched. They would then have the package returned to the prison as undeliverable.

Question: Can inmates get drugs whenever they want?

Kevin: Yes, to marijuana. Other drugs were more difficult to get. Often, inmate trustees were providers because they worked outside the prison fences and had access to the roadside. Family members would drive close to where the unit was working, throw a bag of drugs in the ditch, and inmates who worked on tractors could pick it up.

Eventually, tobacco products were outlawed for prisoners, and COs would smuggle various products. That often would lead to escalating involvement, sometimes because inmates would threaten to turn them in for the original tobacco smuggling.

Question: How prevalent is homosexuality in prisons?

Kevin: There are enough inmates who are willing homosexuals that there was not much forced violent homosexual rape. Some of the homosexuality involved people who would not be homosexual on the outside. Some engaged in it as a way to make a living, some for protection, and some for fear of violent consequences if they did not. Others sought out relationships because it was the only option for sex that they had. The sex between inmates usually resulted from a predatory inmate coercing a weaker one to have sex. The homosexual relationships were primarily about a feeling of dominance over the other inmate. Part of the common culture is that when two men are having sex only one of them is a homosexual. The masculine role is not considered by some to be homosexual.

Most of the time, it wasn't forcible rape, but sex was gained through coercion, such as a mechanism to pay off a debt. Sometimes the predator orchestrated the situation to put the person in debt, with the intention of receiving payment through services. Usually, it was with a dominant male pressuring a weaker male, so the weaker inmates gave in because they were afraid or unwilling to fight for themselves. Often, there was a seduction of sorts at first, and then they were coerced into sex.

There really wasn't much likelihood of gang rape like in the scene from *The Shawshank Redemption* because it would cause too much attention. Current legislation leaves prisons liable for this kind of assault. Most homosexual activity was below the radar screen. Inmates were pretty secretive about what they did. From the way sex occurred in prison to my knowledge, I don't think the PREA (Prison Rape Elimination Act) legislation will be very successful with the more subtle types of coercive sex.

Question: What do inmates think about getting involved in prison programs?

Kevin: Most would participate because that's what they have to do to be paroled. Some programs are operated in air-conditioned space, and since most prisons had little air conditioning, it encouraged attendance during the summer. Programs also were a way to have contact with people from outside the prison. Some inmates felt they were out of the prison when they were in the programs, and there was a feeling that people cared about them.

I am not sure that many prison programs are effective. But, for guys locked up for seven to ten years, teaching life skills is helpful. The college program in prison saved me. I realized I had to do something to get out of prison, and the aging out process woke me up. I no longer personally have a criminal identity and don't even think of committing a crime. It has been nineteen years since my last conviction, but my felony status is still a primary consideration of everything in my life. There is no number of years of doing the right thing that can fix a time when they did the wrong thing.

Prison Life for Female Offenders

In many ways, women's prisons have many of the same situations, issues, and relationships that occur in male prisons. The history of women's prisons is very similar to that of men's prisons; however, there was a time lag of several decades before reforms spread from men's to women's prisons. Much of that was due to the gender-related policies that resulted in operating women's prisons to reinforce gender stereotypes by providing programming to prepare women for domestic housekeeping and parenting roles. It was more than seventy-five years after the invention of the prison in the United States before the first separate women's facility was opened. And it was almost another century before women received vocational training in areas other than cooking, sewing, and cleaning. However, modern prison environments for women have caught up to some extent. Facilities for both men and women are similar, there is drug abuse and homosexuality in prisons for both sexes, and prisons are not the best situation for preparing to return to the community

The History of Women's Prisons

Male and female offenders were housed in the same facilities in early U.S. jails. Although women were separated in different cells, the institutions were not designed to provide specific security or programs to meet the special needs of female offenders. Both male and female prisoners were under the supervision of male staff, and it was not uncommon for female prisoners to be raped by their guards. The need to separate male and female offenders was a concern of the Quakers, who devised and opened the first prison in a portion of the Walnut Street Jail in the late 1700s, and women were then housed in a separate section. However, while male inmates were housed in single cells and kept separate from other male inmates, female inmates did not receive the same separation and were housed together in large cells within the jail.[58]

Over the next several decades, it was recognized that female prisoners should be housed and dealt with separately. The first of these reforms for female prisoners was prompted by an English woman named **Elizabeth Fry,** a Quaker who formed the Ladies Society for Promoting the Reformation of Female Prisoners in 1816 and tried to convince officials that the special needs of women required hiring female guards and making other reforms.[59] Her efforts finally resulted in Parliament's passing three of Fry's requests, but not until some thirty years after she made them. The suggestions included (1) segregation of prisoners by sex, (2) using female guards to supervise female prisoners, and (3) decreasing the amount of hard labor required of female prisoners.[60] Soon after Parliament passed these acts, the first prison for housing only female offenders was opened in England.

Fry traveled to the United States and pushed for similar reforms for female prisoners there as well. Partly as a result of her efforts, the New York House of Refuge was opened in 1825 with a totally separate building to house female juvenile offenders, who were to be supervised by female staff. A major step forward in the treatment of female offenders occurred in 1863, when Zebulon Brockway, then-superintendent of the Detroit House of Correction, opened a separate unit for women and hired women as guards or matrons. Brockway also divided the inmates into small family groups, used the matrons as role models for the women, and provided domestic training. He used the concepts of the reformatory movement described in Chapter 1 in creating programs for women.

Elizabeth Fry
a Quaker who formed the Ladies Society for Promoting the Reformation of Female Prisoners in 1816; she tried to convince officials that women prisoners should be separated from male prisoner and that female guards should be hired to supervise them

Elizabeth Fry was a Quaker who formed the Ladies Society for Promoting the Reformation of Female Prisoners in 1816. Courtesy of Hulton Archive/Getty Images.

The emphasis was on education and training to prepare inmates for release and successful return to society.

The reformatory model continued for women (and for youthful male offenders) for the next hundred years and continues today for many women's prisons.[62] The Indiana Reformatory for Women and Girls, opened in 1873, was the first separate state prison for women. Soon thereafter, Massachusetts and New York opened reformatories for women, and other states gradually followed their lead and had totally separate facilities for female prisoners.

The design of the reformatories for women was different from the prisons for men; it used a **cottage-style architecture,** with several small housing units holding approximately thirty inmates, and each cottage included kitchens, living rooms, and sometimes nurseries for inmates with children. The design was created as a basis to train women prisoners in the female role of domesticity, through vocational training in cooking, sewing, and cleaning.[63] These types of prisons for women continued into the middle of the twentieth century, when the continuation of promoting gender stereotypes in vocational training and the management of women's prisons was questioned, although some authors suggest that these gender stereotypes continued to influence the operation of women's prisons even into the 1980s.[64]

Over the past twenty years, women's prisons have begun to look like and be operated in a manner very similar to men's prisons. The cottage design is no longer used, although campus-style prisons (for both men and women) have housing buildings separate from other program and service buildings. Physical security has increased as well. Many early women's reformatories did not have a secure fence to keep inmates from escaping, relying instead on the inmates' being trustworthy and not a risk to the community if they did escape. Today, prisons for women have the same perimeter security, with fences, razor ribbon, and electronic detection

cottage-style architecture

a style of prison design used for women's prisons, with several small housing units holding approximately thirty inmates; each cottage included kitchens, living rooms, and sometimes nurseries for inmates with children

The Federal Reformatory for Women, opened in 1927, was one of the first prisons created for women and originally had no fence or other perimeter security.
Courtesy of the Federal Bureau of Prisons.

devices to reduce escape attempts. Modern women's prisons also are built with program space to accommodate nontraditional vocational training programs such as carpentry and electronics. They also include special housing units to separate and manage disorderly and potentially violent inmates from the remainder of the population. The "An Insider's Experience" box in *MyCrimeKit* describes the challenges faced when attempting to modernize a women's prison based on the traditional methods of managing female prisoners.

mycrime**kit**

Insider's Experience: Changing a Women's Prison.

Culture in Women's Prisons

The culture in a women's prison is considerably different from that in a men's prison, with a different style of inmate communications with each other and with staff.[65] Most studies report that women also have an inmate code, emphasizing similar guidelines for women as for men, such as "do your own time" and "don't rat (tell) on other inmates." However, the code is not as important to women as to men. The important difference between male and female inmate culture is in the relationships that women form. Male inmates stay as independent and isolated as possible and avoid any emotional or personal relationships. Female prisoners, on the other hand, seek close personal and emotional relationships with other inmates. They also are not as concerned about being labeled a "snitch" by other inmates because of interacting with staff.

Much of the culture of a women's prison has to do with the fact that approximately 65 percent of female inmates are mothers, and much of their thoughts while in prison are about release and reestablishing their family and role as mothers. Owens notes that the importance of women's relationships with their children "has an impact on the values shaping prison culture in several ways, such as making conversations about children sacred, acknowledging the intensity and grief attached to these relationships, sanctioning those with histories of hurting children, and other child-specific cultural beliefs or behaviors."[66]

Female inmates often form pseudofamilies, in which each inmate plays a role as mother, father, children, and even nieces.
Courtesy of AP/Wide World Photos.

pseudofamilies

family organizations formed by female inmates who have roles of parents and children

Both because women enjoy and need the support resulting from sharing personal facts regarding their children and lives with others and because they have been socialized to play a specific role within a family structure, female inmates often tend to form what are called **pseudofamilies**. In these organizations, inmates play actual roles of parents and children. Some but not all pseudofamilies have a romantic dyad or a couple that acts as parents; there may be two mothers or a father and a mother. Parents are usually the older and more prisonwise inmates, and younger inmates take the role of children. The parental partners in these prison families are not always sexual in nature. Propper suggests that they are based on asexual pairing and do not present a greater likelihood of homosexual activity.[67] Pollock-Byrne, in describing these families, suggests that most prison lesbian relationships are based not so much on actual sexual activity as on affection with a sexual connotation.[68]

These pseudofamilies become the focus of much of the activity for family members. Family members make a great effort to try to live in the same housing unit, work together on the same jobs, and recreate together. The parents act as mentors for the younger inmates, protect them, and maintain a discipline of order and control. The families also provide mutual support and protection, an aid network, and an opportunity for fun and laughter.[69] Although most of the younger (children) inmates take on the role of daughters, some "women who take on the 'butch' or the aggressive role may be a dad, a son, or a brother, yet these designations can often be fluid."[70] Diaz-Cotto contends that these family relationships are now in decline in many prisons, primarily because inmates have more access to family, friends, and others outside prison and therefore do not have to invest as much in prison-developed relationships.[71]

The sexual relationships that develop in a women's prison are also much different from the homosexuality that occurs in men's prisons. Men must continually show their masculinity through sexual conquest of weaker inmates, and the risk of rape is much greater in men's prisons. The male sexual aggressor is not interested in a relationship, but simply in sexual gratification, power, and dominance. Sexuality for female offenders is altogether different in that it is a search for affection, emotional support, and sharing. The desire for power and dominance and the potential for rape are minimal, and "butches" in women's prisons are sought after by women who want to play a woman's role in a relationship.[72] Early research indicated that one out of four female inmates reports involvement in a lesbian relationship,[73] but it has more recently been estimated that "between 30 and 60 percent of incarcerated women are in lesbian relationships."[74]

In response to the Prison Rape Elimination Act of 2003, a survey was conducted to specifically examine sexual violence that occurs in female prisons and how if differs from that which occurs in male prisons. Violence between female inmates was found to be a part of the "constellation of overlapping individual, relational, institutional, and societal factors," and that violence occurs on a continuum ranging from verbal intimidation to homicide (extremely rare).[75] The report confirmed that violence in women's prisons is not as severe or prevalent as in men's prisons. Women were unlikely to discuss sexual violence unless prompted, and described sexual victimization as ranging from sexual comments and touching to sexual assault by aggressors. Although their threat of unanticipated sexual violence appears to be less likely than in men's prisons, it related more to a build up of the types of relationships described above and can be the result of the relationship going bad through disrespect or jealousy.

The world in which women live in prison is, in many ways, similar to that faced by male inmates. Their special needs, situations, and characteristics create unique management challenges and lead to the development of different cultures within prisons for female inmates. As described by Fleisher and colleagues, after a review of the development of culture within a new women's prison, "A key issue in the development of gender-based distinctions in organizational culture is learning how to create, implement, and then perpetuate a set of organizational values and beliefs that meets women's programming needs and styles of interpersonal interaction."[76]

Summary

CHAPTER REVIEW

The society of a prison has a unique culture. Few if any other environments are so isolated from normal living and society that they result in such a distinct culture. This results from the forced stay, the need for routine and control by staff, the adaptation to living with many other people and many heterogeneous groups, the interdependence of inmates on other inmates, and the anger and bitterness that inmates feel as a response to their situation. As prison culture has developed over the past two centuries, in some ways it has changed little, whereas in other ways it has changed dramatically.

Prisons still operate with at least a cursory understanding of and sensitivity to an inmate code, particularly the tenets to "be tough" and "don't trust the guards." However, the trusted old con, which lived by the code and was respected by other inmates, is a thing of the past. Younger inmates, many of whom are gang members whose loyalty is to the gang and who follow gang requirements over the inmate code, deal with issues through strength rather than guile and do not respect the "old con," whom they see as weak and not willing to take what they want. Women's prisons have more of an accepted respect and hierarchy related to both how long and how well time is served. However, for women, the status associated with this comes not so much from adherence to the inmate code, but from knowledge and relationships and the ability to mentor and protect younger inmates.

As much as prison staff want to be aware and in control of everything within a prison, much occurs in the life of prison inmates that staff do not understand and have little influence over. Although staff do not ignore drug use, gang activity and violence, or homosexuality, many honestly admit that they cannot totally control or prevent these activities. In fact, staff never find out about all the drug use, violent acts, and homosexual activity. Well-managed institutions are said to be "controlled by staff, and not by inmates." Even though this is true, the actions and relationships of inmates usually have a much greater influence on the development of prison culture than the policies and procedures of staff.

Key Terms

total institution

inmate code

prisonization

convicts

thieves

square johns

interpersonal violence

collective violence

prison gangs

gang validation process

debrief

gang intelligence officers

sexual triangle

conjugal visiting

random drug testing

Elizabeth Fry

cottage-style architecture

pseudofamilies

Review Questions

1. Define what Goffman meant with the concept of "total institutions."

2. Describe the Zimbardo experiment and its results.

3. What are the two theories regarding how inmate culture becomes a part of prison life?

4. How has following the inmate culture in a prison changed, and what are the potential reasons for the change?

5. List five reasons for violence in prisons.

6. What methods do correctional agencies use to control prison gangs?

7. List three of the major gangs in prisons today.

8. Why, does Hassine suggest, do most prison sexual assaults occur?

9. What do correctional officials do to prevent sexual assaults in prison?

10. What is the Prison Rape Elimination Act and what types of sexual assault occur in prison?

11. What percentage of inmates in state and federal prisons are serving sentences for drug offenses?

12. How do drugs get into prisons?

13. What role does Terry suggest that humor plays in a prison environment?

14. How does the inmate culture in a women's prison differ from that in a prison for men?

15. According to PREA surveys, how is sexual assault for female inmates different than for males?

You Make the Decision...

Implement Conjugal Visiting?

There are several pros and cons regarding conjugal visiting. When I worked for the Federal Bureau of Prisons (BOP), it became a topic of heavy discussion during one administration. The deputy attorney general (number two in command in the Department of Justice) favored conjugal visits for the BOP and asked Director Norman Carlson to consider it. The BOP had always taken the approach that conjugal visits in prisons were not a normal situation, and the BOP preferred extensive, furlough programs to allow inmates to earn the privilege of going home for a weekend to have a more natural setting and time for a relationship with their spouse. There was also the concern that since only married inmates were allowed conjugal visits in states, it would discriminate against unmarried and homosexual inmates and that there would likely be "jailhouse" marriages (those done out of convenience rather than for a long-term loving situation) just to get the chance for conjugal visits.

However, the deputy attorney general countered that the BOP often expressed concern for the level of violence in prisons, and some of the violence resulted from forced homosexual activities and fights between sexual triangles. It was difficult to counter the bosses' argument, but the leadership of the BOP was against their implementation. They decided to conduct a study, but before it was completed, there was a change in leadership in the Department of Justice, and the deputy left his position. The BOP did not pursue the issue with his replacement, and it was never raised again.

In this "You Make the Decision," decide whether you will implement conjugal visiting. In doing so, consider the pros and cons and try to imagine the logistical problems that would be encountered by the implementation of such a program. But then decide, either by yourself or in a small classroom group, whether you favor or oppose the implementation of conjugal visiting.

Chapter Resources on mycrimekit™

Go to mycrimekit.com to explore the following study tools and resources specific to this chapter:

- **Practice Quiz:** multiple-choice, true/false, short-answer, and essay questions to help students test their knowledge
- **WebQuests:** learning activities built around Web searches
  - Inside Prison: www.insideprison.com

- **Insider's Experiences:** "Changing a Women's Prison"
- **Seiter Videos:**
  - See inmates discuss prison life
- **Flashcards:** Eighteen flashcards to test knowledge of the chapter's key terms

The World of

After reading this chapter, you should be able to:

1. Know the types and functions of jobs available in a prison.
2. Understand how prisons are organized.
3. Explain the role of a prison warden.
4. Describe the importance of organizational culture and understand how culture is formed in a prison.
5. Know the role a correctional officer plays in a prison, and consider the pros and cons of this job for yourself.
6. Understand the daily activities of a correctional officer, how they gain inmate compliance, and the stress and danger of the job.
7. Describe the role of treatment and services staff within a prison.
8. Discuss prison culture for staff.
9. Know the history of female correctional officers in men's prisons and understand the challenges that face them in modern prisons.

Introduction

Just as there is a definite culture and hierarchy of status for prison inmates, there is also a culture and organizational hierarchy for prison staff. Some penologists would argue that prison staff are also influenced by the prison environment and become even more "prisonized" than inmates. That argument does not seem all that unreasonable. Most career prison staff spend more time "behind bars" than all but a small percentage of inmates. A correctional officer, who works for twenty-five years prior to retirement, 2,080 hours (40 hours for 52 weeks) per year, spends a total of 52,000 hours in the prison. This is almost six full years in prison, and the impact of this time on the officer personally is extended over twenty-five years before he or she leaves the prison for good.

Consider also that most staff in prison interact extensively with inmates, to a much greater proportion than they do with other staff. Their job is to gain control and compliance without the use of weapons, threats, or intimidation. To do this requires adaptation to (not cooptation by) the prison environment and understanding the most efficient way to maintain control over inmates. The world of prisons is unlike any other social organization. Words and deeds have different meanings inside prisons than outside, and due to the need for constant interaction and communication, there is no hiding anyone's real personality or approach to the job. Inmates quickly see through staff who try to take on a demeanor that is not really theirs.

In a prison there is considerable and continuous stress, the threat of assault and injury, and the need to never let down one's guard or fail to be attentive to the detail of one's work assignment. Most people on their jobs can have a "bad day at the office," be unproductive, or lose their temper or handle some issue poorly or unprofessionally. However, serious problems can result from having a similar bad day when working in a prison. When your work consists of supervising and maintaining control over possibly a hundred offenders, who are not the most cooperative and likable people in the world and who look for staff weaknesses and take advantage of improper behavior, having a bad day at work can put people at risk or undermine the security of a prison. Prison staff have to be professional, use their interpersonal skills, rely on one another to do their jobs well, leave the prison environment no worse than they found it, and be prepared to come back the next day to begin their eight-hour shift all over again.

In Chapter 10 the organization of a prison was described, and the elements of the organization that make a prison operate effectively were presented. This chapter focuses on the people rather than the organization: the world in which prison staff work, the issues they face, the ways they handle them, and the culture that develops as a result of stressful and challenging working conditions. Descriptions and functions of some of the primary prison staff positions are described, but the chapter focuses on the environment and culture that results from working in a prison setting.

There may be no more demanding job than working in a prison. I spent more than twenty years working for correctional agencies, was assigned to four different prisons, was warden of two prisons, was responsible for more than 30,000 inmates and 7,000 staff as director of a state prison system, oversaw a prison industry program that employed 15,000 inmates and sold $400 million in products each year, and supervised the operation of 65 correctional facilities with 80,000 inmates and 17,000 staff for a private prison company. From this work, I have a great appreciation for those staff who every day enter the world of imprisoned felons, serve the public in difficult and underappreciated positions, face uncertainty and danger, and maintain a professional approach to their jobs, the inmates, and the agencies for which they work.

The Jobs of Prison Staff

When most people think of prison staff, they think of wardens and correctional officers. However, many different positions make up the complement of prison staff. Some of these are listed here:

Chaplain	Counselor or case manager
Computer specialist	Institution administrator
Substance abuse counselor	Employee development specialist
Facility maintenance worker	Financial manager
Food service worker	Health care worker (physician or nurse)
Industrial supervisor	Laundry supervisor
Psychologist	Personnel manager
Recreation specialist	Safety manager
Secretary/clerical worker	Classification specialist
Teacher	Staff training instructor

In many ways, a prison is like a small city, requiring many of the same services and employees. Just like cities, prisons have schools, lodging accommodations, jails, eating establishments, convenience stores, places of worship, recreation facilities, sewer/sanitation/street service departments, facility and vehicle maintenance departments, barbershops, generators or electrical and power resources, laundry services, financial institutions, and administrative offices. All the types of employees that are often found in a small community (except for many retail shops) are found in a prison, because prisons must be fairly self-sustaining and able to provide for themselves in most situations.

Each of these jobs requires specialists, both to manage the functions and to provide the service. Prisons have teachers certified to teach in the public school systems and education supervisors who are usually accredited by the state as school principals. These supervisors carry out many of the functions of a principal in creating a learning environment, supervising teachers, and maintaining discipline of students. Food services administrators must prepare menus, order food,

Prison staff include a variety of positions, such as correctional officer, administrator, medical person, and counselor. Photo by Richard P. Seiter.

and oversee the preparation of meals, and food service workers oversee inmates preparing and serving food. Prison physicians provide patient care and manage prison infirmaries that are very similar in operations to a typical general-practice doctor's office. In many ways, the jobs within a prison setting are very similar to the same functions carried out in the community, except that they are within a secure environment and all the clients are incarcerated felons.

The Organization of a Prison

The organization and administration of prisons is in some ways very simple, and in other ways very complex. It is simple in that there is a very clear and military-like chain of command. Yet prisons are very complex organizations in that they rely on most staff members operating individually, while following the same policies and, hopefully, subscribing to the same operational values and principles of the organization as a whole. Modern prison operations have moved well beyond the past years' emphasis on "lock them up, work them, and feed them." Expansion of inmate rights, the inclusion of rehabilitative programs, and many more prison service options have broadened the internal management puzzle for administrators to piece together. In addition, the interest of the public, the media, and other government agencies has required that prison administrators manage the "external environment" as well as they manage within the prison. Political and public interest in corrections puts additional demands on administrators, both for their time and for their sensitivity to what they do and how they do it.

From their inception in the early 1800s until approximately the 1960s, prisons were closed systems. **Closed systems** consist of only the internal environment and, for prisons, this meant what happened within the walls or fences, under the direct control of the warden and without much interest or any interference from external groups. The organization of a closed system, often with autocratic leadership, is usually very simple, and the mission and goals of the organization are determined and the leader enforces compliance. However, as a result of the external interest in the management of prisons and the fact that no modern entity

closed systems
prison systems that consist of only the internal environment, under the direct control of the warden, and without much interest or any interference from external groups

Prison staff and prison operations have changed since these staff worked at the United States Penitentiary in Leavenworth, Kansas, c. 1895. Courtesy of the Federal Bureau of Prisons.

operates by itself and without interacting with many others, correctional agencies have changed from closed systems to open systems. **Open systems** have frequent interactions between the organization and other groups to obtain resources, gain support, and accomplish goals. Snarr describes the open system of prisons as receiving numerous inputs from external government units and being held accountable for certain expected outputs from taxpayers and elected officials.[1] Prisons today interact with the local community; with their headquarters organization; with interest groups of employees, citizens, vendors, and other public agencies; and with other providers of correctional or counseling services to offenders.

open systems

prison systems that have frequent interactions between the organization and other groups, in order to obtain resources, gain support, and accomplish goals

Prison Chain of Command

Chain of command and unity of command are very critical to every organization, especially a paramilitary organization such as a prison. The chain of command in military organizations has ranks of individuals (privates, sergeants, lieutenants) relating to their place in the chain of command. The **chain of command** represents the vertical hierarchy in an organization, is identified in terms of authority, and is the order through which people receive directives from the person immediately above them and pass these directives to the person immediately below them. Most prisons have a military chain of command and use ranks such as sergeant, lieutenant, and captain. Figure 12.1 illustrates a simple prison chain of command from a warden to a correctional officer.

chain of command

the vertical hierarchy in an organization, identified in terms of authority, and the order through which persons receive directives from the person immediately above them and pass these directives to the person immediately below them

In a pure chain of command, wardens give orders to the associate warden in charge of security, who passes them on to the chief of security, who passes them on to security supervisors, who pass them on to correctional officers. Although prisons are adopting more modern management practices such as staff empowerment and participatory management, they are still (and will always remain to a great extent) very structured in the use of a chain of command; one of the most revered management practices within a prison is to use and not circumvent the chain of command. Wardens certainly interact with all levels of staff and seek their input on a variety of issues. However, prison operations rely on everyone completing their responsibilities in a consistent manner, and all levels of supervision must know what others are doing. Therefore, wardens would not directly instruct a correctional officer to carry out some function without advising or passing the instruction through correctional supervisors.

In a much more complex sense, prison administrators realize that policies and orders cannot cover every act and decision that must be made by a correctional

FIGURE 12.1 A Prison Chain of Command

officer or the way they react to a new experience not covered by policy. Therefore, wardens attempt to instill in all levels of the organization the important principles and values that should be considered when staff act independently. Through this *empowerment,* staff do not just receive orders continuously through the chain of command. They are trained in and follow policy, yet they are informed about and understand the approach and philosophy expected for carrying out their duties and therefore make decisions and perform duties consistent with these expectations.

The Warden

The earlier era of autonomous wardens running their prisons as they desired and answering to almost no one is over. However, most people still associate that style with the role of a warden, primarily as a result of the way wardens are portrayed in movies and on television. In the classic description of the rule of a strong warden in *Stateville: The Penitentiary in Mass Society,* Jacobs described the way Warden Joseph Ragen ran that prison for more than thirty years until the 1960s.[2] Stateville is a maximum-security prison in northern Illinois, and in the middle 1900s it held almost 4,000 inmates in a space designed for 1,600. The prison was filled with violent inmates and had a reputation as one of the toughest prisons in the United States.

Ragen ruled the prison with an iron fist and demanded strict adherence to rules by both staff and inmates. He maintained the prison as clean and spotless, made inmates march in straight lines when moving about the prison, and prohibited staff and inmate communication.[3] A 1996 book by Kantrowitz regarding Stateville and Warden Ragen further describes how Ragen meted out severe punishment to staff and inmates who violated his rules. Kantrowitz notes that Ragen believed his function was to synchronize men and their behavior in time and space, so the prison ran smoothly daily.[4] Jacobs further describes how Ragen was one of the last of the warden "village chieftains" who vanish as their society modernizes.

When Ragen retired, Stateville moved to a more modern management style, forced partly by federal court interventions, and shifted from discipline to

Warden Joseph Ragen of Stateville (Illinois) Penitentiary ran this overcrowded prison with an iron fist, answering to no one and representing a management style long gone in the governing of prisons. Courtesy of Corbis/Bettmann.

rehabilitation. Unfortunately, the change was too much and too fast for the prison, and the education programs that replaced the work programs were not enough to keep inmates productively busy. By 1978, conditions had deteriorated to utter anarchy; inmate gangs ran the prison, declaring certain areas of the prison off-limits to other inmates and staff under threat of death. It took several years to get Stateville orderly, clean, and under the control of staff again. This description is not to support an authoritarian style of prison management as under Ragen, but to point out how fragile the control and authority of staff can be in prison, how inmate groups will quickly move forward to fill any void in leadership and control, and how careful wardens and administrators must be as they attempt to change the culture of such a complex organization.

The Role of Modern Wardens

Today, there are no Warden Ragens, and that type of management and strict adherence to discipline would no longer work. Staff control prisons, but not through threats and intimidation. Control in modern prisons is maintained through a fair and just disciplinary system holding inmates accountable for their behavior, physical security and use of technology, work and treatment programs to keep inmates busy, consistent operations according to policy, and professional staff communication with inmates.

The move away from autonomous operations of each individual prison to more of a centralization of authority has greatly influenced the organization and operation of prisons. Freeman characterizes this development as the "era of bureaucratic wardens," in which wardens must now take responsibility for maintaining a safe, secure, humane prison environment in accordance with accepted standards (constitutional mandates, centralized policies, accreditation standards of professional organizations, and so on), and suggests several specific activities for the bureaucratic warden:

1. Development of the mission statement for the organization
2. Coordination of the budget process
3. Strategic evaluation and emergency planning
4. Management of daily activities
5. Management of labor relations
6. Formulation of policy
7. Supervision and professional development of staff[5]

The modern **warden** is a manager of resources, a role model for staff, and a juggler of priorities; he or she balances custody and treatment, is firm but fair, and knows how to manage the environment external to the prison as well as that within. When people would ask me what it is like to be a warden, I used to kiddingly say, "It is simple, all you have to do is know how to say no." Seriously, however, the role of a modern warden is one of the most complex management jobs in today's society.

Currently, the public has much more interest in and much higher expectations for corrections than in the past. This requires new roles for wardens in terms of how they provide leadership to their agency. Historically, wardens had much greater control over the *internal* operations of the prison and very little *external* interference. Traditional wardens were very autocratic, not just because they wanted to be, but because processes and procedures were not spelled out in a step-by-step manner by a centralized bureaucracy. In the early years of correctional administration, there were few written policies and wardens were often left

mycrimekit

Media—Video: **Modern Prison Operations.**

warden
the chief executive officer of a prison, responsible for the day-to-day operations

Modern prison administrators such as Warden Jesse Williams of the Allen Correctional Institution in Ohio have jobs as complex as CEOs of large organizations. Courtesy of the Ohio Department of Rehabilitation and Correction.

to their own devices and whims as to what should be accomplished and how it should be done. Today there are rules and regulations for every activity, from hiring staff to spending a budget to supervising an offender.

Previously, wardens had few demands on them to be *external managers* because corrections was of little interest to elected officials, the courts, or the media. Now prison administration is of interest to everyone. Crime is an important domestic priority, and the fact that we have so many prisons that require a large percentage of the annual state budgets means that their operation is of great interest to the public and elected officials. Only a few decades ago, federal courts would not get involved in correctional management issues. Today they are regularly and intensively involved in corrections and have even taken over and dictated how some correctional agencies must be managed. Media sources seldom reported on activities or occurrences in a prison. However, print and television media now regularly have stories about criminal justice and prison programs and operations.

These changes require wardens to have different skills and different leadership styles than in the past. Wardens were leaders at the top of their organizations who exercised power by giving orders and making decisions. Wardens maintained control by offering rewards and resources to staff in exchange for assistance in reaching the organization's goals and punished those who did not assist. James MacGregor Burns defined this type of leadership as "transactional," involving exchange relationships between leaders and followers.[6] **Transactional leaders** were the traditional authorities: those with position, power, and knowledge of a substantive area. They were able to provide answers and give direction for any issue the agency confronted. Staff respected them and looked to them for guidance and direction. Transactional leadership worked well in a prison with a relatively stable environment and with routine situations within the experience of the leader.

However, the challenges of modern times within a prison are not so routine, and the environment is not so stable. Change and changing situations are more

transactional leaders
traditional authorities within an organization who were involved in exchange relationships between leaders and followers; they provided answers and direction for any issue the agency confronted

Transformational leaders communicate constantly with staff, help them to learn and understand the values of the organization, and seek their input on policies and procedures. Photo by Richard P. Seiter.

the "routine," and it is impossible to have policies to guide how to deal with every new issue. Therefore, wardens cannot be the substantive experts for everything that goes on in the prison, because there are always new issues to confront that they have never experienced before. These factors require wardens to be less transactional and more like **transformational leaders**. Transformational leadership is much broader than transactional leadership. It is based on principles rather than practice and on motivating people to jointly address challenges and find solutions to new problems. Transformational leaders emphasize the set of values and principles to be used as guidelines in responding to issues. They help staff and the organization to learn and to work through problems in an adaptive manner. They involve staff in finding creative and innovative solutions to new problems. Wardens as transformational leaders must encourage managers and line staff to work together and must empower staff to be able to adapt to change and deal with new challenges and issues.[7]

One important role of a warden is to help set, define, and reinforce the desired culture of the prison. **Organizational culture** includes the values, beliefs, and behaviors that form the way of life within the organization. From the first day of recruiting a prospective staff member and throughout the basic training employees receive before they begin work in a prison, correctional agencies instill the desired organizational culture. For effective correctional agencies, the culture includes being professional, striving to meet high standards, being ethical, positively interacting with inmates, rewarding staff for good performance, and using state of the art correctional practices. Wardens as leaders of their prisons play critical roles in setting and reinforcing the organizational culture. Wardens are the role models for how to put the organizational culture in effect in the workplace. Staff take their cues on meeting standards, communicating with inmates, and rewarding excellence from the warden. The "An Insider's Experience" segment in *MyCrimeKit* illustrates this role of a modern warden.

It is sometimes thought that with all the court intervention, political oversight, centralized control from the state department of corrections, and extensive policies

transformational leaders
organizational leadership based on principles, while motivating staff to jointly address challenges and find solutions to new problems

organizational culture
the values, beliefs, and behaviors that form the way of life within that organization

mycrimekit
Insider's Experience: My Job as a Warden.

and procedures, the role of a warden as a leader has been watered down, and wardens do not have as much impact today as in the past. However, one thing that never changes about organizations is that they reflect the personality of the leader. The warden sets the tone for a prison, defines professional expectations, creates the level of standards for performance, and has a tremendous impact on the morale of staff and inmates. DiIulio, in *Governing Prisons*, writes, "the individual who heads a prison, or a prison system, can shape the organization in ways that help to determine the quality of prison life."[8]

When I was a warden, I was regularly reminded of the attention that inmates and staff pay to the warden: his or her mannerisms, behaviors, tone of voice, and way of speaking. Staff and inmates watch where a warden goes and what he or she does. As I walked around the prison yard and buildings, staff monitored where I was going. I would regularly overhear on someone's communications radio (I did not carry one), "Number 1 [call sign for the warden] on his way to the recreation yard." Staff closely watch what the warden does and says. On one occasion, a correctional officer asked me, "Are you feeling okay today? You don't seem to be walking with the speed and bounce you usually have." Prisons are like most organizations in that the leader sets the tone and contributes to the culture. But prisons, probably more than most other organizations, genuinely reflect the personality and professionalism of the warden.

Life for a Correctional Officer

correctional officer

staff person in a prison or jail who accomplishes the institution's mission by maintaining control and order within the prison

The role of **correctional officers** is critical within a prison and perhaps a role unique to prisons and jails. Their role is unlike other law enforcement jobs and unlike the treatment, services, or administrative functions within a prison. In 2005, there were 295,261 correctional officers working in state and federal prisons in the United States.[9] Correctional officers and supervisors make up approximately two-thirds of all staff in state and federal prisons. Of correctional officers in state prisons, 74 percent were male.[10] Between 2000 and 2005, the number of inmates grew at a faster rate than the number of correctional officers. The ratio of inmates to correctional officers increased from 4.8 to 1 in 2000 to 5.1 to 1 in 2005.[11]

The job of a correctional officer is to assist in the accomplishment of the mission of the prison by maintaining control and order within the prison. While prisons and jails have a considerably different mission, there is relatively little difference in the role that correctional officers play in the two types of facilities. Correctional officers are responsible for constant supervision of inmates and implementation of security procedures within a prison. Their world is both highly technical (in that security procedures require strict adherence to policy and attention to detail) and highly interactive (through personal communications) with inmates.

Officers have to be a variety of things to a variety of people. Their bosses expect them to be exact in performing their security duties, while being professional in their interaction with inmates. Their peers expect them to support each other and not show any weakness in how they do their job and supervise inmates. And inmates expect them to be fair and not hassle them for minor things that don't make a difference. Prout and Ross write, "The most successful [correctional officers] have a genuine interest in their work and a real desire to serve the needs of the correctional system, on the one hand, and the requirements of the inmates on the other . . . They recognize the social and political position of the prison in the larger society beyond the prison walls."[12]

Correctional officers and supervisors make up 60 percent of prison staff. Their role of maintaining order and control is basic to accomplishing the prison's mission. Photo by Richard P. Seiter.

The Daily Grind

The job of correctional officer can become a daily grind of routine duties, while dealing with stressful and possibly dangerous situations. Routine is not a negative in a prison; in fact, it is very important to the successful operation of a correctional facility. Routine in a prison environment is the consistent, scheduled, and expected activities that make up the day within a prison. Officers have to be consistent in the performance of required functions, and inmates have to know what is required of them in terms of such routines as count, locking down in cells, work call, and going to meals.

Correctional officers receive a specific assignment in a prison that can be anything from supervising inmates on a work crew or in a housing area to a non–inmate contact job in a tower or control center. Lombardo lists seven different categories of correctional officer assignments:

1. Living units—officers assigned to supervise housing areas
2. Work detail supervisors—officers who oversee work details such as sanitation or lawn maintenance details
3. Industrial shop and school officers—those who provide security and inmate accountability in these areas
4. Yard officers—the patrol and supervision of inmate movement in the compound or center yard of a prison
5. Administration building assignments—checking in visitors or working in the prison control center (opening doors, watching camera monitors, and maintaining radio communications)
6. Perimeter security—the armed posts of perimeter towers or mobile patrol vehicles
7. Relief officers—those who fill in a variety of assignments for officers who are sick or on a day off[13]

Each specific assignment has **post orders,** a detailed description of the activities that are required to be performed throughout the day that often includes the

post orders
the detailed description of the activities that are required to be performed throughout the day, often including the time they are to occur

Correctional officers must be consistent and follow policy in the performance of their required security duties. Photo by Richard P. Seiter.

time at which they are to occur. Post orders are different from general policies that spell out how to do an activity (such as handling security keys or conducting an inmate count) in that they are specific to the assignment and detail what to do rather than how to do it. As an example, the post orders for a housing unit officer on the day watch may include a schedule similar to the following list:

- 7:00 A.M.—Report for duty and read the logbook of the prior shift's activities.
- 7:30 A.M.—Open the housing unit doors for ten minutes to let inmates go to work.
- 8:00 A.M.—Start sanitation assignment by inmate crew.
- 10:30 A.M.—Open the housing unit doors for inmates returning from work.
- 11:00 A.M. to noon—Allow inmates to go to the dining room for lunch.
- 12:30 P.M.—Open housing unit door for ten minutes for inmates to go to afternoon work call.
- 1:00 P.M.—Do a census count. Inmates who are off duty may be allowed to go to recreation yard.
- 3:00 P.M.—Enter day's activities into the logbook, and sign over housing unit keys to evening shift officer.

The typical day for a correctional officer is a mix of routine activities and constant communication with inmates. Correctional officers' routine is described as follows: "One minute an officer is handing out toilet paper, the next he is explaining court papers. An officer is joking with two inmates playing checkers, and in an instant he is ordering everyone to their cells."[14] Even with a regular routine of activities, there is constant tension and uncertainty as well. An officer in the Nassau County Jail thinks of his role as the following: "One unarmed correction officer and 60 inmates, the jailer and the jailed, warily taking each other's measure, sparring for control."[15] Farkas and Manning suggest that correctional work is at times routine and monotonous, and at other times it is risky and unpredictable.[16]

Although most correctional officers enjoy the challenge of their jobs and have a considerable amount of pride in and loyalty for the correctional agency for which they work, there are always officers who are bitter and feel at odds with the mission of their agency. They may feel that their agency does not appreciate them, they may have been passed over for promotion, or they just may not be happy in their job. A good example of this is described in the book *The Keepers of the Keys,* in which Dickenson expresses the view of many activities within a prison from the eyes of a line correctional officer. He makes fun of the word PRIDE, the corrections department motto that stands for Professionalism, Respect, Integrity, Dignity, and Excellence. Dickenson sarcastically suggests that a better application of this motto is Perfunctory, Reaction, Indecision, Deny, and Excuse.[17]

mycrimekit

Media—Review: Daily
Life of a Correctional
Officer.

Stress and Danger

Stress is common among law enforcement personnel and particularly among correctional officers. This is not surprising because correctional officers must supervise individuals who are confined, yet do not want to be, and who constantly try to manipulate staff to make their confinement as interesting (many inmates enjoy the challenge of manipulating staff) and tolerable as possible. Stress results from many elements of the correctional officers' working situation. In a recent review of the nature and extent of stress among correctional officers, the National Institute of Justice found the following causes of stress:[18]

- Organizational sources of stress include understaffing, overtime, shift work, and supervisor demands. Understaffing results from high turnover or officers taking excessive sick leave and forces too much work on correctional officers in too little time, apprehension about the supervision of large numbers of inmates without potential backup support, and an inability to get time off for special occasions or family crises. Many officers say they welcome the extra pay of overtime, but too much overtime work quickly burns out staff. Officers in many states have to rotate the shifts they work (going from day to evening to night shifts), and this causes havoc with family life and problems with fatigue. And officers report that their supervisors are "always on you to do the job right, but you can't do it right [because of staff shortages]."[19]

- Work-related sources of stress include the threat of violence, inmate demands and manipulations, and problems with co-workers. Although there is no data available for the past decade, inmate assaults against correctional staff in state and federal prisons increased between 1990 and 1995 by nearly one-third (10,731 to 14,165), while the number of correctional officers increased by only 14 percent.[20] And the number of deaths in the line of duty has also increased. Data from the Correctional Peace Officers Foundation (an organization created to support surviving families of correctional officers slain in the line of duty at the hands of incarcerated felons), shows there were fourteen deaths between 1965 and 1979, 27 between 1980 and 1989, 98 between 1990 and 1999, and 76 from 2000 to 2007.[21] The constant challenge by inmates to correctional officer authority also causes stress. Problems with co-workers include competition for promotion and choice assignments, sexist attitudes from male to female officers, and concern for other officers' inappropriate or unprofessional behavior.

- There is stress from outside the system such as poor public image and poor pay. Many officers feel that their work is not understood or appreciated by the public, and low pay causes financial stress even for officers who enjoy their jobs and would like to make corrections a career.

Although stress is never going to be removed from staff working in a prison, some methods and programs have been identified to reduce the damage that stress can have on both employees and their families. Those believed most successful are staff training on stress reduction, family counseling services, and postincident counseling. Most correctional agencies conduct training for staff on the causes of stress, how to attempt to avoid stressful situations, and techniques for managing your own stress levels. Staff learn the benefits of an overall healthy lifestyle of diet, exercise, and seeking stability in financial and family issues and are trained in stress reduction techniques such as breathing exercises. Many agencies provide counseling and services for families, both so that they can better understand the work environment of the officer and to deal with stressful home situations that result in adding stress to the employee. Finally, after a critical incident such as an assault on a staff member, immediate and follow-up counseling is provided employees to give them the opportunity to recognize and manage the natural stress that results from such an incident.

Gaining Compliance of Inmates

The most important skill for correctional officers to learn is how to gain compliance from inmates without having to resort to threats, coercion, or taking disciplinary action and without risking the eruption of violence from an inmate refusing to abide by the orders of an officer. It is not easy to gain compliance from inmates already in prison, many of whom rebel against all authority and are serving long sentences with very little to lose. The overall prison disciplinary system creates the backdrop for gaining compliance by listing expected behavior and the penalties for failure to follow prison rules. Inmate classification systems also provide inmates

Correctional officers gain inmates' compliance through communication rather than threats and intimidation.
Photo by Richard P. Seiter.

A Case Study

Gaining Compliance

A new, young, and aggressive correctional officer (Robert Dole) at a high-security prison wants to establish himself as tough and unwilling to take anything from inmates. He is assigned as a yard officer, and as such watches inmates move across the prison compound from one building to another. As a part of his duties, Dole is to randomly pat-search inmates (similar to frisking by the police). With a pat search, officers move their hands over inmates' bodies to search for concealed weapons, drugs, or other contraband under their clothing. One day, Dole sees an inmate (Jones) he wants to pat-search, he points at Jones and calls out, "Hey, you come over here," and tells him, "Hold your arms out for a pat search," in a brusque and terse manner. When finished and finding nothing prohibited, he orders the inmate, "Ok, keep moving."

Jones realizes he will be searched from time to time, but doesn't like the attitude of disrespect he believes that Dole presented. He is angry about it, and when he arrives at his work area, he is confronted by his work supervisor who wants to discuss his recent poor performance with him. Jones is not a very responsible or mature person and reluctantly begins the conversation with his supervisor. When the supervisor asks why he did not complete a task assigned the previous day, Jones angrily responds, "You guys are just looking for me to screw up, and this is a bunch of bullshit." The supervisor tries to calm him down, but Jones just seems to get madder, and starts yelling at the supervisor. Soon, other correctional staff have to intervene, and while trying to move Jones away, Jones strikes one of them. He is forced to the ground by staff, handcuffed, and taken to the special housing unit.

This incident can happen almost anytime with Jones because of his lack of maturity and responsibility. However, when correctional officer Peter Smith is working as the yard officer, there are fewer such problems. Smith has been working at the prison for a few years and has become comfortable in gaining compliance through courtesy and respect. Smith handles pat searches as follows. When Jones approaches, and Smith decides to pat him down, he looks at Jones and says, "Mr. Jones, could you step over here please, I need to pat you down." When Smith finishes the search without discovering anything, he says, "That's it, Mr. Jones, thank you." Jones is not thrilled with being searched, but leaves feeling that Smith respects him through his courtesy. Both Dole and Smith accomplish their pat-down tasks, yet both create an outcome (Dole's bad, and Smith's good) as a result of how they did their job.

who behave the opportunity to move to less secure prisons with more privileges for inmates. Inmates are aware of these incentives and disincentives and understand that failing to follow orders of staff can result in punishment.

Therefore, staff do not have to *individually* take responsibility for making inmates follow rules. Correctional officers know they will win any war of wills, because an inmate who continues to refuse to comply with rules or a direct order from staff will be punished through the inmate disciplinary system. This allows correctional officers to be relaxed and confident in dealing with inmates. Effective officers use interpersonal communication skills to simply treat inmates as individuals, or as a work supervisor would treat an employee. Inmates know what they are to do and what the rules of a prison are, and reminding them of their responsibilities usually results in proper behavior.

The "A Case Study" box illustrates a good example of the do's and don'ts of gaining compliance.

Correctional Officer Careers

Many college students do not think about a career in corrections or seriously consider becoming a correctional officer after graduation, but a job as correctional officer is a tremendous experience and can provide a valuable foundation for future career opportunities. In fact, many states and the federal prison system expect staff to begin their prison employment as a correctional officer, and officers with a college degree may later move into a job as a counselor or case manager. However, the skills in security, interacting with inmates, and understanding the overall functioning of the prison that are gained in a correctional officer job make employees more valuable in any other role. The "Your Career in Corrections" box describes the role and functions of a correctional officer.

Your Career in Corrections

Correctional Officers

Correctional officers are the front line of prisons, jails, and other correctional facilities. Long ago, the term *guard* was used for the people in charge of overseeing inmates in prisons and jails. The role of guards, also referred to as *turnkeys* or *hacks,* was to simply guard inmates, unlock and lock their cells when necessary, march inmates from the cellhouses to another location for work or eating, and brutally enforce rules and discipline. The role of custodial staff in modern prisons has changed considerably, even to the point to which it is now a misnomer to refer to them as merely "custodial" staff. The contemporary term of *correctional officer* is used to describe the complex role of staff who carry out security functions within a prison. In 1993, the American Correctional Association (ACA) passed a resolution to encourage the use of the term *correctional officer,* because it much better describes their responsibilities of custody and control, which "require extensive interpersonal skills, special training and educations, and . . . correctional personnel are skilled professionals."[22]

Correctional officers (COs) are responsible for overseeing individuals who are detained in jail while awaiting trial or who have been convicted of a crime and are serving a sentence in prison. Their basic responsibility is to maintain order and contribute to the secure operation of the institution. They oversee various sections of an institution, such as a housing unit, yard or compound, perimeter fence, or inmate work or program area. Many tedious custodial functions must be carried out by COs for the maintenance of security and order. They must control doors and grills and lock and unlock them to allow only approved inmate movement. They must search inmates and areas, being alert for contraband such as drugs and weapons that can endanger staff and inmates. They also must conduct inmate counts to maintain inmate accountability and prevent escapes. They make inmates obey the rules and initiate disciplinary action. They often oversee inmate work crews, such as those assigned sanitation responsibilities, and ensure that the inmate crew performs the work at the accepted standard.

Even though some of the details of the CO job may seem unexciting and uninteresting, they are basics that must be accomplished. There are also many challenging roles for correctional officers. Officers must mediate between inmates, educate inmates about rules and procedures, and be a link between the inmate culture and staff management of a prison. COs cannot show favoritism in handing out discipline or enforcing prison rules or policy. Yet they also must use understanding and communication, while recognizing the individualism of every inmate. A major challenge of their role is that correctional officers must maintain order and gain compliance from offenders who are incarcerated against their will and who have a natural inclination to resent those who try to control them. If COs have to force inmates to comply with rules by using disciplinary actions or using force on a regular basis, prisons become the tense, violent, and dangerous world that people envision. Effective correctional officers gain compliance by communicating expectations, fairly enforcing rules, and treating inmates with respect and dignity.

Correctional officers also contribute to the rehabilitation of inmates in three ways: (1) by contributing to an environment of control without threats and tension, (2) by communicating with inmates in a relaxed and professional manner, and (3) by providing human services such as overseeing the feeding of inmates, referring sick inmates to medical staff, or assisting with recreational programs. COs do not have to be counselors or treatment specialists, but they contribute to rehabilitation through the manner in which they conduct themselves. While correctional officers maintain order and provide security, the manner in which they perform their tasks and communicate with inmates has a major impact on the overall prison environment. A brusque and harsh manner, an unwillingness to recognize genuine inmate issues, or a lack of respect for inmates creates an environment with constant tension between inmates and staff. But fair and impartial upholding of prison rules, a pleasant personality, respect for individual dignity, and understanding of the correctional officers' role in prisoner rehabilitation contribute to a relaxed environment with positive interaction between staff and inmates. The role of correctional officer has moved well beyond that of guarding inmates and now requires knowledge, training, good interpersonal communications, and sound decision making.

In 2005, there were 295,261 correctional officers working in state and federal prisons in the United States.[23] In a 2002 survey of officers, 78 percent were male, 70.4 percent were white, and 21.2 percent black. Seventy-seven percent of female COs and 3.5 percent of male COs worked in a prison with inmates of the opposite gender.[24] In 2008, annual salaries for correctional officers ranged from $27,540 for Texas to $45,288 for California.[25] In addition, correctional officers also regularly work overtime, and it is not unusual for officers to make an additional 20 percent of their base salary. Most prison systems do not require a college education for officers, but many require either experience or a two- or four-year degree. Many states and the federal prison system use correctional officer jobs as the entry level into the prison system; staff who are successful as officers gain communications and security skills that serve them well throughout their careers and often help them get promotions and additional career opportunities. Many college students do not think of using their degrees to become correctional officers. However, the job is excellent for gaining experience, developing skills, and beginning a successful career in corrections.

Not everyone will make a good correctional officer, and therefore correctional agencies must thoughtfully recruit, screen, and retain only people who have the talents and characteristics to contribute to the agency mission. It seems reasonable to believe that during good economic times, it is very difficult to recruit and hire outstanding individuals to serve as correctional officers, yet in difficult economic times, the recruitment process would be easier. The reality is that states work hard to recruit correctional officers all the time. In a recent article describing recruitment efforts by the Illinois Department of Corrections, Snyder describes the efforts of the agency to host recruitment and informational sessions to maximize the number of possible applications, yet also do rigorous physical and academic screening to ensure that individuals are appropriate candidates.[26] And Riley and Wilder point out that the key to hiring and retaining qualified officers includes the following: "Agencies must take the time at the beginning of the [hiring] process to identify the characteristics they desire in their staff."[27]

Correctional officers are the positions most critical to the day-to-day management of a prison. They constantly interact with inmates. They carry out the vital security functions that form the basis of safe operations. They set the tone for the prison by how professionally they carry out their duties. And they cannot have an "off" day without it being felt by inmates and other staff who interact with them throughout the workplace. Their jobs are challenging, stressful, and sometimes dangerous. Yet every day approximately 220,000 state and federal line correctional officers perform their jobs in a quality fashion, serve the public, and contribute to the overall criminal justice system in America.

The following "An Interview With" is a good illustration of how professional correctional officers see and do their jobs.

An Interview With...

A Correctional Officer

James Hall has been in corrections three years. He took a job as a correctional officer (CO) as a steppingstone to get into law enforcement. After working in a prison in Tennessee, he realized that he was safer than if he were in law enforcement. He started as a CO, held the position for thirteen months, and then was promoted to a sergeant (senior correctional officer) position. Seven months later, he was again promoted to lieutenant. In this role, he is an assistant shift commander. He enjoys his job, but finds it challenging.

Question: Can you describe your job and what you do as a correctional officer?

Lt. Hall: As a CO, I supervised inmates and made sure they did what they were allowed to do and behaved appropriately. Basically, my job was to develop rapport with the inmates to keep the unit functioning smoothly. It was not all that much different from a past job when I supervised people. Once you develop rapport with inmates, they are much more cooperative. This doesn't mean being a friend; it just means developing a relaxed and respectful way of communicating. Other responsibilities include keeping good counts, maintaining sanitation, and safety and security. I recognize inmates are human beings, and a little recognition promotes a large amount of cooperation from inmates. My first CO job was in segregation, the highest security unit of a prison, which holds inmates who break rules or need to be separated from others. I realized that the inmates will try to push my buttons just to get under my skin. But when they realize they depend on me, they knock it off and will behave appropriately.

Question: And what is your job like as a lieutenant?

Lt. Hall: As a lieutenant or assistant shift commander, I maintain the daily facility schedule. This includes direct supervision of COs and sergeants and responding to any type of facility emergency that might occur. An example of a facility emergency would be responding to inmates in a fight. There are many variables that I must consider to make sure the emergency is handled correctly, like the staff available, type of disturbance, and the location within the prison. Also, I make sure sanitation is high and that inmates handle all inside and outside maintenance and cleaning responsibilities. Also, I serve discipline against inmates. When an inmate breaks a rule, I start the disciplinary due process, everything occurs before the disciplinary officer receives the report.

Question: You said you came into corrections as a bridge for getting into law enforcement. What did you find that you expected or liked about the job?

Lt. Hall: The job is pretty much what I expected. I didn't realize that I could advance as quickly as I did. My mind-set was that I was going to do my job and do it well. The job requires hard work and commitment. I was interested in law enforcement because I wanted to serve the public, and law enforcement was a great way to do that. If we didn't stay on top of our jobs and keep the facility safe and secure, we would not be serving the public.

Question: You work among violent felons. Do you every feel threatened?

Lt. Hall: I feel safe in my job. There have been times when I was assigned to work with a partner that I felt did not care as much about safety and security as I did. That creates a dangerous situation. A safe environment is created by being security oriented, paying attention to detail, and observing what experienced officers do to maintain that environment. An unsafe environment can result from officer complacency. For example, during the night shift, when people are supposed to be asleep, a CO might believe there is no gang activity occurring and lets down his guard, but that really is when gang activity could occur.

Question: It has been said that a good day is one that is dull and routine. Do you every feel the daily grind becomes boring?

Lt. Hall: I don't think of it that way because a person will never experience the same day twice. Things change so much and can change so fast. Inmates and officers change a lot. And facility emergencies change things every day.

Question: How do you handle the stress of the job?

Lt. Hall: The job will be as stressful as you allow it to be. If you are relaxed and take what comes, then there is less stress. I don't allow it to affect my family life. I think it's a personality thing. I try not to stress about things in general. I don't bring stress from home to work or stress from work to my home.

Question: What are some of the keys to success in your job?

Lt. Hall: This is where rapport comes in. I respect inmates as people, they respect me and are willing to do tasks I ask them to do. Inmates already know what their jobs and responsibilities are, whether it's something as simple as making their beds before daily inspections and being ready for inspection. I don't get a lot of grief from the inmates because I don't give out a lot of grief.

Question: You sound as if you like your job. Would you recommend it to others?

Lt. Hall: I would recommend this job to others. There are some of my friends, however, I would not recommend this job to because I know they wouldn't survive. Some people are cut out for this type of work and some are not. A person will do well as a CO if they can make good decisions, are team oriented, and are not biased by different types of people. You have to deal with people from all walks of life. But it is a good job and can lead to a good career.

Recruiting and Retaining Correctional Officers

One of the very difficult challenges faced by correctional agencies is the recruitment of quality individuals as correctional officers who are interested in corrections as a career and committed to giving the job a fair trial to see if it works before quitting. As noted above, the job of a correctional officer can be stressful, dangerous, and tedious. There is little positive recognition and pay is often low for the challenge. A New York state correctional officer noted, "Police and firefighters are recognized as heroes. It's not as glamorous to be a correctional officer."[28]

Correctional agencies have experienced high turnover and low officer morale over the past decade. In 2005, Oklahoma starting pay for a correctional officer was $21,000, and the state prison system had five hundred vacant positions. In New York state, correctional officers were paid between $30,000 and $50,000 per year, but this was not adequate to draw qualified applicants in counties near New York City.[29] During 2000, correctional officers in the North Carolina prison system were paid approximately $21,000 per year, the vacancy rate was approximately 11 percent, and turnover was approximately 37 percent per year. The salary was the primary concern among officers, as a survey of those separating from employment found that 68.5 percent left because they were dissatisfied with the salary, and 37 percent would have stayed if the salary and shift schedules could have improved.[30] In 2001, the Texas prison system had 3,300 vacancies in its complement of 26,000 correctional officers.[31]

A 2003 survey by the American Correctional Association found that the average national turnover of correctional officers was 16.1 percent, and noncompetitive compensation was the most frequently cited reason for recruitment difficulty and the second most cited reason for retention. Demanding work hours, stress and burnout, and employees not understanding and finding they were not suited for the job were other factors in turnover.[32] Another survey of correctional staff in forty-five correctional systems identified recruitment problems as the failure to compete monetarily with law enforcement agencies and the rural location of correctional facilities.[33]

As problematic as these issues seem, they appear to be improving, as correctional agencies are addressing the most serious issues to recruitment and retention, and the recession and rising unemployment rates are making more people consider working as a correctional officer. To avoid retention problems and recruit people who want a career, the Michigan correctional system has consistently paid correctional officers higher rates than neighboring states. And in recent years, Delaware, Louisiana, North Dakota, Vermont, Virginia, and West Virginia have raised pay for correctional officers to make them more comparable to law enforcement officers. Delaware reported that after raising pay by 18 percent in 2006, their vacancy rate was the lowest in five years.[34] The state of Alaska is attempting to improve hiring practices by shortening the time it takes to get hired, as they have discovered that they lost many qualified candidates because of the long lag time between application and hiring. Correctional Commissioner Marc Antrim noted, "The goal is to keep the hiring process to no more than 60 days . . . a successful applicant generally should be able to walk in for their first day of work within 60 days of applying for the job."[35] In 2008, the Texas prison system increased correctional officer starting pay by 10 percent to just over $25,000 and within six months officers are paid approximately $28,500. In addition, in 2009, Texas also provided a $1,500 recruiting bonus if an applicant agrees to work at one of four designated understaffed correctional institutions.

Another way correctional agencies are improving recruitment and retention is positively changing the culture of their organizations. In a case study of Florida and Pennsylvania departments of corrections, it was noted that assessing and enhancing the workplace could reduce staff turnover.[36] And Corrections Corporation of America, the largest private prison company with over 17,000 staff, conducted interviews with staff to determine workplace satisfaction, and identified that the way correctional officers were treated by their first-line supervisors had a major impact on turnover. As a result, the company implemented a values-based training program for supervisors and have seen their retention rates improve as a result.[37]

Although recruitment and retention are improving among many correctional agencies as a result of thoughtful improvements in pay, culture, and working conditions, perhaps the biggest impact in reduced turnover is the recession. With severe economic times comes layoffs and high unemployment. During these times, individuals look for what they consider to be more stable employers, and correctional agencies are perceived to be "recession proof." What remains to be seen is if the improvements made by these agencies will help in retaining employees as the economy improves and jobs in non-correctional agencies are again available.

The Roles of Other Prison Staff

As can be seen from the extensive listing of prison jobs given earlier, there are many more than the two positions (warden and correctional officer). The warden provides leadership and sets the tone for the prison and correctional officers are key to successfully accomplishing day-to-day activities, but many other staff contribute to the accomplishment of the prison mission. Prison staff work either in an administrative capacity or in one of the three operational areas of security, programs or treatment, and service. Some of these roles are described next.

Other Security Personnel

uniformed staff
those prison or jail staff who work in the security or custody department and are responsible for the implementation of security policies and procedures

Prisons operate using a very clear chain of command, and nowhere in the prison is this clearer than with security or custody personnel. Most prisons (particularly high- and maximum-security prisons) have a deputy, associate, or assistant warden in charge of security. This is such an important part of prison operations and includes such a high number of staff (50 to 60 percent of all staff) that it is important to have a senior manager responsible for these functions. The next level of management is a midlevel manager and the highest-ranking **uniformed staff** person in the prison, often assigned the rank of major. This person supervises all security personnel and is the substantive expert on custodial policies and practices. The next level is the rank of uniformed security staff that oversee each eight-hour shift of operations in the prison. Assigned the rank of captain, they oversee the daily functioning and routine within the prison, assign work, and ensure that there are the required number of officers to cover all posts or assignments. Lieutenants are usually assigned to some of the most sensitive and explosive areas of the prison, such as the recreation area, industrial complex, and housing complex. Sergeants act either as senior correctional officers who are assigned the most difficult posts or as the direct supervisors of correctional officers who are responsible for ensuring consistency and quality implementation of policies.

Treatment and Program Staff

Treatment and program staff deliver programs (education, vocational, recreation, substance abuse, religious, psychological) to inmates. The following program or treatment departments are found in most prisons.

Psychological services	Education
Vocational training	Religious services
Substance abuse	Recreation

Each department includes midlevel managers who are substantive experts and manage each area and line staff who are primarily responsible for working with inmates in their specialty areas. The education program has teachers and vocational specialists, the religious programs have chaplains, and the psychological and substance abuse programs have counselors. These are usually specialty areas that require special training and education, and some require professional certification (to do a specific type of drug or mental health counseling) to deliver the programs.

In some prisons, these staff are called **professional staff**, although correctional administrators would rather call all their staff *professional* and use *program* or *treatment* to refer to this category of staff. There is also often a deputy/associate/assistant warden of programs or treatment who supervises these

professional staff
prison or jail staff in a specialty area that requires distinctive training and education and may also require a professional certification to deliver a program

Chaplains are responsible for making religious worship opportunities available to inmates. They lead services, counsel inmates, and oversee services provided by contract ministers. Photo by Richard P. Seiter.

functions. The role of the program and treatment staff is to deliver programs that assist inmates in their rehabilitation and preparation for reentry to the community. Inmates may take general education, English as a second language (ESL), or general equivalency diploma (GED) programs from teachers. They may receive individual or group counseling from staff psychologists, participate in substance abuse programs with drug and alcohol counselors, receive a vocational certificate from a class taught by a certified vocational instructor, or participate in a religious program overseen by a prison chaplain or a contracted priest, imam, rabbi, Protestant minister, or any other religious leader.

Services Staff

The third category of prison staff includes staff who operate departments providing inmate services within a prison. Included departments are prison industries, facility maintenance, business operations, food services, and medical care. The staff organization for each of these departments is different, but they are usually led by a deputy/associate/assistant warden for services (or operations). Service departments include the following:

Prison industries	Business administration
Facility maintenance	Human resources
Safety and sanitation	Health services
Staff training and development	Food services

Each department has a midlevel manager who provides substantive expertise and manages the budget, staff, and delivery of services within the department. Prison industries departments have factory managers to oversee the production of goods and several industrial specialists who supervise inmate workers. Similarly, facilities maintenance departments have managers and trades supervisors (electrical, carpentry, plumbing, heating and air conditioning) who supervise inmate workers. The food services department is organized similarly, with a manager and food service supervisors responsible for overseeing inmates who prepare and serve food. In most prisons,

Maintenance workers train and supervise inmates in performing work to maintain the prison. Photo by Richard P. Seiter.

the business offices operate the inmate commissary and laundry and have staff who supervise inmates in providing these services. Finally, the medical services department has a chief medical officer (physician) as the department head and nurses, pharmacy staff, and other health care delivery personnel to operate the prison infirmary.

This wide variety of jobs provides career opportunities for students with many different majors. In the "You Make the Decision" box, students must weigh the pros and cons and make a decision as to whether they would consider working in a prison.

The Prison Culture for Staff

Staff and inmates quickly learn the culture of a prison. Staff may say, "That's not the way things are done here," or tell inmates, "You need to forget how things were at your last prison, and get used to our way." They are talking about organizational culture, which is reflected in the way policies and procedures are actually carried out. State correctional agencies require the same policies to be implemented at every prison, yet the way policy is implemented differs based on the culture of the prison. Stojkovic and Farkas suggest that there is a "nexus between prison leadership and prison culture," meaning that the leadership of the prison directly influences the culture of the prison.[38] But in some prisons the culture may have continued so long or be so strong that leadership of the prison fails to affect it without lengthy and aggressive efforts.

Many models of prison organizational culture are based on a single focus, whether it varies by characteristics of officers or whether multiple cultures exist within the different levels of staff.[39] In the latter, a "three-cultures" model is presented by Farkas and Manning, suggesting that values, sentiments, and modes of thinking vary between three organizational levels: the lower participant or officer segment, the middle management segment, and the top command segment.[40] In this model, the perspective from which the group looks at their jobs influences the culture of the job level. The line officer level is influenced by their union or labor organization and most influenced by the internal organization of what occurs as they carry out the daily tasks in the prison. The middle management level identifies with either the line officer or top command level and is influenced by the internal orientation of their jobs and working environment. The top command level is consumed with administrative duties, must respond to and is influenced by external audiences (their agency bosses, the public, politicians), and looks beyond the daily activities to longer-term objectives.

Even though all three levels may have a distinct culture, the levels may also influence each other so that there is a merger of cultures, resulting in one blended rather than three distinct cultures. This blending is considered a positive development, and strong and visionary leaders work to bring convergence among the cultures of the three levels. A desired result is that the top command influences the other two to see the long-term good (vision) of the agency and prison, rather than reflect that of the day-to-day activities and strictly internal culture of the line officers. The most effective prisons have only one dominant culture, although there is no denying that all individuals and groups are most strongly influenced by what they desire from their job and the way they look at their work.

Two types of culture develop within a prison, one dealing with the management style of command to line staff and one dealing with the relationship between staff and inmates. The style of **management culture** has to do with the way leadership deals and communicates with subordinate staff and falls into a continuum between *autocratic* and *empowered*. The **relationship culture** is the style by which staff view and communicate with inmates and falls into a continuum between *authoritarian* (gaining compliance by threats and intimidation) and *reasoned* (gaining compliance

management culture
a culture based on the way prison leadership deals and communicates with subordinate staff; it falls into a continuum between autocratic and empowered

relationship culture
a culture based on how staff view and communicate with inmates; it falls into a continuum between authoritarian and reasoned

Autocratic	Moderate	Empowered
Staff must follow policy or check with supervisors before making decisions		Staff make decisions with full knowledge and consistent with prison principles and values

FIGURE 12.2 A Continuum of Management Cultures in a Prison

through incentives and disincentives). Both types of prison culture greatly affect the overall tone in which the prison is operated. Staff and inmates are aware of the culture and adapt and respond as expected, and their behavior therein perpetuates the continuation of the culture.

The management culture of a prison is represented in Figure 12.2. There is no question that the culture of Stateville under Warden Ragen was one of autocratic rule. Staff never made a decision that was not checked with their supervisors. In an autocratic prison culture, staff strictly follow the rules and cannot make decisions to address issues outside of policy. In an empowered culture, employees are knowledgeable about the principles, values, policies, and expected outcomes in the prison, and make decisions consistent with the expected outcome. Seiter writes,

> Empowerment involves providing employees with the principles and values of the organization, along with the desired outcomes (vision and mission), and allowing them to make decisions and respond to situations that are consistent with the principles and values, and move toward the desired outcomes.[41]

Throughout history, most prisons have operated toward the autocratic end of the management culture continuum, partly because of their development as paramilitary organizations, but also because of fear that line staff would make mistakes that could result in dire consequences of loss of life, escapes, or riots. However, a style of empowerment is important in modern prisons for several reasons. First, there is continuous change, and correctional agencies have difficulty developing routine procedures that can be counted on to work over time. Second, rapid changes result in situations that have never before been encountered, and no guidelines on how to respond are available. Third, prison employees are better educated and better trained than in the past, have experienced a world of rapid change, and are prepared to meet never before confronted challenges. Finally, today's employees demand to be involved in the organization and cringe at a rigid bureaucracy that expects them to follow orders and carry out prescribed functions without knowing the reasons behind them.

The prison culture reflecting the relationship between staff and inmates is also critical within a prison environment. This cultural continuum is depicted in Figure 12.3. In the authoritarian culture, staff are threatened by inmates and believe that they cannot maintain control of the prison unless they constantly reinforce their position of authority by threats and intimidation. In such a prison, staff are seen as "weak" if they are polite or show respect and courtesy to inmates. In the reasoned culture, staff know that they have the power of sanctioning inmates with

Authoritarian	Moderate	Reasoned
Staff demand compliance from inmates through threats and intimidation		Staff use agency incentives and disincentives for gaining compliance from inmates

FIGURE 12.3 A Continuum of Staff-Inmate Cultures in a Prison

disincentives and rewarding inmates with incentives, and they maintain control through fairness in making these decisions. Therefore, they interact with inmates in a relaxed and congenial fashion, without losing authority or appearing weak. Prisons that operate on the more reasoned end of the continuum develop a less stressful and tense long-term environment.

Leaders are responsible for creating the culture within an organization. Wardens set the tone and culture by the management style they adopt and the style of staff-inmate interaction they support. The "A Case Study" box gives a good example of a warden taking a leadership role in creating a positive culture within a prison. It represents a real situation I faced after a riot at a prison where I was the warden.

A Case Study

Setting the Tone

After the riot at the prison, the warden observed that staff were taking a much more authoritative approach in their interactions with inmates. More staff elevated their voice and took on a tone of discipline when talking to inmates, and statements by staff to direct an inmate to change their behavior became more like "barking orders" than reminders of the rules. Although these types of interactions are necessary in certain situations and with certain noncompliant inmates, when they tend to become the regular rather than infrequent method of interaction, it sets a climate of tension and hostility that can make the environment more stressful and less stable for both staff and inmates. The warden felt that this behavior was the result of the riot, the fact that staff had witnessed a few inmates destroying property and assaulting staff, and that some staff were fearful and less confident. As a result, staff began to treat all inmates as violent and dangerous and became more terse and disrespectful in their communications. The warden, in conjunction with his top staff, developed a plan to change this interaction style into one that was more relaxed and positive. First, he initiated activities to directly respond to staff members' fear of further victimization by inmates. This included "hardening" the prison by replacing wooden doors with metal ones and putting bars over windows to create "safe havens" for staff if another dangerous situation broke out. Staff were trained in disturbance control methods, boosting their confidence that they could handle a violent situation if one occurred.

As staff felt more comfortable with their personal safety, the warden set out to improve the positive communication between staff and inmates. Additional training was provided to staff regarding positive interactions and proper interpersonal communication. The warden made a videotape shown to all staff of him discussing the importance of positive staff-inmate interactions. On the video, the warden explained the reasons for such positive interaction, emphasizing that it was not to be soft on inmates, but that this approach in effect enhanced the security and safety of the institution. As well as reducing tension and lessening the likelihood of an inmate spontaneously responding with violence in a confrontational situation with staff, positive communication opened the door to inmates sharing important intelligence with staff about planned inmate misconduct or potential inmate gang activities. Supervisors were asked to immediately correct communication that did not comply with this approach by line staff and use this as a key discussion point in all staff evaluations. The warden also appealed to line staff to recognize the problems that inappropriate communication caused and to correct their fellow employees who destabilized the environment and made it more dangerous for everyone else.

These activities worked well over time. Fewer staff used harsh and authoritative tones of voice when unnecessary. More staff began to repeat the importance of positive communication and prided themselves on their ability to gain inmate compliance without having to "bark orders" and demand it. As staff learned that they maintained order more effectively through treating inmates with courtesy and respect, while still consistently and fairly enforcing rules, they operated with increased skill and success. The overall climate of the institution returned to one of positive staff and inmate interaction, a relaxed and less stressful environment, and actually a reduced level of disciplinary infractions for failure to follow orders or insubordination by inmates.

Female Correctional Officers in Men's Prisons

Two or three decades ago, women were not allowed to work in men's prisons as correctional officers; it was believed they would not be able to perform effectively and safely. The arguments against women working as correctional officers included "(1) women weren't strong enough, (2) their presence would be disruptive to prison operations (inmates would not follow their orders or would fight for their attention) and (3) the privacy of male inmates would have to be violated."[42] The only female employees in men's prisons held jobs with no inmate contact, such as clerks, secretaries, or mail workers.

However, Title VII of the 1964 Civil Rights Act, amended in 1972, proscribes employment discrimination on the basis of race, religion, sex, and national origin and therein granted women the legal right to seek employment as correctional officers in men's prisons. Women quickly filed several cases with the Equal Employment Opportunity Commission (EEOC), claiming discrimination on the basis of sex by criminal justice agencies. A provision of Title VII, however, states that some discriminatory practices might be allowed if there is "a bona fide occupational qualification (**BFOQ**) reasonably necessary to the normal operation of that particular business or enterprise."[43] Therefore, correctional agencies hesitated to hire women for correctional officer positions, believing that the risk to security and loss of privacy for inmates would be considered an acceptable BFOQ exception.

In 1977, the U.S. Supreme Court decided the case of **Dothard v. Rawlinson** and first addressed the BFOQ exception.[44] Rawlinson was a woman who was denied a position as a correctional officer in an Alabama men's prison because the state prohibited women in any position that would require contact with male inmates. The Court ruled that a BFOQ prohibiting female correctional officers was allowable because of the deplorable conditions of the Alabama prisons and the presence of predatory male sex offenders as inmates. In *Dothard*, however, the Court did not address the issue of privacy for inmates with regard to the presence of female correctional officers. In 1979, in **Gunther v. Iowa**, the U.S. District Court of Iowa did not find the same predatory environment in a medium-security Iowa prison that was believed to exist in the *Dothard* case within a maximum-security Alabama prison. The court therefore determined that inmate privacy was not a valid reason to refuse to hire women as correctional officers, finding that the state could create staffing and assignment patterns to avoid infringing on inmate privacy. The *Gunther* decision eliminated the major reason that states claimed a BFOQ in not hiring female correctional officers, and most states moved quickly to hire women.

By January 1, 1993, women represented 17.3 percent of the approximately 169,000 correctional officers in state and federal prisons; by January 1, 2002, 22.7 percent of the 218,000 total U.S. correctional officers were women, and 39,059 (77 percent of the total employed) of these female officers worked in men's prisons.[45] By 2005, 26 percent of all correctional officers in state prisons were women.[46] This progress did not come easily, however, as the historical bias against and assumption that female officers would have different attitudes and carry out their duties differently from their male counterparts persisted. Some of the early negative reaction by male correctional officers to women working as co-workers is apparent in the following survey results:

> Out of a hundred men interviewed, only a handful were at all supportive of [women working as correctional officers] . . . . The most frequently voiced reasons for opposing the presence of women were that they impair the security of the institutions as a whole and jeopardize male guards' own safety.[47]

BFOQ
a bona fide occupational qualification reasonably necessary to the normal operation of that particular business or enterprise that may allow for some discriminatory practices to occur

Dothard v. Rawlinson
a 1977 U.S. Supreme Court case regarding a woman who was denied a position as a correctional officer in an Alabama male prison; the Court ruled that a BFOQ against women correctional officers was allowable because of the deplorable conditions of the Alabama prisons and the presence of predatory male sex offenders as inmates

Gunther v. Iowa
a 1979 case in the U.S. District Court of Iowa in which the court determined that inmate privacy was not a valid reason to refuse to hire women as correctional officers; the *Gunther* decision eliminated the major support used for the BFOQ by states in not hiring female correctional officers

Female correctional officers are now a regular part of and play a valuable role in prisons for male inmates. Photo by Richard P. Seiter.

However, studies have found either no or only minor differences in relation to the attitudes and job performance of women compared to men.[48] A study of female correctional officers in California in 1983 found that women performed as well as men as correctional officers. However, men continued to perceive women as less effective when the situation required physical strength or a violent emergency existed.[49] A study within the Federal Bureau of Prisons also found no lapse in performance, but did find that female correctional officers experienced hostility and sometimes sexual harassment from male staff and inmates.[50]

Interesting findings resulted from a survey of male inmates who were asked to rate female correctional officer performance compared to male correctional officers. Cheeseman and colleagues found that higher-security inmates were more likely to favorably rate the performance of female officers than lower-security inmates. The authors write, "Specifically, prisoners classified as close custody

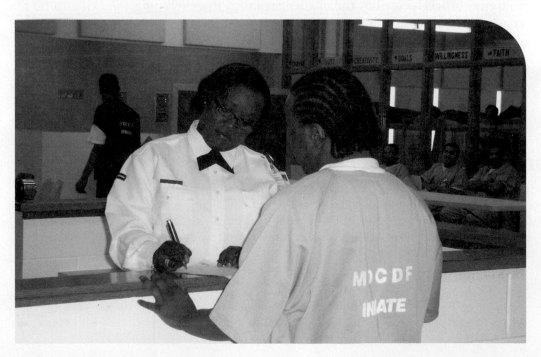

Although many women now work as correctional officers in men's prisons, they still face challenges because they are women working in a predominantly male environment. Photo by Deborah L. O'Brien.

were significantly more likely than minimum or medium custody inmates to agree that female staff performed as well as male staff when responding to stabbings, responding to physical fights, settling verbal disputes among inmates, and preventing riots or disturbances."[51]

In a report of interviews with female jail officers published in 1998, the findings were that female officers believed that they received paternalistic treatment, were excluded from work socialization opportunities, had higher job stress, and had more limited career prospects.[52] The findings further suggested that female correctional officers experience various problems stemming from sexism and sexual harassment by their male co-workers, which could be reduced if the jail administrators demonstrated a commitment to the thorough integration of women within the formal and informal organizational structure. With the passing of time, women have been more openly accepted into male prison environments, and in most states and county jails women receive the same work and promotional opportunities as men.

In fact, there are many benefits to women working as correctional officers. One is that the style of supervision by female correctional officers of male inmates may bring a calming and normalized influence to a prison. Pollock writes:

> *Women officers tend to ask inmates to do things rather than tell them. Female correctional officers foster personal interest in the inmate and use the relationships they develop as a technique of control. This relieves some of the tension found in prisons for men and encourages male prisoners to interact with correctional officers rather than cultivating isolation and separate subcultures.*[53]

Although modern correctional administrators accept women as able to effectively perform the role of correctional officers in men's prisons, some stereotypes still exist, and women in some correctional facilities are forced to endure a lack of respect that is given to male officers by inmates or even other correctional officers. Even though these attitudes are not based on fact or performance, prisons for male inmates are very male-dominated places, and these stereotypes and perceptions will be difficult to totally overcome. The "A Look Into" box reflects the challenges women still face in a predominantly male environment. A female correctional officer describes the challenges faced in developing the skills to be an effective female officer in a men's prison.

A Look Into...

Female Correctional Officers in Male Prisons

Even though there are benefits in having female correctional officers working in prisons housing male inmates, there are naturally challenges to those women who choose to work as officers in this setting. Janel Gonzales is a correctional officer at the Madison Correctional Institution in London, Ohio. As a new officer (employed approximately nine months), she provided this look into the challenges faced by a woman correctional officer. Officer Gonzales lists some of the issues faced when working with male inmates and in an almost all-male work environment.

"I did not plan to be a correctional officer, but was looking for a career with a stable job and good benefits. A friend worked at the Ohio Reformatory for Women as a correctional officer (CO), and she said the job was a 'piece of cake,' even though she said you had to be on your toes and do your job correctly.

"I got hired by the state of Ohio and went through the Correctional Training Academy basic course. My training included courses on security, interpersonal skills, and self-defense. The most useful thing at the Academy was the opportunity to spend time with two instructors who had been COs. They were really honest and told me what to expect. They said that inmates will constantly try to play with you or get things over on you. And they were right. They advised me that when working as a CO supervising a housing unit never let inmates do things outside policy, such as hang out in the television rooms, have inmates from other dorms come into the dorm to braid their hair, or leave the back fire door open for ventilation. So I would tell inmates that if it wasn't policy, they couldn't do it, even if other officers allowed them to do it. I was glad I listened to the instructors, because I soon discovered that inmates will lie, just to see if they could get me to violate a minor policy. If I had done so, it would have led to more major requests for violations.

"One of the most challenging things is to learn how to get compliance from inmates. All correctional officers are different in how they do their jobs; you have to find out and do what works for you. I am a type that if what an inmate is asking just doesn't sound right (and everything they ask isn't covered by policy), I just don't let them do it. Once they find out that you won't vary on your answers, they make it easier on you.

"There are different issues for women than for men correctional officers. First, inmates want to get physically close to you when they talk to you. I just tell them to 'get back' to talk to me. The inmates get male attention all day long, but since there are not that many female officers, it provides something different and they seek female attention. They will come up and ask questions just to talk to you: 'Do you have a kite?' [a form to make a request to staff] or 'Has legal mail been delivered?' Usually they already know the answer to the question. This is not threatening, as I know why they do it. I do not feel stalked, that they just want attention because I am a woman. Female COs face stress different than male COs. From the first day you come into the prison, inmates watch and expect certain things of you. You have to be careful

about joking around with inmates or spending any extra time talking to a particular inmate. They may get the wrong impression that you are being too friendly, and it doesn't take long for other inmates and staff to start wondering if there isn't something going on. That's why I won't joke around with inmates.

"There is additional stress because inmates will try to become romantically involved with female staff. You just have to be very careful about not doing anything that would give inmates an impression that you are that kind of person. But you also have the opposite challenge in that many male inmates don't want a woman telling them what to do. They will look at you funny, or sideways, or second guess it. I just look back and say, 'Oh yeah, I said it.' That never changes, because every time I go into a dorm, there are new inmates. They always want to try you, and you always have to prove yourself.

"People ask me if I am fearful for my personal safety, but I never have been. I know that I can't stop everything from happening. An inmate could walk up behind me at any time and do something. But officers quickly become very resourceful. We have these 'man down,' or Spider alerts, that immediately let other staff know you are in trouble. That is a safeguard that gives me confidence. And I am just not afraid of the inmates. I don't even acknowledge inmates who try to be intimidating. There are some times when an inmate sits somewhere and just stares at you. When they do this, I believe you have to be loud with them and embarrass them. I will ask them if they have something to ask me, and when they say no, I tell them to take their eyes off me; look somewhere else.

"There are also issues female COs face with male staff. When I started work, a male CO told me, 'I disagree with women being in a male prison.' I just looked at him and said, 'Well, I am here.' You cannot be worried about what others think, you just have to do your job. Really, most staff see me and the other women just as other COs.

"The bottom line is that to be successful as a woman in a male prison, you first have to enforce the rules consistently. You can't let anyone take advantage of you. Keep your eyes and ears open. If you learn how to successfully work with inmates, you can probably do anything. I encourage women to work as a CO. It is definitely hard to do and to get comfortable with the job, but once you do, it is worth it."

Summary

In this chapter, the people who work in prisons were described and discussed. The goal of the chapter is for students to better understand the challenges these staff face, the contributions they make, and the environment and culture in which they work. Although most people think of wardens and correctional officers as staff of prisons, there are many more categories of job specialties within a prison. A prison needs almost every category of specialist that it takes to operate a small city. There must be staff to maintain the facility, provide food services and health care to inmates, offer rehabilitative programs, hire and train other staff, manage the finances and budget, and maintain a secure and safe environment.

At the top of the prison chain of command is the warden. Wardens have become almost mythical individuals in the American culture. Partly because of their challenging job of maintaining order among hundreds or thousands of convicted felons, partly because they must direct a diverse workforce often represented by a union and sometimes at odds with the mission of the agency, and partly because of the way in which they are portrayed in movies and television shows, wardens are usually thought of as autocratic, harsh and insensitive to inmates and staff, and often unethical. However, modern wardens have to be outstanding managers of people and resources and must rely on education, intelligence, and experience more than simply a dominating personality.

Correctional officers make up the line position that is critical to the day-to-day operation of a prison and deals directly with inmates. Their job is not glamorous, not easy, and generally underappreciated. Correctional officers have challenging jobs because inmates are constantly trying to manipulate and challenge them and to avoid following rules. Officers must enforce security procedures, and lapses can cause escapes, assaults, and even riots. Officers are key in setting the tone of interaction between staff and inmates. They can perform their duties in a brusque and authoritative manner or act with more respect and courtesy toward inmates. The latter is much more effective in maintaining a more relaxed and less tense environment, yet requires maturity and confidence by the officers to communicate effectively.

Two key issues in a prison are the overall culture and the role of female correctional officers in men's prisons. The culture is the approach or manner in which policies and procedures are carried out within a prison. A prison adopts a culture regarding how staff communicate with each other and how staff communicate with inmates. The warden and other leadership within a prison are critical to establishing and maintaining a positive organizational culture. The use of women as correctional officers has also become a controversial issue in men's prisons. Although banned from working in men's prisons only twenty-five years ago, female officers are now recognized as valuable employees both in how they perform their jobs and in how they contribute to a positive organizational culture.

Key Terms

closed systems
open systems
chain of command
warden
transactional leaders
transformational leaders

organizational culture
correctional officer
post orders
uniformed staff
professional staff
management culture

relationship culture
BFOQ
Dothard v. Rawlinson
Gunther v. Iowa

Review Questions

1. Prisons have many staff other than correctional officers. List five other staff positions within a prison.

2. What is a closed and open system of a prison?

3. How does staff empowerment expand the effectiveness of prison operations beyond the traditional use of issuing orders through the chain of command?

4. What is the role of a modern prison warden?

5. How does transformational leadership differ from transactional leadership?

6. What percentage of all prison staff are correctional officers or correctional supervisors?

7. Describe the job of a correctional officer.

8. What is a post order?

9. What are three causes of stress for correctional officers?

10. How do correctional officers gain the compliance of inmates?

11. List three types of treatment departments within a prison.

12. What are service departments within a prison?

13. What are the two types of culture that can develop within a prison?

14. What did the case of *Gunther v. Iowa* decide, and how did it affect employment of women as correctional officers in men's prisons?

15. Approximately what percentage of state and federal correctional officers is female?

You Make the Decision...

Do I Want to Work in a Prison?

One issue that confronts students considering a career in corrections is whether they want to work in a prison. Often the first reaction is negative. Students think, "i don't want to work in a prison. I didn't get my college degree to work in that type of environment. I want a more professional job." However, if they become more familiar with prisons, their operation, the jobs and roles of various staff, and the quality of the people who work there, they often reconsider their earlier hesitancy to work in a prison.

In this "You Make the Decision," you are to consider the pros and cons of working in a prison.

Think of the various roles and issues for staff that work in a prison described in this chapter. Create a list of all the good things about prison jobs, such as stability, benefits, and opportunities for advancement. Then create a list of the things that are not so positive about working in a prison, such as danger, stress, and relatively low pay.

Once you have created your lists, imagine what it would really be like to work in a prison, and decide (individually or in a group) whether you would take a job working in a prison.

Chapter Resources on mycrimekit™

Go to mycrimekit.com to explore the following study tools and resources specific to this chapter:

- **Practice Quiz:** multiple-choice, true/false, short-answer, and essay questions to help students test their knowledge
- **WebQuests:** learning activities built around Web searches
  - **Bureau of Labor Statistics:** www.bls.gov
- **Insider's Experiences:** "My Job as a Warden"

- **Seiter Videos:**
  - See wardens discuss prison management
  - See the role of a correctional officer discussed
- **Career Center:** A Career as a Correctional Officer
- **Flashcards:** Sixteen flashcards to test knowledge of the chapter's key terms

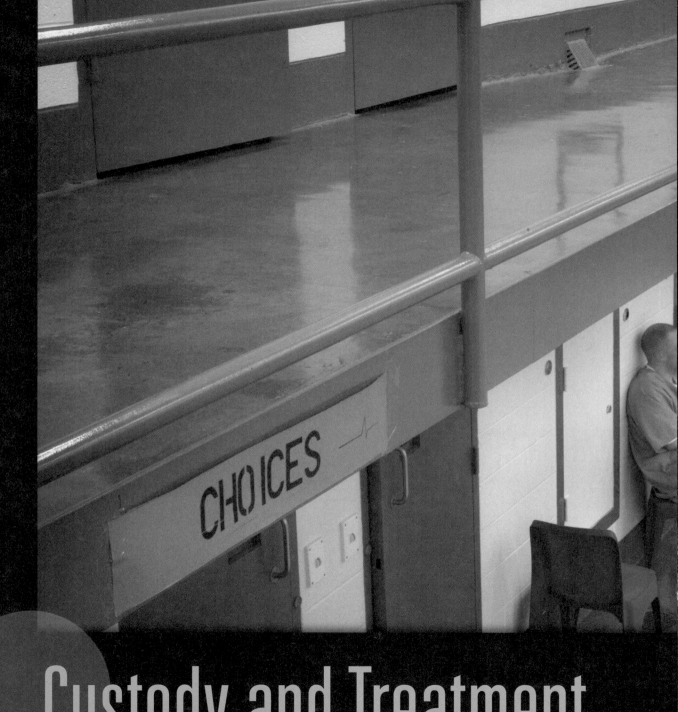

CHOICES

Custody and Treatment

After reading this chapter, you should be able to:

1. List the eight types of activities that contribute to the security and custody functions within a prison.

2. Define inmate accountability and describe the activities by which prison officials ensure that inmates are accounted for.

3. Identify the three types of counts and how they are carried out in a prison.

4. Explain how contraband comes into the possession of inmates and specify procedures to prevent this from occurring.

5. Describe the two categories of inmate assignments in a special housing unit.

6. Discuss the environmental factors and precipitating events that can combine to cause an inmate riot.

7. Outline the functions and operations of the three types of emergency teams in a prison.

8. Define *rehabilitation* and describe its evolution throughout the history of prisons in the United States.

9. Describe the various types of education and vocational programs provided in prisons.

10. Explain the scope of mental health needs of inmates and how prisons provide programs that meet these needs.

11. Identify the level of substance abuse among the inmate population and the level of program opportunities provided in prisons.

12. Trace the history of prison industry programs in terms of the way inmate labor was used and the markets that were available.

13. Describe the importance of prison religious programs and how they are delivered.

Introduction

The mission of prisons is to create a safe and secure environment, while offering inmates programs that can help them in their rehabilitation and reentry to the community. The mission has two dominant themes: custody and treatment. Custody and treatment are the principal functions within a prison, and rather than being two parallel prison functions, they often seem in total conflict with each other. To create a safe and secure environment, *custody*, the activities within a prison that control inmate behavior and maintain order, must be accomplished in a way that reduces the likelihood of escape or violence. Prisons must be secure to prevent escapes and must be safe so that inmates and staff can live and work in the prison without constant fear of assault and injury.

The task of controlling behavior and maintaining order envisions a picture of total and absolute control by correctional officers and an environment in which inmate rights and individual characteristics must be secondary to security. Can behavior be controlled and order maintained at the same time that treatment occurs within a prison? *Treatment* is the creation of an environment and provision of rehabilitative programs that encourage inmates to accept responsibility and to address personal disorders that make success in the community more difficult. The image of treatment within prisons is envisioned as just the opposite of custody. How can prison counselors and treatment staff treat inmates in a "soft and caring" manner, get inmates to acknowledge their weaknesses, and initiate a program of rehabilitation within an environment that is totally controlled and focused on order? The reality is that neither of these suggested images of prisons is accurate. The challenge for prison management is to prudently balance custody and security with treatment and rehabilitation. This balance is not easy to accomplish, and a movement in emphasis to either custody or treatment can upset the balance and lead to serious problems.

In this chapter, the activities prison officials undertake to create a safe and secure environment and to provide inmates the opportunity to address problems and prepare for release are described. Also, the difficulty of maintaining the delicate

Physical security, such as a secure perimeter fence with razor ribbon, is one of the many elements essential to a safe and secure prison. Photo by Richard P. Seiter.

balance between custody and treatment is explained, and the methods by which prison administrators attempt to maintain a dual emphasis on both is presented. For prisons to be safe and secure there must be sufficient physical security, consistent implementation of security practices, methods to control behavior and prevent inmates from possessing dangerous items, and preparation to reduce the likelihood of or to respond to inmate unrest. For prisons to provide effective rehabilitative services there must be assessment of needs and provision of a variety of programs (substance abuse, mental health, religious services, education and recreation, and work opportunities) to address these needs and prepare inmates for release. And, for prisons to accomplish their dual mission in a balanced fashion there must be skilled prison leadership guiding the delicate balance for both security and treatment.

Security and Custody within a Prison

What are security and custody within a prison? Most experts would suggest that they include all the activities that provide for the overall control of inmate behavior, in a way that reduces the likelihood of escape or violence. The most immediate goal of prison operators is to have a safe and secure prison. A safe prison is one in which staff and inmates are relatively safe from assaults or other violent acts. A secure prison is one in which inmates are prevented from escaping and unable to get to prohibited areas of the prison.

The question of how to maintain security and custody within a prison is one that many people think should be very simple, because they perceive that inmates are locked in cells most of the time; people believe that when inmates are out of the cells, they are under the close supervision of many correctional staff. Yet those who work inside correctional institutions recognize that maintaining security and custody is very complicated and requires an integration of several functions and activities within a prison. In reality, inmates are in their cells only a few hours a day and, at other times, they actively participate in work, programs, and leisure activities. Seiter writes,

> There are no simple solutions to creating a safe and secure environment. . . . Inmates are serving longer sentences, often have little hope for a quick release, and may see few incentives for positive behavior. Long sentences can also create frustration and a sense of bitterness and unfair treatment on the part of inmates toward staff. The increasing percent of the inmate population that are youthful, impulsive and gang affiliated heightens the likelihood of violence. . . . Maintaining a safe and secure prison involves the integration of several elements within the prison.[1]

The following eight types of activities combine to contribute to the security and custody functions within a prison and are more fully described in this book.

1. *Effective inmate classification systems.* The goal of an inmate classification system is to separate offenders according to risk of violence and escape, and to match offender needs with correctional resources. The physical security of a prison should be designed to match these risks of violence and escape.
2. *Physical security within a prison.* Prisons are categorized as minimum-, medium-, or maximum-security in terms of the physical security provided,

including the type of fences and perimeter security, housing, and construction material used. Physical security also includes the use of modern technology and physical barriers to keep inmates in or out of certain locations within the prison. Although many observers tend to over rely on physical security, more than that is required to have a safe and secure prison, as prison design and technology "cannot substitute for well-trained staff and good security practices. . . ."[2]

3. *Consistently implemented security policies and procedures.* The importance of professionally developed and consistently implemented policies and procedures for controlling inmate behavior was noted previously. The performance of sound security practices is one of the most critical elements in accomplishing security and custody within a prison.

4. *Control of inmate movement and accountability.* Inmates are allowed to move from one prison location to another for much of the normal day. Yet these movements must be established in a manner that allows staff to maintain inmate accountability at any time during the day.

5. *Control of contraband items.* There are several items that inmates are not allowed to possess (called contraband), including items that can assist in an escape, are dangerous, can sabotage or subvert prison physical security, or create an unhealthy or unsanitary condition. Custody practices call for thorough procedures to keep such items from falling into inmate hands.

6. *Implementation of an effective inmate disciplinary system.* Inmates must be told what behaviors are not allowed within a prison and must be punished and held accountable if they commit these acts. An inmate disciplinary system is therefore an important tool for controlling inmate behavior and effecting prison custody and security.

7. *Methods to separate unruly inmates or inmates at risk.* Prisons use special housing units (SHUs) to separate inmates who are being investigated for misconduct, are at risk of being assaulted, or are being punished for violating prison rules. The operation of SHUs is a key activity in the security and custody function within a prison.

8. *Control and reduction of the likelihood of a prison riot or disturbance.* The greatest fear within a prison is that inmates (who outnumber staff by perhaps twenty to one at any time) will stop following prison policy and rules, act out in a violent manner, injure prison staff, or take over control of the prison. Prison administrators go to great lengths to understand the causes of prison unrest, take action to reduce the likelihood of riots, and prepare to respond to inmate disturbance quickly and efficiently to reduce the potential of serious injury to staff or inmates and the destruction of the prison or government property.

Security and Custody Functions

Many activities are critical security and custody functions within a prison, and eight of these have been listed. Four were described earlier in this book, and inmate accountability, control of contraband, management of special housing units, and prevention of and preparation to respond to inmate unrest and prison riots are presented shortly. Security and custody functions are often tedious and time consuming, yet must be accomplished in a thorough and conscientious fashion in order not to undermine the overall goal of creating a safe and secure prison environment.

Inmate accountability is a principal component of a prison custody operation. Even though physical barriers such as fences, walls, and cells keep inmates in a specific location, the procedures used to account for them during the many hours a day they are out of their cells and involved in work or other programs are perhaps even more important in preventing escapes and maintaining prison order. A prison cannot be safely managed without control of contraband or items that can assist in an escape or be used as dangerous weapons. Prison staff sometimes must separate inmates, either as punishment or for their protection, in special housing units (sometimes thought of as a jail within the prison). And correctional officials can never forget the potential danger that can result from inmates deciding to riot or take control of a prison and its staff and can never waver in their efforts to prevent such incidents and prepare in case they do occur.

Inmate Accountability

Henderson and colleagues define **inmate accountability** as "the staff's ability to locate and identify inmates at any point in time . . . the very heart of institution security, from minimum-security camps to maximum-security penitentiaries."[3] It would be simple to know where inmates are at any time if they were always locked in their cells or dormitories. However, inmates are out of their cells almost eighteen hours a day, and therefore policies and procedures must exist to identify where inmates should be, to control their movement, to supervise them to the greatest extent possible, and to have a system of "counting" them to ensure that they are all where they are supposed to be. The following are key components of inmate accountability policies and procedures:

inmate accountability
the staff's ability to locate and identify inmates at any point in time within a prison

- Inmates are assigned to work and programs on a daily basis. These assignments place them under the supervision of staff responsible for that program or work activity.
- There is a system of inmate movement from one location to another within the prison that reduces the likelihood that inmates can go to other than their assigned location.
- Staff provide both casual and direct inmate supervision when inmates are not in their housing units.
- There are counts of inmates at regular and random times to ensure that they are where they are supposed to be within the prison.

Program and Work Assignments

Prison work and program assignments not only aid in inmate rehabilitation, but are also critical security functions in that they keep inmates active, limit time inmates might use to plan an escape or violation of rules, and place inmates under the direct supervision of staff. For example, inmates assigned to participate in an education program are assigned to the classroom of a specific teacher, who checks inmates in as class begins and is responsible for the inmates until the end of the assignment. This contributes to security and custody, because inmates are assigned to a correctional staff member who maintains responsibility for them, supervises them, and knows where they are during that time.

Prison work and program assignments are also an important part of the normal routine of the prison day. The "A Case Study" box illustrates how a routine of work and programs contributes to inmate accountability.

A Case Study

The Daily Routine

The daily routine for a prison is an important part of inmate accountability and contributes greatly to the overall security of a prison. The day begins early and continues late; prison officials desire to have scheduled activities during which inmates are under the direct supervision of staff for as many hours a day as possible. A typical prison workday is presented here.

On workdays, inmates awake between 5:30 A.M. and 6:00 A.M. and leave their cells at 6:00 A.M. to shower and prepare for the workday. They are allowed to go to the dining hall for breakfast from 6:30 to 7:00 and must return to their housing unit by 7:15 A.M. There is a **work call** at 7:30 A.M., and inmates move to their assigned jobs or programs. They are at their assigned location until 10:30, when they are to return to their housing unit, to be released to move to the dining hall for lunch from 11:00 until 12:00 noon.

After lunch, there is an afternoon work call at 12:30 P.M., and inmates remain at their assignments until 3:30. They then return to the housing unit, have a formal "count," and then go to the dining hall for dinner. After dinner, there are evening programs and leisure activities until 8:30 when inmates return to the housing unit and are locked in. They usually have time in the unit until approximately 11:30 P.M., when they are locked in their cells until let out the next morning. The work and program routine serves as the foundation for inmate accountability. Both staff and inmates know the schedule and adhere to it. Inmates know and move to where they are to be, and prison staff know the inmates they have assigned to them and for whom they are responsible. Staff then directly supervise those inmates and maintain their accountability during the six to eight hours per day of their assignment.

work call
the time when inmates move to their assigned jobs or programs assignments

controlled movement
the procedure used by prisons to maintain accountability for inmates as they move throughout the prison

Inmate Movements

As illustrated in the case study, inmates move throughout the prison during the day and evening. How they move and the way these movements are controlled and supervised is an essential element of inmate accountability. Many people imagine that inmates move individually in a prison, with at least one staff person walking with them from one point to another. However, this is not accurate, and inmates usually move in large groups from their housing units to work, meals, or education or recreation programs. To maintain inmate accountability during these mass movements, prisons use a controlled system for inmate moves.

Controlled movement is the procedure used by prisons to maintain accountability for inmates as they move throughout the prison. The most common form of controlled movement is to schedule inmates to move from one point to another at a specific time, according to the daily routine and schedule. For example, at the 7:30 A.M. work call, a controlled movement begins with the unlocking of doors to the housing units and program and work areas. The staff who unlock the doors stand by the doors and watch inmates exit and enter. Inmates usually have a short time (say, ten minutes) to move from one location to another. After the ten minutes, inmates are expected to have reached their designated destination, and the doors are all relocked. Inmates who are not in their required location are subject to disciplinary action.

Controlled movement contributes to inmate accountability in that it limits the time in which inmates have freedom to move or walk around the prison and prevents them from standing and communicating with other inmates to organize gang activities or pass information. Efficient controlled movement gives staff both real and perceived control over inmates; it not only maintains accountability, but

Inmates are out of their cells most of the day and move across the prison compound using a variety of controlled movement methods. Photo courtesy of Corrections Corporation of America.

also has specific policies and procedures to form the habit of inmate compliance with prison rules.

Even with ideal schedules and routines, there are times other than during mass movements when inmates must move individually. They may have a visit from a family member, may have an appointment with the prison doctor or psychologist, or may be required to meet with a staff member who is not their work or program supervisor. These individual movements are usually handled either through the use of a *call out* or a *pass system*. With the **call out**, inmates are scheduled for their appointments at least a day in advance. A schedule of all the appointments and required moves for the day is prepared and distributed to staff, naming the inmate, the time, and the beginning and ending points of the move. Supervising staff allow inmates to move according to the call-out schedule.

Instead of, or sometimes in addition to, a call-out system, some prisons use a pass system for individual inmate movement. A prison **pass system** is similar to that used in many high schools; an inmate is issued a pass by the work or program supervisor to go to the scheduled appointment. The pass includes a place for staff members to write the time the inmate leaves their supervision and for receiving staff members to write the time the inmate arrives and leaves the appointment. Upon the inmate's return to the work or program supervisor, the time of return is also written on the pass. Staff are aware of the time it takes to move from one area of the prison to another and recognize any deviation from the expected time to move. If inmates take longer than they should during the move, they are subject to disciplinary action. During the time inmates are walking from one location to another, staff who see them will often ask to see their pass and double-check that the inmate is in possession of a pass and is moving toward the intended destination. Through the use of controlled mass movements and either a call-out or pass system for individual movement, staff control inmate movement within the prison without having to escort them.

call out
a schedule of all the appointments and required moves for a day, including the name and expected times of the moves

pass system
a form of inmate movement in which an inmate is issued a pass by the work or program supervisor to go to a scheduled appointment

Casual and Direct Inmate Supervision

Casual and direct supervision of inmates by staff is another critical component of inmate accountability. Work and program supervisors are responsible for inmates during the times of their assignment, and correctional officers are responsible for inmates assigned to areas that they supervise. This supervision is *direct* in that assigned staff can directly see and watch inmates and their activities. Inmate accountability is also enhanced through *casual* supervision, or supervision by staff who are not responsible for inmates, but still have the opportunity to see their movements or activities. Prison staff are trained to constantly watch inmates and look for suspicious behavior. Staff who are walking across the prison compound see inmate movements, and even though they are not directly responsible, they monitor inmate behavior for anything unusual. Staff working in their offices look out windows and also monitor inmates' movements and activities.

Modern prisons are designed to aid in the casual supervision of inmates. For example, in the education areas within prisons, education administrators and teachers often have offices with windows with a view into the central compound of the prison and can see inmates move from one area to another. They also have windows between their offices and adjacent classrooms or library areas, so they can casually monitor inmates in those locations and see if any other staff are having trouble with an inmate. Classrooms have large windows into the corridor, into adjacent classrooms, and on the outside of the building. Not only can teachers see inmates outside their classrooms, but other staff can also see them and their interactions with inmates in their classrooms. These easy viewing situations provide additional supervision and security and keep staff from feeling isolated, insecure, and unprotected.

Inmate Counts

Another element of inmate accountability is the actual counting of inmates at various locations and times. Counts are done to determine that all inmates are where they should be and that no inmates either are out of bounds (in an unauthorized location) or have escaped. A series of daily counts reduces the amount of time an inmate may be unaccounted for, reducing the opportunity to escape (or quickly finding out if an escape has occurred) or to plan any other act that threatens the

Prison classrooms, staff offices, and program areas often have several large windows so that casual supervision can occur. Photo by Richard P. Seiter.

secure and orderly operation of a prison. Prisons use three different types of counts: regular, census, and random. **Regular counts** consist of the scheduled counting of inmates in their housing units to ensure that they are in the prison and have not escaped. At these counts, inmates must be in their cell or on their beds, and correctional officers walk by and count how many are in the housing unit. They then call in the number to a central location, at which staff add up all the counts to be sure that they have the correct number of inmates.

American Correctional Association standards require a minimum of one count per eight-hour correctional shift; however, most agencies have at least five scheduled counts during a twenty-four-hour period. With this many counts, inmates are quickly discovered missing if they have escaped or are trying to escape. Prison regular counts usually occur at midnight, at 3:00 A.M. when inmates are asleep in their cells, before work call at approximately 7:00 A.M., after return from work for the day (approximately 4:00 P.M.), and when inmates are required to return to their housing units after evening programs or recreation (approximately 9:00 P.M.). The 4:00 P.M. count is often a **stand-up count,** the most formal count of the day, at which inmates must stand at their cell door or by their dormitory bed to be counted and matched to the number of and identification of inmates assigned to each housing area.

A second type of count is a **census count,** a less formal count conducted at program and work assignments by the staff responsible for supervising inmates. They are usually held at the beginning and end of each work period to ensure that the work and program details have the correct number of assigned inmates. A third type of count is a **random count**. Random counts are done at any time and wherever inmates are when the random count is called. The warden or a high-ranking prison official will determine that a random count is needed (just to keep everyone honest) and put out an order for all inmate movement to cease, for all doors to be locked, and for all inmates to be counted where they are at the time. Since inmates know when the regular and census counts are held, random counts

regular counts
the scheduled counting of inmates in their housing units to ensure that they are in the prison and have not escaped

stand-up count
the most formal count of the day, at which inmates must stand at their cell door or by their dormitory bed to be counted and matched to the number of inmates assigned to each housing area

census counts
a less formal count conducted at program and work assignments by the staff responsible for supervising inmates

random counts
counts done at any time, freezing inmates at whatever location they are in when the random count is called

Correctional officers perform counts in prison housing units by going to every cell door and counting the number of inmates to be sure that all are accounted for. Photo by Richard P. Seiter.

keep inmates from planning to leave their assigned area right after a count and give themselves the maximum expected time between regular and census counts.

Control of Contraband

A second component of prison custody and security is to control contraband. **Contraband** is defined simply as any item that inmates are not allowed to possess and can include items that can assist in an escape (ladders or ropes), are dangerous (weapons or drugs), can sabotage or subvert prison physical security (wire cutters that can cut a security fence), or are nuisance items that create unhealthy or unsanitary conditions (unsealed food that can spoil in an inmate cell). Since contraband undermines the safe and secure operation of a prison, custody and security staff have many specific policies and spend considerable time implementing them to avoid possession of contraband by inmates.

Prisons have policies clearly identifying contraband items, or the limits on the number of items that inmates are allowed to have. Contraband policies also categorize contraband by risk, with the risk levels requiring different methods for storage and use. For example, tools are classified by their risk to prison security. Class A tools are those that can be a weapon, aid in escape, or undermine the security of a prison and include items such as files, knives, saw blades, ladders, ropes, extension cords, lift devices, and grinders. Class A tools are only to be used under the direct supervision of staff and must be placed in a secure storage area when not in use. Class B tools are less risky, and include light pliers, short power cords, or other hand tools that are not likely to be used as a weapon or aid in an escape. They may be stored and used by inmates under less stringent conditions, but must still be controlled and accounted for.[4]

Contraband items may end up in possession of inmates in at least four ways. First, inmates may receive prohibited items hidden in mail or packages. Prisons allow inmates to send and receive letters; sometimes inmates may receive packages with reading material or other allowable items. To keep small items such as drugs from being mailed into a prison, inmate mail is not read, but is opened and searched for contraband items. Hardback books and magazines (in which it is easy to hide drugs or other small contraband) may be purchased and delivered only directly from the publisher, thereby reducing the opportunity for a friend or family member to hide contraband in these publications.

Class A tools such as ladders are a serious security risk in prisons and therefore are locked so that inmates cannot take them to use as an aid in escape. Photo by Richard P. Seiter.

Second, inmate visitors may bring contraband items into the prison and give them to an inmate. Visiting by friends and family is important to maintain inmates' community ties and helps in their successful reintegration upon release. Visiting rooms are designed to allow as relaxed as possible contact and conversation between inmates and their visitors. Also, if there is no reasonable suspicion, visitors may not be searched. Visitors pass through a metal detector upon entry to the prison, and they are permitted to take only limited personal items into the visiting room, such as money and unopened packages of cigarettes. However, in the normal visiting setting, it is difficult to control the introduction of contraband such as drugs. During the visit, correctional staff monitor the visiting room and the conduct of inmates and visitors. Unfortunately, it is unlikely that staff (unless tipped off by another inmate) will notice passing of small contraband between a visitor and inmate. The best protection against entry of contraband through the visiting room is a thorough search of inmates after the visit and before they return to the general area of the prison. As they leave their visit, inmates are strip-searched, and when all visiting ends for the day, the visiting room is thoroughly searched before any more inmates enter the area.

Third, inmates may gain possession of contraband that is available in the prison, but should not be in possession of inmates without staff supervision. Inmates often attempt to smuggle items out of the allowed area of supervision. Some seemingly nonthreatening examples of such contraband are those that can cause a health and sanitation problem, such as food that is served in the dining room. Inmates try to obtain extra food, hide it, and take it to their housing units, sell it to others, or keep it for their own use at a later time. More serious examples of such contraband are the Class A tools described previously. Inmate food services workers often must be issued knives to prepare food; inmate maintenance workers may sometimes be issued tools that can cut wires or even bars. Prison contraband control procedures reduce the chance of such dangerous tools or utensils falling in an inmate's possession or being removed from the assigned area.

Class A tools and food service knives are hung on a **shadow board,** a light-colored background with the outline of the tool painted on it. This enables staff

shadow board
a light colored background with the outline of the tool painted on it, allowing for a missing tool or knife to be quickly noticed

One way to control hazardous tools or knives is to use a shadow board and lock them in a cage so inmates cannot get to them. Photo by Richard P. Seiter.

to quickly identify a missing tool or knife. When a tool or knife is issued to an inmate, a record of the staff member who issued the tool and the inmate to whom it was given is created. Before the end of the work period, all tools must be accounted for and back on the shadow board before inmates may leave the area. And, as inmates are released from a work area that uses such tools or knives, they are searched and, in some situations, must walk through a metal detector.

Finally and unfortunately, unethical staff may provide contraband items to inmates. Some staff may do this to make money. Inmates will arrange payment to the staff member by someone in the community if they bring drugs or possibly weapons into the prison. Other naive staff may do it "to be nice," bringing an inmate only nuisance items such as food or cigarettes that an inmate cannot get in prison. After a staff member has agreed to do this, however, manipulative inmates then threaten to tell prison officials about the staff violation of rules, knowing that the staff member will be punished for violating rules, unless the staff member agrees to bring more serious and dangerous contraband into the prison in exchange for the inmate's silence.

To deter such actions by staff, some prisons search their staff or require them to walk through metal detectors as they come to work. Since staff are well aware of these procedures and can easily avoid detection of bringing contraband into a prison, many prisons do not even attempt such searches. Instead, they rely on hiring the right kind of people and treating staff as trusted professionals, while encouraging all staff to share in the responsibility of identifying staff who may be smuggling items into the prison. Prison training programs for new staff present the dangers of providing contraband to inmates and how it undermines the safety of all staff. Although these efforts work for most staff, there is always a staff member who fails to heed the warning and, whether for money or because of poor judgment, is a target for inmates who try to get them to bring contraband into the prison.

Prison officials not only take many precautions to prevent contraband from getting into the hands of inmates, but also require regular efforts to search for contraband that an inmate may have acquired. A considerable amount of time every day is devoted to searching areas of the prison or shaking down inmates to find contraband and deter its possession. Correctional officers assigned to housing units have post order requirements to search a certain number of cells every day, and teams of staff may be assigned to an area (such as prison industries or a recreation building) for a complete search. Inmates are randomly selected for shakedowns or frisk searches of their bodies (similar to the standard pat downs performed by police officers on criminal suspects) as they move across the compound. And all inmates leaving work areas where Class A tools are used (food services, maintenance, or industries) are patted down and may walk through a metal detector.

Special Housing Units

special housing unit
a temporary housing assignment for inmates who present a danger to the security of the prison, need protection from other inmates, or are being punished for violating prison rules

A critical security and custody function is to be able to separate certain inmates from the rest of the general inmate population, either for their protection, as punishment, during an investigation, or because they are a threat to the orderly operation of the prison. For these situations, prisons have a **special housing unit** (SHU), similar to the operation of a jail in the community. An SHU is a temporary housing assignment for inmates who present a danger to the security of the prison, need protection from other inmates, or are being punished for violating prison rules. A stay in the SHU can be only a few days or up to twelve months. Inmates who need longer separation from a prison's inmate population are either transferred to another prison or placed in a supermax facility.

Correctional officers must be constantly on the lookout for contraband. Reprinted with permission of the Correctional Corporation of America.

Two categories of inmates are assigned to the SHU. The first category is **administrative detention** (AD), a "non-punitive confinement used to house inmates whose continued presence in the general population may pose a serious threat to life, property, self, staff, or other inmates, or to the security or orderly running of the institution."[5] Inmates may be placed in administrative detention if they are charged with violating a serious rule in the prison and allowing them to remain in the general prison population could undermine security or for their own safety. For a minor charge of violating a prison rule, such as the possession of nuisance contraband, inmates remain in the general population pending a disciplinary hearing. However, for more serious violations, such as fighting or possession of a weapon, they are held in administrative detention until the hearing and a determination of guilt and decision regarding punishment.

Inmates may also be placed in administrative detention for their own safety. Inmates who are being threatened or believe they are at risk of being assaulted often notify staff and seek protection, for example, if the inmate has a co-defendant in the prison against whom he or she testified or if the inmate is being pressured to participate in homosexual activity or to have a visitor bring drugs into the prison. In these situations, the inmate is placed in administrative detention, an investigation is completed, and officials decide whether to transfer the inmate to another prison. There is no predetermined time to hold inmates in administrative detention; they remain until the investigation is complete and appropriate action is taken. The "You Make the Decision" box at the end of the chapter illustrates the difficult decision prison staff have to make regarding inmates potentially at risk in a prison.

administrative detention

a nonpunitive confinement in SHU used to house inmates whose continued presence in the general population may pose a serious threat to the security or orderly running of the prison

The inside of a cell in the SHU has minimal comforts, and inmates do not like placement there and separation from the rest of the inmate population.
Photo by Richard P. Seiter.

disciplinary segregation

a punitive assignment in SHU after a finding of guilt for a serious prison rule violation; disciplinary segregation is for a set amount of time established by the authorized hearing official

The second category of SHU placement is **disciplinary segregation** (DS), a status of punishment after a finding of guilt for a serious prison rule violation. Disciplinary segregation is for a set amount of time established by the person or committee that considers the violation. In the Bureau of Prisons disciplinary policy, infractions of greatest severity can result in disciplinary segregation of up to sixty days, infractions of high severity can result in up to thirty days, and those of moderate severity can result in up to fifteen days.[6] Once inmates complete their disciplinary segregation time, they are returned to the general population, unless the disciplinary sanction also included a transfer to another prison.

The SHU is a separate building within a prison, usually located so that inmates in the SHU cannot communicate with general-population inmates. It is physically very secure; cells have metal doors and metal furnishings. Furnishings include a stainless steel toilet and sink and a bed and writing table secured to the floor or walls. Outside but adjacent to the SHU is a small, fenced recreation area in which inmates are allowed to exercise between five and ten hours per week. Operating procedures for the SHU are similar for both statuses. Inmates come out of their cells only when handcuffed and escorted by staff. Meals are brought to each cell. Medical and program (education or religious) staff visit inmates in the SHU, as all services are brought to the unit. SHU inmates do have access to correspondence, limited reading material, and visiting privileges.

Inmate Riots and Disturbances

The most feared event at a prison is an inmate riot or disturbance. No matter how well staff follow policy or do their jobs, emergency situations such as riots, escapes, hostage taking, and nonviolent food or work strikes can occur. Therefore, prison officials implement security and custody procedures in prisons to reduce the likelihood of such emergencies and to be prepared if emergencies do occur. Preparation includes developing contingency plans, training staff in their proper response, and creating and training special teams for hostage negotiations and responding to a disturbance.

The Attica (New York) riot in 1971, one of the most deadly in the history of prisons, highlighted many factors that can create tension and increase the potential for disturbances within a prison. Courtesy of Corbis/Bettmann.

Inmate disturbances have a devastating impact on a prison, the staff, and even the inmates. The last thirty years have seen several serious riots.[7] One of the most serious riots, and one that captured the interest of the U.S. public, was the 1971 riot at the state prison in Attica, New York.[8] Tensions had been building at Attica for several months, as inmates complained about poor food and medical service and discrimination by staff. A large proportion of the Attica inmates were African Americans from New York City, whereas staff members were predominantly white and from rural upstate New York. In September 1971, inmates took control of a large section of the prison and held several staff members as hostages. Negotiations between correctional officials and inmates continued for four days until the governor of New York and the director of corrections decided it was time to end the siege. The New York State Police were sent into the prison and authorized to use deadly force to regain control. After they retook the prison, thirty-two inmates and eleven staff members were found killed. The investigation discovered that the state police killed thirty-nine of those during the retaking of the prison.

Another serious riot occurred in February 1980, when prisoners took over the entire prison in Santa Fe, New Mexico. Inmates held twelve staff members as hostages, controlled the prison for thirty-six hours, and caused more than $100 million in damage.[9] Inmates got control of other inmates' records and found that some had acted as informants. Rioting inmates tortured and killed thirty-three inmates they believed to have aided staff.

Another serious riot took place in 1993 at the Southern Ohio Correctional Facility in Lucasville, Ohio. In an article regarding this riot, Ohio correctional executives wrote:

On Easter Sunday 1993, inmates returning to L-block from recreation at the maximum security Southern Ohio Correctional Facility in rural Lucasville assaulted the entry officer. Minutes later, L-block was overrun, and the longest prison siege in U.S. history where lives were lost was underway. Eleven days later the riot ended. Corrections Officer Robert Vallandingham and nine inmates had been murdered. Thirteen corrections officers had been taken hostage. Five were held for the duration of the disturbance. L-block was virtually destroyed.

environmental factors

factors that create tension and an underlying unrest among inmates; they can include hot weather, reduction in budgets for recreation equipment, prison crowding, poor food service or medical care, a perceived pattern of unfairness in the management of the prison, or poor security procedures that allow inmates to create an unsafe environment

precipitating event

the "spark in the haystack" that sets off an inmate riot; usually must be preceded by the right environmental factors before a precipitating event creates the beginning of a prison riot

As the more than 200 media reporters packed up their cameras and satellite dishes, Ohioans breathed a collective sigh of relief that the carnage was over. But for the 11,000 employees of the Ohio Department of Rehabilitation and Correction, the end of the riot signaled fundamental changes at every level of the operation.[10]

Investigations of inmate riots and disturbances have discovered that most are not planned or precisely initiated by inmate leaders. Disturbances more often result from the coalescing of two types of factors and events. The first are **environmental factors** that create tension and an underlying unrest among inmates. They can include hot weather, reduction in budgets for recreation equipment, prison crowding, poor food service or medical care, a perceived pattern of unfairness in prison management, or poor security procedures that allow inmates to create an unsafe environment. The second is a **precipitating event,** often thought of as the "spark in the haystack," that sets off an inmate riot. It usually takes both the right environmental factors and a precipitating event to create the beginning of a prison riot.

Preventive actions that prison administrators can take to reduce inmate unrest and lessen the chance that a single precipitating event will result in a riot include the following:

- Understanding the importance to both staff and inmates of managerial visibility and approachability
- Performing effective security audits that discover security deficiencies so they can be corrected before inmates exploit them
- Consistently enforcing all rules and regulations
- Maintaining effective communications between inmates and staff, among staff, and particularly between line and supervisory personnel
- Providing appropriate programs and services of all types (food, medical care, and so forth)

Rioting inmates at the Southern Ohio Correctional Facility in Lucasville, Ohio, in 1993 did severe damage to the facility and murdered ten people. Courtesy of the Ohio Department of Rehabilitation and Correction.

- Implementing effective management systems, such as sanitation, safety and security inspections, contraband deterrence and detection, tool and key control, and inmate accountability
- Developing sensitivity to changes in inmate actions or the institution atmosphere
- Using risk-assessment programs to identify possible trouble spots and correcting them as soon as possible; such systems may include the use of objective indicators (tests, review of incident data, sick call data) or more subjective elements (staff and inmate interviews) to assign levels of risk to a situation or institution[11]

The "A Look Into" box gives an example of a riot that occurred while I was the warden of the Federal Correctional Institution in Greenville, Illinois. It illustrates how environmental factors and a precipitating event can combine to result in a serious riot culminating in staff injury and major destruction of the prison.

A Look Into...

Causes of a Riot

In October 1995, the Federal Correctional Institution in Greenville, Illinois, was a new federal prison. It was constructed using Federal Bureau of Prisons (BOP) standard medium-security guidelines, with solid wood cell doors and card tables and folding chairs used by inmates in the housing units' common areas. The prison first accepted inmates in early 1994. The prison had just over 500 cells, but because of severe overcrowding in other federal prisons, it rapidly filled to twice that capacity to more than 1,000 inmates, with two inmates in every cell and even three inmates in some cells. Most inmates were transferred to Greenville from Southeast and West Coast federal prisons, which were experiencing the most overcrowding. These inmates were moved away from their families and friends, could not receive visits, and did not want to be in southern Illinois.

As is the practice in federal prisons, some experienced staff members are transferred to new prisons, but the majority are hired locally and have no prison experience. Procedures were new, and some were still changing and developing. The newly hired correctional officers and other staff were learning to deal with medium-security inmates, almost all of whom had been transferred from other prisons and knew how to try to take advantage of new staff and untried procedures.

Throughout 1995, there was considerable public discussion about changing the federal drug laws regarding crack cocaine. There was a ten-to-one ratio of crack to powder cocaine, meaning that to receive a mandatory ten-year prison sentence, crack cocaine offenders had to possess only one-tenth the amount required for powder cocaine offenders. Since crack cocaine was primarily used in African American communities, more than 95 percent of the crack cocaine offenders at Greenville were African American. This became an issue of racial injustice and was being reconsidered by the U.S. Sentencing Commission. In fact, in the summer of 1995, the commission recommended to Congress that the two drugs should be equalized in their weight and corresponding sentence. Through rumor, African American inmates convicted of crack cocaine trafficking believed that a change would be made, it would be retroactive, and that many would receive an immediate reduction of their sentences.

In the fall of 1995, a report issued by the U.S. Department of Justice, Bureau of Justice Statistics, noted the much higher percentage of black men between ages 19 and 30 who were incarcerated at a much greater rate compared to their percentage in the overall U.S. population. This also became a rallying cry for racial injustice. Over the summer and fall of 1995, much media attention was given to a call for a "Million Man March" by Minister Louis Farrakhan, the controversial leader of the Nation of Islam. The Million Man March called attention to

...continued

the need for African American men to take responsibility for their families. However, it also emphasized, especially in the minds of inmates, the issue of racial injustice regarding the disparity between crack and powder cocaine sentencing.

The Million Man March occurred on Monday of the third week of October. On Wednesday evening of the same week, Congress rejected the recommendation by the sentencing commission to reduce the disparity between crack and powder cocaine sentences. The next day riots broke out in federal prisons in Alabama, Tennessee, and Pennsylvania. There was national media coverage of the fires and destruction from these riots, and inmates in Greenville watched these events unfold on television news coverage.

On Friday of that week, the Bureau of Prisons took peremptory action to prevent more riots, ordering a national lockdown of all federal prisons. At Greenville, inmates were called back to their housing units around 3:00 P.M., about one hour earlier than usual. Arriving in the housing units, inmates were told to go into their cells to be locked down. Several inmates refused to go into their cells and began assaulting staff. A riot ensued and resulted in injury of thirteen staff members and massive destruction of two housing units. Four or five other federal prisons also experienced smaller disturbances during the next few weeks.

Environmental factors in this riot included inexperienced staff implementing new procedures. Many inmates were extremely unhappy about being in Greenville. Feelings of racial injustice were heightened by the Million Man March, and there were expectations that the injustice would be ended by congressional action. The congressional action to maintain current sentences was unexpected by prison officials and was disappointing to inmates. The precipitating event was the attempted lockdown, in a time when external (societal) tensions were high. The inmates were extremely upset because they did not know the duration or reasons for the lockdown or even if this action was warranted.

Planning for Emergency Situations

Inmate disturbances can occur in any prison. Knowing this, all prisons develop contingency or emergency plans to identify the responses and procedures to be put in place in case of a disturbance. These plans describe how to prevent disturbances and, if a riot occurs, the initial reactions, communications, staff response, the potential use of firearms and crowd control ordinances, managing the media, and postemergency actions. Emergency plans are a guide for actions in a time when emotions are high, staff and inmates may be in danger or already injured, things seem chaotic and out of control, and the warden and top prison officials may be out of the prison. The plan is detailed to the point that it provides the order of steps to take to respond to certain events. Staff are required to read the plan and are trained in its implementation in the event of an emergency. Well-coordinated, appropriate, and timely reaction at the beginning of a disturbance is critical. Boin and Van Duin write, "As prison authorities find themselves confronted with a riot, . . . [they] will have to take some sort of action in order to cope with the threat and restore a state of normalcy. It is in this stage that the actions of prison authorities may make the difference between a food strike in an isolated cell block (a riot you will never hear about) and the overtaking of an entire institution (a riot you might never forget)."[12]

Emergency Response Teams

In preparation for inmate disturbances, emergency plans require creation, staffing, and training of at least three teams, capable of using all the options available in crisis situations, including negotiation, controlling the disturbance, and use of deadly force. The three teams include a hostage negotiation team, disturbance control team, and special emergency response team. The key is for the decision maker to decide which team to use and how to react. It has been suggested that "negotiation, the option involving the least amount of force, is the preferred option when time permits."[13]

In some riots, staff members are taken hostage, creating a very difficult and stressful situation that eliminates or delays many of the activities that could be used to respond to a nonhostage emergency. **Hostage negotiation teams** (HNTs) are used to respond to a hostage taking. The HNT is made up of eight to ten prison employees with excellent communication skills and ability to perform under stress. The team's principal role is to open lines of communication with the hostage takers as quickly as possible so that inmates see an option to injuring the hostage and begin to consider how to resolve the situation. The HNT goal is to preserve life and regain control of the prison and inmates. Once they open communication lines, they attempt to "reduce stress and tension with the hostage takers, build rapport, obtain intelligence, stall for time, allow hostage takers to express emotion and ventilate, and establish a problem-solving atmosphere."[14] Over the period of negotiations, a rapport builds between the negotiators and the hostage takers, and the Stockholm Syndrome develops between the captors and the hostages. The Stockholm Syndrome is thought to result in the hostages and captors beginning to identify with each other; hostage takers see the hostages as people rather than just objects, and they are therefore less likely to physically harm or kill their hostages.

The second type of emergency team is the **disturbance control team** (DCT). The DCT has a primary mission of controlling inmates during riot situations by using defensive tactics and equipment to move them, isolate them, and get them to give up and stop the disturbance. The team wears helmets, ballistic-resistant vests, and baseball catcher-style shin guards and carries riot batons, gas masks, handcuffs, chemical agents such as tear and pepper gas, and ordnance such as smoke grenades, stun and flash rounds, and Sting-Ball grenades. The DCT responds to a riot with a deliberate, orderly, and disciplined approach. Through this "show of force," inmates often end the confrontation, recognizing that the DCT is well trained and the inmates are likely to be hurt if they do not capitulate.

Unfortunately, some riots and hostage situations do not end successfully through negotiation or the use of the DCT. In these cases, the third type of team,

hostage negotiation teams
a team of eight to ten prison employees, with excellent communication skills and ability to perform under stress, with the principle role to open lines of communications between staff and hostage takers

disturbance control team
an emergency team with the primary mission of controlling inmates during riot situations by using defensive tactics and equipment to move, isolate, and get them to give up and stop the disturbance

This picture shows the burned-out center of the U.S. Penitentiary in Atlanta, Georgia, after rioting Cuban inmates took over the entire prison and held several staff members as hostages for several days in 1987. Courtesy of the Federal Bureau of Prisons.

SERT members must train regularly with weapons to be used in serious prison emergency situations. Courtesy of the Ohio Department of Rehabilitation and Correction.

special emergency response team

an emergency team trained in the use of lethal force for when all else fails to resolve an emergency situation

the **special emergency response team** (SERT), may be called upon. A SERT, similar to a police SWAT team, is trained in the use of weapons, explosives, entry procedures, and snipers. They will be authorized to use lethal force when all else fails to resolve an emergency situation. It is a difficult decision for correctional officials to commit to the use of a SERT assault with deadly force. Hostage takers always give deadlines and threaten to kill hostages if their demands are not met. It is good strategy to have the negotiating team try to talk hostage takers past deadlines, while hoping that they will not injure hostages. Yet hostage takers may reach a point at which they are about to kill or injure hostages, and the order must be given and the SERT prepared to begin an assault.

Before the SERT assaults, they prepare a detailed plan that must receive the approval of the emergency decision maker. Once the plan is approved, the team moves into position and stays ready to begin the assault upon receiving the "go" order. If force is necessary, it must be overwhelming, but only in the amount necessary to restore order. Prison officials' goal is to develop a tactical action that ensures total control of the inmates as the final outcome so that inmates cannot take the weapons and have SERT members as more hostages.

In the *MyCrimeKit* is an "Insider's Experience" box regarding the shattered confidence of staff after a riot. After the riot of FCI-Greenville we realized that the prison had to return to normal operations, but in the aftermath of the riot this occurred only after changes in the style of management and improvement in the security and operation of the prison were made. Thankfully, the staff responded, and FCI-Greenville became one of the best correctional institutions in the Federal Bureau of Prisons.

mycrimekit™

Insider's Experience: Rebuilding Staff Confidence after a Riot.

Treatment and Programs within a Prison

While creating a safe and secure environment, prisons also have the mission of providing inmates the opportunity to participate in programs that can help in their rehabilitation and successful reentry to the community. Although it has always been acknowledged that rehabilitation is a valid correctional goal, support for it and the emphasis that rehabilitative programs receive in prisons have ebbed and flowed over the history of U.S. corrections. However, the public continues to support and correctional officials continue to encourage programs that are designed to improve offenders' deficiencies that may have contributed to their past criminality.

Rehabilitation, at that point better termed "redemption," was a primary focus of the first U.S. prison (the Walnut Street Jail), opened in Philadelphia in 1790. Inmates were expected to read the Bible and reflect on their wrongdoings. They were also required to work on trade products in their cells so that these products could be sold to help support the prison. Over the next 150 years, work became the primary program within prisons, although counseling and religious services remained a mainstay of every prison. In the history of U.S. corrections, programs for the rehabilitation of offenders have always been considered important.

The heyday of the goal of rehabilitation came during the middle of the twentieth century when corrections adopted a *medical model*, in which crime was believed to be the result of an underlying pathology of offenders that could be diagnosed and treated. Offenders were considered sick and in need of treatment to prepare them to return to the community as productive, law-abiding citizens. Correctional agencies implemented a variety of treatment programs to improve offenders and to provide them with the tools necessary to be successful members of society. The need for rehabilitation of offenders was emphasized by the Commission on Law Enforcement and the Administration of Justice, appointed by President Lyndon Johnson in 1966, which noted a need for "substantial upgrading" of the correctional system and its reorientation "toward integration of offenders into community life."[15]

By the 1980s, however, public support of rehabilitation was declining, partly the result of the publication of an early 1970s study of the effectiveness of correctional treatment. In a review of findings from 231 correctional treatment programs, Lipton and colleagues found no common themes in correctional interventions that consistently reduce recidivism.[16] In an earlier article regarding the review that became known as the "nothing works" conclusion, Martinson stated that "with few and isolated exceptions, the rehabilitative efforts that have been reported so far have had no appreciable effect on recidivism."[17]

During this time, correctional philosophy reverted to Darwinism and the *classical model*, in which offenders are seen as rational individuals with free will who chose to commit and are personally accountable for their crimes. With this philosophy, punishment and deterrence are considered more important as goals than rehabilitation. However, rehabilitative programs have continued in prison and community corrections settings, although medical terms such as *treatment* and *diagnosis* have been replaced with *programming* and *assessment*. In the current era of accountability, offenders must take responsibility for their criminal acts. Although there is recognition of and support for self-improvement of offenders, these programs are often voluntary, prisons provide them as "opportunities" rather than treatment for deficiencies, and offenders are seen not as ill but in need of modifying their willingness to commit crimes.

Currently, the public expects criminals to be punished, yet supports providing rehabilitation programs to inmates. The public wants to be protected, but it also wants the correctional system to improve inmates' likelihood of success upon release. Innes found "no evidence in the available survey data that the general public shares the view that there is any necessary incompatibility among the goals of justice in society, punishment of criminals, and teaching or training programs for inmates."[18] A 2006 public opinion survey indicated that 87 percent of those surveyed favor rehabilitative services for prisoners as opposed to a punishment-only system,[19] and greater than 90 percent of those surveyed rated as "important" that prison inmates receive job training, drug treatment, mental health services, family support, and housing assistance.[20]

In this textbook, the term *rehabilitation* will continue to be used. Rehabilitation, by definition, means "to return to a previous form." For correctional purposes, Senese and Kalinich define rehabilitation as "a programmed effort to alter attitudes and behaviors of inmates, which is focused on the elimination of their future criminal behaviors."[21] Prisons offer a variety of programs, including education, vocational training, recreation, religious, substance abuse, mental health, work, and a variety of other self-improvement modalities. These programs are valued, not only because they improve the offender, but also because they have been found to result in less idleness, disruption, and violence within prisons. This more practical than altruistic emphasis continued for crime-prevention purposes. Cullen and Applegate suggest that "the rehabilitative paradigm requires that government invest in lawbreakers. The goal is to improve offenders both as an end in itself and as a means of reducing recidivism and of protecting society."[22]

The following sections describe the process and programs that are ordinarily provided within prisons, which include assessing the program needs of inmates and creating a plan for them to follow during their period of incarceration. These programs can include education and vocational, recreational, substance abuse, mental health, and work programs.

Identifying Inmate Needs

Once an offender is sentenced to prison, a reception and classification process begins. Many states have correctional reception centers to which inmates are initially assigned to assess their risk of violence and escape and their need for rehabilitative programs. The risk assessment is normally done through the use of objective classification systems, with a determination of the security level of prison (based primarily on the physical security available) to which an inmate will be assigned. The identification of program needs is determined through a combination of assessment instruments, interviews with psychologists or other mental health professionals, and educational and vocational testing.

From these assessments, testing, and interviews, inmate needs for various types of programs are identified. Educational proficiency exams give an indication of an inmate's level of literacy, regardless of the grade completed in school, and indicate whether additional educational programming is needed. Psychological assessments identify any mental illness, suicide proclivity, or need for special mental health placements or programs. And through interviews and review of past histories, the need for substance abuse treatment is determined. Since most offenders have limited work histories and poor work skills, the program plan also addresses the types of vocational training or prison work experience that may help the inmate.

Once needs are identified, inmates move from the reception process to the regular incarceration stage of their sentence. If they were originally in a reception center, they are transferred to a prison to begin service of their sentence. Once transferred, inmates meet with the unit management or program team to develop a program plan to follow during their sentence. If the inmates' functional literacy is below a certain level, they are assigned to go to school. If a mental health or substance abuse problem has been identified, they are referred to the mental health department for treatment or placement in a substance abuse program. They will be assigned to a vocational program or prison job to develop work skills. And they will be informed of leisure programs and other programs within the prison believed to be of interest or assistance to them.

The unit or treatment team normally meets with inmates every six months thereafter to review the progress and current status of their program, but if an inmate requests a change in program, the team will schedule a review early. At these reviews, the team examines reports from the various program departments and discusses progress, concerns, or successes with the inmate. Most treatment programs are voluntary, yet the team may strongly suggest the inmate's involvement and commitment. Other programs may be required by statute (in several states and the federal government, inmates testing below a certain literacy level must enroll in school) or as a part of their sentence (some states allow judges to require inmates to participate in a substance abuse program during their sentence).

Types of Prison Programs

Inmates have a variety of needs, and no two inmates are exactly the same. However, there are a few inmate programs that most inmates need and participate in. Approximately half of entering prison inmates have graduated from high school. Nearly 70 percent of state prison inmates have a drug or alcohol problem. Very few inmates have an extensive work history or marketable vocational skills. And approximately 16 percent of incarcerated offenders are mentally ill. Prisons therefore attempt to create programs to meet the general needs of inmates and deal with individual requirements within these programs. Educational and vocational, mental health, substance abuse, work, religious, and recreational programs within prisons are presented next.

Educational and Vocational Programs

Education is recognized as critical to everyone's success in modern U.S. society. The achieved educational level of the general population of the United States has increased steadily in the past few decades, and criminal offenders have consistently been found significantly less educated than their law-abiding peers. In a 2003 publication of the Bureau of Justice Statistics, it was reported that in 1997, only 18.4 percent of the general population had not completed high school or received a GED, whereas 39.7 percent of state prison inmates, 26.5 percent of federal prison inmates, 46.5 percent of jail inmates, and 30.6 percent of probationers had only some high school or less.[23] Although the percentages of inmates entering prison who have not completed high school or earned a GED remained about the same between 1991 (40 percent) and 1997 (41 percent), the number of such inmates entering state prisons increased from 293,000 in 1991 to 420,000 in 1997.[24] Table 13.1 illustrates the educational attainment levels for various correctional populations and the general public.

Inmates have a significant need for educational programs and, appropriately, most prisons provide these programs. In a recent survey of adult correctional facilities, about nine in ten state prisons and all federal prisons provided educational programs for inmates.[25] As indicated in Table 13.2, prisons offer a variety of education programs, with secondary education programs to prepare inmates to take the GED the most prevalent during 2000.

A high proportion of inmates participate in education programs; more than half (52 percent of state and 57 percent of federal inmates) report taking education classes since their most recent admission (Table 13.3). Even though the percentages of inmates participating in such programs decreased from 1991 to 1997, the actual number of inmates who were educated in prison increased during this period from 402,500 to 550,000.[26] As noted in Table 13.3, vocational programs and high school or GED programs were the most popular among inmates, with about one-third participating in vocational programs and one-fourth participating in high school classes.

mycrimekit

Read about Careers in Corrections as a Correctional Programs Supervisor.

TABLE 13.1

Educational Attainment for State and Federal Prison Inmates in 1997 and 1991, Local Jail Inmates in 1996 and 1989, Probationers in 1995, and the General Population in 1997

Educational Attainment	Prison Inmates				Local Jail Inmates		Probationers	General Population
	State		Federal					
	1997	1991	1997	1991	1996	1989	1995	1997
8th grade or less	14.2%	14.3%	12.0%	11.0%	13.1%	15.6%	8.4%	7.2%
Some high school	25.5	26.9	14.5	12.3	33.4	38.2	22.2	11.2
GED*	28.5	24.6	22.7	22.6	14.1	9.2	11.0	...
High school diploma	20.5	21.8	27.0	25.9	25.9	24.0	34.8	33.2
Postsecondary/ some college	9.0	10.1	15.8	18.8	10.3	10.3	18.8	26.4
College graduate or more	2.4	2.3	8.1	9.3	3.2	2.8	4.8	22.0
Number	1,055,495	706,173	88,705	53,677	503,599	393,111	2,029,866	192,352,084

Note: Probationers have been excluded from the general population. General population includes the noninstitutional population 18 or older. Detail may not add to 100% due to rounding.

*General educational development certificate.

... Not available in the Current Population Survey.

Source: Caroline Wolf Harlow, *Education and Correctional Populations* (Washington, D.C.: U.S. Department of Justice, Bureau of Justice Statistics, January 2003), p. 1.

TABLE 13.2 Educational Programs Offered in State, Federal, and Private Prisons, 2000 and 1995, and Local Jails, 1999

Educational Programs	State Prisons		Federal Prisons		Private Prisons		Local Jails
	2000	1995	2000	1995	2000	1995	1999
With an education program	91.2%	88.0%	100.0%	100.0%	87.6%	71.8%	60.3%
Basic adult education	80.4	76.0	97.4	92.0	61.6	40.0	24.7
Secondary education	83.6	80.3	98.7	100.0	70.7	51.8	54.8
College courses	26.7	31.4	80.5	68.8	27.3	18.2	3.4
Special education	39.6	33.4	59.7	34.8	21.9	27.3	10.8
Vocational training	55.7	54.5	93.5	73.2	44.2	25.5	6.5
Study release programs	7.7	9.3	6.5	5.4	28.9	32.7	9.3
Without an education program	8.8	12.0	0.0	0.0	12.4	28.2	39.7
Number of facilities	1,307	1,278*	*	*	242	110	2,819

Note: Detail may not add to total because facilities may have more than one educational program.

*Changed definitions prevent meaningful comparisons of the numbers of federal facilities, 1995 and 2000.

Source: Caroline Wolf Harlow, *Education and Correctional Populations* (Washington, D.C.: U.S. Department of Justice, Bureau of Justice Statistics, January 2003), p. 4.

TABLE 13.3 Participation in Educational Programs Since Most Recent Incarceration or Sentence, for State and Federal Prison Inmates, 1997 and 1991, for Local Jail Inmates, 1996, and for Probationers, 1995

Educational Programs	Prison Inmates				Local Jail Inmates	Probationers
	State		Federal			
	1997	1991	1997	1991	1996	1995
Total	51.9%	56.6%	56.4%	67.0%	14.1%	22.9%
Basic	3.1	5.3	1.9	10.4	0.8	0.4
GED/high school	23.4	27.3	23.0	27.3	8.6	7.8
College courses	9.9	13.9	12.9	18.9	1.0	6.1
English as a second language	1.2	. . .	5.7	. . .	. . .	. . .
Vocational	32.2	31.2	31.0	29.4	4.8	7.0
Other	2.6	2.6	5.6	8.4	2.1	3.4
Number of inmates	1,046,136	709,042	87,624	53,753	501,159	2,055,942

Note: Detail may not add to total due to rounding or inmates' participation in more than one educational program.

. . . Not available

Source: Caroline Wolf Harlow, *Education and Correctional Populations* (Washington, D.C.: U.S. Department of Justice, Bureau of Justice Statistics, January 2003), p. 4.

Education has been a part of prison programming for more than a century. One of the most famous U.S. penologists, Zebulon R. Brockway, argued that law-abiding behavior was attainable through legitimate industry and education and advocated it for inmates at the American Prison Association conference in 1870. The current American Correctional Association standard for correctional educational programs states that:

> *written policy, procedure, and practice provide for a comprehensive education program, available to all inmates who are eligible, that includes the following: educational philosophy and goals, communications skills, general education, basic academic skills, GED preparation, special education, vocational education, postsecondary education, and other education programs as dictated by the needs of the institutional population.*[27]

mandatory prison educational

many states and the Federal Bureau of Prisons require inmates without a high school diploma or GED to attend school

Historically, most prison education programs have been voluntary; however, many states and the Federal Bureau of Prisons (BOP) now have a requirement of **mandatory prison education** programs. In 1983, the BOP implemented the first mandatory literacy program for inmates who functioned at less than a sixth-grade educational level. The standard was raised to the eighth-grade level in 1986, and in 1991, the Crime Control Act of 1990 (Public Law 101–647) directed the BOP to have a mandatory functional literacy program for all mentally capable inmates, and the BOP raised their educational standard to the twelfth grade. Many states have since adopted such standards, and the mandatory requirement has much to do with the increasing participation over the past few years.

There have been mixed results concerning the impact of correctional education on postrelease recidivism. Several studies have indicated a positive relationship between participating in prison education programs and lower recidivism.[28] A study of postrelease recidivism of inmates released from Texas prisons during 1991 and 1992 found that inmates at the lowest levels of educational achievement benefited most from participation in academic programs as indicated by lower recidivism rates.[29] Vito and Tewksbury evaluated a program in Kentucky

Prison libraries are important to aid the education program and provide leisure reading opportunities to inmates.

Photo by Richard P. Seiter.

to increase the literacy levels of state and local inmates and to reduce recidivism. Although graduates of the program increased their reading and math competencies by up to three grade levels, the educational component did not seem to have an effect on their recidivism rates when compared to nongraduates measured twelve to fifteen months after program involvement.[30]

Most prisons also offer vocational training programs to improve inmates' vocational skills. **Vocational training** is specific training in a trade area such as carpentry, electronics, welding, office equipment and word processing, food services, or horticulture and landscaping. Vocational training has been shown to be effective in reducing recidivism. Saylor and Gaes found that "those who participated in either vocational or apprenticeship training were 33 percent less likely to recidivate through the observation period," which was as long as twelve years and as short as eight years.[31] Lattimore and colleagues also found a reduction in recidivism rates by vocational training participants in two North Carolina prisons for young offenders. Inmates who participated in the Vocational Delivery System program were less likely (36 percent) to be arrested following release from prison than the control group (46 percent).[32]

Currently, few prisons have extensive postsecondary education programs, even though several thousand inmates took college classes and earned college degrees in the past. State and federal prisons previously used **Pell grants** to fund inmate college programs. Pell grants were enacted and funded by Congress in the 1970s as a way for "disadvantaged populations" to receive funds to take college courses. Inmates met the definition of disadvantaged, and most prisons arranged with local colleges to offer courses in the prison and qualify inmates to receive Pell grant funds to pay their tuition. When I was the director of corrections in Ohio, almost every prison had more than one hundred inmates attending college classes as full-time students. These college programs were considered a productive use of inmate time and were found to motivate inmates and improve morale.

However, in 1994, after complaints that inmates should not get a "free" college education in prison, Congress specifically eliminated inmates from receiving Pell grants, and many active and proven college programs in prisons were eliminated.[33] Some states were able to provide limited funding and keep college-level programs going on a minimal basis. However, in 2000, the Federal Bureau of Prisons proposed modifying its own rules to make inmates responsible for all college-degree tuition costs.[34] Prisons now will help inmates arrange to take correspondence courses, but

vocational training
specific training in a trade area to prepare students to work in that trade

Pell grants
grants for disadvantaged individuals used to cover tuition costs for college courses

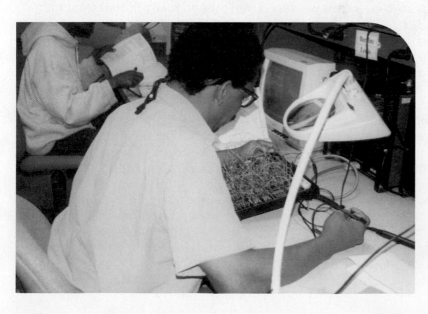

Prison vocational training classes teach inmates skills that are current and often high-tech. Photo by Richard P. Seiter.

all costs must be borne by the inmate. Even ten years after the end of the Pell grants, most correctional educators still bemoan their loss as a step back in correctional education and the ability to encourage inmates to maximize their education potential, at a time when they have little else to do.

The "Your Career in Corrections" box highlights the role that correctional educators play in prisons.

Your Career in Corrections

Correctional Educators

Correctional educators are the people who teach, oversee, or coordinate education and sometimes vocational training programs within prisons. Education is one of the oldest and largest programs in any prison; most prisons have between five and ten education staff members. Correctional education formed as early as the 1800s, with prison chaplains considered the first "teachers," as they used the Bible (often the only book allowed in early prisons) to teach inmates how to read. As the earliest prison reformers began to push for improvements in the operations of U.S. prisons, one of their first initiatives was to push for more education programs to give inmates the literacy skills seen as critical to success after release.

Correctional education is a nontraditional occupation; it is not an area that people specifically study or prepare for. Not many teachers begin thinking that they want to work in a prison; they seem to fall into it through one way or another. Most find that they love teaching, but are not completely happy with the traditional school system and begin to look for other options. They also don't always plan to make it a career, but often find it a challenging and rewarding job and decide to continue correctional work until retirement.

Correctional educators have a nontraditional setting in that in some ways, it is like a "one-room" school. Teachers are not divided into grades, but have specialty areas such as English, math, or reading, and have students at all levels in their classes at one time. Adult learners are tested to determine their proficiency and then work at their own level under the guidance of the teacher. Many correctional educators really like the adult learner approach as well as the structure and order of a prison education program. They find the work very rewarding, as they do not lose students each year (as they move to another grade), but see them continue until they reach a milestone of success (such as getting their GED). Most inmates enroll in

school because they see it as their only means of not coming back, and they have a true motivation to learn. They (and their teachers) get almost immediate gratification, because they do not have to wait twelve years to graduate from high school, and they can get their GED in a matter of months in many cases. Another positive factor in many correctional educators' minds is that they do not worry about security in the prison environment; many say they actually feel safer teaching in a prison than in many public schools. They have control over inmates and the inmates face consequences if they misbehave.

There are also some disadvantages and frustrations teaching in a prison. First, inmates have many issues in their own backgrounds that can affect their ability to learn: special learning disorders, family problems, drug addiction, or a long sentence. One frustrating thing (especially for correctional education administrators) is that teachers are not trained in working with this type of student in a prison environment. Special training and professional development must be provided to teachers until they become accustomed to the special circumstances they will face. Even though many inmates are motivated, others are not, so teachers have to be creative with limited resources. Their students did not succeed in traditional school systems, and correctional educators must get them past this failure and do things differently. Finally, and only partly seriously, correctional educators do not get the summers off. Prison education programs go year round, unlike the traditional school calendar.

Overall, correctional educators are a very satisfied, motivated, and dedicated group of professionals. They do a difficult job, but feel that they are really helping people who understand the importance of their education and generally recognize that they do not have too many more chances to be successful. It can be a good career for those who like to teach and help others.

Mental Health Programs

Providing programs for inmates with mental illness represents a very difficult problem within correctional institutions. First, a relatively high percentage of inmates have mental health problems. Second, the security demands to control these inmates can be obstacles to program efforts. Finally, correctional agencies are not designed to provide mental health programs to the same extent as mental health agencies. Unfortunately, in many states, the link between correctional and mental health agencies is often not as strong as it could be, and some mental health agencies (in many states, the mental health agencies are charged with the responsibility) do not give provision of mental health services within a prison a high priority.

A 2006 U.S. Department of Justice, Bureau of Justice Statistics, survey of prisoners estimated that more than half of all prison and jail inmates experienced a mental health problem within the past twelve months.[35] And, 15 percent of state prisoners and 24 percent of jail inmates reported symptoms classified as psychotic disorders.[36] This is consistent with an earlier estimate that 16.2 percent of all prisoners were identified as mentally ill.[37] Beck and Maruschak found that on June 30, 2000, 1,394 of the nation's 1,558 public and private adult prisons provided mental health services to inmates, yet only one in eight prisoners were receiving mental health therapy or counseling services.[38] Although still too low, this appears to have marginally improved. A 2006 review indicated that 34 percent of state inmates, 24 percent of federal inmates, and 17 percent of jail inmates received mental heath treatment since their admission.[39]

Even though almost all prisons provide mentally ill inmates with outpatient treatment, a 2000 census found that there were 155 prisons that were designed for and had an operational mission to provide mental health programming for inmates.[40] Some of these facilities house mentally ill inmates for long periods or throughout their incarceration. Others are used to house and treat inmates who have experienced acute episodes of mental illness for short terms, stabilize them with medication and treatment, and then return them to the general-population prison. A few states have agreements with the state mental health agencies to transfer the most severely mentally ill inmates to secure psychiatric hospitals for long-term treatment. In most cases, this requires a probate hearing by a court to determine that the inmate's illness is so acute that he or she must be hospitalized in such a facility.

Table 13.4 illustrates the number of inmates who were receiving mental health treatment while confined in state correctional facilities on June 30, 2000. The treatment is categorized in three types: twenty-four-hour care, therapy/counseling, and receiving psychotropic medication. In the table, the percentages represent the number receiving mental health services of the total inmates housed in the prisons that provide these services. There are 16,986 state prisoners housed in a mental health unit and receiving twenty-four-hour care. As indicated in Table 13.4, nearly 13 percent of state inmates (about 79 percent of those identified as mentally ill) receive mental health therapy or counseling services from a trained professional on a regular basis. This treatment was received by the highest percentage of female-only prisons (with more than one in four female inmates receiving therapy). Nearly 10 percent of all state inmates were receiving psychotropic medications such as antidepressants, stimulants, sedatives, or tranquilizers.

One key to successfully providing mental health treatment to inmates is a positive partnership between state and local correctional agencies and state and local mental health service agencies. In many states, the correctional

TABLE 13.4	Inmates Receiving Mental Health Treatment in State Confinement Facilities, by Facility Characteristic, June 30, 2000

| | Number of Inmates Receiving— | | | | | |
| | 24-hour Mental Health Care | | Therapy/ Counseling | | Psychotropic Medications | |
Facility Characteristic	Number	Percent	Number	Percent	Number	Percent
Total[a]	16,986	1.8%	122,376	12.9%	95,114	9.8%
Facility operation						
Public	16,270	1.8%	116,296	13.0%	90,721	10.0%
Private	716	1.3	6,080	10.8	4,393	7.7
Authority to house						
Males only	13,064	1.5%	100,371	11.9%	74,736	8.7%
Females only	830	1.5	14,744	27.1	12,119	22.1
Both	3,092	5.9	7,261	14.3	8,259	15.2
Security level						
Maximum/high	6,928	2.4%	44,637	14.9%	35,069	11.5%
Medium	9,608	1.8	65,726	12.6	52,208	9.8
Minimum/low	448	0.4	11,593	9.3	7,355	5.8
Facility size[b]						
1,500 or more	6,298	1.4%	59,970	12.8%	45,283	9.3%
750–1,499	5,140	1.6	41,953	13.0	31,816	9.9
250–749	4,582	3.5	16,831	13.4	14,866	11.6
100–249	888	3.3	3,309	12.4	2,867	10.9
Fewer than 100	78	2.3	313	11.0	282	8.8

[a]Excludes inmates in mental health treatment in Florida for whom only statewide totals were reported.

[b]Based on the average daily population between July 1, 1999, and June 30, 2000.

Source: Allen J. Beck and Laura J. Maruschak, *Mental Health Treatment in State Prisons, 2000* (Washington, D.C.: U.S. Department of Justice, Bureau of Justice Statistics, July 2001), p. 3.

agency creates the physical setting for treatment within prisons, and the state mental health department provides staff, training, and other resources to carry out the treatment. In Ohio, a team of individuals from both the correctional and mental health agencies has developed a conceptual model of *holistic health care* that provides the following:

- Integrated medical, psychiatric, psychological, and chemical dependency service delivery
- Continuity of care within DRC (the correctional agency) and upon release
- An array of services
- Delivery of services by self-directed multidisciplinary work teams[41]

Particularly important is the **continuum of care** to provide various levels of mental health treatment based on the intensity of needs for each inmate as inmates prepare for movement from prison to release to the community. The most intensive level of care is an inpatient prison hospital, in which inmates

continuum of care
provision of mental health programs based on the intensity of needs for each inmate, including as inmates prepare for release to the community

with acute needs who represent a risk to themselves or others can receive aggressive treatment. For inmates who have severe mental illness symptoms but do not require a hospital setting, short-term crisis units are designed to stabilize their symptoms and return them to a general-population prison. The third level is a residential unit within a general-population prison, in which mentally ill inmates live and receive treatment in a therapeutic milieu, yet interact with other inmates for work, food services, and other program participation. Finally, general-population prisons provide outpatient therapy and counseling for mentally ill inmates who can live and function in a general-population prison.

Mental health programs within prisons are critical to accomplishing the mission of a correctional facility. Without the types of integrative and multileveled programs described here, mentally ill inmates can be disruptive and undermine the safe and secure operation of a prison. Without effective treatment, these inmates will be unable to prepare for release and successfully reenter the community. The final step in an effective correctional mental health program is transition to the community. In preparation for release, prison and postrelease staff contact community mental health programs, identify resources for continuing mental health treatment from prison to the community, and encourage the offender to seek care from these programs.

Substance Abuse Programs

Substance abuse treatment programs are also critical activities within prisons because such a high proportion of inmates have a history of drug or alcohol abuse. In a recent survey of the drug and alcohol abuse patterns of incarcerated offenders, the Bureau of Justice Statistics categorized inmates based on their substance abuse involvement (see Table 13.5). Fifty-three percent of state and 45.5 percent of federal prison inmates were classified as having any dependence or abuse. Of these, most (56 percent of those in state prisons and 50 percent of those in federal

TABLE 13.5	**Prevalence of Drug Dependence or Abuse among State and Federal Prisoners, 2004**	
Diagnostic Criteria	**Percent of Prison Inmates—**	
	State	**Federal**
Any dependence or abuse	53.4%	45.5%
Dependence and abuse	34.9	27.5
Dependence only	1.2	1.2
Abuse only	17.3	16.8
No dependence or abuse*	46.6	54.5

*Includes inmates who did not use drugs.

Source: Christopher J. Mumola and Jennifer C. Karberg, "Drug Use and Dependence, State and Federal Prisoners, 2004," *Bureau of Justice Statistics Special Report* (Washington, D.C.: U.S. Department of Justice, October 2006), p. 7.

prisons) were regular drug users in the month prior to their arrest.[42] In addition, 9 percent of state and 5 percent of federal inmates were determined to have been involved in alcohol abuse at the time of their offense.

Substance abuse treatment in prisons is critically important, as the Office of National Drug Control Policy reports that treatment while in prison and during postincarceration supervision can reduce recidivism by roughly 50 percent.[43] Historically however, the treatment needs of drug abusing inmates has gone unmet while they are in prison. In a 1991 study by the U.S. General Accounting Office, it was estimated that fewer than 20 percent of identified substance abusers were enrolled in a prison substance abuse program.[44] And in a 1998 report, only 24 percent of state inmates were estimated to receive treatment over the course of a year.[45] The percentage of inmates receiving treatment has improved over the past decade.

Table 13.6 illustrates the types of drug abuse treatment that are provided to state and federal prisoners, and in 2004, about 39 percent of state prisoners and 45 percent of federal prisoners those who were drug dependent or abusing in the year before their admission to prison took part in a drug abuse program.[46]

Residential treatment is the most intensive, in which inmates live in a unit entirely focused on a substance abuse milieu, and is often considered the most effective treatment for substance abuse. In a study of Federal Bureau of Prisons residential treatment programs, only 3.3 percent of those receiving treatment (compared to 12.1 percent of a similar group that did not receive treatment) were rearrested in the first six months after release.[47] This type of treatment is also the most expensive, and that explains why only 9.2 percent of state and 8.7 percent of federal inmates participate in residential programs.

In the following "An Interview With" feature, a substance abuse coordinator illustrates the challenges of providing substance abuse programs in prisons.

mycrimekit

Media—Video: Substance Abuse Programs

TABLE 13.6 Drug Treatment or Program Participation since Admission among State and Federal Prisoners who Used Drugs in the Month before the Offense, 1997 and 2004

| Type of Drug Treatment or Program Since Admission | Percent of Prisoners Who Used Drugs in the Month Before the Offense— | | | |
| | State | | Federal | |
	2004	1997	2004	1997
Any drug treatment or programs	39.2%	34.3%	45.3%	38.8%
Treatment	14.1%	14.6%	15.2%	15.4%
Residential facility or unit	9.2	8.8	8.7	10.9
Counselling by a professional	6.0	6.0	6.8	5.5
Detoxification unit	0.9	1.0	0.8	0.3
Maintenance drug	0.3	0.3	0.2	0.4
Other programs	33.7%	28.3%	38.8%	31.7%
Self-help group/peer counseling	26.9	23.1	20.8	15.8
Education program	17.0	14.1	28.1	23.8

Source: Christopher J. Mumola and Jennifer C. Karberg, "Drug Use and Dependence, State and Federal Prisoners, 2004," *Bureau of Justice Statistics Special Report* (Washington, D.C.: U.S. Department of Justice, October 2006), p. 9.

Substance abuse inmates participate in group counseling sessions. Reprinted with permission of the Corrections Corporation of America.

An Interview With...

A Substance Abuse Coordinator

Don Murray has been a coordinator of substance abuse programs in prisons for almost twenty-five years. He has worked in three different prisons, as chief of mental health services for the Federal Bureau of Prison and as director of substance abuse programs for Corrections Corporation of America. In these roles, he has developed an understanding of the problems facing substance abusers and the characteristics of the types of programs that best work for this difficult population.

Question: What percentage of prison inmates have a serious substance abuse problem, and why are substance abuse and crime so closely correlated?

Dr. Murray: There are substantial substance abuse problems in prisons, and the issues are even greater in jails. Studies show that 90 percent of individuals are under the influence of alcohol or drugs at the time of their crimes. They may be diagnosed as abusing or being dependent on drugs. Fifty to sixty percent of inmates (this is probably a conservative number) entering a prison have substance abuse problems. The more areas of life that drug abuse affects, the more likely criminal activity will occur. The reason substance abuse and crime are so closely correlated was determined by David Nurco, who developed the multiplier effect, which

states that using drugs can lead to selling them, addiction, and other problems.

Question: Can you describe the addiction issues that relate to substance abusers?

Dr. Murray: I like to conceptualize addicts along two paths, although this is a very simplified dichotomy. The first category of addict is the primary addict, who was an addict and resorted to crime as a way to support their habit. They don't necessarily have many character disorders, but just commit crimes to get money. For men, their crimes are often robbery, theft, and breaking and entering. For women, it is usually prostitution. The secondary type was not an addict to begin with. Their initial use was part of their sensation-seeking world. These people are usually antisocial personalities. Their drug use led to addiction, which led to other illegal acts. In most of these cases, there were character impairments, and drugs were a way to self-medicate and were part of their lifestyle.

Question: How do you have to attack substance abuse in prisons?

Dr. Murray: The most important thing is to have a comprehensive assessment of all people. Successful

...continued

addiction treatment is not a one-stop, one-program reaction. People become addicted for many reasons, and treatment programs must address their individual problems. The approaches must be as different as are the effects of different drugs. It is very difficult to offer the variety of programs in prisons due to funding limitations. People often do not receive the treatment they need in prison, and re-addiction is too common immediately after they leave prison. If we were better able to develop individual treatment programs and postprison monitoring programs, we would be more successful in treatment. The most important treatment time is during reentry. Having individual treatment does not require 3,000 treatment programs. But it does require individual assessments (the most important aspect of treatment) that assign offenders to the types of programs that fit their issues. The more comprehensive and consistent the programs, the more effective they will be. During incarceration, unit-based individual treatment programs (separate units for people with addictions) have been found to be most effective and must be of duration of six to nine months. Also, it is extremely important to have a monitoring program that occurs as part of the aftercare monitoring as the individuals return to the community. Reentry often causes anxiety and negative emotional states, and this is a critical time as offenders are likely to return to drug use as a way of coping.

Question: What are the ranges of substance abuse program types for prisoners?

Dr. Murray: There are many programs, and no single treatment program is appropriate for all addicts. There are very traditional twelve-step programs that offer a spiritual or moral basis. There are also scientific-based programs that help people recognize negative emotional states and other triggers that lead to addictive behavior and then deal with those issues. Finally, there are cognitive behavioral programs that attack the underlying faulty thinking pattern of addicts. One example of that is the frustration someone feels at not having a great job and the great life they feel entitled to them, and they then take what they want. Finally, there is methadone maintenance for heroin addicts.

Question: What types of programs seem most effective?

Dr. Murray: Research tends to show that cognitive-based and relapse-prevention programs (both deal with behavior therapy) are the most effective. Success of treatment is determined by what happens after inmates' release. It is important to have a good assessment and consistent programs and skilled providers to be successful.

Question: Can you describe any success stories or failures that give students a realistic understanding of the challenge of trying to treat substance abuse?

Dr. Murray: The Federal Bureau of Prisons is just one of many agencies that has developed successful addiction programs. One study (which is one of many) shows that 76 percent of inmates treated versus not treated in prisons are much more likely not to return to drug use during the first year after prison. Addiction is a chronic problem and often requires participation in many different programs before the individual recovers. In the long run, for people who recover from drug use, the cost of their treatment is much less expensive than the other problems caused by their drug use, for example, hepatitis, incarceration, and law enforcement activities.

I have the pleasure of working with someone I knew as a federal inmate in a prison where I was chief of Psychological Services. He received treatment and now is a treatment leader in one of our facilities. He has helped many, many people recover from their addictions.

Question: What types of jobs are available for students who wish a career in corrections working in substance abuse programs?

Dr. Murray: Many counseling and program director jobs are available, and there is a tremendous need for filling these positions. For mental health professionals, there always are opportunities to work in corrections. This need will continue as prison populations increase and prisons continue to house individuals with addictions and mental health problems. It is helpful to have a background either in psychology or criminal justice, and substance abuse treatment knowledge is very important, as is being a licensed chemical dependence counselor.

Prison Work Programs

Just as rehabilitative programs have been an accepted component of prisons throughout their history, so has the importance of work. In the Walnut Street Jail, inmates labored in their cells at spinning, weaving, and shoemaking. Not only was such work considered important for the inmate, but early prison labor also benefited the state, as goods were sold to help prisons be self-sufficient. In the early 1800s, state prisons leased out prisoners to the private sector. Companies would bid for control of the prison and its labor, and the winning leaseholder worked the inmates in their industrial operations and, to maximize profits, spent as little as possible to house and feed the inmates. The **lease system** ended in the early twentieth century, and states began to operate their own prison industries to keep inmates busy and make a profit from the sale of produced goods.

As prison industry programs expanded during the early 1900s, organized labor began to complain about the unfair competition resulting from prisons' sale of goods using free inmate labor. As a result, Congress passed the Hawes-Cooper Act in 1929, requiring that prison products be subject to the laws of any state to which they were shipped. Opponents of prison-made products argued that this did not go far enough, and in 1935 Congress passed the Ashurst-Sumners Act, mandating that prison products be marked as prison-made goods, and then amended the act in 1940 to fully prohibit the interstate shipment of prison goods.

These acts ended the sale of prison products on the open market and, as an alternative, prisons began to produce goods that could be used by the state and federal governments. This **state-use system** resulted in prison industries producing inmate clothing, office furniture, and other products that could be sold to government agencies. In 1934, Congress established Federal Prison Industries (FPI) as a wholly owned government corporation to produce prison goods for sale to the federal government. FPI is currently the largest prison industry program and is a major producer of goods for government agencies (primarily the military) with sales of almost $500 million a year.

Although thousands of inmates work in prison industries, the majority work in other areas of prison operations to help run the prison. In most prisons, staff supervise inmates who actually do the work, such as preparing and serving food, doing laundry, doing electrical or plumbing work to maintain the facility, and cutting grass or doing other landscape work. The public supports prison work programs both to assist in rehabilitation and to prepare inmates for the work environment in the community. Prison officials consider work programs essential for managing a correctional institution, because they keep inmates productively busy and help maintain control and order.

lease system
state prisons accepted bids and leased out prisoners to the private sector, which would work the inmates in their industrial operations

state-use system
only allowing prison-made goods to be sold to and used by the state and federal government agencies

Many prison inmates work in trades areas such as heating and air conditioning, learning skills that can help them find jobs after release. Photo by Richard P. Seiter.

Inmates are assigned to several different areas of the prison. Some work in the prison laundry washing sheets, blankets, and inmate clothing. In food service, inmates prepare food, serve it to the inmate population, and clean dishes and cooking equipment for the next meal. Other inmates work in the prison maintenance department in such areas as plumbing, electrical, heating and air conditioning, carpentry, and maintenance of prison landscaping and grounds. Finally, prisoners are used to constantly clean the prison. Sanitation is very important to prevent unsanitary conditions and the spread of infectious diseases in a prison with such large numbers of people living in congested, overcrowded conditions. Overall, between 75 and 90 percent of prisoners work in these types of job assignments to maintain the prison and its daily operations.

Prison Industries

Even with criticism from labor and trade organizations resulting in restrictions for the markets, prison industries continue to be very important to prison operations and for inmate rehabilitation. Prison industries has several benefits:

1. Industrial work assignments that are similar to private-sector operations provide inmates realistic work experience and instill positive work habits.
2. Work experience can provide valuable training and skill development that inmates can use after release.
3. Inmate earnings can be used to support families, pay fines and restitution, and provide inmates money to purchase their own personal items allowed in prison.
4. Earnings by the industry can be used to offset the cost of incarceration.
5. Industrial work assignments are a positive way to reduce idleness and serve as an incentive for good behavior; therefore, they are valuable for inmate management.[48]

After surviving the challenges presented by the congressional acts of the 1930s, prison industry programs have grown significantly. On January 1, 2002, there were 78,881 inmates (7.8 percent of the prison population) working in prison industries in the fifty states, the District of Columbia, and the Federal

Prison industry programs keep inmates productively busy while in prison and have been shown to reduce recidivism after release by inmate participants. Photo by Richard P. Seiter.

Bureau of Prisons. In 2001, these programs had sales of $1.7 billion and profits of nearly $19 million.[49] Inmates work under the supervision of staff, which must maintain a close watch over security and quality. Some of the most common products produced and sold for state use include garments and textile products, wood furniture, printing services, metal products, and other services such as laundry, warehousing, data entry, and construction. Inmates are paid between $2.63 and $7.64 per day.[50]

In addition to the state-use programs of prison industries, Congress in 1979 passed the Private Sector Prison Industry Enhancement Certification (PIE) Program, which allowed for the sale of prison goods on the open market if the program is certified as meeting several conditions, including the following:

- Paying the inmates wages comparable with similar jobs in the community
- Consulting with representatives of private industry and organized labor
- Certifying that the PIE industry does not displace employed workers in the community
- Collecting funds for a victim assistance program
- Providing inmates with benefits in the event of injury in the course of employment
- Ensuring that inmate participation was voluntary
- Providing a substantial role for the private sector[51]

Almost two-thirds of the states are involved in the **PIE Program,** in which private companies hire inmates to produce goods inside the prisons. In 2001, there were 5,103 inmates employed in over 200 PIE industry programs. Since they must pay inmates wages comparable to private-sector workers, the daily wage as of January 1, 2002, for inmates working in PIE ranged from $21.43 to $36.50.[52] Another requirement is that a share of the inmates' salary is withheld for fines, victim compensation, room and board, support of families, and payment of taxes. From the beginning of the PIE Program until June 2003, on wages of $264 million, more than $146 million was withheld from pay, of which 48 percent was for room and board, 24 percent for taxes, 17 percent for victim restitution, and 11 percent for family support.[53]

Prison industry programs are an asset to prison operations, provide funds to operate, and reduce recidivism. Saylor and Gaes conducted the Post-Release Employment Project, collecting data on more than 7,000 federal offenders for a four-year period, comparing those participating in prison industries work programs with similar offenders who did not participate in programs. The results demonstrated significant and substantive effects on both in-prison (misconduct reports) and postprison (employment and arrest rates) outcome measures.[54] As beneficial and successful as prison industries is to a prison operation, it is unfortunate that such a low percentage of inmates are able to participate in these programs.

PIE Program
prison industry programs operated by private companies, with prison goods authorized to be sold on the open market if the program is certified as meeting certain conditions

Religious Programs

Since their inception, prisons have been places for religious reformation. Even though religion used to reform offenders is not the focus in modern prisons that it was in the Walnut Street Jail, religious programming continues to be an important rehabilitative opportunity within prisons. Whether due to the history of prisons or because U.S. society values religion, we will probably never give up the belief that the practice of religion is valuable for inmates and that offenders who develop a foundation of religious beliefs are more likely to be successful upon their return to the community. Today, prisons strive to provide religious programs for any group or individual who wants to worship and follow the tenets of a recognized faith.

Most inmates are Muslim, Jewish, Protestant, or Catholic, yet there are dozens of other religious sects and worship groups. In most prisons, religious services and activities are coordinated by one or two full-time chaplains (usually Protestant and Catholic) who contract with ministers of other sects to hold services and provide religious guidance for prisoners of those faith groups. In addition to regular services, activities may include Bible study or religious discussion groups. With usually fifteen to twenty different religious groups, the schedule for religious programs is usually very full, and there are often two or three faith groups meeting on any given night. Volunteers play a particularly important role in providing religious programming; they are used to lead study or discussion groups.

Recreation Programs

Another important but far more controversial area of prison programming is recreation or leisure activities. Although it is certainly reasonable to recognize that inmates cannot be in their cells or working the entire day, and therefore some types of organized and supervised activities are important to maintain order, the public does not like the image of inmates with too much idle time, watching color television or lifting weights. Therefore, prison officials attempt to have active recreation programs that reduce idleness, promote health and fitness, and allow inmates to "burn off steam" through exercise.

Most inmates are required to work approximately six hours per day, five days per week, but there could be far too much idle time without extensive recreational

Recreation is considered critical to a controlled and orderly prison. Photo by Richard P. Seiter.

programming to keep inmates busy. Prison recreation programs include outside sports such as soccer, basketball, or softball; less active recreation such as table games or card playing, billiards, or Ping-Pong; art and craft activities such as painting, leather crafts, or pottery making; and fitness programs such as running or calisthenics. Organized athletic activities, such as intramural teams, also have positive rehabilitative benefits, in that they require inmates to work together, develop teamwork, and follow rules and procedures. Recreational programs are also an incentive for good behavior, because inmates can be disciplined by restriction of their participation in such activities.

The most controversial recreational activity is weight lifting, which has been a staple of prisons for decades. Recently, many state legislatures, county governments, and Congress have passed legislation ending or limiting weight lifting in prisons and jails. The first effort to ban weight lifting in prison came after inmates, in a 1993 riot at the Southern Ohio Correctional Facility, used weight equipment to break into rooms in which staff were hiding and take them hostage. As a result, an Ohio congresswoman proposed legislation to ban weight lifting in prison, arguing that the elimination of weights would protect staff from harm. Along with banning weight lifting, many of these legislative acts have also banned the use of electronic musical instruments, paid programming such as HBO movies, and leisure activities such as pool and billiards.

Opponents of weight lifting in prisons argue that inmates who get stronger represent a danger to correctional and law enforcement personnel who may have to physically control them. They suggest that the public does not like the image of inmates spending their time getting stronger by working out with weights, and this image reinforces the stereotypes of a leisurely prison life that does not serve as a punishment and deterrent to crime. However, most correctional officials oppose any ban on the use of weight equipment, arguing that such exercise is an important incentive for good behavior and that there are very few cases in which staff

With the controversy regarding weights in prisons, several prisons have removed weights and replaced them with "dip" bars or other exercise equipment. Photo by Richard P. Seiter.

must physically confront a stronger inmate. They point out that weight-lifting inmates seldom get into trouble; they are usually very self-disciplined and do not want to lose the opportunity to exercise. Also, prison staff are trained not to attempt to break up a fight or get into a physical confrontation unless they have a definite physical advantage or staff greatly outnumber inmates.

Over the past decade, and partially as a result of the ban on weight lifting in many jurisdictions, prisons have started recreation programs focusing on educating inmates regarding health and diet to encourage them to develop healthy lifestyles. Offenders enter prison with histories of poor medical care, nutrition, and eating habits and a lack of understanding of the importance of exercise and aerobic activities to reduce fat and improve heart functioning. As prison sentences lengthen and inmates age while in prison, the costs of medical care increase significantly. Health education programs are a negligible investment in improving the long-term health of offenders and thereby reducing health care costs for inmates in the future.

Even though there is significant opposition to recreation programs for inmates, they will continue to be an important part of prison programming. There is no alternative to increased idleness if inmates have nothing to do with the time they are not at work or participating in a self-improvement program. Prison administrators fear idleness as a precursor of violence and inmate unrest, especially in today's overcrowded prisons, and forcibly argue this point to elected officials, and prisons will continue to have active recreational programs to encourage good behavior and maintain order.

Summary

Custody and treatment make up the two key emphases in the mission of prisons. Prisons attempt to create a safe and secure environment through the implementation of professional security policies and provide inmates many program opportunities that can aid in their successful reentry to the community. In many ways, the two components of the prison mission seem in competition with each other. How can a prison maintain security and order while encouraging inmates to participate in self-improvement programs? And how can positive programs operate within an environment that must control every inmate activity? However, in other ways, these two emphases seem to complement and support one another, because active programs help develop self-control and encourage inmate good behavior.

In this chapter, the approaches and activities undertaken within prisons to ensure security and custody while promoting participation in inmate programming are described. Important practices for maintaining security and order include effective classification systems, adequate physical security, consistent implementation of policy and procedure, inmate accountability and control of contraband, a fair and equitable disciplinary system, methods to separate inmates when necessary, and preparation to respond to inmate disturbances and riots. Valuable program activities include education and vocational programs, mental health treatment, substance abuse programs, work activities including prison industries, religious programs, and leisure activities.

No one questions the importance of security and custody practices within a prison. Few would doubt the need to control inmate behavior and mandate compliance with rules and policies to create a safe environment for staff and inmates and fashion such habits among inmates. However, there is considerable controversy regarding the importance of many prison programs in terms of their cost and potential to undermine the punitive and deterrent aspects of a prison sentence. Yet prison programs reduce idleness, teach inmates to live and work in groups, open staff-inmate channels of communication, increase the confidence and self-esteem of offenders, encourage them to accept challenges and strive for success, and increase the educational and vocational skills of inmates.

Many correctional programs have proved effective in reducing recidivism. Several studies over the past decade have affirmed the value of prison rehabilitation programs[55] and bode well for their future. Even with an emphasis on "punishment" of criminals, the public expects them to return to the community better prepared to become law-abiding citizens. Rehabilitative programs are a reasonable investment in saving money associated with continued offender criminality. We know that simply enhancing criminal sanctions and increasing the level of punishment do not reduce recidivism. However, correctly classifying offenders and providing them with quality treatment interventions result in a significant reduction in recidivism.

Key Terms

inmate accountability

work call

controlled movement

call out

pass system

regular counts

stand-up count

census count

random count

contraband

shadow board

special housing unit

administrative detention

disciplinary segregation

environmental factors

precipitating event

hostage negotiation team

disturbance control team

special emergency response team

mandatory prison education

vocational training

Pell grants

continuum of care

lease system

state-use system

PIE Program

Review Questions

1. What is the definition of custody and treatment?
2. List the eight types of activities that contribute to the security and custody functions within a prison.
3. Define inmate accountability and list the key components to maintaining inmate accountability in a prison.
4. What is the difference between controlled movement and a pass system?
5. What is a stand-up count?
6. How do random counts prevent inmates from planning escape around the other two types of counts?
7. What is contraband?

8. List five Class A tools under prison security policies.

9. What is a shadow board and how is it used to control contraband?

10. What is the purpose of an SHU and what are the two categories of assignment to an SHU?

11. What does it take for a precipitating event to cause a prison riot?

12. Name the three types of teams included in prison emergency plans.

13. What is the Stockholm Syndrome?

14. What percentage of inmates have basic literacy needs?

15. What are mandatory education programs in prisons?

16. How are mental health programs delivered in prisons and what is the continuum of care?

17. Describe the various types of substance abuse programs in prisons.

18. Define the state-use system for prison industries.

19. Outline the conditions required to be certified as a PIE Program.

20. List the arguments against weight lifting in prison.

You Make the Decision...

Lock Him Up?

Inmates may be placed in administrative detention (AD) if determined a risk to their safety if they remain in general population. The difficult decision is when to lock up inmates, or place them in the SHU, when there is no definite evidence that they are at risk. The following situation is not uncommon.

An inmate comes into the captain's office and tells the officer in charge that he is being pressured to have his wife bring drugs into the prison by a group of inmates. He thinks the inmates are in a gang. He says they told him if he doesn't do it, he will be killed. He will not identify the inmates, because he is afraid that if he does, their fellow gang members will kill him. He won't give any more or any specific information, saying that anything he says that can be traced back to him and result in the other inmates being locked up for investigation will also result in his being killed. None of the security staff have had previous encounters with this inmate, can vouch for his credibility, or have any information to support his story. His case manager, when contacted, says the inmate had been seeking a transfer to a prison closer to his home where his wife lives. The case manager told the inmate that that prison was very overcrowded and that there was a moratorium on transfers for twelve months.

You could decide to place him in AD to separate him from the threatening inmates and transfer him to another prison. However, two problems can result. First, inmates sometimes create a story like this to get a transfer. They know that if they are at risk, they can expect to be moved to another prison, so they can manipulate the system. Second, just transferring the inmate does nothing to deal with a gang that is pressuring inmates to bring in drugs, and they will just try another inmate if this doesn't work out. So, most prison officials will push the inmate to give more specific information to act on the allegation; but do not want him to be in danger, even if he won't provide any details.

So, what do you do? You have to decide whether you would place him in AD. You do not want to give in to his manipulations for a transfer if he is not telling the truth. If you do, other inmates will do the same thing. Yet you can't ignore his request. Consider this, and decide either individually or in a small classroom group whether to lock him up or not.

Chapter Resources on mycrimekit™

Go to mycrimekit.com to explore the following study tools and resources specific to this chapter:

- **Practice Quiz:** multiple-choice, true/false, short-answer, and essay questions to help students test their knowledge
- **WebQuests:** learning activities built around Web searches
  - Community Corrections-Programs that Work: http://community.nicic.org
  - Justice Policy Institute: www.justicepolicy.org
  - Washington State Institute of Public Policy: www.wwsipp.wa.gov

- **Insider's Experiences:** "Rebuilding Staff Confidence after a Riot"
- **Seiter Videos:**
  - See a prison administrator discuss prison riots
  - See an expert discuss substance abuse programs
- **Career Center:** A Career as a Correctional Programs Supervisor
- **Flashcards:** Twenty-six flashcards to test knowledge of the chapter's key terms

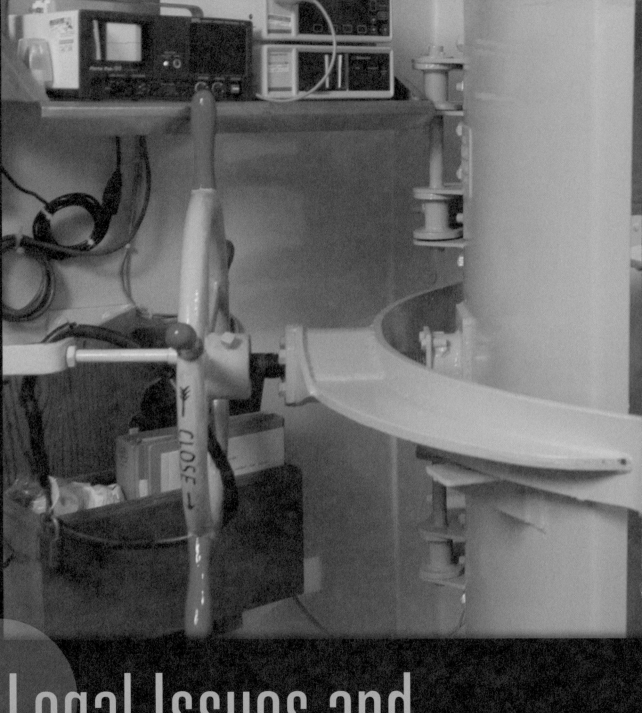

Legal Issues and the Death Penalty

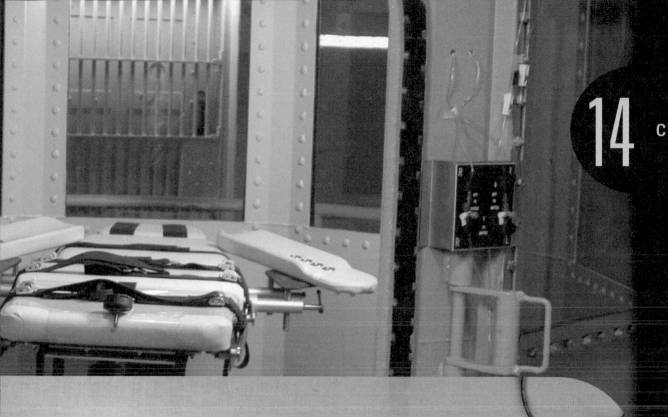

After reading this chapter, you should be able to:

1. Describe the historical development of the legal rights of inmates and the creation and then abandonment of the hands-off doctrine by federal courts.

2. Explain how the First, Fourth, Eighth, and Fourteenth Amendments to the U.S. Constitution create a basis for inmate lawsuits.

3. Identify the types of tests the courts have created to consider whether prison conditions of confinement violate the Eighth Amendment rights of inmates.

4. Specify the legal cases and constitutional standards regarding inmate religious practice, delivery of medical care, and inmate discipline within prisons.

5. Explain how recent court decisions and congressional actions have limited the filing of inmate lawsuits.

6. Specify the legal decisions that have affected the use of capital punishment in the United States and describe the requirements for capital trials under *Furman v. Georgia*.

7. List and describe court rulings regarding the use of capital punishment with juveniles, the mentally ill, the mentally retarded, and for noncapital crimes.

8. Detail the number of inmates under sentence of death, the number of executions each year, and the manner in which inmates are executed in each state.

9. Explain the various reasons cited by proponents of capital punishment and the counterarguments of its opponents.

10. Describe the current and any changes in public attitude regarding the death penalty.

Introduction

This chapter discusses the complex issues of the legal rights of inmates and the use of capital punishment. There are, perhaps, no more emotional topics than these in the overall operations of correctional agencies. Few people would argue that inmates should lose every right they have, as citizens of the United States, as a result of committing a felony and being imprisoned. It is uncomfortable to think about the unfair treatment, torture and excessive use of force, discrimination, and failure to provide basic due process to inmates that has occurred during the history of correctional institutions. Although most agree that inmates do not deserve such treatment, many people also believe that inmates today receive too many rights and unduly burden correctional officials and cost taxpayers money with petty claims, and that the pendulum has swung too far in providing inmates more rights than they should have. The first section of this chapter addresses the evolution of inmate rights, the foundation for prisoner rights provided by the U.S. Constitution, a description of the specific areas of inmate rights, and some movements to limit litigation by inmates against correctional agencies and officials.

The second section of this chapter addresses another emotional issue: the use of capital punishment. Even though our country has a long history of the use of the death penalty as a sanction for serious crimes, the majority of the public supports it, and the U.S. Supreme Court has ruled that capital punishment in itself is not cruel and unusual, there is still deep concern and persevering debate on the topic. The historical use of capital punishment in the United States and the very active consideration of capital punishment laws by the federal courts over the past thirty years are presented. Arguments for and against the need for capital punishment are described, as well as the constant concern about error in conviction and the irrevocability of a sentence of death.

Legal Issues Regarding Inmates

As much as is heard about inmates suing the state, the governor, the prison warden, or any number of other prison staff, we tend to believe that lawsuits have always been a part of the history of prisons, and inmates have always had, as some people think, more rights than law-abiding citizens. However, that is not the case. The truth is that inmates are still citizens of the United States and therefore come under the protection of the Constitution and the Bill of Rights, just like any other U.S. citizen. However, certain security and safety concerns in the operation of a prison allow prison administrators to limit inmates' full enjoyment of the rights they would have if they were not in prison.

Inmates have not been hesitant to file suits against correctional agencies or prison staff. In 1995, there were more than 40,000 civil rights lawsuits filed by inmates against state correctional agencies. The number of lawsuits began to slow soon thereafter, and there were fewer (24,463) lawsuits filed against a correctional agency or its staff in 2000.[1] On January 1, 2002, twenty-two states had seventy-eight class-action lawsuits in effect; court orders concerning conditions of confinement affected 143 prisons; and limits on how many inmates could be housed in prisons were in effect at 135 prisons in ten states.[2] Since 2000, the number of prisoner-initiated lawsuits in federal courts has continued to drop, with approximately 25,000 filed in 2006, even though the number of inmates is much higher than in the decade before.[3]

The Development of Inmate Legal Rights

Historically, until fifty years ago, there was little consideration of the rights of people confined in correctional institutions, as federal courts did not want to intervene in the administration of prisons. This avoidance was primarily the result of the 1871 decision of *Ruffin v. Commonwealth of Virginia*,[4] in which the U.S. Supreme Court enunciated the **slave-of-the-state doctrine** holding that inmates were, for all intents and purposes, slaves of the state and had no rights that were not granted them by the state. With this decision, the Court created what became known as the *hands-off doctrine* and did not accept lawsuits regarding violation of inmates' constitutional rights. The Court believed it good policy to continue this approach due to (1) the Court's lack of expertise in corrections and showing deference to the judgment of prison administrators, (2) the need for separation of powers between the judicial and the executive branches of government, and (3) a concern that accepting prisoner rights cases would open a Pandora's box of further litigation, and the courts would be flooded with prisoner lawsuits. The hands-off doctrine was supported in the 1948 decision of *Price v. Johnston*, when the Court ruled that convicted inmates must expect that as a part of their punishment they lose the freedoms that free citizens take for granted.[5]

Federal courts adhered to the hands-off doctrine for most of the next two decades. However, after reading complaints by inmates that seemed like a continuing escalation of the violation of basic tenets of the Constitution, the Court decided that it needed to give some guidance to correctional officials. In 1964, it accepted and heard *Cooper v. Pate*,[6] a case regarding religious freedom in prison. Black Muslim inmates claimed that they were not being allowed to congregate, eat their prescribed religious diet, or wear distinctive items of clothing, all of which were basic tenets of their religious practice and therefore a violation of Section 1983 of the Civil Rights Act of 1871. The Court, recognizing the Black Muslim faith as constituting an established religion, ruled that Black Muslims should be allowed to follow the prescribed practices of that religion, if those practices did not present a clear and present danger to the security and orderly running of a prison.

With their decision in *Cooper v. Pate*, the Court effectively ended the hands-off doctrine by recognizing that inmates could sue prison officials for violation of their rights under the Constitution. With this decision, the world of inmate lawsuits and legal issues for inmates changed forever. The floodgates were opened; the federal courts spend considerable time and resources handling inmate complaints and correctional administrators must constantly stay attuned to new decisions by the courts and the impact that such decisions have on prison operations. New decisions clarify the rights that are not lost by being convicted of a felony and incarcerated and guide correctional officials in following the earlier court **precedents** and revising policies and procedures to be consistent with such decisions. As a result, instead of the early belief that inmates lose their rights, it is now believed that inmates retain their constitutional rights as citizens when incarcerated unless the necessity for security and order in a prison deems otherwise.

Since the U.S. Supreme Court abandoned the hands-off doctrine, the number of cases filed has increased tremendously. In a 1994 review of the use of litigation by inmates under Section 1983 of the Civil Rights Act, Hanson and Daley note, "The Administrative Office of the U.S. Courts counted only 218 cases in 1966, the first year that state prisoners' rights cases were recorded as a specific category of litigation. The number climbed to 26,824 by 1992. . . . Finally, there is approximately one lawsuit for every thirty state prison inmates."[7] Figure 14.1 illustrates the increase in the number of lawsuits in comparison with the number of

slave-of-the-state doctrine
as decided in the 1871 decision of *Ruffin v. the Commonwealth of Virginia*, that held inmates were slaves of the state and had no rights that were not granted them by the state

precedents
decisions of the courts that come before and are therefore binding on later decisions of courts within the same jurisdiction

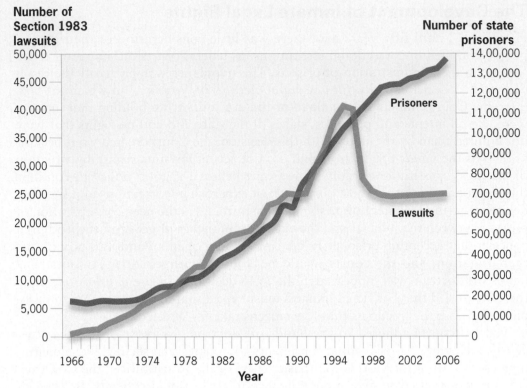

Source: John Scalia, "Prisoner Petitions Filed in U.S. District Courts, 2000, with Trends 1980–2000," *Bureau of Justice Statistics Special Report* (Washington, D.C.: U.S. Department of Justice, January 2002), updated with David Crary, "Law Curbing Inmates' Lawsuits Questioned," *USA Today*, February 13, 2008, http://www.usatoday.com/news/nation/2008-02-13-3685431048_x.htm (accessed August 16, 2009).

FIGURE 14.1 National Trends in the Number of State Prison Lawsuits

inmates from 1966 until 2006. Following a description of the development of prisoner legal issues in a variety of areas, there is a further explanation of the slowdown of lawsuits by inmates over the past decade.

The Bill of Rights and Congressional Actions Providing Inmate Rights

The source of all inmate rights is the Constitution of the United States (ratified in 1788) and the Bill of Rights (added in 1791), just as they are the source of the rights granted to all citizens of the United States. The primary amendments that are used as a basis of lawsuits by prison inmates are the Eighth (prohibiting cruel and unusual punishment) and the Fourteenth (providing due process to individuals charged with crimes). Other amendments, as well as specific laws passed by Congress, are used less frequently, but are still the basis of many inmate rights.

The **Eighth Amendment** states that no cruel or unusual punishment may be inflicted and is a broad opening for a variety of inmate lawsuits over aspects such as prison overcrowding, life and safety issues, use of force against inmates by staff, or poor food or medical care. It is difficult for a court or correctional administrators to determine what level of restrictions in a prison constitutes "cruel and unusual punishment." Obviously, torture or physical punishment are not allowed, but less obvious allegations of cruel and unusual punishment are more difficult to define specifically because almost every case has individual situations and presents varying facts. Over the past three decades, the federal courts have provided some guidance in defining cruel and unusual punishment in three major prisoner-rights cases.

Eighth Amendment
states that no cruel or unusual punishment may be inflicted

In the 1970 case of *Holt v. Sarver*, a federal district court looked at conditions throughout the Arkansas prison system and created a standard of cruel and unusual punishment under the Eighth Amendment. Going beyond the concept of torture or physical punishment, the court found that if people of *reasonable sensitivity* found the treatment shocking or disgusting, it would also be considered cruel and unusual. The court ruled that in general terms, cruel and unusual punishment is that which "amounts to torture, when it is grossly excessive in proportion to the offense for which it is imposed, or that is inherently unfair, or that is unnecessarily degrading, or that is shocking or disgusting to people of reasonable sensitivity."[8]

In the 1979 case of *Bell v. Wolfish*, the Court reviewed conditions and practices at a federal jail for short-term offenders in New York City. Even though the jail was recently constructed, it was already overcrowded, with two inmates held in most cells at the time of the inmates' complaints leading to this decision. Inmates also complained that prohibiting them from receiving hardback books not mailed directly from a publisher, not allowing them to observe searches of their cells, and requiring them to submit to visual searches of body cavities after visits with family members or friends constituted cruel and unusual punishment. The Court ruling adopted the *punitive intent standard*, stating that the case should turn only on whether the practices in question violated detainees' right to be free from punishment, using a standard of whether the individual restrictions were punitive or merely regulatory restraints, whether the practice is reasonably related to a legitimate goal other than punishment, and whether it appears to be excessive in relation to that alternative purpose.[9]

In *Solem v. Helm*, the Court in 1983 developed the *test of proportionality*, declaring the following:

> [W]e hold as a matter of principle that a criminal sentence must be proportionate to the crime for which the defendant has been convicted. . . . In sum, a court's proportionality analysis . . . should be guided by objective criteria, including (i) the gravity of the offense and the harshness of the penalty; (ii) the sentences imposed on other criminals in the same jurisdiction; and (iii) the sentences imposed for commission of the same crime in other jurisdictions. . . .[10]

The **Fourteenth Amendment** asserts that no state shall deprive any person of life, liberty, or property without the due process of law and also prohibits states from denying any person the equal protection of the law. When initially passed, the Constitution and Bill of Rights applied only to the federal courts and federal law in defining the relationship between citizens and government. The Fifth and Sixth Amendments guarantee due process in the course of legal proceedings, and the Fourteenth Amendment expanded these rights to states. Inmates who claim that prison officials have taken action against them for disciplinary reasons without providing them due process or that they have not had access to legal materials and therefore access to the courts often cite the Fourteenth Amendment.

Inmate lawsuits also regularly cite the First Amendment as the basis for their complaints. The First Amendment guarantees that no law shall be enacted that restricts or abridges an individual's freedom of religion, speech, and the press. These were seen by our founding fathers as such basic and fundamental rights (thus, the "First" Amendment) that the federal courts require very compelling reasons for prison officials to deny such freedoms to inmates. In the 1974 case of *Pell v. Procunier*, the U.S. Supreme Court created the **balancing test,** declaring that "[a] prison inmate retains those First Amendment rights that are not inconsistent with

Fourteenth Amendment
no state shall deprive any person of life, liberty, or property without the due process of law; states may not deny any person the equal protection of the law

balancing test
established in *Pell v. Procunier*, finding that prison inmates retain those First Amendment rights that are not inconsistent with their status as prisoner or with legitimate penological objectives

Civil Rights Act of 1871
this act of Congress
guaranteed the rights of freed
slaves and provided access to
federal courts for violations of
the act

Section 1983
a section of the Civil Rights
Act that prohibits any person
acting under the color of any
statute, ordinance, or
regulation (color of law) from
depriving another of his or
her constitutional rights

**Americans with
Disabilities Act**
a law that prohibits any entity
from discriminating against an
individual with a disability in
regards to employment,
public service and
transportation, public
accommodations, and
telecommunications services

his status as prisoner or with the *legitimate penological objectives* of a correctional system."[11] The Court recognized that correctional officials have legitimate concerns in trying to provide security and safety within a correctional institution and that these should be weighed (or balanced) against the restriction of rights. In more recent decisions, courts often have required prison officials to make reasonable accommodations to practices and procedures to allow for such rights. Issues under the First Amendment of use of the mail, access to outside publications, and access to the press are described next.

Not every right was anticipated or addressed in the U.S. Constitution or the Bill of Rights. Therefore, over the years, Congress has passed several acts to protect individuals against discrimination. The earliest was the **Civil Rights Act of 1871,** which guaranteed the rights of freed slaves and provided access to federal courts for violations of the act. **Section 1983** of the Civil Rights Act prohibits any person, acting under the color of any statute, ordinance, or regulation (color of law), from depriving another of his or her constitutional rights. The use of Section 1983 of the Civil Rights Act has expanded beyond the original use intended by Congress, and inmates regularly use it to sue government employees in their individual capacity for restricting religious practice, failing to provide proper medical care, or not protecting an inmate from assault by another inmate.

Another act of Congress that affects correctional institutions is the **Americans with Disabilities Act** (ADA) of 1990. The ADA prohibits any entity from discriminating against an individual with a disability in regard to employment, public services and transportation, public accommodations, and telecommunications services. The most difficult issues for correctional agencies arise in the sections dealing with employment and accommodation. Many prisons (like most law enforcement agencies) have physical conditions of employment that some disabled individuals cannot meet. And inmates can sue regarding the requirement that all areas of a prison be accessible to people with disabilities. The courts have continually (against strenuous objections by prison officials and governors from almost every state) held that the ADA applies to correctional institutions as well as other

The Americans with Disabilities Act of 1990 requires prisons to make accommodations for inmates with all types of physical disabilities.

Photo by Richard P. Seiter.

public entities. The states often argue that the ADA was not intended for prisons, but for public buildings, and that prisons, although funded with public money, are not public in that not everyone has access to them. However, in *United States v. Georgia* (2006), the Court unanimously ruled that under Title II of the ADA, the state has a duty to accommodate the needs of disabled persons, and that prisoners whose rights have been violated under the act may sue for monetary damages if the ADA violation also involves a violation of a prisoner's constitutional rights.[12]

Specific Rights of Prisoners

The Constitution, Bill of Rights, and other acts of Congress form the basis of rights provided to inmates and guide correctional officials as they struggle to maintain security and order in prisons without violating the basic rights of inmates. The next several sections describe specific areas in which inmate rights are often argued in courts and in which there has been an evolution of practice in correctional facilities. These include overcrowding and overall conditions of confinement, religious freedom, medical care, freedom of speech, use of the mail and receipt of publications, access to the press, access to the courts, privacy and search and seizure, and inmate discipline.

Conditions of Confinement

Inmates often complain about overcrowding and poor overall conditions of confinement (poor food, lack of satisfactory health care, unsanitary conditions) that can result from overcrowding or from simple neglect by prison officials. Courts use the **totality-of-conditions test** to determine whether the overall conditions within a prison constitute cruel and unusual punishment. The totality-of-conditions test examines the aggregate of circumstances in a prison to determine whether they, as a whole, are cruel and unusual, even if no single condition of the prison is cruel and unusual. This test was created in *Pugh v. Locke* in 1976, when Alabama prison conditions were found so debilitating that they deprived inmates of the opportunity to rehabilitate themselves or even maintain skills they already possessed.[13]

> **totality-of-conditions test**
> a test created in *Pugh v. Locke* that examines the aggregate of circumstances in a prison to determine whether cruel and unusual conditions exist

However, the U.S. Supreme Court has clearly determined that overcrowding (having more than one person in a cell) is not cruel and unusual punishment in violation of the Eighth Amendment. In *Bell v. Wolfish* in 1979, the Court held that there is no one-person, one-cell guarantee within a prison.[14] Shortly thereafter (in 1981), the Court in *Rhodes v. Chapman* determined that double celling in itself does not constitute cruel and unusual punishment, in that it does not "inflict unnecessary or wanton pain."[15] And finally, in 1991, the Court in *Wilson v. Seiter* (a significant corrections decision with the author of this text as the named defendant) noted that uncomfortable conditions are a part of the penalty that inmates pay for their criminality and that inmates must prove that conditions are objectively cruel and unusual and that they exist due to the **deliberate indifference** of prison administrators.[16] Deliberate indifference thereafter became the standard for individual liability under conditions of confinement suits brought under Section 1983. The "A Case Study" box illustrates some of the background issues that can lead to the development of inmate lawsuits.

> **deliberate indifference**
> as established in *Wilson v. Seiter*, the standard that conditions at prison are not unconstitutional unless prison administrators show deliberate indifference toward inmates' basic needs

A Case Study

The Development of an Inmate Lawsuit

Two significant cases regarding conditions of prison confinement are *Rhodes v. Chapman* and *Wilson v. Seiter*. As director of the Ohio Department of Corrections, I was directly involved in one of these lawsuits; I became director shortly after the U.S. Supreme Court decided *Rhodes v. Chapman*. The following case study illustrates some of the issues that can lead to inmate lawsuits and affect a court decision regarding the cases.

Rhodes v. Chapman involved the Southern Ohio Correctional Institution (SOCF) located in Lucasville, Ohio. SOCF was opened in the early 1970s to replace the century-old Ohio Penitentiary (OP). Its design was to be state of the art in that it would be all single cells in three different sections so that different groups of inmates could be separated. However, the prison opened with a large percentage of new staff, and some of the worst prisoners from the OP were transferred to the new prison. Too many inmates were transferred to SOCF too fast, and the staff competence and procedures could not keep up with the rapid growth in the number of inmates, many of whom were violent and disruptive.

The prison experienced several problems, including inmate riots, hostage takings, escapes, and staff union strikes. The upper management was changed and while things improved, there were still many problems. Inmate Kelly Chapman and others decided to sue the Ohio Department of Corrections, complaining primarily that the prison held many more inmates than the 1,600 single cells were designed to hold. Prison officials were unconcerned about double-celling, as the cells were fairly large (approximately 80 square feet), and the prison had ample space for programs and services.

The department won the case at the federal district court level, but the inmates appealed and won in the U.S. Court of Appeals. Ohio decided to appeal to the U.S. Supreme Court, believing that one person per cell would not be upheld. The case was won at this level, but only because the "totality of conditions" at SOCF indicated that inmates were out of their cells all but eight hours per day, many programs (education, vocational, and work) kept inmates busy during the day, and services (food services and medical) were adequate.

In *Wilson v. Seiter*, we had opened an old tuberculosis hospital that had been closed for several years as the Hocking Correctional Facility (HCF). Housing was dormitory-style, and the prison had just over three hundred inmates. We decided to place older inmates in the prison, as there was limited program and recreation space, believing that these inmates would need less space for such activities. Although the prison seemed to meet our needs, inmates complained that the old facility was too hot (it was not air conditioned) in the summer, and in the winter (due to rows of windows similar to an elementary school) it was not warm enough for the older inmates who lived there.

The case was quickly thrown out at the U.S. district court level, as the court did not believe that inmate "Pearly" Wilson and others involved in the lawsuit had complained about issues that breached their constitutional rights as prisoners. When the inmates appealed, the upper-level court determined that the lower court had used the wrong standard for determining that we as prison administrators had not violated the constitutional standard against cruel and unusual punishment. The case went to the U.S. Supreme Court not on the conditions that existed at HCF, but on the standard that prison administrators must be held to when conditions that were "uncomfortable" but possibly not "unconstitutional" existed. The decision by the Supreme Court that conditions at a prison are not unconstitutional unless prison administrators show "deliberate indifference" toward inmates' basic needs was a good win and very important for future defenses of inmate lawsuits by correctional agencies.

Religious Freedom

The practice of religious freedom was so fundamental in the founding of the United States that courts hold correctional officials to a high standard in the restriction of the practice of inmates' duly recognized religion. The First Amendment to the Constitution states that "Congress shall make no law respecting an establishment of religion, or prohibiting the free exercise thereof . . . ." In the 1964 case of *Cooper v. Pate*,[17] the Court determined that inmates should be allowed to practice their religion when the following conditions are met: (1) The religion claimed is a duly established religion, (2) the practices desired by inmates are part of the basic tenets of the religion, and (3) the practices do not present a clear and present danger to the security and orderly running of a prison.

Several cases since *Cooper v. Pate* have further refined this ruling. In terms of the religion being duly established, it is not for prison officials to determine which religions inmates may practice, yet inmates cannot just create some religion to subvert prison restrictions. In *Cruz v. Beto* (1972), the Supreme Court stated that inmates must be given a "reasonable opportunity" to practice their religion, even if the inmates' faith is not traditional or conventional.[18] Yet when a group of inmates at the Atlanta federal penitentiary created a new religion called the Church of the New Song (CONS) and demanded that steak and wine be included on the prison menu, the federal court disagreed (*Theriault v. Silber*, 1977), because it was not a religion entitled to First Amendment protection.[19]

If the religion is a valid one, inmates can practice activities that are determined to be based on basic tenets of the religion. For example, Jewish inmates must be provided kosher food as a part of the prison menu (*Kahane v. Carlson*, 1975).[20] Yet the court ruled in *O'Lone v. Estate of Shabazz* (1987) that prison officials do not have to rearrange inmate work schedules to allow a Muslim inmate to attend Friday worship services, even though Jumu'ah is a central part of the Islamic religious faith.[21] Another clarification of what is required for provision of religious activities is how in 1996, the Eighth Circuit ruled that prison officials must provide sweat lodges and the opportunity to use them to Native American inmates (*Hamilton v. Schriro*, 1996).[22] However, this was modified in the Eighth Circuit in 2008 when the court considered the potential future security problems that could occur with sweat lodges and the equipment and materials that go along with it (*Fowler v. Crawford*, 2008).[23] In this case, if prison officials reasonably believe that security and safety is compromised, they do not have to provide a sweat lodge to inmates.

When a religious practice can present a danger to the security and orderly running of a prison is difficult to generalize. In the *O'Lone* case, prison officials were successful partly because they argued that modifying the work schedules

Although federal courts initially ruled that prisons must provide sweat lodges for Native American inmates to practice their religious tradition of going into a small lodge (the branches forming an igloo-like structure are covered with blankets), a later decision allowed that if prison officials believe this undermines security, they can prohibit sweat lodges. Photo by Richard P. Seiter.

for inmates would undermine security. The courts often use a "reasonableness" test, established in the 1987 case of *Turner v. Safley*, in which the restriction of practice must reasonably be related to a legitimate penological interest, such as security or safety, but possibly including conserving resources.[24] And while the court recognized that it is not practical to provide every inmate a member of the clergy (*Gittlemacker v. Prasse*, 1970),[25] Muslim inmates have been allowed to have a special meal to end Ramadan, despite prison officials' argument that provision of special food served after sunset would be cost prohibitive (*Walker v. Blackwell*, 1969).[26]

An attempt to clarify the religious rights of prisoners through legislation came with the passing by Congress of the Religious Land Use and Institutionalized Persons Act (RLUIPA) in 2000. RLUIPA says that for the government to impose a substantial restriction on an inmate's right to exercise religion, it bears the burden to justify the restriction furthers a compelling government interest and is implemented in the "least restrictive means" of furthering that interest.[27] This was challenged by the State of Ohio, but in *Cutter v. Wilkinson* (2005), the Supreme Court found that RLUIPA did not violate the First Amendment and the least restrictive test continues. The decision of *Fowler v. Crawford* is likely to be further examined by the Supreme Court as to whether it modifies this standard.

An interesting case (*Americans United for Separation of Church and State v. Prison Fellowship Ministries*) decided recently has to do with prisons using public funds to offer faith-based programs to inmates. An Iowa state prison provided inmates a chance to live together and participate in the InnerChange program operated by Prison Fellowship Ministries that was dominated by Bible study, religious revivals, and church services. In 2006, the Southern District Court of Iowa ruled that the program was "pervasively sectarian" and therefore unconstitutional as it violated the separation of church and state.[28] Inmates in the program received privileges other inmates did not (more privacy, family visits, and computer time), and there were no equivalent nonreligious programs. The Eighth U.S. Circuit Court of Appeals affirmed the district court decision, noting that inmates had "no genuine and independent private choice" to receive rehabilitation services from an organization other than the one run by Prison Fellowship.[29]

Medical Care

The provision of adequate medical care is another basic right for inmates, established through court decisions responding to inmate suits alleging that failure to provide such care was a violation of the Eighth Amendment prohibition of cruel and unusual punishment. In 1970, the court looked at conditions throughout the Arkansas prison system, including medical care, and created a test of cruel and unusual punishment within the Eighth Amendment. Instead of including only the concept of torture or physical punishment, the court found that if people of reasonable sensitivity found the treatment shocking or disgusting, it would also be considered cruel and unusual (*Holt v. Sarver*).[30]

In *Estelle v. Gamble* (1976), the Supreme Court determined that prison officials have a duty to provide medical treatment to inmates, since inmates are dependent on them to provide for their medical needs. In this case, the Court prohibited "deliberate indifference" in responding to inmate medical needs, and neither medical staff in responding to needs nor correctional staff by denying, interfering with, or delaying access to medical care can be deliberately indifferent to such needs without the unnecessary or wanton infliction of pain.[31] In *Ramos v. Lamm* (1980), the court further suggested that deliberate indifference can also result from "repeated examples of negligent acts which disclose a pattern of

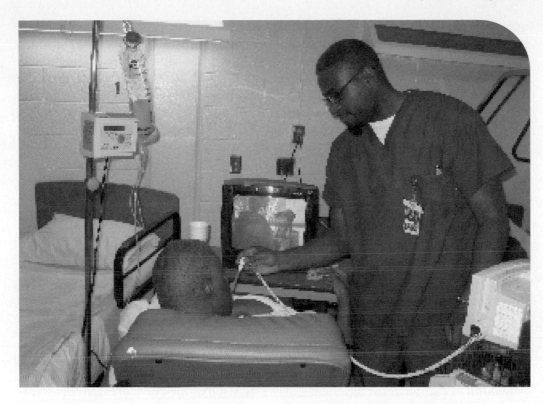

Prison medical care is an area of great sensitivity to inmates, who regularly complain about it. Photo by Richard P. Seiter.

conduct" by the correctional and medical staff.[32] And in 1991, the Court established that medical care in prisons must be "reasonably commensurate with modern medical science and of a quality acceptable within prudent professional standards" (*Fernandez v. United States* [1991]).[33] The principle of **community standards** seems reasonable in providing medical care, because inmates should expect to get the same quality of treatment for their health needs as they would receive if they were in the community. This does not mean that prisons must take every possible step in responding to medical needs, but they cannot deny inmates care that they would have received if not incarcerated. Medical care continues to be the topic that receives the most inmate complaints and suits. In addition to challenging a lack of adequate medical care under the Eighth Amendment, inmates often sue prison officials personally through Section 1983 of the U.S. Code, established in the Civil Rights Act of 1871.

community standards
the test established in *Fernandez v. United States* that medical care for inmates must be reasonably commensurate with medical care they would receive if not imprisoned

First Amendment Rights

The First Amendment of the Constitution prohibits Congress from "abridging the freedom of speech, or of the press, or the right of the people peaceably to assemble. . . ." Yet in terms of freedom of speech, almost everyone has heard that "you can't yell fire in the middle of a crowded theater" and recognizes that there are some restrictions to the common citizen's rights to free speech. It is easy to imagine that many such restrictions would apply to free speech, access to the press, or freedom to assemble in a prison environment. The balancing test created in *Pell v. Procunier* is the guideline used in determining the reasonableness of restricting First Amendment rights to inmates.

An example of the use of the balancing test is in the handling of inmate mail. Mail is recognized as important in communicating with family and friends outside prison, and such contact aids in rehabilitation and success after release. However, in the case of *Procunier v. Martinez* (1974), the U.S. Supreme Court acknowledged that there was a valid security interest in prison officials reading inmate mail, but determined that they could not censor it.[34] Prison officials also cannot prevent inmates from writing letters that are vulgar or disparaging about prison staff (*McNamara v. Moody*, 1979).[35] In *Turner v. Safley* (1987), the Supreme Court also allowed prison officials to continue to ban inmates from writing to inmates in other correctional institutions.[36] And in regard to restricting the right of assembly, the Supreme Court in 1977 supported the ban on inmates soliciting other inmates to join an inmate union, having union meetings, and doing bulk mailings regarding the union (*Jones v. North Carolina Prisoners' Labor Union, Inc.*).[37]

Freedom of access to the press as a First Amendment right has also been the subject of many inmate legal cases. In the *Pell v. Procunier* case, California prison officials were allowed to ban press and other media interviews with specific inmates when they believed it could endanger prison security. The Court found that there were alternative channels for inmates to communicate with the media other than in-person interviews. However, most correctional agencies do allow inmates to have interviews with the press, either by telephone or in person. The greater concern regarding media interviews is the inmate's right to privacy, and prison officials usually require that an inmate request such an interview, rather than a media person seek an interview with an inmate through prison officials.

Receipt of publications (magazines and books) is also an issue of First Amendment rights. In the 1971 case of *Sostre v. Otis*, the court created the "clear and present danger" standard.[38] Because there are publications that could detail how to saw prison bars with mess hall utensils, make a bomb, or provoke a prison riot, the court noted that such material could be inflammatory or dangerous, and its presence in a prison could create a clear and present danger. A ban of publications that wardens thought were detrimental to good order and institutional discipline or that might facilitate criminal activity was also upheld in *Thornburgh v. Abbott* (1989).[39] Prison officials are also concerned about publications such as magazines and books that, due to the nature of how they are assembled, could be used to hide small contraband items such as drugs. For that reason, the courts have upheld a restriction that allows inmates to receive such publications only directly from the publisher (*Guajardo v. Estelle* [1978]).[40]

Access to the Courts

Another basic right for U.S. citizens is that they have access to the courts to address any injustice. This holds true for inmates. In 1969, the Supreme Court in *Johnson v. Avery* recognized that inmates, to have full access to the courts, must often have legal assistance.[41] In its decision, the Court ruled that inmates have a right to consult other inmates for legal advice if trained legal advisors are not available. And shortly thereafter, the Court added that prisons must provide sufficient legal materials to enable inmates to conduct legal research in order to have reasonable access to the courts (*Younger v. Gilmore*, 1971).[42] This was further established in 1977, when the Court decided *Bounds v. Smith*, requiring prisons to provide adequate law libraries or adequate assistance from trained legal people.[43]

Fourth Amendment Rights

The Fourth Amendment provides that people be secure "against unreasonable searches and seizures." This affects prison officials, who must closely watch inmates, monitor their behavior, and control the importation of dangerous contraband (principally weapons and drugs) to maintain safety and security. The

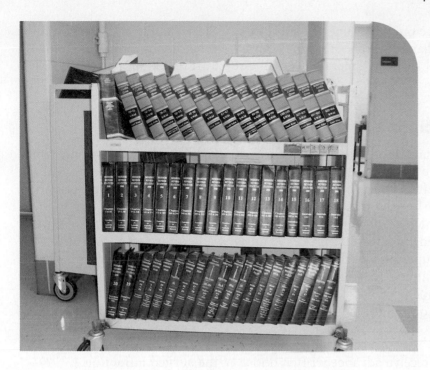

Even in jails or if inmates are held in an SHU, they have access to legal materials. Some institutions deliver legal books to these inmates on a cart. Photo by Richard P. Seiter.

practices of searches of inmates, their belongings, and their housing areas are basic to good prison security practices. The legal issue is how much privacy from searches is reasonable within a prison. The courts have clearly ruled that inmates do not have an expectation of privacy while in prison. In *Hudson v. Palmer* (1984), the Supreme Court dismissed the claims of inmate Palmer that searches of his cell were just to harass him and held that "the Fourth Amendment proscription against unreasonable searches does not apply within the confines of the prison cell."[44] Prison officials may do searches randomly and without providing specific justification. However, they are expected to leave inmates' cells orderly (not to trash them in the search), or inmates may sue under the Eighth Amendment for destruction of their property.

Inmates are also personally searched on a regular basis. In *Bell v. Wolfish* (1979), routine strip searches of inmates were deemed not to be a violation of the Fourth Amendment because they are reasonable to maintain security within a prison.[45] Searches of body cavities are more sensitive than a visual search of an inmate's naked body. However, it is not unusual for inmates to hide drugs, handcuff keys, weapons (bullets for guns), or even hacksaw blades in the rectum to smuggle them into a prison. Therefore, while these searches must be done, the courts require that there must be information that an inmate is hiding contraband in a body cavity, medical staff must conduct the search, and the search must be done in a manner that respects the inmate's dignity and privacy (*Tribble v. Gardner*, 1988).[46]

The courts have also addressed the issue of searches by prison staff of the opposite sex. In *Grummett v. Rushen* (1984), the court agreed with California prison officials that prohibiting female correctional officers from being assigned to housing areas in which inmates could be seen in partial or total nudity did not outweigh the women's equal employment opportunity rights.[47] The need for privacy can easily be accommodated by inmates wearing robes and by installing privacy screens in front of showers that do not totally block the view and therefore reduce security. Additionally, in *Johnson v. Phelan* (1995), the court also allowed searches of inmates by opposite-sex correctional staff, noting how impractical it would be to have only the same sex conduct searches of inmates.[48] However, the courts lecture against searches that may harass, humiliate, or intimidate inmates, and correctional agencies generally use same-sex staff to conduct searches, unless in an emergency.

Inmate Discipline

Inmate disciplinary processes are guided by the Fourteenth Amendment, which states, "No State shall . . . deprive any person of life, liberty, or property, without due process of law." Due process as it relates to disciplinary processes for inmate misbehavior within the prison was first considered in the 1974 case *Wolff v. McDonnell*, which dealt with a claim that the state of Nebraska disciplinary processes denied inmates due process and were therefore unconstitutional.[49] However, the Supreme Court differentiated between due process required by a defendant at trial and that of a prison inmate. Although prison inmates do not receive all the due process of someone not yet proved guilty, the Court enumerated the steps required for prisoner due process when facing a prison disciplinary hearing:

- The right to receive advance written notice of the alleged infraction
- The right to have sufficient time (at least twenty-four hours) to prepare a defense
- The right to present documentary evidence and to call witnesses on his or her behalf, unless permitting this would be unduly hazardous
- The right to have assistance (by an inmate or staff representative) when the circumstances of the case are complex or if the prisoner is illiterate
- The right to a written statement of the findings of an impartial disciplinary committee of the evidence relied on to support the finding of fact and the reasons the disciplinary action was taken

A later 1995 Supreme Court case clarified and gave new guidance to inmate disciplinary procedures requiring due process. In *Sandin v. Conner*, the Court, noting

Inmates have the right to limited due process in prison inmate disciplinary processes, and hearing officers not from the inmates' prison often decide guilt and punishment. Courtesy of Corbis/Bettmann.

that the purpose of prison disciplinary actions is to maintain good prison management and achieve rehabilitative goals, determined that disciplinary actions in pursuit of those goals that do not add to the sentence being served or change the conditions contemplated in the sentence being served do not create a liberty interest and do not require due process.[50] Thus, under *Sandin*, an inmate who violates a prison rule and receives a punishment of placement in disciplinary segregation for a temporary period does not trigger the need for due process, whereas loss of good time that subsequently extends the sentence (by delaying the release date) does trigger the need for due process. Even with the *Sandin* decision, most prisons find it more efficient and continue to provide the full *Wolff* due-process rights for handling inmate discipline.

All these areas regarding inmate rights are constantly developing and practices are changing based on the latest legal precedent. The greatest time of change was from 1965 until 1980, the first fifteen years after the U.S. Supreme Court abandoned the hands-off doctrine. Correctional agencies began to be somewhat more proactive in dealing with issues that often were found to be of concern to federal courts. However, in the early 1990s, public sentiment indicated a frustration and disenchantment with the high number of inmate lawsuits, and Congress took action to limit lawsuits filed by inmates.

Limiting Litigation by Inmates

Over the past twenty years, there have been a number of actions have led to a reduction in the number of lawsuits filed by inmates. First, some Supreme Court decisions seem to have "turned the tide" of decisions away from inmates and toward support for prison administrators. The beginning of the restrictions on inmates' rights was the 1987 case of *Turner v. Safley*, when the Supreme Court ruled that correctional administrators can restrict inmates' constitutional rights to reasonably further a legitimate penological interest such as security, order, or rehabilitation.[51] The 1991 case of *Wilson v. Seiter* is considered a key decision for correctional agencies; the Court stated that prison conditions, while they may be uncomfortable, are not unconstitutional unless administrators acted with "deliberate indifference" to the basic needs of inmates.[52] Also, the 1995 decision regarding the due process that should be provided to inmates in the disciplinary process in *Sandin v. Conner* considerably lessened the requirements of earlier cases by determining that only disciplinary actions that add to the sentence being served or change the conditions of the sentence require due process.[53]

Second, the courts have moved back toward the hands-off doctrine of allowing prisons to deal with problems themselves, rather than have inmates file lawsuits that are expensive to the correctional agencies and taxpayers. In 1980, Congress revised the Civil Rights of Institutionalized Persons Act, requiring inmates to exhaust their administrative remedies before filing a petition in federal court. If correctional agencies provide an administrative remedy process and give inmates a chance to informally resolve a problem or have a complaint dealt with by prison officials, the courts will require this process to be used before they accept an inmate lawsuit. Many federal courts require inmates to certify that they have exhausted these administrative appeals and include a copy of the response from the agency.

Finally, Congress has acted to make it more difficult for inmates to file successful suits against correctional agencies. In the Violent Crime Control Act of 1994, Congress (1) specified that federal courts find a violation of the Eighth Amendment only if the inmate filing the suit demonstrates that he or she has personally suffered from overcrowding conditions, (2) prohibited federal courts from imposing a population cap on a prison unless the "cruel and unusual punishment" is clearly harming particular identified inmates, and (3) allow a review of any court orders or consent decrees based on violations of the Eighth Amendment. In 1996, Congress passed the Prison Litigation Reform Act, requiring inmates filing prison suits to pay a filing fee unless they claim pauper status, limiting awards of attorney fees, punishing inmates with loss of good time for filing frivolous suits, and prohibiting inmates from suing for mental or emotional distress unless they have suffered a physical injury.

Although these actions do not eliminate the filing of lawsuits by inmates, many critics suggest that legitimate inmate cases are being blocked and cite the fact that even with an increase in the number of inmates from 1.5 million to over 2 million, the number of prisoner-initiated lawsuits in federal courts has dropped from about 41,000 in 1995 to 25,000 in 2006,[54] and fewer correctional facilities are under court directives than in past years. In 2000, one in five adult prisons were operating under a court order or consent decree, and by 2005, there was only one in eight.[55] The federal courts once were so actively involved in inmate legal actions that they often had to appoint a court monitor or special master to oversee their decisions. Correctional agencies now have the opportunity to thoughtfully address valid inmate claims and do not have to spend so much time and money responding to frivolous claims.

As we conclude this review of legal rights of inmates, the "Your Career in Corrections" box describes the role of correctional attorneys.

Your Career in Corrections

Correctional Attorneys

Although it is not a position that most people think about in a correctional agency, with all the inmate lawsuits it is obvious that correctional agencies need attorneys to advise and represent them. In most state and federal correctional systems, the agencies have full-time staff attorneys who work with staff and administrators, and the office of the attorney general (AG) then handles the actual litigation. The role of the attorney general is to direct the case and its defense and argue it in court if it goes that far before being dismissed or settled. The staff attorneys who work for the agencies have a very different role.

When an inmate sues a correctional agency, a big part of the function of the staff attorney is fact finding: digging for documentation, talking to witnesses, and finding out what really happened. It usually takes a combination of finding the right documents and talking to people to discover the true facts. Then the staff attorney works with the AG office to assess the case and determine the legal position of the agency. In most cases, there is no or limited basis for the inmate claim, and the agency

takes a position to fight the case and is usually successful in getting it dismissed before it goes to trial. In other cases, there may actually be the potential for liability, and the correctional agency must decide whether to fight the case or settle it (agree to some conditions or payment for the liability). In some cases, an inmate is asking only for a minor amount ($50 for a pair of shoes that were damaged or lost), and even though the agency does not feel responsible, it is more expensive to fight the case. Correctional agencies do not want to settle too many cases on this "nuisance value" situation, as it can encourage other inmates to file similar suits just because the agency will not fight it, but it is sometimes good practice to settle such nuisance cases.

Another role of the staff attorney is preventive, to watch for issues (policies or procedures) that may incur potential legal liabilities and try to get the policy or procedure changed. The staff attorney brings the issue to the decision makers, expresses the legal concerns, and advises them on the potential problems. In a way, the attorney helps administrators determine the most important aspects or outcomes of the policy or procedure and then works to find a more legally defensible way to accomplish what they want.

Correctional attorneys note that the best thing about their job is the variety of issues they address and variety of cases they work. At any time, they may have cases involving use of force, freedom of religion, medical malpractice, or conditions of confinement. In private practice, young attorneys are often pigeonholed into one particular area of the law and do nothing except work on these types of cases. The negative things about the job are that it sometimes seems as though much time is wasted dealing with minor or trivial cases, such as the nuisance value cases noted earlier.

Most people do not go to law school thinking about working for a correctional agency. Somehow they fall into the position and, once involved, most people stay with the correctional agency, obviously enjoying the variety and challenge of their work.

Capital Punishment

Many people, in discussing inmate rights, suggest that the ultimate right is to "life, liberty, and the pursuit of happiness." They go on to suggest that no discussion of the rights of inmates should fail to address the issue of *capital punishment*, the legal killing of someone by the government as punishment for serious criminal misconduct. The topic of capital punishment is one of the most hotly debated, emotionally charged, and controversial components of our criminal justice system. Some people oppose it on a moral basis, claiming that government never has the right of retribution by taking someone's life. Others argue that capital punishment is a deterrent and that executing a few people saves many other lives. The

The electric chair has been used throughout the history of capital punishment and is still in use in some states today.

Courtesy of the Ohio Department of Rehabilitation and Correction.

practical-minded propose that the overall cost to the criminal justice system should be considered in any decision regarding capital punishment. However, many disagree about whether capital punishment or a sentence of life in prison is less expensive.

In this section, we examine the history of capital punishment in the United States, the legal cases and developments regarding the use of the death penalty, the current status of capital punishment, the number of people on death row, and the methods of execution that are currently used. Also described are issues regarding capital punishment, including the potential for error in the finding of guilt, execution of juveniles and the mentally ill or retarded, the deterrent value, and the cost of capital punishment versus a lengthy prison sentence. Finally, the public's view and opinion of the death penalty are discussed, and the most recent actions by state officials regarding the death penalty are described.

The History of Capital Punishment in the United States

As noted in Chapter 1, capital punishment was used extensively in England and in the early American colonies, as many crimes (not just murder) carried a penalty of death. Brutal corporal punishments also regularly resulted in death, as the imposition of such torture so seriously injured the offender as to be a cause of his or her death. Both torture and executions were often carried out in public, as a deterrent to others with the threat of the punishment they would receive if committing similar crimes. Public executions continued until 1936, when several thousand people witnessed the execution by hanging of a black man convicted of raping and murdering a white woman in a small town in Kentucky.

With the creation of the prison as a criminal sanction, the reliance on corporal and capital punishment lessened, and the number and types of crimes that could result in capital punishment were reduced. Even though we believe that the criminal justice system became more "enlightened" and "merciful" during the twentieth century, the 1930s and 1940s still saw more than 150 executions per year. However, as indicated in Figure 14.2, the number of executions declined to zero in the late 1960s and did not rise until the late 1970s. Since the mid-1980s, the number of executions has climbed rapidly, and from January 1 to December 31, 2008, thirty-seven inmates were executed in nine states.[56]

Legal and Statutory Provisions for the Death Penalty

Figure 14.2 illustrates the dramatic decline in the number of people executed from 1940 to 1967. Peaking at 199 executions in 1935, the graph looks like a mountain range with peaks up and down, but with a consistent decline through the next three decades. Only two executions took place in 1967, and none were performed in 1968 or for the next ten years. This decline was primarily the result of the courts' willingness to consider appeals from death row inmates and continued legal challenges to the constitutionality of the death penalty. At this time, the public was not in a retributive mood; we were coming out of a war with a considerable number of fatalities, there was a strong belief in rehabilitation and that people could change, and crime was not a serious concern among the public.

Persons executed, 1930–2004

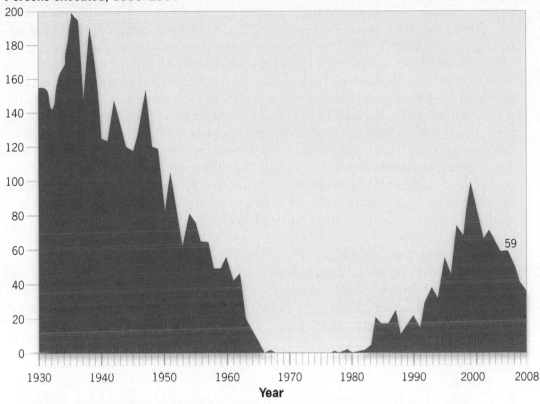

Source: Bureau of Justice Statistics, "Executions, 1930–2008," *Capital Punishment: Facts at a Glance*, www.ojp.usdoj.gov/bjs/glance/exe.htm (accessed August 16, 2009).

FIGURE 14.2   Executions, 1930–2008

The increasing amount of litigation regarding capital punishment culminated with the 1972 landmark decision by the U.S. Supreme Court in *Furman v. Georgia*.[57] Furman (a 26-year-old black man with a sixth-grade education) was burglarizing a home. When discovered by the homeowner, Furman tried to escape, shot back into the house through a closed door once outside, and killed the homeowner. Before his trial, Furman was committed to a state psychiatric hospital for evaluation. The hospital staff concluded that Furman had a mild to moderate mental deficiency, with psychotic episodes and a convulsive disorder. However, the staff concluded that Furman was not psychotic at the time of his trial, knew right from wrong, and was able to cooperate with his attorney to prepare a defense. Therefore, he was able to stand trial, and the jury found him guilty of first-degree murder and sentenced him to death.

The case was appealed and made its way to the U.S. Supreme Court, at which several critical decisions were made regarding the death penalty. First, the Court did not determine that capital punishment in itself is unconstitutional as cruel and unusual punishment, although two of the justices voted that it was. Without such a determination, the Court's decision did not put an overall ban on capital punishment throughout the United States. Second, in a 5–4 vote, the Court determined that due to the arbitrary, capricious, and unfair manner in which it was applied, the death penalty as then administered was cruel and unusual. However, the Court's decision (even with, or perhaps because of, each justice writing a separate opinion) provided no clear guidance to states as what would be considered not arbitrary and capricious. Within months after the decision, states began to rewrite their death penalty statutes to make them less arbitrary and constitutionally acceptable.

bifurcated trial

used in capital cases, with guilt first established at a traditional trial, and if found guilty, a second stage of sentencing considers between death or life imprisonment

States took two approaches to try to overcome the "arbitrary" concerns of the Supreme Court. The first approach was to adopt mandatory requirements for a sanction of the death penalty when a specific crime was committed, thereby eliminating discretion altogether. Both Louisiana and North Carolina had such mandatory statutes found unconstitutional in the 1976 cases of *Robert v. Louisiana* and *Woodson v. North Carolina*.[58] Most states passed guided-discretion statutes that provided for **bifurcated trials,** in which guilt was first established at a traditional trial. If found guilty, the trial moved to a second stage of sentencing, at which the jury would decide between death and life imprisonment, using statutory guidelines to consider both aggravating and mitigating circumstances of the crime. Aggravating circumstances could include the killing of a law enforcement officer, committing murder during commission of another felony such as rape or robbery, previous convictions of murder, or multiple killings. Mitigating circumstances could be emotional stress that impaired decision making, mental deficiencies, playing a secondary or minor role in the murder, or developmental problems that bring sympathy from the jury.

The first case in which a guided-discretion statute was considered and found constitutional by the U.S. Supreme Court was the 1976 case of *Gregg v. Georgia*.[59] Through its decision in this case, the Supreme Court laid out the expected elements of a state's death penalty to pass constitutional muster:

- The death penalty can be considered only for specific and the most serious crimes.

- The trial must be bifurcated into two stages: one to determine guilt and the other to consider the sentence.

- During the sentencing stage, the jury will hear evidence regarding both mitigating and aggravating circumstances surrounding the crime, the victim, and the defendant.

- There must be an automatic appeal and review of the death sentence to consider whether the sentence could have been arbitrary due to prejudice, passion, or some other factor; whether the evidence supports the finding during sentencing of statutory aggravating circumstances; and whether the death penalty has been similarly imposed for similar crimes and similar defendants.

Since *Gregg v. Georgia*, thirty-eight states and the federal government passed capital murder statutes. However, at this time, the District of Columbia and fourteen states (listed in Table 14.1) have either not passed or passed and later abolished death penalty statutes.

TABLE 14.1	States That Have Not Adopted the Death Penalty	
Alaska	New Jersey
Hawaii	New Mexico
Iowa	North Dakota
Maine	Rhode Island
Massachusetts	Vermont
Michigan	West Virginia
Minnesota	Wisconsin

Several other federal court decisions have addressed the death penalty since *Gregg v. Georgia*, some clarifying and addressing the death penalty regarding certain groups of offenders. As noted in *Gregg v. Georgia*, the death penalty can be imposed only for specific, serious crimes, and several cases have dealt with the issue of what is an acceptable crime for which to impose death as a sanction. In *Coker v. Georgia* (1977), the Court said that the death penalty was excessive for rape of an adult.[60] In *Godfrey v. Georgia* (1980), the Court decided that statements of aggravating circumstances that define the crime being "outrageously or wantonly vile, horrible, or inhumane" are too broad and vague.[61] And in 1987, the Court determined that the death penalty could be imposed on offenders who do not specifically intend to kill their victims (*Tison v. Arizona*).[62] Table 14.2 indicates the specific offenses in each state that can receive capital punishment.

TABLE 14.2	Capital Offenses by State, 2007
State	**Offense**
Alabama	Intentional murder with 18 aggravating factors (Ala. Stat. Ann. 13A-5-40(a)(1)-(18)).
Arizona	First-degree murder accompanied by at least 1 of 14 aggravating factors (A.R.S. § 13-703(F)).
Arkansas[a]	Capital murder (Ark. Code Ann. 5-10-101) with a finding of at least 1 of 10 aggravating circumstances; treason.
	Revision: Amended the definition of capital murder to include murder committed in the course of robbery, aggravated robbery, residential burglary, or commercial burglary (Ark. Code Ann. § 5-10-101 (Supp. 2007)), effective 7/31/2007.
California	First-degree murder with special circumstances; trian wrecking; treason; perjury causing execution.
Colorado[b]	First-degree murder with at least 1 of 17 aggravating factors; first-degree kidnapping resulting in death; treason.
Connecticut	Capital felony with 8 forms of aggravated homicide (C.G.S § 53a–54b).
Delaware	First-degree murder with at least 1 statutory aggravating circumstance (11 Del. C. § 4209).
Florida	First-degree murder; felony murder; capital drug trafficking; capital sexual battery.
Georgia	Murder; kidnapping with bodily injury or ransom when the victim dies; aircraft hijacking; treason.
Idaho	First-degree murder with aggravating factors; aggravated kidnapping; perjury resulting in death.
Illinois	First-degree murder with 1 of 21 aggravating circumstances.
Indiana	Murder with 16 aggravating circumstances (IC 35-50-2-9).
Kansas	Capital murder with 8 aggravating circumstances (KSA 21-3439, KSA 21-4625).
Kentucky	Murder with aggravating factors; kidnapping with aggravating factors (KRS 32.025).
Louisiana	First-degree murder; aggravated rape of victim under age 13; treason (La. R.S. 14:30, 14:42, and 14:113).
Maryland	First-degree murder, either premeditated or during the commission of a felony, provided that certain death eligibility requirements are satisfied.
Mississippi	Capital murder (Miss. Code Ann. § 97-3-19(2)); aircraft piracy (Miss. Code Ann. § 97-25-55(1)).

Continued

TABLE 14.2 **Continued**

State	Offense
Missouri[a]	First-degree murder (565.020 RSMO 2000).
	Revision: Added to the capital statute provisions for selecting members of the execution team and prohibiting disclosure of the identity of anyone who has been on the execution team (Mo. Rev. Stat § 546.720), effective 8/28/2007.
Montana	Capital murder with 1 of 9 aggravating circumstances (Mont. Code Ann § 46-18-303); aggravated sexual intercourse without consent (Mont. Code Ann. § 45-5-503).
Nebraska	First-degree murder with a finding of at least 1 statutorily-defined aggravating circumstance.
Nevada	First-degree murder with at least 1 of 15 aggravating circumstances (NRS 200.030, 200.033, 200.035).
New Hampshire	Six categories of capital murder (RSA 630:1, RSA 630:5).
New York	First-degree murder with 1 of 13 aggravating factors (NY Penal Law § 125.27).
North Carolina	First-degree murder (NCGS §14-17).
Ohio	Aggravated murder with at least 1 of 10 aggravating circumstances (O.R.C. secs. 2903.01, 2929.02, and 2929.04).
Oklahoma	First-degree murder in conjunction with a finding of at least 1 of 8 statutorily-defined aggravating circumstances; sex crimes against a child under 14 years of age.
Oregon	Aggravated murder (ORS 163.095).
Pennsylvania	First-degree murder with 18 aggravating circumstances.
South Carolina[a]	Murder with 1 of 12 aggravating circumstances (§ 16-3-20(C)(a)); criminal sexual conduct with a minor with 1 of 9 aggravators (§ 16-3-655).
	Revision: Added as an aggravating circumstance murder committed while in the commission of first-degree arson (§ 16-3-20(C)(a)(1)(j)), effective 6/8/2007.
South Dakota[a]	First-degree murder with 1 of 10 aggravating circumstances.
	Revision: Amended the code of criminal procedure to allow for use of a 3-drug protocol in administering lethal injection (SDCL § 23A-27A-32), effective 7/1/2007.
Tennessee[a]	First-degree murder with 1 of 15 aggravating circumstances (Tenn. Code Ann § 39-13-204).
	Revision: Amended the definition of first-degree murder to include killing in the perpetration of rape or aggravated rape of a child (Tenn Code Ann. § 39-13-202(a)(2)), effective 7/1/2007.
Texas[a]	Criminal homicide with 1 of 9 aggravating circumstances (Tex. Penal Code § 19.03); super aggravated sexual assault (Tex. Penal Code § 12.42(c)(3)).
	Revision: Revised the penal code and the code of criminal procedure to allow the death penalty for aggravated sexual assault of victims under the age of 14 when the offender has a previous conviction for a similar offense (TX Penal Code § 12.42(c)(3) and Tex. Code Crim. Proc. Art 37.072), effective 9/1/2007.
Utah[a]	Aggravated murder (76-5-202, Utah Code Annotated).
	Revision: Amended the criminal code to allow for an automatic sentence of life without parole if the death penalty is ruled unconstitutional (Utah Code Ann. § 76-3-207) and added to the definition of aggravated murder intentional killing when the victim is younger than 14 years of age (Utah Code Ann. § 76-5-202(t)). Both changes became effective 4/30/07.

Continued

TABLE 14.2	Continued

State	Offense
Virginia[a]	First-degree murder with 1 of 15 aggravating circumstances (VA Code § 18.2-31).
	Revision: Added to the definition of capital murder willful, deliberate, and premeditated killing of a judge or a witness when the killing is for the purpose of interfering with the person's duties in a criminal case (Va. Code § 18.2-31(14) and (15)), effective 7/1/2007.
Washington	Aggravated first-degree murder.
Wyoming[a]	First-degree murder.
	Revision: Added as a capital offense murder during the commission of sexual abuse of a minor (W.S. § 6-2-101), effective 7/1/2007.

Note: New Mexico abolished the death penalty in early 2009.

[a]Nine states revised statutory provisions relating to the death penalty during 2007.

[b]The Colorado Supreme Court struck a portion of that state's capital statute on April 23, 2007 (*Peopel v. Montour,* 157 P.3d 489 (Colo. 2007)). The statue (*Colo. Rev. Stat.* § 18-1.3-1201(1)(a)) specified that defendants pleading guilty to a class 1 felony be sentenced by the judge, thereby requiring defendants to waive their right to a jury trial on all facts essential to determining death penalty eligibility as established in *Ring v. Arizona.* The court ruled that this was unconstitutional under Sixth and Fourteenth Amendments.

Source: *National Prisoner Statistics Program (NPS-8)* (Washington, D.C.: U.S. Department of Justice, December 2008), www.ojp.usdoj/gov/bjs/pub/html/cp/2007/tables/cp07st01.htm (accessed April 16, 2009).

The U.S. Supreme Court has also considered the use of the death penalty for offenders who are insane, those with mental illness, and juveniles. In 1986, the Court considered the case of *Ford v. Wainwright* and ruled that mentally ill people cannot be executed.[63] When convicted, Ford was not judged mentally ill and not until he was on death row did he display conditions of mental illness. The Court considered the case and concluded that executing an insane person was a violation of the Eighth Amendment, in that the accused must comprehend both the fact that he or she has been sentenced to death and the reason for the sentence.

The Court, in addressing the issue of the death penalty for the mentally retarded, has only recently reversed itself. In 1989, it decided *Penry v. Lynaugh.*[64] Penry had an IQ of approximately 70, yet was considered able to stand for trial. The Court decided that the execution of mentally retarded offenders does not violate the Eighth Amendment; at that time only two states (Maryland and Georgia) prohibited executing the mentally retarded. However, in 2002, the Court heard the case of *Atkins v. Virginia* and, by a 6–3 vote, determined that executions of mentally retarded criminals were "cruel and unusual punishment" under the Eighth Amendment.[65] Atkins was convicted of shooting a man for beer money in 1996. At that time, he had an IQ of 59. The majority acknowledged a reversal of *Penry,* but noted that there has been a growing national consensus since 1989 that executions of the mentally retarded may be unacceptable, even though only eighteen of the thirty-eight states that allow capital punishment had disallowed such executions. With the ruling, inmates on death row who can prove mental retardation (usually an IQ less than 70) will have their sentences commuted to life imprisonment.

The Supreme Court has also considered the use of the death penalty for juvenile offenders, and there has been an evolution of case law similar to that developed

In *Atkins v. Virginia*, the U.S. Supreme Court determined that executions of mentally retarded criminals (like Rodney Atkins) were cruel and unusual punishment under the Eighth Amendment. Courtesy of Daily Press/AP Wide World.

regarding the death penalty for the mentally retarded. Until recently, juveniles could be executed for capital crimes. In *Eddings v. Oklahoma* (1982), the Court held that the youthful age of a defendant should be considered as a mitigating factor during the sentencing stage of a capital punishment trial.[66] In 1989, the Court ruled in *Stanford v. Kentucky* that the minimum age to impose a death sentence on a juvenile is age 16.[67] In 2002, the Court refused to consider *In re Stanford*, declining to reconsider the issue of capital punishment for juveniles,[68] and on January 27, 2003, the Court also declined to consider the death penalty for Scott Allen Hain, a 17-year-old Oklahoma offender, even though four justices wrote that they believed executing juveniles "is a relic of the past and is inconsistent with evolving standards of decency."[69] At that time, 16 remained the age for which juvenile offenders could be considered for a sentence of death. In 2004, of the thirty-eight states that allow the death penalty, only twenty states allowed for the execution of juveniles; six jurisdictions did not specify a minimum age; and fourteen others indicated an age between fourteen and seventeen for which the death penalty could be imposed.[70]

On October 3, 2004, the U.S. Supreme Court heard the case of *Roper v. Simmons*[71] and considered evidence of a national consensus against the death penalty for juveniles that was in some respects parallel to the evidence used in *Atkins* to demonstrate a national consensus against the death penalty for the mentally retarded. On March 1, 2005, the Court by a 5–4 vote held that "the Eighth and Fourteenth Amendments forbid the imposition of the death penalty on offenders who are under the age of 18 when their crimes were committed."[72] The Court believed that a lack of maturity and an underdeveloped sense of responsibility are found in youth more often than in adults, juveniles are more vulnerable or susceptible to negative influences and outside pressures, and the character of a juvenile is not as well formed as that of an adult. The Court's ruling removed seventy-two juveniles in twelve states from death row, substituting life in prison for execution.

The most recent case concerning who can be executed was *Kennedy v. Louisiana*,[73] in which the Supreme Court by a 5–4 vote found that a Louisiana state statute allowing persons convicted of raping a child to be sentenced to death violated the Eighth Amendment prohibition against cruel and unusual punishment.

The Court recognized the horrific nature of the crime, but questioned whether the death penalty met society's current standards of decency. Using their logic in *Roper* and in *Atkins*, the Court found a societal consensus against the death penalty for child rape, as while nine states still allowed the death penalty as a punishment, there had been no execution for such a crime since 1964. The Court ruled that capital punishment is a violation of the Eighth Amendment unless it is consistent with the current standards of decency, and there is a difference between intentional first-degree murder and non-homicide crimes, including child rape. Although child rape is devastating in harm, it does not compare to murder in its "severity and irrevocability."[74]

Current Statistics Regarding Capital Punishment

Death Row Prisoners

At year-end 2007, thirty-five states and the federal prison system held 3,220 prisoners (all of whom had committed murder) under sentence of death, which was six fewer than at year-end 2006.[75] As can be seen in Figure 14.3, the number of inmates on death row declined immediately after the 1972 Supreme Court decision in *Furman v. Georgia*, holding that the death penalty as then administered was unconstitutional. Even with that decision, not every state emptied its death row, so the number did not reduce to zero. Soon thereafter, the number on death row began to climb significantly as the Court in *Gregg v. Georgia* and other cases upheld the revised capital punishment laws.

Of those on death row at year-end 2007, two of three had prior felony convictions, one in twelve had prior homicide convictions, fifty-six were women, and

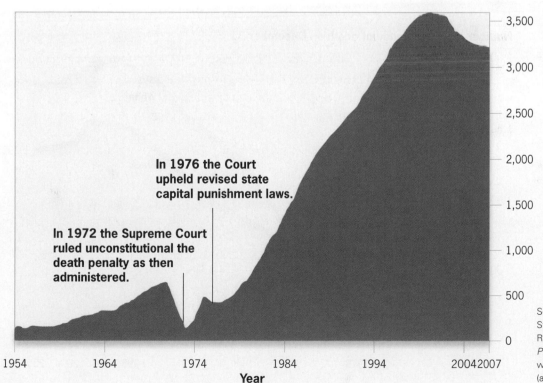

In 1976 the Court upheld revised state capital punishment laws.

In 1972 the Supreme Court ruled unconstitutional the death penalty as then administered.

Source: Bureau of Justice Statistics, "Prisoners on Death Row, 1954–2007," *Capital Punishment: Facts at a Glance*, www.ojp.usdoj.gov/bjs/glance/dr.htm (accessed August 16, 2009).

FIGURE 14.3   Prisoners on Death Row, 1954–2007

the youngest and oldest inmates were 19 and 92, respectively.[76] Race has been an issue in the capital punishment debate for the past several decades, as minorities continue to be overrepresented among those sentenced to death, on death row, and executed. Of people under sentence of death in 2007,

- 1,766 (56 percent) were white,
- 1,330 (42 percent) were black,
- 30 (0.8 percent) were American Indian,
- 35 (0.6 percent) were Asian, and
- 10 (0.3 percent) were of unknown race.

Also, 356 Hispanic inmates (13 percent) of either white or black origin were under sentence of death.[77]

Figure 14.4 illustrates the proportions of people on death row by race. The fact that minorities are on death row at a rate well above their representation in the U.S. population has opened the door to an argument of the continuation of racial bias in the administration of the death penalty. However, in the 1987 case of *McCleskey v. Kemp*, the Supreme Court heard an argument of race discrimination in the death penalty. McCleskey was a black man convicted of murdering a white police officer. McCleskey's attorneys, in their arguments to the Supreme Court, used a study by Baldus, Woodworth, and Pulaski that examined the role of race in the imposition of the death penalty in Georgia. The study found that defendants charged with killing whites were 4.3 times more likely to receive the death penalty than those convicted of killing blacks.[78] The attorneys argued that this disproportionate sentencing to death of killers of whites indicated a denial of the equal protection clause under the Fourteenth Amendment and likely an arbitrary and capricious use of the death penalty in violation of the Eighth

Number under sentence of death on December 31

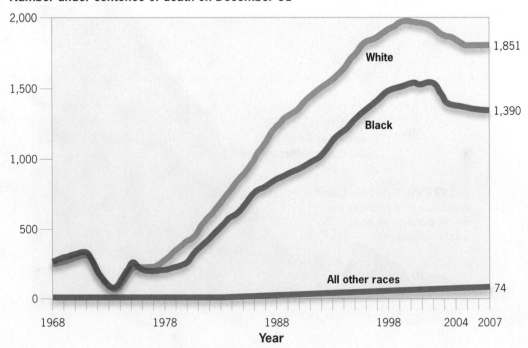

Source: Bureau of Justice Statistics, "Prisoners on Death Row by Race, 1968–2007," *Capital Punishment: Facts at a Glance*, www.ojp.usdoj.gov/bjs/glance/drrace.htm (accessed August 16, 2009).

FIGURE 14.4 Prisoners under Sentence of Death by Race, 1968–2004

TABLE 14.3	Executions during 2008
Texas	18
Virginia	4
Georgia	3
South Carolina	3
Florida	2
Mississippi	2
Ohio	2
Oklahoma	2
Kentucky	1
Total	37

Source: Bureau of Justice Statistics, *Capital Punishment Statistics: Summary Findings*, www.ojp.usdoj.gov/bjs/cp.htm (accessed April 16, 2009).

Amendment. However, by a 5–4 vote, the Court rejected these claims, noting that a statistical study did not establish discrimination in this particular case.

Executions

As indicated in Figure 14.2, the number of executions has risen over the past twenty years, and in 2008, thirty-seven were executed in nine states. Table 14.3 lists the number of people executed by state. Texas, by far, leads with eighteen, and no other state has more than four executions. Of the persons executed in 2008, twenty (54 percent) were white and seventeen (46 percent) were black; all were men. Thirty-six executions were carried out by **lethal injection** and one was carried out by electrocution.[79]

Table 14.4 illustrates all of the executions both from 1930 to 2007 and from 1977 through 2007 by state. Overall, from 1977 through 2007, there have been 1,099 executions carried out in the United States. Again, Texas has by far more (405 since 1977) than any other state. Table 14.5 also illustrates the methods of execution used by various states. In some states, more than one

lethal injection
a method of execution in which drugs are injected into a person's body, making the heart stop and causing death

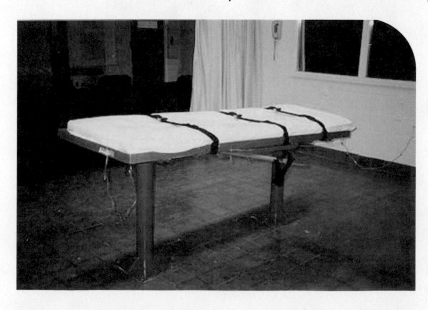

Lethal injection is now the most widely used method of execution. Courtesy of the Ohio Department of Rehabilitation and Correction.

TABLE 14.4 **Number of Persons Executed, by Jurisdiction, 1930–2007**

Jurisdiction	Number Executed	
	Since 1930	Since 1977
U.S. total	4,958	1,099
Texas	702	405
Georgia	406	40
New York	329	0
North Carolina	306	43
California	305	13
Florida	234	64
South Carolina	199	37
Ohio	198	26
Virginia	190	98
Alabama	173	38
Mississippi	162	8
Louisiana	160	27
Pennsylvania	155	3
Oklahoma	146	86
Arkansas	145	27
Missouri	128	66
Kentucky	105	2
Illinois	102	12
Tennessee	97	4
New Jersey	74	0
Maryland	73	5
Arizona	61	23
Indiana	60	19
Washington	51	4
Colorado	48	1
Nevada	41	12
District of Columbia	40	0
West Virginia	40	0
Federal system	36	3
Massachusetts	27	0
Delaware	26	14
Connecticut	22	1
Oregon	21	2
Utah	19	6
Iowa	18	0
Kansas	15	0
Montana	9	3
New Mexico	9	1
Wyoming	8	1
Nebraska	7	3
Vermont	4	0
Idaho	4	1
South Dakota	2	1
New Hampshire	1	0

Note: Military authorities carried out an additional 160 executions between 1930 and 1961.

Source: Tracy L. Snell, *Capital Punishment, 2007—Statistical Tables,* Table 9, http://www.ojp.usdoj.gov/bjs/pub/html/cp/2007/tables/cp07st09.htm (accessed April 16, 2009).

TABLE 14.5   Method of Execution, by State, 2007

Lethal Injection	Electrocution	Lethal Gas	Hanging	Firing Squad
Alabama[a]	Alabama[a]	Arizona[a,b]	Delaware[a,c]	Idaho[a]
Arizona[a,b]	Arkansas[a,d]	California[a]	New Hampshire[a,e]	Oklahoma[f]
Arkansas[a,d]	Florida[a]	Missouri[a]	Washington[a]	Utah[g]
California[a]	Illinois[a,h]	Wyoming[i]		
Colorado	Kentucky[a,j]			
Connecticut	Nebraska			
Delaware[a,c]	Oklahoma[f]			
Florida[a]	South Carolina[a]			
Georgia	Tennessee[a,k]			
Idaho[a]	Virginia[a]			
Illinois[a]				
Indiana				
Kansas				
Kentucky[a,j]				
Louisiana				
Maryland				
Mississippi				
Missouri[d]				
Montana				
Nevada				
New Hampshire[a]				
New York				
North Carolina				
Ohio				
Oklahoma[a]				
Oregon				
Pennsylvania				
South Carolina[a]				
South Dakota				
Tennessee[a,k]				
Texas				
Utah[a]				
Virginia[a]				
Washington[a]				
Wyoming[a]				

Note: The method of execution of Federal prisoners is lethal injection, pursuant to 28 CFR, Part 26. For offenses under the Violent Crime Control and Law Enforcement Act of 1994, the execution method is that of the State in which the conviction took place (18 U S.C. 3596).

[a]Authorizes two methods of execution.

[b]Authorizes lethal injection for persons sentenced after November 15, 1992; inmates sentenced before that date may select lethal injection or gas.

[c]Authorizes lethal injection for those whose capital offense occurred on or after June 13, 1986; those who committed the offense before that date may select lethal injection or hanging.

[d]Authorizes lethal injection for those whose offense occurred on or after July 4, 1983; inmates whose offense occurred before that date may select lethal injection or electrocution.

[e]Authorizes hanging only if lethal injection cannot be given.

[f]Authorizes electrocution if lethal injection is held to be unconstitutional, and firing squad if both lethal injection and electrocution are held to be unconstitutional.

[g]Authorizes firing squad if lethal injection is held unconstitutional. Inmates who selected execution by firing squad prior to May 3, 2004, may still be entitled to execution by that method.

[h]Authroizes electrocution only if lethal injection is held illegal or unconstitutional.

[i]Authorizes lethal gas if lethal injection is held to be unconstitutional.

[j]Authorizes lethal injection for persons sentenced on or after March 31, 1998; inmates sentenced before that date may select lethal injection or electrocution.

[k]Authorizes lethal injection for those whose capital offense occurred after December 31, 1998; those who committed the offense before that date may select electrocution by written waiver.

Source: Tracy L. Snell, *Capital Punishment, 2007—Statistical Tables*, Table 2, http://www.ojp.usdoj.gov/bjs/pub/html/cp/2007/tables/cp07st09.htm (accessed April 16, 2009).

method of execution is authorized, although currently almost every state authorizes only the use of lethal injection.

In early 2006, death penalty opponents and lawyers for death row inmates began to challenge the use of lethal injection as a violation of the Eighth Amendment prohibiting cruel and unusual punishment. Most states use a three-drug protocol for lethal injection. The three-drug "cocktail" administered uses sodium thiopental to render the person unconscious, pancuronium bromide to paralyze breathing muscles, and potassium chloride to stop the heart. Even though death penalty supporters and attorneys for states using lethal injection argue that no evidence exists, inmate attorneys suggest that the use of the first two drugs may not always fully work, and the inmate can suffer during the process.

In February 2006, the Eighth U.S. Circuit Court of Appeals delayed the execution of Michael Taylor until an April 2006 hearing on the issue of whether lethal injection is unconstitutionally cruel and unusual. California (with 650 inmates on death row) had to postpone executions because they could not recruit appropriately trained and licensed medical personnel to mix the drugs and insert intravenous lines into inmates to be executed. This issue also brings up the conflict between the American Medical Association and other medical groups that oppose licensed medical personnel administering drugs to end life and state requirements that such licensed personnel oversee the executions.

This issue was settled as the U.S. Supreme Court accepted and heard the case of *Baze et al. v. Rees*. The petitioners were convicted murderers sentenced to death in Kentucky. The state trial court held fact-finding hearings and ruled that there was minimal risk of the improper administration of the drug protocol and upheld its use as constitutional. This was affirmed by the Kentucky Supreme Court. On April 16, 2008, the U.S. Supreme Court voted 7–2 to affirm the decision.[80] The Court noted that the inmates conceded that the procedure was "humane" when carried out correctly and failed to prove the incorrect administration of the drugs would violate the Eighth Amendment. Of interest was that although Justice John Paul Stevens concurred with the decision, he wrote a separate opinion in which he, for the first time, stated his opposition to capital punishment, writing that he did not believe adequate procedures were in place to minimize bias and error. He had, since 1976, upheld the death penalty as constitutional, but over the years found the protections for death penalty cases to be removed to a point where fairness could no longer be guaranteed.

The following "An Interview With" box describes the issues that must be considered and the personal feelings that result as correctional officials plan for an execution.

mycrimekit

Media—Video:
Executions

An Interview With...

A Warden Who Oversees Executions

Stephen Huffman is a twenty-five-year veteran of the Ohio Department of Rehabilitation and Correction. He started his career in the business office at the London (Ohio) Correctional Institution. He rose to assistant warden and then became security administrator of the South Region. In 1997, he became warden of the Southern Ohio Correctional Institution in Lucasville. Lucasville was the highest security prison in Ohio and has housed the execution chamber since the 1970s. Mr. Huffman was promoted to regional director of the North Region in 2000 and one year later was assigned as regional director of the South Region, where Lucasville is located. He has held that job for the past five years. As warden at

Lucasville, he oversaw the first execution to take place in Ohio in thirty-six years and has witnessed nineteen more executions in his current job.

Question: Director Huffman, can you describe what you had to do when you had to prepare for the first execution in Ohio to take place in thirty-six years?

Mr. Huffman: When I first arrived at Lucasville as warden, death row inmates had the choice of execution between the electric chair and lethal injection. Forty-eight hours before the execution was scheduled, the inmate had to decide which method of execution he wanted used. All chose lethal injection. Since 2001, inmates do not have a choice, and lethal injection is the sole method now used in Ohio. Because of the choice, we had to prepare for both means of execution. For several years before the first execution, we selected the execution teams, and they would practice quarterly. Within the last month before a scheduled execution, we practiced weekly. The practices were done in as real a situation as possible, with someone in the chair and someone on the table as a part of practice.

Question: What are some of the key things you have to consider and practice for an execution?

Mr. Huffman: For the electric chair, we had several physical and maintenance types of activities. First, we had to make sure there was proper ventilation in the death house. Our electricians and maintenance staff had to make sure the voltage regulator worked properly so that the flow of electrical voltage was regulated at the level specified. We carefully selected people to be on the team, and practice was just like the real thing. We had twelve members and a leader on the team. Each person had a specific assignment. Some staff would monitor the inmate and respond to all requests he had. Others were assigned to death house and had to escort the inmate into the chamber and strap him to the chair or table.

Staff had to volunteer for the assignment, and we were careful to choose only staff that would not be overly sensitive and could not handle the process and were also not overeager to do it. Everyone had to be extremely professional at all times. Since the first execution on February 19, 1999, only one member has asked to be removed from the execution team. Unless you go to the facility and work with these people daily, you do not realize what they do and how well they perform their job. As an example, it is not unusual for families of the executed inmate to write to the warden and thank him for how the staff treated their family member and did their job with such dignity.

Question: What are some of the unexpected issues that come up in preparing for an execution?

Mr. Huffman: One difficulty for the first execution was finding a physician that would participate and pronounce the inmate as dead. At this early time, the American Medical Association had not taken a position on involvement by physicians in an execution, and physicians feared they might lose their license for such involvement.

Another issue arose in the witnesses for the inmate and for the victim. Both the inmate and the victim families get three witnesses at the actual execution. Staff are assigned to each family group. One of the toughest things is to keep the families calm and avoid any animosity between them. They are all in the same small room to witness the execution and, as you can imagine, emotions are quite high. It takes a special person with the right demeanor to deal with both families. The media are also with the families in the witness room. Three media (one radio, one television, and one print journalist) are allowed as witnesses. When the execution is over, both families and the media are given the opportunity to speak to the rest of the media and, almost all the time, all speak to the media.

Question: What is the process up to the execution time?

Mr. Huffman: That depends on the time of the execution. Executions used to be at midnight, then at 9:00 P.M., and they are now at 10:00 A.M. This changed in part so that the attorney general's office has time to work on last-minute appeals. The AG's office must respond if a state or federal judge requests a stay of execution. This is a very sensitive and difficult time, and the AG's office tries to respond quickly so that the execution is not delayed too long. In 1998, an inmate was being transported to the facility and received a stay. This particular inmate had volunteered to be executed, meaning he did not seek any appeals after his sentence. It still took six years before the process was finished and he was executed. When he got the stay, I was being interviewed by the media who told me of the stay and asked me what we would do. I responded something like we had to stay prepared, because the execution "may" still go on. I got in a lot of trouble with my bosses for that comment, because

...continued

the legal process was responding rapidly with the belief that the sentence was both legal and just and "would" go on.

During the time before the first execution, death row inmates in Ohio were housed at the Mansfield Correctional Institution where death row had been moved from Lucasville. Death row is now at the Ohio State Penitentiary, our supermax prison. Death row was placed somewhere other than where the execution was to take place to avoid the Stockholm syndrome, where staff begin to get too close and empathize with the inmate. We don't release the date or time that inmates will be transported to Lucasville for the execution. When they are, they are escorted by our special emergency response team (SERT). At Lucasville, they are placed in a cell within the death house with a television, radio, a telephone, or a typewriter. They are dressed in special clothing noting death row. This may seem odd, but the biggest thing for the warden is to give the inmate confidence that you will carry out the execution in a dignified manner and abide by his wishes. Up to the last few hours, the inmate is counting on the warden and focusing on the execution. A few inmates stay awake all night, but most sleep very little and spend time talking to their family or the execution team members. The family of the inmate can visit up to two hours before the execution and then only three (chosen by the inmate) are allowed to stay to witness the execution. We don't call it the last meal, but they get a preferred meal, which can be almost anything we can fix within the prison.

The warden is always going between the victim and the inmate's families to talk to them and be sure their needs are met. You also have to deal with protesters. The Ohio Highway Patrol assists and keeps the protesters separated by those who are for and those who are against the death penalty. There are usually pretty large crowds, although with each execution, the number of protesters and of media is reduced.

Question: Can you describe some personal feelings about an execution?

Mr. Huffman: During one of the early executions that I oversaw, I was standing next to the execution table, and the inmate asked me if he would be able to see his mother and sister while he was on the table. I told him yes, if he turned his head to the left, they would be just a few feet away. He never looked at them, but that is when reality hit me that he was a human being who had a mother and sister who loved him unconditionally, just like the rest of us. His family was a victim of the crime as well.

Question: What is the role of the warden in dealing with the media regarding an execution?

Mr. Huffman: Now, the warden seldom meets with the media. The public information officer does most of it, as it is just too much for the warden to manage the media and the execution. At that first execution in 1999, we had over 200 news media at the institution. There is a lot of pressure on the warden. But some of the news media will only talk to the warden. What is tough is that there is a small percentage of the media that want to paint a negative picture of a "killer squad" or "death squad." I received hate mail from other countries, telling me I was no better than Hitler. When I speak to college students about my job, I tell them the toughest thing is dealing with media that want to paint a picture that is negative of you and your staff. We are just trying to carry out the law and do it professionally.

Personally, I often get asked what my own position is on the death penalty. I just respond that it is the law and I have no problems carrying out the law. What does bother me, however, is that I often see other people not on death row who did not get the death penalty, but who have done as bad or worse acts as those under sentence of death. It just does not seem fair that they will not be executed just because of plea bargaining or whatever else. That is the only thing I have a problem with.

When I was going through that first execution, it was very hard on me personally. It is not easy to be called a Nazi or killer when you are just trying to do what is right and do it with dignity for all involved. I owe a lot to my church, which supported and helped me through all this.

Question: What happens in the rest of the prison during the time of an execution?

Mr. Huffman: On the day of an execution, all inmates are locked down after breakfast. We go under the incident command system with an incident commander in charge of the operation of the prison. That leaves the warden free to concentrate on the execution. We have not had a single incident during an execution. The other inmates stay calm and don't interfere.

The most important thing for everyone, the other prisoners, families, the inmate, and the staff, is to maintain organization and make everything very routine. You must keep that routine with staff so that everyone knows their role and their place. It is a very difficult situation, but I believe that Ohio does a very good job at it.

Operational Problems

People seldom think about it, but how do you manage offenders who have already proved that they have a propensity for violence and are in prison facing execution? They obviously have little to live for, and correctional administrators can threaten them with no penalty that is worse than what they already face. This creates the dilemma of how to operate death rows. They must be secure to protect staff and other inmates. Yet these prisoners have not (in most cases) violated any prison rule to deserve to be isolated in an SHU-type situation.

Most administrators decide to err on the safe side and operate a very secure death row, with inmates in single cells most of the time. Death row is operated like an SHU in that all services come to the unit, inmates are in their cells most of the time, and they recreate and do almost everything by themselves. A few states allow inmates on death row to work, and some even have a prison industry as a part of the death row. However, security and safe operations have to be constant at all times. The "An Insider's Experience" box in *MyCrimeKit* illustrates the danger of operating a death row.

mycrimekit

Insider's Experience: Hostages on Death Row.

Reasons for Capital Punishment

Proponents of the death penalty argue for its existence for several reasons, which usually include deterrence, retribution, incapacitation, and cost.

Deterrence

Proponents of the death penalty argue that, by having capital punishment laws, additional murders are prevented through general deterrence. Reflecting back to Bentham's hedonistic calculus that crimes will be prevented if the punishment outweighs the pleasure from the crime, it is difficult to understand how a rational person would commit a murder knowing that he or she will be executed in return. This logic seems to challenge theories of the deterrent effect of the death penalty. It can first be argued that fully rational people do not commit many murders. Although a few early studies have found evidence of capital punishment as deterrence, these have been criticized as methodologically flawed and are not recognized as credible evidence.[81] There is far more evidence that capital punishment does not deter other murders. A 1984 study by Decker and Kohfeld of homicide rates in Illinois from 1933 to 1980 did not identify any differences in rates depending on whether there was a death penalty allowed, a death penalty was allowed but not used, or the death penalty was abolished.[82] A 2006 research report used "model averaging" to weigh averages of a wide set of possible models of deterrence, and concluded there is little empirical evidence of a deterrent effect from capital punishment.[83] Other studies of homicide rates from various states have also not found a deterrent effect with the death penalty.[84] The general public is inconclusive in its views of the deterrent effect of capital punishment. In a 2006 public opinion poll, 34 percent responded that they believed that executing people who commit murder deters others from committing murder, 64 percent believed that it has "no" deterrent effect, and 2 percent were not sure or refused to answer.[85]

Some proponents argue that capital punishment can be a deterrent, but will have increased deterrent value if executions are carried out in public, or at least receive a considerable amount of publicity. However, researchers argue that such publicity brings about a "brutalization" rather than a deterrent effect, in that some people identify with the executioner, and executions can promote imitation rather than deterrence for individuals already prone to violence.[86] A study by Cockran and colleagues and a replication of the study by Bailey of the impact of the Oklahoma capital punishment law found that a brutalization effect seems to occur as the media cover executions.[87]

Retribution

Most people believe that punishment is important to show that "bad acts result in bad outcomes." People generally do not want criminals to get off without punishment adequately matched to the severity of their crime. The concept of retribution is that offenders get their just deserts, a punishment that fits their crime (an eye for an eye). As described by Bohm in writing of capital punishment and retribution, revenge for taking a life is based on a belief that a killer deserves to be executed.[88] Many people believe that capital punishment is the only just punishment for the taking of a life. However, opponents point out that even with bifurcated trials as a result of *Gregg v. Georgia*, there is still racial and ethnic discrimination in the application of capital punishment,[89] undermining a retributive argument.

Incapacitation

The incapacitation argument regarding capital punishment is that the only sure way to protect the public from a criminal so vicious that he or she would kill someone is to execute the person. However, it is also generally accepted that murderers have very low rates of recidivism. Studies by Sorensen and colleagues and by Vito and Wilson of inmates who had committed murder and then had their death sentences commuted indicate that offenders who commit murder have a very low rate of recidivism, and less than 1 percent later committed another murder.[90] Opponents of the death penalty also argue that life in prison without the chance of parole equally protects society through incapacitation rather than execution.

Cost

A common argument when considering the death penalty is cost. Proponents of the death penalty argue that it is less expensive than life imprisonment, whereas opponents point out that the additional costs of a capital trial and appeals make the death penalty more expensive. Depending on the assumptions made, both sides can show evidence to support their position. Bedau[91] and Bohm[92] point out that capital punishment is more expensive due to the high cost of the trial and subsequent litigation. A 1993 study found that capital trials in North Carolina are significantly more costly than noncapital trials and, when comparing the cost of incarceration on death row for ten years, found that it was less costly than regular imprisonment for twenty years.[93] And a review of several state comparisons of the cost of the death penalty compared to life imprisonment reported much greater expense for a death penalty trial and imprisonment than for a life sentence (in New York, $1.4 million compared to $602,000; in Florida, $3.2 million or six times the cost of life imprisonment).[94]

In addition, a 2008 report by the Urban Institute found that in Maryland, the average capital-eligible case in which prosecutors did not seek the death penalty had a lifetime cost of $1.1 million, to include $870,000 for incarceration and

$250,000 for adjudication. A capital-eligible case resulting in the death penalty cost approximately $3 million, with prison costs for holding on death row of $1.3 million and $1.7 million for adjudication.[95] Cost was one of the factors sited as Governor Bill Richardson signed legislation repealing the death penalty in New Mexico in early 2009, and when New Jersey abolished its death penalty in 2007.[96]

Public Opinion Regarding the Death Penalty

Over the past forty years, public opinion regarding the death penalty has changed significantly. In surveys of the U.S. public in 1965, the Harris Poll reported that only 38 percent believed in the death penalty;[97] the Gallup Poll reported that only 45 percent were in favor of it.[98] Over the next four decades, public attitudes continuously became more supportive of the use of capital punishment. By 2004, the Harris Poll reported that 69 percent of those surveyed believed in the use of capital punishment.[99] These opinions have consistently varied by the gender and race of those surveyed. In 2000, the National Opinion Research Center reported that while 63 percent of a national sample favored the death penalty for crimes of murder, it was supported by 71 percent of men and 57 percent of women, and 69 percent of whites and only 42 percent of nonwhites.[100]

Since that time, there appears to be a weakening of support for the death penalty. Although still showing strong support, in an October 2008 Gallup Poll of American opinion on the death penalty, 64 percent of those polled supported the death penalty, down from 69 percent in 2007, and those opposing capital punishment rose from 27 to 30 percent.[101] And a Harris poll of over 1,000 American adults found that opposition to the death penalty has increased since 2003, as 30 percent of those sampled oppose the death penalty, an 8 percent increase in the past five years. Some of this movement is due to the fact that 95 percent of those polled believed that innocent people are sometimes convicted of murder.[102]

Another interesting fact is the moderation of support for the death penalty when compared to life in prison without possibility of parole. The Gallup Poll found that in 2006, when respondents were asked, "What do you think is the better penalty for murder?" 47 percent responded "the death penalty" and 48 percent responded "life in prison."[103] The reasons that individuals favor the death penalty provide a varied response. As indicated in Table 14.6, attitudes changed from 2000 to 2003. The latest survey indicates most people support it for "just deserts" or "eye for an eye" reasons (40 percent), and 12 percent favor it because it saves taxpayer money.

The Potential for Error

One serious concern regarding the death penalty is the potential for error, or the fallibility of the death penalty. We tend to have faith in our justice system and want to believe that it makes very few errors, especially in capital murder trials when the death penalty is a possible sanction. There is considerable debate as to how many mistakes are made in findings of guilt in death penalty trials and whether the potential for a mistake (with the irrevocability of the death penalty) puts in question the use of capital punishment. Proponents of the death penalty suggest that few errors have occurred since *Gregg v. Georgia*, with bifurcated

TABLE 14.6 Reported Reasons for Favoring the Death Penalty for Persons Convicted of Murder, United States, 1991, 2000, 2001, and 2003

Question: "Why Do You Favor the Death Penalty for Persons Convicted of Murder?"

Reason for Favoring	1991	2000	2001	2003
Any eye for an eye/they took a life/fits the crime	40%	40%	48%	37%
	12	12	20	11
Deterrent for potential crimes/set an example	8	8	10	11
Depends on the type of crime they commit	6	6	6	4
Fair punishment	6	6	1	3
They deserve it	5	5	6	13
They will repeat their crime/keep them from repeating it	4	4	6	7
Biblical reasons	3	3	3	5
Serve justice	2	3	1	4
Don't believe they can be rehabilitated	1	1	2	2
If there's no doubt the person committed the crime	NA	NA	2	3
Would help/benefit families of victims	NA	NA	1	2
Support/believe in death penalty	NA	NA	6	2
Life sentences don't always mean life in prison	NA	NA	2	1
Relieves prison overcrowding	NA	NA	2	1
Other	10	10	3	4
No opinion	3	3	1	2

Note: This question was asked only of persons who stated they favor the death penalty. Percentages may add to more than 100 because up to two responses were recorded from each respondent.

Source: The Gallup Organization, Inc., *The Gallup Poll* [Online], www.gallup.com/poll/tb/religvalue/20030603c.asp (June 10, 2003). Table adapted by *Sourcebook* staff. Reprinted by permission.

trials and automatic reviews. However, Dieter has reviewed the risk of error and identified several reasons that error still exists:

- *General reasons:* The overall expansion in the authorization of the death penalty and the fact that it has become a political issue
- *Investigative reasons:* The pressure on the police to solve murders and on prosecutors to win trials, along with lack of resources by defense attorneys for investigation
- *Reasons during trial:* The fact that juries are often influenced by publicity, there are mistaken identities, and the heinous nature of many murders increases the likelihood of conviction
- *Plea bargaining and failure to dismiss:* There are more guilty pleas by innocent defendants, and there are fewer dismissals of charges for innocent people[104]

A study by Bedau and Radelet reviewed thousands of death penalty cases during the twentieth century and concluded that twenty-three innocent people had been executed since 1900.[105] The Death Penalty Information Center also reported that, between 1973 and 2008, 131 inmates under sentence of death have been released with evidence of their innocence.[106] In the past decade, the use of DNA evidence has provided a credible source for review of the guilt of some death row inmates. The use of DNA as evidence is a fairly recent technology, was not available at the time of trial for some death row inmates, but can now be used to reconsider questionable cases of guilt.

Over the past decade, perhaps the greatest attention to the fallibility of the death penalty has occurred in Illinois. From 1976 to 2000, Illinois executed twelve people and released thirteen from death row due to actual innocence. Death row proponents suggest that this proves that the system and layers of appeals work. Law students at Northwestern and DePaul Universities have for several years been researching death row cases, looking for evidence of innocence. If not for their efforts, most of these death row inmates would not have been freed. In 2000, Governor George H. Ryan declared a moratorium on executions in Illinois over concerns regarding the possible execution of innocent people. In doing so, he created a blue-ribbon task force to examine how death penalty investigations and trials worked in Illinois, and the task force made eighty-five recommendations for improvement in the administration of the death penalty.

On January 11, 2003, Governor Ryan took a dramatic step. Condemning the capital punishment system as fundamentally flawed and unfair, he announced that he was commuting the death sentences of 167 people (163 men and 4 women), primarily to life in prison. A few days earlier, he had pardoned four death row inmates, freeing them from death row and from prison. Ryan left office as governor on January 13, 2003, just two days after he emptied the state's death row, setting the stage for further debate over potential errors. There were cheers for his actions from many anti-death-penalty groups and the families of those on death row. Meanwhile, there were jeers and considerable bitterness from the families of the more than 250 victims of Illinois death row inmates, pro-death-penalty groups, and Illinois prosecutors and legislators. Prosecutors say that, although they cannot undo Governor Ryan's blanket commutations, they plan to start refilling death row immediately. They claim that they will not let Ryan's action hinder their pursuit of capital punishment in pending cases, but they acknowledge that there will be new challenges in convincing juries that the death penalty is just and fair. As an interesting aside, in September 2006, former governor Ryan was himself sentenced to 6 1/2 years in prison for conspiracy and fraud for taking payoffs from political insiders in exchange for state business.

In 2003, Illinois Governor George Ryan was acclaimed by capital punishment foes as he commuted the sentences of or gave pardons to all inmates on death row, citing the risk of error by executing innocent people.

Courtesy of AP/Wide World Photos.

Capital punishment has been a hotly debated topic in the United States for years. Proponents call it just and cite the general support of the public. Opponents call it brutal and immoral and cite the number of innocent defendants who have been convicted and executed. Even though a majority of Americans continue to support its use, there is a softening of support for capital punishment, especially with more information available on potential errors in convicting innocent defendants. This perplexing dilemma is apparent in a recent speech given by Renee Cardwell Hughes, a common pleas judge in Philadelphia, Pennsylvania. Judge Hughes noted, "I am a trial judge and there are two people on death row whose commitment papers bear my signature." However, continuing the speech, Judge Hughes commented that the death penalty "is in fact a cruel and unusual form of punishment which violates the laws which assure equal protection to all of our citizens."[107] After reading the arguments for and against the death penalty, students must now struggle with their own beliefs regarding the death penalty in the "You Make the Decision" box at the end of the chapter.

Summary

Have we as a society gone too far in recognizing the legal rights of inmates? Many people believe we have, yet few would argue that inmates should lose all protections of the Constitution and Bill of Rights because they have committed a felony and been incarcerated. This chapter has described the emergence and then abandonment of the hands-off doctrine regarding suits by inmates and the evolution of recognition by the courts of specific rights of confined individuals. Many legal decisions have created guidelines for the provision of medical care, opportunity to practice one's religion, conditions of confinement, and due process during inmate disciplinary hearings.

For twenty-five years after the landmark decision of *Cooper v. Pate* opened a Pandora's box of inmate lawsuits, federal court decisions seemed to expand the requirements for prison officials to grant additional privileges and rights for inmates. However, over the past ten years this trend has reversed somewhat and, in fact, the number of lawsuits by prisoners has actually declined significantly since 1995. Proactive policy implementations by prison administrators, congressional actions, and some court decisions have all contributed to this changing trend.

This chapter has also addressed the complex and emotional issue of the use of capital punishment in the United States. Although long a part of sentencing for serious criminal behavior, the use of capital punishment declined significantly during the 1950s and 1960s and ended for a short period after the Supreme Court ruled in *Furman v. Georgia*. This case did not declare capital punishment in itself as cruel and unusual punishment, but did create general guidelines that must be followed for capital punishment statutes to be considered constitutional. Since *Furman*, thirty-six states and the federal government have reenacted capital punishment statutes, and more than 3,500 prisoners are currently on death rows awaiting execution.

The reasons for support of capital punishment are also addressed. Proponents usually cite the value of capital punishment as a deterrent and provide the need for retribution, protection of society from further crimes, and reduced costs as arguments for their support. However, opponents counter these arguments, and there have been few, if any, conclusive studies on the impact of capital punishment in any of these areas. The biggest concern regarding capital punishment is its fallibility, or the chance of error in finding an innocent person guilty. Recent uses of DNA evidence have led to the exoneration and release of several inmates previously found guilty of murder and sentenced to death. For this reason, public support for capital punishment has diminished, especially when considering an option of life imprisonment without parole.

This chapter brings an end to our look into life in prisons and our examination of the world in which inmates live and prison staff work. We have reviewed the approaches taken by prison administrators to manage prisons and create a safe and secure environment while offering inmates the opportunity to participate in rehabilitative programs. In the final section of this book, we turn to recent and developing correctional challenges, including increasing correctional populations, the impact of politics on correctional policy, tightening public budgets, determining effectiveness, and future questions for correctional students and officials to deliberate.

Key Terms

slave-of-the-state doctrine

precedents

Eighth Amendment

Fourteenth Amendment

balancing test

Civil Rights Act of 1871

Section 1983

Americans with Disabilities Act

totality-of-conditions test

deliberate indifference

community standards

bifurcated trial

lethal injection

Review Questions

1. What is the hands-off doctrine, and in what case did the U.S. Supreme Court abandon it?

2. Define *cruel and unusual punishment* of the Eighth Amendment as it relates to prison conditions.

3. What is the *deliberate indifference* test regarding conditions of confinement as established in *Wilson v. Seiter*?

4. How did *Cooper v. Pate* change the reluctance of the federal courts to get involved in prisoner lawsuits?

5. What standards are used to determine whether the level and quality of medical care provided to inmates are constitutionally acceptable?

6. List the due process principles established for inmate discipline in the case of *Wolff v. McDonnell*.

7. How did the Prison Litigation Reform Act of 1996 limit litigation by inmates?

8. Define a bifurcated trial as established by *Furman v. Georgia*.

9. How many states currently have a statute allowing the death penalty?

10. What 2005 case dealt with the death penalty for juveniles under age 18, and what was the outcome of the decision?

11. Of all death row inmates, what percentage is white?

12. How many inmates were executed and by what method in 2007, and what state executed the most offenders?

13. Describe evidence of the deterrent effect of the death penalty.

14. What percentage of the public supports the death penalty?

15. What dramatic step did Governor George Ryan of Illinois take in 2003 while expressing concerns about the fallibility of the death penalty?

You Make the Decision...

Support the Death Penalty?

The reasons for and against capital punishment related to deterrence, retribution, incapacitation, and cost are listed in the preceding sections. Public support and the potential for error are also described. At this time, students must decide, if they do not already have a position, whether they support the death penalty. Even if you have a firm position, go through the exercise of considering all factors and see if it leads you to the same conclusion.

Either by yourself or in a small classroom group, list all the areas that are discussed as reasons for capital punishment. Then list other factors you think should be considered part of the capital punishment equation. These may be religious or humanistic, desires by the victims' families, or any other factor you think is important. Weigh all these factors and decide whether you support capital punishment. This exercise is much more fun if done in a small group, and students can argue their points and try to convince others of the strength of their positions.

Chapter Resources on mycrimekit™

Go to mycrimekit.com to explore the following study tools and resources specific to this chapter:

- **Practice Quiz:** multiple-choice, true/false, short-answer, and essay questions to help students test their knowledge

- **WebQuests:** learning activities built around Web searches
  - Americans for Effective Law Enforcement: www.aele.org
  - Death Penalty Information Center: www.deathpenaltyinfo.org

- **Insider's Experiences:** "Hostages on Death Row"

- **Seiter Videos:**
  - See an expert discuss inmate medical care
  - See a warden discuss executions

- **Flashcards:** Thirteen flashcards to test knowledge of the chapter's key terms

Correctional Challenges

Issues in Corrections

After reading this chapter, you should be able to:

1. Describe the trend regarding the number of individuals under correctional supervision over the past twenty years and specify the trend over the past five years.

2. Identify the forces that have caused an increase in the prison population and compare the growth of the states to the federal prison system.

3. Discuss the involvement of politics in correctional policy over the past twenty years.

4. Describe the public's attitude regarding correctional sanctions and treatment programs.

5. Specify the status of state budgets and the impact of funding for corrections.

6. Explain the approaches states are taking to make up for budget shortfalls.

7. Identify issues debated regarding private operation of prisons.

8. Compare the effectiveness of public versus private prisons.

9. Discuss the benefits of correctional accreditation.

10. Explain the importance of staff diversity and how correctional agencies accomplish it.

11. Describe recent advances in research methodology and findings of the reviews of correctional treatment effectiveness.

Introduction

Corrections is a constantly evolving discipline. Although it could be argued that we still do what was done centuries ago (incarcerate criminals and supervise them in the community), it can also be argued that everything has changed (prison architecture and management, styles of community supervision). Something certain about the field of corrections is that things do change. New issues develop. New pressures are brought to bear. New factors enter into old problems. And, quite frankly, old issues or programs reappear, sometimes with a different name or a different "spin." Yet, often it is (as the saying goes) the same old car, just a new wax job.

In this chapter, we review some of the most recent developments, issues, and challenges facing corrections today and tomorrow. First, trends in prison and jail populations are examined. Both have continued to grow, but the growth has slowed significantly for prisons and could result in a very different situation for correctional agencies in the next ten years than they faced ten years ago. Second, correctional policy has become increasingly driven by politics over the past fifteen years. Corrections and the operations surrounding it had little public importance in the political agenda just two decades ago. However, with the increase in spending, the public's concern about crime, and politicians' belief that they had to show a "tough on crime" posture, this has forever changed. Correctional policy is now, unfortunately, too often the result of political rhetoric and media sound bites than it is a thoughtful dialogue and planning based on research and prioritizing resources.

In addition, with the growth in the number of correctional clients, there has been a tremendous increase in budget allocations to correctional agencies. Yet with the downturn in the economy during the early 2000s, governments are seeking to reduce correctional spending. This chapter examines some options that can be used to reduce budget allocations.

Another issue for correctional management is the use and utility of accreditation. Developed as a means to enhance credibility and professionalism of correctional agencies, accreditation is seen by most correctional officials as a worthy endeavor, yet others see it as a bureaucratic nuisance. The accreditation process is described and the pros and cons are discussed. A critically important emphasis for correctional agencies is the diversity of staff. With a majority of clients coming from minority groups, correctional agencies have attempted to change their staff's makeup to be more reflective of the client population and thereby reduce the likelihood of problems that could result from a perception of racism and insensitivity. Finally, corrections is, now more than ever, being held accountable for the outcomes of its programs and activities. Therefore, the current understanding of the effectiveness of correctional treatment is examined.

Prison and Jail Populations

At midyear 2002, the population of the nation's prisons and jails for the first time reached 2 million. As of June 30, 2008, there were 2,396,120 offenders incarcerated in the fifty states, the District of Columbia, and federal government prisons and local jails. One-third of these were in jails (785,556), and two-thirds were in prison (1,610,584).[1] Even though both prison and jail numbers have continued to grow over the past decade, there has been a declining percentage of growth in the number of people incarcerated in state prisons, federal prisons, and local jails. During the 1990s, the inmate population grew an average of 8.7 percent per year.[2] Then from 2000 to 2006, the total incarcerated population increased 2.6 percent per year, with state prison populations increasing by 1.7 percent, federal prisons by 5.3 percent, and local jails by 3.6 percent. However, during the six months ending June 30, 2008, the prison population increased by only 0.8 percent compared to a 1.6 percent increase during the same six months in 2007. As well, the jail populations increased only 0.7 percent over twelve months ending June 30, 2008, the lowest growth in jail populations in twenty-seven years. And, sixteen states actually had a decline in their prison population during the first half of 2008.[3]

Table 15.1 illustrates the overall growth in the number of people held in prisons, yet also notes a slowly increasing rate of incarceration. Between 2000 and

TABLE 15.1 **Prisoners Under the Jurisdiction of State or Federal Prisons, Imprisonment Rates and Incarceration Rates, December 31, 2000–2007 and June 30, 2007 and 2008**

Year	Prisoners Under Jurisdiction[a]					Sentenced Prisoners[b]	Imprisonment Rate[c]	Incarceration Rate[d]
	Total	Federal	State	Male	Female			
2000	1,391,261	145,416	1,245,845	1,298,027	93,234	1,331,278	478	684
2001	1,404,032	156,993	1,247,039	1,311,053	92,979	1,345,217	470	685
2002	1,440,144	163,528	1,276,616	1,342,513	97,631	1,380,516	476	701
2003	1,468,601	173,059	1,295,542	1,367,755	100,846	1,408,361	482	712
2004	1,497,100	180,328	1,316,772	1,392,278	104,822	1,433,728	486	723
2005	1,527,929	187,618	1,340,311	1,420,303	107,626	1,462,866	491	737
2006[e]	1,569,945	193,046	1,376,899	1,457,486	112,459	1,504,660	501	751
2007[e]								
June 30	1,594,611	199,118	1,395,493	1,479,297	115,314	1,528,384	509	762
December 31	1,598,242	199,618	1,398,624	1,483,835	114,407	1,532,847	506	756
2008[e]								
June 30	1,610,584	201,142	1,409,442	1,494,805	115,779	1,540,805	509	762
Annual change								
Average annual change, 12/31/2000–12/31/2007	2.0%	4.6%	1.7%	1.9%	3.0%	2.0%	0.8%	1.4%
Percent change, 06/30/2007–06/30/2008	1.0	1.0	1.0	1.0	0.4	0.8	0.0	0.0
Six-month change								
12/31/2006–06/30/2007	1.6%	3.1%	1.4%	1.5%	2.5%	1.6%	1.5%	1.5%
12/31/2007–06/30/2008	0.8	0.8	0.8	0.7	1.2	0.5	0.6	0.8

[a]Jurisdiction refers to the legal authorty over a prisoner, regardless of where the prisoner is held.

[b]Includes prisoners under the authority of state or federal correctional officials with sentences of more than one year, regardless of where they were held.

[c]Imprisonment rate is defined as the number of prisoners sentenced to more than one year under state or federal jurisdiction per 100,000 U.S. residents. Imprisonment rates are based on U.S. Census Bureau population estimates per 100,000 U.S. residents. Resident population estimates are as of January 1 for yearend and July 1 for midyear.

[d]Includes all inmates held in custody in state or federal prisons or local jails. Incarceration rate is defined as the total number of inmates in custody per 100,000 U.S. residents.

[e]Includes estimates for Illinois for 2006, 2007, and 2008 and Nevada for December 31, 2007. See *Methodology*.

Source: Heather C. West and William J. Sabol, *Prison Inmates at Midyear 2008—Statistical Tables* (Washington, D.C.: U.S. Department of Justice, Bureau of Justice Statistics, March 2009), p. 2.

TABLE 15.2 | **Inmates Confined in Local Jails at Midyear, Average Daily Jail Population, and Incarceration Rates, 2000–2008**

Year	Inmates Confined at Midyear		Average Daily Population[a]		Incarceration Rate[b]
	Number	Percent	Number	Percent	
2000	621,149	2.5%	618,319	1.7%	226
2001	631,240	1.6	625,966	1.2	222
2002	665,475	5.4	652,082	4.2	231
2003	691,301	3.9	680,760	4.4	238
2004	713,990	3.3	706,242	3.7	243
2005	747,529	4.7	733,442	3.9	252
2006[c]	765,819	2.4	755,320	3.0	256
2007[d]	780,174	1.9	773,138	2.4	259
2008	785,556	0.7	776,573	0.4	258
Average annual increase					
2000–2007		3.3%		3.2%	
2007–2008		0.7		0.4	

[a]Average daily population is the sum of the number of inmates in jail each day for a year, divided by the number of days in the year.
[b]Number of inmates confined at midyear per 100,000 U.S residents.
[c]Based on revised data from selected jail jurisdictions for the number of inmates confined at midyear 2006. See *Methodology* for a description of revised data.
[d]Based on revised data from selected jail jurisdictions for the number of inmates confined at midyear 2007 and the average daily population in 2007. See *methodology* for a description of revised data.

Source: Todd D. Minton and William J. Sabol, *Jail Inmates at Midyear 2008—Statistical Tables* (Washington, D.C.: U.S. Department of Justice, Bureau of Justice Statistics, March 2009), p. 2.

June 30, 2008, the incarceration rate grew from 684 to 762 per 100,000 U.S. residents (11.4 percent). That rate increase has slowed since the 31 percent reported from 1990 to 1995. Table 15.2 illustrates the same information regarding the jail population. Jail incarceration rates grew from 226 per 100,000 in 2000 to 258 per 100,000 residents on June 30, 2008 (a 14 percent growth).

As noted above, the growth of the prison population has been steadily slowing over the past several years. This overall slowdown in the growth of the prison population can be somewhat misleading, however, as the federal prison population continues to experience high growth rates, while the state prison population has slowed in growth. The U.S. Congress has continued to federalize several crimes that had previously been handled at the state level, with the war on drugs and gun crimes having the most significant effect. In addition, over the past few years, the federal government has taken responsibility for housing inmates who were previously incarcerated by the District of Columbia, increasing the federal prison population by almost 7,000 inmates as a result. As noted in Table 15.1, the average annual change in the number of federal prisoners from 2000 to 2007 was 4.6 percent, whereas the average annual state growth was 1.7 percent for the same time period.

An interesting result of the changing prison population has been the impact on private prisons. As indicated in Table 15.3, from 2000 to midyear 2008, the number of inmates held in privately operated prisons increased from 90,542 to

TABLE 15.3	Number of Prisoners Held in Private Facilities, December 31, 2000–2007 and June 30, 2007 and 2008

| Year | Number of Prisoners | | | Percent of all Prisoners |
	Total	Federal	State	
2000	90,542	15,524	75,018	6.5%
2001	91,953	19,251	72,702	6.5
2002	93,912	20,274	73,638	6.5
2003	95,707	21,865	73,842	6.5
2004	98,628	24,768	73,860	6.6
2005	107,940	27,046	80,894	7.1
2006	113,697	27,726	85,971	7.2
2007				
June 30	118,239	30,379	87,860	7.4%
December 31	125,997	31,310	94,687	7.9
2008				
June 30	126,249	32,712	93,537	7.8%
Annual change				:
Average annual change, 12/31/2000–12/31/2007	4.0%	10.5%	3.4%	
Percent change, 06/30/2007–06/30/2008	6.8	7.7	6.5	:

Note: Includes estimates for Illinois for 2006, 2007, and 2008 and Nevada for December 31, 2007. See *Methoodology*.

: Not calculated.

Source: Heather C. West and William J. Sabol, *Prison Inmates at Midyear 2008—Statistical Tables* (Washington, D.C.: U.S. Department of Justice, Bureau of Justice Statistics, March 2009), p. 12.

126,249, an increase of 39 percent. What seems to be occurring is much of the new growth in prison inmates are going into private prisons, most likely because the private companies provide the funding to add capacity without government agencies having to sell bonds and budget all the capital construction money up front. In a 2001 review of the status of private prisons, the authors projected that "[t]he number of privatized prisons is likely to increase, but not at the pace exhibited during the past decade."[4] However, another argument is noted in a 2003 paper, as the author suggested that there is considerable evidence that prison privatization is now in decline, a result of declining incarceration rates, overbuilding of prison beds, legislation antagonistic to the private prison industry, and a number of well-publicized serious incidents.[5]

As noted in Table 15.2, the jail population has also increased, with an average annual growth of 3.3 percent from 2000 to 2007, but slowed in 2008. Trends in the size and growth in local jail populations are difficult to analyze, because the number of jailed inmates has continued to rise over the past several years, but with no consistent pattern in its growth. Figure 15.1 illustrates the growth by percentage for jails during each twelve-month period between 2000 and 2008. Jail incarceration rates have a trend similar to prisons in that they rose significantly from 193 per 100,000 in 1995 to 231 per 100,000 in 2002.[6] Since that time, there has been a slower increase as the jail incarceration rate grew to only 258 per 100,000 in 2008.[7]

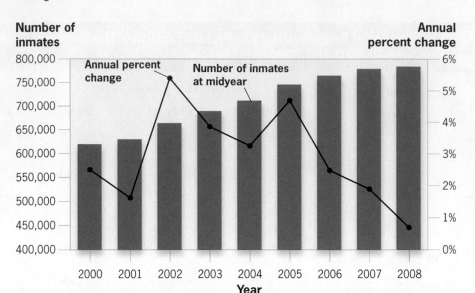

Source: Todd D. Minton and William J. Sabol, *Jail Inmates at Midyear 2008—Statistical Tables* (Washington, D.C.: U.S. Department of Justice, Bureau of Justice Statistics, March 2009), p. 2.

FIGURE 15.1   Inmates Confined in Local Jails at Midyear and Annual Percent Change in the Jail Population, 2000–2008

There are several reasons for the slowdown in the growth of incarcerated offenders that has continued (seemingly unabated) over the past twenty years. First, it is only natural that after such growth there would be a slowdown at some time. If, as proponents of the use of incarceration argue, incapacitating offenders in prison reduces crime, then at some point a large number of potential criminals will be in jail and prison, and the increase in new admissions will have to slow down. Although reducing the inmate population by shortening sentences or eliminating mandatory prison terms for some offenses does not seem politically popular, recent incarceration trends do note some relief.

After the era of lengthening sentences over the past twenty years, it is difficult to comprehend that legislative bodies will significantly roll back sentencing codes to the "less tough" levels that existed before the mid-1980s. However, most states have a constitutional requirement to balance their budgets and are not allowed to operate at a deficit, as does the federal government. Therefore, as addressed in a section below regarding the impact of tightening budgets on correctional policy, there may now be a political opportunity to modify statutes to reduce the number of people in prison. In addition, there has been considerable publicity about the questionable merit of tough sentencing laws such as California's three-strikes legislation. In a review of this process, Greenwood and colleagues suggest that legislators who found voting for the legislation politically attractive later reversed themselves and found that voting against funding the act's implementation was just as politically attractive.[8]

Second, many states have increased their use of alternatives to incarceration, and these efforts are finally having some impact. There has been an increasing concern that continued increases in the use of incarceration have failed to concurrently increase public safety,[9] yet this policy has undoubtedly increased the cost to taxpayers. Therefore, many states have looked for and implemented sanctions between probation and incarceration. Many of these have proved effective and less costly when the risk of offenders is properly identified and matched to correctional sanctions.[10] As well, jail pretrial release programs have been added in many local jurisdictions and have also effectively slowed the increase in the number of jail inmates. The Pretrial Services Resource Center, in a review of methods used to alleviate jail overcrowding conducted for the U.S. Department of Justice, reported,

> *In response to increased jail populations, probation agencies are working with other criminal justice agencies to develop alternative programs. Many counties opt for increasing the number of community-based alternatives, instead of the rate of incarceration, because the former is a more cost-effective means of alleviating jail crowding while maintaining public safety.*[11]

Finally, the continually increasing costs to government for building and operating correctional facilities challenges a jurisdiction's budget, and as the recession of 2008 moves forward, it is likely that there will be an even greater slowing of the population. In a report regarding methods to alleviate jail overcrowding (that is also relevant to prisons), the authors noted, "Construction and operation of local jails are extremely expensive propositions. Over the years, the view that a jurisdiction can solve its jail crowding problem through building has proved to be wrong."[12] There are many factors that influence correctional policy, including politics and budgetary challenges. Both of these issues are addressed below.

Politics and Policy

Why has the U.S. prison population risen so dramatically over the past twenty years, and why may its growth be beginning to slow down? It is important to examine the impact of politics on the formation of correctional policy. Although citizens would like to believe that policy is developed from painstaking research, analysis of costs and benefits, and weighing of many alternatives, unfortunately that is seldom the case. Especially in regard to issues in which there is emotion and strong sentiment, elected officials more often respond by making decisions that will be seen by the public as the "right thing to do" and that will likely win them votes and reelection.

When it comes to the use of incarceration as a sanction for criminal offending, changes in sentencing and incarceration policies had significantly more impact than other changes. Blumstein and Beck examined the growth of imprisonment between 1980 and 1996 and concluded that 88 percent was due to changes in policy, including sentencing to prison rather than probation (51 percent) and lengthening time served by offenders (37 percent). Only 12 percent of the growth was the result of changes in the crime rate or the makeup of criminal offenders.[13]

Why have elected officials moved aggressively toward "tough on crime" policies, even where there is little evidence of their effectiveness and with the knowledge that they are extremely expensive in relation to community alternative sanctions? Perhaps the watershed political event regarding politics and criminal justice policy occurred during the 1988 presidential campaign, when Vice President George Bush successfully used the public's fear of crime as a campaign tool against his opponent, Governor Michael Dukakis of Massachusetts. Bush used campaign ads presenting Dukakis as soft on crime for allowing a Massachusetts **furlough** program and suggesting that it led to the commission of a tragic murder by Willie Horton, a furloughed inmate, while he lived in a halfway house.

Other candidates for public office saw the effectiveness of "tough on crime" policies and the dangers of being labeled "soft on crime." Therefore, campaign promises to keep dangerous offenders in prison longer became the rallying cry for elections from Virginia to California, resulting in tough sentencing laws and

mycrimekit

Media—Video: Public Attitudes—What the Public Wants

furlough
a program in which prison inmates are allowed to leave the prison early to reside in a halfway house and prepare for reentry to the community

The "politicizing" of corrections was believed to have reached its watershed during the presidential campaign between George Bush and Michael Dukakis. Courtesy of Dennis Cook/AP Wide World Photos.

funding for prison construction passed by state legislatures across the country. Such legislation includes the California three-strikes law, resulting from a similar public campaign to toughen laws after the 1993 murder of 12-year-old Polly Klaas by Richard Allen Davis, who was on parole after serving only eight years of a sixteen-year sentence for kidnapping.

Another example is the nation's war on drugs, in which President Ronald Reagan pushed through legislation to toughen drug laws, allocate more resources to investigating and prosecuting drug laws, and require mandatory prison terms for federal drug offenders. The dramatic increase in the federal prison population resulted primarily from these policies, to the point that almost two-thirds of the federal prison population is currently drug offenders. A 1999 article in *Newsweek* noted, "We are developing a powerful 'prison–industrial complex,' a national growth industry exploiting today's hostility toward wrongdoers."[14]

Unfortunately, once political rhetoric forces correctional policy to move in this direction, it is difficult to change directions and turn back the clock. Increasing costs of correctional budgets usually take money from other public services, such as education, social service programs, and improvement of deteriorating infrastructures. As an example, the National Conference of State Legislatures reported that state spending on higher education experienced the highest reduction in its history during the 1990s, during which state correctional spending had its fastest growth.[15] Addressing this dilemma, Irwin and Austin argue that society must turn away from the excessive use of prisons, which is diverting money from education, child care, mental health, and medical services, all of which have a greater impact on reducing crime than does building more prisons.[16]

One interesting thing in the linkage of politics and correctional policy is that the public is not nearly as strongly in favor of "get tough" policies as elected officials believe. A major result of the **"tough on crime"** political mentality has been the implementation of sentencing guidelines, determinate sentencing to replace the use of parole boards, and mandatory sentencing. All these reduce discretion by judges and correctional professionals, resulting in an inability to distinguish among offenders by their risk and chance for successful rehabilitation. As Petersilia writes, "One of the most distinguishing characteristics of U.S. crime policy since the 1980s has been the gradual chipping away on individualized decision making and its replacement with one-size-fits-all laws and policies."[17]

"tough on crime"
an attitude that criminals should be severely punished for their wrongdoings, and long prison sentences are the most effective criminal sanction

Public attitudes are becoming less punitive in their belief about the most effective way to handle criminal offenders than in the past. In 1994, only 48 percent of Americans favored addressing the causes of crime and 42 percent preferred the punitive approach.[18] By 2002, a public opinion poll conducted by Peter D. Hart Research Associates found the public favored addressing the root causes of crime over strict sentencing, by 65 percent to 32 percent. Poll respondents also favor a more rational sentencing for offenders. Only 28 percent of Americans surveyed believed that the most effective way to reduce crime is to keep offenders off the street as long as possible. Nearly two-thirds of those surveyed believed that the most effective way to reduce crime is to rehabilitate prisoners by requiring education and job training.[19] And in 2006, a National Council on Crime and Delinquency poll found that 87 percent of the U.S. voting public favored rehabilitative services for inmates as opposed to a punitive approach to sentencing.[20]

Americans have also expressed concern with the punitive approach taken by the war on drugs. In the Hart survey, respondents recognized drug abuse as a medical problem, and 63 percent favored handling it primarily through counseling and treatment, whereas only 31 percent believed that it is a serious crime that should be handled mainly by the courts and prison system. Respondents also expressed concern with the overreach of three-strikes laws; 56 percent favored elimination of these policies and other mandatory sentencing laws, and giving judges more discretion to choose the appropriate sentence. In general, only 35 percent supported the direction of the nation's crime approach, and 54 percent believed we are on the wrong track.[21]

Elected officials continuously evaluate public opinion in their consideration of support or opposition for correctional policies. In the following "An Interview With" box, former U.S. Senator Mike DeWine is a good example of how elected officials look at correctional policies and programs.

Public opinion surveys have discovered that the primary interest of the public is to be protected. They do not support sanctions that do not punish offenders and

An Interview With...

An Elected Official, U.S. Senator Mike DeWine

Correctional policy has become very visible, and public interest and involvement in the creation of correctional policy are much higher than in the past. Elected officials, therefore, become actively involved in the formulation of correctional policy. One elected official who is very knowledgeable and involved in corrections is Mike DeWine, former U.S. senator from Ohio. In his more than thirty years of public service, Senator DeWine has worked at all levels of government. He has been a county prosecuting attorney, an Ohio state senator, a four-term U.S. congressman, and Ohio's fifty-ninth lieutenant governor. As lieutenant governor, he oversaw the operations of all of the state criminal justice departments, including the adult corrections and youth services departments. He was first sworn into the U.S. Senate on January 4, 1995, and served two terms until 2007. Senator DeWine was very gracious in sharing his time to be interviewed regarding corrections and public policy.

Question: Senator DeWine, do elected officials care or show much interest in correctional policies?

Senator DeWine: As an elected official who has been closely involved in the criminal justice system throughout my public life, I am very concerned about correctional operations, public opinion, and protection of society. Politicians listen closely to

...continued

public attitude and opinion regarding corrections and criminal justice. Public opinion is an element in shaping policy, since elected officials have a responsibility to address the concerns of those we serve. Everyone has an opinion, cares about, and wants more information about corrections. Crime is one of the most important issues to the public.

Question: What is most important to the public regarding correctional policy?

Senator DeWine: There are several things. First, the public has an interest in whether prisons have too many amenities and therefore do not really punish or correct offenders. It is clear that the vast majority of the public thinks that prisoners are treated too well. Correctional officials must be proactive and illustrate to the public the many good things going on in prisons that contribute to public safety, benefit the community, and can even improve the chance of offenders returning to society as productive and law-abiding citizens. A good example is the use of community service. In Ohio, we reach out to the communities to identify needs that can be met with prison labor. The state department of corrections provides over a million hours of community service work to local communities per year. The prison staff go to the local community and ask, "What can we do for you? Are there bookcases we can build? Are there teaching tools or kits that you need but cannot afford to have made?" These programs matter, they make a difference, they are good justice, and they are win–win situations for everyone. They keep prisoners occupied and busy, and inmates are able to give something back to the community. This changes the public perception of prisoners sitting in a comfortable place, watching television, eating three meals a day, and living off the taxpayers.

Something else important to the public and elected officials is to have a focus on victims of crime. When I started as a prosecuting attorney, victims of crime were literally the forgotten people in the criminal justice system. It was the State of Ohio versus Defendant. The victim was not even mentioned in the title of the case. We need to involve victims at every step of the criminal justice process. Victims need to be informed and active participants at the sentencing hearing as well as during the parole or release decision process. We also find ways to give something back to victims and require offenders to be accountable for their actions and the pain and loss they have caused. The public expects offenders to give something back to society.

Question: What do elected officials think of rehabilitative correctional programs?

Senator DeWine: Knowing that virtually every offender will be released from prison and living among us, it makes sense to give offenders the tools to make a legitimate living and give them the opportunity to deal with some of the underlying problems that may have contributed to their involvement in crime. The public knows that such programs will not be successful with everyone, but no one supports not doing anything to let inmates improve themselves and prepare for release. It is estimated that up to 80 percent of offenders have a substance abuse problem, and we need to somehow deal with this while they are under correctional supervision.

Question: What would you advise correctional officials regarding understanding and responding to the matters that the public wants regarding correctional operations?

Senator DeWine: First, correctional officials must make an effort to reach out to the public, educate them about how prisons are run, and involve them as much as possible in the correctional process. I do not believe that public opinion and professional correctional judgment are adversarial in regards to correctional policy. I suggest that correctional professionals be more proactive regarding public sentiment when establishing correctional policy. Being consistent with and sensitive to issues that are red flags for the public can go a long way in gaining support from elected officials and their constituencies.

protect society. However, if they believe that community sanctions effectively protect them, the public supports the use of community sanctions over imprisonment. In an Ohio survey, when informed that prison space is scarce and expensive, the public supported the use of community corrections instead of paying for new prison construction.[22] A National Opinion Survey on Crime and Justice (NOSCJ) survey also found support for community correctional programs: 73 percent of those surveyed indicated that intensive probation supervision was either "very effective" or "somewhat effective," 55 percent similarly supported house arrest,

73 percent supported electronic monitoring of offenders, and 78 percent supported the use of boot camps as alternatives to traditional prison sentences.[23]

Even though there is momentum to slow the growth of incarceration, continued building of new prisons, and additional increases in the budgets of correctional agencies, there are also factors that encourage a continuation of that policy. We have developed a prison-industrial complex that requires monetary commitments and has political support for its continuation. Once the capital outlay for building a new prison is committed, it is not realistic to project that it will be closed and abandoned. Rural communities depend on the economic value of the jobs and purchases resulting from a prison in their area. Labor unions such as the California Correctional Peace Officers Association (CCPOA) have become a major lobbying influence for maintaining correctional officer jobs. This union has tremendous power in California politics, having contributed $2.3 million to the successful 1998 campaign of the California governor.[24] And some writers have argued that private prison companies, which will benefit from continued policies of incarceration, also influence criminal justice legislation.[25]

It will be interesting to observe whether elected officials will continue to spend money that the state does not have to further toughen criminal sanctions. Unfortunately, we often fail to learn from our past mistakes when it comes to

A Case Study

Politics and Policy Regarding Prison Industries

When I was an assistant director of the Federal Bureau of Prisons, I had responsibility for Federal Prison Industries (FPI), a government corporation that manufactured products in prisons, and thereby provided inmates with real-world work opportunities and sold the products to the federal government. The last year I was in the position, FPI had more than $400 million in sales of prison-made products. FPI was authorized by Congress in the 1930s, recognizing that inmates could not sit idly in their cells all day, the goods could be sold to the government at a fair or reduced price, and profits could be used to assist in managing federal prisons. Government agencies were to buy from FPI if they produced a product that met the agencies' specifications, could be delivered on time, and was sold at a fair market price.

FPI was the model of a government corporation for the next fifty years. It was started with a grant of buildings, machinery, and raw materials valued at approximately $3 million. Over the years, it returned some $80 million in profits back to the U.S. Treasury. There was never another penny of taxpayer dollars appropriated to its operation, because it proved profitable and able to operate successfully. Inmates received excellent training and developed valuable work skills, contributing to a reduction of recidivism for participants. The policy of operating

FPI by this method was effective and led to efficiencies in government.

However, in the late 1980s, private companies and trade associations that produced products similar to FPI, as well as labor unions, became concerned about the size of FPI in terms of sales to the government. They began to approach their members of Congress and argued that it was unfair to let inmates work and sell products that competed with the private sector and therefore cost law-abiding citizens jobs. Even though FPI had a minuscule share of any market for the products they sold, these associations and individuals lobbied Congress to take away the "mandatory source" policy, in which agencies were supposed to first see if FPI had the product available before they purchased it from the private sector.

Members of Congress are aware that there are few if any votes to be received from supporting an inmate work program. Yet they can lose votes by seeming to not support their constituents who believe that jobs are lost due to the FPI work program. To this day, bills are annually introduced to limit the opportunity of FPI to sell inmate-made goods to the federal government. Although the merits of both the private sector and FPI arguments are debatable, this is truly a situation of politics competing with effective public policy.

crime policy. Although it is hoped that elected officials will turn away from political rhetoric and emotion and toward research, analysis, and careful planning to shape our crime policies in the future, we have not always seen that to be the case. At this time, however, the difficult budget decisions facing public officials may create a backdrop for more rational decision making. The "A Case Study" box is a good example of how politics and correctional policy can clash.

The Impact of Budgets on Correctional Policy

As noted above, the recession and budget challenges at the federal, state, and local levels have had an impact on incarceration rates as governments try to reduce the cost of corrections. The economic downturn over the past few years has resulted in reduced tax receipts by states and the federal government. When the economy was strong and governments were experiencing budget surpluses, it was an easy decision to expand prison space and other correctional services to meet the burgeoning population under supervision. With tightening budgets, it is now a much more complicated decision as to whether to increase taxes, reduce the correctional population, or eliminate some services or supervision to meet budget shortfalls. Freeman observes, "Tax revenues are not unlimited and, as correctional budgets have grown at the expense of other state agencies, elected officials have increasingly demanded that corrections assume a proactive role in reducing the burden on the taxpayer."[26]

Over the past twenty years, the number of clients served by adult correctional agencies has grown significantly. At the end of 2007, nearly 7.3 million individuals were under correctional supervision of probation, prison, jail, or parole (see Figure 15.2). Correspondingly, expenditures for correctional agencies have also

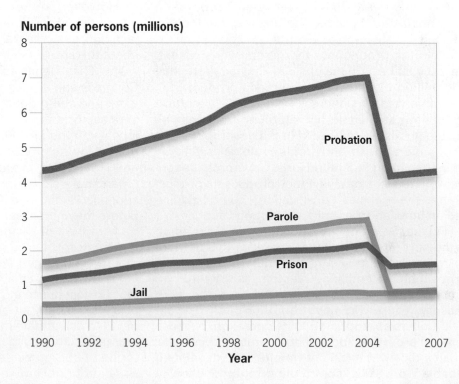

Source: Bureau of Justice Statistics Correctional Surveys (Annual Probation Survey, National Prisoner Statistics, Survey of Jails, and Annual Parole Survey) as presented in *Probation and Parole in the United States, 2007*, p. 2.

FIGURE 15.2 Number of Persons under Correctional Supervision, by Type of Supervision, 1990–2007

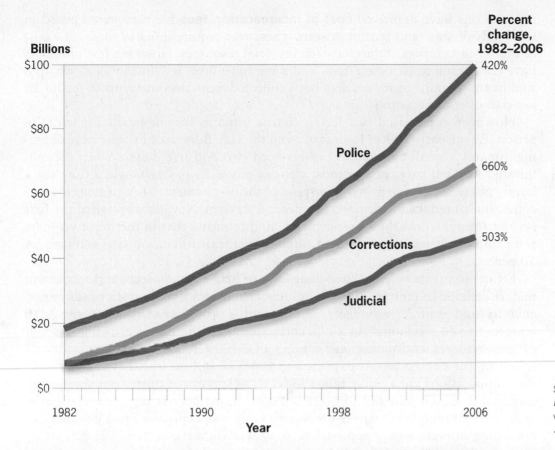

FIGURE 15.3   Direct Expenditure by Criminal Justice Function, 1982–2007

Source: Bureau of Justice Statistics, *Expenditure Facts at a Glance*, www.ojp.usdoj.gov/bjs/glance/exptyp .htm (accessed April 15, 2009).

grown. As indicated in Figure 15.3, expenditures for all three components of the criminal justice system (police, judicial, and corrections) have expanded from 1982 to 2006. However, even though police expenditures rose by 420 percent and judicial expenditures by 503 percent, corrections led the increase, rising by 660 percent. In fiscal year 1991, state and federal adult correctional agencies' budgets totaled $18.1 billion.[27] By fiscal year 2006, these budgets, with the inclusion of local jails, more than tripled to $68.7 billion.[28]

State correctional agencies consumed 6.8 percent of state general funds in 2007,[29] and by 2011, continued prison growth is expected to cost an additional $25 billion.[30] Figures vary widely, but the average per prisoner operating cost was $28,816 ($78.95 per day) in 2008.[31] Key drivers of increased cost per inmate are health care and salaries for staff, as "prisons are struggling mightily to keep a full complement of officers on staff. The result—the extensive use of overtime—is one of the biggest budget busters confronting corrections."[32]

Over the past few years, states have tried to identify ways to **create revenues** to reduce the government costs for program operations. Charging offenders for some aspects of their supervision was not new, particularly for community corrections. As a condition of probation, offenders have regularly been charged a fine or had to pay victim restitution, and many probation agencies charge offenders for services such as drug counseling, halfway house stays, or participation in work release programs, as well as for their supervision costs of electronic monitoring, intensive supervision, or drug testing. Almost all county probation departments and forty-one states report using such fees.[33]

A rather unique approach but one with much political appeal has been to attempt to get inmates to contribute to the cost of their incarceration, and many

create revenues
the idea that governments can charge for certain services, even for correctional supervision or programs provided to offenders

cost of incarceration fee

fees charged to prisoners in local jails or prisons to cover the cost to taxpayers for their incarceration

jurisdictions have approved **cost of incarceration fees** for prisoners housed in local jails or state and federal prisons. These fees require inmates to pay the cost of their incarceration, if they have the financial resources. However, few offenders have the means to pay these fees, and there have been few instances in which a significant amount of money has been collected from an inmate to cover his or her cost of confinement.

However, often used is a fee to charge inmates for medical care while in prison. By the early 2000s, forty states and the U.S. Bureau of Prisons were charging inmates a small **co-payment** of between two and five dollars when they requested medical care, just as most citizens pay a co-payment when they see a family physician.[34] The primary purpose of the co-payment is not to generate revenues, but to reduce the demand for medical services. Nevada was one of the first states to begin to use these co-payments, and reported that in the first two years after implementing a co-payment, inmate medical utilization was reduced by 50 percent.[35]

co-payment

a minimal charge for inmates to see a physician or receive medical care; in most states, the charges are two to three dollars

Efforts to create revenue have done little to help states overcome their current budget deficits. In January 2009, states reported over $50 billion shortfalls in revenue to fund their 2009 budgets, and the gap is projected to widen in the 2010 budgets to $84.3 billion.[36] In 2008, corrections was the fastest growing segment of state budgets, consuming one in every fifteen discretionary dollars, and state spending for corrections is expected to top $52 billion in fiscal year 2008.[37] Prison operations are a prime target for cuts, as surveys of thirty-four states indicate that in 2008, nine out of every ten corrections dollars were spend on prisons.[38] Community alternatives are significantly less expensive, and jurisdictions are taking unprecedented approaches to try to reduce the costs of corrections by moving more of the population from prison to community supervision. As noted above, historically, no politician wanted to be painted as "soft on crime." In these tight budget times, however, fiscal issues are beginning to trump politics.

The Pew Report *One in 31* notes, that "Some policy makers are questioning the wisdom of devoting an increasingly large slice of the budget pie to incarceration, especially when recidivism rates have remained discouragingly high."[39] As a result, many policy makers are looking to lower correctional costs, and if possible, reduce recidivism. The most frequent solution for reducing the cost of corrections is to blend incarceration for high-risk and violent offenders with the increased use of community punishments for lawbreakers guilty of less serious crimes. A good example is Texas, which avoided spending an estimated $523 million in more prison beds by expanding drug treatment and diversion beds, many of them in secure facilities. Texas also changed parole practices and expanded drug courts. These reforms are expected to save Texas $210 million over the next two years, and double that if the recidivism rate drops as expected. Senator John Whitmire of Houston noted that, "It's always been safer politically to build the next prison. . . . But, we're at a point where I don't think we can afford to do that anymore."[40]

There are several targets to reduce the costs of incarceration. One is on the "front end" by using more community diversion programs to give offenders another chance to stay in the community rather than be imprisoned. There are also efforts to change how those who violate rules of probation and parole are handled. In 2005, parole violators accounted for more than one-third of all prison admissions.[41] Many of these revocations are for "technical" violations—failing a drug test or missing an appointment with their parole officer—rather than commission of a new crime. States are increasingly opting to punish technical parole violators with community-based sanctions, such as day reporting centers, electronic monitoring systems, and community service. And states are giving inmates the chance to earn more good time in order to reduce the length of sentence served. And on the "release end," there is a renewed focus on prisoner reentry. Every state is focusing on ways to improve the programming and transition for inmates coming out of prison, hoping to reduce recidivism and thereby reduce the costs for incarceration. Examples of some of these are noted below.

In California, Governor Arnold Schwarzenegger proposed to release 22,000 nonviolent inmates early and place them on unsupervised parole. In Rhode Island, lawmakers expanded good time to move more offenders from prison to postprison supervision. In Kentucky, nonviolent offenders were allowed to service up to 180 days of their prison sentence at home. In Mississippi, Governor Haley Barbour signed into law a measure to make nonviolent inmates eligible for release after serving 25 percent of their sentences. In South Carolina, there was a proposal to abolish parole to slow the return of parole violators to prison.[42]

One common target for diversion is nonviolent offenders with drug addictions. Since 2004, at least thirteen states have adopted legislation creating or expanding community corrections options for nonviolent offenders, including the use of drug courts.[43] In March 2009, the New York state legislature reached agreement on repealing the 1970s Rockefeller drug laws that required mandatory prison terms for low-level drug felons. In its place, the state would give judges more authority to send nonviolent drug offenders to community treatment instead of prison. A spokesperson for Governor David A. Paterson said these reforms "reflect the governor's core principle to focus on treatment rather than punishment to end the cycle of addiction."[44] The state faces a $16 billion budget deficit for fiscal year 2009, and although the treatment in lieu of prison would cost $80 million per year, in the long run, the repeal is expected to save money as the treatment program would be less expensive than the $45,000 it costs per year to confine a prisoner in New York.

Kansas and Texas, states with reputations for being tough on crime, are gaining considerable recognition for their efforts to save money by diverting offenders from prisons to less expensive community alternatives. While governor for Kansas, Kathleen Sebelius signed into law a plan to reduce prison admissions by providing counties with financial incentives to create community correctional systems and to provide opportunities for low-risk inmates to reduce their sentences by participating in prison programs. A large percentage of prison admissions are probation or parole violators, and if counties reduce their recidivism rates by 20 percent or more, they qualify for grants from the state. The law also allows early release of up to sixty days for qualified offenders who successfully complete education and counseling programs that are expected to decrease their chances of returning to prison.[45]

In Texas, the state legislature approved a plan to divert thousands of inmates from prison to rehabilitation facilities designed to help them reenter society and funded a new 500-bed treatment facility for offenders sentenced for driving while intoxicated (DWI) at which they are provided substance-abuse treatment rather than being sent to prison where they would receive little or no counseling. The goal of this is to reduce the need for construction of costly new prisons. "We have changed the course of the ship substantially in the state of Texas," said Representative Jerry Madden, chairman of the House Corrections Committee and an engineer of the prison plan.[46]

Hawaii found that it was increasing the cost of its prison system by failing to successfully deal with its offenders on probation, and some judges were sentencing inmates to ten years in prison because they missed appointments with their probation officers. Judge Steven Alm was one of those judges, but thought, "there has to be a better way to change offender behavior." Alm created a new approach

The Orient (Ohio) Correctional Institution was closed during 2003 due to insufficient budgets to pay for staff salaries. Its closure resulted in increasing overcrowding at other prisons. Courtesy of the Ohio Department of Rehabilitation and Correction.

and sends probation violators from his court immediately to jail— but he keeps them there for only a few days. As they comply with their probation expectations, they get more freedom and have fewer check-ins with their probation officer. A four-year study of the program found there are more than 80 percent fewer violations, and more importantly, the number of new crimes committed by the people on probation has been cut in half.[47]

In Wisconsin, there is hope that dollars coming from the Recovery Act funds (the stimulus bill passed by the Obama administration) will help with budget challenges and with diverting offenders from prison. The state is emphasizing public safety along with cost cutting and is using the governor's budget and Recovery Act funds to keep the most serious offenders in prison while increasing supervision for nonviolent and lower-risk offenders in the community. Governor Doyle believes that additional focus on reentry, community treatment, and diversion programs will reduce recidivism and the number of offenders that must be held in prisons.[48]

The question is how many of these proposals will become a reality and how significantly the changes in policy or law will reduce prison populations. Several times in the past three decades, there have been modest efforts to restructure sentences and use more alternatives to prison in an effort to either reduce costs or create a system that seems to provide more equity and fairness. However, political reaction has always been strongly negative, and the sponsors of such legislation have backed down with few changes and very little change in policy or budgets. If the current recession deepens and continues, the likelihood that these efforts will this time lead to more significant and longer-lasting change increases.

Private Prisons

A growing method used by correctional agencies to reduce their costs is to contract some services or the entire operation of prisons to the private sector. During the Reagan and George H. W. Bush presidential terms, governments began to consider use of the private sector to provide many services that had previously been provided solely by government. Some contracting for services outside government had been done for years by correctional agencies, but some ideas were relatively new. Halfway houses had historically been private,

Private prisons now hold over 125,000 inmates in adult prisons, more than 7 percent of the total population, and more beds are being built.
Reprinted with permission of the Corrections Corporation of America.

nonprofit operations, and community correctional agencies also began to contract for electronic monitoring, drug testing, and some program services. However, during the 1980s, prisons began to consider contracting with private companies to provide food services, medical and mental health care, educational programming, and substance abuse counseling, and by the turn of the century, there were 126 state and federal prisons contracting for food services and 397 for medical care for inmates.[49] Another 300 prisons had private contractors providing mental health services, and 226 prisons contracted for substance abuse services.[50]

Agencies also began to consider contracting total housing, services, security, and programs for inmates with the private sector. Since the first contract with a private prison to house offenders for a public correctional agency in the early 1980s, the use of such contracts has grown significantly. On June 30, 2008, there were 126,249 state, District of Columbia, and federal inmates in private prisons across the United States.[51] At an average cost per day of $53.38, these contracts equate to almost $2.5 billion per year.[52]

After twenty-five years of private prisons contracting with government agencies, there is little question as to whether this is a policy decision that will continue. However, there remains debate regarding the costs, benefits, quality of service, and ethical concerns of an offender's freedom being taken away by a for-profit company. Logan identified ten issues that are key to any deliberations regarding the use of private prisons:

1. The propriety of proprietary prisons—can the punishment of offenders be delegated to nonpublic agencies?

2. Cost and efficiency—are private prisons operated less expensively than public prisons?

3. Quality—does the profit motive diminish the drive for delivery of quality services and programs to inmates?

4. Quantity—does the involvement of the private sector to make a profit encourage the expansion of imprisonment beyond what is in the public interest?

5. Flexibility—does the fact that the private sector does not have to follow bureaucratic government policies for purchasing and personnel management increase efficiency?

6. Security—does an emphasis on profits and cost-cutting undermine security for inmates, staff, and the community?

7. Liability—what impact does a government's contracting with a private firm for housing inmates have on the liability of the government for violation of inmates' constitutional rights?

8. Accountability and monitoring—how will the private contractor be monitored to fulfill requirements and be held responsible if it does not?

9. Corruption—without the restraints inherent in government to reduce the likelihood of corruption, will there be an increase in corruption in private prisons?

10. Dependence—will the public sector become dependent on the private-sector contract and, if so, how does this affect decision making?[53]

A critical issue for private prisons concerns cost efficiency, as states and the federal governments expect to save money by contracting with private prison companies. In purely monetary terms, the average cost of private-sector contracts for 2008 of $54.75 per inmate per day compares very favorably to the average daily cost per inmate in a public prison of $79.00.[54] However, it is difficult to make an "apples to apples" comparison, as the public costs include all security levels and operation of expensive prison hospitals, but do not include the cost of construction.

Several studies have compared the cost of privately operated prisons, but few controlled for comparable security levels for the evaluated prisons. The earliest review of the Hamilton County, Tennessee, private prison suggested that it saved from 4 to 15 percent annually over county-operated penal farm costs.[55] A study comparing costs of public and private prisons in Kentucky and Massachusetts found that private prisons appeared to be better managed than public prisons.[56] A 1992 study comparing costs for public and private facilities housing parole violators in California found a lower cost per day for private facilities.[57]

Several recent studies have found that private prisons house offenders at less cost than their public counterparts. A study initially funded by private prisons determined that between 1999 and 2004, "states that have some of their prisoners in privately-owned or -operated prisons experience lower growth in the cost of housing their public prisoners."[58] A *Harvard Law Review* article concluded that "what imperfect empirical evidence there is suggests that private prisons cost less than public prisons and that their quality is no worse."[59] A literature review in 2002 by the Reason Foundation identified seventeen studies that measure quality of operations by government and private prisons, and fifteen of those conclude that "the quality at the private facilities is as good or better than at government-run facilities."[60] However, Segal and Moore, in a review of the costs of outsourcing correctional services, conclude, "Policymakers should be wary of over-reliance on cost-comparison data in making privatization decisions, and be certain that cost analysts do not take it upon themselves to make

mycrimekit

Media—Video: Prison Privatization

policy assumptions in determining cost figures."[61] Further, there are still many concerns with states contracting with for-profit companies to incarcerate offenders. Dolovich questions the legitimacy of this approach, even if private prisons can operate for less money without a drop in quality.[62]

Another reason correctional agencies turn to privatization is to eliminate having to appropriate funds for the enormous capital outlay required to build prisons. During the period of tremendous growth in the inmate population from the late 1980s through the early 2000s, the private sector was able to fund, build, and provide prison beds more rapidly than the public sector. Austin and Coventry note that, because private companies are not subject to government regulations regarding construction of buildings, the private sector can build prisons for nearly 25 percent less and in half the time compared to public governments.[63] Culp also notes that some states were approaching their debt ceilings or did not have the time to issue bonds to fund new prison construction.[64] A 2004 analysis of Oklahoma's use of private prisons found that the state succeeded in housing a substantial number of offenders, without spending a penny on building new facilities.[65]

Several studies have examined postrelease outcomes between public and private prison inmates, with mixed reviews. Results from a Florida study comparing recidivism of releasees from private and public prisons favored the private prisons. Recidivism of releasees from the private prisons was lower than for those released from public prisons, and of those who reoffended; the crimes were less serious for the private prison releasees.[66] However, when the General Accounting Office (GAO) conducted a comprehensive review of five outcome studies of private prisons completed since 1991 in Texas, New Mexico, California, Tennessee, and Louisiana, analysts did not believe that three of these studies were sufficiently designed to use results, but found that outcomes from the remaining two indicated minimal or no differences between the public and private prison operations.[67] Other studies have also failed to find any significant differences between the outcomes of offenders released from public versus private prisons.[68] In a national survey to compare private and public prison operations that analyzed the types of inmates, inmate misconduct, and general characteristics of prisons and their staff, Camp and Gaes concluded that private prisons had higher escape rates and more positive results from drug tests and did not enhance staff or community safety.[69]

There has not yet been a sufficient number of "apples to apples" comparisons of quality and cost between public and privately operated prisons to draw decisive conclusions. The most recent and perhaps most comprehensive is a review of the Taft, California, private prison, which found that inmates and staff were provided a safe living and working environment and the private facility cost less to operate, but it had lower rates of assault, more escapes, higher rates of drug use, and higher rates of inmate grievances.[70]

Opponents of the use of private prisons cite the lack of firm data as undermining the argument by the private sector that they can be more effective than their public counterparts. However, proponents suggest the evidence proves that the private sector can operate prisons as effectively as the public sector, and there are many other reasons (including cost) why the private sector plays a valuable role in providing correctional services across the nation. Even without firm cost and quality comparisons, it is expected that the use of contracts by public correctional agencies with the private sector will continue at a substantial level for the foreseeable future.

The "You Make the Decision" box asks students to decide whether they would turn to the private sector to house prisoners for their state agency.

Accreditation of Correctional Programs

As noted in Chapter 1, in the first 150 years of corrections, correctional institutions and agencies usually lacked professional standards, central management, and consistency of operations. Therefore, as correctional organizations moved to improve their performance, professionalism, and perception by the public, a process was created to identify operational procedures that met modern professional standards. The aspects subscribed to a **profession** include the following: (1) a systematic body of theoretical knowledge acquired through lengthy academic study and not possessed by those outside the profession, (2) community interests rather than self-interest as a motivator of professional behavior, (3) self-regulation, and (4) a system of rewards.[71] Correctional agencies desired to follow the model of the American Bar Association and the American Medical Association by furthering the professional development of members while guiding and regulating their performance to the greatest extent possible.

In this regard, the American Correctional Association (ACA) has been instrumental in encouraging professional development and accrediting correctional agencies. The ACA is the major correctional professional organization, with more than 30,000 members internationally. An important element of being self-regulating is to have a professional code of ethics. As illustrated in Figure 15.4, the ACA Code of Ethics was adopted in 1975 and lists expectations of professional performance and practice by correctional professionals.

In addition, the ACA was used as the vehicle to create standards for professional practice of corrections as a profession, and the **Commission on Accreditation for Corrections** (CAC) was formed to administer national accreditation programs for all components of adult and juvenile correctional agencies in the early 1970s. The first step was to develop standards that are the accepted professional practice for correctional agencies. Groups of correctional professionals were recruited to write dozens of standards that apply to correctional operations. For instance, the most recent version of the standards for adult correctional institutions identifies 463 standards regarding operational facets such as staff training, safety and emergency procedures, food services operations, health care, inmate programs, security procedures, and correctional industries.[72]

profession

correctional agencies desire to be seen as a profession, and therefore create standards for ethical behavior, promote their community interests, and fashion a process for self-regulation

Commission on Accreditation for Corrections

formed to administer a national accreditation programs for all components of adult and juvenile correctional agencies

ACA standards are very specific regarding all areas of prison operations, and even include standards on the number of seats required (as a percentage of the inmate population) in the dining room so that meals can be served in a reasonable time. Photo by Richard P. Seiter.

American Correctional Association
Code of Ethics

Preamble

The American Correctional Association expects of its members unfailing honesty, respect for the dignity and individuality of human beings, and a commitment to professional and compassionate service. To this end, we subscribe to the following principles.

Members shall respect and protect the civil and legal rights of all individuals.

Members shall treat every professional situation with concern for the welfare of the individuals involved and with no intent to personal gain.

Members shall maintain relationships with colleagues to promote mutual respect within the profession and improve the quality of service.

Members shall make public criticism of their colleagues or their agencies only when warranted, verifiable, and constructive.

Members shall respect the importance of all disciplines within the criminal justice system and work to improve cooperation with each segment.

Members shall honor the public's right to information and share information with the public to the extent permitted by law subject to individual's right to privacy.

Members shall respect and protect the right of the public to be safeguarded from criminal activity.

Members shall refrain from using their positions to secure personal privileges or advantages.

Members shall refrain from allowing personal interest to impair objectivity in the performance of duty while acting in an official capacity.

Members shall refrain from entering into any formal or informal activity or agreement which presents a conflict of interest or is inconsistent with the conscientious performance of duties.

Members shall refrain from accepting any gifts, services, or favors that are or appear to be improper or imply an obligation inconsistent with the free and objective exercise of professional duties.

Members shall clearly differentiate between personal views/statements and views/statements/positions made on behalf of the agency or Association.

Members shall report to appropriate authorities any corrupt or unethical behaviors in which there is sufficient evidence to justify review.

Members shall refrain from discriminating against any individual because of race, gender, creed, national origin, religious affiliation, age, disability, or any other type of prohibited discrimination.

Members shall preserve the integrity of private information; they shall refrain from seeking information on individuals beyond that which is necessary to implement responsibilities and perform their duties; members shall refrain from revealing nonpublic information unless expressly authorized to do so.

Members shall make all appointments, promotions, and dismissals in accordance with established civil service rules, applicable contract agreements, and individual merit, rather than furtherance of personal interests.

Members shall respect, promote, and contribute to a work place that is safe, healthy, and free of harassment in any form.

Adopted August 1975 at the 105th Congress of Correction
Revised August 1990 at the 120th Congress of Correction
Revised August 1994 at the 124th Congress of Correction

Source: American Correctional Association, Adopted at the 124th Congress of Corrections in 1994.

FIGURE 15.4   American Correctional Association Code of Ethics

Correctional agencies must decide whether they believe that adopting these standards and using them as the basis for their own policies and procedures is in their best interests. According to the American Correctional Association, the purpose of the standards and accreditation process is

> to promote improvement in the management of correctional agencies through the administration of a voluntary accreditation program and the ongoing development and revision of relevant, useful standards. The recognized benefits from such a process include improved management, a defense against lawsuits through documentation and the demonstration of a "good faith" effort to improve conditions of confinement, increased accountability and enhanced public credibility for administrative and line staff, a safer and more humane environment for personnel and offenders, and the establishment of measurable criteria for upgrading programs, personnel, and physical plant on a continuing basis.[73]

If an agency decides that it wants to be accredited, it first must apply to the ACA for consideration. The ACA and CAC will send a team of evaluators to the agency or institution to conduct a comprehensive evaluation of the agency's operations in line with the documented standards. To be accredited, an agency must meet all mandatory standards (those representing life safety issues) and 90 percent of all nonmandatory standards. If the agency is accredited, there is a reaccreditation process in which a less intensive evaluation occurs every three years thereafter to ensure that the agency continues to meet these professional standards in its operation. Agencies often use their accreditation as a defense to inmate lawsuits and to demonstrate to constituents or political oversight groups that they are performing at an acceptable level of professional operations.

The first accreditation of correctional agencies occurred in 1978, and by January 1, 2002, 501 state and federal prisons in twenty-eight state or federal correctional agencies had been accredited by the ACA.[74] Since then, the number of facilities accredited has continued to grow, and by March 2009, there were 612 of the 1,697 (36 percent) adult prisons accredited by ACA. At this time, there were also 254 community residential facilities (halfway houses) and 199 juvenile correctional facilities that were accredited.[75] Even though many facilities are not accredited by ACA, this does not mean that they are not being operated professionally or do not meet constitutional standards. Many agencies simply do not believe that the accreditation process is necessary or worth the time and effort to go through the process. Accreditation is strictly voluntary, as the ACA has no regulatory authority. The disadvantages to accreditation include cost, time, stress, and extra work by the staff to prepare for the process.[76] Although it is believed to be beneficial for those agencies that have gone through the policy, others recognize the standards as an indication of quality, yet choose to forgo the time-consuming process to become accredited.

Importance of Staff Diversity

staff diversity
the representation of a wide variety (in gender, race, and ethnicity) of people working for a correctional agency

An extremely important factor within the operation of correctional agencies is **staff diversity**. Having a staff that is diverse in terms of gender, race, and ethnicity is important for many reasons. First, having women within a correctional workforce brings a calming and normalized influence to men's prisons and doubles the available pool for recruiting talented individuals. Second, with such a large percentage of offenders under correctional supervision being minorities, race and ethnic diversity aid in the management of prisons and community correctional agencies. Finally, staff members constantly learn from each other. Diversity in terms of gender, race, and ethnicity provides experiences for staff that make them better able to more effectively supervise a diverse group of offenders. The role of women working in men's prisons was described in Chapter 12, and issues of staff diversity in terms of race and ethnicity are presented next.

Over the years, there has been a shift in the racial makeup of adults under correctional supervision, and there is now an **overrepresentation of minorities** under correctional supervision. In 1986, whites made up a majority (65 percent) of offenders under correctional supervision (in prisons and jails and under community supervision). However, by the end of 2007, the imprisonment rate of men per 100,000 population was 955 for whites, 3,138 for blacks, and 1,259 for Hispanics.[77] Since 2000, however, the black imprisonment rate has actually declined from 3,188.[78] This proportion of minorities increases when considering the seriousness of the criminal punishment. Of the 2,311,200 inmates in prison and jail on June 30, 2008, 807,000 (34.9 percent) were white, 913,800 (39.5 percent) were black, and 460,400 (19.9 percent) were Hispanic.[79]

This disproportionate number of minorities in prison and jails makes it important that correctional agencies aggressively recruit minority staff in order to have the staff be somewhat representative of the offender makeup. The problems resulting from an almost all-white workforce supervising an inmate population that was primarily minority became expressly clear after the riot in the New York State Penitentiary in Attica in 1971. In a review of the causes of the riot, one significant problem was found to be the guarding of urban black and Hispanic inmates by rural white staff, which were separated by culture, mistrust, and a lack of communication. Not only was the staff from the rural area of New York State in which Attica is located, but also they had no understanding of the culture of the urban black and Hispanic inmates. Neither side made much effort to communicate; they let the cultural and racial differences grow into hostility and inmates believed race and discrimination to be the basis for many of the prison policies.

Even though there is no conclusive evidence that the criminal justice system is inherently racist in practice or policy, the high numbers of minorities in correctional systems create a phenomenon that causes management problems for correctional officials. In response, correctional agencies have created **affirmative action programs** to recruit and develop a workforce that mirrors, to some extent, the client base. Although race and ethnicity do not have to be a barrier to communication between inmates and staff, a diverse workforce enhances the potential for positive communication by reducing the perception by offenders that the system is racist and taking away one rationale of inmates that they have a "right" to misbehave or not follow prison rules.

The people who are responsible for implementing affirmative action programs (as well as a variety of other staff functions) for a correctional agency are human resources managers. The "Your Career in Corrections" box describes the functions of these positions.

Since the Attica riot, there has been progress in the hiring of minority staff by correctional agencies. On January 1, 2002, of the total of 435,688 staff employed by adult correctional agencies, 69.0 percent were white, 20.1 percent were black, and 7.6 percent were Hispanic.[80] Even though these percentages are still predominantly white, the percentage of nonwhite employees has increased from 28.8 percent in 1994 to 30.8 percent in 2002.[81] Probation and parole agencies have done even better than prisons. For sixty probation and parole

overrepresentation of minorities
a greater percentage of certain racial and ethnic groups in the correctional population than in the general U.S. population

affirmative action programs
activities to aggressively recruit and provide opportunities for employment to women and minorities

Your Career in Corrections

Human Resources Managers

Professional staff are critical to a successful correctional agency, and most of the budget dollars go toward staff salaries. The people responsible for all the administrative and personal contacts to hire staff are human resources managers (HRMs). These people were called *personnel managers* several years ago, but the more descriptive term is *human resources*. This is because the role of human resources is so varied and broad, including payroll (making sure staff members are paid correctly), benefits (life and health insurance, retirement), staffing (recruiting and hiring), labor–management relations, classification (determining the correct levels for pay of positions), staff training, performance evaluations, staff development, and affirmative action. There are so many different areas that an HRM has to be a generalist and knowledgeable in many different areas.

Although a few corrections HRMs major in human resources in college and then look for jobs, most do not begin their careers with a plan to work in this field. As entry-level HR jobs become available, HRMs look for individuals with good people, computer, and organizational skills to move into HR jobs as assistants, where they learn a lot about this area through specific training and work on the job.

HRMs note that the good things about the jobs include the variety, because there are not many routine, day-to-day things; they get to work on all the previously listed areas. They also enjoy dealing with staff, helping them with benefits, working out problems, and planning their retirements. HR staff get to know all the other staff, because they work with them on many issues. The "not so good" things about the job include dealing with disciplinary actions (when staff members violate rules and are penalized) and with some very good people who just made a mistake and may be ashamed, humiliated, or even angry.

The kind of person who makes a good HR staffer has a lot of patience, is a little outgoing but not aggressive, and is seen as approachable, dependable, and reliable. HRMs give important advice to people—staff members who are planning to retire, wardens considering a new policy, managers who need to hire someone for a job—so they must be seen as credible. HRMs represent another correctional job that people seldom think about, but that is critical to the success of a correctional institution.

agencies surveyed, it was reported that on January 1, 2002, they employed 50,640 people, of whom 66.7 percent were white, 23.5 percent were black, and 7.2 percent were Hispanic.[82]

These advances have not always been easy. Irwin points out that when minority staff were first recruited to rural prisons with predominantly white staff, some white staff felt that the nonwhite, urban officers would be more pro-inmate and less trustworthy and might undermine security and did not easily accept them.[83] Some studies have suggested that nonwhite correctional officers experience more stress than their white counterparts, and black officers are more likely to quit their jobs than white officers, primarily because of conflicts with their supervisors.[84] Just as inmates become bitter and perceive many actions as racist when there is not a diverse workforce, minority staff can have some of the same feelings when they represent a small minority of the staff and do not feel fully accepted into their workplace.

Today, very few jurisdictions experience tension among their staff due to differences in race or ethnicity. There will always be charges of discrimination even within diverse correctional staffs, but the issue of the importance of diversity is not in question, and correctional staff recognize the safety needs to work together regardless of background, attitude, or philosophies. The challenge of supervising offenders is the common ground for all correctional staff and binds them as one to accomplish their mission.

The "An Insider's Experience" in *MyCrimeKit* illustrates the challenges I faced in trying to increase diversity in the Ohio department of corrections.

mycrimekit
An Insider's perspective: Increasing Minority Staff

Effectiveness of Treatment Programs

One issue that has created controversy and influenced correctional policy over the past twenty-five years is the evaluation of the outcome of correctional treatment programs. Although the public supports the concept of rehabilitation and correctional officials value treatment programs for the stabilizing effect they have on offender populations, the bottom line is that there is an expectation that such programs reduce recidivism. Elected officials and advocates and opponents of rehabilitation all agree that, in exchange for the dollars they are spending on such programs, there should be a crime reduction payback.

Support for rehabilitation dwindled after an early 1970s review by Martinson and colleagues of the effectiveness of correctional treatment. While finding a few isolated correlations between a treatment program and a reduction in recidivism, they identified no consistent findings that any single treatment program significantly reduced recidivism.[85] Therefore, their conclusion that "nothing works" led to the abandonment of the medical model of corrections and began the momentum for many states to move from indeterminate sentencing with a focus on changing the individual offender to determinant sentencing with an emphasis on deterrence and incapacitation.

There have been many methodological concerns about the early work of Martinson and the ability to actually evaluate correctional treatment programs based on recidivism. Many question the validity of using recidivism as a measure of the effectiveness of correctional programs, considering it unfair to expect correctional treatment to have a long-term impact by reducing recidivism. Recidivism can have varying definitions, including the commission of any new crime, commission of a felony during the period of community supervision, and return to prison. A reasonable length for posttreatment follow-up is also a concern. Can a correctional sanction or program be expected to have an impact on an offender for three or even five years after the termination of the sanction or program? Another concern is that social science research designs often have difficulty controlling for the many external and internal factors that can affect recidivism rates.

In a recent review of the effectiveness of correctional treatment, Cullen and Gendreau point out several limitations in the review by Martinson.[86] First, since the initial study, there have been developments in researchers' abilities to quantitatively synthesize and assess the impact of research findings, particularly through the use of **meta-analysis**. Meta-analysis statistically measures the average effect an intervention has on recidivism across all studies, while identifying and controlling for various conditions such as the characteristics of the offenders treated, the type of setting, and the study methodology. Second, although the review by Lipton and colleagues was comprehensive for that time, there were a limited number of studies per treatment category: "7 for casework/individual counseling; 15 for skill development; 12 for individual psychotherapy; 19 for group methods; and 20 for milieu therapy."[87] Third, the Lipton review did not include cognitive–behavioral therapy programs, which have been found to be successful treatment approaches for offenders.[88] Finally, the review did not consider any impact or outcome other than recidivism, such as prison behavior or educational achievement.

meta-analysis
a statistical measure of the average effect an intervention has on recidivism across all studies, while identifying and controlling for various study conditions

Later studies revisit and question the "nothing works" concept regarding correctional treatment. In a 1975 analysis of the studies reviewed by Martinson, Palmer noted that 48 percent of the studies cited found a positive effect on recidivism.[89] And in 1990, Andrews and colleagues found that of the better-controlled studies, 40 percent found that treatment had a "positive effect."[90] In addition, the more recent use of meta-analysis has identified positive success of correctional treatment programs in reducing recidivism. A meta-analysis allows a much more sensitive consideration of the results of several studies considered together. Rather than, as Martinson and colleagues did, just tallying the number of studies that showed a statistically significant impact on recidivism caused by the correctional intervention, the computations of a meta-analysis allow the calculation of the effect of all studies, even if they individually do not result in a statistically significant outcome.

In a 1993 analysis of the impact of correctional treatment, Lipsey and Wilson reviewed ten meta-analyses and identified a 25 percent reduction of recidivism by psychological, educational, and behavioral correctional treatment programs.[91] And, in 1995, Losel reviewed thirteen meta-analyses and found that the average impact from the treatment intervention would result in a recidivism rate of 45 percent for the treatment group and 55 percent for the control group.[92] These findings make one reconsider the 1972 Martinson conclusion that "nothing works."

Fortunately for those who support the correctional goal to rehabilitate offenders, there has been resurgence in support for rehabilitation programs. Partially due to tightening budgets and partly due to the belief that we cannot continue to "recycle" offenders through correctional programs only to have them continue to fail when returned to the community or once leaving parole or probation supervision, many jurisdictions search for and implement programs that are "evidence based." This means there is evidence of success, generally defined as reducing recidivism. Over the past decade, there has been a renewed focus on determining whether a program works or not.

An excellent example of how focusing on program evaluation can lead to better policy decisions and savings has been in Washington State. The state faced

Rehabilitative programs are believed to reduce recidivism. Reprinted with permission of the Corrections Corporation of America.

forecasts that they would need to construct several new prisons in the coming decades, and in 2005, the Washington legislature directed the Washington State Institute for Public Policy to find "evidence-based" options that could reduce recidivism and avoid the need for expensive prison construction. The Institute conducted a review of 571 program evaluations within corrections, estimated the benefits and costs of them, and created an alternative policy of putting money into effective programs rather than new prison construction. The findings are being implemented, and the estimated savings for avoiding prison construction in the state is approximately $2 billion.[93] In this era of tightening budgets, a critical question for the future is whether positive research findings and fiscal challenges will result in increased funding for rehabilitative programs in other jurisdictions. This topic is addressed in Chapter 16.

Summary

CHAPTER REVIEW

It is interesting to theorize why the growth in the prison population has been slowing. As a result of "tough on crime" legislation to send more offenders to prison for longer times and initiatives such as the war on drugs, the prison population in the United States grew by almost 600 percent in twenty years. Yet several factors now seem to be slowing that trend. Whether it is simply a demographic change with a lower percentage of the nation's population in the high-crime age, a need to find alternatives to incarceration to reduce budget demands, the incapacitative effect of incarcerating so many people, or a combination, for the first time in decades some states are actually experiencing a reduction in their prison population.

One definite truth is that the formation of correctional policies has become much more politicized than in the past. Elected officials (or those seeking office) are constantly espousing how they will take aggressive actions to protect citizens from dangerous criminals. Such rhetoric encourages sending more people to prison and makes it more difficult for those under community supervision to stay out of prison. Some individuals speculate that tightening budgets may force officials to reconsider constantly arguing for increased use of incarceration as a criminal sanction. Yet a variety of activities (enhancing the use of community alternatives, creating revenues, and contracting with the private sector) are being considered to try to reduce the budget crunch in order to fund correctional agencies.

Two very positive developments in corrections over the past twenty years that are expected to continue into the next decade are accreditation of correctional agencies and an increasing number of minority staff. During the late 1970s, correctional agencies searched for methods to increase their credibility and professionalism, both for management purposes and in the minds of the courts and with other public officials. The formation of a process of self-regulation and certification of meeting professional standards was developed and has been adopted by a large percentage of agencies and institutions. Yet this process is expensive and time consuming, and several agencies have not yet decided that it is worth the investment.

As a result of riots, charges of racism, and an increasing sensitivity to the fact that correctional clients are predominantly minority group members, correctional agencies have aggressively targeted the recruitment and hiring of minority staff. This development is recognized as an effective management tool to better and more fairly handle offenders.

The results of more recent research into the effectiveness of correctional treatment programs are also significant for the future of corrections. The next question to be answered is this: "If correctional treatment reduces recidivism and crime, is it not wise to invest more funds into treatment programs for offenders?" This significant question is further addressed in Chapter 16 regarding the future of corrections.

In the final chapter of this text, we look further into the future to investigate how these and other developments will affect correctional management and operations in the next two decades. The current paradigms are challenged and promising new approaches are examined. Many believe that the past twenty-five years represented a step backward in correctional thought and invention, but many also believe that the future is very promising for those who want to shake up the status quo, reverse the "lock 'em up" mentality, and find new ways to better manage criminal offenders.

Key Terms

furlough
"tough on crime"
create revenues
cost of incarceration fees
co-payment
profession

Commission on Accreditation for Corrections
staff diversity
overrepresentation of minorities
affirmative action programs
meta-analysis

Review Questions

1. What has occurred in regard to the size of the state prison population over the past five years?

2. How has the federalization of many crimes affected the populations of state and federal prisons?

3. Who is Willie Horton, and what role did he play in politicizing correctional policy?

4. What is the public's opinion regarding correctional sanctions and treatment programs?

5. Describe the status of state budgets.

6. In what ways can correctional agencies raise revenues by providing their services?

7. How are states using community alternatives to bring down the cost of corrections?

8. What percentage of inmates are housed in private prisons?

9. Are private prisons less expensive and more effective?

10. What is the role of the Commission on Accreditation for Corrections?

11. How many prisons are accredited by the American Correctional Association?

12. What does it mean that minorities are overrepresented in the correctional population?

13. How much diversity is there in correctional agencies staff?

14. What is a meta-analysis?

15. Summarize the outcome of evaluations of effectiveness of correctional treatment programs.

You Make the Decision...

Use the Private Sector to Operate Prisons?

You are the director of a state department of corrections with no history of contracting entire prison operations to the private sector. Several of your fellow state administrators have used the private sector to house their inmates, and no one has expressed a serious concern about price or quality. However, you are aware of several serious incidents (riots, escapes, and inmate brutality) that have occurred in a few private prisons across the country and are sensitive to the negative publicity that these incidents brought. You are also aware of all the studies that are inconclusive in terms of the benefits of the private sector in comparison to the public sector for cost and outcome.

Yet your legislative budget committee is pushing for the state to try privatization. With tightening budgets, they want to find less expensive ways to manage the burgeoning correctional population in the state. You have a good relationship with the labor union representing state correctional officers, and they are firmly opposed to privatization, as they fear the loss of public, union jobs with privatization.

You are caught in the middle of the budget committee and the labor union in regards to whether you will support privatization. You are going to make one of them very unhappy with whatever decision you make.

You have decided to go through the list of ten issues regarding privatization that have been presented in this chapter, weigh these factors as good or bad, and decide whether you will support privatizing a new prison in your state. For this exercise, either by yourself or in a small classroom group, go through each of these ten issues, determine whether they are favorable or unfavorable to the private sector, and then score your overall view either for or against the privatization of prisons. Use this score to decide whether you will support privatizing a state prison and what statement you will make as to your reasons for the decision. Once you make this decision, determine how you will deal with the party (budget committee or labor union) you will anger with your decision.

Chapter Resources on mycrimekit™

Go to mycrimekit.com to explore the following study tools and resources specific to this chapter:

- **Practice Quiz:** multiple-choice, true/false, short-answer, and essay questions to help students test their knowledge
- **WebQuests:** learning activities built around Web searches
  - Corrections Technology: www.correctionstech.org
  - Office of Justice Programs, Reentry: www.reentry.gov
  - Urban Institute–Reentry: www.urban.org

- **Insider's Experiences:** "Increasing Minority Staff"
- **Seiter Videos:**
  - See an elected official discuss public attitudes
  - See an administrator discuss prison privatization
- **Flashcards:** Eleven flashcards to test knowledge of the chapter's key terms

Questions Regarding
the Future of

After reading this chapter, you should be able to:

1. Identify some of the key questions facing corrections in the next ten years.

2. List the pros and cons for our current approach to sentencing criminal offenders.

3. Discuss whether the current approach to sentencing can be successful and continue as is.

4. Identify the recent methodological advancements that aid researchers in determining whether correctional treatment programs are successful.

5. Outline current strategies for supervising offenders in the community and discuss forces that will push them to continue as is or change in some manner.

6. Describe how technology will impact corrections over the next decade.

7. Define restorative justice and list its benefits over current sentencing approaches.

8. Explain how prisonization is an obstacle to successful reentry to the community.

9. List methods and changes in procedures that will counteract or reduce the impact of prisonization on inmates.

10. Identify the positive benefits of a career in corrections.

11. Decide whether a career in corrections is right for you.

Introduction

At this point in the textbook, we have covered all of the basic operational approaches and issues facing corrections today. In Part I of the text ("Putting Corrections into Perspective"), we reviewed the history of crime and punishment and our traditional and current approaches to sentencing. In Part II ("Correctional Policy and Operations"), we examined how correctional programs and policies developed and are currently operated, including jails, probation, intermediate sanctions, prisons, postrelease supervision, and prisoner reentry. In Part III ("Correctional Clients"), we learned about adult males and females, juveniles, and other special clients of correctional agencies. Part IV ("Prison Life") was written to give students a realistic appreciation for life either working or living in a prison. Topics included how prisons are managed and how inmates and staff cope with the authority and control necessary for accomplishing the mission of prisons. We also read about the approaches for providing custody and treatment within a prison, the legal issues in prison operations, and the controversies around the imposition of the death penalty. In Part V ("Correctional Challenges"), we examined the current issues facing corrections and will try to answer some of the most critical questions regarding the future of correctional operations.

Correctional textbooks take a variety of approaches in examining the future of corrections. Most identify issues that are unresolved or continue to confront correctional policymakers and practitioners. Others recite facts and figures regarding crime and correctional practice and leave it to the reader to interpret what these mean. In this textbook, a different approach is taken; we address some of the most critical questions regarding the future of corrections, including the following:

- Can our current approach to sentencing and corrections be successful and continue?
- Will rehabilitation continue as a primary correctional goal?
- Will supervision of offenders in the community change in approach?
- How will technology impact corrections in the future?
- Do we need a new paradigm for sentencing and corrections?
- Can we reduce the impact of prisonization and improve the successful reentry of prisoners to the community?
- Is corrections a good career choice for me?

To consider these questions, students are given the opportunity to review relevant data and developing controversies. These questions are addressed fully and then an answer is given. There are no assurances that this is the "right" or "correct" answer, and only the future will reveal the true result. However, by asking and then answering these questions, students, instructors, and others have an avenue to debate for themselves how these issues will be addressed. We know for certain that corrections will continue to change. We also may be able to project the forces that will affect change in corrections. What is less certain is the result of correctional operations and how these questions may be shaped in the future. For that matter, it is even somewhat uncertain that these questions will continue to be critical issues ten or fifteen years from now. The challenge (and fun) is speculating and developing contingencies for the future of corrections.

Before addressing each of these questions and as a beginning look at the future of corrections, an interview with a correctional expert regarding the future of corrections is presented in the "An Interview With" box.

mycrimekit

Media—Video: Changes in Corrections

An Interview With...

A Correctional Expert

For the final chapter of this book on the future of corrections, the following interview is presented with someone who is truly an expert in corrections today and a visionary into what corrections can be in the future. Dr. Reginald A. Wilkinson is the longest tenured state correctional administrator in the country. He has been the director of the Ohio Department of Rehabilitation and Corrections for more than fifteen years and has served the department in many capacities since 1973. He has been the president of the American Correctional Association (ACA), the Association of State Correctional Administrators (ASCA), and the International Association of Reentry, as well as vice-chair for North America of the International Corrections and Prison Association. He is currently chair of the National Institute of Corrections Advisory Board. He is perhaps the most visible and respected voice regarding corrections in the United States.

Question: Dr. Wilkinson, thank you for taking the time for this interview. To begin, can you describe what you think are some of the most significant developments in corrections over the past ten years.

Dr. Wilkinson: First, I would say that the movement to emphasize prisoner reentry has been huge. When the president of the United States remarks that "America is the land of the second chance" and mentions the importance of prisoner reentry in his 2004 State of the Union address, this puts major emphasis behind it. In Ohio we espouse that the reentry process begins the day a person arrives at prison, not two or three weeks or months before they are scheduled for release. When we receive someone at a reception center that is when we begin to prepare him or her to go home. Our reentry planning is not a program; instead, it's a way to integrate the reentry of offenders into the basic constructs (muscle memory) of everything we do. Our reentry philosophy has become our operating system (like Windows 2000 for a computer) that is the underpinning of our correctional operations.

Second, there has been a major change in prison litigation and regulation by the federal courts. As an example, the impact of court rulings such as religious freedoms has had a major impact on how we govern prisons. We are no longer seeing consent orders that last for fifteen to twenty years. Today, even with the medical receivership example in California, most agencies have gained ground in proving to the court that we know how to run professional and constitutional prisons. As we have increased our sophistication, our knowledge, and our proactivity, the courts have recognized the role they played in the 1970s and 1980s is no longer necessary. We are regulating ourselves more and more, especially with the popularity of correctional standards.

Another concept that is really big is the notion of restorative justice. This notion suggests that correctional and other justice agencies should partner with other critical stakeholders such as victims of crime. Today, we focus everything we do on a collaborative basis. Until the last few years, our relationships with victims, for instance, were relegated to parole notification. Ohio created a very active Office of Victims Services. We literally receive thousands of phone calls and hits on our victims' website. We have moved away from just treating victims as a political necessity; instead, the relationship and involvement of victims are critical to the orderly operation of our prisons and the effective supervision of offenders in the community. Victims even participate in policy matters. We collaborate with many community stakeholders as full partners, not just crime victims.

Finally, I think there has been a broadening of the entire framework upon which we think about corrections work. In fact, I seldom use the phrase "criminal justice," because it is such a misnomer. The criminal element of justice is just a small piece of what is important in our society. Today, we have victims' justice, community justice, and restorative justice. And perhaps most important is the overall focus on social justice, which is more descriptive of what we should be all about. The justice system cannot solve the crime problem or the drug problem alone. Quite frankly, government is not equipped to adequately address these concerns without collaborative relationships. It takes a combination of employers, social service agencies, community leaders, and other nongovernmental agencies in order to be effective. Without involving all these other entities, we will merely be putting Band-Aids

...continued

on the problems that we have. We have to look differently at what we do.

Question: And what do you think are likely to be some of the most significant developments in the future?

Dr. Wilkinson: From my perspective it's neither a defined activity nor a traditional program. The future success of corrections work will reside with talented staff that has made this work a career. There are correctional professionals now who are really beginning to "get it." Also, we will continue to do a better job at harnessing best practices and promising programs that work. We will furthermore do much more sharing important data within and between jurisdictions. A good example is the Association of State Correctional Administrator's Performance-Based Measurement System. The PBMS will allow us to compare apples to apples and to define true uniform measures. As a result of improved information technology and data, we will be able to make well-informed decisions. I believe that if you can't measure something, then you shouldn't do it. We will be measuring much more of what we do in the future. Legislators and public officials will not accept anything less than that. Our management will be the result of evidence-based practices.

Question: What types of metrics make sense for monitoring the management of corrections?

Dr. Wilkinson: The first and foremost is money. It used to be that correctional agencies were just a blip on the fiscal radar screen. Nowadays corrections agencies consume large portions of taxpayer dollars. Public officials are extremely interested in how much money we can save without compromising public safety. Another metric will be exactly how effective we are. For instance, rates of recidivism must be reduced. Thus, victimization is reduced. Prisoners must become better prepared to go home "for good." Public officials must understand that rehabilitation is achievable. Another measure is how we manage offenders with special needs, such as the mentally ill. We need to ensure that clinical and social services are available to those who need them. The price of not doing this will mean more crime and more incarceration and, therefore, the need for more correctional funds.

Question: How do you encourage public or elected officials to pay more attention to corrections?

Dr. Wilkinson: This is already happening. For the past several years, my approach has been that correctional administrators should not just be administrators of corrections operations. We must be advocates for what is right and we must help influence the community and public officials as to what we should be doing. We can't just talk about running prisons, but how crime and corrections problems can be solved. We must go well beyond correctional systems' capabilities to solve criminality by truly implementing a social justice movement. We are better prepared today to effect positive change than when I began my corrections career in 1973. At that time in Ohio, we had 7,800 inmates and eight prisons. Today, we have 46,000 inmates in thirty-two prisons.

Question: What can be done to stop the "tough on crime" rhetoric by elected officials?

Dr. Wilkinson: The key is that we in corrections must have credibility with public officials. Correctional administrators must be respected as public servants who want to improve the quality of life of all citizens. We must show them we are good stewards of the public trust and that we care about public safety.

I am proud of and believe we in corrections have had many successes in this area, but we still have many challenges as well. For instance, in Ohio we have 600 people in prison merely for not paying child support. Now, putting them in prison for six months seems meaningless. They aren't going to be paying child support while they sit in prison. We would be better off to assign them to some type of work program so that they can learn job skills and pay their debts. Ohio is one of a few states that is incarcerating these "dead beat dads," and there are many constituent groups that support locking up these types of people. But we have to question whether or not it is good public policy. A success in Ohio is that we have all but stopped sending offenders back to prison solely because they used drugs and had a positive drug use. Again, it would not be cost-effective to send them to prison for a few months and then re-release them no better able to avoid drugs in the community than when they were first released. But to do any of these things, correctional officials must have credibility and a relationship with legislators to get them to take you seriously.

Question: What things do you see regarding corrections that make you most proud of your profession?

Dr. Wilkinson: It is probably that we are employing and promoting better educated persons to run our correctional systems. This is true of staff at all levels. This means there will be continuous improvement in what we do.

The more sophisticated our staff the better decision making will be. Decisions made will not be based on a hunch but on data, experience, and identifying best practices. The more academic we become about our work, the better the choices we will make on how to solve our critical challenges. The notion of workforce development and continuing education for corrections staff is made easier by the advancements in web-based applications and professional development. Despite the many challenges we face in the justice business, we will continue to improve our processes.

Can Our Current Approach to Sentencing and Corrections be Successful and Continue?

The answer to this question first depends on what we are trying to accomplish. As suggested in Chapter 1, the five goals of punishment, deterrence, incapacitation, rehabilitation, and restitution have varied in emphasis over the years. The past two centuries have seen many swings in sentencing approaches and philosophies. During the 1800s, sentencing was a mix of punishment and rehabilitation. For offenders considered to have the potential to be productive and law-abiding citizens, probation was granted, with an emphasis on helping them find work and deal with the problems that led to their criminality. More hardened criminals were sent to prison for determinate terms, subject to hard labor and strict discipline, with few rehabilitative programs to prepare them for release.

By the twentieth century, the concept of parole was being adopted in most states and with that came the emphasis on rehabilitation. Over the last two decades, an emphasis on offender accountability has precipitated the reemergence of determinate sentencing as the primary sentencing approach. Although this emphasis continues, there has more recently been additional consideration of the victim and focus on restitution as a sentencing goal and correctional practice.

Currently, the predominant approach to sentencing and corrections is based on punishment, deterrence, and incapacitation. Many states have opted to abolish indeterminate sentencing and have abandoned the rehabilitative philosophy. Sentences are continually enhanced with the belief that if we lengthen sentences, at some point potential offenders will recognize that crime does not pay, and they will be deterred from future criminality. Even if deterrence does not work, advocates suggest that long sentences will at least incapacitate offenders and result in their inability to commit further crimes against society. As a result of these changes, state and federal prison populations grew more rapidly than in any other period since prisons were first established, and reached 1,610,584 on June 30, 2008.[1] Figure 16.1 illustrates the overall increases in the number of persons under correctional supervision for the past twenty-five years.

This approach to sentencing has placed far more people under correctional supervision than we have ever had in the past, and the incarceration rate has continued to climb. By the end of the twentieth century, more than 6 million offenders were either in prison, in jail, or under supervision in the community. The Bureau of Justice Statistics Correctional Surveys report a 260 percent increase in the number of offenders on probation, a 235 percent increase in the number of offenders in jail, a 211 percent increase in the number of inmates in prison, and a 267 percent increase in the number of offenders on parole between 1980 and 2007.[2]

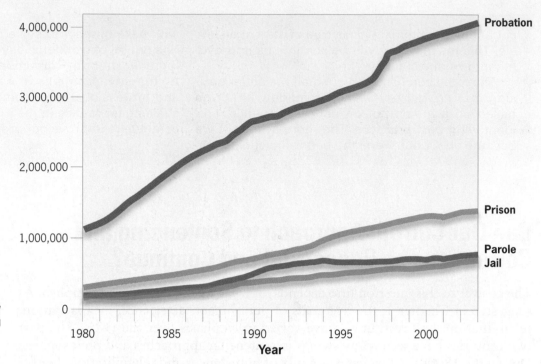

Source: Bureau of Justice Statistics, *Correctional Surveys 1980–2007: Correctional Populations in the United States, Annual, Prisoners in 2007,* and *Probation and Parole in the United States, 2007.*

FIGURE 16.1 Adult Correctional Populations

With the increase in the number of offenders has come a comparable growth in the dollars committed to operate correctional agencies. In fiscal year 1994, the combined budgets for local, state, and federal adult correctional agencies totaled $34.9 billion. By fiscal year 2007, these budgets increased 100 percent to $68.8 billion.[3] The Bureau of Justice Statistics reports that, from 1982 through 2006, spending for corrections increased 660 percent, far exceeding the increase in police and judicial spending. Correctional agency spending is expected to continue to increase, as by 2011, continued prison growth is expected to cost an additional $25 billion.[4]

The bottom line is that the current "tough on crime" approach to sentencing has significantly increased the number of prisoners, the number of people under correctional supervision, and the budgets allocated to correctional agencies. But has this policy made citizens safer or less likely to be victims of street crime? From 1991 to 2007, crime decreased significantly, from a Crime Index rate of 5,897 to 3,730 offenses per every 100,000 citizens (a decrease of 37 percent), reducing it to rates not seen since 1975.[5] Unfortunately, perhaps due to extensive media coverage of crime, citizens continue to believe that crime is increasing.[6] But should the credit for the decrease in crime be attributed to the deterrent or incapacitative effect of current sentencing practices, or are there other reasons why crime rates have decreased?

In an interesting analysis of the impact of the increased use of incarceration on the decline of crime rates during the 1990s, Spelman estimates that about one-quarter of the declining crime rates during the 1990s can be attributed to the increase in the number of offenders incarcerated during that period.[7] Other authors suggest that the rest of the crime drop is attributable to making it more difficult for potential youthful offenders to obtain guns, a reduction in the number of new users of crack cocaine and therefore a reduction in the demand (and therefore number of dealers) for the drug, and a good economy with available employment for those who want to work.[8]

The increase in the number of inmates has led to the construction and opening of several new prisons across the United States. *Courtesy of the Ohio Department of Rehabilitation and Correction.*

The answer to the question of whether this sentencing approach can be successful is "yes, marginally." There is no question that by locking up all the people whom we have imprisoned over the past fifteen years we do reduce crime to some extent. However, these sentencing practices and the budget required to maintain them come at a very high cost. Not only are taxpayers pouring billions more dollars into the correctional system than two decades ago, but there is high "opportunity cost" as well. Every dollar that must be directed to correctional agencies cannot be directed toward programs believed to prevent future crimes, such as prenatal care, improved nutrition for poor families, improvements in educational opportunities and achievement, substance abuse treatment, enhanced job training and employment development, and mental health treatment.

The further question of whether these sentencing approaches will continue is intermingled with the first answer. During the 1990s, when the economy was strong and the federal government and most states had a budget surplus, legislatures did not have to make tough budget choices of what to fund. However, with the downturn in the economy, lower tax revenues, and spending deficits running across almost every governmental unit, these budget decisions are much more difficult. Government officials are now seeking **accountability;** they are challenged to consider how to get the best "bang for their buck" and must take into account how effective programs are in achieving their overall goals. Today, federal, state, and local governments are looking for ways to reduce the cost of corrections and are more willing to consider alternatives to incarceration or even different sentencing approaches that result in shorter time served for nonviolent offenders.

On August 9, 2003, in a speech to the annual meeting of the American Bar Association in San Francisco, U.S. Supreme Court Justice Anthony M. Kennedy became the most visible and prominent individual to question the efficacy of our sentencing practices. Justice Kennedy, a moderate conservative appointed to the Court by former President Ronald Reagan, stated, "Our resources are misspent,

accountability
holding one responsible for accomplishing objectives in a cost-efficient manner

our punishments too severe, our sentences too long."[9] Kennedy described the fifteen-year-old federal sentencing guidelines that give judges a narrow range of punishments for crimes as leading to longer terms than were previously common and needing to be revisited and revised downward.

The current budget challenge and an increasing number of views such as those by Justice Kennedy are likely to result in a marginal change to the current "tough on crime" approach and overall reliance on deterrence and incapacitation. The minimal reduction of crime and the high cost of imprisonment and community supervision require a reconsideration of the success of current sentencing practices. The answer to the second part of the question, "Can our current approach to sentencing and corrections be successful *and continue?*" is no, it cannot continue. It is poor public policy to continue an approach that returns to the taxpayer so little for the resources committed. That leads to an even more difficult question: What can replace the current sentencing approach? One area receiving attention and consideration (described in the next section) has been the potential to decrease crime and recidivism through rehabilitative programs.

Will Rehabilitation Continue as a Primary Correctional Goal?

As noted in Chapter 15, since Martinson and colleagues reviewed the success of correctional treatment programs and concluded that "nothing works" in the early 1970s, rehabilitation gradually took a backseat to other correctional goals such as punishment, deterrence, and incapacitation.[10] The reasoning was simple and difficult to argue. Corrections had been following the medical model of corrections for the previous twenty years. Under this model, it was believed that offenders have underlying problems that are the cause of their criminality that must be diagnosed and treated. However, if there is no evidence that correctional treatment results in a reduction of recidivism, why continue to invest dollars and staff resources in it? Why not give up on rehabilitation, let potential offenders know that they will be held accountable for their criminal acts, and punish law violations severely with lengthy periods of incarceration? It is obvious that society is best protected when offenders are removed from the community and put in prison. Therefore, incapacitating offenders through imprisonment enhances public safety in the short term. And in the longer term, it was argued that public safety is enhanced by the deterrent value that these lengthy sentences have both on individual offenders and on society as a whole.

Proponents of rehabilitation and the medical model in the late 1970s and early 1980s found that they were losing ground. Many elected officials and policymakers met their arguments that we cannot give up on rehabilitation with understanding. However, with continuous media reports on the increase in violence and other crimes during this period resulting in an increased fear of crime and anger toward criminals by the public, these elected officials were not likely to risk their chances of reelection by arguing against longer sentences for criminals. As a result, fifteen states and the federal government ended the use of indeterminate sentencing and parole, twenty states severely limited the parole-eligible inmate population, and only fifteen states continued the use of full discretionary parole. In 1977, more than 70 percent of prisoners were released on discretionary parole. Yet by 2006, only 33 percent of inmates were released by a parole board after serving an indeterminate sentence, as fifteen states and the federal government abolished parole and twenty others restricted the number of inmates eligible for parole.[11]

Rehabilitative programs such as training in computers and office skills are important to prepare inmates for work and success after release. Courtesy of the Ohio Department of Rehabilitation and Correction.

Since the mid-1980s, criminal sentencing has focused on public safety rather than on changing behavior through treatment of the offender. And indeterminate sentencing has been replaced with determinate sentencing, often based on the justice model, in which the individual characteristics of the offender are unimportant in the sentencing decision; the sentence is based almost totally on the severity of the crime and the past criminal history of the offender. Many states also implemented mandatory minimum sentences, three-strikes laws, and truth-in-sentencing provisions in their sentencing codes.

Mandatory minimum sentences require that for certain crimes (violent crimes, crimes using a gun, distribution of narcotics) or certain types of offenders (habitual criminals, sexual predators), there must be a sentence to prison for a minimum term. The sentencing judge does not have an option to impose a sentence of probation or a fine or to suspend the sentence. Three-strikes laws are a legislative mandate that judges must sentence third-time felons to extremely long or life prison sentences. These laws were intended to protect society from habitual law violators by incapacitating them with long sentences in prison. And truth-in-sentencing (TIS) laws require inmates to serve 85 percent of their sentence before they are eligible for release. TIS statutes dramatically reduce the amount of good time that prison officials may grant inmates as incentives for good behavior or program participation.[12] The purpose of these laws is again to satisfy the public that offenders are getting their "just deserts" from their criminal law violation, and not getting their sentences cut short through administrative decisions by prison administrators or parole boards.

The result of these sentencing changes has been a gradual reduction in the proportion of inmates serving an indeterminate sentence and a change in philosophy to deterrence and incapacitation rather than rehabilitation. Inmates are serving significantly longer prison terms and participate in fewer rehabilitative or prerelease programs. Lynch and Sabol found that the average time served by inmates released in 1990 was twenty-two months; those released in 1998 served an average of twenty-seven months.[13] The authors also examined program participation between 1991 and 1997 prison release cohorts. They found that from 1991 to 1997 the percentage of inmates participating in vocational training declined from 32 to 27 percent, and education participation declined from 42 to 34 percent.

In addition, a recent survey indicated that a relatively small percentage of inmates is currently participating in rehabilitative programs. On January 1, 2002, state and federal prisons reported only 117,945 inmates (12.9 percent) in drug treatment programs, a decline of more than 50,000 inmates since 2000.[14] On the same date, only 78,881 inmates (7.8 percent) were assigned to prison industries, a program extremely successful in improving work skills and reducing recidivism.[15] Only 12,192 inmates (1.0 percent) were enrolled in sex offender programs on January 1, 2002.[16] Only 31,390 inmates were placed in halfway houses during 2001, only 4.7 percent of the 669,132 inmates released from state and federal prisons that year.[17] And during 2001 only 35,458 inmates were placed in work or study release.[18] And a recent review of inmate programming in California indicates these trends continue, as 50 percent of all exiting California prisoners did not participate in *any* rehabilitation or work programs during their entire prison term. This failure to provide programming extended into parole as 56 percent of parolees had no formal programs while under parole supervision.[19]

Even with this reduction in the number of inmates participating in rehabilitative programs, there have been positive developments for advocates of rehabilitation. First, there is still public support for rehabilitation. Over the past two decades, as a punitive attitude about crime, sentencing, and offenders developed, there has never been a total withdrawal of support for rehabilitation. In a recent survey, 87 percent of the U.S. voting public is in favor of rehabilitative services for prisoners as opposed to a punishment-only system.[20] There is strong support for a variety of inmates programming, as greater than 90 percent of those surveyed rating as "important" job training, drug treatment, mental health services, family support, and housing guidance to be provided to inmates.[21]

Second, there is increasing evidence of positive results from treatment programs. This evidence has come from additional evaluations of the success of rehabilitative programs, as well as improved methods of measuring the effect of such research outcomes. The Martinson study found 231 evaluations in which the result was examined independently, with the conclusion that "with few and isolated exceptions, the rehabilitative efforts that have been reported so far have had no appreciable effect on recidivism."[22] However, the use of more sophisticated techniques for reviews of research has provided evidence of the success of correctional treatment. One technique is the use of meta-analysis to quantify research results. As noted in Chapter 15, meta-analysis allows researchers to examine many different outcome studies of programs, identify their individual indicators of success, and link those to each other to determine overall success of any particular treatment modality. Gendreau and colleagues explain what meta-analysis is:

> *Consider how one would assess an individual's academic performance. . . . If the grades were poor, was it due to poor study habits, "tough" courses, and so on? In order to obtain a more accurate assessment of the magnitude of the results (i.e., average grade) and how they may vary by age, study habits, and so forth across all undergraduates, then the data could be assessed on a sample of 100 students. Essentially, this is what meta-analysis does, but in this case, the individual represents one "research study."*[23]

Another new approach to analyzing the effect of correctional treatment is the use of systematic reviews of evaluations, identifying studies on a particular modality, and analyzing their modality impact through the group of studies. Farrington and colleagues describe how systematic reviews can be useful in identifying key indicators of treatment success across several studies.[24] Finally, researchers have also begun to measure the quality of correctional programs in assessing their effectiveness. High-quality treatment programs are based on identified offender needs, are targeted at high-risk offenders, are delivered outside the correctional environment, are fully implemented, and include follow-up after completion of treatment.[25] Using techniques to quantify the quality of a treatment program and include quality as a variable influencing program outcome has provided additional evidence of the success of high-quality treatment programs. Using these updated methods, many reviews of treatment programs now conclude that certain categories of treatment programs are effective when implemented in a quality fashion.[26]

The new information regarding the effectiveness of correctional treatment has led to increased support by elected officials and policymakers and to a **rebirth in rehabilitation**. The public wants criminals punished, but is sympathetic to rehabilitative programs. Elected officials recognize this and are willing to fund rehabilitation programs that make a difference. However, rehabilitative programs have to prove that they are cost-effective and save the government at least as much money as they cost. It is much easier for a correctional official to argue for expending funds for correctional programs by citing data that illustrate how investing in the program reduces recidivism and protects society. Elected officials find it easy to promote and vote to fund programs on this basis, rather than because they may help offenders improve their deficiencies. Therefore, it is expected that rehabilitation will experience a rebirth, receive additional funds, and expand in its importance as a goal of corrections and as an essential element of correctional operations. The "An Insider's Experience" box in *MyCrimeKit* provides readers with a little background in forming my personal opinion regarding rehabilitation.

rebirth in rehabilitation
a return to support for correctional treatment programs due to a realization that such programs can reduce recidivism by offenders

mycrimekit
An Insider's Experience: Education Really Does Work.

Will Supervision of Offenders in the Community Change in Approach?

Even though many more offenders are supervised in the community than are in prison and jail, the style of supervision is changing, affecting the number of revocations and subsequent imprisonment. Current supervision strategies show little tolerance for risk, special surveillance and types of conditions have expanded, and offenders are classified and supervised as aggregate groups of risk categories rather than as individuals. These changes have some very negative collateral consequences, yet it is difficult to envision how these changes can be reversed. Throughout history, probation and parole supervision used a casework approach; officers considered it their responsibility to work with offenders in finding jobs, getting into treatment programs, dealing with problems, and successfully completing supervision. However, the casework focus of helping offenders has been slowly transitioning into one in which officers use a surveillance approach to supervision of community offenders. This approach emphasizes monitoring and enforcing compliance with the conditions of supervision, timely detection of violations, and expeditious revocation when violations occur.

This transition has occurred for many reasons. First, over the past twenty years, more conditions have been placed on offenders under community supervision, and therefore a violation and its detection are more likely. Adams and Roth found that between 1987 and 1996 the percentage of federal offenders with at least one special condition (participation in substance abuse, drug testing, and electronic monitoring) increased from 67 percent to 91 percent.[27] During 2001, states involved in probation and parole supervision reported conducting 6,403,990 drug tests and revoked 90,796 offenders as a result of a positive test for drug use.[28] In 2007, agencies reported that 70 percent of probationers and 84 percent of parolees were on active supervision with weekly or monthly face-to-face contact with their supervision officer.[29] Second, there has been very limited tolerance for risk to the community. Instead of focusing on rehabilitation and characteristics of individual offenders, parole and probation agencies now use actuarial methods to classify offenders and manage risk for aggregate populations. There are many positives to these actuarial methods, such as matching offender risk to reoffend to the allocation of resources. However, these actuarial assessments can result in a psychology of adding surveillance techniques rather than treatment programs to an individual's supervision.

Third, the hiring and training of community supervision officers has changed. Historically, officers had a social work or clinical background and were trained in counseling and rehabilitation of offenders. Today, the majority of entering officers have a college degree with a major of criminal justice, with less than one-third majoring in psychology, sociology, or social work.[30] Training and orientation for officers is increasingly in line with that of law enforcement officers. In a recent survey, thirty-seven of forty-eight responding agencies authorize their parole or probation officers to carry weapons;[31] in twenty-one of forty-three agencies, probation and parole officers have full peace officer status, carrying weapons and having arrest powers.[32]

Finally, community officers and supervisors must be sensitive to public safety. Even the most professional staff are cautious when it comes to handling even minor technical violations by community offenders. There is limited benefit, yet significant risk, if an officer tries to work with an offender, allowing a minor violation, in an attempt to deal with a more significant issue such as substance abuse. If that offender later commits a serious crime, the actions of the officer for not acting on the minor violation will be called into question, and in some jurisdictions the officer or agency can be liable to the victim of a subsequent crime.

As a result of these changes in community supervision, the rate of revocations and resulting incarcerations has increased significantly, and most revocations are for only technical violations of supervision, rather than commitment of a new felony. According to West and Sabol, 697,975 offenders were admitted to state prisons during 2007.[33] Of this number, 62,510 (9.2 percent) were probation violators, 183,896 (31 percent) were parole violators, and 13,109 (2.2 percent) were violators of some other type of postrelease supervision.[34] Overall, approximately four in ten prison admissions were offenders revoked from community supervision. This contrasts with 1980, when parole violators constituted only 18 percent of all admissions.[35] In 2006, 50 percent of probationers violated and sent to prison, and two-thirds of parole violators reimprisoned were for technical violations instead of to serve a new sentence.[36]

This trend of moving community supervision more toward a surveillance approach and the resulting increase in the number of violations and revocations represents an **invisible policy,** not passed by legislatures or formally adopted as a policy by correctional agencies. More so, these practices result from a natural and gradual move in emphasis by individual officers to avoid risk and lessen the likelihood of criticism or legal responsibility. Although it can be argued that this is a positive development for public safety, it can also be argued that it is expensive and short-sighted. Offenders who are violated for technical reasons (not a new crime) usually are returned to prison for from ninety days to one year. These offenders, once released, are seldom better prepared for successful reentry and have

invisible policy

a practice that is not formalized in statute or written policy, but that develops through a consistent set of pressures that influence the practice in a specific manner

One example of additional conditions and methods of surveillance is the regular use of a Breathalyzer to detect whether an offender supervised in the community has been drinking. Photo by Richard P. Seiter.

probably done little to reduce any personal problem such as substance abuse, poor work habits, or family problems. This is a catch-22 for community officers who do not want to risk a chance of new crimes by those they supervise, yet recognize that such revocations do little to reduce recidivism in the long run.

It is difficult to answer the question of whether supervision of offenders in the community will change, but it is proposed that this approach to supervision will have to change for many reasons. First, no level of supervision in the community can prevent offenders from committing further crimes. We have created intensive supervision caseloads with only twenty-five offenders under the supervision of an officer. We have used electronic monitoring to know when offenders are not at home. We have begun to use **global positioning systems** (GPSs) to track offenders throughout their community. However, the role of probation, parole, or other community sentences is not to "incapacitate" offenders and totally prevent them from committing crimes. Offenders placed in the community are there either because they are not such a serious criminal or serious risk to society as to warrant incarceration or because they have served their prison sentence and are ready to return to the community. An understanding of community supervision is that these offenders have a level of responsibility (reinforced with supervision) that reduces the likelihood of their committing crimes. It is impractical to expect community supervision to stop determined offenders from committing more crimes, no matter what intensity of supervision or what technologies are used.

The second reason we must change our supervision approach is that it is resulting in too much expense with no proof that it is worth the cost. Through our increase in the intensity of supervision, we discover more technical violations of probation, parole, or other community placement. These technical violations, without commission of a new crime, therefore result in thousands of offenders being sent to prison each year. It is difficult to say how many would have committed a serious crime if allowed to remain in the community. However, we do know that these incarcerations are costing taxpayers hundreds of millions of dollars each year. We must reconsider what price we are willing to pay to potentially prevent future crimes, particularly when the violation and imprisonment last only a few months and then we must again face the issue of successfully supervising the same offender in the community.

Finally, there are examples of success with moving away from a surveillance style of supervision back to a more proactive supervision approach. A good example is Maryland's move to an evidence-based supervision model that begins with a risk and

global positioning system
a system that uses a satellite to receive a signal from a transmitter and identify its location to a monitoring station

The use of GPSs is not unusual in modern supervision of offenders in the community. The only equipment needed for the offender is a somewhat larger ankle bracelet and small bag, as illustrated by this probation officer. Photo by Richard P. Seiter.

need assessment to identify treatment and control needs and makes the supervision officer an instrument for facilitating offender change. This Proactive Community Supervision (PSC) model has resulted in fewer rearrests (30 percent for the PCS and 42 percent for traditional models) among offenders. The conclusion is that supervision styles can be transformed and achieve public safety goals by focusing on positive offender change.[37]

Changing the approach to community supervision will not be easy. We have created a "prison recycling monster," in that it is often considered irresponsible for community officers to not act on these technical violations and can even result in the agency being found legally and financially responsible for further crimes committed by an offender whose supervision is not revoked after technical violations. Therefore, we send violators to prison because we have so few options. Yet a change in supervision will occur. It will be based on the finding that success in the community measured by reductions in recidivism is more likely through a balance of casework or treatment and monitoring than by increases in surveillance.[38] Therefore, community supervision will gradually move back toward the casework style, in which officers emphasize treatment for meeting offender needs but still hold offenders accountable for their failure to meet conditions of their community placement.

How Will Technology Impact Corrections in the Future?

Today, correctional agencies have several technologies to review and consider whether they have applications to correctional operations to improve their efficiency or effectiveness. There are many standard technology applications that are used in the noncorrectional world such as data storage or generation, electronic medical records, office applications to order supplies and pay bills in a paperless fashion, computerized time clocks that automatically create payroll, and identification systems to allow and record employee access. These innovations will continue to make the "business" operations of corrections more efficient just as they do any other government agency or private company. However, this section is focused on the available or developing technologies and how their use might change the traditional way that corrections has supervised or programmed offenders.

Several applications will be described, and then the question will be posed as to whether these technological advancements will have an impact on corrections to the extent that they will significantly change the way that correctional agencies go about their work. Some of the applications below include how to collect and share criminal or gang intelligence between correctional and law enforcement agencies, how inmates communicate with people outside the prison, how contraband can be prevented or detected within a prison, the potential improvements in staff safety, and how technology can aid in supervision of offenders in the community. Fabelo suggests that correctional agencies taking advantage of new technologies to reduce the costs of supervising criminal offenders and minimizing the risk they pose to society is called "technocorrections."[39]

The nation's prisons and jails hold millions of offenders, many of whom are part of criminal networks or gangs in the community. The intelligence that is collected by observing and recording their prison behavior can be useful to law enforcement and homeland security efforts. The Department of Homeland Security spent more than $380 million by the end of 2007 to provide Fusion Centers to state and local governments to collect intelligence information and use it to proactively identify threats to our security.[40] Correctional agencies are beginning to contribute to these Fusion Centers so that their data on criminal or potential terrorist networks can be linked with law enforcement information. Complicated computer systems and programs can sort through large volumes of information and find relevance to a small piece of information at one location and another piece of information at another one.

An interesting development is the use of e-messaging by inmates. A few states are beginning to allow electronic messages to be sent into prisons and may soon allow inmates to respond electronically. Traditional mailrooms had to open all incoming letters and search them for contraband. In 2006, Colorado implemented a system in which inmate families and friends can pay a small fee and can e-mail a letter to the prison, which prints it off and delivers it to the inmate just as they would regular mail.[41] There is no time wasted to open the letters, and an intelligence program looks for key words that can look for criminal or gang activity. Colorado is planning to create kiosks in the prisons by which inmates can send e-letters out through a secure system, so they do not have access to the Internet. Colorado corrections officials point out this type of system improves security, reduces staff time, does not cost money as the rates charged pay for the system, and increases the contact between inmates and their families.[42]

Another way technology is helping prison operations is through the improved detection of contraband. Inmates often try to have drugs smuggled into a prison through the mail, by injecting cocaine into the ink of a gel pen, or placing drops of liquid LSD on the envelope glue. A team from the Sandia National Laboratories developed both a hand-portable and a fixed drug detector that can detect trace amounts of drugs and identify it in under ten seconds.[43] A serious problem for prisons has been the use of cell phones by inmates. As cell phones are cheaper and smaller, they are more easily brought into a prison (staff or visitors smuggle them in or they get them mailed in and hidden in other objects) and they are difficult to find and detect. The Federal Communications Commission (FCC) does not allow cell phone communications to be blocked, even in a prison. Technology innovations attempt to detect signals and find and confiscate the cell phone, overpower the signal with a stronger one, or intercept the signal, which requires a judicial order.[44] The technology available is expensive and not too successful, and further advances are required before prisons can be effective at preventing inmate use of cell phones.

Supervision of offenders in the community is being improved by the use of technology. This includes GPS tracking of offenders and outlining geographic areas in which they cannot go, with an alarm going off if the offender ventures into a prohibited area. In New Mexico, parole agents use active tracking via GPS technology that allows the officer to draw an "invisible fence" or exclusion zone around an area such as a playground that is forbidden for the offender to enter.[45] A Sex Offender Registry Information System allows police or correctional officials to identify registered sex offenders who fit descriptions or drive cars similar to those used in a crime.[46] The system reduces time to investigation when a sex offender is suspected of committing a crime. Parole and probation officers use remote kiosks similar to video conferencing to make more frequent checks on offenders in rural or faraway places.[47]

Perhaps the most popular use of technology is to make prison staff safer. In a recent update by the National Institute of Justice, it was noted that technology can make corrections work safer with body armor to protect staff from stabbings, devises to detect drugs in the mail, and technology to monitor inmate behavior.[48] Corrections has worked with the U.S. Department of Defense to develop the Staff Alarm and Inmate Tracking (SAINT) program to help pinpoint the location and nature of problems such as an assault on an officer within seconds of its occurrence. These systems are a combination of cameras throughout a facility and a duress alarm worn by an officer that can be triggered by the officer or automatically goes off if the officer is knocked down. When triggered, it not only sends an alarm, but also identifies the location on a map of the prison and can direct a pan-and-tilt camera to automatically focus on that spot and begin recording.[49] These types of systems are believed to be a deterrent to assault by inmates and a stronger perception of safety by staff working in a prison.

The question is whether these technologies will have a significant impact on the operation of correctional agencies and add to their safety or efficiency. The answer is yes, they will. We are in a highly fluid and rapidly developing period of technological advancement. If there is a problem to be solved and the will and finances to address it, a technological advancement can be developed to aid in the solution to the problem. Corrections is a prime target for greater use of technology. With over 2 million inmates incarcerated and several more million supervised in the community, there is a great need and opportunity. The types of innovations described above will continue to be funded, improved, and expanded in their correctional use.

Do We Need a New Paradigm for Sentencing and Corrections?

In many people's minds, we do need a new paradigm for sentencing and corrections. We have been using the same sentencing model for two centuries, and over the past twenty years, we have increasingly relied on incarceration as a sanction for crimes. This continued reliance on imprisonment is costing society a tremendous amount of money, wasting lives, and doing little to prepare offenders to be successful in the community. But what options make sense in meeting the many goals of corrections? One model that seems to deserve consideration is the use of community justice or restorative justice.

Community or restorative justice is an alternative model for sentencing offenders. *Restorative justice* is a sentencing approach that is future oriented, focuses on restoration for the victim and society, and is less expensive for the taxpayer. This model is seen as more desirable than traditional sentencing and punishing offenders, which does little for society and the victims of crimes and focuses only in a reactive way on offenders. Victims have historically been left out of the criminal justice process, and only recently have there been programs to assist victims and ensure that their voices are heard throughout the process. Restorative justice also looks to avoid the high cost to taxpayers of imprisonment, particularly for nonviolent offenders. Instead of spending large amounts of money to punish and incarcerate those offenders who represent little risk to their communities, restorative justice emphasizes that they "make right" the harm they have caused.

Restorative justice sentencing models shift the focus from being reactive and punishment oriented, from cost to the taxpayers, and from a lack of involvement by the victims. The first of two major elements of restorative justice is to hold offenders accountable for the harm they have done and find ways for them to repair the damage. With restorative justice, offenders are forced to face and understand the damage their crime has caused and to actively participate in repairing the injury from their crime. The second element is the active involvement of the victim in determining the proper sanction for the crime. Minnesota was one of the first jurisdictions to implement restorative justice sentencing and describes this victim focus as follows:

> *Restorative justice is a philosophical framework that . . . balances the needs of three primary stakeholders: the victim, the offender, and the community. This is contrasted with a justice system that seeks as its primary aim to catch, convict, and punish offenders . . . . Restorative values include responsibility, accountability, and participation by all who have a stake in the outcome, repairing the harm, making things right, and supporting the victim.*[50]

In a pure restorative justice model, the offender and victim both participate in the decision regarding sentencing for the offense, focusing on what the offender can do to repair the damage. The victim provides input, in that he or she may want an apology, restitution, or a punitive sentence of imprisonment. The offender must accept responsibility, recognize the harm he or she has caused, and agree to a reparative approach to correct the harm. Some victims are hesitant to be fully involved in the process or particularly to have any direct interaction with offenders. Therefore, it is not necessary for the parties to be together to discuss **reparation;** yet a face-to-face discussion is believed to go a long way in furthering the feeling of involvement by the victim and forcing the offender to put a face to the crime committed.

An interesting sidebar of the use of restorative justice is the benefit it can have in the public's confidence in the justice system. In the mid-1990s, the Vermont Department of Corrections recognized that it had a lack of confidence and support from the general public and implemented a restorative justice sentencing model with one objective being to improve its image. Vermont created "two kinds of sentencing tracks, each to address a different sentencing purpose."[51]

reparation
the acts by offenders to repair the damage done from their crimes; it may be in the form of money, community service, or some other act seen as valuable to the victim

These inmates are performing community service work to build a home for Habitat for Humanity. Courtesy of the Ohio Department of Rehabilitation and Correction.

As illustrated in Figure 16.2, offenders who commit serious crimes are placed in the risk management track, which focuses on incapacitating the offender by providing a range of security, treatment, supervision, and surveillance to manage that risk and protect the public.

Nonviolent offenders are placed in the reparative track. Community boards create programs and sanctions that can be used to repair damage from the crime while holding offenders accountable for their offense. Probation sanctions include acts such as making an apology, paying restitution to the victim, and performing community service. Intermediate sanctions include more intensive community supervision under the supervision of the parole board. Offenders failing to perform the reparative acts or meet the conditions of this community supervision are violated and sent to prison. In the reparative track, a sentence of imprisonment is usually in a minimum-security facility, and even the imprisonment maintains a focus on reparation through community work.

Apart from the overall sentencing process included in the restorative justice model, restoration and community justice can also be emphasized throughout the correctional process. Most correctional agencies have implemented ways to inform victims regarding the offenders' classification, assignments, and potential release

	Probation	Intermediate Sanction	Prison
Risk Management	Supervision Counseling Referral	Day treatment center Intensive substance abuse Life management Supervision Community restitution	Incapacitation and treatment (violent, sex, education, mental health)
Reparative	Reparative board Apology Restitution Community service	Reparative board, supervised Community service Work crew	Community Service work Camp

Source: John G. Perry and John F. Gorczyk, "Restructuring Corrections: Using Market Research in Vermont," *Corrections Management Quarterly* 1, no. 3 (1997): 33.

FIGURE 16.2 Vermont Department of Corrections Sentencing Tracks

from prison. For most states and the Federal Bureau of Prisons, victims are notified of the impending release of an offender. Some states provide the opportunity for victims to make their views known before a parole hearing or even to attend the hearing and make a personal statement. In addition to continued involvement of victims in the correctional process, many jurisdictions find other ways for offenders to focus on reparation during their sentence.

The Federal Bureau of Prisons (BOP) has been very successful in collecting fines and restitution from inmates and from offenders under community supervision. Inmate financial responsibility is considered in decisions regarding preferred housing or job assignments. Ohio is one of many states that extensively use prison inmates for community service. Over the first eight years of this program, it was reported that Ohio inmates performed 4.2 million hours of community service work.[52] In addition to the benefits of performing this work, a study of Ohio inmates performing community service indicated a "positive statistical significance with regard to participation in community service and recidivism. In essence, prisoners with *any* experience in community service were reimprisoned less often than those who had none."[53]

Restorative justice concepts have the support of and are seen as effective by the general public. Restorative justice models are seen as more proactive than traditional sentencing, focusing on the community rather than just the offender, and emphasizing repairing the damage from the crime more than punishing the offender. In a recent review of the success of the Vermont community justice model, Karp found that 81 percent of offenders successfully completed their reparative probation. Only 31 percent of reparative probationers were rearrested within one year, and only 1.5 percent were rearrested for violent offenses.[54] Because community or restorative justice approaches have the support of the public and are promising in their effectiveness, they represent a new paradigm for sentencing and corrections that will be expanded in the future.

This inmate is involved in a community service program that repairs and rebuilds wheelchairs to ship to impoverished foreign countries, where those unable to afford them can be granted the gift of mobility. The program is called Wheels for the World. Photo by Richard P. Seiter.

Can We Reduce the Impact of Prisonization and Improve the Successful Reentry of Prisoners to the Community?

One of the most debilitating problems undermining offenders' successful return to the community is the impact of prisonization. As described in Chapter 11, Clemmer noted that inmates take on the customs and cultures of the prison and, as they identify with and incorporate these behaviors, they find it increasingly more difficult to return to the community and adapt to the behaviors of free society.[55] Terry describes how inmates actually become bound by an informal set of inmate rules called the inmate code. Inmates who live by the inmate code are said to have a convict identity.[56] This convict identity is difficult to shed when returning to the community and makes the free world and the behavior of law-abiding citizens seem even more surreal than would be expected.

Is there a way to reduce the likelihood of prisonization and taking on a convict identity and thereby improve the transition from prison to community? This area is difficult to study and has received little research attention over the past decade. However, there are many theories about how the prison experience and the community transition can be changed to improve the likelihood of success in reentry. These include finding ways to have inmates practice community-based values and customs, utilizing transitional programs to assist in preparation for release, and shortening prison sentences to the minimum necessary to provide appropriate punishments.

First, prison operations should be guided by a principle of encouraging inmates to practice values and customs that are important in the community. Prisons have significantly changed for the better since the 1960s, when Goffman wrote about "total institutions" and how their isolated nature, location, and separation from normal society resulted in inmates losing their identity and ability to make decisions for themselves.[57] Goffman had suggested that the overwhelming control of inmates' behavior can result in some inmates becoming confused, hostile, and bitter and can actually reduce an individual's capacity for independent living. In the late 1950s, Cressey noted that staff authority required inmates to spend most of every day with other inmates with whom they do not choose to associate and that the control of their activities gives them little chance to succeed or fail.[58]

Today's prisons are not nearly so regimented and authoritarian as to isolate inmates from their own identity or their ability to make decisions. Yet meeting the prison goals of custody and control forces prisons to operate in a way that is naturally very different from independent living in the community. However, it is possible to operate prisons with a clear emphasis on encouraging the types of behaviors that make for success in the community. The Missouri Department of Corrections recently adopted an approach it calls the **parallel universe** to accomplish this.

The department recognized the problems with successful reentry and attempted to re-create its prisons similar to the outside world, through interacting with the environment outside prisons and replicating the requirements and rewards of the free world. The goal for the parallel universe is to "cultivate in offenders the skills that yield civil, productive conduct. Essentially, the parallel universe is a corrections-based reentry program."[59] The parallel universe encourages inmates to make choices and assume responsibility by putting them in

parallel universe
an approach to operating prisons focusing on cultivating in offenders the skills that yield civil, productive conduct, encouraging inmates to make choices and assume responsibility by putting them in situations that are similar to real life in the community

situations that are similar to real life in the community. There are four interactive strategies:

> *First, every offender is engaged during work and nonworking hours in productive activities that parallel those of free society. In work hours, offenders go to school and work and, as applicable, to treatment for sex offenses, chronic mental health problems, and drug and alcohol dependencies. In nonworking hours they participate in community service, reparative activities, and recreation. Second, every offender must adopt relapse prevention strategies and abstain from unauthorized activities, including drug and alcohol consumption and sexual misconduct. Third, most offenders can earn opportunities to make choices and are held accountable for them. Fourth, offenders are recognized for good conduct and can improve their status by obeying the rules and regulations.*[60]

The Missouri program is not unique in how most modern correctional agencies operate. Yet it is unique in that the department's total focus is to change the prison culture in a way that is designed to improve the chance of successful reentry rather than be an obstacle to it.

Other ways that prisons can reduce the difficulty in the community transition include efforts to maintain family and community ties, maintain work skills, and have inmates associate with citizens other than inmates and correctional staff. Prisons encourage visiting and allow telephone calls to family members and friends. However, these do not go far enough to avoid losing touch with the real issues facing inmates as family members or parents. Parenting programs as described previously are important in this regard. Yet it is also important to create programs that maintain inmates' conscious involvement in the issues that face their families. Why is my son having problems in school, and what can we as parents do about it? Now that my daughter is of dating age, what should she know about sex and the chance of contracting a sexually transmitted disease? Inmates feel unable to deal with these types of issues and therefore do not try to get involved in most normal family and parenting decisions. Yet being involved in the struggle about how to address these types of concerns is exactly what can help them stay linked to the community rather than to the problems of prison life.

As inmates stay in prison for long periods of time, they lose any positive work habits and skills they may have. When they return to the community, they feel even more unable to perform or compete in the world of work and often quickly give up trying. Prison industry programs are extremely valuable in maintaining or developing skills, creating good work habits, and building confidence in one's ability to produce in the competitive working environment. It has also been shown that work in prison industries not only improves prison behavior, but also reduces recidivism rates following release.[61] Unfortunately, on December 30, 2005, only 562 (31 percent of total number) correctional facilities provided prison industry programs.[62]

Inmates also need to associate with individuals who are not inmates or prison staff. Most prisons have volunteer programs in which citizens come into the prison to assist with educational, religious, substance abuse, or other programs or activities. Volunteers in this regard can be excellent mentors and role models for inmates. It is not necessary that they work with individual inmates. Just the association gives inmates an opportunity to talk about normal issues in the community and avoid the focus on the prison that results from conversations with other inmates or prison staff.

The second way to reduce the effect of prisonization is through the use of transitional programs in preparation for release. Several programs have been found effective in improving the success of prisoner reentry and reducing recidivism. Vocational training and work release programs are effective in reducing recidivism and improving job readiness skills for ex-offenders. Drug rehabilitation programs are effective in reducing arrests, drug-related offenses, continued drug use, and parole violations. Halfway house programs reduce the frequency and severity of future crimes. There are promising results for sex and violent offender programs. Unfortunately, these programs still are not provided to a high percentage of the inmate population.

The final method for reducing the impact of prisonization is to shorten prison sentences to only a term that meets the need for society to be assured that inmates receive appropriate punishment for their crime and not to go beyond this point to reflect society's anger and frustration over our inability to solve the crime problem. During the past twenty years, we have attacked the crime problem through enhancing sentences. A serious crime that received considerable publicity usually resulted in state legislatures lengthening the term served by offenders. Unfortunately, this usually occurred without any firm evidence that the enhancement would reduce crime and often without an estimate of the cost of the enhancement. The impact of this approach to sentencing has been addressed previously, and crime has been reduced by lengthening criminal sentences. However, the question addressed in this section is how to reduce the impact of prisonization on inmates so that it is less of an obstacle to successful reentry. When asked to cite the most important change that can be made to improve the likelihood of successful reentry for prisoners, Terry responded, "to keep time spent in prison to the least possible time, thereby reducing the likelihood and impact of prisonization."[63] This is only common sense. Even with the suggested modifications in prison programs and operations to reduce the likelihood and strength of prisonization, there will still be a continued idealization of the prison way of life the longer someone lives in a prison environment.

The answer to the question of whether we can reduce the impact of prisonization and improve the successful reentry of prisoners to the community is yes. We can if we find ways to have inmates practice community-based values and customs, utilize transitional programs to help inmates prepare for release from prison, and shorten prison sentences to the minimum necessary to provide appropriate punishments. The key feature to successfully implementing these approaches is to have an objective of minimizing the deleterious effect of imprisonment on inmates. A program such as the parallel universe in Missouri is an excellent example of how this can be accomplished.

The concept of prisoner reentry brings to mind the integration of correctional, community, and social services resources that are also necessary to aid in the successful reintegration of prisoners returning to the community. Many staff positions in community and social service agencies also contribute to the reentry of offenders and are the topic of the "Your Career in Corrections" box.

Is Corrections a Good Career Choice for me?

This text has presented various jobs that are available to those seeking a career in corrections. There have been discussions regarding the pay, working conditions, challenges, benefits, and issues that people face while working in corrections. With this information, it is time for students to consider whether a **career in corrections** is right for them. Correctional jobs are difficult to perform, and not every person who expresses an interest in corrections is suited for this type of work.

mycrimekit

Media—Video:
Prisonization of Inmates

career in corrections
beginning work for a correctional agency with a possibility of working in corrections from now until retirement

Your Career in Corrections

Community Social Service Staff

Throughout this textbook, students have been provided ideas and information for careers working for correctional agencies. However, corrections cannot operate in a vacuum and successfully punish offenders, treat them, and deter them from committing further crimes. The relationship of offenders to many other factors (employment, family, their environment in the neighborhood, availability of drugs, mental competence) all affect whether they will avoid further criminal behavior. In this regard, many other types of jobs work with correctional agencies and may be of interest to students of corrections.

First are the many community and social service agencies that work with offenders. Every community has job training and development agencies, community mental health departments, family counseling organizations, and substance abuse counselors. Some of these are private organizations that receive grants or contract with public agencies. Some are religious organizations, linked to and supported by churches. Others are federal, state, or local public agencies created to help disadvantaged citizens find jobs or receive counseling or treatment. Students majoring in criminal justice or corrections often do not consider these public or quasi-public social service agencies. However, there are many jobs as counselors or program developers in all these types of agencies that work with correctional clients and do work similar to correctional staff. Finding these jobs is not as easy as applying to work for a large public correctional agency; they are often small agencies that do not have a central job clearinghouse, and therefore students must develop networks through internships and faculty contacts to hear of the availability of jobs and know where and how to apply for positions.

A second category of jobs that relate closely to correctional staff positions are the other two elements of the criminal justice system: the police and the courts. Although traditional police work is similar in some ways to the security functions of correctional officers, their role is substantially different. The work of correctional staff is based on using interpersonal skills to deal with clients over a significant period of time. Police officers use many of the same skills, but their interactions with citizens or clients of the criminal justice system are usually made up of single transactions or situations. However, police departments usually have school patrol officers or community relations officers who have a role that is more long term and preventive in nature. These staff learn to work with the community or school, getting to know the citizens and students and often advising or counseling them on issues regarding criminal justice. Courts also have victim services officers and drug court staff who play a very similar role to correctional staff.

Finally, many other social and community service positions may appeal to someone interested in a career in corrections. People drawn to corrections usually have an interest in helping others and in serving the public; they enjoy interacting with people, like jobs with a lot of variety that are not "desk-bound," and want a career that has opportunities for advancement and can lead to a variety of different career moves. Family and children's services, housing, public assistance, recreation, and legal services are a variety of agencies that need these kinds of people to work and perform roles very similar to correctional staff. If you are drawn to correctional work, your job possibilities are as endless as your imagination.

It is important to seriously consider the roles and specific duties of these jobs before applying for a job and committing to a career in corrections.

Corrections is a people business, meaning that it is not the bars, fences, policies, or equipment that successfully carry out the goals of a correctional sanction. It is the staff. Positive, professional correctional staff can make any program or policy effective. Yet unprofessional, poorly trained, or uncaring staff will cause any policy or program to fail. Because of the mission of corrections, the role of staff in correctional agencies is even more critical than the role of staff in most other public agencies or private-sector companies. Correctional agencies are responsible for protecting the public by limiting offenders' freedoms. This is a serious responsibility.

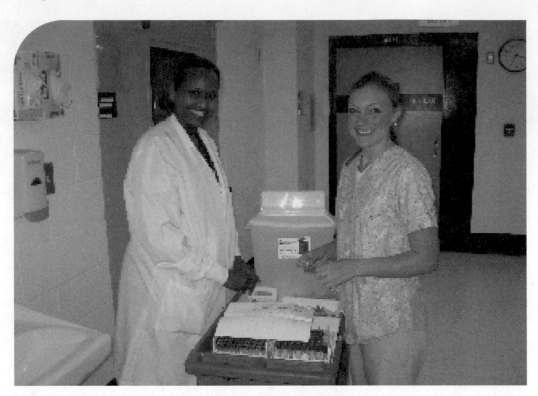

There are several positions in health care in corrections.

Photo by Richard P. Seiter.

When correctional staff fail to effectively do their jobs, innocent citizens may be victims of crime. Correctional staff have considerable discretion in how they carry out their duties and take away offenders' individual freedoms. Therefore, staff members doing these difficult jobs must follow the highest of ethical standards.

It is not unusual for people to apply for and get a job with a correctional agency and then determine that it is not the right type of position for them. This leads to a high turnover of correctional staff, especially during the first few months of employment and especially in the difficult role of correctional officer. As indicated in Table 16.1, turnover rates for correctional officers between 1993 and 2001 increased from a low of 11.6 percent to a high of 16.6 percent.[64]

TABLE 16.1 **Correctional Officer Average Annual Turnover Rate, 1993–2001**

Year	Percent
1993	12.0
1994	11.6
1995	12.7
1996	12.9
1997	14.9
1998	15.4
1999	16.0
2000	16.1
2001	16.6

Source: Adapted from Camille Graham Camp and George M. Camp, *The 2002 Corrections Yearbook: Adult Systems* (Middletown, Conn. : Criminal Justice Institute, 2003), p. 171.

Correctional officers make up the highest percentage of jail and prison staff and conduct a variety of custody and security functions. Photo by Richard P. Seiter.

Wright examined correctional turnover and suggests, "Prisons experience high rates of turnover among employees, averaging 16 percent nationwide and reaching over 40 percent in some settings."[65]

One reason for a high turnover rate in these and other correctional jobs is the stressful and dangerous nature of the positions. Correctional staff in prison and the community work with difficult clients who regularly challenge them, attempting to avoid compliance and detection of violations. There is also always the risk of assault and serious injury. Although many job-related functions lead to stress for correctional workers (understaffing, rotating shift work, inmate demands and manipulations, and poor public image), officers mentioned the threat of violence more frequently than any other single feature of their occupation.[66]

Even with these challenges and concerns, there are many reasons to consider corrections as a career. First, there are many available jobs. The most recent report (May 2004) by the Bureau of Justice Statistics reported there were 747,061 correctional employees working at the federal, state, and local levels in the United States in 2001.[67] This is almost a 30 percent increase since 1992, when there were 556,500 correctional employees.[68] Second, these jobs are very stable, and there are many career opportunities. Seldom does a correctional agency have a layoff or have to reduce its number of staff. Staff with the proper educational requirements who work hard and do a good job will be promoted and given opportunities for advancement. With the growth that has occurred in corrections over the past two decades, there is a continuous requirement for new staff. As new staff are hired, those currently working are considered for promotion to take the new middle-management positions.

Third, the pay is better than most people believe, and the benefits are very good. In 2008, examples of annual salaries for correctional officers were $27,540 for Texas and $45,288 for California.[69] Public-sector correctional agencies usually have excellent vacations, days off, and health care coverage. Many have a special retirement system, similar to those of law enforcement agencies, in which employees can retire after twenty-five to thirty years of service at any age. This seems like a long time for students today thinking about a career, but retiring at age fifty or fifty-five is an outstanding benefit.

mycrimekit

Media—Video:
Recruiting People into Corrections

Finally, corrections is an interesting and enjoyable career. There is seldom a boring day in a correctional job. You deal with people, you face new challenges, and you have to make decisions as you go. Even though corrections is not a career for everyone, it is a career for people who do not want to be desk-bound, who enjoy working with people, who are not afraid of a challenge, and who want to serve the public. People with these characteristics will be making the right choice to select a career in corrections. This textbook was written to provide students a real-life understanding of what corrections is really all about. Students should seriously consider all the issues raised in this book as they consider whether a career in corrections is right for them. But the answer, in this author's opinion, to the question of whether corrections is a good career choice is a definite yes. I have enjoyed it for more than twenty-five years and would recommend it to anyone.

Summary

With this summary, your study of an introduction to corrections is coming to a close. Corrections has an interesting history, currently faces significant challenges, and has a difficult to predict future. One thing that is known about the future of corrections, however, is that the discipline will continue to grow in importance, visibility, and interest to the public. Only fifty years ago, the public and elected officials had little interest in or knowledge of correctional operations. Today, it is one of the most hotly debated areas of public policy.

In this final chapter, seven questions have been proposed. First, can our current approach to sentencing and corrections be successful and continue? The answer to this question is yes and no. The "tough on crime" approach to sentencing, with lengthy sentences and an emphasis on deterrence and incapacitation, can reduce crime, but only marginally. It cannot continue, however, if taxpayers demand a greater return on the tremendous amount of money they are pumping into the nation's correctional system.

Second, will rehabilitation continue as a primary correctional goal? The answer to this question is yes, it will continue and will even expand in importance. The public supports rehabilitation programs, and there is increasing evidence of their success in reducing recidivism. Therefore, rehabilitation will experience a rebirth in importance as a correctional goal of correctional operations.

Third, will supervision of offenders in the community change in approach? A change in supervision will occur. Just as evidence of the success of rehabilitation will prompt its reemphasis, there is evidence of potential reductions in recidivism through a balance of casework and monitoring. These findings will lead to a gradual move back toward the casework style, rather than a focus on surveillance.

Fourth, what technological developments will be implemented and how will they impact corrections? We are living in a time of rapidly changing uses for technology and innovations are continuously being considered for use in corrections. Some of these will definitely change how we conduct the business of corrections and there are other technologies that while useful, can never replace the human element of people supervising, treating, and working with other people.

Fifth, do we need a new paradigm for sentencing and corrections? The old paradigms have been relatively unchanged over two hundred years, and we do need to find new approaches. Community justice or restorative justice represents just such an approach. It is supported by the public, appears promising in effectiveness, and is a new sentencing and correctional paradigm that warrants expansion in the future.

Sixth, can we reduce the impact of prisonization and improve the successful reentry of prisoners to the community? Again, the answer to this question is yes. Through finding ways to have inmates practice community-based values and customs, utilizing transitional programs to assist in preparation for release, and shortening prison sentences to the minimum necessary to provide appropriate punishments, we can reduce the negative effects of prisonization and increase the chance of successful reentry to the community.

Seventh, and perhaps the most important question for readers, is corrections a good career choice? The answer is a resounding yes. In regard to this question, I admit a lack of objectivity and a total bias to the positive. I have had a career working in corrections for more than twenty-five years. I have found fulfillment from meeting difficult challenges and disappointment from failures. However, I have seldom had a dull moment and never a second thought about whether corrections was the right choice for me. Correctional jobs are available, they are stable, they pay better than most people think, and they are interesting and enjoyable. You meet hundreds of dedicated people, and you make plenty of friends. By reading this book and studying corrections, it is hoped that students will agree that it is an honorable career that deserves a close look as a possible future.

To conclude our look into the future of corrections, students are to read the "You Make the Decision" box and consider the answers to the seven questions posed in this chapter, as well as others they consider important to the future of corrections.

Key Terms

accountability
rebirth in rehabilitation
invisible policy
global positioning system

reparation
parallel universe
career in corrections

Review Questions

1. What current correctional goals most influence sentencing policy, and how has a focus on these goals influenced the number of offenders under correctional supervision?

2. How will tightening budgets influence future sentencing policies?

3. How has the development of meta-analysis influenced researchers examining the effectiveness of correctional treatment?

4. What does it mean to have a "rebirth in rehabilitation"?

5. What has been the result of a movement toward surveillance of offenders in the community?

6. What "invisible policy" is being used in the supervision of community offenders?

7. List and describe three new technologies that have a positive use for corrections.

8. In what way can e-messaging by inmates help prison administrators?

9. Define *restorative justice*.

10. How are sentences determined within a restorative justice approach?

11. Why do inmates become prisonized and why does prisonization reduce the successful reentry of prisoners?

12. How can the process of prisonization be reduced?

13. What are the positive and negative factors of working in corrections?

14. Is a career in corrections right for you?

You Make the Decision...

What Will the Future Bring?

In this chapter, seven questions regarding the future of corrections have been asked:

- Can our current approach to sentencing and corrections be successful and continue?
- Will rehabilitation continue as a primary correctional goal?
- Will supervision of offenders in the community change in approach?
- How will technology impact corrections in the future?
- Do we need a new paradigm for sentencing and corrections?
- Can we reduce the impact of prisonization and improve the successful reentry of prisoners to the community?
- Is corrections a good career choice for me?

As author, I answered them from my perspective, providing some of the data and situations that I believed would lead to each of the questions being answered as I did. However, it is now time for you to try to provide answers to these same questions *and* identify other questions you think are relevant for the future.

In this "You Make the Decision," discuss each question in a small group. List the three or four arguments for and against answering the question the way I answered it. Then, decide whether you agree with the answer I provided or not, and present the reasons for your decision. If you disagreed, give the answer you think is most likely to happen and the reasons you believe it to be true.

Then think back on our study of corrections throughout this book and consider what other questions you believe are important to ponder for the future. I picked only seven "big picture" issues. You can add to that or get more "micro" in your questions, such as "Will supermax prisons incur any successful 'cruel or unusual' legal challenges?" or "Will correctional agencies have to significantly increase salaries in order to attract qualified staff in the future?" There may be no right or wrong answers to your questions. However, the fun is in thinking about the future, the types of issues that will occur, and what you think the outcome will be.

Chapter Resources on mycrimekit™

Go to mycrimekit.com to explore the following study tools and resources specific to this chapter:

- **Practice Quiz:** multiple-choice, true/false, short-answer, and essay questions to help students test their knowledge
- **WebQuests:** learning activities built around Web searches
  - Restorative Justice: www.restorativejustice.org
- **Insider's Experiences:** "Education Really Does Work"

- **Seiter Videos:**
  - See an administrator discuss changes in corrections
  - See experts discuss sentences and rehabilitation
  - See inmates discuss prisonization
  - See an administrator discuss recruiting people into corrections
- **Flashcards:** Seven flashcards to test knowledge of the chapter's key terms

Glossary

ACA accreditation: a process to promote and recognize improvement in the management of correctional agencies through the administration of voluntary standards

accountability: holding one responsible for accomplishing objectives in a cost-efficient manner

adjudicate: to find a juvenile guilty of a delinquent act

administrative appeals process: an informal process for inmates to appeal a disciplinary sanction or to seek remedy of any other injustice they feel they have received at the hands of correctional officials

administrative detention: a nonpunitive confinement in SHU used to house inmates whose continued presence in the general population may pose a serious threat to the security or orderly running of the prison

administrative form of sentencing: administrative bodies (correctional officials and parole/release boards) have primary discretion in granting good time and determining the release time of offenders

affirmative action programs: activities to aggressively recruit and provide opportunities for employment to women and minorities

aftercare: supervision of a juvenile in the community after serving time in a juvenile correctional institution; similar to parole for adults

age of original jurisdiction: the upper or oldest age that a juvenile court will have jurisdiction over categories of offenders

Alexander Maconochie: the superintendent of the British penal colony on Norfolk Island from 1841 to 1844 who created a system of marks for good behavior that could lead to a graduated release from prison

American Correctional Association: the largest professional organization for corrections in the United States

Americans with Disabilities Act: a law that prohibits any entity from discriminating against an individual with a disability in regards to employment, public service and transportation, public accommodations, and telecommunications services

antipsychotic drugs: drugs administered to mentally ill individuals to counteract the symptoms of their mental illness, often allowing them to live successfully in the community rather than needing to be institutionalized

asset forfeiture: the authorized seizure by the government of money, negotiable instruments, securities, or other things of value that were obtained through illegal activities

Atavism: the existence of features common in the early stages of human evolution, implied the idea that criminals are born, and criminal behavior is *predetermined*

Auburn system: the congregate and silent operation of prisons, in which inmates were allowed to work together during the day, but had to stay separate and silent at other times

bail: the pledge of money or property in exchange for a promise to return for further criminal processing

balancing test: established in *Pell v. Procunier*, finding that prison inmates retain those First Amendment rights that are not inconsistent with their status as prisoner or with legitimate penological objectives

Barefield v. Leach: a 1974 federal court decision that a disparity of programs for female inmates could not be justified because the smaller number of female inmates made it more costly to provide program parity

Bell v. Wolfish: a 1979 U.S. Supreme Court case in which the punitive intent standard was adopted for considering violations of the Eighth Amendment regarding jail operations

BFOQ: a bona fide occupational qualification reasonably necessary to the normal operation of that particular business or enterprise that may allow for some discriminatory practices to occur

bifurcated trial: used in capital cases, with guilt first established at a traditional trial, and if found guilty, a second stage of sentencing considers between death or life imprisonment

blended sentencing: a middle ground between juvenile and adult sentences that allows judges to choose from a broad array of both juvenile and adult sanctions

brig: a military term meaning a correctional facility

Bruscino v. Carlson: a 1985 federal court decision that the lockdown of inmates at the U.S. Penitentiary in Marion, Illinois, was not a violation of the Constitution

call out: a schedule of all the appointments and required moves for a day, including the name and expected times of the moves

capital punishment: punishment for the most serious crimes (generally first-degree murder); most states and the federal government provide for the death penalty

career in corrections: beginning work for a correctional agency with a possibility of working in corrections from now until retirement

case manager: sometimes called social worker or case worker; responsible for developing the program of work and rehabilitation for inmates assigned to him or her

casework style of supervision: a style of supervising community offenders that places emphasis on assisting the offender with problems, counseling, and working to make sure the offender successfully completes supervision

census counts: a less formal count conducted at program and work assignments by the staff responsible for supervising inmates

Cesare Beccaria: an Italian theorist who in the eighteenth century first suggested linking crime causation to punishments and became known as the founder of the Classical School of criminology

Cesare Lombroso: the Italian physician who in the nineteenth century founded the Positive School

chain of command: the vertical hierarchy in an organization, identified in terms of authority, and the order through which persons receive directives from the person immediately above them and pass these directives to the person immediately below them

Civil Rights Act of 1871: this act of Congress guaranteed the rights of freed slaves and provided access to federal courts for violations of the act

Classical School: the theory linking crime causation to punishment, based on offenders' free will and hedonism

closed systems: prison systems that consist of only the internal environment, under the direct control of the warden, and without much interest or any interference from external groups

collective bargaining: the formal recognition of employee organizations and their right to negotiate with management regarding workplace issues

collective violence: prison violence that is between and initiated by groups of inmates and includes prison riots and disturbances; it can be groups of inmates against staff or against one another, as this violence stems from the fundamental difference in values and positions of the two groups

Commission on Accreditation for Corrections: formed to administer a national accreditation programs for all components of adult and juvenile correctional agencies

community classification systems: risk assessments that predict the chance of new crimes being committed; they are used to determine the level of supervision an offender will receive in the community

community corrections: those criminal sanctions that involve community supervision of offenders, make use of correctional and program resources available in the community, and require offenders to abide by specified conditions to remain in the community

community residential centers: houses in which offenders live in the community that provide supervision, room and board, and some treatment as an alternative to prison

community service: an economic sanction used when offenders do not have funds from which to pay a fine or make restitution; referred to as a "fine on their time," so that indigent offenders do not have to serve prison or jail time merely because they lack the fiscal ability to pay a fine

community standards: the test established in *Fernandez v. United States* that medical care for inmates must be reasonably commensurate with medical care they would receive if not imprisoned

concurrent sentences: sentences that run at the same time

conjugal visiting: sometimes referred to as family visiting, these are private visiting opportunities between inmates and their spouses, and it is expected that they will engage in sexual relations

consecutive sentences: sentences that run one after the other

consent decree: an informal handling of a juvenile justice case, in which the delinquent juvenile admits to wrongdoing and agrees to specific conditions of behavior; sometimes called informal probation

containment model: an approach to managing sex offenders that includes treatment to develop internal control over deviant thoughts, supervision and surveillance to control external behaviors, and polygraph examinations to monitor conformance to treatment plans and supervision conditions

continuum of care: provision of mental health programs based on the intensity of needs for each inmate, including as inmates prepare for release to the community

contraband: any item that inmates are not allowed to possess, including items that can assist in an escape, are dangerous, can undermine prison physical security, or are nuisance items

controlled movement: the procedure used by prisons to maintain accountability for inmates as they move throughout the prison

convicts: long-term inmates who become used to the prison society and find a way to live in this environment with a minimal amount of problems and disruptions

co-payment: a minimal charge for inmates to see a physician or receive medical care; in most states, the charges are two to three dollars

Cornell Correctional Companies: a private correctional company headquartered in Texas that operates sixty-nine correctional facilities in the United States.

correctional counselor: a former correctional officer who works with inmates on prison issues such as creating a visiting or telephone list or getting a prison job assignment

correctional officer: staff person in a prison or jail who accomplishes the institution's mission by maintaining control and order within the prison

Corrections Corporation of America: the largest of the private prison corporations that opened the first private, for-profit correctional facility in 1984 in Tennessee; currently operates seventy correctional facilities

corrections: the range of community and institutional sanctions, treatment programs, and services for managing criminal offenders

cost of incarceration fee: fees charged to prisoners in local jails or prisons to cover the cost to taxpayers for their incarceration

cost of supervision: offenders have to pay for some costs associated with their supervision in the community, such as drug testing or electronic monitoring

cottage-style architecture: a style of prison design used for women's prisons, with several small housing units holding approximately thirty inmates; each cottage included kitchens, living rooms, and sometimes nurseries for inmates with children

create revenues: the idea that governments can charge for certain services, even for correctional supervision or programs provided to offenders

custody: the functions within a prison that come under the security activities and includes all "uniformed" employees such as correctional officers and correctional supervisors

debrief: gang members tell correctional officials everything they know about the gang operations and membership; once inmates debrief, they become an enemy of the gang

deinstitutionalize: the move to remove juveniles from correctional institutions and place them in community alternatives

deliberate indifference: as established in *Wilson v. Seiter*, the standard that conditions at prison are not unconstitutional unless prison administrators show deliberate indifference toward inmates' basic needs

delinquent children: children who have committed an act that would be considered criminal if committed by an adult

dependent children: children who, although committing no legal offense, may be without a parent or guardian, possibly because the parent is physically or mentally unable to act in that capacity

determinate sentences: sentences of fixed terms

direct supervision: a style of inmate supervision with staff located in direct contact with inmates; requires staff to continuously supervise and communicate with inmates, reducing tension and avoiding the development of conflicts between inmates or inmates and staff

director: the chief executive officer of a state or federal department of corrections

disciplinary segregation: a punitive assignment in SHU after a finding of guilt for a serious prison rule violation; disciplinary segregation is for a set amount of time established by the authorized hearing official

discretionary parole: Release of inmates in which the decision to release is made by a parole board

disturbance control team: an emergency team with the primary mission of controlling inmates during riot situations by using defensive tactics and equipment to move, isolate, and get them to give up and stop the disturbance

Dothard v. Rawlinson: a 1977 U.S. Supreme Court case regarding a woman who was denied a position as a correctional officer in an Alabama male prison; the Court ruled that a BFOQ against women correctional officers was allowable because of the deplorable conditions of the Alabama prisons and the presence of predatory male sex offenders as inmates

drug courts: an alternative to traditional court models to deal with the underlying drug problem as the basis of the offenders' criminality

drug offenders: those convicted of crimes regarding the possession or sale of drugs

drug use forecasting: surveys of jailed inmates by the U.S. Department of Justice to determine the extent of drug use related to criminality

economic sanction: a requirement that an offender pay a fine or restitution

to the victim as a part of his or her sentence

Eighth Amendment: states that no cruel or unusual punishment may be inflicted

electronic monitoring: the use of technology to monitor an offender's location

Elizabeth Fry: a Quaker who formed the Ladies Society for Promoting the Reformation of Female Prisoners in 1816; she tried to convince officials that women prisoners should be separated from male prisoner and that female guards should be hired to supervise them

Elmira Reformatory: the first reformatory in the United States; it opened in 1876 and used the principles of the Irish system, indeterminate sentences, and parole

employee awards program: a program to recognize and reward staff who perform beyond their expected level

environmental factors: factors that create tension and an underlying unrest among inmates; they can include hot weather, reduction in budgets for recreation equipment, prison crowding, poor food service or medical care, a perceived pattern of unfairness in the management of the prison, or poor security procedures that allow inmates to create an unsafe environment

Federal Bureau of Prisons: an agency within the U.S. Department of Justice charged with housing and managing federal law offenders

federalized: the making of a crime a federal rather than a state offense; results when the U.S. Congress decides that it desires federal law enforcement and prosecution of certain offenses

felony: crime that is punishable by a year or more of incarceration

female offenders: women who are convicted and sentenced; just over 6 percent of prison inmates are females

fines: a requirement that offenders pay some dollar amount to the court as punishment for committing the offense

first-generation jails: a linear design was used for housing inmates, in which cells are aligned in long, straight rows, with walkways in the front of the cells for jail correctional officers to walk intermittently to observe what is going on in the cells

Fourteenth Amendment: no state shall deprive any person of life, liberty, or

property without the due process of law; states may not deny any person the equal protection of the law

furlough: a program in which prison inmates are allowed to leave the prison early to reside in a halfway house and prepare for reentry to the community

Gagnon v. Scarpelli: a 1973 U.S. Supreme Court decision that created the due process requirements for revoking probation

gang intelligence officers: prison staff charged with collecting intelligence and advising administrators regarding strategies to manage and contain prison gang activity

gang validation process: an identification of the number of identifiers of gang activity used to confirm individuals' gang involvement level

gaol: an early English term for a jail

general deterrence: the recognition that criminal acts result in punishment, and the effect of that recognition on society that prevents future crimes

general population: inmates in prison who do not have any specific designation as a special type of offender

Girl Scouts Behind Bars: Girl Scout troops that have their chapter based in a prison so inmates with children can participate as Scout parents

global positioning system: a system that uses a satellite to receive a signal from a transmitter and identify its location to a monitoring station

good time: affords inmates the opportunity to reduce their eligibility for release by good behavior in prison

graduated incarceration: a system in which juveniles handled by adult courts are placed in juvenile facilities until they reach the age of 18; they are then transferred to an adult prison to complete the sentence

Gunther v. Iowa: a 1979 case in the U.S. District Court of Iowa in which the court determined that inmate privacy was not a valid reason to refuse to hire women as correctional officers; the *Gunther* decision eliminated the major support used for the BFOQ by states in not hiring female correctional officers

hands-off doctrine: an avoidance by the U.S. Supreme Court of judicial intervention in the operations of prisons and the judgment of correctional administrators

hearing officers: Officials who are not appointed parole board members, yet they hold parole hearings and make recommendations to the parole board regarding inmates'release

hedonistic calculus: the idea that the main objective of an intelligent person is to achieve the most pleasure and the least pain and that individuals are constantly calculating the pluses and minuses of their potential actions

hostage negotiation teams: a team of eight to ten prison employees, with excellent communication skills and ability to perform under stress, with the principle role to open lines of communications between staff and hostage takers

house arrest: offenders live at home and must be at home except for times they are to be at work or participating in other activities approved by their probation officer

human immunodeficiency virus (HIV): a virus that attacks the body's immune system, increasing the chance of infection and other diseases

Immigration and Customs Enforcement (ICE): formerly the U.S. Immigration and Naturalization Service (INS), responsible for housing illegal aliens pending a hearing or deportation back to their home country

imprisonment: a sentence in a prison of a year or more

In re Gault: a 1967 U.S. Supreme Court case requiring that, in hearings in which a juvenile may be committed to an institution, they must have the right to counsel, to notice of the charges against them, to question witnesses, and to protection against self-incrimination

incapacitation: reducing offenders' ability or capacity to commit further crimes

incarceration rates: the number of persons per 100,000 that are in jail or prison

indeterminate sentences: sentences that have a minimum and maximum time to serve; a decision by a release authority determines the actual time served within that range

Industrial Prison Era: prison operations with emphasis on having inmates work and produce products that could help to make the prisons self-sustaining

inmate accountability: the staff's ability to locate and identify inmates at any point in time within a prison

inmate code: the expected rules and behaviors represented by the model prisoner and reflecting the values and norms of prison society

inmate disciplinary system: a policy that clearly prescribes the process required to find that an inmate committed a proscribed act and identifies allowable punishments for each act; a key to controlling inmate behavior

inspector: a person in a department of corrections who investigates allegations by inmates against staff

intake: determination if a juvenile case should be dismissed, handled informally, or referred to the juvenile court

integrity interview: interviews of candidates for correctional employment used to determine if the candidate has issues or conditions that could put them in a compromising situation or make them more likely to accept a bribe to show favored treatment to an inmate

intensive supervised probation (ISP): supervision of community offenders with higher than average risk, through smaller caseloads and very close monitoring of activities

intensive-supervision caseload: caseload for offenders with too high a risk or need to be on regular supervision; created as an alternative to sending these offenders to prison

intermediate sanctions: midrange dispositions that fall between probation and imprisonment

internal classification system: instruments used to assign inmates to housing or programs after they are placed in a particular prison

interpersonal violence: prison violence that occurs between two or more individual inmates; the reason for the violence is a personal issue between the individuals

invisible policy: a practice that is not formalized in statute or written policy, but that develops through a consistent set of pressures that influence the practice in a specific manner

Irish system: a four-stage system of graduated release from prison and return to the community; the stages were solitary confinement, special prison, open institutions, and ticket of leave

jails: locally operated correctional facilities that confine persons before or after adjudidication

Jeremy Bentham: creator of the hedonistic calculus suggesting that punishments outweigh the pleasure criminals get from committing their crime

John Augustus: the Boston shoemaker who became the "father" of probation

John Howard: the sheriff of Bedfordshire, England, who encouraged reform of English jails in the late 1700s

judicial form of sentencing: judges have primary discretion in creating the sentence

just deserts model: a model for sentencing proposed by von Hirsch that had fixed sentences for each crime so that the punishment fit the crime

justice model: the model for sentencing proposed by Fogel that would use flat, determinate sentences, eliminate parole boards, and make all treatment voluntary

juvenile detention: the temporary care of children in physically restricted facilities pending court disposition or transfer to another jurisdiction or agency

juvenile gangs: groups of adolescents or young adults who see themselves as a group and have been involved in enough crime to be of considerable concern to law enforcement and the community

juvenile justice system: a system to handle juveniles separate from adult offenders, based on the concept of *parens patriae*, which was used as the basis for giving the court the authority to take over supervision of children when their parents failed to provide proper care and guidance

lease system: state prisons accepted bids and leased out prisoners to the private sector, which would work the inmates in their industrial operations

legislative form of sentencing: legislative bodies create very structured sentencing codes, and therefore have primary discretion in the length of time served by offenders

length of stay: the time served in a jail or prison by any inmate

lethal injection: a method of execution in which drugs are injected into a person's body, making the heart stop and causing death

lockup: refers to a small jail with only a few cells and no accommodations for food services, medical care, or recreation

male offenders: men who are convicted and sentenced; they constitute over 93 percent of all prison inmates

management culture: a culture based on the way prison leadership deals and communicates with subordinate staff; it falls into a continuum between autocratic and empowered

mandatory minimum sentences: a requirement that for certain crimes or for certain types of offenders, there must be a sentence to prison for at least a minimum term

mandatory prison educational: many states and the Federal Bureau of Prisons require inmates without a high school diploma or GED to attend school

Manhattan Bail Project: a program started in the 1960s to assist judges in identifying individuals who were good candidates to be released on their own recognizance without commercial or monetary bond

mark system: credits against a sentence that allowed for inmates to be released once they earned the required level of marks through work and good behavior

medical model: a theory of corrections that offenders were sick, inflicted with problems that caused their criminality, and needed to be diagnosed and treated, and that rehabilitative programs would resolve offenders' problems and prepare them for release into the community able to be productive and crime-free

meta-analysis: a statistical measure of the average effect an intervention has on recidivism across all studies, while identifying and controlling for various study conditions

misdemeanors: crimes that are punishable by less than a year of incarceration

mission: a statement of an organization's major function and what it is to accomplish, or its basic purposes, to include general outcomes that it is committed to achieving

Morrissey v. Brewer: A 1972 U.S. Supreme Court decision that once parole is granted, a liberty interest is created and offenders must have certain due process to revoke that liberty

neglected children: children who have a family or guardian, but are not receiving proper care or the situation in the home is harmful to them and their upbringing

Neoclassical School: a compromise between Classical and Positive Schools; while holding offenders accountable for their crimes, allowing for some

consideration of mitigating and aggravating circumstances

net widening: the overlapping of criminal sanctions and added supervision for community-placed offenders, rather than diversion of offenders from prison

new penology: an emphasis on the rational and efficient deployment of control strategies for managing and confining high-risk criminal populations

new-crime violations: violation of the condition of probation prohibiting the commission of any additional crimes

"nothing works": a conclusion by Robert Martinson that no correctional treatment program reduces recidivism; it effectively spelled the end to the medical model

objective classification systems: statistical approaches to consider the risk of escape and violence by inmates

offender restitution: a requirement that offenders repay society for the harm created by the offense

open systems: prison systems that have frequent interactions between the organization and other groups, in order to obtain resources, gain support, and accomplish goals

order: the sanction for a juvenile found delinquent by juvenile court; similar to the sentence for an adult

organizational culture: the values, beliefs, and behaviors that form the way of life within that organization

overrepresentation of minorities: a greater percentage of certain racial and ethnic groups in the correctional population than in the general U.S. population

parallel universe: an approach to operating prisons focusing on cultivating in offenders the skills that yield civil, productive conduct, encouraging inmates to make choices and assume responsibility by putting them in situations that are similar to real life in the community

parens patriae: means "parents of the nation," established in 1601 to allow officials to take change of delinquent children and place them in poorhouses or orphanages to gain control of them; in more modern times, this doctrine was expanded as the basis for juvenile court and correctional systems to take responsibility for educating and nurturing delinquents, with an emphasis on reform and rehabilitation

parenting programs: prison programs to assist inmates to improve their parenting skills, even while in prison

Pargo v. Elliott: the 1985 Eighth Circuit Court case that allowed that differences in programs between male and female prisons does not necessarily violate the equal protection clause of the Constitution

parole guidelines: similar to sentencing guidelines, these use predictive factors to determine the offenders' risk to the community and chance for success; guidelines prescribe a presumptive time to be served based on the seriousness of the crime and the factors predictive of success for each inmate

parole: the conditional release of inmates by a parole board prior to the expiration of their sentence

pass system: a form of inmate movement in which an inmate is issued a pass by the work or program supervisor to go to a scheduled appointment

pedophile: someone who is sexually attracted to and molests children

Pell grants: grants for disadvantaged individuals used to cover tuition costs for college courses

penal code: a legislative authorization to provide a specific range of punishment for a specific crime

penitentiary: the term first used to describe secure facilities used to hold offenders serving a criminal sentence; still used today for some older or highly secure prisons

Pennsylvania system: the "separate and silent" system of prison operations emphasizing reformation and avoidance of criminal contamination

penology: the study of the use of punishment for criminal acts

Period of Transition: an era of prison operations in which enforced idleness, lack of professional programs, and excessive size and overcrowding of prisons resulted in an increase in prisoner discontent and prison riots

PIE Program: prison industry programs operated by private companies, with prison goods authorized to be sold on the open market if the program is certified as meeting certain conditions

plea bargaining: an agreement in which the defendant enters a plea of guilty in exchange for a reduced sentence in comparison to the sentence allowable for the charged offense

podular designs: a design of prisoner housing that provides common day room areas in the center of the unit to allow inmates to watch television or play table games, thereby getting out of their cells and reducing idleness and tension; podular designs make it easier for officers to view inmate activities in the cells and the dayrooms from one central location

policy audit: a review to ascertain whether broad agency policy is in place at the prison

policy implementation audit: a review to identify whether the procedures prescribed by policy are consistently being carried out by staff in their daily duties

positive contact: Face to face contact between a parole officer and an offender

Positive School: the belief that criminals do not have complete choice over their criminal actions and may commit acts that are beyond their control

post orders: the detailed description of the activities that are required to be performed throughout the day, often including the time they are to occur

precedents: decisions of the courts that come before and are therefore binding on later decisions of courts within the same jurisdiction

precipitating event: the "spark in the haystack" that sets off an inmate riot; usually must be preceded by the right environmental factors before a precipitating event creates the beginning of a prison riot

presentence investigation: a report used during the sentencing process that details the background of a convicted offender, to include criminal, social, education, employment, mental and physical health, and other significant factors

presumptive parole date: a date the inmate can expect to be released on parole, even if it is five or ten years later than the hearing

presumptive sentencing: a predetermined range of a minimum, average, and maximum term for a specific crime for a "typical" offender, with allowances for mitigating and aggravating circumstances to be considered

pretrial diversion: the suspension of criminal process while the offender is provided the chance to participate in treatment programs and avoid further criminal activity

preventive detention: detaining an accused person in jail to protect the community from crimes they are

likely to commit if set free pending trial

prison gangs: groups that form in prison and use the threat of violence to intimidate other inmates, control drug sales and prostitution, and gain power and influence

prisoner reentry: the process of an inmate leaving prison and returning to the community

prisonization: the process whereby inmates take on the folkways, mores, customs, and general culture of the penitentiary

prisons: institutions designed to house convicted, adult felons, serving a sentence of one year or more

private prison: any secure correctional facility, operated by other than a governmental agency and usually in a for-profit manner, which contracts with a governmental entity, to provide security, housing, and programs for adult offenders

probation: a prison sentence that is suspended on the condition that the offender follows certain prescribed rules and commits no further crimes

probation supervision: the role of a probation or parole officer in monitoring an offender's behavior through office visits; contacts with family, friends, bosses, or treatment providers; and visits to their home or place of work

profession: correctional agencies desire to be seen as a profession, and therefore create standards for ethical behavior, promote their community interests, and fashion a process for self-regulation

professional staff: prison or jail staff in a specialty area that requires distinctive training and education and may also require a professional certification to deliver a program

pseudofamilies: family organizations formed by female inmates who have roles of parents and children

Punishment: the correctional goal emphasizing the infliction of pain or suffering

racial disparity: the fact that minorities make up a greater percentage of those under correctional supervision than their makeup in the U.S. population

random count: counts done at any time, freezing inmates at whatever location they are in when the random count is called

random drug testing: randomly selecting a percentage of inmates to urine

test to see whether they have used any drug recently; a good deterrent to and source of data about prisoner drug use

rebirth in rehabilitation: a return to support for correctional treatment programs due to a realization that such programs can reduce recidivism by offenders

recidivism: the state of relapse that occurs when offenders complete their criminal punishment and then continue to commit crimes

referral: the formal processing of a juvenile offense through the juvenile court

Reformatory Era: an environment emphasizing reformation that expanded education and vocational programs and focused offenders' attention on their future

Refuge Period: a period from 1824 to 1899 when delinquent or neglected children were placed in a home for training and discipline

regional jail: a jail that serves more than one county and is overseen by a regional jail commission

regular caseload: caseload made up of standard probationers, requiring no special program or supervision

regular counts: the scheduled counting of inmates in their housing units to ensure that they are in the prison and have not escaped

rehabilitation: a programmed effort to alter the attitudes and behaviors of inmates and improve their likelihood of becoming law-abiding citizens

Rehabilitative Era: an era of prison management emphasizing the professionalizing of staff through recruitment and training and implementation of many self-improvement programs of prison management

reintegration: a belief that after offenders complete their treatment in prison they need transitional care, and that the community must be involved in their successful return to society

relationship culture: a culture based on how staff view and communicate with inmates; it falls into a continuum between authoritarian and reasoned

release on recognizance: release from jail based only on the defendant's promise to appear for further court procedures

reparation: the acts by offenders to repair the damage done from their crimes; it may be in the form of money, community service, or some other act seen as valuable to the victim

restitution: acts by which criminals make right or repay society or their victims for their wrongs

restorative justice: models of sentencing that shift the focus away from punishment of the offender and emphasize the victim by holding offenders accountable for the harm they caused and finding opportunities for them to repair the damage

Retribution: infliction of punishment on those who deserve to be punished

Retributive Era: an era of corrections that emphasizes holding offenders accountable for their acts and being tough on criminals while keeping them isolated from law-abiding citizens and making them serve "hard" time

Rhodes v. Chapman: a 1981 U.S. Supreme Court decision that overcrowded conditions resulting in two inmates housed in cells designed for one person was not a violation of the Eighth Amendment right of protection from cruel and unusual punishment

salient factor score: a point determination for each inmate for use with parole guidelines; the score is based on factors predictive of success on parole

Sanford Bates: the first director of the Federal Bureau of Prisons

second-generation jails: jails using podular housing designs and remote supervision; officers are located in a secure control room overlooking the cells and day room, with electronic controls to open and close individual cell doors

Section 1983: a section of the Civil Rights Act that prohibits any person acting under the color of any statute, ordinance, or regulation (color of law) from depriving another of his or her constitutional rights

security classification: to match offenders to institutions that have the physical security and staff resources to prevent escapes and control their behavior

security levels: levels such as minimum, low, medium, high, or maximum are distinct by such features such as the presence of towers and other perimeter security barriers (fences or walls) with detection devices, the type of housing for prisoners (cells or dormitory), and the staff-to-inmate ratio

segregated incarceration: a form of incarceration in which juveniles handled by adult courts are assigned to an adult prison, yet they are housed separately and placed in specialized educational, vocational, life skills training, and substance abuse programs that meet their age and needs

selective incapacitation: incarceration of high-risk offenders for preventative reasons based on what they are expected to do, not what they have already done

seniority: the use of the length of employment to determine an employee's assignment, days off, or other job-related functions

sentencing: the imposition of a criminal sanction by a judicial authority

sentencing guidelines: structured sentences, based on measures of offense severity and criminal history, to determine the length of the term of imprisonment

Sentencing Reform Act of 1984: the act of Congress that abolished parole, established determinate sentencing, and reduced the amount of good time available to federal offenders

services: the functions required to operate a prison such as budget and financial, maintenance, human resource management, food and health services, work programs, commissary function, and laundry operations

sex offenders: offenders who have committed a legally prohibited sexual act or in some states any offender who commits any crime that was statutorily defined as sexually motivated

sexual triangles: two inmates become jealous and fight over another one

shadow board: a light colored background with the outline of the tool painted on it, allowing for a missing tool or knife to be quickly noticed

sheriff: the elected official who oversees both policing activities within the county and the operation of the jail

shock incarceration/boot camp: alternatives to traditional incarceration that are operated similar to a military boot camp; offenders are required to have short hair, shine their shoes, wear uniforms, do extensive physical exercise, and perform hard physical labor; at times, these are complemented with education or

drug programming, but the major components of boot camps are military regimentation, discipline, exercise, and hard work

shock probation: a short period of imprisonment to "shock" the offender, with a return to the community within a few weeks to continue supervision on probation

short-term confinement: a sentence in a jail for one year or less

Sir Walter Crofton: the director of Irish prison system in 1854, who began to implement many of the ideas of Maconochie's work

slave-of-the-state doctrine: as decided in the 1871 decision of *Ruffin v. the Commonwealth of Virginia*, that held inmates were slaves of the state and had no rights that were not granted them by the state

special caseload: caseload is made up of offenders with a particular type of problem, such as substance abuse, mental illness, or a history of sex offenses

special conditions of probation: conditions of probation tailored to meet the needs for a particular offender; they can be imposed to meet the specific risks or needs of an individual offender

special emergency response team: an emergency team trained in the use of lethal force for when all else fails to resolve an emergency situation

special housing unit: a temporary housing assignment for inmates who present a danger to the security of the prison, need protection from other inmates, or are being punished for violating prison rules

special offenders: offenders whose circumstances, conditions, or behaviors require management or treatment outside of the normal approach to supervision

specific deterrence: the effect of punishment on an individual offender that prevents that person from committing future crimes

split sentence: a combination of a short jail sentence and then return to the community on probation

square johns: inmates who are usually first-time offenders and have more identification with "straight" society and norms of the noncriminals

staff diversity: the representation of a wide variety (in gender, race, and ethnicity) of people working for a correctional agency

standard conditions of probation: conditions that must be followed by every probationer

stand-up count: the most formal count of the day, at which inmates must stand at their cell door or by their dormitory bed to be counted and matched to the number of inmates assigned to each housing area

state-use system: only allowing prison-made goods to be sold to and used by the state and federal government agencies

status offense: an activity that is considered a crime only because the offender is under the age of 18 and would not be a crime if committed by an adult; includes acts such as running away from home, ungovernability, truancy, or underage drinking

straight adult incarceration: a form of incarceration in which juveniles handled by adult courts are placed in adult prisons with no separate housing or differentiation in programming or job assignments

street crimes: traditional reference to crimes with little sophistication required, such as murder, robbery, burglary, assault, and theft

substance abuse programs: programs for offenders to reduce their likelihood of further abuse of alcohol or drugs

suicide prevention programs: jail and prison programs that include early detection of suicide risks, staff education to recognize signs of potential suicide, and procedures for managing inmates that are now suicidal

suicide watch: management of suicidal inmates who are placed in a specially designed cell and have constant supervision

supermax prisons: either freestanding or distinct units within other prisons that provide for the management and secure control of inmates designated as violent or seriously disruptive in other prisons

superpredator: a term created by DiIulio to describe a generation of violent youths who practiced almost indiscriminant violence on the streets

supervised mandatory release: a type of release in which inmates serve a determinate sentence and are then released, but with a period of supervision to follow

supervised pretrial release programs: supervision of offenders released on their own recognizance, similar to supervision while on probation

surety: a person who is legally liable for the conduct of another; someone who guarantees the accused person's appearance in court

surveillance style of supervision: a style of supervising community offenders that places emphasis on monitoring and enforcing compliance with the rules or supervision and the detection of violations leading to revocation and return to custody

technical violations: violations of conditions of community supervision, without commission of a new crime

test of proportionality: the result of the 1983 case of *Solem v. Helm*; a test used to guide sentencing based on the gravity of the offense and consistency of the severity of punishment

The GEO Group, Inc.: a private correctional company headquartered in Florida that operates fifty-one correctional facilities in the United States.

thieves: inmates who have adopted a career of crime and are doing their prison time until they can get out and hit the "big score"

third-generation jails: jail designs without remote control centers, in which correctional officers are located in the housing unit in direct contact with inmates

Three Penitentiary Act: the 1891 act of Congress that authorized the construction of the first three federal prisons

three-strikes laws: a legislative mandate that judges sentence third-time felons to extremely long or life prison sentences

ticket of leave: a form of release used by Maconochie; once prisoners earning the required level of marks, they received a conditional pardon and were released to the community

total institution: Goffman's concept of a setting isolating people from the rest of society and unnecessarily manipulating them through the actions of the administrative staff

totality-of-conditions test: a test created in *Pugh v. Locke* that examines the aggregate of circumstances in a prison to determine whether cruel and unusual conditions exist

"tough on crime": an attitude that criminals should be severely punished for their wrongdoings, and long prison sentences are the most effective criminal sanction

transactional leaders: traditional authorities within an organization who were involved in exchange relationships between leaders and followers; they provided answers and direction for any issue the agency confronted

transformational leaders: organizational leadership based on principles, while motivating staff to jointly address challenges and find solutions to new problems

transportation: used in England during the seventeenth and eighteenth centuries to remove criminals from society by sending them to British colonies such as America

treatment: the creation of an environment and provision of rehabilitative programs that encourage inmates to accept responsibility and to address personal disorders that make success in the community more difficult

truth in sentencing: requires completion of 85 percent of the sentence before prisoners are eligible for release

unconditional mandatory release: a type of release in which inmates serve the full portion of their sentence and have no supervision after release from prison

uniformed staff: those prison or jail staff who work in the security or custody department and are responsible for the implementation of security policies and procedures

unit management: organizing a prison into smaller components by decentralizing the authority to manage the inmate population while making staff more accessible to inmates

unit manager: the staff person who is in charge of the unit, including housing, security, and treatment issues

victim compensation: offenders repay their victims directly for their losses and harm caused by the offense

victims' movement: the criminal justice system's recognition that victims should be involved in the process of sentencing criminals

violation: Failure to follow conditions of parole supervision

vocational training: specific training in a trade area to prepare students to work in that trade

waiver to adult courts: because of the serious nature of a juvenile offender's crime, statutory exceptions were granted to allow the movement from juvenile to adult courts for criminal processing

Walnut Street Jail: the first penitentiary in the United States

War on Drugs: a Reagan initiative to reduce the availability and dependence on illicit drugs through interdiction, criminal sanctions, and treatment

warden: the chief executive officer of a prison, responsible for the day-to-day operations

work call: the time when inmates move to their assigned jobs or programs assignments

Zebulon R. Brockway: a leading U.S. penologist in the mid-1800s who was a proponent of adopting the Irish system in the United States and who became the first superintendent of the Elmira Reformatory

Endnotes

Chapter 1

1. Douglas C. Eadie, "Strategic Management by Design," in *Strategic Planning for Local Government: A Handbook for Officials and Citizens,* edited by Roger L. Kemp (Jefferson, N.C.: McFarland, 1993), p. 85.

2. Adapted from the Bureau of Justice Statistics, *Sourcebook of Criminal Justice Statistics,* 2001 (Washington, D.C.: U.S. Department of Justice, 2003); and Matthew R. Durose and Patrick A. Langan, *Felony Sentences in State Courts, 2000* (Washington, D.C.: U.S. Department of Justice, Bureau of Justice Statistics, June 2003).

3. Pew Center on the States, *1 in 100: Behind Bars in America,* 2008, p. 6.

4. Bureau of Justice Statistics, Direct Expenditures by Level of Government 1982–2006, http://www.ojp.usdoj.gov/bjs/glace/tables/exgovtab.htm (accessed March 29, 2009).

5. Bureau of Justice Statistics, *Sourcebook of Criminal Justice Statistics,* http://www.albany.edu/sourcebook/pdf/t6132007.pdf (accessed November 20, 2008).

6. Pew Center on the States, Public Safety Performance Project, *One in 31: The Long Reach of American Corrections,* March 2009, p. 11.

7. Lauren E. Glaze and Thomas P. Bonczar, *Probation and Parole in the United States, 2006.* (Washington, D.C.: U.S. Department of Justice, Bureau of Justice Statistics, 2007), p. 2.

8. Pew Center on the States, 2009, p. 12.

9. Camille Graham Camp and George M. Camp, *The 2002 Corrections Yearbook: Adult Corrections* (Middletown, CN: Criminal Justice Institute, 2000), pp. 76; Camp and Camp, 2001, p. 89; Camp and Camp, 2002, p. 89.

10. James J. Stephan, "Census of State and Federal Correctional Facilities, 2005," *National Prisoner Statistics Program,* (Washington, D.C.: U.S. Department of Justice, Bureau of Justice Statistics, October 2008), pp. 1 and 2.

11. Bureau of Justice Statistics, *Sourcebook of Criminal Justice Statistics, 1994,* (Washington, D.C.: US Department of Justice, 1995), p. 26.

12. Kristin Hughes, *Criminal Justice Expenditure Extracts, 2005, Sourcebook of Criminal Justice Statistics* (Washington, D.C.: U.S. Department of Justice, Bureau of Justice Statistics, 2005),Table 2.

13. Jody K. Spertzel, "A Correctional Career Guide," *Corrections Today* 55, no. 1 (1993), p. 37.

14. U.S. Department of Justice, Federal Bureau of Investigation, *Crime in the United States 2007—Table 1,* http://www/fbi.gov/ucr/cius2007/data/table_01.html (accessed October 13, 2008).

15. Harry Elmer Barnes and Negley K. Teeters, *New Horizons in Criminology,* 3rd ed. (Upper Saddle River, N.J.: Prentice Hall, 1959), p. 322.

16. See Richard Louis Dugsdale, *The Jukes: A Study in Crime Pauperism, Disease, and Heredity,* 3rd ed. (New York: G. P. Putnam's Sons, 1985); and Henry Herbert Goddard, *The Kallikak Family: A Study in the Heredity of Feeblemindedness* (New York: Macmillan, 1912).

17. For more information, see Richard Herrnstein, "Crime File: Biology and Crime" (study guide, National Institute of Justice, n.d.).

18. For an overview of this issue, see Frank Schmalleger, *Criminology Today: An Integrative Introduction,* Fourth Edition, (Upper Saddle River,NJ, Pearson Prentice Hall, 2006), pp. 152–155.

19. Gabriel Tarde, *Penal Philosophy,* translated by R. Howell (Boston: Little, Brown, 1912). Originally published in 1890.

20. Randy Martin, Robert J. Mutchnick, and W. Timothy Austin, *Criminological Thought: Pioneers Past and Present* (New York: Macmillan, 1990).

21. A good overview of these theories of crime can be found in Hugh D. Barlow, *Criminal Justice in America* (Upper Saddle River, N.J.: Prentice Hall, 2000), pp. 84–117.

22. *The American Prison: From the Beginning . . . A Pictorial History* (College Park, Md.: American Correctional Association, 1983), p. 16.

23. Ibid., p. 24.

24. Barnes and Teeters, op. cit.

25. For the complete list of principles of the 1870 National Prison Association, see Enoch C. Wines, ed., *Transactions of the National Congress on Penitentiary and Reformatory Discipline* (Albany, N.Y.: Argus, 1871).

26. Margaret Cahalan, *Historical Corrections Statistics in the United States: 1850–1984* (Washington, D.C.: U.S. Department of Justice, 1986), p. 36.

27. *The American Prison,* p. 208.

28. Douglas Lipton, Robert Martinson, and Judith Wilks, *The Effectiveness of Correctional Treatment and What Works: A Survey of Treatment Evaluation Studies* (New York: Praeger, 1975).

29. *Bell v. Wolfish,* 441 U.S. 520 (1979).

30. *Solem v. Helm,* 463 U.S. 277 (1983).

31. Todd R. Clear and George R. Cole, *American Corrections,* 5th ed. (Belmont, Calif.: West/Wadsworth, 2000), p. 59.

32. Norman A. Carlson, Karen M. Hess, and Christine M. H. Orthmann, *Corrections in the 21st Century* (Belmont, Calif.: West/Wadsworth, 1999), p. 16.

33. Alfred Blumstein, "Selective Incapacitation as a Means of Crime Control," *American Behavioral Scientist* 27, no. 1 (1983): 93.

34. Ibid., p. 94.

35. Marianne W. Zawitz, ed., *Report to the Nation on Crime and Justice* (Washington, D.C.: U.S. Department of Justice, Bureau of Justice Statistics, 1983), p. 35.

36 Peter Greenwood, *Selective Incapacitation* (Santa Monica, Calif.: RAND Corporation, 1983).

37 Stuart Miller, Simon Dinitz, and John Conrad, *Careers of the Violent* (Lexington, Mass.: Lexington Books, 1982).

38 Michael R. Gottfredson and Travis Hirschi, "The Methodological Adequacy of Longitudinal Research on Crime," *Criminology* 25 (1987): 581–614.

39 Harry E. Allen and Clifford E. Simonsen, *Corrections in America: An Introduction,* 9th ed. (Upper Saddle River, N.J.: Prentice Hall, 2001), pp. 58–59.

40 Barbara A. Sims, "Questions of Corrections: Public Attitudes toward Prison and Community-Based Programs," *Corrections Management Quarterly* 1, no. 1 (1997): 55.

41 Robert M. Freeman, *Correctional Organization and Management: Public Policy Challenges, Behavior, and Structure* (Boston: Butterworth-Heinemann, 1999), p. 397.

42 Myron Steele and Thomas J. Quinn, "Restorative Justice: Including Victims in Community Corrections," in *The Dilemmas of Corrections: Contemporary Readings,* edited by Kenneth C. Haas and Geoffrey P. Alpert (Prospect Heights, Ill.: Waveland Press, 1995), p. 530.

Chapter 2

1 National Association of Pretrial Services Agencies Diversion Committee, *Pretrial Diversion Abstract: Information Report,* www.napsa.org/docs/divabst.htm (accessed September 25, 2002), pp. 2–3.

2 For a discussion of TASC, see "Treatment Alternatives to Street Crimes," *Bureau of Justice Assistance Fact Sheet* (Washington, D.C.: U.S. Department of Justice, 1992).

3 For a discussion of diversion and recidivism, see Dean J. Champion, *Probation, Parole, and Community Corrections,* 4th ed. (Upper Saddle River, N.J.: Prentice Hall, 2002), p.162.

4 National Association of Pretrial Services Agencies Diversion Committee, pp. 3–4.

5 *United States v. Salerno,* 481 U.S. 739 (1987).

6 William Rhodes, Raymond Hyatt, and Paul Scheiman, "Predicting Pretrial Misconduct with Drug Tests of Arrestees," *in Research in Brief* (Washington, D.C.: National Institute of Justice, 1996), pp. 1–6.

7 Wayne Welsh, "Changes in Arrest Policies as a Result of Court Orders Against County Jails," *Justice Quarterly* 10, no. 1 (March 1993).

8 Mary T. Phillips, "Bail, Detention, and Nonfelony Case Outcomes," *Research Brief,* no. 14, (New York: New York City Criminal Justice Agency, 2007).

9 For a good description of pretrial supervision programs, see Thomas J. Wolf, "What United States Pretrial Service Officers Do," *Federal Probation* 61, no. 1 (March 1997): 19–24.

10 In Phillips, op. cit., offense history and arrest charges explained 30 percent of the variations of conviction, and detention decisions explained an additional 6 percent.

11 *Williams v. New York,* 337 U.S. 241 (1949).

12 Robert C. Davis and Barbara E. Smith, "The Effects of Victim Impact Statements on Sentencing Decisions: A Test in an Urban Setting," *Justice Quarterly* 11, no. 3 (September 1994): 453–470.

13 As cited in Joan Petersilia, "Parole and *Prisoner* Reentry in the United States," in Prisons, edited by Michael Tonry and Joan Petersilia (Chicago: University of Chicago Press, 1999), pp. 489–490.

14 P. Ditton and D. J. Wilson, Truth in *Sentencing in State Prisons* (Washington, D.C.: U.S. Department of Justice, Bureau of Justice Statistics, 1999).

15 Timothy A. Hughes, Doris James Wilson, and Allen J. Beck, *Trends in State Parole,* 1990–2000 (Washington, D.C.: U.S. Department of Justice, Bureau of Justice Statistics, October 2001).

16 J. Furniss, "The Population Boom," *Corrections Today* 58, no. 1 (1996): 38–43.

17 Heather C. West and William J. Sabol, *Prison Inmates at Midyear 200—Statistical Tables,* (Washington, D.C.: U.S. Department of Justice, Bureau of Justice Statistics, March 2009), p. 2.

18 Bureau of Prisons, Website: www.bop.gov. (August 2005).

19 Walter J. Dickey, *Evaluating Mandatory Minimum Sentences* (Washington, D.C.: Campaign for Effective Crime Policy, 1993), p. 3.

20 For an overview of three-strikes laws across the country, see Walter J. Dickey and Pam Hollenhorst, "Three-Strikes Laws: Five Years Later," *Corrections Management Quarterly* 3, no. 3 (1999): 1–18.

21 For a good review of the three-strikes law in California, see Kevin E. Meehan, "California's Three-Strikes Law: The First Six Years," *Corrections Management Quarterly* 4, no. 4 (2000): 22–33.

22 F. Zimring, S. Kamin, and G. Hawkins, *Crime and Punishment in California* (Berkeley, Calif.: Institute of Government Studies Press, 1999), p. 83.

23 For a discussion of sentencing guidelines, see Bureau of Justice Statistics, *Report to the Nation on Crime and Justice,* 2nd ed. (Washington, D.C.: U.S. Department of Justice, 1988), p. 92.

24 Drug Court Programs Office, *Defining Drug Courts: The Key Components* (Washington, D.C.: U.S. Department of Justice, Office of Justice Programs, 1997).

25 John A. Fagan, "Do Criminal Sanctions Deter Drug Crimes?" in *Drugs and Crime: Evaluating Public Policy Initiatives,* edited by Doris L. MacKenzie and C. D. Uchida (Thousand Oaks, Calif.: Sage, 1994).

26 C. West Huddleston III, Karen Freeman-Wilson, Douglas B. Marlowe, and Aaron Roussell, "A National Report Card on Drug Courts and Other Problem Solving Court Programs in the United States," *Painting the Current Picture* 2, no. 1 (May 2008), Bureau of Justice Assistance.

27 Aubrey Fox and Greg Berman, "Going to Scale: A Conversation About the Future of Drug Courts" (National Criminal Justice Reference Service), *Court Review,* Fall 2002, 4.

28 John Roman, Wendy Townsend, and Avinash Singh Bhati, Recidivism Rates for Drug Court Graduates: *Nationally Based Estimates, Final Report* (Washington, D.C.: U.S. Department of Justice, National Institute of Justice, July 2003).

29 J. S. Goldkamp, "Miami's Treatment Drug Court for Felony Defendants: Some Implications of Assessment Findings," *Prison Journal* 74, no. 2 (1994): 110–157.

30 R. H. Peters and M. R. Murrin, "Effectiveness of Treatment-Based Drug Courts in Reducing Criminal Recidivism," *Criminal Justice and Behavior* 27, no. 1 (2000): 72–96.

31 *Adult Drug Courts: Evidence Indicates Recidivism Reduction and Mixed Results for Other Outcomes* (Washington, D.C.: U.S. Government Accountability Office, February 2005).

32 A good overview of the drug court model can be found in Shelly Johnson, Dana Jones Hubbard, and Edward J. Latessa, "Drug Courts and Treatment: Lessons to Be Learned from the 'What Works' Literature," *Corrections Management Quarterly* 4, no. 4 (2000): 70–77.

33 Henry J. Steadman, Susan Davidson, and Collie Brown, "Mental Health Courts," *Psychiatric Services* 52 (2001): 457.

34 Michael Thompson, Fred Osher, and Denise Tomasini-Joshi, *Improving Responses to People with Mental Illnesses:* The Essential Elements of a Mental Health Court (New York: Council of State Governments Justice Center, 2007).

35 Criminal Justice/Mental Health Consensus Project, *Mental Health Courts: A Primer for Policymakers and Practitioners* (New York: Council of State Governments Justice Center, 2008).

36 E. Trupin, H. Richards, D. Werthheimer, and C. Bruschi, *Seattle Municipal Court, Mental Health Court: Evaluation Report* (Seattle, Wash.: City of Seattle, 2001); H. A. Herinckx, S. C. Swart, S. M. Ama, C. D. Dolezal, and S. King, "Rearrest and Linkage to Mental Health Services among Clients of the Clark County Mental Health Court Program," *Psychiatric Services* 56 (2005): 853–857.

37 Dale E. McNiel and Renee L. Binder, "Effectiveness of a Mental Health Court in Reducing Criminal Recidivism and Violence," *American Journal of Psychiatry* 164 (2007): 1395–1403; Marlee E. Moore and Virginia Aldiage Hiday, "Mental Health Court Outcomes: A Comparison of Re-arrest and Re-arrest Severity between Mental Health Court and Traditional Court Participants," *Law and Human Behavior* 164 (2006): 659–674.

Chapter 3

1 Data from the Bureau of Justice Statistics indicates that a total of 4.2 million offenders were admitted to probation (2.3 million), prison (0.70 million), and parole (0.5 million) in 2006, whereas 9.8 million were admitted to jails. See *Sourcebook of Criminal Justice Statistics 2006* (Washington, D.C.: U.S. Government Printing Office, 1995), pp. 524, 533, 537, 575.

2 David Rothman, *The Discovery of the Asylum: Social Order and Disorder in the New Republic* (Boston: Little, Brown, 1971), p. 56.

3 The Reason Foundation, Annual Privatization Report 2008, *Public Safety*, p. 106.

4 There were 3,376 jails in the United States on June 30, 1999, according to Bureau of Justice Statistics, *Sourcebook of Criminal Justice Statistics, 2003* (Washington, D.C.: U.S. Department of Justice, 2003), p. 91.

5 Todd D. Minton and William J. Sabol, *Jail Inmates at Midyear 2008—Statistical Tables* (Washington, D.C.: U.S. Department of Justice, Bureau of Justice Statistics, March 2009), p. 2.

6 Bureau of Justice Statistics, *Key Facts at a Glance*, http://www.ojp.usdoj.gov/bjs/glance/tables/corr2tab.htm (accessed December 22, 2008); and Minton and Sabol, p. 2.

7 Paige M. Harrison and Allen J. Beck, *Prison and Jail Inmates at Midyear 2004 (*Washington, D.C.: U.S. Department of Justice, Bureau of Justice Statistics, April 2005), p. 2.

8 Minton and Sabol, p. 5.

9 Ibid., p. 5.

10 Criminal Justice Policy Council, *The State Jail System Today* (Austin, Texas: Criminal Justice Policy Council, March 2000).

11 D. Alan Henry, "The Impact of Financial Conditions of Release on Jail Populations," *Corrections Management Quarterly* 3, no. 2 (1999): 30.

12 James J. Stephan, *Census of Jails, 1999* (Washington, D.C.: U.S. Department of Justice, Bureau of Justice Statistics, August 2001), p. 4.

13 Minton and Sabol, p. 5.

14 Craig Perkins, James J. Stephan, and Allen J. Beck, *Jails and Jail Inmates, 1993–94* (Washington, D.C.: Bureau of Justice Statistics, U.S. Department of Justice, April 1995), p. 13.

15 Federal Bureau of Investigation, *Crime in the United States 2007*, Persons Arrested, U.S. Department of Justice, p. 1.

16 Doris J. James, *Profile of Jail Inmates, 2002*, Bureau of Justice Statistics Special Report NCJ 201932 (Washington, D.C.: U.S. Government Printing Office, July 2004).

17 Bureau of Justice Statistics, 2003, p. 342.

18 Tennessee Bureau of Investigation, *Crime in Tennessee 2007*, p. 6

19 Heather C. West and William J. Sabol, "Prisoners in 2007," *Bureau of Justice Statistics Bulletin* (Washington, D.C.: U.S. Department of Justice, December 2007), p. 25.

20 Ibid., p. 24.

21 R. Durose , P. A. Langan, *Felony Sentences in State Courts, 2004,* NCJ 215646 (Washington, D.C.: Bureau of Justice Statistics, July 2007).

22 West and Sabol, p. 3.

23 William J. Sabol, Todd D. Minton, and Paige M. Harrison, "Prison and Jail Inmates, Midyear 2006," *Bureau of Justice Statistics Bulletin* (Washington, D.C.: U.S. Department of Justice, January 2007), pp. 2–3.

24 William J. Sabol and Todd D. Minton, "Jail Inmates at Midyear 2007," *Bureau of Justice Statistics Bulletin* (Washington, D.C.: U.S. Department of Justice, June 2008), p. 3.

25 See James Austin, "An Overview of the Nation's Jails," *Corrections Management Quarterly* 3, no. 2 (1999): 3.

26 Michael O'Toole, "The Numbers Say They Are More Different Than Normally Assumed," *American Jails*, May–June 1997, p. 37.

27 During 2005, the Fayetteville, NC, County Jail had serious problems in this regard: five prisoners were released accidentally, resulting in significant negative press.

28 Vernon Fox, *Correctional Institutions* (Englewood Cliffs, N.J.: Prentice Hall, 1983), p. 61.

29 Tim Brennan, "Implementing Organization Change in Criminal Justice: Some Lessons from Jail Classification Systems," *Corrections Management Quarterly* 3, no. 2 (1999): 12.

30 Ibid., p. 14.

31 Bureau of Justice Statistics, Data Online, Expenditure and Employment, http://www.bjsdata.ojp.usdoj.gov/dataonline/Search/EandE/state_emp_next.cfm (accessed December 29, 2008).

32 Ibid., p. 10.

33 Sabol, Minton, and Harrison, p. 6.

34 Ibid., p. 26.

35 Ibid., p. 27.

36 Bureau of Justice Statistics, "Employment National Estimates," *BJS Data Online: Expenditures and Employment,* http://bjsdata.ojp.usdoj.gov/dataonline/Search/EandE/state_emp_next.cfm (accessed April 12, 2009).

37 Stephan, p. 25.

38 Ibid, p. 31.

39 As cited in Robert W. Duffy, "City's $101 Million Justice Center Is State-of-the-Art in Jail Design," *St. Louis Post-Dispatch,* November 17, 2002, p. B5.

40 G. J. Bayens, J. Williams, and J. O. Smykla, "Jail Type Makes a Difference: Evaluating the Transition from a Traditional to a Podular Direct Supervision Jail across Ten Years," *American Jails,* May/June 1997, pp. 33–39.

41 Bureau of Justice Statistics Correctional Surveys, *Correctional Populations in the United States* and *Prison and Jail Inmates at Midyear* (Washington, D.C.: U.S. Department of Justice, various years).

42 Darrell Gilliard, *Prison and Jail Inmates at Midyear 1998* (Washington, D.C.: U.S. Department of Justice, 1999), p. 7.

43 Minton and Sabol, p. 3.

44 Harrison and Beck; and Minton and Sabol, p. 3.

45 Minton and Sabol, p. 7.

46 For a good overview of the issues regarding privatization, see Charles Logan, *Private Prisons: Cons and Pros* (New York: McGraw-Hill, 1996).

47 Stephan, p. 6.

48 *Bell v. Wolfish,* U.S. 520 (1979).

49 Stephan, p. 5.

50 "Prisons Replace Hospitals for the Nation's Mentally Ill," *New York Times,* March 5, 1998, p. A26.

51 William M. DiMascio, *Seeking Justice: Crime and Punishment in America* (New York: Edna McConnell Clark Foundation, 1997), p. 22.

52 Doris J. James and Lauren E. Glaze, *Mental Health Problems of Prison and Jail Inmates* (Washington, D.C.: U.S. Department of Justice, Bureau of Justice Statistics, September 2006), p. 1.

53 Ibid., p. 10.

54 Christopher J. Mumola, *Suicide and Homicide in State Prisons and Local Jails* (Washington, D.C.: U.S. Department of Justice, Bureau of Justice Statistics, August 2005), p. 1.

55 Ibid., p. 8.

56 Ibid., p. 1.

Chapter 4

1 David Dressler, *Practice of Probation and Parole* (New York: Columbia University Press, 1962).

2 Ibid., p. 18.

3 Joan Petersilia, *Reforming Probation and Parole in the 21st Century* (Lanham, Md.: American Correctional Association, 2002), p. 20.

4 Dressler, op. cit.

5 Lauren E. Glaze and Thomas P. Bonczar, *Probation and Parole in the United States,* 2007 Statistical Tables (Washington, D.C.: U.S. Department of Justice, December 2008), p. 1.

6 Comptroller General of the United States, *State and County Probation: Systems in Crisis, Report to the Congress of the United States* (Washington, D.C.: U.S. Government Printing Office, 1976.)

7 Glaze and Bonczar, pp. 1–3.

8 Richard P. Seiter and Angela West, "Supervision Styles in Probation and Parole: An Analysis of Activities," *Journal of Offender Rehabilitation* (forthcoming).

9 Camille Graham Camp and George M. Camp, *The 2002 Corrections Yearbook: Adult Corrections* (Middletown, Conn.: Criminal Justice Institute, 2003), p. 214.

10 Ibid., p. 191.

11 Paula M. Ditton, *Mental Health and Treatment of Inmates and Probationers* (Washington, D.C.: U.S. Department of Justice, Bureau of Justice Statistics, 1999).

12 Jennifer Eno Louden, Jennifer L. Skeem, Jacqueline Camp, and Elizabeth Christenson, "Supervising Probationers with Mental Disorder: How do Agencies Respond to Violations?," *Criminal Justice and Behavior* 35, no. 7 (July 2008): 832–847.

13 Camp and Camp, p. 191.

14 Peter Finn and Sarah Kuck, "Stress among Probation and Parole Officers and What Can Be Done About It," *NIJ Research for Practice* (Washington, D.C.: U.S. Department of Justice, June 2005).

15 Lauren E. Glaze and Thomas P. Bonczar, "Probation and Parole in the United States, 2006," *Bureau of Justice Statistics Bulletin* (Washington, D.C.: U.S. Department of Justice, December 2007), p. 2.

16 *Bearden v. Georgia,* 461 U.S. 660 (1983).

17 *United States v. Birnbaum,* 421 F.2d 993 (1970).

18 *Mempa v. Rhay,* 389 U.S. 128 (1967).

19 *Morrissey v. Brewer,* 408 U.S. 271 (1972).

20 *Gagnon v. Scarpelli,* 411 U.S. 778 (1973).

21 R. I. Cohen, *Probation and Parole Violators in State Prison, 1991* (Washington, D.C.: U.S. Department of Justice, 1995), p. 2.

22 Calculated from Glaze and Bonczar (December 2007), p. 2.

23 *Bureau of Justice Statistics National Update* (Washington, D.C.: U.S. Department of Justice, 1994), p. 10.

24 Joan R. Petersilia, Susan Turner, James Kahan, and Joyce Peterson, Executive Summary of *Granting Felons Probation: Public Risks and Alternatives* (Santa Monica, Calif.: RAND, 1985), p. 1.

25 Glaze and Bonczar (December 2007), p. 2.

26 Todd Clear and Anthony Braga, "Community Corrections," in *Crime,* edited by James Q. Wilson and Joan R. Petersilia (San Francisco, Calif.: Institute for Contemporary Studies, 1995), pp. 421–444.

27 Patrick Langan and Mark A. Cunniff, *Recidivism of Felons on Probation, 1986–89* (Washington, D.C.: U.S. Department of Justice, Bureau of Justice Statistics, 1995).

28 Michael Geerken and Hennessey D. Hayes, "Probation and Parole: Public Risk and the Future of Incarceration Alternatives," *Criminology* 31, no. 4 (1993): 549–564.

29 Joan R. Petersilia and Susan Turner, *Prison versus Probation in California: Implications for Crime and Offender Recidivism* (Santa Monica, Calif.: RAND, 1986), pp. 27–33.

30 Camp and Camp, p. 86.

31 The Pew Center on the States, Public Safety Project, *One in 31: The Long Reach of American Corrections* (March 2009), p. 12.

32 Ibid.

33 Daniel Glaser, *The Effectiveness of a Prison and Parole System* (New York: Bobbs-Merrill, 1964), p. 423.

34 P. T. Alberty, *A Study of the Relationship between Styles of Supervision and Parole Officer's Violations Rate* (master's thesis, University of Missouri, 1969), p. 3.

35 David I. Rothman, *Conscience and Convenience: The Asylum and Its Alternatives in Progressive America* (Boston: Little, Brown, 1980).

36 Edward E. Rhine, "Probation and Parole Supervision: In Need of a New Narrative," *Corrections Management Quarterly* 1, no. 2 (1999): 72.

37 Dan Richard Beto, Ronald P. Corbett, Jr., and John J. DiIulio, Jr., "Getting Serious about Probation and the Crime Problem," *Corrections Management Quarterly* 4, no. 2 (2000): 3.

38 Kevin Johnson, "To Save Money on Prisons, States Take a Softer Stance," *USA Today*, March 18, 2009, p. 1.

39 Reinventing Probation Council, "'Broken Windows' Probation: The Next Step in Fighting Crime," *Civil Report* 7 (1999): 2.

40 General Accounting Office, *State and County Probation Systems in Crisis* (Washington, D.C.: U.S. Government Printing Office, 1976), p. 53.

41 Vincent O'Leary and Todd R. Clear, *Directions for Community Corrections in the 1990s* (Washington, D.C.: U.S. Department of Justice, June 1984), p. 11.

42 The Pew Center on the States, *One in 31: The Long Reach of American Corrections* (Washington, D.C.: The Pew Charitable Trusts, March 2009), p. 2.

43 Camp and Camp, p. 190.

44 Ibid., p. 195.

45 Joan Petersilia and Susan Turner, "Intensive Probation and Parole," in *Crime and Justice: An Annual Review of Research*, edited by Michael Tonry (Chicago: University of Chicago Press, 1993).

46 Paul Gendreau and Tracy Little, *A Meta-Analysis of the Effectiveness of Sanctions on Offender Recidivism* (University of New Brunswick, 1993).

47 A good description of the current use of electronic monitoring can be seen in Randy R. Gainey and Brian K. Payne, "Understanding the Experience of House Arrest with Electronic Monitoring: An Analysis of Quantitative and Qualitative Data," *International Journal of Offender Therapy and Comparative Criminology* 44, no. 1 (February 2000): 84–96.

48 Camp and Camp, pp. 191, 206.

49 Michael Brown and Preston Elrod, "Electronic House Arrest: An Examination of Citizen Attitudes," *Crime and Delinquency* 41, no. 3 (1995): 332–346.

50 A. W. Cohn, L. Biondi, L. C. Flaim, M. Paskowski, and S. Cohn, "Evaluating Electronic Monitoring Programs," *Alternatives to Incarceration* 3, no. 1 (January-February 1997): 16–24.

51 Voncile Gowdy, *Intermediate Sanctions* (Washington, D.C.: U.S. Department of Justice, 1993), pp. 6–7.

52 Pierre du Pont, *Expanding Sentencing Options: A Governor's Perspective* (Washington, D.C.: U.S. National Institute of Justice, 1985).

53 The Pew Center (March 2009), p. 2.

54 Ibid., p. 145.

55 James J. Stephan, "Census of State and Federal Correctional Facilities, 2005," *National Prisoner Statistics Program*, (Washington, D.C.: US Department of Justice, October 2008), p. 2.

56 Bureau of Justice Statistics, Key Facts at a Glance, *Correctional Populations*, http://www.ojp.usdoj.gov/bjs/glance/tables/corr2tab.htm (accessed April 11, 2009).

57 California Department of Justice, *Crime and Delinquency in California, 2001* (Sacramento: California Department of Justice, 2001).

58 D. MacKenzie and C. Souryal, "Multisite Evaluation of Shock Incarceration," in *National Institute of Justice: Research Report* (Washington, D.C.: U.S. Department of Justice, 1994).

59 Camp and Camp, pp. 106, 132.

60 For an overview of evaluations of correctional boot camps, see Jeanne B. Stinchcomb, "Recovering from the Shocking Reality of Shock Incarceration—What Correctional Administrators Can Learn from Boot Camp Failures," *Corrections Management Quarterly* 3, no. 4 (1999): 43–52.

61 U.S. General Accounting Office, *Prison Boot Camps: Short-Term Prison Costs Reduced, but Long-Term Impact Uncertain* (Washington, D.C.: U.S. Government Printing Office, 1993).

62 MacKenzie and Souryal, p. 28.

63 Gennaro Vito, "Developments in Shock Probation: A Review of Research Findings and Policy Implications," *Federal Probation* 50, no. 1 (1985): 23–25.

64 Edward J. Latessa and Harry E. Allen, *Corrections in the Community*, 2nd ed. (Cincinnati, Ohio: Anderson, 1999), pp. 403–404.

65 Joan Petersilia, "A Decade of Experimenting with Intermediate Sanctions: What Have We Learned?" *Corrections Management Quarterly* 3, no. 4 (1999): 23–24.

66 Benedict Carey, "Drug Rehabilitation or Revolving Door?" *New York Times*, December 23, 2008, p. D4.

67 Ibid.

Chapter 5

1 President's Commission on Law Enforcement and Administration of Justice, *The Challenge of Crime in a Free Society* (Washington, D.C.: U.S. Government Printing Office, 1967), p. 165.

2 Ibid.

3 David Shichor, *Punishment for Profit* (Thousand Oaks, Calif.: Sage, 1995), p. 9.

4 Pete Wittenberg, "Power, Influence, and the Development of Correctional Policy," *Federal Probation* 60, no. 2 (1996): 46.

5 Heather C. West and William J. Sabol, *Prison Inmates at Midyear 2008—Statistical Tables,* (Washington, D.C.: U.S. Department of Justice, Bureau of Justice Statistics, March 2009), p. 1.

6 *Rhodes v. Chapman,* 29 Cr. L. Rptr. 3061 (1981).

7 *Bruscino v. Carlson* (Civil Action No. 84-4320), D.C.S.D. III (1987).

8 Cisco Lassiter, "Roboprison," *Mother Jones* (September/October 1990): 76.

9 Douglas C. Eadie, "Strategic Management by Design," in *Strategic Planning for Local Government: A Handbook for Officials and Citizens*, edited by Roger L. Kemp (Jefferson, N.C.: McFarland, 1993), p. 85.

10 Federal Bureau of Prisons website, www.bop.gov (accessed October 2005).

11 Camille Graham Camp and George M. Camp, *The 2002 Corrections Yearbook: Adult Systems* (Middletown, Conn.: Criminal Justice Institute, 2003), pp. 151, 75.

12 Ibid.

13 Sourcebook of Criminal Justice Statistics Online, *Table 2.36. 2008, Attitudes toward Level of Crime in Own Area*, http://wwwalbany.edu/sourcebook/pdf/t2362008.pdf (accessed March 5, 2009).

14 Camille Graham Camp and George M. Camp, *The Corrections Yearbook, 2002* (Middletown, Conn.: Criminal Justice Institute, 2003), p. 39.

15 Michael Tonry, "Why Are U.S. Incarceration Rates So High?" *Crime and Delinquency* 45, no. 14 (October 1999): 445.

16 Bureau of Justice Statistics, *National Prisoner Statistics* (Washington, D.C.: U.S. Department of Justice, 1977).

17 Ibid.

18 P. Ditton and D. J. Wilson, *Truth in Sentencing in State Prisons* (Washington, D.C.: U.S. Department of Justice, Bureau of Justice Statistics, NCJ 170032, January 1999).

19 Edward E. Rhine, "Probation and Parole Supervision: In Need of a New Narrative," *Corrections Quarterly* 1, no. 2 (1997): 73.

20 Heather C. West and William J. Sabol, *Prisoners in 2007* (Washington, D.C.: U.S. Department of Justice, Bureau of Justice Statistics, December 2008), p. 3.

21 Camp and Camp, *2002 Corrections Yearbook*, pp. 198–199.

22 Bureau of Justice Statistics, *Drugs, Crime and the Justice System* (Washington, D.C.: National Institute of Justice, 1993), p. 2.

23 Office of National Drug Control Policy, *National Drug Control Strategy: FY 2005 Budget Summary* (Washington, D.C.: The White House, March 2004), p. 13; Office of *National Drug Control Policy, National Drug Control Strategy: FY 2003 Budget Summary* (Washington, D.C.: Executive Office of the President, 2003), pp. 10–11.

24 West and Sabol, *Prison Inmates at Midyear 2008*, p. 2.

25 Ibid.

26 Ibid.

27 Ibid., p. 8.

28 Ibid.

29 Camille Graham Camp and George M. Camp, *The 2002 Corrections Yearbook: Adult Systems* (Middletown, Conn.: Criminal Justice Institute, 2003), pp. 82–83, 84, 97, 98, 118.

30 James J. Stephan, "Census of State and Federal Correctional Facilities, 2005," *National Prisoner Statistics Program*, (Washington, D.C.: U.S. Department of Justice, Ocober 2008), pp. 1–2.

31 U.S. Department of Justice, Bureau of Justice Statistics, Key Facts at a Glance, *Direct Expenditures by Criminal Justice Function, 1982–2006*.

32 James J. Stephan, *Census of State and Federal Correctional Facilities, 2005* (Washington, D.C.: U.S. Department of Justice, Bureau of Justice Statistics, October 2008), pp. 1–2.

33 Ibid., p. 7.

34 This act was officially known as "An Act for the Erection of United States Prisons and for the Imprisonment of United States Prisoners, and for Other Purposes."

35 The U.S. Penitentiary in Leavenworth was built with convict labor, from inmates housed at the U.S. Disciplinary Barracks for Military Prisoners in Leavenworth, and took several years to complete. It was finally finished in 1928, but it housed inmates shortly after the beginning of the twentieth century.

36 Federal Prison System, *The Bureau in Brief*, www.bop.gov/ (accessed April 2002).

37 Harry E. Allen and Clifford E. Simonsen, *Corrections in America: An Introduction*, 8th ed. (Upper Saddle River, N.J.: Prentice Hall, 1998), p. 538.

38 West and Sabol, *Prisoners in 2007*, p. 2, and the Bureau of Prisons website at www.bop.gov, accessed on April 13, 2009.

39 Brian A. Reaves and Lynn M. Bauer, *Federal Law Enforcement Officers, 2002*, NCJ 199995 (Washington, D.C.: U.S. Department of Justice, Bureau of Justice Statistics Bulletin, August 2003), p. 1.

40 Ibid., p. 2.

41 West and Sabol, *Prison Inmates at Midyear 2008*, p. 2

42 Ibid.

43 Federal Bureau of Prisons website, www.bop.gov/ (accessed August 9, 2009).

44 Ibid.

45 *State of the Bureau of Prisons, 2007* (Washington, D.C.: U.S. Department of Justice, 2008), p. 26.

46 West and Sabol, *Prison Inmates at Midyear 2008*, p. 2.

47 Ibid., p. 3.

48 Stephan, *Census of State and Federal Correctional Facilities, 2005*, Appendix Table 1.

49 Chase Riveland, "The Correctional Leader and Public Policy Skills," *Corrections Management Quarterly* 1, no. 3 (1997): 23.

50 Camp and Camp, *2002 Corrections Yearbook*, p. 5.

51 West and Sabol, *Prison Inmates at Midyear 2008*, p. 7.

52 West and Sabol, *Prisoners in 2007*, p. 3.

53 Matthew R. Durose and Patrick A. Langan, *Felony Sentences in State Courts, 2004*, (Washington, D.C.: U.S. Department of Justice, Bureau of Justice Statistics, July 2007), p. 1.

54 West and Sabol, (December 2008), p. 22.

55 Allen Beck and Darrell Gilliard, *Prisoners in 1994* (Washington, D.C.: U.S. Department of Justice, 1995), p. 10.

56 West and Sabol, *Prisoners in 2007*, p. 22.

57 West and Sabol, *Prison Inmates at Midyear 2008*, p. 2.

58 Stephan, *Census of State and Federal Correctional Facilities, 2005*, Appendix Table 4.

59 Ibid.

60 Ibid., p. 4.

61 The remainder were pending charges or disposition. West and Sabol, *Prisoners in 2007*, p. 26.

62 Harrison and Beck, *Prisoners in 2004*, p. 11.

63 West and Sabol, *Prisoners in 2007*, p. 26.

64 Harry Allen, Evelyn Parks, Eric Carlson, and Richard Seiter, *Program Models, Halfway Houses* (Washington, D.C.: U.S. Department of Justice, 1978).

65 Edmund R. McGarrell and Timothy Flanagan, *Sourcebook of Criminal Justice Statistics, 1984* (Washington, D.C.: U.S. Department of Justice, 1985).

66 Michael Welch, *Corrections: A Critical Approach* (New York: McGraw-Hill, 1996), p. 416.

67 Charles Logan, *Private Prisons: Cons and Pros* (New York: Oxford University Press, 1990), p. 20.

68 West and Sabol, *Prison Inmates at Midyear 2008*, p. 12.

69 Stephan, *Census of State and Federal Correctional Facilities*, 2005.

70 Voncile B. Gowdy, "Should We Privatize Our Prisons? The Pros and Cons," *Corrections Management Quarterly* 1, no. 2 (1997): 61.

Chapter 6

1 W. B. Taylor, "Alexander Maconochie and the Revolt against the Penitentiary," *Southern Journal of Justice* 3, no. 1 (1978): 18.

2 R. Hughes, *The Fatal Shore* (New York: Knopf, 1987), p. 468.

3 As cited in Norval Morris, *Maconochie's Gentlemen: The Story of Norfolk Island and the Roots of Modern Prison Reform* (New York: Oxford University Press, 2002), p. 156.

4 H. E. Barnes and N. D. Teeters, *New Horizons in Criminology* (Upper Saddle River, N.J.: Prentice Hall, 1959).

5 A. A. Bruce, *Parole and Indeterminate Sentences* (Springfield: Illinois Parole Board, 1928).

6 M. S. Sherrill, "Determinate Sentencing: History, Theory, Debate," *Corrections Magazine*, no. 3 (September 1977): 3–13.

7 E. Lindsey, "Historical Origins of the Sanction of Imprisonment for Serious Crimes," *Journal of Criminal Law and Criminology* 16, no. 1 (1925): 9–26.

8 David Dressler, *The Parole Chief* (New York: Viking Press, 1951).

9 Margaret Werner Cahalan, *Historical Corrections Statistics in the United States*, 1850–1984 (Washington, D.C.: U.S. Government Printing Office, 1986).

10 Edward J. Latessa and Harry E. Allen, *Corrections in the Community*, 2nd ed. (Cincinnati, Ohio: Anderson, 1999), p. 159.

11 Seymour Halleck, *The Politics of Therapy* (New York: Science House, 1971).

12 Norval Morris, *The Future of Imprisonment* (Chicago: University of Chicago Press, 1974).

13 John Irwin, "Adaptation to Being Corrected: Corrections from the Convict's Perspective," in *Sociology of Corrections*, edited by R. G. Legar and J. R. Stratton (New York: Wiley, 1977), pp. 276–300.

14 Howard Abadinsky, *Probation and Parole: Theory and Practice*, 8th ed. (Upper Saddle River, N.J.: Prentice Hall, 2001), p. 218.

15 Douglas Lipton, Robert Martinson, and Judith Wilks, *The Effectiveness of Correctional Treatment and What Works: A Survey of Treatment Evaluation Studies* (New York: Praeger, 1975).

16 David Fogel, *We Are the Living Proof* (Cincinnati, Ohio: Anderson, 1975).

17 Andrew von Hirsch and Kathleen J. Hanrahan, *Abolish Parole?* (Washington, D.C.: U.S. Government Printing Office, 1978).

18 Twentieth Century Task Force on Sentencing, *Fair and Certain Punishment* (New York: McGraw-Hill, 1976).

19 Bureau of Justice Statistics, *National Prisoner Statistics* (Washington, D.C.: U.S. Department of Justice, 1977).

20 Alvin Blumstein, "Prisons: A Policy Challenge," in *Crime: Public Policies for Crime Control*, edited by James Q. Wilson and Joan Petersilia (Oakland, Calif.: Institute for Contemporary Studies, 2002), pp. 451–452.

21 J. Furniss, "The Population Boom," Corrections Today 58, no. 1 (1996): 38–43.

22 Heather C. West and William J. Sabol, *Prison Inmates at Midyear 2008—Statistical Tables*, (Washington, D.C.: U.S. Department of Justice, Bureau of Justice Statistics, March 2009), p. 2.

23 Lauren E. Glaze and Thomas P. Bonczar, *Probation and Parole in the United States, 2006* (Washington, D.C.: U.S. Department of Justice, Bureau of Justice Statistics, December 2007), p. 6.

24 J. Monahan, *Predicting Violent Behavior: An Assessment of Clinical Techniques* (Beverly Hills, Calif.: Sage, 1981).

25 During the 1980s, several states were under federal court order to keep their prison population at less than full capacity. When the population grew to a certain point (perhaps 98 percent), an emergency release would be mandated, and the parole board could review all inmates within so many months of parole eligibility and release those most deserving and presenting the least community risk.

26 Glaze and Bonczar, *Probation and Parole*, p. 4.

27 Ibid., p. 6.

28 Ibid., p. 4.

29 *Greenholtz v. Inmates of the Nebraska Penal and Correctional Complex*, 99 S. Ct. 2100 (1979).

30 Edward E. Rhine, William R. Smith, and Ronald W. Jackson, *Paroling Authorities: Recent History and Current Practice* (Laurel, Md.: American Correctional Association, 1991), p. 54.

31 President's Commission on Law Enforcement and Administration of Justice, Task Force Report: Corrections (Washington, D.C.: U.S. Government Printing Office, 1967), p. 67.

32 Timothy A. Hughes, Doris James Wilson, and Allen J. Beck, *Trends in State Parole, 1990–2000* (Washington, D.C.: U.S. Department of Justice, Bureau of Justice Statistics, October 2001), p. 7.

33 Ohio Department of Rehabilitation and Correction, "APA Offender Classification," Policy Section 501, Number 28, February 15, 2001, p. 3.

34 Ibid., pp. 5–6.

35 Glaze and Bonczar, p. 4.

36 Camille Graham Camp and George M. Camp, *The 2002 Corrections Yearbook: Adult Systems* (Middletown, Conn.: Criminal Justice Institute), p. 191.

37 Glaze and Bonczar, *Probation and Parole*, p. 7.

38 Ibid., p. 3.

39 Ibid., p. 221.

40 Ibid., p. 225.

41 "Parole Officer Job Description, Career as a Parole Officer, Salary, Employment—Definition and Nature of the Work, Education and Training Requirements, Getting the Job," available at http://careers.stateuniversity.com/pages/728/Parole-Officer.html (accessed April 14, 2009).

42 *Morrissey v. Brewer*, 408 U.S. 471 (1972).

43 *Gagnon v. Scarpelli*, 411 U.S. 778 (1973).

44 Glaze and Bonczar, *Probation and Parole*, p. 7.

45 Ibid., p. 8.

46 Heather C. West and William J. Sabol, *Prisoners in 2007* (Washington, D.C.: U.S. Department of Justice, Bureau of Justice Statistics, December 2008), p. 3.

47 Patrick A. Langan and David J. Levin, "Recidivism of Prisoners Released in 1994," *Bureau of Justice Statistics Special Report* (Washington, D.C.: U.S. Department of Justice, June 2002), p. 1.

48 Howard R. Sacks and Charles H. Logan, "Does Parole Make a (Lasting) Difference?" in *Criminal Justice: Law and Politics*, 4th ed., edited by George F. Cole (Pacific Grove, Calif.: Brooks/Cole, 1984), pp. 362–378.

49 William J. Sabol, William P. Adams, Barbara Parthasarathy, and Yan Yuan, *Offenders Returning to Federal Prison, 1986–1997, Special Report* (Washington, D.C.: U.S. Department of Justice, Bureau of Justice Statistics, September 2000), p. 6.

50 Joan Petersilia, "When Prisoners Return to the Community: Political, Economic, and Social Consequences," *Corrections Management Quarterly* 5, no. 3 (2001): 4.

51 West and Sabol, *Prisoners in 2007*, p. 3.

52 Joan R. Petersilia, "The Collateral Consequences of Prisoner Reentry in California: Effects on Children, Public Health, and Community" (monograph, April 2000), p. 1. Also, Glaze and Bonczar, *Probation and Parole*, p. 26.

53 Marta Nelson, Perry Deess, and Charlotte Allen, "The First Month Out: Post–Incarceration Experiences in New York City," (monograph, the Vera Institute, September 1999).

54 G. G. Gaes, T. J. Flanagan, L. L. Motiuk, and L. Stewart, "Adult Correctional Treatment," in *Prisons*, edited by Michael Tonry and Joan Petersilia (Chicago: University of Chicago Press, 1999), pp. 361–426.

55 Charles M. Terry, "From C-Block to Academic: You Can't Get There from Here," in *Convict Criminology*, edited by Jeffrey Ian Ross and Stephen C. Richards (Belmont, Calif.: Wadsworth, 2003), p. 105.

56 P. Ditton and D. J. Wilson, *Truth in Sentencing in State Prisons* (Washington, D.C.: U.S. Department of Justice, Bureau of Justice Statistics, 1999).

57 Christopher J. Mumola, *Substance Abuse and Treatment, State and Federal Prisoners, 1997* (Washington, D.C.: U.S. Department of Justice, Bureau of Justice Statistics, 1999).

58 James J. Stephan, "Census of State and Federal Correctional Facilities, 2005," *Bureau of Justice Statistics: National Prisoner Statistics Program* (Washington, D.C.: U.S. Department of Justice, October 2008), p. 5.

59 Camp and Camp, *2002 Corrections Yearbook*, pp. 136–137.

60 Ibid., p. 119.

61 Ibid., p. 134.

62 Ibid., pp. 71, 146.

63 Camp and Camp, *2002 Corrections Yearbook*, p. 144.

64 Joan R. Petersilia, "Parole and Prisoner Reentry in the United States," in *Prisons*, edited by Michael Tonry and Joan Petersilia (Chicago: University of Chicago Press, 1999), pp. 479–529.

65 Lauren E. Glaze and Thomas P. Bonczar, *Probation and Parole in the United States, 2005*, (Washington, D.C.: U.S. Department of Justice, Bureau of Justice Statistics, November 2006), p. 8.

66 See Gwen Rubenstein and Debbi Mukamal, "Welfare and Housing—Denial of Benefits to Drug Offenders," in *Invisible Punishment: The Collateral Consequences of Mass Imprisonment*, edited by Marc Mauer and Meda Chesney-Lind (New York: New Press, 2002), pp. 37–58.

67 Donald Burman, "Families and Incarceration," in *Invisible Punishment: The Collateral Consequences of Mass Imprisonment*, edited by Marc Mauer and Meda Chesney-Lind (New York: New Press, 2002), p. 117.

68 Christopher J. Mumola, *Bureau of Justice Statistics Special Report: Incarcerated Parents and Their Children* (Washington, D.C.: U.S. Department of Justice, 2000).

69 S. Bushway and P. Reuter, "Labor Markets and Crime Risk Factors," in *Preventing Crime: What Works, What Doesn't, What's Promising*, edited by L. W. Sherman, D. Gottfredson, D. MacKenzie, J. Eck, P. Reuter, and S. Bushway (Washington, D.C.: U.S. Department of Justice, Office of Justice Programs, 1998).

70 Christopher Uggen and Jeremy Staff, "Work as a Turning Point for Criminal Offenders," *Corrections Management Quarterly* 5, no. 4 (2001): 1–16.

71 Nancy La Vigne, Elizabeth Davies, Tobi Palmer, and Robin Halberstadt, *Release Planning for Successful Reentry* (Washington, D.C.:Urban Institute Justice Policy Center, September 2008).

72 *The Report of the Re-Entry Policy Council*, The Justice Center, Council of State Governments, (New York, 2005).

73 In the Senate there were 33 cosponsors, including Senators Joseph Biden (D-DE), Arlen Specter (R-PA), Sam Brownback (R-KS), and Patrick Leahy (D-VT). In the House there were 92 cosponsors, including Representatives Danny Davis (D-IL), Chris Cannon (R-UT), John Conyers (D-MI), Lamar Smith (R-TX), Bobby Scott (D-VA), Randy Forbes (R-VA), Stephanie Tubbs Jones (D-OH), and James Sensenbrenner (R-WI).

74 Donald J. Farole, *Harlem Parole Reentry Court Evaluation: Implementation and Primary Impacts* (New York: Center for Court Innovation, 2003).

75 A good overview of these courts is available in Shadd Maruna and Thomas P. LeBel, "Welcome Home? Examining the 'Reentry Court' Concept from a Strengths-based Perspective," *Western Criminology Review* 4, no. 2 (2003): 91–107.

76 U.S. Department of Justice, "Survey of Inmates in State and Federal Correctional Facilities," (Ann Arbor, Mich.: Inter-University Consortium for Political and Social Research, 2004).

77 Bruce Western, *Punishment and Inequality in America*, Chapter 5 (New York: Russell Sage Foundation, 2006).

78 For a summary of the three evaluations, see Bruce Western, *From Prison to Work: A Proposal for a National Prisoner Reentry Program* (Washington, D.C.: The Brookings Institution, December 2008), pp. 10–11.

79 Richard P. Seiter and Karen R. Kadela, "Prisoner Reentry: What Works, What Doesn't, and What's Promising," *Crime and Delinquency* 49, no. 3 (April 2003): 360–388.

80 Washington Department of Corrections, *A Re-Entry Focused Correctional System* (Olympia, Wash.: Government Management, Accountability, and Performance Forum, November 2006).

81 Jeremy Travis, "But They All Come Back: Rethinking Prisoner Reentry," Corrections *Management Quarterly* 5, no. 3 (2001): 23–33.

82 Victoria C. Myers, currently Division Director of Human Services for the Missouri Department of Corrections, and formerly a member of the Missouri Parole Board, developed these scenarios.

Chapter 7

1 Heather C. West and William J. Sabol, *Prison Inmates at Midyear 2008—Statistical Tables* (Washington, D.C.: U.S. Department of Justice, Bureau of Justice Statistics, March 2009), p. 2.

2 Ibid., p. 11.

3 Lawrence A. Greenfeld and Tracy L. Snell, *Women Offenders* (Washington, D.C.: U.S. Department of Justice, Bureau of Justice Statistics, 1999), p. 6.

4 West and Sabol, p. 2; and Heather C. West and William J. Sabol, "Prisoners in 2007," *Bureau of Justice Statistics Bulletin* (Washington, D.C.: U.S. Department of Justice, December 2008), p. 3.

5 Lauren E. Glaze and Thomas P. Bonczar, *Probation and Parole in the United States, 2007 Statistical Tables* (Washington, D.C.: U.S. Department of Justice, December 2008), pp. 1–6.

6 West and Sabol, *Prison Inmates at Midyear* 2008, pp. 4–5.

7 Ibid., p. 2.

8 Ibid.

9 Ibid., p. 10.

10 Bureau of Justice Statistics Correctional Surveys (*National Probation Data Survey, National Prisoner Statistics, Survey of Jails, and National Parole Data Survey*) as presented in *Correctional Populations in the United States*, 1997 (Washington, D.C.: U.S. Department of Justice, 1998).

11 West and Sabol, *Prison Inmates at Midyear* 2008, p. 18.

12 Lauren E. Glaze and Seri Palla, *Probation and Parole in the United States*, 2004 (Washington, D.C.: U.S. Department of Justice, Bureau of Justice Statistics Bulletin, November 2005), p. 6.

13 The Pew Center on the States, Public Safety Performance Project, *One in 31: The Long Reach of American Corrections* (March 2009), p. 34.

14 National Urban League, State of Black America: Message to the President, *Executive Summary* (2009), p. 1.

15 William Wilbanks, *The Myth of a Racist Criminal Justice System* (Monterey, Calif.: Brooks/Cole, 1987), pp. 5, 6.

16 Uniform Crime Report, *Crime in the United States* 2007, Table 43 (Washington, D.C.: U.S. Department of Justice, Federal Bureau of Investigation).

17 J. M. Klofas, "Drugs and Justice: The Impact of Drugs on Criminal Justice in a Metropolitan Community," *Crime and Delinquency* 39, no. 2 (1993): 204.

18 West and Sabol, *Prisoners in* 2007, p. 19.

19 Camille Graham Camp and George M. Camp, *The Corrections Yearbook*, 1998 (Middletown, Conn.: Criminal Justice Institute, 1999), p. 25.

20 Kenneth Moritsugu, "Inmate Chronological Age versus Physical Age," in *Long-Term Confinement and the Aging Inmate Population* (Washington, D.C.: Federal Bureau of Prisons, 1990).

21 Kevin Strom, *Profile of State Prisoners under Age 18, 1985–1997*, NCJ 176989 (Washington, D.C.: U.S. Department of Justice, Bureau of Justice Statistics, February 2000), p. 1.

22 Paige M. Harrison and Jennifer C. Karberg, *Prisons and Jail Inmates at Midyear* 2004 (Washington, D.C.: U.S. Department of Justice, Bureau of Justice Statistics, April 2005), p. 5.

23 West and Sabol, *Prisoners in* 2007, p. 21.

24 Ibid.

25 Camp and Camp, *Corrections Yearbook*, 1998, p. 57.

26 Camille Graham Camp and George M. Camp, *Corrections Yearbook, Adult Corrections* 2002, (Middletown, CN: Criminal Justice Institute, 2003), p. 39.

27 Ibid., p. 41.

28 Bureau of Justice Statistics, *Sourcebook of Criminal Justice Statistics*, 2003 (Washington, D.C.: U.S. Department of Justice, 2004), p. 354.

29 West and Sabol, *Prison Inmates at Midyear* 2008, p. 2.

30 Lauren E. Glaze and Thomas P. Bonczar, *Probation and Parole in the United States, 2007 Statistical Tables* (Washington, D.C.: U.S. Department of Justice, Bureau of Justice Statistics, December 2008), pp. 1, 6.

31 Federal Bureau of Investigation, *Crime in the United States*, 2007 (Washington, D.C.: U.S. Department of Justice, 2007), Table 33.

32 West and Sabol, *Prisoners in* 2007, p. 22.

33 James J. Stephan, "Census of State and Federal Correctional Facilities, 2005," *National Prisoner Statistics Program* (Washington, D.C.: U.S. Department of Justice, October 2008), Appendix Table 11.

34 Peter M. Carlson, "Case Management/Unit Management," in *Prison and Jail Administration: Practice and Theory*, edited by Peter M. Carlson and Judith Simon Garrett (Gaithersburg, Md.: Aspen, 1999), p. 83.

35 Harold Williamson, *The Corrections Profession* (Newbury Park, Calif.: Sage, 1990), p. 137.

36 Federal Bureau of Investigation, *Crime in the United States*, 2007, Table 35.

37 Greenfeld and Snell, *Women Offenders*, p. 5.

38 Federal Bureau of Investigation, *Crime in the United States*, 2007, http:www.fbi.gov/ucr/cius2007/data/table_42.html (accessed April 2, 2009).

39 David E. Olson, Arthur J. Lurigio, and Manus Seng, "Comparison of Female and Male Probationers: Characteristics and Case Outcomes," *Women and Criminal Justice* 11, no. 4 (2000): 65–79.

40 Ibid.

41 West and Sabol, *Prisoners in* 2007, p. 21.

42 D. Steffensmeier, J. Kramer, and C. Streifel, "Gender and Imprisonment Decisions," *Criminology* 31, no. 3 (1993): 411–449.

43 Meda Chesney-Lind, "The Forgotten Offender, Women in Prison: From Partial Justice to Vengeful Equity," in *Exploring Corrections: A Book of Readings*, edited by Tara Gray (Boston: Allyn & Bacon, 2002), p. 8.

44 Reported in Greenfeld and Snell, *Women Offenders*, p. 11.

45 Ibid.

46 Allen J. Beck, *Prisoners in* 1998 (Washington, D.C.: U.S. Department of Justice, 1999).

47 West and Sabol, *Prison Inmates at Midyear* 2008, p. 2.

48 Ibid., p. 21.
49 Camp and Camp, *Corrections Yearbook*, 2002, p. 38.
50 Greenfeld and Snell, *Women Offenders*, pp. 1, 9.
51 Ibid.
52 Lauren E. Glaze and Laura M. Maruschak, *Parents in Prison and Their Minor Children* (Washington, D.C.: U.S. Department of Justice, Bureau of Justice Statistics, August, 2008), p. 3.
53 Ibid.
54 George Church, "The View from behind Bars," *Time* 22 (September 1990): 20–22.
55 Merry Morash, Timothy S. Bynum, and Barbara A. Koons, "Women Offenders: Programming Needs and Promising Approaches," *National Institute of Justice: Research in Brief* (August 1998): 7.
56 Glaze and Maruschak, *Parents in Prison*, pp. 3, 4, 16.
57 Phyllis Jo Baunach, *Mothers in Prison* (New Brunswick, N.J.: Transaction, 1984).
58 M. Moses, "The Girl Scouts Behind Bars Program: Keeping Incarcerated Mothers and Their Daughters Together," in *Maternal Ties: A Selection of Programs for Female Offenders*, edited by C. Blinn (Lanham, Md.: American Correctional Association, 1997), pp. 35–49.
59 Christopher C. Mumola and Jennifer C. Karberg, "Drug Use and Dependence, State and Federal Prisoners, 2004," *Bureau of Justice Statistics Special Report* (Washington, D.C.: U.S. Department of Justice, October 2006), p. 3.
60 Greenfeld and Snell, *Women Offenders*, p. 8.
61 Ibid.
62 Center for Substance Abuse Treatment, *Substance Abuse Treatment for Incarcerated Women Offenders: Guide to Promising Practices* (Rockville, Md.: Department of Health and Human Services, Public Health Service, 1997), p. 2.
63 Stephan, Appendix Table 19.
64 Camp and Camp, *Corrections Yearbook*, 2002, p. 136.
65 Jennifer C. Karberg and Doris J. James, *Substance Dependence, Abuse, and Treatment of Jail Inmates*, 2002 (Washington, D.C.: U.S. Department of Justice, Bureau of Justice Statistics Bulletin, July 2005), p. 10.
66 Bureau of Justice Statistics, *Substance Abuse and Treatment: State and Federal Prisons*, 1997 (Washington, D.C.: U.S. Department of Justice, 1999).
67 Chesney–Lind, *Exploring Corrections*, p. 11.
68 Jacqueline M. Moore, "Privatization of Inmate Health Care: A New Approach to an Old Problem," *Corrections Management Quarterly* 2, no. 2 (1998):46.
69 Ibid., p. 47.
70 Robert R. Ross and Elizabeth A. Fabiano, *Female Offenders: Correctional Afterthoughts* (Jefferson, N.C.: McFarland, 1986).
71 Greenfeld and Snell, *Women Offenders*, p. 8.
72 John D. Wooldredge and Kimberly Masters, "Confronting Problems Faced by Pregnant Inmates in State Prisons," *Crime and Delinquency* 39 (1993): 195–203.
73 Richard P. Seiter, *Correctional Administration: Integrating Theory and Practice* (Upper Saddle River, N.J.: Prentice Hall, 2002), p. 282.
74 Patricia Van Voorhis and Lois Presser, *Classification of Women Offenders: A National Assessment of Current Practices* (Washington, D.C.: U.S. Department of Justice, National Institute of Corrections, 2001).
75 *Barefield v. Leach*, No. 10282 (D. N.M., 1974), 196.
76 *Pargo v. Elliott*, 49 F.3d 1355 (8th Cir. 1995), 196.
77 Nicole H. Rafter, *Partial Justice: Women, Prison, and Social Control*, 2nd ed. (New Brunswick, N.J.: Transaction, 1990).

Chapter 8

1 Howard N. Snyder, Office of Juvenile Justice and Delinquency Prevention, *Juvenile Arrests 2006, OJJDP Bulletin* (November 2008), p. 3.
2 John J. Wilson and James C. Howell, *Comprehensive Strategy for Serious, Violent, and Chronic Juvenile Offenders: Program Summary* (Washington, D.C.: U.S. Department of Justice, Office of Juvenile Justice and Delinquency Prevention, 1993), p. 2.
3 Snyder, *Juvenile Arrests* 2006, p. 4.
4 Ibid., p. 5.
5 H. N. Snyder, M. Sickmund, and Y. Poe-Yamagata, *Juvenile Offenders and Victims: 1996 Update on Violence* (Washington, D.C.: U.S. Department of Justice, 1996), p. 21.
6 Alfred Blumstein, "Youth, Violence, Guns, and the Illicit-Drug Industry," *Journal of Criminal Law and Criminology* 86, no. 1 (1995): 14.
7 Snyder, *Juvenile Arrests* 2006, p. 4.
8 A description of the Refuge Period and other developments in the juvenile justice system can be found in Todd R. Clear and George F. Cole, *American Corrections*, 5th ed. (Belmont, Calif.: Wadsworth, 2000), pp. 395–399.
9 Howard N. Snyder and Melissa Sickmund, *Juvenile Offenders and Victims: 1999 National Report* (Washington, D.C.: U.S. Department of Justice, National Center for Juvenile Justice, September 1999), p. 86.
10 The Juvenile Justice and Delinquency Prevention Act of 1974 (Public Law 93–415) encouraged removing status offenders from the juvenile court system.
11 John J. Dilulio, Jr., "The Question of Black Crime," *Public Interest* (Fall 1994): 3–12.
12 Melissa Sickmund, *Juveniles in Court* (Washington, D.C.: U.S. Department of Justice, Office of Juvenile Justice and Delinquency Prevention, June 2003).
13 James A. Gondles, Jr., "Kids Are Kids, Not Adults," *Corrections Today* (June 1997): 3.
14 Melissa Sickmund, *Offenders in Juvenile Court, 1997* (Washington, D.C.: U.S. Department of Justice, Office of Juvenile Justice and Delinquency Prevention, October 2000), p. 6.
15 Charles Puzzanchera and Melissa Sickmund, *Juvenile Court Statistics 2005* (Washington, D.C.: National Center for Juvenile Justice, Office of Juvenile Justice and Delinquency Prevention, July 2008), p. 72.
16 Sickmund, *Juveniles in Court*, p. 5.
17 State of Missouri Department of Corrections website, www.doc.missouri.gov/overview (accessed April 2001).
18 State of Missouri Department of Social Services website, www.dss.mo.gov/dys (accessed April 2006).
19 Puzzanchera and Sickmund, p. 31.
20 Snyder and Sickmund, *Juvenile Offenders*, p. 97.
21 National Council on Crime and Delinquency, *Juvenile Justice Policy Statement* (San Francisco: NCCD, 1991).
22 Puzzanchera and Sickmund, p. 58.
23 Puzzanchera and Sickmund, p. 55.
24 Ibid.

25 Howard Snyder and Melissa Sickmund, *Juvenile Offenders and Victims: 2006 National Report* (Washington, D.C.: Office of Juvenile Justice and Delinquency Prevention, 2006), p. 197.

26 Ibid., p. 197.

27 Ibid.

28 Ibid.

29 Ibid.

30 James Austin, Kelly Dedel Johnson, and Ronald Weitzer, "Alternatives to the Secure Detention and Confinement of Juvenile Offenders," *Juvenile Justice Bulletin* (Washington, D.C.: Office of Juvenile Justice and Delinquency Prevention, 2005).

31 *Kent v. United States*, 383 U.S. 541, 86 S. Ct. 1045 (1966).

32 *In re Gault*, 387 U.S. 1, 87 S. Ct. 1428 (1967).

33 *In re Winship*, 397 U.S. 358, 90 S. Ct. 1068 (1970).

34 *McKeiver v. Pennsylvania,* 403 U.S. 528, 91 S. Ct. 1976 (1971).

35 *Breed v. Jones*, U.S. 519, 95 S. Ct. 1779 (1975).

36 *Fare v. Michael C.,* 442 U.S. 707 (1979).

37 *Schall v. Martin*, 467 U.S. 253, 104 S. Ct. 2403 (1984).

38 *Eddings v. Oklahoma*, 455 U.S. 104 (1982).

39 *Stanford v. Kentucky,* 492 U.S. 361 (1989).

40 In re Stanford, *123 S. Ct. 472 (2002).*

41 Quoted in Associated Press, "Supreme Court Appears One Vote Shy of Rejecting Death Penalty for Young Killers," *St. Louis Post Dispatch,* January 28, 2003, p. 2.

42 *Roper v. Simmons*, 000 U.S. 03-633 (2005).

43 Sarah R. Battin-Pearson, Terence P. Thornberry, J. David Hawkins, and Marvin D. Krohn, *Gang Membership, Delinquent Peers, and Delinquent Behavior* (Washington, D.C.: U.S. Department of Justice, Office of Juvenile Justice and Delinquency Prevention, October 1998), p. 1.

44 C. L. Maxson, K. J. Woods, and M. W. Klein, "Street Gang Migration: How Big a Threat," *National Institute of Justice Journal* 230 (February 1996): 26–31.

45 Arlen Egley, Jr., and Christina E. O'Donnell, *Highlights of the 2006 National Youth Gang Survey* (Washington, D.C.: U.S. Department of Justice, Office of Juvenile Justice and Delinquency Prevention, July 2008), p. 1.

46 Ibid.

47 Arlen Egley, Jr., James C. Howell, and Aline K. *Major, National Youth Gang Survey 1999–2001* (Washington, D.C.: U.S. Department of Justice, Office of Juvenile Justice and Delinquency Prevention, July 2006), p. 21.

48 For a description of how police organize to target the suppression of youth gang activity, see Vincent J. Webb and Charles Katz, "Policing Gangs in an Era of Community Policing," in *Policing Gangs and Youth Violence,* edited by Scott Decker (Belmont, Calif.: Thompson-Wadsworth, 2003), pp. 17–49.

49 Curtis C. VanderWaal, Duane C. McBride, Yvonne M. Terry-McElrath, and Holly VanBuren, *Breaking the Juvenile Drug-Crime Cycle: A Guide for Practitioners and Policymakers* (Washington, D.C.: U.S. Department of Justice, National Institute of Justice, May 2001), p. 2.

50 Shay Bilchik, "A Juvenile Justice System for the 21st Century," *Juvenile Justice Bulletin* (May 1998), p. 1.

Chapter 9

1 Howard N. Snyder, Melissa Sickmund, and Eileen Poe-Yamagata, *Juvenile Transfers to Criminal Courts in the 1990s: Lessons Learned from Four Studies* (Washington, D.C.: U.S. Department of Justice, Office of Juvenile Justice and Delinquency Prevention, August 2000), p. xi.

2 Patricia Griffin, Patricia Torbet, and Linda Szymanski, *Trying Juveniles as Adults in Criminal Courts: An Analysis of State Transfer Provisions* (Washington, D.C.: U.S. Department of Justice, Office of Juvenile Justice and Delinquency Prevention, December 1998), p. 1.

3 Melissa Sickmund, *Juveniles in Court* (Washington, D.C.: U.S. Department of Justice, Bureau of Justice Statistics, June 2003), p. 7.

4 Charles M. Puzzanchera and Melissa Sickmund, *Juvenile Court Statistics 2005* (Washington, D.C.: U.S. Department of Justice, National Center for Juvenile Justice, July 2008), p. 40.

5 Ibid.

6 Kevin J. Strom, *Profile of State Prisoners under Age 18, 1985–97* (Washington, D.C.: U.S. Department of Justice, Bureau of Justice Statistics, February 2000), p. 1.

7 Heather C. West and William J. Sabol, *Prison Inmates at Midyear 2008—Statistical Tables, National Prisoner Statistics* (Washington, D.C.: U.S. Department of Justice, March 2009), p. 20.

8 Ibid.

9 Paige M. Harrison and Jennifer C. Karberg, *Prison and Jail Inmates at Mid-Year 2002* (Washington, D.C.: U.S. Department of Justice, Bureau of Justice Statistics Bulletin, April 2003), p. 10.

10 Attapol Kuanliang, Jon S. Sorensen, and Mark D. Cunningham, "Juvenile Inmates in an Adult Prison System: Rates of Disciplinary Misconduct and Violence," *Criminal Justice and Behavior: An International Journal* 35, no. 9 (September 2008): 1186–1201.

11 National Drug Control Strategy, Office of *Nation Drug Control Policy, Federal Drug Control Spending by Function, FY 2007–FY 2009*, p. 11.

12 National Institute of Justice, Drug Use Forecasting: *Drugs and Crime, 1990, Annual Report* (Washington, D.C.: U.S. Department of Justice, 1991).

13 Jennifer C. Karbetg and Doris J. James, *Substance Dependence, Abuse, and Treatment of Jail Inmates, 2002* (Washington, D.C.: U.S. Department of Justice, July 2005), p. 1.

14 Christopher J. Mumola and Jennifer C. Karberg, "Drug Use and Dependence, State and Federal Prisoners, 2004," *Bureau of Justice Statistics Special Report* (Washington, D.C.: U.S. Department of Justice, October 2006), p. 5.

15 Ibid., p. 6.

16 Ibid., p. 2.

17 Bureau of Justice Statistics, *Mental Health and Treatment of Inmates and Probationers* (Washington, D.C.: U.S. Department of Justice, July 1999).

18 Bureau of Justice Statistics, *Profile of Jail Inmates, 1996* (Washington, D.C.: U.S. Department of Justice, April 1998).

19 Bureau of Justice Statistics, "Number of Persons under Jurisdiction of State Correctional Authorities by Most Serious Offense, 1980–2005" *Bureau of Justice Statistics Key Facts at a Glance* (Washington, D.C.: U.S. Department of Justice, revised December 11, 2008), available at http://ojp.usdoj.gov/bjs/glance/tables/corrtyptab.htm.

20 Heather C. West and William J. Sabol, *Prisoners in 2007* (Washington, D.C.: U.S. Department of Justice, December 2008), p. 22.

21 Substance Abuse and Mental Health Services Administration, *National Household Survey on Drug Abuse, 2004* (Washington, D.C.: U.S. Government Printing Office, 2005). In addition, the most recent survey by the Substance Abuse and Mental Health Services Administration reported teenage use of illicit drugs in the past month declined from 11.4 percent to 10.9 percent between 2002 and 2004. See Douglas Wright and Neeraja Sathe, *State Estimates of Substance Use from the 2003–2004 National Surveys on Drug Use and Health* (Rockville, Md.: Department of Health and Human Services, March 2006).

22 The Pew Research Center for the People and the Press, included in *Sourcebook of Criminal Justice Statistics, 2001* (Washington, D.C.: U.S. Department of Justice, 2003), p. 129.

23 Ibid.

24 Mumola and Karberg, p. 9.

25 Bernadette Pelissier, William Rhodes, William Saylor, Gerry Gaes, Scott D. Camp, Suzy D. Vanyur, and Sue Wallace, "Triad Drug Treatment Project," *Federal Probation 65,* no. 3 (December 2001): 3–7.

26 Federal Bureau of Prisons, "Drug Treatment Programs in Federal Prisons," in *Best Practices: Excellence in Corrections,* edited by Edward E. Rhine (Lanham, Md.: American Correctional Association, 1998), pp. 427–430.

27 Ibid., p. 429.

28 Gregory P. Falkin, Sheila Strauss, and Timothy Bohen, "Matching Drug-Involved Probationers to Appropriate Drug Interventions: A Strategy for Reducing Recidivism," *Federal Probation* (June 1999): 4.

29 Ibid., p. 5.

30 Frank S. Pearson and Douglas S. Lipton, "A Meta-Analytic Review of the Effectiveness of Correctional-Based Treatment for Drug Abuse," *Prison Journal 79,* no. 4 (1999): 384–410.

31 The National Task Force on Correctional Substance Abuse Strategies, *Intervening with Substance Abusing Offenders: A Framework for Action* (Washington, D.C.: U.S. Department of Justice, National Institute of Corrections, June 1991), p. 27.

32 "Prisons Replace Hospitals for the Nation's Mentally Ill," *New York Times,* March 5, 1998, p. A-26.

33 Doris J. James and Lauren E. Glaze, *Mental Health Problems of Prison and Jail Inmates* (Washington, D.C.: U.S. Department of Justice, Bureau of Justice Statistics, September 2006), p. 1.

34 Ibid.

35 Ibid., p. 9.

36 Ibid., p. 1.

37 Ibid.

38 U.S. Census Bureau, "Quick Facts" (Washington, D.C.: U.S. Census Bureau) http://quickfacts.census.gov/qfd/states/00000.html (accessed April 11, 2009).

39 Kenneth Moritsugu, "Inmate Chronological Age versus Physical Age," in *Long-Term Confinement and the Aging Inmate Population* (Washington, D.C.: U.S. Department of Justice, Federal Bureau of Prisons, 1990).

40 Camille Graham Camp and George M. Camp, *Corrections Yearbook: Adult Corrections, 2002,* (Middletown, CN: Criminal Justice Institute, 2003), pp. 32, 33.

41 West and Sabol, *Prisoners in 2007,* p. 19.

42 Tammerlin Drummond, "Cellblock Seniors: They Have Grown Old and Frail in Prison. Must They Still Be Locked Up?" Time 153, no. 24 (June 21, 1999): 60.

43 West and Sabol, *Prisoners in 2007* p. 22.

44 Robert Perkinson, "Shackled Justice: Florence Federal Penitentiary and the New Politics of Punishment," *Social Justice* 21, no. 3 (1994): 119.

45 *Bruscino v. Carlson,* 854 F.2d 162 (7th Cir. 1988).

46 Chase Riveland, *Supermax Prisons: Overview and General Considerations* (Washington, D.C.: U.S. Department of Justice, National Institute of Corrections, January 1999), p. 3.

47 Sarah Lawrence and Daniel P. Mears, *Benefit-Cost Analysis of Supermax Prisons: Critical Steps and Considerations* (Washington, D.C.: Urban Institute Justice Policy Center, August 2004).

48 Bureau of Justice Statistics, *Sourcebook of Criminal Justice Statistics Online* (Washington, D.C.: U.S. Department of Justice, 2007) www.albany.edu/sourcebook/pdf/t322007.pdf (accessed April 11, 2009).

49 Bureau of Justice Statistics, *Sourcebook of Criminal Justice Statistics 2003* (Washington, D.C.: U.S. Department of Justice, March 2004) p. 192.

50 Lawrence A. Greenfeld, *Sex Offenses and Offenders: An Analysis of Data on Rape and Sexual Assault* (Washington, D.C.: U.S. Department of Justice, Bureau of Justice Statistics, February 1997).

51 National Alert Registry, www.registeredoffenderslists.org (accessed December 9, 2005).

52 Kim English, Suzanne Pullen, and Linda Jones, *Managing Adult Sex Offenders in the Community—A Containment Approach* (Washington, D.C.: U.S. Department of Justice, National Institute of Justice, January 1997).

53 West and Sabol, *Prisoners in 2007,* p. 21.

54 Ibid.

55 Bureau of Justice Statistics, *Sourcebook of Criminal Justice Statistics, Sourcebook 2003* (Washington, D.C.: U.S. Department of Justice, 2004), p. 511.

56 English, Pullen, and Jones, p. 3.

57 Ibid., p. 2.

58 Greenfeld, p. 25.

59 Ibid., pp. 25–26.

60 Rebecca L. Jackson and Derek T. Hess, "Evaluation of Civil Commitment for Sex Offenders: A Survey of Experts," *Sexual Abuse: A Journal of Research and Treatment* 19, no. 4 (December 2007): 425–448.

61 *Kansas v. Hendricks,* 117 U.S. 2072 (1997); *Seling v. Young,* 531 U.S. 215 (2001); *Kansas v. Crane,* 534 US 407 (2002).

62 Theodore M. Hammett, Cheryl Roberts, and Sofia Kennedy, "Health Related Issues in Prisoner Reentry," *Crime & Delinquency* 47, no. 3 (July 2001): 390–409.

63 Laura M. Maruschak, *HIV in Prisons, 2004* (Washington, D.C.: Bureau of Justice Statistics, November 2006), p. 1.

64 Ibid.

65 Ibid., p. 2.

66 Theodore M. Hammett, Sofia Kennedy, and Sarah Kuck, *National Survey of Infectious Diseases in Correctional Facilities: HIV and Sexually Transmitted Diseases* (Washington, D.C.: National Institute of Justice, March 2007).

67 Ibid.

68 Christopher P. Krebs, "Inmate Factors Associated with HIV Transmission in Prison," *Criminology and Public Policy 5*, no. 1 (February 2006): 113–136.

69 Theodore M. Hammett, M. P. Harmon, and W. Rhodes, "The Burden of Infectious Disease among Inmates and Releasees from U.S. Correctional Facilities," *American Journal of Public Health* 92 (1997): 189–194.

70 Theodore Hammett, "Editorial Introduction: HIV in Prisons," *Criminology and Public Policy 5*, no. 1 (February 2006): 108.

71 Karen Wilcock, Theodore M. Hammett, Rebecca Widom, and Joel Epstein, *Tuberculosis in Correctional Facilities 1994–95* (Washington, D.C.: U.S. Department of Justice, 1996), p. 5.

72 Jessica R. MacNeil, Mark N. Lobato, and Marisa Moore, "An Unanswered Health Disparity: Tuberculosis among Correctional Inmates, 1993 through 2003," *American Journal of Public Health* 95, no. 10 (2005): 1800–1805.

73 Laura Maruschak, *Medical Problems of Prisoners* (Washington, D.C.: U.S. Department of Justice, April 2008).

74 Centers for Disease Control, "Screening for Tuberculosis and Tuberculosis Infection in High Risk Populations: Recommendations of the Advisory Council for the Elimination of Tuberculosis," *Morbidity and Mortality Weekly Report* 44, no. RR-11 (1994): 19–34.

75 Theodore M. Hammett, *Public Health/Corrections Collaborations: Prevention and Treatment of HIV/AIDS, STDs, and TB* (Washington, D.C.: U.S. Department of Justice, National Institute of Justice, July 1998), p. 9.

76 Allen J. Beck and Laura Maruschak, "Hepatitis Testing and Treatment in State Prisons," *Bureau of Justice Statistics Special Report* (Washington, D.C.: U.S. Department of Justice, April 2004).

77 H. J. Alter and L. B. Seeff, "Recovery, Persistence, and Sequelae in Hepatitis C Viral Infection: A Perspective on Long-Term Outcome," *Seminars in Liver Disease* 20, no. 1 (2000): 17–35.

78 S. A. Allen, A. C. Spaulding, and A. M. Osei, "Treatment of Chronic Hepatitis C in a State Correctional Facility," *Annals of Internal Medicine* 138 (2003): 187–190.

79 Scott A. Allen, Josiah D. Rich, Beth Schwartzapfel, and Peter D. Friedmann, "Hepatitis C among Offenders: Correctional Challenges and Public Health Opportunity," *Federal Probation* 67, no. 2 (September 2003): 22–26.

Chapter 10

1 James J. Stephan, "Census of State and Federal Correctional Facilities, 2005," *National Prisoner Statistics Program* (Washington, D.C.: U.S. Department of Justice, October 2008), p. 1.

2 Ibid., p 2.

3 Ohio Department of Rehabilitation and Correction website, www.drc.state.oh.us/web/Reports/FactSheet/October (accessed December 2005).

4 Heather C. West and William J. Sabol, *Prison Inmates at Midyear 2008—Statistical Tables*, (Washington, D.C.: U.S. Department of Justice, Bureau of Justice Statistics, March 2009), p. 3.

5 Ohio Department of Rehabilitation and Correction website, www.drc.state.oh.us/web/Reports/FactSheet/February 2006 (accessed February 2006).

6 Tracey Kyckelhahn and Thomas H. Cohen, *Civil Rights Complaints in U.S. District Courts, 1990–2006* (Washington, D.C.: U.S. Department of Justice, Bureau of Justice Statistics, August 2008), p. 8.

7 Ibid., pp. 82–83, 84, 97, 98.

8 Stephan, pp. 1 and 2.

9 Data taken from West and Sabol, p. 2, and The Pew Center on the States, *One in 31: The Long Reach of American Corrections* (Washington, D.C.: Pew Charitable Trusts, March 2009), pp. 1–2.

10 Camille Graham Camp and George M. Camp, *The 2002 Corrections Yearbook, Adult Systems*, (Middletown, Conn.: Criminal Justice Institute, 2002), pp. 7, 154, 187, 92.

11 For a discussion of the history of unit management in the Bureau of Prisons, see Robert Levinson and Roy Gerard, "Functional Units: A Different Correctional Approach," *Federal Probation* 37, no. 4 (1973): 8–16.

12 Federal Bureau of Prisons, *Unit Management Manual* (Washington, D.C.: U.S. Department of Justice, Bureau of Prisons, 1977), p. 6.

13 Robert Freeman, "Management and Administrative Issues," in *Prisons: Today and Tomorrow*, edited by Jocelyn M. Pollock (Gaithersburg, Md.: Aspen, 1997), p. 300.

14 E. C. Hughes, "Professions," in *The Professions in America*, edited by Kenneth S. Lynn (Boston: Houghton-Mifflin, 1965), p. 4.

15 American Correctional Association, *Standards for Adult Correctional Institutions*, 3rd ed. (Laurel, Md.: American Correctional Association, 1990), p. vii.

16 Mary Dallao, "Keeping Classification Current," *Corrections Today* 59, no. 4 (July 1997): 87.

17 Tim Brennan, "Classification for Control in Jail and Prisons," in *Prediction and Classification: Criminal Justice Decision Making*, edited by Don M. Gottfredson and Michael Tonry (Chicago: University of Chicago Press, 1987), p. 343.

18 Stephan, p. 2.

19 Joan Mullen, *American Prisons and Jails, Volume I: Summary and Policy Implications of a National Survey* (Washington, D.C.: U.S. Department of Justice, 1980), p. 57.

20 Federal Bureau of Prisons, "Inmate Discipline and Special Housing Units," Federal Prison System, Policy Statement #5270.07 (Washington, D.C.: U.S. Department of Justice, December 29, 1987), chapter 1, p. 1.

21 Ibid., chapter 4, p. 4.

22 Ibid., chapter 2, p. 3.

23 Clair A. Cripe, "Inmate Disciplinary Procedures," in *Prison and Jail Administration: Practice and Theory*, edited by Peter M. Carlson and Judith Simon Garrett (Gaithersburg, Md.: Aspen, 1999), p. 214.

24 Steven W. Perry, "Justice Expenditure and Employment Extracts 2006," *Criminal Justice Expenditure and Employment Extracts Program* (Washington, D.C.: U.S. Department of Justice, August 2008), available at www.ojp.usdoj.gov/bjs/eande.htm

25 Donald Cressey, "Prison Organizations," in *Handbook of Organizations*, edited by J. March (New York: Rand McNally, 1965), p. 1024.

26 Kelsey Kauffman, *Prison Officers and Their World* (Cambridge, Mass.: Harvard University Press, 1988), p. 167.

27 John J. DiIulio, *Governing Prisons: A Comparative Study of Correctional Management* (New York: Free Press, 1987), p. 95.

28 M. Robert Montilla, *Prison Employee Unionism: Management Guide for Correctional Administrators* (Washington, D.C.: U.S. Department of Justice, National Institute of Law Enforcement and Criminal Justice, 1978), p. 2.

29 James B. Jacobs and Norma Meacham Crotty, *Guard Unions and the Future of Prisons* (Ithaca, N.Y.: Institute of Public Employment, 1978), p. 41.

30 Andrew A. Peterson, "Deterring Strikes by Public Employees: New York's Two-for-One Salary Penalty and the 1979 Prison Guard Strike," *Industrial and Labor Relations Review* 34, no. 4 (July 1981): 545–562.

31 Lynn Zimmer and James B. Jacobs, "Challenging the Taylor Law: Prison Guards on Strike," *Industrial and Labor Relations Review,* 34, no. 4 (July 1981): 531–544.

Chapter 11

1 Erving Goffman, *Asylums: Essays on the Social Situation of Mental Patients and Other Inmates* (New York: Doubleday, 1961).

2 Phillip G. Zimbardo, "Pathology of Imprisonment," *Society* 9 (April 1972): 4–8.

3 Ibid., p. 4.

4 Donald Clemmer, *The Prison Community* (New York: Rinehart, 1940), p. 8.

5 Gresham Sykes, *The Society of Captives: A Study of a Maximum Security Prison* (Princeton, N.J.: Princeton University Press, 1958).

6 John Irwin and Donald Cressey, "Thieves, Convicts, and the Inmate Culture," *Social Problems* 10 (1962): 145–157.

7 This list of selected prison terms was collected by Kate King, professor of criminal justice at Murray State University.

8 Heather C. West and William J. Sabol, *Prisoners in 2007,* Bureau of Justice Statistics Bulletin (Washington, D.C.: U.S. Department of Justice, December 2008), p. 21.

9 Karen F. Lahm, "Inmate-On-Inmate Assault: A Multilevel Examination of Prison Violence," *Criminal Justice and Behavior* 35, no. 1 (January 2008): 120–137.

10 S. Ekland-Olson, "Crowding, Social Control, and Prison Violence: Evidence from the Post-*Ruiz* Years in Texas," *Law and Society Review* 20, no. 3 (1986): 289–421. Also see Gerald G. Gaes and W. J. McGuire, "Prison Violence: The Contribution of Crowding versus Other Determinants of Prison Assault Rates," *Journal of Research in Crime and Delinquency* 22, no. 1 (1985): 41–65.

11 John Irwin, *Prisons in Turmoil* (Boston: Little, Brown, 1980).

12 James B. Jacobs, *Statesville, a Penitentiary in Mass Society* (Chicago: University of Chicago Press, 1977).

13 Mark S. Fleisher, *Warehousing Violence* (Newbury Park, Calif.: Sage, 1989), p. 198.

14 Victor Hassine, *Life without Parole: Living in Prison Today,* 2nd ed. (Los Angeles: Roxbury, 1999), p. 39.

15 Michael C. Braswell, Reid H. Montgomery, and Lucien X. Lombardo, *Prison Violence in America*, 2nd ed. (Cincinnati, Ohio: Anderson, 1994).

16 Robert Johnson, *Hard Time: Understanding and Reforming the Prison*, 3rd ed. (Belmont, Calif.: Wadsworth, 2002), p. 149.

17 Charles M. Terry, *The Fellas: Overcoming Prison and Addiction* (Belmont, Calif.: Wadsworth, 2003), p. 72.

18 Christopher A. Innes and Vicki D. Verdeyen, "Conceptualizing the Management of Violent Inmates," *Corrections Management Quarterly* 1, no. 4 (1997): 1–9.

19 Christopher J. Mumola, "Suicide and Homicide in State Prisons and Local Jails," *Bureau of Justice Statistics Special Report* (Washington, D.C.: U.S. Department of Justice, August 2005), p. 1.

20 Erika Harrell, "Violence by Gang Members, 1993–2002," *Bureau of Justice Statistics Crime Data Brief* (Washington, D.C.: U.S. Department of Justice, June 2005), p. 1.

21 National Gang Intelligence Center and the National Drug Intelligence Center, *2009 National Gang Threat Assessment*, www.fbi.gov/pressrel09/ngta020209.htm (accessed April 16, 2009).

22 Gerald G. Gaes, Susan Wallace, Evan Gilman, Jody Klein-Saffran, and Sharon Suppa, "Influence of Prison Gang Affiliation on Violence and Other Prison Misconduct," *Prison Journal* 82, no. 3 (2002): 359–385.

23 National Institute of Corrections, *Management Strategies in Disturbances and with Gangs/Disruptive Groups* (Washington, D.C.: U.S. Department of Justice, 1991), p. 2.

24 George M. Camp and Camille Graham Camp, *Prison Gangs: Their Extent, Nature, and Impact on Prisons* (Washington, D.C.: U.S. Government Printing Office, 1985).

25 American Correctional Association, *Gangs in Correctional Facilities: A National Assessment* (Laurel, Md.: American Correctional Association, 1993).

26 Camille Graham Camp and George M. Camp, *The 2002 Corrections Yearbook* (Middletown, Conn.: The Criminal Justice Institute, 2003), p. 37.

27 Gregory Scott, "Broken Windows behind Bars: Eradicating Prison Gangs through Ecological Hardening and Symbol Cleansing," *Corrections Management Quarterly* 5, no. 1 (2001): 23–36.

28 Ibid., p. 24.

29 Sykes, *Society of Captives*.

30 Mark S. Fleisher and Scott H. Decker, "An Overview of the Challenge of Prison Gangs," *Corrections Management Quarterly* 5, no. 1 (2001): 5.

31 Richard P. Seiter, "Winning a Battle of Wills: Correctional Administrators and Prison Gangs," *Corrections Management Quarterly* 5, no. 1 (2001): iv.

32 Tony Lesce, "How to Cope with Prison Gangs," *Corrections Technology & Management* 4, no. 2 (March/April 2000): 22–25.

33 National Institute of Corrections, *Management Strategies* (Washington, D.C.: U.S. Department of Justice, 1991), p. 2.

34 Ibid., pp. 5–6.

35 Intelligence Section, Federal Bureau of Prisons, *Gang Interdiction Strategies Briefing Guide* (Washington, D.C.: U.S. Department of Justice, April 29, 1996), p. 17.

36 *Johnson v. California*, 321 F.3d 791 (2005).

37 Peter L. Nacci and Thomas R. Kane, "The Incidence of Sex and Sexual Aggression in Federal Prisons," *Federal Probation* 47, no. 4 (December 1983): 31–36.

38 Victor Hassine, *Life without Parole: Living in Prison Today* (Los Angeles: Roxbury, 1997), p. 138.

39 T. J. Fagan, D. Wennerstrom, and J. Miller, "Sexual Assault of Male Inmates: Prevention, Identification, and Intervention," *Journal of Correctional Health Care* 3, no. 1 (1996): 49–63.

40 Allen J. Beck and Paige M. Harrison, "Sexual Violence Reported by Correctional Authorities, 2006," *Bureau of Justice Statistics Special Report* (Washington, D.C.: U.S. Department of Justice, August 2007).

41 Allen J. Beck and Paige M. Harrison, "Sexual Victimization in State and Federal Prisons Reported by Inmates, 2007," *Bureau of Justice Statistics Special Report* (Washington, D.C.: U.S. Department of Justice, December 2007).

42 John Blackmore and Janine Zweig, "Developing State Prison Policies to Respond to Sexual Violence," *Corrections Today* 70, no. 4 (August 2008): 78–81.

43 R. Alan Thompson, Lisa S. Nored, and Kelly Cheeseman Dial, "Prison Rape Elimination Act: An Evaluation of Policy Compliance with Illustrative Excerpts," *Criminal Justice Policy Review* 19, no. 4 (December 2008): 414–437.

44 Aviva N. Moster and Elizabeth L. Jeglic, "Prison Warden Attitudes toward Prison Rape and Sexual Assault," *The Prison Journal* 89 (April 2009): 65–78.

45 The Urban Institute, "Strategies to Prevent Prison Rape by Changing the Correctional Culture," *NIJ Research in Practice* (Washington, D.C.: U.S. Department of Justice, October 2008).

46 Camp and Camp, *2002 Corrections Yearbook*, p. 149.

47 Heather C. West and William J. Sabol , *Prisoners in 2007* (Washington, D.C.: U.S. Department of Justice, Bureau of Justice Statistics Bulletin, December 2008), p. 22.

48 Ibid., p. 9.

49 Christopher J. Mumola and Jennifer C. Karberg, *Drug Use and Dependence, State and Federal Prisoners, 2004* (Washington, D.C.: U. S. Department of Justice, Bureau of Justice Statistics, October 2006), p. 1.

50 C. W. Harlow, *HIV in U.S. Prisons and Jails* (Washington, D.C.: U.S. Department of Justice, 1993).

51 Camp and Camp, 2002 *Corrections Yearbook*, pp. 138–139.

52 Ibid., p. 140.

53 Mumola and Karberg, p. 9.

54 Charles M. Terry, "The Function of Humor for Prison Inmates," *Journal of Contemporary Criminal Justice* 13, no. 1 (February 1997): 23–40.

55 Goffman, *Asylums*.

56 S. Ungar, "Self-Mockery: An Alternative Form of Self-Presentation," *Symbolic Interaction* 71, no. 1 (1984): 121–133.

57 Terry, "Function of Humor," p. 24.

58 Henry Elmer Barnes, *The Evolution of Penology in Pennsylvania: A Study in American Social History* (Montclair, N.J.: Patterson Smith, 1968).

59 Russell P. Dobash, R. Emerson Dobash, and Sue Gutteridge, *The Imprisonment of Women* (Oxford, England: Basil Blackwell, 1986), p. 52.

60 Allison Morris, *Women, Crime and Criminal Justice* (Oxford, England: Basil Blackwell, 1987).

61 Nicole H. Rafter, *Partial Justice: Women, Prison, and Social Control*, 2nd ed. (New Brunswick, N.J.: Transaction, 1990).

62 Nicole H. Rafter, "Gender and Justice: The Equal Protection Issues," in *The American Prison*, edited by Lynne Goodstein and Doris MacKenzie (New York: Plenum Press, 1989), pp. 89–109.

63 Clarice Feinman, "A Historical Overview of the Treatment of Incarcerated Women: Myths and Realities of Rehabilitation," *Prison Journal* 63 (1983): 12–26.

64 Clarice Feinman, "Sex-Role Stereotypes and Justice for Women," in *Women and Crime in America*, edited by L. H. Bowker (New York: Macmillan, 1981), pp. 383–391.

65 See Mark S. Fleisher, Richard H. Rison, and David W. Helman, "Federal Inmates: A Growing Constituency in the Federal Bureau of Prisons," *Corrections Management Quarterly* 1, no. 4 (1997): 28–35.

66 Barbara Owens, *In the Mix: Struggle and Survival in a Women's Prison* (Albany: State University of New York Press, 1998), p. 120.

67 A. Propper, "Make Believe Families and Homosexuality among Imprisoned Girls," *Criminology* 20, no. 1 (1982): 120.

68 Joycelyn M. Pollock-Byrne, *Women, Prison, and Crime* (Belmont, Calif.: Wadsworth, 1990).

69 C. B. Hart, "Gender Differences in Social Support among Inmates," *Women and Criminal Justice* 6 (1995): 67–68.

70 Ira J. Silverman, *Corrections: A Comprehensive View*, 2nd ed. (Belmont, Calif.: Wadsworth, 2001), p. 200.

71 J. Diaz-Cotto, *Gender, Ethnicity, and the State: Latina and Latino Prison Politics* (Albany: New York State University Press, 1996).

72 Katherine Stuart Van Wormer and Clemens Bartolas, *Women and the Criminal Justice System* (Boston: Allyn and Bacon, 2000), p. 66.

73 Imogene L. Moyer, "Differential Social Structures and Homosexuality among Women in Prison," *Virginia Social Science Journal* 13 (1978): 13–19.

74 Owens, *In the Mix*, p. 198.

75 Barbara Owen, James Wells, Joycelyn Pollock, Bernadette Muscat, and Stephanie Torres, *Gendered Violence and Safety: A Contextual Approach to Improving Security in Women's Facilities* (Washington, D.C.: U.S. Department of Justice, November 2008), p. vi.

76 Fleisher, Rison, and Helman, "Federal Inmates," p. 34.

Chapter 12

1 Richard W. Snarr, *Introduction to Corrections*, 3rd ed. (Madison, Wis.: Brown & Benchmark, 1996), p. 179.

2 James B. Jacobs, *Stateville: The Penitentiary in Mass Society* (Chicago: University of Chicago Press, 1977).

3 "At Stateville: The Calm Is Tense," *Corrections Magazine* 61, no. 3 (June 1980): 6–10, 15–19.

4 Nathan Kantrowitz, *Close Control: Managing a Maximum Security Prison; the Story of Ragen's Stateville Penitentiary* (Albany, N.Y.: Harrow and Heston, 1996).

5 Robert Freeman, "Management and Administrative Issues," in *Prisons: Today and Tomorrow*, edited by Jocelyn M. Pollock (Gaithersburg, Md.: Aspen, 1997), p. 279.

6 James MacGregor Burns, *Leadership* (New York: Harper & Row, 1978).

7 M. Kay Harris, "A Call for Transformational Leadership for Corrections," *Corrections Management Quarterly* 3, no. 1 (1997): 22–25.

8 John J. DiIulio, Jr., *Governing Prisons: A Comparative Study of Correctional Management* (New York: Free Press, 1987), pp. 188–189.

9 James J. Stephan, "Census of State and Federal Correctional Facilities, 2005," *National Prisoner Statistics Program* (Washington, D.C.: U.S. Department of Justice, October 2008), p. 4.

10 Ibid.

11 Ibid., p. 5.

12 Curtis Prout and Robert N. Ross, *Care and Punishment: The Dilemmas of Prison Medicine* (Pittsburgh, Pa.: University of Pittsburgh Press, 1988), p. 152.

13 Lucien X. Lombardo, *Guards Imprisoned*, 2nd ed. (Cincinnati, Ohio: Anderson, 1989).

14 Andrew Metz, "Life on the Inside: The Jailers," in *Exploring Corrections: A Book of Readings* (Boston: Allyn and Bacon, 2002), p. 65.

15 Ibid., p. 64.

16 M. A. Farkas and P. K. Manning, "The Occupational Cultures of Corrections and Police Officers," *Journal of Crime and Justice* 20, no. 2 (1997): 51–68.

17 Lee Dickenson, *The Keepers of the Keys* (Fort Bragg, Calif.: Lost Coast, 1999), pp. 142–143.

18 Peter Finn, *Addressing Correctional Officer Stress: Programs and Strategies* (Washington, D.C.: U.S. Department of Justice, National Institute of Justice, December 2000).

19 Ibid., p. 13.

20 Cited in Finn, *Correctional Officer Stress*, p. 11.

21 From the Correctional Peace Officer Foundation website at www.cpof.org/page/3361250.htm (accessed April 7, 2009).

22 American Correctional Association, "Resolution on the Term 'Correctional Officer,'" *Corrections Today* (April 1993): 60.

23 James J. Stephan, "Census of State and Federal Correctional Facilities, 2005," *National Prisoner Statistics Program* (Washington, D.C.: U.S. Department of Justice, October 2008), p. 4.

24 Camille Graham Camp and George M. Camp, *Corrections Yearbook, Adult Systems*, 2002 (Middletown, CN: Criminal Justice Institute, 2003), pp. 158, 159, 165.

25 Texas Department of Criminal Justice (Corrections) website at http://www.tdcj.state.tx.us/vacancy/coinfo/cosalary.htm and California Department of Corrections and Rehabilitation website at http://www.cdcr.ca.gov/Career_Opportunities/POR/docs/payandbenefits.pdf.

26 Donald N. Snyder, Jr., "Recruitment and Retention Programs: Important during Economic Ups and Downs," *Corrections Today* (June 2000): 92–95.

27 Frank E. Riley and Beverly A. Wilder, "Hiring Correctional Staff with the Right Stuff," *Corrections Today* (June 2000): 91.

28 Quoting correctional officer Donna Verrastro in an AP National article by David Crary, "High Stress, Low Glamor: Correctional Officers Struggle with Workplace Strains," *PoliceOne.com News* (May 8, 2005), www.policeone.com/pc_print.asp?vid=100392 (accessed April 12, 2009).

29 Ibid.

30 North Carolina Department of Corrections, "DOC Addresses Correctional Officer Recruitment and Retention Issues," April 2000, ww2w.doc.state.nc.us/NEWSZ/cnews/0007/recruit.htm (accessed April 12, 2009).

31 Glen Castlebury, "Correctional Officer Recruitment and Retention in Texas," *Corrections Today* 64, no. 3 (June 2001): 80–83.

32 Jane Lommel, "Turning Around Turnover," *Corrections Today* 66, no. 5 (August 2004): 54–57.

33 Cece Hill, "Staff Recruitment and Workforce Issues," *Corrections Compendium* 31, no. 3 (May/June 2006): 15–32.

34 Pew Center on the States, *Ten Steps Corrections Directors Can Take to Strengthen Performance* (Washington, D.C.: The Pew Charitable Trusts, May 2008).

35 Alaska Department of Corrections Press Release, "Department of Corrections Actively Recruiting Alaskans for Correctional Officer Positions" (Juneau, Alaska: Department of Corrections, January 26, 2005).

36 Brian E. Cronin, Ralph Klessig, and William D. Sprenkle, "Recruiting and Retaining Staff through Culture Change," *Corrections Today* 70, no. 4 (August 2008): 48–51.

37 Gary C. Mohr, "Samberg Program Improves Leadership and Addresses Turnover," *Corrections Today*, 71, no. 2 (April 2009), 56–58.

38 Stan Stojkovic and Mary Ann Farkas, *Correctional Leadership: A Cultural Perspective* (Belmont, Calif.: Wadsworth/Thompson, 2003), p. 5.

39 For a good discussion of the various models of prison organizational culture, see Stojkovic and Farkas, *Correctional Leadership*, pp. 37–47.

40 M. Farkas and P. K. Manning, "The Occupational Cultures of Policing and Correctional Work," *Journal of Crime and Justice* 22, no. 2 (1997): 51–68.

41 Richard P. Seiter, *Correctional Administration: Integrating Theory and Practice* (Upper Saddle River, N.J.: Prentice Hall, 2002), p. 365.

42 Norman A. Carlson, Karen M. Hess, and Christine M. H. Orthmann, *Corrections in the Twenty-First Century: A Practical Approach* (Belmont, Calif.: Wadsworth, 1999), p. 441.

43 42 U.S.C. 2000e-2 (1976), p. 703(e).

44 *Dothard v. Rawlinson*, 433 U.S. 321 (1977).

45 Camp and Camp, *2002 Corrections Yearbook*, pp. 159, 164, 165.

46 Stephan, p. 4.

47 Lynn E. Zimmer, *Women Guarding Men* (Chicago: University of Chicago Press, 1986), pp. 53–54.

48 See Nancy C. Jurik and Gregory J. Halembia, "Gender, Working Conditions and the Job Satisfaction of Women in a Non-Traditional Occupation: Female Correctional Officers in Men's Prisons," *Sociological Quarterly* 25 (1984): 551–566. Also see Lincoln J. Fry and Daniel Glaser, "Gender Differences in Work Adjustment of Prison Employees," *Journal of Offender Counseling, Services and Rehabilitation*, 12 (1987): 39–52.

49 Herbert Holeman and Barbara Krepps-Hess, *Women Correctional Officers in the California Department of Corrections* (Sacramento: California Department of Corrections, Research Unit, 1983).

50 See Kevin Wright and William Saylor, "Male and Female Employees' Perceptions of Prison Work: Is There a Difference?" *Justice Quarterly* 8 (1991): 505–524.

51 Kelly A. Cheeseman, Janet L. Mullings, and James W. Marquart, "Inmate Perceptions of Security Staff across Various Custody Levels," *Corrections Management Quarterly* 5, no. 2 (2001): 44.

52 Mark R. Pogrebin and Eric D. Poole, "Sex, Gender, and Work: The Case of Women Jail Officers," *Sociology of Crime, Law, and Deviance* 1 (1998): 105–124.

53 Joycelyn M. Pollock, "Women in Corrections: Custody and the 'Caring Ethic,'" in *Women, Law, and Social Control*, edited by Alida V. Merlo and Joycelyn M. Pollock (Boston: Allyn and Bacon, 1995), p. 111.

Chapter 13

1 Richard P. Seiter, *Correctional Administration: Integrating Theory and Practice* (Upper Saddle River, N.J.: Prentice Hall, 2002), pp. 205–206.

2 *The Security Audit Program: A "How To" Guide and Model Instrument for Adaptation to Local Standards, Policies, and Procedures* (Washington, D.C.: U.S. Department of Justice, National Institute of Corrections, 1999), p. 1.

3 James D. Henderson, W. Hardy Rauch, and Richard L. Phillips, *Guidelines for the Development of a Security Program*, 2nd ed. (Lanham, Md.: American Correctional Association, 1997), p. 21.

4 Ibid., pp. 143–144.

5 Ibid., p. 129.

6 Federal Bureau of Prisons, "Inmate Discipline and Special Housing Units," Policy Statement Number 5270.07 (Washington, D.C.: U.S. Department of Justice, Bureau of Prisons, December 29, 1987), chapter 4, pp. 4–10.

7 For a good historical overview, see Reid H. Montgomery, Jr., and Gordon A. Crews, *A History of Correctional Violence: An Examination of Reported Causes of Riots and Disturbances* (Lanham, Md.: American Correctional Association, 1998).

8 There are several official and government reports on this riot. However, a source of interesting reading is Tom Wicker, *A Time to Die* (New York: Quadrangle/New York Times Book Company, 1975).

9 Attorney General's Office, *Report of the Attorney General on the February 2 and 3, 1980 Riot at the Penitentiary of New Mexico* (Santa Fe: State of New Mexico, Office of the Attorney General, 1980).

10 Reginald A. Wilkinson and Thomas J. Stickrath, "After the Storm: Anatomy of a Riot's Aftermath," *Corrections Management Quarterly* 1, no. 1 (1996): 16.

11 Henderson, Rauch, and Phillips, *Guidelines*, pp. 180–181.

12 R. Arjen Boin and Menno J. Van Duin, "Prison Riots as Organized Failures: A Managerial Perspective," *Prison Journal* 75, no. 3 (1995): 365.

13 Earnest A. Stepp, "Preparing for Chaos: Emergency Management," in *Prison and Jail Administration: Practice and Theory*, edited by Peter M. Carlson and Judith Simon Garrett (Gaithersburg, Md.: Aspen, 1999), p. 371.

14 Gothriel Lafleur, Louis Stender, and Jim Lyons, "Hostage Situations in Correctional Facilities," in *Prison and Jail Administration: Practice and Theory*, edited by Peter M. Carlson and Judith Simon Garrett (Gaithersburg, Md.: Aspen, 1999), p. 376.

15 President's Commission on Law Enforcement and the Administration of Justice, *The Challenge of Crime in a Free Society* (Washington, D.C.: U.S. Government Printing Office, 1967), p. 183.

16 Douglas Lipton, Robert Martinson, and Judith Wilks, *The Effectiveness of Correctional Treatment* (New York: Praeger, 1975).

17 Robert Martinson, "What Works? Questions and Answers about Prison Reform," *The Public Interest* 35 (1974): 25.

18 Christopher A. Innes, "Recent Public Opinion in the United States toward Punishment and Corrections," *Prison Journal* 73, no. 3 (1993): 232.

19 Barry Krisberg and Susan Marchionna, "Attitudes of US Voters toward Prisoners Rehabilitation and Reentry Policies," *Focus: Views from the National Council on Crime and Delinquency* (Washington, D.C.: National Council on Crime and Delinquency, April 2006).

20 Ibid.

21 J. Senese and David B. Kalinich, "Activities and Rehabilitation Programs for Offenders," in *Corrections: An Introduction,* edited by S. Stojkovic and R. Lovell (Cincinnati, Ohio: Anderson, 1992), p. 223.

22 Francis T. Cullen and Brandon K. Applegate, eds., *Offender Rehabilitation: Effective Correctional Intervention* (Aldershot, England: Ashgate, Dartmouth, 1998), p. xiv.

23 Caroline Wolf Harlow, *Education and Correctional Populations* (Washington, D.C.: U.S. Department of Justice, Bureau of Justice Statistics, January 2003), p. 1.

24 Ibid.

25 Ibid., p. 4.

26 Ibid., p. 5.

27 Commission on Accreditation for Corrections, "Comprehensive Education Program, Standard 3–34410," in *Standards for Adult Correctional Institutions* (College Park, Md.: American Correctional Association, 1990), p. 14.

28 See J. Gerber and E. J. Fritsch, "Adult Academic and Vocational Correctional Education Programs: A Review of Recent Research," *Journal of Offender Rehabilitation* 22 (1995): 199–242; M. D. Harer, "Recidivism among Federal Prisoners Released in 1987," *Journal of Correctional Education* 46, no. 3 (1995): 98–128; M. Jancic, "Does Correctional Education Have an Effect on Recidivism?" *Journal of Correctional Education* 49, no. 4 (1998): 152–161.

29 K. Adams, K. J. Bennett, T. J. Flanagan, J. W. Marquart, S. J. Cuvelier, E. Fritsch, J. Gerber, D. R. Longmire, and V. S. Burton, Jr., "Large-Scale Multidimensional Test of the Effect of Prison Education Programs on Offenders' Behavior," *Prison Journal* 74, no. 4 (December 1994): 433–449.

30 G. F. Vito and R. Tewksbury, "Improving the Educational Skills of Inmates: The Results of an Impact Evaluation," *Corrections Compendium* 24, no. 10 (1999): 1–17.

31 William G. Saylor and Gerald G. Gaes, "Training Inmates through Industrial Work Participation and Vocational and Apprenticeship Instruction," *Corrections Management Quarterly* 1, no. 2 (1997): 40.

32 Pamela K. Lattimore, Ann Dryden Witte, and Joanna R. Baker, "Experimental Assessment of the Effect of Vocational Training on Youthful Property Offenders," *Evaluation Review* 14, no. 2 (1990): 115–133.

33 John Linton, "Inmate Education Makes Sense," *Corrections Today* 60, no. 3 (1998): 18.

34 Steve Peacock, "BOP Proposes Inmates Pay All Tuition Costs for College," *Corrections Journal* 4, no. 10 (2000): 7.

35 Doris J. James and Lauren E. Glaze, "Mental Health Problems of Prison and Jail Inmates," *Bureau of Justice Statistics Special Report*, (Washington, D.C.: U.S. Department of Justice, September 2006), p. 1.

36 Ibid.

37 Paula M. Ditton, *Mental Health and Treatment of Inmates and Probationers* (Washington, D.C.: U.S. Department of Justice, Bureau of Justice Statistics, 1999).

38 Allen J. Beck and Laura J. Maruschak, *Mental Health Treatment in State Prisons, 2000* (Washington, D.C.: U.S. Department of Justice, Bureau of Justice Statistics, July 2001).

39 James and Glaze, p. 9.

40 Ibid.

41 "Mental Health Care in Ohio Corrections" (Columbus: Ohio Department of Rehabilitation and Correction, 1997), p. 4.

42 Christopher J. Mumola and Jennifer C. Karberg, *Drug Use and Dependence, State and Federal Prisoners, 2004* (Washington, D.C.: U.S. Department of Justice, Bureau of Justice Statistics, October 2006), p. 1.

43 Office of National Drug Control Policy, *The National Drug Control Strategy: 1998* (Washington, D.C.: The White House, February 1998).

44 U.S. General Accounting Office, *Drug Treatment: State Prisons Face Challenges in Providing Treatment: A Report to the Committee on Government Operation, U.S. House of Representatives* (Washington, D.C.: U.S. General Accounting Office, 1991).

45 National Center on Addiction and Substance Abuse at Columbia University, *Behind Bars: Substance Abuse and America's Prison Population* (New York: National Center on Addiction and Substance Abuse at Columbia University, 1998).

46 Mumola and Karberg, p. 9.

47 Federal Bureau of Prisons, *TRIAD Drug Treatment Evaluation Six-Month Report: Executive Summary* (Washington, D.C.: U.S. Department of Justice, 1998).

48 Seiter, *Correctional Administration*, p. 126.

49 Camille Graham Camp and George M. Camp, *The 2001 Corrections Yearbook* (Middletown, Conn.: The Criminal Justice Institute, 2002), pp. 118 and 124.

50 Ibid., p. 120.

51 National Institute of Justice, *Developing Private Sector Prison Industries: From Concept to Start Up* (Washington, D.C.: U.S. Government Printing Office, 1990), p. 22.

52 Camp and Camp, *2001 Corrections Yearbook*, p. 120.

53 Bureau of Justice Assistance, "Prison Industry Enhancement Certification Program," *Bureau of Justice Assistance: Program Brief* (Washington, D.C.: U.S. Department of Justice, March 2004).

54 William G. Saylor and Gerald G. Gaes, "The Post-Release Employment Project: Prison Work Has Measurable Effects on Post-Release Success," *Federal Prisons Journal* 2, no. 4 (1992): 33–36.

55 Robert Martinson, *Offender Rehabilitation: Effective Correctional Intervention*, edited by Francis T. Cullen and Brandon K. Applegate (Aldershot, England: Ashgate, Dartmouth, 1998), chapter 4; D. A. Andrews and J. Bonta, *The Psychology of Criminal Conduct* (Cincinnati, Ohio: Anderson, 1994); Paul Gendreau, "The Principles of Effective Intervention with Offenders," in *Choosing Correctional Options That Work: Defining the Demand and Evaluating the Supply,* edited by A. Harland (Thousand Oaks, Calif.: Sage, 1996), pp. 117–130; M. W. Lipsey, "Juvenile Delinquency Treatment: A Meta-Analytic Inquiry into the Variability of Effects," in *Meta-Analysis for Explanation,* edited by T. D. Cook, H. Cooper, D. S. Cordray, H. Hartmann, L. V. Hedges, R. J. Light, T. A. Louis, and F. Mosteller (New York: Russell Sage, 1992), pp. 83–127; D. S. Andrews, I. Zinger, R. D. Hoge, J. Bonta, P. Gendreau, and F. T. Cullen, "Does Correctional Treatment Work? A Psychologically Informed Meta-Analysis," *Criminology* 28 (1990): 369–404.

Chapter 14

1 John Scalia, "Prisoner Petitions Filed in U.S. District Courts, 2000, with Trends 1980–2000," *Bureau of Justice Statistics Special Report* (Washington, D.C.: U.S. Department of Justice, January 2002).

2 Camille Graham Camp and George M. Camp, *The 2002 Corrections Yearbook: Adult Systems* (Middletown, Conn.: Criminal Justice Institute, 2003), pp. 72–73.

3 David Crary, "Law Curbing Inmates' Lawsuits Questioned," *USA Today*, February 13, 2008, http://www.usatoday.com/news/nation/2008-02-13-3685431048_x.htm (accessed August 16, 2009).

4 *Ruffin v. Commonwealth of Virginia*, 62 Va. (21 Gratt.) 790, 796 (1871).

5 *Price v. Johnston*, 334 U.S. 266 (1948).

6 *Cooper v. Pate*, 378 U.S. 546 (1964).

7 Roger A. Hanson and Henry W. K. Daley, *Challenging the Conditions of Prisons and Jails: A Report on Section 1983 Litigation* (Washington, D.C.: U.S. Department of Justice, Bureau of Justice Statistics, 1994), pp. 1–2.

8 *Holt v. Sarver*, 309 F. Supp. 362 [E.D. Ark. 1970], aff'd 442 F.2d 304 9th Cir. (1971).

9 *Bell v. Wolfish*, 441 U.S. 520 (1979).

10 *Solem v. Helm*, 463 U.S. 277 (1983).

11 *Pell v. Procunier*, 417 U.S. 817 (1974).

12 *United States v. Georgia*, 546 U.S. 151 (2006).

13 *Pugh v. Locke*, 406 F. 2d 318 (1976).

14 *Bell v. Wolfish*, 441 U.S. 520 (1979).

15 *Rhodes v. Chapman*, 452 U.S. 337 (1981).

16 *Wilson v. Seiter*, 111 S. Ct. 2321 (1991).

17 *Cooper v. Pate*, 378 U.S. 546 (1964).

18 *Cruz v. Beto*, 405 U.S. 319 (1972).

19 *Theriault v. Silber*, 391 F. Supp. 579 (1977).

20 *Kahane v. Carlson*, 527 F.2d 492 (2d Cir. 1975).

21 *O'Lone v. Estate of Shabazz*, 482 U.S. 342 (1987).

22 *Hamilton v. Schriro*, 74 F.3d 1545 (8th Cir. 1996).

23 *Fowler v. Crawford*, U.S. App. LEXIS 15841 (8th Cir. 2008).

24 *Turner v. Safley*, 482 U.S. 78 (1987).

25 *Gittlemacker v. Prasse*, 428 F.2d 1 (3d Cir. 1970).

26 *Walker v. Blackwell*, 411 F.2d 23 (1969).

27 42 U.S.C. 2000cc-1(a)(1)-(2).

28 *Americans United for Separation of Church and State v. Prison Fellowship Ministries*, 432 F. Supp. 2d 862.

29 *Americans United for Separation of Church and State v. Prison Fellowship Ministries*, 509 F.3d 406 (2007).

30 *Holt v. Sarver*, 309 F. Supp. 362 [E.D. Ark. 1970], *aff'd* 442 F.2d 304 9th Cir. (1971).

31 *Estelle v. Gamble*, 429 U.S. 97 (1976).

32 *Ramos v. Lamm*, 639 F.2d 559, 576 (1980).

33 *Fernandez v. United States*, 941 F.2d 1488 (1991).

34 *Procunier v. Martinez*, 416 U.S. 396 (1974).

35 *McNamara v. Moody*, 606 F. Supp. 2d 621 (5th Cir. 1979).

36 *Turner v. Safley*, 482 U.S. 78 (1987).

37 *Jones v. North Carolina Prisoners' Labor Union, Inc.*, 433 U.S. 119 (1977).

38 *Sostre v. Otis*, 330 F. Supp. 941 (1971).

39 *Thornburgh v. Abbott*, 109 S. Ct. 1874 (1989).

40 *Guajardo v. Estelle*, 580 F.2d 748 (1978).

41 *Johnson v. Avery*, 393 U.S. 483 (1969).

42 *Younger v. Gilmore*, 404 U.S. 15 (1971).

43 *Bounds v. Smith*, 430 U.S. 817 (1977).

44 *Hudson v. Palmer*, 468 U.S. 517 (1984).

45 *Bell v. Wolfish*, 441 U.S. 520 (1979).

46 *Tribble v. Gardner*, 860 F.2d 321 (9th Cir. 1988).

47 *Grummett v. Rushen*, 587 F. Supp. 913 (9th Cir. 1984).

48 *Johnson v. Phelan*, 69 F.3d 144 (7th Cir. 1995).

49 *Wolff v. McDonnell*, 418 U.S. 539 (1974).

50 *Sandin v. Conner*, 515 U.S. 472 (1995).

51 *Turner v. Safley*, 482 U.S. 78 (1987).

52 *Wilson v. Seiter*, 111 S. Ct. 2321 (1991).

53 *Sandin v. Conner*, 515 U.S. 472 (1995).

54 Crary, "Law Curbing Inmates' Lawsuits Questioned."

55 James J. Stephan, "Census of State and Federal Correctional Facilities, 2005," *National Prisoner Statistics Program* (Washington, D.C.: U.S. Department of Justice, October 2008), p. 3.

56 U.S. Department of Justice, Bureau of Justice Statistics, *Capital Punishment, 2007—Statistical Tables*, Advance Count of Executions, Table 7, http://www.ojp.usdoj.gov/bjs/pub/html/cp/2007/tables/cp07sta.htm (accessed March 2, 2009).

57 *Furman v. Georgia*, 408 U.S. 238 (1972).

58 *Robert v. Louisiana*, 428 U.S. 325 (1976); *Woodson v. North Carolina*, 428 U.S. 280 (1976).

59 *Gregg v. Georgia*, 428 U.S. 153 (1976).

60 *Coker v. Georgia*, 433 U.S. 584 (1977).

61 *Godfrey v. Georgia*, 446 U.S. 420 (1980).

62 *Tison v. Arizona*, 107 S. Ct. 1676 (1987).

63 *Ford v. Wainwright*, 477 U.S. 399 (1986).

64 *Penry v. Lynaugh*, 45 Cr. L. Rptr. 3188 (1989).

65 *Atkins v. Virginia*, 536 U.S. 304 (2002).

66 *Eddings v. Oklahoma*, 455 U.S. 104 (1982).

67 *Stanford v. Kentucky*, 492 U.S. 361 (1989).

68 *In re Stanford*, 123 S. Ct. 472 (2002).

69 As quoted in a story by the Associated Press, "Supreme Court Appears One Vote Shy of Rejecting Death Penalty for Young Killers," *St. Louis Post-Dispatch*, January 28, 2003, p. 2.

70 Thomas P. Bonczar and Tracy L. Snell, "Capital Punishment, 2004," *Bureau of Justice Statistics Bulletin*, (Washington, D.C.: U.S. Department of Justice, 2005), p. 4.

71 *Roper v. Simmons*, 000 U.S. 03–633 (2005).

72 Bonczar and Snell, *Capital Punishment*, p. 1.

73 *Kennedy v. Louisiana*, 554 U.S.___2008.

74 Ibid.

75 U.S. Department of Justice, Bureau of Justice Statistics, *Demographic Characteristics of Prisoners under Sentence of Death*, 2007, Capital Punishment, 2007—Statistical Tables, Table 5, http//www.ojp.usdoj.gov/bjs/pub/html/cp/2007/tables/cpo7st05.htm (accessed March 2, 2009).

76 U.S. Department of Justice, Bureau of Justice Statistics, *Capital Punishment Statistics: Summary Findings*, www.ojp.usdoj.gov/bjs/cp.htm (accessed April 16, 2009).

77 U.S. Department of Justice, *Demographic Characteristics*.

78 David C. Baldus, George F. Woodworth, and Charles A. Pulaski, Jr., *Equal Justice and the Death Penalty: A Legal and Empirical Analysis* (Boston: Northeastern University Press, 1990).

79 Bonczar and Snell, *Capital Punishment*, p. 1.

80 *Baze et al. v. Rees*, 553 U.S.___(2008).

81 As an example, see Isaac Ehrlich, "The Deterrent Effect of Capital Punishment: A Question of Life and Death," *American Economic Review* 65 (1975): 397–417.

82 S. Decker and C. Kohfeld, "A Deterrence Study of the Death Penalty in Illinois," *Journal of Criminal Justice* 12 (1984): 367–377.

83 Ethan Cohen-Cole et al., *Reevaluating the Deterrent Effect of Capital Punishment: Model and Data Uncertainty* (Washington, D.C.: U.S. Department of Justice, December 2006).

84 See S. Decker and C. Kohfeld, "The Deterrent Effect of Capital Punishment in the Five Most Active Execution States: A Time Series Analysis," *Criminal Justice Review* 15 (1990): 173–191; W. C. Bailey, "Desegregation in Deterrence and Death Penalty Research: The Case of Murder in Chicago," *Journal of Criminal Law and Criminology* 74 (1983): 827–859.

85 The Gallup Organization, Inc., *The Gallup Poll* [Online], http://poll.gallup.com/ [June 1, 2006]. Table adapted by SOURCEBOOK staff. Reprinted by permission.

86 For a discussion of brutalization theory, see W. J. Bowers and G. Pierce, "Deterrence or Brutalization: What Is the Effect of Executions?" *Crime and Delinquency* 26 (1980): 453–484.

87 See John K. Cockran, Mitchell B. Chamlin, and Mark Seth, "Deterrence or Brutalization? An Impact Assessment of Oklahoma's Return to Capital Punishment," *Criminology* 31 (1994): 107–134; William C. Bailey, "Deterrence, Brutalization, and the Death Penalty: Another Examination of Oklahoma's Return to Capital Punishment," *Criminology* 36, no. 4 (1998): 711–733.

88 R. M. Bohm, "Retribution and Capital Punishment: Toward a Better Understanding of Death Penalty Opinion," *Journal of Criminal Justice* 20 (1992): 227–236.

89 T. J. Keil and G. F. Vito, "Race and the Death Penalty in Kentucky Murder Trials," *American Journal of Criminal Justice* 20, no. 1 (Fall 1995): 17–36; R. A. Rofferty, "In the Shadow of *McClesky v. Kemp:* Discriminatory Impact of the Death Sentencing Process," *New England Journal on Criminal and Civil Confinement* 21, no. 1 (Winter 1995): 271–312; R. N. Stone, "Killing of Charles Walker: Racial Bias and the Death Sentence," *Criminal Justice* 7, no. 2 (Summer 1992): 22–27, 54–55; J. R. Sorensen and D. H. Wallace, "Capital Punishment in Missouri: Examining the Issue of Racial Disparity," *Behavioral Sciences and the Law* 13, no. 1 (Winter 1995): 61–80.

90 J. Sorensen, R. Wrinkle, V. Brewer, and J. Mauquaut, "Capital Punishment and Deterrence: Examining the Effect

of Executions on Murder in Texas," *Crime and Delinquency* 45, no. 4 (October 1999): 481–493; Gennaro F. Vito and Deborah G. Wilson, "Back from the Dead: Tracking the Progress of Kentucky's *Furman*-Commuted Death Row Population," *Justice Quarterly* 5, no. 1 (1988): 101–111.

91 Hugo A. Bedau, *The Case Against the Death Penalty* (Washington, D.C.: American Civil Liberties Union, Capital Punishment Project, 1992).

92 Bohm, "Retribution and Capital Punishment."

93 P. J. Cook and D. B. Slawson, *The Costs of Processing Murder Cases in North Carolina* (Durham, N.C.: Duke University, Jerry Sanford Institute of Public Policy, 1993).

94 R. S. Spangenberg and E. R. Walsh, "Capital Punishment or Life Imprisonment? Some Cost Considerations," *Loyola University of Los Angeles Law Review* 23, no. 1 (November 1989): 45–58.

95 John Roman et al., *The Cost of the Death Penalty in Maryland* (Washington, D.C.: The Urban Institute, March 2008), Abstract.

96 Globe Editorial writers, "The Cost of Capital Punishment," *Boston Globe.com*, April 15, 2009, www.boston.com/bostonglobe/editorial_opinion/editorials/articles/2009/04/15/the_cost_of_capital_punishment/ (accessed August 16, 2009).

97 *The Harris Poll*, 2001.

98 Gallup Poll, www.gallup.com/content/default.asp?ci = 6031 (accessed May 20, 2002).

99 Lydia Saad, *Support for Death Penalty Study at 64%*, the Gallup Poll, December 8, 2005, p. 1.

100 National Opinion Research Center, *General Surveys, 1972–2000* (Storrs: Roper Center for Public Opinion Research, University of Connecticut, 2001).

101 Linda Saad, "Americans Hold Firm to Support the Death Penalty," *Gallup Poll: Death Penalty* (November 17, 2008), http://www.gallup.com/poll/111931/Americans-Hold-Firm-Support-Death-Penalty.aspx (accessed August 16, 2009).

102 Harris Interactive, "Over Three in Five Americans Believe in the Death Penalty," *Business Wire*, March 18, 2008, http://www.deathpenaltyinfo.org/national-polls-and-studies (accessed August 16, 2009).

103 The Gallup Organization, Inc., *The Gallup Poll* [Online] http//poll.gallup.com/ [June 1, 2006]. Table adapted by SOURCEBOOK staff. Reprinted by permission.

104 R. Dieter, *Innocence and the Death Penalty: The Increasing Danger of Executing the Innocent* (Washington, D.C.: Death Penalty Information Center, 1997).

105 Hugo Adam Bedau and Michael L. Radelet, "Miscarriages of Justice in Potentially Capital Cases," *Stanford Law Review* 40 (1987): 21–181.

106 Death Penalty Information Center, http://www.deathpenaltyinfo.org/innocence-and-death-penalty (accessed April 19, 2009).

107 Renee Cardwell Hughes, "The Death Penalty: A Failed System," in *The State of Corrections: 2001 Proceedings of the ACA Annual Conference* (Lanham, Md.: American Correctional Association, 2002), p. 123.

Chapter 15

1 Bureau of Justice Statistics, Press Release, "Growth in Prison and Jail Populations Slowing: 16 States Report Declines in the Number of Prisoners" (Washington, D.C.: U.S. Department of Justice, released March 31, 2009), http://www.ojp.usdoj.gov/bjs/pub/press/pimjim08stpr.htm (accessed August 16, 2009).

2 See *Prisoners in 2000, Bureau of Justice Statistics Bulletin* (Washington, D.C.: U.S. Department of Justice, 2001).

3 Bureau of Justice Statistics, Press Release.

4 James Austin and Garry Coventry, *Emerging Issues on Privatized Prisons* (Washington, D.C.: U.S. Department of Justice, Bureau of Justice Assistance, February 2001), p. xi.

5 Richard F. Culp, "The Rise and Stall of Prison Privatization" (paper presented at the Academy of Criminal Justice Sciences, Boston, Mass., March 2003).

6 Paige M. Harrison and Allen J. Beck, "Prisoners in 2004," *Bureau of Justice Statistics Bulletin* (Washington, D.C.: U.S. Department of Justice, April 2005), p. 8.

7 Todd D. Minton and William J. Sabol, *Jail Inmates at Midyear 2008—Statistical Tables*, (Washington D.C.: U.S. Department of Justice, March 2009), p. 2.

8 Peter Greenwood et al., "Estimated Benefits and Costs of California's New Mandatory Sentencing Law," in *Three Strikes and You're Out*, edited by David Shichor and Dale K. Sechrest (Thousand Oaks, Calif.: Sage, 1996).

9 For a good review of this issue, see Joseph W. Rogers, "The Greatest Correctional Myth: Winning the War on Crime through Incarceration," in *Public Policy, Crime, and Criminal Justice*, 2nd ed., edited by Barry W. Hancock and Paul M. Sharp (Upper Saddle River, N.J.: Prentice Hall, 2000), pp. 308–321.

10 For a description of intermediate sanctions that have proved effective, see Richard P. Seiter, *Correctional Administration: Integrating Theory and Practice* (Upper Saddle River, N.J.: Prentice Hall, 2002), pp. 446–447.

11 Pretrial Services Resource Center, *A Second Look at Alleviating Jail Overcrowding: A Systems Perspective* (Washington, D.C.: U.S. Department of Justice, Bureau of Justice Assistance, October 2000), p. 2.

12 Ibid., p. 66.

13 Alfred Blumstein and Allen J. Beck, "Population Growth in U.S. Prisons: 1980–1996," in *Prisons: A Review of Research*, edited by Michael Tonry and Joan Petersilia (Chicago: University of Chicago Press, 1999), pp. 17–62.

14 Rufus King, "It's Time to Open the Doors of Our Prisons," *Newsweek*, April 19, 1999, p. 10.

15 Sam C. Proband, "Corrections Leads State Budget Increases in FY 1997," *Overcrowded Times* 8, no. 4 (1997): 4.

16 John Irwin and James Austin, *It's About Time: America's Imprisonment Binge* (Belmont, Calif.: Wadsworth, 1994).

17 Joan Petersilia, *When Prisoners Come Home: Parole and Prisoner Reentry* (New York: Oxford University Press, 2003), p. 221.

18 As cited in Peter D. Hart Research Associates, *Changing Pubilc Attitudes toward the Crimninal Justice System* (New York: Open Society, February 2002).

18 Ibid.

19 Barry Krisberg and Susan Marchionna, "Attitudes of U.S. Voters toward Prisoners Rehabilitation and Reentry Policies," *Focus: Views from the National Council on Crime and Delinquency* (San Francisco, Calif.: NCCD, April 2006).

20 Ibid.

21 S. E. Skovan, J. E. Scott, and E. T. Cullen, "Prison Crowding: Public Attitudes toward Strategies of Population Control," *Journal of Research in Crime and Delinquency* 25, no. 2 (1988): 150–169.

22 Barbara A. Sims, "Questions of Corrections: Public Attitudes toward Prison and Community-Based Programs," *Corrections Management Quarterly* 1, no. 1 (1997): 54.

23 Daniel Weintraub, "State Prison Guards Set to Ratify Rich New Contract," *Sacramento Bee*, February 10, 2002, p. E5.

24 See Joe Hallinan, *Going Up the River: Travels in a Prison Nation* (New York: Random House, 2002); Joel Caplan, "Policy for Profit: The Private-Prison Industry's Influence over Criminal Justice Legislation," *ACJS Today* 26, no. 1 (January/February 2003): 15–20.

25 Robert M. Freeman, *Correctional Organization and Management: Public Policy Challenges, Behavior, and Structure* (Boston: Butterworth-Heinemann, 1999), p. 108.

26 Bureau of Justice Statistics, *Expenditure Facts at a Glance*, www.ojp.usdoj.gov/bjs/glance/tables/exptyptab.htm (accessed January 17, 2006).

27 Camille Graham Camp and George M. Camp, *The 2002 Corrections Yearbook: Adult Corrections* (Middletown, Conn.: Criminal Justice Institute, 2003), p. 92.

28 National Association of State Budget Officers, "State Expenditure Report FY 2006," December 2007, http://www.nasbo.org/Publications/PDFs/fy2006er.pdf (accessed August 16, 2009).

29 *Public Safety, Public Spending: Forecasting America's Prison Population, 2007–2011*, Public Safety Performance Project (Washington, D.C.: The Pew Charitable Trust, February 2007), p. ii.

30 Pew Center of the States, *One in 31: The Long Reach of American Corrections* (Washington, D.C.: Pew Charitable Trusts, March 2009), p. 2.

31 Ibid., p. 13.

32 C. S. Baird, D. A. Holien, and J. A. Bakke, *Fees for Probation Services* (Washington, D.C.: U.S. Department of Justice, National Institute for Justice, 1986).

33 Camp and Camp, 2002 *Corrections Yearbook*, pp. 105–106.

34 M. Nolan, "Medical Co-Payment System: Nevada Department of Prisons" (paper presented at the annual conference of the American Correctional Health Services Association, Salt Lake City, Utah, April 1992).

35 National Conference of State Legislatures, *Update on State Budget Gaps: FY 2009 & FY 2010* (Denver, Colo.: National Conference of State Legislatures, January 2009).

36 Pew Center on the States, *One in 31*.

37 Ibid., p. 11.

38 Ibid., p. 15.

39 Ibid., p. 18.

40 William J. Sabol et al., *Prison and Jail Inmates at Midyear 2006* (Washington, D.C.: U.S Department of Justice, Bureau of Justice Statistics, June 2007).

41 All of these examples were taken from Keith B. Richburg and Ashley Surdin, "Fiscal Pressures Lead Some States to Free Inmates Early," *Washington Post*, May 5, 2008, p. A01.

42 Vera Institute of Justice, *Managing State Prison Growth: Key Trends in Sentencing Policy* (New York: Vera Institute of Justice, January 2008).

43 Jeremy W. Peters, "Albany Reaches Deal to Repeal '70s Drug Laws," *The New York Times*, March 26, 2009, p. A21.

44 John Gramlich, "States Seek Alternatives to More Prisons," Stateline.org, June 18, 2007, http://www.stateline.org/live/details/story?contentId=217204 (accessed August 16, 2009).

45 Ibid., p.3.

46 Laura Sullivan, "Shrinking State Budgets May Spring Some Inmates," *National Public Radio Legal Affairs Report*, April 1, 2009, http://www.npr.org/templates/story/story.php?storyId=102536945 (accessed August 16, 2009).

47 "$30 million in Stimulus for Public Safety," a report WKOW television in Madison, Wisconsin, April 9, 2009, www.wkowtv.com/Gloval/story.asp?S=10157862 (accessed August 16, 2009).

48 Camp and Camp, *2002 Corrections Yearbook*, pp. 100 and 101.

49 Ibid., pp. 103 and 104.

50 Heather C. West and William J. Sabol, *Prison Inmates at Midyear 2008—Statistical Tables* (Washington, D.C.: U.S. Department of Justice, Bureau of Justice Statistics, March 2009), p. 12.

51 Average revenue per worker-day was calculated from the annual reports of the three publicly traded companies (CCA, GEO, and Cornell).

52 Charles Logan, *Looking at Hidden Costs: Public and Private Corrections* (Washington, D.C.: National Institute of Justice, 1989).

53 The cost of private prison operations per day was calculated from the 2008 earnings report of the three publicly traded private prison companies (CCA, GEO, Cornell). The public prison cost was from a survey of thirty-four states for their 2008 costs, as reported in The Pew Center on the States, *One in 31: The Long Reach of American Corrections* (Washington, D.C.: Pew Charitable Trusts, March 2009).

54 Logan, *Looking at Hidden Costs*, pp. 52–54.

55 J. Hackett et al., *Issues in Contracting for the Private Operation of Prisons and Jails* (Washington, D.C.: U.S. Department of Justice, 1987).

56 Dale K. Sechrest and David Shichor, "Comparing Public and Private Correctional Facilities in California: An Exploratory Study," in *Privatization and the Provision of Nashville, TN: Correctional Services: Context and Consequences*, edited by G. Larry Mays and Tara Gray (Cincinnati, Ohio: Anderson, 1996), p. 135.

57 James F. Blumstein, Mark A. Cohen, and Suman Seth, "Do Government Agencies Respond to Market Pressures? Evidence from Private Prisons," *Virginia Journal of Social Policy & the Law*, 15, no. 3 (Spring 2008), p. 466.

58 "Developments in the Law of Prisons: A Tale of Two Systems: Cost, Quality, and Accountability in Private Prisons," *Harvard Law Review* 115, no. 7 (May 2002): 1891.

59 Geoffrey F. Segal, *Comparing Public and Private Prisons on Quality* (Los Angeles: The Reason Foundation, 2005), http://www.reason.org/ps290.pdf (accessed August 16, 2009).

60 Geoffrey F. Segal and Adrian T. Moore, *Weighing the Watchmen: Evaluating the Costs and Benefits of Outsourcing Correctional Services* (Los Angeles: Reason Public Policy Institute, January 2002), p. 17.

61 Sharon Dolovich, "State Punishment and Private Prisons," *Duke Law Journal* 55, no. 3 (2005): 439–546.

62 J. Austin and G. Coventry, *Emerging Issues on Privatized Prisons* (San Francisco: National Council of Crime and Delinquency, March 1999).

63 Culp, "Rise and Stall."

64 Douglas McDonald and Carl Patten, *Governments' Management of Private Prisons* (Washington, D.C.: U.S. Department of Justice, January 2004), p. 102.

65 Lonn Lanza-Kaduce, Karen F. Parker, and Charles W. Thomas, "A Comparative Recidivism Analysis of Releasees from Private and Public Prisons," *Crime and Delinquency* 45, no. 1 (1999): 28–47.

66 U.S. General Accounting Office, *Private and Public Prisons: Studies Comparing Operational Costs and/or Quality of Service* (Washington, D.C.: GAO, 1996).

67 Studies showing little evidence of cost savings include A. Cheung, *Prison Privatization and the Use of Incarceration* (Washington, D.C.: Sentencing Project, January 2002); P. Mattera and M. Khan, *Jail Breaks: Economic Development Subsidies Given to Private Prisons* (Washington, D.C.: Institute on Taxation and Economic Policy, October 2001).

68 Scott D. Camp and Gerald G. Gaes, "Growth and Quality of U.S. Private Prisons: Evidence from a National Survey," *Criminology and Public Policy* (July 2002): 427–449.

69 Douglas C. McDonald and Kenneth Carlson, *Contracting for Imprisonment in the Federal Prison System: Cost and Performance of the Privately Operated Taft Correctional Institution* (Washington, D.C.: U.S. Department of Justice, November 2005).

70 E. C. Hughes, "Professions," in *The Professions in America*, edited by Kenneth S. Lynn (Boston: Houghton Mifflin, 1965), p. 4.

71 American Correctional Association, *Standards for Adult Correctional Institutions*, 3rd ed. (Lanham, Md.: American Correctional Association, 1990).

72 Ibid., p. vii.

73 Camp and Camp, *2002 Corrections Yearbook*, p. 90.

74 These numbers were received by the author from Mark Flowers, Executive Director of the ACA Commission on Accreditation, via email on March 26, 2009.

75 Elizabeth Ward, "Accreditation: A Positive Step toward Facility Improvement," *Corrections Today* (February 1995): 78–80.

76 Heather C. West and William J. Sabol, "Prisoners in 2007," *Bureau of Justice Statistics Bulletin* (Washington, D.C.: U.S. Department of Justice, December 2008), p. 19.

77 Ibid,. p. 4.

78 Bureau of Justice Statistics, *Prison Inmates at Mid-Year 2008—Statistical Tables* (Washington, D.C.: U.S. Department of Justice, March 2009), http://www.ojp.usdoj.gov/bjs/abstract/pim08st.htm (accessed August 16, 2009).

79 Camp and Camp, 2002 *Corrections Yearbook*, p. 154.

80 Ibid., p. 155.

81 Ibid., p. 219.

82 John Irwin, "The Changing Social Structure of the Men's Correctional Prison," in *Corrections and Punishment*, edited by D. Greenberg (Beverly Hills, Calif.: Sage, 1977), pp. 21–40.

83 Susan Philliber, "Thy Brother's Keeper: A Review of Literature on Correctional Officers," *Justice Quarterly* 4, no. 1 (1987): 9–33.

84 Douglas Lipton, Robert Martinson, and Judith Wilks, *The Effectiveness of Correctional Treatment and What Works: A Survey of Treatment Evaluation Studies* (New York: Praeger, 1975).

85 Francis T. Cullen and Paul Gendreau, "Assessing Correctional Rehabilitation: Policy, Practice, and Prospects," in *Policies, Processes, and Decisions of the Criminal Justice System*, edited by Julie Horney (Washington, D.C.: U.S. Department of Justice, National Institute of Justice, 2000), pp. 109–175.

86 Ibid., p. 127.

87 See D. A. Andrews, Ivan Zinger, Robert D. Hoge, James Bonta, Paul Gendreau, and Francis D. Cullen, "Does Correctional Treatment Work? A Clinically Relevant and Psychologically Informed Meta-Analysis," *Criminology* 28 (August 1990): 369–404; D. A. Andrews and James Bonta, *The Psychology of Criminal Conduct*, 2nd ed. (Cincinnati, Ohio: Anderson, 1998).

88 Ted Palmer, "Martinson Revisited," *Journal of Research in Crime and Delinquency* 12 (July 1975): 133–152.

89 Andrews et al., "Does Correctional Treatment Work?" p. 374.

90 Mark W. Lipsey and David B. Wilson, "The Efficacy of Psychological, Educational, and Behavioral Treatment," *American Psychologist* 48, no. 12 (1993): 1181–1209.

91 Friedrich Losel, "The Efficacy of Correctional Treatment: A Review and Synthesis of Meta Evaluations," in *What Works: Reducing Reoffending*, edited by James McGuire (West Sussex, England: Wiley, 1995).

92 Steve Aos, Marna Miller, and Elizabeth Drake, *Evidence-Based Public Policy Options to Reduce Future Prison Construction, Criminal Justice Costs, and Crime Rates* (Olympia: Washington State Institute for Public Policy, 2006).

Chapter 16

1 Heather C. West and William J. Sabol, *Prison Inmates at Midyear 2008—Statistical Tables* (Washington, D.C.: U.S. Department of Justice, Bureau of Justice Statistics, March 2009), p. 2.

2 Bureau of Justice Statistics, U.S. Department of Justice, *Key Facts at a Glance, Correctional Populations*, http//www/ojp/usdoj.gov/bjs/glance/tables/corr2tab.htm (accessed March 10, 2009).

3 Bureau of Justice Statistics, U.S. Department of Justice, *Key Facts at a Glance, Direct Expenditures by Criminal Justice Function, 1982–2006*, http//www.ojp.usdoj.gov/bjs/glance/tables/exptyptab.htm (accessed March 10, 2009).

4 *Public Safety, Public Spending: Forecasting America's Prison Population, 2007–2011*, Public Safety Performance Project (Washington, D.C.: The Pew Charitable Trust, February 2007), p. ii.

5 Federal Bureau of Investigation, U.S. Department of Justice, Uniform Crime Reports, *Crime in the United*

States, 2007, Table 1-Crime in the United States, by Volume and Rate per 100,00 inhabitants, 1988–2007, http://www/fbi.gov/ucr/cius2007/offenses/standard_links/ national-estimates.html (accessed March 10, 2009).

6 Gallup Poll, *Public Grows More Pessimistic about U.S. Crime,* Lydia Saad, October 20, 2005.

7 William Spelman, "The Limited Importance of Prison Expansion," in *The Crime Drop in America,* edited by Alfred Blumstein and Joel Wallman (Cambridge, Mass.: Cambridge University Press, 2000).

8 Alfred Blumstein and Joel Wallman, eds., *The Crime Drop in America* (Cambridge, Mass.: Cambridge University Press), 2000.

9 As reported by the Associated Press, "Supreme Court Justice Says Prison Terms Are Too Long," *St. Louis Post-Dispatch,* August 10, 2003, p. A7.

10 Douglas Lipton, Robert Martinson, and Judith Wilks, *The Effectiveness of Correctional Treatment and What Works: A Survey of Treatment Evaluation Studies* (New York: Praeger, 1975).

11 Lauren E. Glaze and Thomas P. Bonczar, "Probation and Parole in the United States, 2006," *Bureau of Justice Statistics Bulletin* (Washington, D.C.: U.S. Department of Justice, December 2007), p. 6.

12 P. Ditton and D. J. Wilson, *Truth in Sentencing in State Prisons* (Washington, D.C.: U.S. Department of Justice, Bureau of Justice Statistics, 1999).

13 James P. Lynch and William J. Sabol, "Prisoner Reentry in Perspective," www.urban.org/url.cfm?ID=410213 (accessed September 18, 2001).

14 Camille Graham Camp and George M. Camp, *Corrections Yearbook: Adult Corrections, 2002* (Middletown, CN: Criminal Justice Institute, 2003), pp. 136–137.

15 Ibid., pp. 118–119.

16 Ibid., p. 135.

17 Ibid., pp. 71, 146.

18 Ibid., p. 146.

19 California Expert Panel on Adult Offender Recidivism Reduction Programming, *A Roadmap for Effective Offender Programming in California: Report to the California State Legislature* (Sacramento, Calif.: California Department of Corrections and Rehabilitation, 2007).

20 Barry Krisberg and Susan Marchionna, "Attitudes of U.S. Voters toward Prisoners Rehabilitation and Reentry Policies," *Focus: Views from the National Council on Crime and Delinquency,* http://www.famm.org/ Repository/Files/Attitudes_of_US_Voters_toward_Prisoner_ Rehabilitation_and_Reentry_Policies%5B1%5D.pdf (accessed August 17, 2009).

21 Ibid.

22 Robert Martinson, "What Works? Questions and Answers about Prison Reform," *Public Interest* 35 (1974): 25.

23 Paul Gendreau, Claire Goggin, and Paula Smith, "Generating Rational Correctional Policies: An Introduction to Advances in Cumulating Knowledge," *Corrections Management Quarterly* 4, no. 2 (2000): 56–57.

24 David P. Farrington, Anthony Petrosino, and Brandon C. Welsh, "Systematic Reviews and Cost-Benefit Analyses of Correctional Interventions," *Prison Journal* 81, no. 3 (2001): 339–359.

25 For discussions of qualitative assessments of treatment programs and matching of offenders to program services, see Sharon Levrant, Francis T. Cullen, Betsy Fulton, and John Wozniak, "Reconsidering Restorative Justice: The Corruption of Benevolence Revisited?" *Crime and Delinquency* 45 (1999): 3–27; Edward J. Latessa and Alexander Holsinger, "The Importance of Evaluating Correctional Programs: Assessing Outcome and Quality," *Corrections Management Quarterly 2,* no. 4 (1998): 22–29; Paul Gendreau and Donald Andrews, *The Correctional Program Assessment Inventory,* 5th ed. (Saint John, Canada: University of New Brunswick, 1994); Gendreau, Goggin, and Smith, "Generating Rational Correctional Policies," pp. 52–60.

26 For examples of studies that indicate a positive treatment effect, see Francis T. Cullen and Brandon K. Applegate, eds., *Offender Rehabilitation: Effective Treatment Intervention* (Aldershot, England: Ashgate, 1997); Gerald G. Gaes, "Correctional Treatment," in *The Handbook of Crime and Punishment,* edited by Michael Tonry (New York: Oxford University Press, 1998), pp. 712–738; Vernon L. Quinsey, "Treatment of Sex Offenders," in *The Handbook of Crime and Punishment,* pp. 403–425; Douglas S. Lipton, "Prison-Based Therapeutic Communities: Their Success with Drug-Abusing Offenders," *National Institute of Justice Journal* (February 1996): 12–20; William G. Saylor and Gerald G. Gaes, "Training Inmates through Industrial Work Participation and Vocational and Apprenticeship Instruction," *Corrections Management Quarterly* 1, no. 2 (1997): 40; Federal Bureau of Prisons, *TRIAD Drug Treatment Evaluation Six-Month Report: Executive Summary* (Washington, D.C.: U.S. Department of Justice, 1998).

27 William Adams and Jeffrey Roth, *Federal Offenders under Community Supervision, 1989–96* (Washington, D.C.: U.S. Department of Justice, Bureau of Justice Statistics, 1998).

28 Camp and Camp, *2002 Corrections Yearbook,* p. 201.

29 Glaze and Bonczar, p. 4.

30 In a study of St. Louis parole and probation officers, Seiter and West found that 54.1 percent of respondents majored in criminal justice, 1.1 percent in psychology, 9.0 percent in sociology, and 4.5 percent in social work. Other majors included education, business, art, and history. See Richard P. Seiter and Angela D. West, "Supervision Styles in Probation and Parole: An Analysis of Activities," *Offender Rehabilitation* 38, no. 2 (2003): 57–75.

31 Camp and Camp, *2002 Corrections Yearbook,* p. 203.

32 Ibid., p. 224.

33 West and Sabol, *Prisoners in 2007,* p. 3.

34 Camp and Camp, *2002 Corrections Yearbook,* pp. 59–61.

35 Joan Petersilia, "When Prisoners Return to the Community: Political, Economic, and Social Consequences," *Federal Probation* 65, no. 1 (June 2001): 3–8.

36 Glaze and Bonczar, pp. 2 and 7.

37 Faye X. Taxman, "No Illusions: Offender and Organizational Change in Maryland's Proactive Community Supervision Efforts," *Criminology and Public Policy* 7, no. 2 (May 2008): 275–302.

38 Francis T. Cullen, John Paul Wright, Paul Gendreau, and D. A. Andrews, "What Correctional Treatment Can Tell Us about Criminological Theory: Implications for Social Learning Theory," in *Social Learning Theory and the Explanation of Crime: A Guide for the New Century*, edited by Ronald L. Akers and Gary F. Jensen (New Brunswick, N.J.: Transaction, 2003), pp. 339–362.

39 Tony Fabelo, "Technocorrections: The Promises, the Uncertain Threats," *Sentencing & Corrections: Issues for the 21st Century*, Papers from the Executive Sessions on Sentencing and Corrections, No. 5 (Washington, D.C.: U.S. Department of Justice, May 2000).

40 Thomas J. Herzog, "If the World Is Flat, How Come Corrections Is Still Round? Integrating Correctional Authorities into the Fusion Center Rubric," an unpublished Whitepaper brief of the Corrections Technology Association, September 2007.

41 National Law Enforcement and Corrections Technology Center, "E-Messaging Saves Time, Improves Security," *Tech Beat* (Summer 2008), http://www.justnet.org/TechBeat%20Files/E-Messaging.pdf (accessed August 17, 2009).

42 Ann Coppola, "In the Year 2028," *The Corrections Connection*, posted March 10, 2008 on-line website, www.justnet.org/Pages/RecordView.aspx?itemid=1581 (accessed August).

43 William Falcon, "Special Technologies for Law Enforcement and Corrections," *NIJ Journal 252* (July 2005): 22–27.

44 National Law Enforcement and Corrections Technology Center, "No More 'Cell' Phones," *Tech Beat* (Winter 2005), http://www.justnet.org/TechBeat%20Files/NoMoreCellPhones.pdf (accessed August 17, 2009).

45 National Law Enforcement and Corrections Center, "On Parole in New Mexico," *Tech Beat* (Spring 2005), http://www.justnet.org/TechBeat%20Files/ParoleNM.pdf (accessed August 17, 2009).

46 Maureen Boyle, "Tracking Sex Offenders Made Easy with New State Computer System," *Enterprise News.com* (March 1, 2008), www.enterprisenews.com/news/x2052203702?view=print (accessed August 17, 2009).

47 Ann Coppola, "Tracking the Event Horizon," *The Corrections Connection* (June 17, 2008), www.justnet.org/Pages/RecordView.aspx?itemid=1633 (accessed August 17, 2009).

48 NIJ Staff, "Making Corrections Safer with Technology," *Corrections Today 70*, no. 1 (February 2008): 62–63.

49 Office of Justice Programs, "Duress Systems in Correctional Facilities," In *Short: Toward Criminal Justice Solutions* (Washington, D.C.: U.S. Department of Justice, June 2006), http://www.ncjrs.gov/pdffiles1/nij/214921.pdf (accessed August 17, 2009).

50 Mark Carey, "Overcoming Fear, Misunderstanding, and NIMBY through Restorative Covenants," *Corrections Management Quarterly 4*, no. 3 (2000): 12.

51 John G. Perry and John F. Gorczyk, "Restructuring Corrections: Using Market Research in Vermont," *Corrections Management Quarterly 1*, no. 3 (1997): 27.

52 Reginald A. Wilkinson, "The Impact of Community Service Work on Ohio State Prisoners: A Restorative Justice Perspective and Overview," *Corrections Management Quarterly 4*, no. 3 (2000): 30.

53 Ibid.

54 David R. Karp, "Does Community Justice Work?" *Perspectives 27*, no. 1 (2003): 32–37.

55 Donald Clemmer, *The Prison Community* (New York: Rinehart, 1940).

56 Charles M. Terry, "The Function of Humor for Prison Inmates," *Journal of Contemporary Criminal Justice 13*, no. 1 (February 1997): 23–40.

57 Erving Goffman, *Asylums: Essays on the Social Situation of Mental Patients and Other Inmates* (New York: Doubleday, 1961).

58 Donald Cressey, "Contradictory Directives in Complex Organizations: The Case of the Prison," *Administrative Science Quarterly* (June 1959).

59 Dora Schriro, "Correcting Corrections: Missouri's Parallel Universe," in *Sentencing and Corrections: Issues for the 21st Century* (Washington, D.C.: U.S. Department of Justice, National Institute of Justice, May 2000), p. 3.

60 Ibid., p. 4.

61 William G. Saylor and Gerald G. Gaes, "The Post-Release Employment Project: Prison Work Has Measurable Effects on Post-Release Success," *Federal Prisons Journal 2*, no. 4 (1992): 33–36.

62 James J. Stephan, "Census of State and Federal Correctional Facilities, 2005," *Bureau of Justice Statistics: National Prisoner Statistics Program* (Washington, D.C.: U.S. Department of Justice, October 2008), p. 5.

63 Charles M. Terry, interview by author, St. Louis University, July 28, 2003.

64 Camp and Camp, *2002 Corrections Yearbook*, pp. 170–171.

65 Kevin N. Wright, *Effective Prison Leadership* (Binghamton, N.Y.: William Neil, 1994), p. 47.

66 Ibid., p. 14.

67 Lynn Bauer and Steven D. Owens, "Justice Expenditure and Employment in the United States, 2001," *Bureau of Justice Statistics Bulletin* (Washington, D.C.: U.S. Department of Justice, May 2004), p. 5.

68 Bureau of Justice Statistics, *Sourcebook of Criminal Justice Statistics, 1994* (Washington, D.C.: U.S. Department of Justice, updated March 2003), p. 26.

69 Texas Department of Criminal Justice (Corrections), http://www.tdcj.state.tx.us/vacancy/coinfo/cosalary.htm and California Department of Corrections and Rehabilitation, http://www.cdcr.ca.gov/Career_Opportunities/POR/docs/payandbenefits.pdf (accessed August 17, 2009).

Index

Note: Page numbers followed by f or t indicate Figures or Tables